PRAISE FOR

Remember the
AFL

I have a hard time believing that the American Football League will soon be celebrating its 50th anniversary. It seems like just yesterday that I was running pass routes in stadiums around the country. Though it was a couple of years old by the time I arrived in San Diego in 1962, the AFL was still struggling to find its niche in the world of professional football. But the league quickly made its mark, with great ballplayers and fantastic teams battling every Sunday. AFL players and fans alike take pride in the fact that when the merger concluded in 1970, the AFL (that "Other League") and NFL were tied with two Super Bowl victories each. If you enjoyed our league in the 1960s, *Remember the AFL*, will be a wonderful trip down memory lane. For those that are not old enough to have their own AFL experience, *Remember the AFL* will give you an in-depth look at the most colorful and exciting football of the era. Thanks to Dave Steidel for putting together this fantastic book!
– Lance Alworth, receiver – San Diego Chargers 1962-1969

I enjoyed reading *Remember the AFL*. Dave Steidel's book is a salute to the AFL and genuinely captures the essence and excitement of the AFL experience. It brought back great memories, and I'm so proud to have been a part of this football era. I believe the players from the 60s were instrumental in making the game what it is today
– Fred Arbanas, tight end – Kansas City Chiefs 1962-1969

Dave Steidel has come up with a great concept: a book that not only tells the fascinating history of the American Football League, team by team, year by year, and also serves as a delightful trivia test to help the reader *Remember the AFL*. The question-and-answer format, the imaginative grouping of facts, and the depth of information should keep even the most avid AFL fans exercising their thinking caps to recall the names, places, and events, as well as the too-seldom seen images that defined the genesis of modern professional football. The unique approach uses a trivia format to UN-trivialize the American Football League.
– Ange Coniglio, AFL Archivist – AFL Hall of Fame www.RemembertheAFL.com

Dave Steidel has written an in-depth book about the American Football League. It highlights the events and players who forged a new path in American sports—a new league that challenged, then gained equality with the established NFL. For the league that welcomed players from all walks of life and all ethnic and racial backgrounds, this book brings back the thrills and memories that everyone will enjoy reliving.
– Abner Haynes, running back – Dallas Texans/Kansas City Chiefs, Denver Broncos, Miami Dolphins, New York Jets 1960-1967

Playing in the AFL was a great experience that will remain for a lifetime as wonderful memories. *Remember the AFL* does much to bring to the surface many of those memories. I guess we all have so many stories to tell that nobody would ever believe. I am AFL. The NFL will never know what we had. They don't deserve us!
– Charlie Hennigan, receiver – Houston Oilers 1960-1966

MORE PRAISE FOR

Remember the
AFL

Reading *Remember the AFL* brought back many good memories. It was fun reliving all those games and even learning some things I didn't know. It was great fun making the history of the American Football League, and this book made it fun to relive it.
– E. J. Holub, linebacker and center – Dallas Texans/Kansas City Chiefs 1961-1969

Remember the AFL is well documented with detail that was enjoyable to read. It covers the AFL in its entirety. As the only AFL player to start in the very first and very last AFL game, I really appreciated being able to have the details brought back to my memory. For anyone who is interested in pro football and its time prior to the merger, this is an excellent book. I really did not like reading about the Bills' loss to Kansas City in the game that decided who played in the first Super Bowl, but so goes life.
– Harry Jacobs, linebacker – Buffalo Bills 1960-1969

I enjoyed reading Dave Steidel's book about the AFL very much. It brought back many great memories of games and the great players from the past who played in the league. I think anyone who reads it will find it enjoyable too.
– Don Maynard, receiver – New York Titans/Jets 1960-1969

Though the first American Football League game was played nearly 50 years ago, love for the old AFL burns as brightly today as it did back then. Those of us who were not around then to enjoy those glorious teams rely on old photos and dedicated historians to help us understand the significance of Lamar Hunt and the "Other League." I speak for football fans young and old when I say that we owe a great debt to Dave Steidel for keeping the AFL's torch burning bright, and helping us all to better understand this wonderful piece of American history.
– Todd Tobias, author of *Charging Through the AFL* and *Bombs Away: The Don Coryell Years*

A very entertaining book. A lot of names mentioned, some I'd forgotten. I remember the Bengals' first game—in San Diego, against the Chargers. It was played at one o'clock on a Friday afternoon because there was a flea market scheduled for the parking lot of the stadium on Sunday. Set up was Saturday. That was life in the AFL. I got a check for $644 on the plane ride home. I was a prrroooo football player.
– Bob Trumpy, tight end – Cincinnati Bengals 1968-1969

Remember the
AFL

THE ULTIMATE FAN'S GUIDE
TO THE AMERICAN FOOTBALL LEAGUE

★ ★ ★ ★ ★ ★ ★ ★ ★ ★ ★

Dave Steidel

CLERISY PRESS

Remember the
AFL

Copyright © 2008 by Dave Steidel

All rights reserved. No portion of this book may be reproduced in any fashion, print, facsimile, or electronic, or by any method yet to be developed, without express permission of the copyright holder.

FOR FURTHER INFORMATION, CONTACT THE PUBLISHER AT:
CLERISY PRESS
1700 MADISON ROAD
CINCINNATI, OH 45206

Library of Congress Cataloging-in-Publication Data:
Steidel, David.
Remember the AFL : the ultimate fan's guide to the American Football League / by David Steidel. -- 1st ed.
    p. cm.
ISBN-13: 978-1-57860-323-7
ISBN-10: 1-57860-323-4
1. American Football League--History. I. Title.

GV955.5.A45S74 2008
796.332'640973--dc22

2008021983

Game action and player photos appear courtesy of the San Diego Chargers, Kansas City Chiefs, Oakland Raiders, Houston Oilers (Tennessee Titans), Boston (New England) Patriots, Miami Dolphins, and New York Jets, Rich Clarkson and Associates, and Robert L. Smith

Football cards appear courtesy of the Topps Company Inc. and Fleer Trading Cards

The *Sports Illustrated* cover appears courtesy of *Sports Illustrated*/Walter Iooss Jr.

AFL and NFL trademarks appear courtesy of NFL Properties

"The Heidi game" photo on page 330 appears courtesy of Corbis Corporation

The photo of Paul Brown on page 434 appears courtesy of the Paul E. Brown Museum

Uniform and helmet graphics provided courtesy of Craig Wheeler

Remember the AFL sticker appears courtesy of Ange Coniglio

The drawing of the Mini-Jet car on page 438 appears courtesy of Alex Selig

Edited by
Jack Heffron

Editorial support by
Trevor Hamilton, Stephanie Morris, Kara Pelicano, Donna Poehner

Cover and interior designed by
Stephen Sullivan

Printed in China by
Everbest Printing Co. through Four Colour Imports, Ltd., Louisville, Kentucky

Distributed by Publishers Group West

Dedicated to my wife, Cara, daughter, Tacie, and son, Tanner, who endured my living in the '60s while researching and writing this book, my parents who graciously financed my passion for collecting football cards back in the day, and all the players, coaches, and owners of the American Football League who forged a magical and lasting imprint on my youth.

Acknowledgements

The history of the American Football League is more than a story about football. It is a celebration of the people and partners who made up the league and played the games. It is about a one-for-all and all-for-one attitude that made the AFL a winner from top to bottom. The same can be said for this book, for I could never have accomplished the goal or completed this project without that same all-for-one approach by a great network of AFL aficionados who assisted in many ways.

First, foremost, and above all is Ange Coniglio, the godfather of American Football League history. He and his Web site (www.remembertheafl.com) were the inspiration and impetus that spurred me toward following my love for the AFL and writing this book. Ange was an invaluable resource, contact, and friend who revived my interest in the AFL and offered many kind words and leads that kept me going when it all seemed impossible. He is undoubtedly America's #1 AFL enthusiast and keeper of the flame. The *Remember the AFL* bumper sticker was created by Ange when he lobbied for retention of the league's identity. A copy of it is in the pro football Hall of Fame.

Thanks also to Craig Wheeler, whose uniform art and helmet renderings are beautiful and add immeasurably to the history of the AFL in this book. But more importantly is his professional expertise and friendship, which helped make this book what we hope is the best remembrance about the AFL to date. Author Todd Tobias was invaluable for the help and advice offered. His assistance, along with John Richards, in locating volumes of AFL films was invaluable. Todd is the author of *Charging Through the AFL*, which is the best Chargers history book ever written. And although not a card-carrying baby boomer, his knowledge of the AFL is right up there with the best of them. Todd also graciously offered his personal collection of

Acknowledgements

1960 Fleer football cards that appear. The New York Mini-Jet art in the trivia section is the work of Alexander Selig.

The Topps Company Inc. and the Fleer Trading Cards Company also have graciously granted permission to use the cards that appear in the book. I can't begin to count the hours of enjoyment collecting their cards has given me while growing up. They are forever special in my heart. The cards that appear were donated from the personal collections of Todd Tobias (1960), Jim Sharp (1964 and Super Bowl), Ange Coniglio (1965) and especially the yeoman work provided by Bob Swick (1962, '63, '66, '67, '68, '69, '70).

Charter member franchises—the San Diego Chargers, Kansas City Chiefs, New York Jets, Oakland Raiders, Tennessee Titans (Houston Oilers), New England (Boston) Patriots—and players Tom Addison, Chuck Shonta, and Robert L. Smith (Buffalo Bills) have also generously offered the use of the many photographs that appear.

Finally, but certainly not lastly, are my sincere thanks to AFL players Chris Burford, E.J. Holub, Fred Arbanas, and Abner Haynes of the Kansas City Chiefs, San Diego Charger Lance Alworth, Houston Oiler Charlie Hennigan, New York Jet Don Maynard, Cincinnati Bengal Bob Trumpy, the Buffalo Bills Harry Jacobs and director of archives Denny Lynch for their time and feedback given in review and endorsement of this book.

For me this book represents the culmination of a nearly fifty-year dream to write a book about what I have known and loved since its birth—the American Football League. It is my sincerest wish that everyone who reads this remembrance enjoys it as much as I did writing it.

★ *Lance Alworth of the San Diego Chargers was the first AFL player elected to the Hall of Fame.*

Table of CONTENTS

	Acknowledgements	6
	Foreword	10
	Introduction	16
	Not So Foolish	22
Part 1	The Progress of the Seasons	28
	1960	31
	1961	63
	1962	95
	1963	129
	1964	160
	1965	186
	1966	222
	1967	260
	1968	298
	1969	340
Part 2	AFL Trivia	384
	Headgear Quiz	386
	In the Trenches	388
	Faces of the Game	400
	By the Numbers	414
	For the Record	423
	It's a Wrap	430
	Lists to Debate	431
	Trivia Answers	440

Remember the AFL

Foreword

The locker room floors were oily, not unlike the old and scarred wood under our desks at Sequoia Grammar School, in Oakland, California, in the 1940's and 50's. But this was New York City, in the famed and fabled Polo Grounds, once home to the baseball and football Giants—Bobby Thompson, Frank Gifford, Y.A. Tittle, and the like. But again, this was 1960, and the glory days of the Polo Grounds were long gone. The walk down the stairs from the showers, that barely dribbled as if water was rationed, was across dirty unkempt floors to the small metal lockers of a bygone era. The field itself was another story. Obviously, those 5-7,000 (overestimated to be 10-15,000) in the stands, counting the ticket takers and the concessionaires, had come to see the new curiosity in town—Harry Wismer's ragtag New York Titans, the precursors of the Jets.

As a player for the visiting Dallas Texans, Lamar Hunt's initial team, I was more concerned about playing the game than in noticing the surroundings, but I still couldn't help but be taken aback during warmups when I saw a 2x4 permanently implanted in the ground, delineating the left field foul line from beyond third base to the left field wall. While running routes during warmup, I also noticed a sharp drop from the infield to the outfield grass. I found myself literally running down and away from the ball as it descended from Cotton Davidson's hand. Apparently baseball drainage patterns were quite a bit different from the manicured perfection of Stanford Stadium, which I'd grown accustomed to over the previous four years.

Of course, it wasn't just the Polo Grounds. There were other less than magnificent stadiums in the first years of the AFL, unlike the pleasure palaces of today. Who among the early players in the AFL can forget that to get to the field in old War Memorial Stadium in Buffalo we actually trotted through

Foreword

the crowd, up the steps from the field to the concourse, past the concession stands, and then filed up the metal stairs to the dingy, small locker room above the hot dog and Coca-Cola stands, all the while chatting with the fans, with the kids trotting along side of us. That entrance and exit was only surpassed by our annual trips to Denver. Bears Stadium, the old baseball park that preceded Mile High where the visiting teams had to enter and exit the field coming out of a door under the end zone stands, hopeful of dodging the beer and soda expeditiously and carefully aimed to christen our comings and goings from the field. Boston University and Fenway Park in Boston were also not known as breathers, with the Red Sox field the hardest surface I'd ever played on except in the frozen snow and ice in Kansas City's old Memorial Stadium Park on Brooklyn Avenue. The third base area at Fenway, with the field tightly compacted to ensure the true roll of those infield grounders, was my unfortunate landing zone on a clean hard tackle from an undersized but big-of-heart cornerback from the Patriots who shortened one of my seasons by four or five games due to a dislocated, separated shoulder that took two surgeries to correct. Cunningham was the guy's name, and I can still recall my cartwheel after he hit me. I also remember the young kid who came to all our Patriot games and helped me to the locker room, as our trainer had to stay on the field with the team. Best part of that circumstance was that it elevated Otis Taylor from his job as my backup to starting the rest of the season, and we then teamed up as the starting wide outs the following two years. Otis went on to be one of the great unrewarded stars of the AFL.

In the early 60's, we played in high school stadiums—Jeppesen Field in Houston, exhibitions at P.C. Cobb in the Dallas-Fort Worth area, two games in two nights (the Oilers and the Broncos) at Wichita Falls

★ Chris Burford, Dallas Texans/Kansas City Chiefs

High School, in North Texas. My oh my, what Abner Haynes, Smokey Stover, Walt Corey, Max Boydston, Sherrill Headrick, Johnny Robinson, Jerry Cornelison, Duane Wood, Curley Johnson, myself and many others did for fifty dollars in those days!

But before ever getting the opportunity to play an exhibition and/or league game, we spent a hellish three to four weeks at training camp in Roswell, New Mexico, at the New Mexico Military Institute. The temperatures were in the high 90s to 100s, and we stayed in rooms without air conditioning and no screens on the windows. The grounds were surrounded by irrigation ditches, and I still have memories of the nightly attacks by the mosquitoes, some big enough to carry two passengers! And they worry about the UFO's there. That's where it all began for most of us on that initial 1960 AFL team. It wasn't just that Roswell was a small town; our only recourse for food (the fare at the military institute appeared to have been left over from Pershing's campaign against Pancho Villa a half century before) and source for entertainment was the Dairy Queen, kitty-corner from the campus, with appetites to be salved with a burger and a serenade by a pre-pigtailed Willie Nelson singing "Hello Walls" and Patsy Cline doing "Crazy Arms," while we took turns thrashing each other on the pinball machine. That exhibition season was further highlighted by trips to Little Rock, Arkansas, at the height of the school desegregation conflagrations, and to fog-bound Kezar stadium, in San Francisco, for our first tussle with the Oakland Raiders before a generously estimated crowd of five to ten thousand, none of which could be seen from the gray-shrouded field. An interesting aside was that eight months before, I'd been fortunate enough to have played in the East-West Shrine Game before sixty thousand screaming Shriners as part of the victorious West team with Don Meredith, Dick Bass, Larry Wilson, Jack Spikes, and Gail Cogdill, most of whom signed with the NFL.

It soon became apparent—and amazing—that those friends who signed with the NFL, as opposed to the fledgling AFL, were automatically considered superior players by the press and media of the day, when we all went to school, played and won and lost together, with a fairly even split proportionately going to each league. It was gratifying for us that those ten tough years of the AFL's existence ended with the Jets and Chiefs, though huge underdogs, knocking off the NFL Champs (Colts and Vikings) in the third and fourth Super Bowls. We went from discounted leftovers to the best the sport had to offer! It only came about by hard work, perseverance, and the knowledge that when talent meets attitude and desire … luck happens! The AFL was now real, competitive, and a force to be reckoned with, and the NFL knew it in spades. To get there took the push of a young, boyish, humble, but driven Texan who was only six years my senior, but was the instigator, dreamer, and guts of the league—Lamar Hunt. To put it together, stick it out, and find others of like mind to buy into his vision of the American Football League was at times a thankless task, but do it he did. It was accomplished with players, coaches, owners, and fans of a like mind, which is what this book is all about. A remembrance of a time gone by that underpins much of the offensive explosiveness and defensive imagination and creativity of the pro game of today.

This book by Dave Steidel highlights the personalities, achievements, and failings of all of us in the 60s who filled out those thirty-three-man rosters, covered those punts and kickoffs, lived the highs and lows, and had the experience of a lifetime bringing something new to the American public. However, I can't leave the topic without expressing the sadness and dissatisfaction I still feel in dealing with the old NFL syndrome of bypassing many of the great AFL players and coaches when considering their Canton annual honors. How is it possible that so few of the All-Time AFL team members (1960-69) have failed to be honored by the Pro-Football Hall of Fame? I played against the best in the AFL and NFL of that day, and it doesn't add up. As good as the NFL players were that have been enshrined from those days, there were as many just as good from the AFL who were overlooked. The writers, broadcasters, and selectors—many of whom never saw an AFL game—continue to ignore many of the greats. This book shines a bit of light on some of those great players and memorializes many of them, though it can't provide what they truly deserve. In chronicling events of each team and calling attention to their on-field exploits, Dave Steidel makes the effort to capture many of the moments that mattered and set the league apart from the then staid NFL. In particular, and with apologies to Art Powell, Charlie Hennigan, Paul Lowe, Cookie Gilcrest, Butch Byrd, Earl Faison, and Ernie Ladd, no Hall of Fame is complete without the likes of many of my former teammates with the Texans and Chiefs, in particular, safety Johnny Robinson, defensive lineman Jerry Mays, guard Ed Budde, tackle Jim Tyrer, tight end Fred Arbanas, running back Abner Haynes, cornerback and returner David Grayson, linebackers Sherrill Headrick and E.J. Holub, wideout Otis Taylor, and punter Jerrell Wilson.

Of course, proper recognition has been achieved and given to quarterback Len Dawson, linebackers Bobby Bell and Willie Lanier, defensive lineman Buck Buchanan, kicker Jan Stenerud, and Head Coach Hank Stram. The other Texan/Chief accorded pro football's highest honor is of course Lamar Hunt, without whom the world of professional and amateur sports as we know it would be much the lesser, and so many lives would have taken a different (and less prosperous and fulfilled) turn. Any creation, rendition, or synopsis of a history of the AFL begins and ends with Lamar, his dream, execution, and fruition of the "league that came in from the cold." Congratulations to Dave Steidel and his efforts to preserve a portion of pro football's past and entertain those who will only know of the AFL through these pages. With regards to all of us, but mainly my teammates, who had a part, large or small, in the birth and rise of the AFL and professional football.

— *Chris Burford*, Texans/Chiefs, 1960-67

BUFFALO BILLS

Texans

OILERS

L A
CHARGERS

BRONCOS

TITANS
OF NEW YORK

Remember the AFL

Who Are These Guys?
Introduction

I'm probably not unlike many other baby boomers who grew up in the 50s and 60s. My parents introduced me to baseball and football card collecting in 1958 when they arrived home from the grocery store one Saturday morning in late summer and pulled two wax packs from one of the bags. I can still remember that All-Star cards of Mickey Mantle and Jackie Jensen emerged from each. I still have them. As the summer turned into fall—and football season made the transition from vacation time to back-to-school time less painful—my rite of passage into second grade included a weekly jaunt to the corner store with my nickel allowance to purchase a pack of football cards. I had a ton by Thanksgiving and invented games and lineups to stretch every ounce of enjoyment of these new heroes. Johnny Unitas, L.G. Dupre, Clarence Peaks, and Pete Retzlaff were just a few of those who greeted me each morning as I awoke and were also my last contacts before my nightly prayers and jumping into bed. I was eight years old and infatuated with the glamour and glory of the sport and time.

The winter came and went, and the arrival of a new spring and summer was filled with collecting empty soda bottles to return to stores to receive a two cents per bottle payback, which went into my baseball card fund. The richest feeling I ever had was exchanging twelve bottles one day and racing to the store to buy a motherload of five packs of baseball cards. In those days Topps disbursed their sets in a series of seven releases spaced over the course of the season. Collecting and trading cards was a science back then, and many of us searched the town for stores that received the latest series first to get a jump on others.

By August of 1960 I was a full-fledged NFL supporter, eager for the first delivery of football cards to arrive at my neighborhood store. That's when the epiphany occurred! All I knew was that the wrapper said they were football cards. And all I was hoping for was a new Jimmy Brown, Lenny Moore, or Tommy McDonald. My initial reaction when I opened my first new pack of the season was confusion, then disappointment, followed by more confusion. The gum was always stale, that was

Introduction

a given, but what was with the college uniforms, and who were the Denver Broncos?

This was not the NFL, even a nine year old knew that. This was something completely different, but I didn't know what, or even why. Was the NFL not issuing football cards this year? Did I just waste a hard-earned nickel that could have been saved for a real set of cards? Was this the Twilight Zone? Some guy named Abner Haynes was wearing a green uniform. Roger Ellis wore a Michigan Wolverine helmet. Bill Kinard appeared to be waving to his mother in the stands as he ran with the ball, and New York Titan lineman Gene Cockrell looked like he was using a blocking dummy as a jousting pole. And then there was Billy Cannon! Now there's a name I knew. This must be that new league that was starting up—the American Football League! Okay, maybe not getting a Jimmy Brown wasn't so bad afterall.

The names of Topps and Fleer were irrelevant to this young football fan, and I had no idea that the two companies even existed. All I knew was that if the pack said they were football cards then I was buying it. It was another two weeks before the NFL cards arrived, but by then I already had a drawer full of cardboard cavaliers from the other league. The Eagles were on the local CBS station that Sunday, but in 1960 our antenna only received NBC and ABC without my father taking me up on the roof and physically turning it so I could see Norm Van Brocklin throw passes to Tommy McDonald through an otherwise scratchy, snowy screen. "Just watch the game that's on the other channel," I was told one Sunday.

Better advice had never been given to me. These were the guys I had on all those cards in my drawer! Although I missed seeing my favorite Eagle wings on the players' helmets, those helmets with the lightning bolts on ABC looked pretty cool. I didn't even notice on our seventeen-inch, black-and-white Motorola that the stripes on Denver's socks were different, only that their helmets looked like most of the colleges of the day—and man, did their quarterback throw a lot of passes. That, too, was pretty cool since my Eagles also passed more than they ran.

17

BILLY
CANNON
HALFBACK

HOUST
OIL

ROGER
ELLIS
CENTER

NEW YORK
TITANS

BILLY KINARD
HALFBACK
BUFFALO BILLS

GENE COCKRELL
GUARD
NEW YORK TITANS

Remember the AFL

With each Sunday, the need to bug my dad to turn the antenna became less and less important, while watching the team with the lightning bolts and their number twenty-three (Paul Lowe) breaking away for long-distance runs or seeing George Blanda in those oil derrick helmets pass to Billy Cannon became the pastime of choice. And it stayed that way for the next ten years. I was there from the get-go, one of the original card-carrying American Football League fans from its inception—and it all started because I bought the wrong pack of football cards.

You might say the league and I came of age together during the '60s. I loved watching the AFL's wide-open style of play. I never really thought Denver's vertically striped socks were that horrible or cared how many seats were empty in the cavernous Polo Grounds. I can still hear Curt Gowdy's voice in my head announcing that "Bobby Janik and Freddy Glick are deep to return the punt for Houston," or Paul Christman telling me that "Charlie Tolar fights oil well fires in the off season," and will forever hear Charlie Jones's distinctive voice reporting that the Raiders have just been penalized fifteen yards for unnecessary roughness. I have considered that maybe, just maybe, Abner Haynes had a secret plan when he decided to "kick to the clock" after winning the sudden-death coin toss in the longest championship game in AFL history and have witnessed countless missiles from John Hadl to Lance Alworth and touchdown bombs from Daryle Lamonica to Warren Wells. I remember going to bed on Sunday night, November 17, 1968, believing that the Jets held off the Raiders, late surge in "the Heidi game," not knowing about Charlie Smith's and Preston Reidlehuber's heroics until I read the newspaper the next morning. And I truly felt emancipated when Joe Willie and the Jets thrashed that horse team from the "other league" in Super Bowl III.

The AFL was more than just a fledgling football league in the '60s; it was anti-establishment, played by players for love of the game and at times, even played without getting paid. For many it was a second chance (and for some, the only chance) to play professional football. And I love to watch those old AFL highlight films and see Hank Stram strutting around the sidelines gloating about calling the "65 toss-power-trap" that Mike Garrett ran for a touchdown in Super Bowl IV. Football in the AFL was a simple game played with a pioneering spirit. It was "the league that came in from the cold." This book is for all those baby boomers and beyond who grew up following the AFL, who have glorious memories like those described above and for those who came to appreciate the American Football League long after it dropped its final curtain following the 1969 season. Three cheers for chief pioneer Lamar Hunt and his "foolish club." And long live the spirit and memory of the American Football League.

★ *Hank Stram, Kansas City Chiefs*

Not so Foolish

The AFL was born in 1959 when twenty-six-year-old Texas oil man Lamar Hunt was shut out in his bid to purchase an NFL franchise by the patriarchal leadership of that league. But the young millionaire would not be denied and set out to create his own professional football league in spite of the opposition. His brainchild would turn into the American Football League, fathered by pioneering businessmen who had the courage and tenacity to invest in a dream and take on the pro football monopoly that was the NFL.

Hunt first pitched his idea to Bud Adams of Houston, another Texas oil man who had been shutout of NFL ownership. Together the two spearheaded the movement to create a league of eight teams to begin play in 1960. On August 14 at an organizational meeting in Chicago, owners Harry Wismer of New York, Barron Hilton of Los Angeles, Max Winter, E. William Boyer and H. P. Skoglund of Minnesota, Bob Howsam of Denver along with Adams and Hunt made the new league a reality. It was officially given its name on August 22 in Dallas. Still seeking a seventh and eighth franchise, the league brought in Ralph Wilson Jr., of Buffalo at a meeting in New York on October 28, 1959, while Billy Sullivan Jr., of Boston came on board a month later, at the player-stocking draft on November 22.

★ *The founding fathers of the AFL dubbed themselves "The Foolish Club."*

The owners were ill-prepared for this significant undertaking, with some teams even turning to preseason college magazines for player information and scouting reports. The first AFL draft was done by offense and defense positions with four quarterbacks, two halfbacks, an end and a center being selected in the first of the thirty-three rounds. Only three of the eight selections—Ger Schwedes of Syracuse, LSU's Billy Cannon, and Penn State's Richie Lucas—signed with the new league. A week later the league endorsed World War II flying ace Joe Foss as its first commissioner.

Few pundits gave the league a chance beyond two years. But thanks in part to ABC and later NBC-TV and to these persistent millionaire owners, the new league stayed afloat amid the many bouts of player sabotage and theft long enough and strong enough to force a merger with those very NFL owners who turned them away. As the eight AFL teams spread throughout the country prepared for their inaugural season, one of their first tasks was to find the right men to lead them on the field. They sought head coaches who could not only organize but who could also draw fans with their style of play and competition. Over the course of the league's history, the original eight franchises grew to ten teams that employed twenty-six head coaches.

They were men who were not afraid to try something new or something different, men who would break the mold and build their own successful brand of football. The wide-open, fill-the-air-with-footballs style of play the league employed in the early years appealed to an equally different kind of fan—young ones. These fans appreciated the AFL's alternative to the NFL's reliance on three yards and a cloud of dust, and they would find new heroes among the castoffs and rookies who stocked the teams of this new league.

The league's first setback occurred shortly after the new year when the NFL fired a shot across the AFL bow in a last ditch effort to sink the fledgling league. Expansion committee chair George Halas offered the Minnesota owners a franchise and at the same time broke ground in Dallas. As the northern-most AFL team accepted the invitation, Hunt and company were suddenly sent scrambling to find an alternative location to host their eighth team. At the insistence of Hilton to bring a rivalry team to California, the owners awarded an eight-man syndicate headed by Chet Soda a franchise in Oakland. More disputes followed, with the courts deciding the fates of All-Americans Billy Cannon, Johnny Robinson, and Charlie Flowers who signed contracts with teams from both leagues while each cried foul on the other. All three went to the AFL.

After Independence Day in 1960, the first AFL training camps opened with more than 800 hopefuls vying for 264 roster spots. And when the exhibition season kicked off in Buffalo on the next to last day of July, the American Football League was finally off and running on a journey that would last through the decade.

In the end, the dream of this Foolish Club of owners would turn the AFL from "the other league," into "the league that came in from the cold."

Not so Foolish

One of the first tasks for the Foolish Club was to hire head coaches to run their new teams. Match the LETTER of the coach, and name him, with questions 1-8 below.

A — LOS ANGELES CHARGERS
B — OAKLAND RAIDERS
C — DALLAS TEXANS
D — NEW YORK TITANS
E — BUFFALO BILLS
F — HOUSTON OILERS
G — BOSTON PATRIOTS
H — DENVER BRONCOS

1. I coached the L.A. Rams in the NFL for five years but was fired after the 1959 season. I coached in more AFL championship games than any other coach. _____

2. I was the only coach to be the head man for three of the original AFL teams and won two AFL titles. My Western Illinois team was undefeated in 1959. _____

3. I was an All-American at Notre Dame and the first AFL coach-of-the-year in 1960 but was fired after five games in 1961. _____

4. I was an assistant coach on three NFL champions in Detroit in the 1950s. My AFL team finished 13-16-1 in 1960 and 1961. _____

5. I had a pretty good run as head coach at the Naval Academy for eight years before coming to the AFL. Unfortunately, I was the first AFL head coach to be fired. _____

6. I was the only coach my AFL franchise had throughout the ten AFL years and my teams played in three AFL championship games and two Super Bowls. _____

7. I coached in the NFL and Canada prior to my AFL stint. Under my direction my team was 7-20-1. _____

8. My eccentric owner at times was a better slinger than I was. After refusing to be demoted to assistant coach I was fired and later surfaced as head coach of another AFL team. _____

Remember the AFL

9. Match each team owner in "The Foolish Club" with his picture.

A. Billy Sullivan, Boston; B. Lamar Hunt, Dallas; C. Cal Kunz, Denver; D. Bud Adams, Houston; E. Harry Wismer, NY; F. Ralph Wilson, Buffalo; G. Barron Hilton, Los Angeles; H. Wayne Valley, Oakland; I. Commissioner Joe Foss

Top row, (l to r)

_____ , _____
_____ , _____
_____ , _____
_____

Bottom row, (l to r)

_____ , _____

10. Match the first players drafted into the AFL with the team that drafted them.
(extra credit if you can also match the college these players played for)

TEAM		PLAYER		COLLEGE
1. Boston	_____	A. Richie Lucas	_____	Syracuse
2. Buffalo	_____	B. Don Meredith	_____	SMU
3. Dallas	_____	C. Billy Cannon	_____	Notre Dame
4. Denver	_____	D. Gerhard Schwedes	_____	LSU
5. Houston	_____	E. Monty Stickles	_____	Penn State
6. Los Angeles	_____	F. George Izo	_____	Trinity
7. Minnesota	_____	G. Dale Hackbart	_____	Notre Dame
8. New York	_____	H. Roger LeClerc	_____	Wisconsin

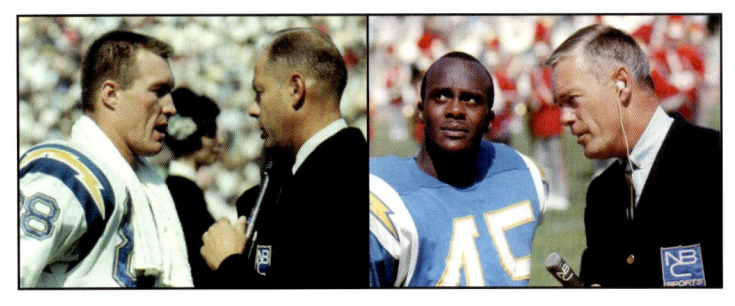

11. In the early days Curt Gowdy was one of the main AFL announcers on TV broadcasts. The other was Jack Buck. Who was Gowdy's, and who was Buck's color man?

_____

_____

26

Not so Foolish

12. The memorably hideous uniforms (at left) of the Denver Broncos in 1960 and 1961 featured the infamous vertically striped socks. The Broncos bought these from a defunct post season All-Star game. What was this bowl game called? The _____ Bowl

13. What preseason magazine did the AFL owners use as their scouting guide for their first team stocking player draft? _____

14. Prior to Pete Rozelle becoming commissioner of the NFL, Lamar Hunt and his fellow owners held meetings for support with Rozelle's predecessor. What former team owner preceded Rozelle as the NFL's commissioner and what team did he once own?
_____

15. In 1959, Heisman Trophy winner Billy Cannon signed to play with the NFL Los Angeles Rams prior to his final game. Then, after his final game, Cannon also signed to play with the AFL Houston Oilers for double the amount that the Rams offered him. The NFL and AFL went to court over the signing dispute with the AFL winning Cannon's rights. What other running back, for Cannon's last game opponent in the Sugar Bowl, also signed with the NFL (Giants) and AFL (Chargers) leading to another AFL court victory? _____

16. Match the AFL teams with the stadium it called home at the start of 1960.

   A. New York Titans   _____   1. War Memorial
   B. Denver Broncos   _____   2. Jeppesen Stadium
   C. Los Angeles Chargers   _____   3. The Cotton Bowl
   D. Houston Oilers   _____   4. Mile High Stadium
   E. Dallas Texans   _____   5. Rice Stadium
   F. Boston Patriots   _____   6. Bears Stadium
   G. Buffalo Bills   _____   7. Braves Field
   H. Oakland Raiders   _____   8. The Polo Grounds
                                            9. Candlestick Park
                                            10. Kezar Stadium
                                            11. The Coliseum

17. Much has been made of the Denver Broncos first year uniforms, but what also lends to the Broncos lore is their accommodations at their first year's training camp. At what Colorado college did Denver set up their first training camp? _____

18. One of Oakland's original owners, Y.C. (Chet) Soda, had a hand in selecting the original (but later rejected) team name. The name referenced the way Soda would greet people, by saying "Hello _____".

19. The AFL's first commissioner, Joe Foss, was decorated with the Congressional Medal of Honor for gunning down twenty-six Japanese planes, and his squadron downed an additional 135 enemy aircraft in World War II. It was the most successful airborne unit in marine history, earning his group this nickname.
   A. The Black Sheep squadron
   B. Joe's Flying Circus
   C. Foss' Fancy Flyers
   D. The Dandy Dozen
   _____

20. When Foss returned from the war he entered politics and served two terms as governor of his home state. Which state was it? _____

Part 1

The Progress of the Seasons

From its beginning on September 9, 1960, through its last game, January 4, 1970, the American Football League was a roller coaster ride through adventureland.

In the early years the Houston Oilers and L. A./San Diego Chargers were the class of the league. Boston and Dallas showed signs of life enough to challenge them, but they always seemed to end up a step behind. The Denver Broncos, Oakland Raiders, and New York Titans had flashes of hope but mostly just a lot of futility.

In their third year, the highpoint for the league was the televised 1962 Championship Game that went into double overtime. It was the longest game in pro football history at the time and was the springboard to a revived emergence for the league. The AFL in 1963 saw Al Davis turn a downtrodden 1-13 Oakland Raider team into an upset-minded challenger with a 10-4 record, coming within a game of winning the Western Division. They even defeated the eventual AFL Champion San Diego Chargers both times they played them.

In the East, the Buffalo Bills and Boston Patriots both overtook the three-time division champion Oilers and were forced to extend their season with a playoff game to break their season-ending tie. A year later, the Bills, Patriots, and Chargers were again the class of the league—Oakland took a slight step backward while the Broncos and the renamed New York Jets were still searching for a winning formula.

By the mid '60s the league's first group of stars that included Abner Haynes, George Blanda, Billy Cannon, Cookie Gilchrist, and Lionel Taylor were showing signs of age, while a new group of youthful phenoms like Lance Alworth, Mike Garrett, Bobby Bell, and Jim Nance were ready to carry the ball to the next level. While the Chargers and Bills were playing in the next two championship games in '64 and '65, Boston and the Kansas City Chiefs continued to dog their heels, waiting for each to slip. And then came Broadway Joe, the Gogolak hijacking, the player raids, and finally, the merger!

San Diego did finally slip in 1966, and the

★ George Blanda, Houston Oilers

Chiefs, always ready, took control of the West. The East again was a nail biter to the end, with Buffalo again edging out the perennial bridesmaid Boston Patriots. Super Bowl I become a reality—but also a humbling defeat.

Then in 1967 Al Davis had his Raiders primed to destroy the rest of the competition. With more balance and force than any AFL team had ever shown, the "pride and poise boys," led by Daryle Lamonica, "The Mad Bomber," surged to the best ever AFL record of 13-1. But again the Super Bowl was a disappointment.

The league truly came of age in 1968. Joe and the Jets ran away from the other Eastern Division teams, "the Heidi game" created a national phenomenon, and a second season-ending division tie had to be broken in a playoff game, this time in the West. The oddsmakers said the NFL's Colts would destroy the Jets by 17 points in Super Bowl III, and Joe Namath guaranteed a New York victory. Joe was right!

On January 4, 1970, the AFL played its final game; the last AFL Championship game between the two most dominant teams over the last three years, the Chiefs and Raiders. It was only fitting that the Chiefs, the franchise owned by the AFL's founding father, would close out the league's existence victoriously. And then in the last AFL vs. NFL Super Bowl, the Chiefs would gain parity and respect for the AFL by defeating the best the NFL had to offer. Super Bowls I and II went to the NFL, Super Bowls III and IV to the AFL. On the following pages the progress of the AFL seasons will once again come to life.

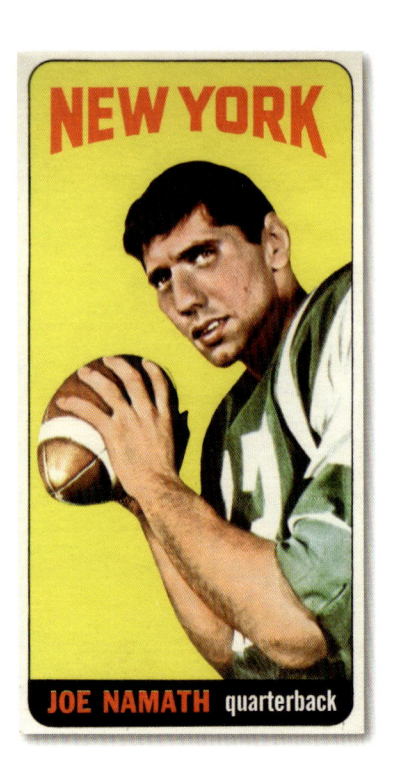

1960

AMERICAN FOOTBALL LEAGUE – 1960 FINAL STANDINGS

EASTERN DIVISION

TEAM	GP	W	L	T	PF	PA	PCT.
HOUSTON OILERS	14	10	4	0	379	285	0.714
NEW YORK TITANS	14	7	7	0	382	399	0.500
BUFFALO BILLS	14	5	8	1	296	303	0.393
BOSTON PATRIOTS	14	5	9	0	286	349	0.357

WESTERN DIVISION

TEAM	GP	W	L	T	PF	PA	PCT.
LOS ANGELES CHARGERS	14	10	4	0	373	336	0.714
DALLAS TEXANS	14	8	6	0	362	253	0.571
OAKLAND RAIDERS	14	6	8	0	319	388	0.429
DENVER BRONCOS	14	4	9	1	309	393	0.321

Depending on who you talk to, Billy Cannon is remembered for many outstanding feats. To some it's his Heisman Trophy college career, to others it's his Halloween run for LSU, to others it's his historic court case that pitted the AFL against the NFL for his playing rights. Others will recall his 88-yard touchdown reception to win the first AFL championship game, and his 35-yard TD reception to win the AFL title again the next year. He also led the league in rushing in 1961. But what no one can debate is that Billy Cannon, everybody's All-American in 1959, was the first big-name signing to give credibility to the AFL.

■ BOSTON PATRIOTS ■

GETTING A JUMP ON THE REST OF THE league, the Boston Patriots' Tony Discenzo put his toe into a Joe Foss-signed J5-V Spalding football on Friday evening, September 9, 1960, on Boston University's Nickerson Field and simultaneously kicked off the history of the American Football League.

The Boston franchise of the AFL was created in late November of 1959, only days before the first AFL player draft. They were the eighth and last team admitted. Without a scouting combine or staff, owner Billy Sullivan and company were hardly prepared to embark on such a monumental task. Yet, after

The Progress of the Seasons – 1960

putting together their original team, the still-to-be-named franchise looked relatively solid.

A contest to name the team ensued with thousands of entries. From the lot, a team of local sportswriters selected the name suggested by no less than seventy-four entrants. Christened the "Patriots" for local historic flavor, it was fitting that the team's first training camp opened on July 4, 1960.

Shortly after the team was named, a *Boston Globe* artist penned a cartoon character logo depicting an offensive center dressed as a minuteman ready to snap the ball. That logo became the team's mascot, "Pat the Patriot."

On July 30, the Patriots faced the Buffalo Bills in the first AFL exhibition game. With Discenzo's kick on September 9, the Pats began the AFL's first regular-season game. By virtue of a 43-6 drubbing of Denver in an exhibition game a few weeks earlier, the Patriots were favored over the Broncos—who failed to win an exhibition game—at home. As could be expected, the Patriots wore red, white, and blue uniforms consisting of red jerseys with white and blue trim. Their white helmets were highlighted with a tri-cornered minuteman hat and the players' numbers on each side.

Armed with thirty-four-year-old Boston College alum Ed "Butch" Songin at quarterback and All-American Ron Burton at halfback, the Patriots scored first on a Gino Cappelletti field goal for a 3-0 lead, but Denver followed with the AFL's first touchdown later in the half. Ahead only 7-3 in the third

★ *Boston's Larry Garron follows his blockers against Denver in the AFL's first game.* ★

quarter, Denver's Gene Mingo returned Tommy Greene's punt 76 yards for the game-winning score. A 10-yard touchdown pass from Songin to Jim Colclough, also a BC grad, drew Boston to within 3 points, but the Pats came up disappointingly short, losing 13-10, thus also becoming the first team to lose an AFL game. Boston won its first game the next week in New York's Polo Grounds 28-24, but not without the AFL's first controversy. Coach Lou Saban relieved Songin with rookie Tommy Greene, another local from Holy Cross, at quarterback, who found split end Colclough in the end zone with one minute left, making the score New York 24 Boston 21. The defense was able to force a punt on the Titans next possession. But with three seconds left, the punt never happened. New York punter Rick Sapienza fumbled the snap, which was recovered by Boston safety Chuck Shonta, after the Pats' defensive back Gino Cappelletti allegedly kicked the fumble forward 10 yards. Shonta returned his pick-up 52 yards into the Titan end zone for the winning touchdown. New York immediately protested to the league office, but Commissioner Joe Foss denied the contention that Cappelletti illegally kicked the ball, and Boston's first victory became official.

The Pats dropped four of their next five games before beating the Raiders, Titans, and Dallas Texans in succession to pull to .500 at 5-5. But losing the last four games of the season dropped them to the bottom of the Eastern Division with a 5-9 maiden season. Noteworthy in the last game of the season against Houston was Gino Cappelletti appearing for the first time on offense. Used as a defensive back throughout the first season, Gino intercepted four passes. He caught one pass against the Oilers, good for 28 yards, and began an offensive career that would end with him being the Patriots all-time leader in receptions over his ten AFL years. Boston's interest at home among the local followers ranged from an attendance low of 8,446 against Oakland to a season high of 27,123 against Houston, an average home crowd of 16,984, which was higher than both of the league venues in New York and Los Angeles.

---

1. The first game in AFL history was played in Boston between the Denver Broncos and the Patriots at Boston University's Braves Field. What other three venues did the Patriots call home in New England during the AFL's ten-year history?

The Progress of the Seasons – 1960

Although Butch Songin threw 22 touchdowns for the season, his performance was inconsistent and disappointing. He completed 47% of his tosses including 15 interceptions. On the year, Lou Saban used no less than four quarterbacks in an effort to generate offense for the lethargic Pats whose 286 points were a league low. Alan Miller and Dick Christy handled the rushing with 416 and 363 yards respectively, while Jim Colclough's 49 receptions were a team high. Miller and Christy chipped in for 29 and 26 catches followed by Ron Burton's 23. Defensive standouts Tom Addison at linebacker and Ross O'Hanley at safety were selected for the All-AFL team.

Leading passers	Attempts	Completions	Pct	TDs	Yards	Int
Ed "Butch" Songin	392	187	48%	22	2476	15
Tommy Greene	63	27	43%	1	251	0

Leading rushers	Attempts	Yards gained	Average	TDs
Alan Miller	108	416	4.1	1
Dick Christy	78	363	4.6	4
Ron Burton	66	280	4.2	1
Jim Crawford	51	238	4.7	2

Leading receivers	Caught	Yards gained	Average	TDs
Jim Colclough	49	666	13.6	9
Alan Miller	29	284	9.8	2
Dick Christy	26	268	10.3	2
Ron Burton	21	196	9.3	0
Tom Stephens	22	320	14.5	3
Oscar Lofton	19	360	18.9	4

Leading scorers	TDs	XPM	XPA	FGM	FGA	PTS
Gino Cappelletti	0	30	32	8	21	60
Jim Colclough	9					54

2. The AFL instituted several new wrinkles in its rookie year, including players' names on the back of their jerseys and the 2-point conversion option. Even the referees got into the act. What was different about the AFL officials uniforms, in contrast to those of the NFL?

■ DENVER BRONCOS ■

CLAD IN MUSTARD-GOLD JERSEYS AND mud-brown pants, the Denver Broncos were not expected to mount much of a challenge to the strong Boston roster on opening night. But riding the crest of the momentum created by a 59-yard touchdown pass and a 76-yard punt return for a touchdown, the Broncos earned themselves the first victory in AFL history by dropping the Patriots 13-10. Posting an early season record of 3-1, the Broncos' passing carnival quickly established that if they were going to win, it would not be by relying on a sustained ground attack.

Using the thin Colorado air to carry their assaults on other AFL teams, they developed a game plan that called strictly for air mail. Quarterback Frank Tripucka and company averaged a league-high 36 passes a game while attempting only 31 rushes per contest. Fullback Dave Rolle's 501 yards accounted for 42 percent of the Broncos ground yardage with Lionel Taylor's 1,235 pass-catching yardage logging 38 percent of the Broncos air traffic. Besides Taylor's league-leading heroics for the Broncos, Denver also boasted all-purpose halfback Gene Mingo, who scored a league-leading 123 points on 18 field goals, 33 extra points, and 6 touchdowns. However, Denver's luck ran out after their first six games, which saw a strong 4-2 record sink to a season ending 4-9-1 record—failing to bring home another win in their last eight games. Denver not only finished last in the AFL West but also ended up last in rushing offense as well as defending against the rush.

The team was the property of the Howsam family, owners of the minor league Denver Bears baseball team of the Pacific Coast League. They also owned the Bears' stadium, aptly called Bears Stadium. The Broncos would also play their home games there. Their coach was Frank Filchock, brought from Saskatchewan of the Canadian League, where general manager Dean Griffing was also recruited. Filchock opened his preseason summer camp in July at the Colorado College of Mines compound where Denver was able to stash some two hundred aspiring professional football recruits on the fourth floor of an army-type barracks. Helping Filchock mold his team was former Notre Dame quarterback Frank Tripucka. Tripucka had played for Detroit and the Chicago Cardinals prior to jumping to the CFL. As it turned out, the play-calling recruits could not hold a candle to the cagy old pro and Tripucka was beckoned into active duty before the season began.

As with several other teams in the new AFL, the Broncos were operating on a shoestring budget. And when it came time to outfit the young Broncos, Griffing went shopping for the cheapest deal he could find. At a price he was willing to pay, Denver's tightwad GM found a set of uniforms in Tucson, Arizona, where a one-time college all-star game known as the Copper Bowl had gone under. Griffing had struck what he thought was gold—the game's brown helmets, gold shirts with brown numbers, and brown pants became the property of the Denver Broncos. To top off the deal, Griffing even took the peculiar-looking, vertically striped socks of alternating gold and brown. The players called them hideous and gaudy, while the NFL simply held their hands

The Progress of the Seasons – 1960

over their mouths and laughed. The socks became famous for their uniqueness and the ridicule heaped on them and would eventually find themselves at the bottom of an exorcising bonfire.

The Broncos played all of their exhibition games and their first three regular-season games on the road while renovations were made to Bears Stadium. After winning their first game in Boston, the Broncs stampeded into Buffalo. The Denver defenders intercepted 6 Bills' passes, 4 by Austin Gonsoulin, with the biggest of the day snared by Johnny Piatt, who grabbed an errant throw midway through the fourth quarter and returned it 40 yards for a Denver score and a 27-21 win. The young Broncos, who started the season with few expectations, already had two wins on the road, and readied themselves to capture a third.

In New York the next week, Denver was ready to make it three straight by leading the Titans 21-17 with 24 seconds left in the game. On fourth down from their own ten, Filchock sent in his punting team to push the Titans deep in their own half of the field, giving them only a remote chance of scoring. With New York sending everyone in on a charge to block the punt, the Broncos were unable to contain it, and the blocked ball rolled loose at the 10. Titan safety Roger Donahoo picked it up and ran into the end zone, and what had looked like an undefeated team suddenly found themselves on the losing end for the first time, 24-21.

October 2 marked the Broncos first home game, and 18,372 fans came out to "the Bear" to watch. The opponents were the 2-1 Oakland Raiders, who also lacked a home field. Multi-talented Gene Mingo started the scoring with a 17-yard field goal in the first quarter, and with Oakland leading 7-3 in the second, Tripucka went to work with his new flanker, Lionel Taylor. Taylor had been cut by the Chicago Bears who were not happy with his performance as a defensive back. Signing with the Broncos, Taylor was on the defensive depth chart until an after-practice touch game in which he caught everything Tripucka threw his way. Looking for some spark for the offense, Filchock chose the first home game to unveil his new find. On a third and six "Trip," he connected for his first of many TD passes to Taylor, a 12-yarder. Later in the period Taylor lined up as a slotback behind the right tackle. After the center snap, Taylor faked a block and circled behind a waiting escort where he snagged Tripucka's up-the-middle screen pass and ran 20 yards for another score. As the half drew to a close defensive end, Bill Yelberton intercepted a Tom Flores pass and pranced 20 yards for a score, giving Denver a 24-7 lead. The Broncs went on to victory by a score of 31-14, and had a 3-1 record on the season.

Four Gene Mingo field goals and a 1-yard plunge by Al Carmichael was not enough to overtake the Chargers in their next game and the Broncs fell to 3-2, but still had the lead in the West. In week seven, Denver held onto its Western Conference lead by beating the Patriots 31-24 in a spectacular comeback. They scored 31 unanswered points in the second half, producing 2 touchdowns in less than 2 minutes. Tripucka found Carmichael for a 21-yard score and followed that up with a 19-yarder to Bill Jessup. In the fourth, the Broncos pulled a flea flicker that Tripucka no doubt drew up in the huddle, hitting Lionel Taylor with a 50-yard hitch pass. Taylor immediately flipped the ball to Carmichael who was trailing the play. Today, it is known as a hook and ladder; back then it just happened. Carmichael went the final 35 yards for 6 points. Still behind 24-21, Tripucka continued to drive his stallions and hit Taylor again for an 8-yard score. Denver had now scored 4 touchdowns in nine and a half minutes. Mingo added a late field goal to make the score 31-24, but Boston's Butch Songin was looking for some payback and had the Patriots marching through Bronco territory. With a chance to win on the last play of the game, Songin fired a bomb into the end zone, but Denver's Bob McNamara nabbed it in front of the waiting Patriot receiver. What looked like a 24-0 defeat at the half miraculously turned into a heart-stopping, crowd-pleasing 31-24 victory in full view of ABC's national audience.

Trailing late in the game the next week in Dallas, Gene Mingo had a shot at tying the Texans at 17-17 with a last-second field goal but missed it, dropping the Broncs to 4-3, but still keeping them on top of the West.

By now, Tripucka and Taylor were one of the hottest passing combinations in the AFL. With the league's worst rushing offense, Tripucka was passing more often than the team was running. Fullback Dave Rolle was their leading ball carrier after running mate Al Carmichael fell prey to injury after rushing for 211 yards, leaving his halfback position to kicker Gene Mingo. Mingo finished second on the team with 323 yards. But it was the passing attack that kept the Broncos in most games, and Tripucka threw more often than anyone. He threw 478 times, completing 248 for 3,038 yards and 24 touchdowns. The rugged veteran completed an astounding 51 percent of his throws but also connected with opponents 34 times for another league high. More often than not his target was the incomparable Lionel Taylor, who didn't start on offense until the third game of the season. Taylor went on to catch an AFL high 92 passes, including 12 for touchdowns. The next best receiver in gold and brown was Carmichael who caught 32 before being injured. After him were Ken Carpenter with 29 and Bill Greer with 22. A loss to Houston dropped Denver to .500 at 4-4, with their biggest margin of defeat coming the next week in Dallas at 34-7. The Broncos were now fading fast.

On November 27, a snow-covered field in Denver hosted one of those classic Western shootouts in which only the fastest guns survive. Buffalo blitzed the Broncos in the first half by outscoring them 17-7, and then bullied them some more in the third with 21 points, holding a 38-7 advantage five minutes into the second half. Denver finally put up 7 points of their own when Frank Tripucka hit his favorite receiver, Lionel Taylor, with a short 5-yard hitch pass. Shaking loose, Taylor was off and running for an 80-yard touchdown. As the fourth quarter began, the Bills led 38-21. Early in the fourth

The Progress of the Seasons – 1960

Taylor again caught one of Denver's deceptive up-the-middle screen passes and had himself another touchdown, this time for 24 yards as the gap closed to 38-28. Moments later Tripucka was moving the Broncs again. And again he connected with Taylor for a 35-yard touchdown pass. Denver's combo of Tripucka-to-Taylor struck for 3 TD's in the second half, and inside of the first seven minutes of the fourth quarter put 14 more points on the board. Taylor was enjoying what would become a patented receiving day. What Taylor lacked in speed he made up for with elusiveness. And today his elusiveness led to 9 catches for almost 200 yards.

With Denver digging into the inch-deep snow that covered the field, the Bills offense went into hibernation. On Denver's next possession Tripucka had them moving again—all the way to the 1 yard line where fullback Don Allen punched across the goal line with a little more than four minutes left. It appeared that all Buffalo could do was sit and watch, and to the 7,785 fans who braved the frigid temperature and snow, sitting and watching the victory unfold was fine with them. A chance to win or tie was all they were hoping for as the clock ticked down to 1:15 left. Then the Broncos got their final chance from their own 33 yard line. Those who were still in the stands had their fingers crossed as Tripucka again took to the air. But many of the fingers were crossed in hopes that he wouldn't find the Bill defenders for a sixth time. Trip connected on 3 quick tosses and then got some help from the officials who flagged Buffalo for pass interference. The Denver drive came to a halt at the Bills 12 yard line with nine seconds remaining. Gene Mingo put the finishing touch on the drive with a 19-yard field goal and the Broncos had a 38-38 comeback tie that in the end seemed like a victory. It was the last bright spot of their season as they failed to record a victory in their last eight games, finishing with a disappointing 4-9-1 record after jumping out to a Western Division-leading 3-1 record. The absence of a consistent running game was partially responsible for the Broncos reliance on the pass. But it was also the inability to keep the opposition off the scoreboard that kept Tripucka throwing. Denver had the worst defense against the run and finished last in total defense. No one gave up more points than the 393 surrendered by the Broncos. Never reaching the 20,000 mark in attendance for any of their home games, the Broncos had the second-lowest attendance among the AFL teams with a 13,048 average.

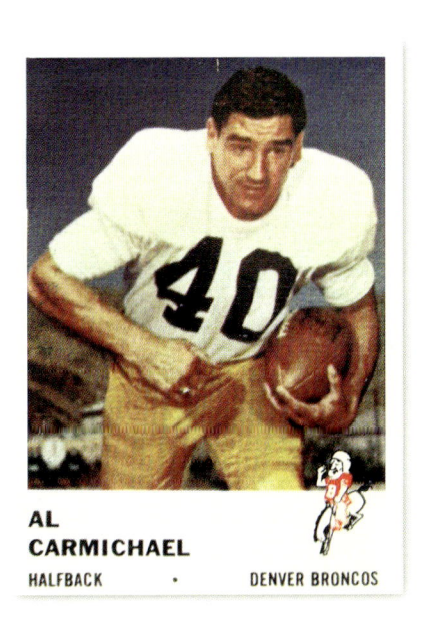

AL CARMICHAEL
HALFBACK • DENVER BRONCOS

Leading passers	Attempts	Completions	Pct	TDs	Yards	Int
Frank Tripucka	478	248	52%	24	3038	34
George Herring	22	9	41%	0	137	1

Leading rushers	Attempts	Yards gained	Average	TDs
Dave Rolle	130	501	3.9	2
Gene Mingo	83	323	3.9	4
Henry Bell	43	238	5.5	0
Al Carmichael	41	211	5.1	2

Leading receivers	Caught	Yards gained	Average	TDs
Lionel Taylor	92	1235	13.4	12
Al Carmichael	32	616	19.2	5
Ken Carpenter	29	350	12.0	1
Jim Greer	22	284	12.9	1
Dave Rolle	21	122	5.8	1
Gene Mingo	19	156	8.2	1

Leading scorers	TDs	XPM	XPA	FGM	FGA	PTs
Gene Mingo	6	33	36	18	28	123
Lionel Taylor	12					72

3. Who scored the first touchdown in AFL history—a 59-yard pass from Frank Tripucka after catching just 1 TD pass in 1958 with Green Bay and not playing at all in 1959?

▪ DALLAS TEXANS ▪

THE DALLAS TEXANS WERE THE FLAGship franchise for the newly formed American Football League. Owned by league founding father Lamar Hunt, they had the resources and determination to make his brainchild a success. Pitted in a head-to-head battle against the NFL expansion Cowboys for the territorial rights of Texas, the Texans shared the Cotton Bowl with their rivals and played to similar attendance numbers all year long. The Texans were the better team, but the Cowboys had better opponents, drawing on marquee visitors

The Progress of the Seasons – 1960

like Jim Brown, Sam Huff, and Norm Van Brocklin to fill their seats. In contrast to the blue-and-white Cowboys, Hunt outfitted his team in red jerseys and white pants. Their helmets were a solid red with the great state of Texas planted on the sides. A gold star inside of the state represented the city of Dallas.

The Texans were the preseason favorite to win the Western Division as the season kicked off. But a disappointing 8-6 record at season's end had everyone scratching their heads to explain what went wrong. Of the 6 losses, 3 were by less than 4 points. In the opener the difference was a mere point to Los Angeles. Week four saw them lose to New York by 2 and by 1 the following week against Oakland. Digging out from a 2-4 start, the team, coached by the venerable Hank Stram, went 6-2 thereafter, finishing two games behind the division-winning Chargers.

Dallas featured the best running game in the AFL, paced by league rushing leader Abner Haynes, who ran for 875 yards, a 5.6-yard average. LSU All-American Johnny Robinson had 458 yards, placing him ninth among all AFL runners. Behind him in tenth place was teammate Jack Spikes, who gained another 457 yards. Haynes was also the team's receiving leader with 55 passes caught, and he picked up the first AFL Rookie of the Year award. Stanford rookie Chris Burford was a close second in receiving with 46 catches and 5 touchdowns. Robinson caught 41 and tight end Max Boydston 29. Noteworthy in the Texan backfield was young Clem Daniels, a third-string runner from Prairie View College. Daniels carried the ball only one time in 1960, a 2-yard loss. A change of venue the next year would be his ticket to stardom as Daniels fled to Oakland where he became the all-time leading rusher in AFL history.

Led by former Baylor quarterback Cotton Davidson, the Dallas team had a definite Texas and Southwest flavor. Besides Davidson in the Dallas backfield were Haynes from North Texas State, Spikes from TCU, and Robinson from LSU. Other "good old boys" from the Lone Star State on the original roster were tackle Jerry Cornelison from SMU, Hunt's alma mater, backup quarterback Hunter Enis, and Sherrill Headrick from TCU, and halfback Curley Johnson from Houston.

Offensively Dallas was in the middle of the pack in scoring points and a lowly seventh of eight in passing. Haynes was selected for the all-league team. He was joined on offense by guard Bill Krisher. The defense gave up fewer points than any other team, a feat they accomplished in four of the ten AFL years. Led by all-league selections Mel Branch from LSU at defensive end and middle linebacker

41

Sherrill Headrick, the Texans were a force to be reckoned with against the run as well as the pass. The secondary of Duane Wood, Don Flynn, Jimmy Harris, and David Webster picked off 32 passes, second only to Buffalo's 33. But Stram grew frustrated by the defense's inconsistency. Of the five league shutouts in 1960, three came at the hands of the Texan defense. The first came in a rematch of their opening season loss against the Chargers, a 17-0 win. But a week later they allowed the New York Titans 37 points. Later in the season the defense fell victim to the Patriots for 42 points, followed by a 41-point offensive performance by the Titans, both losses. Then in a complete turnaround, they shut out both Houston and Boston on successive weeks and ended the season by allowing Buffalo only a single touchdown, winning 24-7. In the last three games Headrick, Branch, and the Texan defense gave up a total of only 7 points.

While battling for both the Western Division lead and the hearts of Texans, Dallas outdrew all the other AFL teams as well as the NFL Cowboys. Their average home attendance was 24,500 with their largest, as expected, coming on their season opener against the Chargers, when 42,000 clicked through the gates.

Leading passers	Attempts	Completions	Pct	TDs	Yards	Int
Cotton Davidson	379	179	47%	15	2474	16
Hunter Enis	54	30	55%	1	357	2

Leading rushers	Attempts	Yards gained	Average	TDs
Abner Haynes	156	875	5.6	9
Johnny Robinson	98	458	4.7	4
Jack Spikes	115	457	4.0	5
Bo Dickinson	35	143	4.1	1

Leading receivers	Caught	Yards gained	Average	TDs
Abner Haynes	55	576	10.4	3
Chris Burfordl	46	789	17.1	5
Johnny Robinson	41	611	14.9	4
Max Boydston	29	357	12.3	3
Jack Spikes	11	158	14.3	0
Curley Johnson	10	174	17.4	1

Leading scorers	TDs	XPM	XPA	FGM	FGA	PTs
Jack Spikes	5	35	37	13	31	103
Abner Haynes	12					72

4. The conception of the American Football League occurred late in 1958 when young millionaire Lamar Hunt tried unsuccessfully to buy an NFL franchise. From that point on, Hunt began carving out a path to form his own league, which became the AFL. Which NFL team did Hunt try to purchase?

■ OAKLAND RAIDERS ■

AS THE OAKLAND RAIDERS GEARED UP for their first game in black, gold, and white, the last addition to the American Football League was a potpourri of names and faces pieced together to fill the team's roster. By virtue of a special draft to stock the team after the original Minnesota franchise dropped out to join the NFL, the Raiders selected players from the other seven AFL teams who could protect eleven players, putting the rest of the roster at the disposal of Oakland.

Together for little more than a month, the Raiders, originally dubbed "The Señors" by lead owner Chet Soda, were at a decided disadvantage for more reasons than one. The city of Oakland had a team—but had to travel across the bay to see them. Overtures to use a stadium on the right side of the bay in Strawberry Canyon owned by the University of California were unsuccessful. On September 11, the Raiders wrote the first chapter of their history with a home game played in a city that really didn't want them. San Francisco's Kezar Stadium, home to the NFL 49ers, was the site for this historic game as the Raiders hosted the Houston Oilers. Led by former Navy coach Eddie Erdelatz, the Raiders lost their first two games at home before gaining their first victory on the road in Houston 14-13. Their first home win was not until October 16, over the Boston Patriots, lifting them to a 3-3 record. With Tony Teresa, Billy Lott, and Jack Larsheid eating up yardage on the ground, quarterback Tom Flores, out of the University of the Pacific, provided the aerial assault, throwing to Lott, Teresa, and rookie ends Gene Prebola from Boston University and Al Goldstein from North Carolina. Lott led the team with 49 catches. The team held together under Erdelatz's fine direction and registered a .500 record through their first ten games. They then lost their next three before closing out the year with a 48-10 thumping of Denver in their second home away from home, San Francisco's Candlestick Park, by scoring 31 points in the fourth quarter to win 48-10. The Raiders played their final three home games of 1960 in Candlestick.

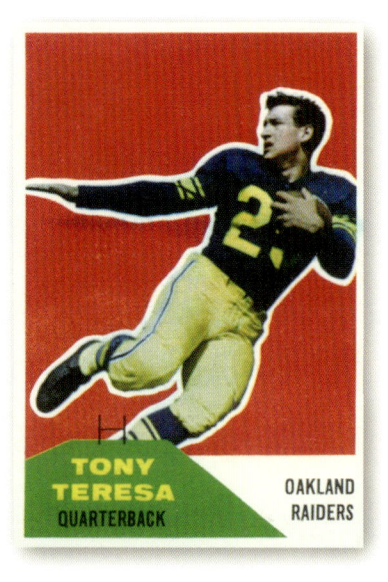

Oakland's forte this first season was their running game, finishing second in the league largely on the tail of halfback Tony Teresa, who gained 608 yards for a 4.37 yards-per-carry average and 10 touchdowns. Lott's 520 yards averaged 5.25 per carry. Tom Flores, the AFL's top-rated passer, hit on 54 percent of his throws and led the Raiders to the fifth-best passing attack. Babe Parilli, an NFL veteran, also assisted in the passing department, giving Flores a lift when needed. Babe connected for 87 of his 187 passes (46.5 percent), while 5 made it over the goal line.

The defense was another story. They were weak against the run and worse against the pass. The Raiders' 6-8 record placed them third in the AFL West and gave the few fans who followed them across the bay reason to believe that if a team built from ruins could muster a near .500 record on such short notice, 1961 could only get better. The Raiders' lone all-league selection was rookie center Jim Otto.

As was expected, the Raiders drew fewer fans than any other AFL team. Playing in San Francisco did not help the team's identity in Oakland. Nor did the fact that they changed venues late in the season. Topping out at 12,703 fans at their first home game, the Raiders claimed over 10,000 at only three of their seven home games with a low of 7,000 for their season-ending game in Candlestick Park against Denver. Their 9,875 average attendance was the only one in the league under 13,000.

After piecing together a roster in the eleventh hour the Raiders never looked back, scoring more points than three of the originals while allowing fewer points than two others. With a new draft on the horizon and a year under their belts, Oakland looked to improve in every department and planned to make a run for the roses in 1961. The Raiders also planned to play all seven home games in 1961 at Candlestick Park, hoping to finally move across the bay to their real home in 1962.

Leading passers	Attempts	Completions	Pct	TDs	Yards	Int
Tom Flores	252	136	54%	12	1738	12
Vito "Babe" Parilli	187	87	46%	5	1003	11

The Progress of the Seasons – 1960

Leading rushers	Attempts	Yards gained	Average	TDs
Tony Teresa	139	608	4.4	6
Billy Lott	99	520	5.3	5
Jack Larsheid	94	397	4.2	1
Jim "Jetstream" Smith	63	214	3.4	6

Leading receivers	Caught	Yards gained	Average	TDs
Billy Lott	49	524	10.7	1
Tony Teresa	35	393	11.2	4
Gene Prebola	33	404	12.2	2
Alan Goldstein	27	354	13.1	1
Charley Hardy	24	423	17.6	3
Jack Larsheid	22	187	8.5	1

Leading scorers	TDs	XPM	XPA	FGM	FGA	PTs
Tony Teresa	10					60
Larry Barnes		37	39	6	25	55

---

5. Which team was so strapped for money during their first year that they did not even outfit their squad with practice attire? Instead each player had to bring his own T-shirt and shorts to practice. Often it was not enough to ward off the cold weather.

■ BUFFALO BILLS ■

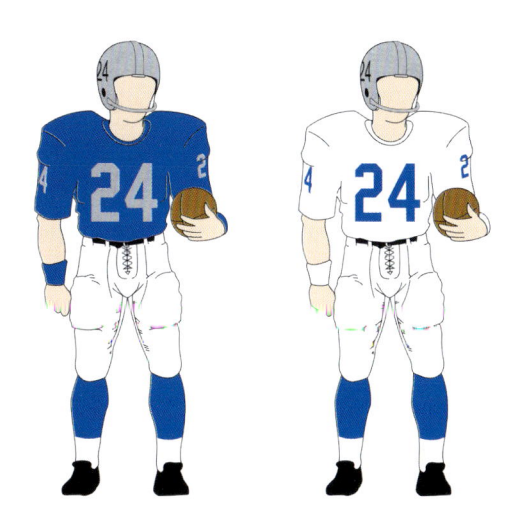

ON OCTOBER 28, 1959, THE BUFFALO Bills officially became the seventh team to join the new American Football League. Ralph Wilson Jr., a Detroit insurance magnate and a stockholder of the NFL Lions, became the principal owner. His first draft selection five weeks later was All-American Penn State quarterback Richie Lucas, and on December 16 Buffalo had their first head coach with Wilson hiring Detroit Lion assistant coach Buster Ramsey. Ramsey was the architect of the rough-and-tumble Lion defense that appeared in four NFL championship games in the fifties, winning three of them. It was no surprise that the Bills became the most rugged defensive team in the AFL and in 1960 ranked as the best in total defense as well as the best against the pass. They placed three players—linebacker Archie Matsos, DE LaVerne Torczon, and DB Richie McCabe—on the all-league defensive unit. The offense was another story, as the other side of the line was within 10 points of finishing last in scoring.

Owner Wilson's Detroit roots were visually apparent from the start as the Bills emerged from the locker room on July 30, 1960, for their first exhibition game against Boston in ancient War Memorial Stadium. Their blue-and-silver uniforms were identical, head to toe, to those of the Detroit Lions. The Bills lack of offense was never more apparent than on September 11 when they kicked off their team's history with a 27-3 loss against the Titans in the dark and dreary New York Polo Grounds.

A week later they put a little more muscle into the offense but still came away winless, losing their home opener 27-21. Buffalo started the season with veteran Tommy O'Connell, the NFL's leading passer in 1957, at quarterback. And when the offense faltered Ramsey turned to another veteran, Johnny Green, for help. Later in the season rookies Richie Lucas and Bob Broadhead also took turns under center.

On September 23, while on the road in New England, the Bills won their first game by shutting out Boston 13-0. It was the first shutout in the AFL's three-week history. In week four the Bills actually won the battle of offensive statistics but not the war on the scoreboard. Gaining 238 total yards to the Chargers 159, they lost 24-10. O'Connell went most of the way, completing 8 of 14 passes but the only Buffalo touchdown, which closed the gap temporarily, came on the end of Richie Lucas's only pass of the day, a 36-yard completion to flanker Elbert Dubenion. Dubenion was the receiving ace for the game with 6 catches for 88 yards and a score. A second loss to New York followed.

It was in week six that the Bills offense took off and scored their highest point total of the year. Johnny Green, taking over for the ineffective O'Connell, completed 14 passes for 243 yards and 4 touchdowns. He scored another himself on a 1-yard plunge as the Bills thundered past Oakland 38-9.

That victory was followed by a thrilling 25-24 win over eventual champions Houston, but Tommy Green banged up his throwing arm in the game and was mostly ineffective thereafter, completing only 39 percent of his passes with 10 touchdowns. Tommy O'Connell fared slightly better, but his 44 percent completion rate was less than expected.

Two more losses put the Bills' record at 3-6 and then suddenly the blue and silver found life in their continually listless offense, scoring over 30 points in each of their final four games to close out the last month of the season going 2-1-1. The first of those wins came at the expense of the Chargers 32-3, with O'Connell and Green each throwing TD passes, one to converted quarterback Richie Lucas for 17 yards and another to rookie end Dan Chamberlain for 49 yards. Fullback Wray Carlton scored on two runs, and linebacker Archie Matsos ran back one of the Bill's 4 interceptions on Charger quarterback Jack Kemp for another. The next week in Denver the Bills led 38-7 after the first three quarters,

The Progress of the Seasons – 1960

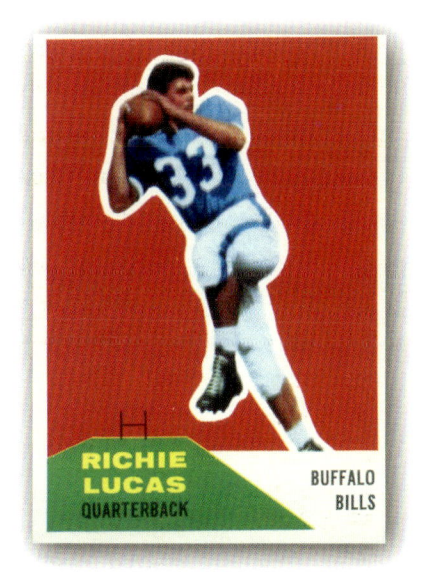

playing well on both sides of the ball. Halfback Wilmer Fowler broke off a 61-yard run early in the game en route to his 120 yards on the day. Elbert Dubenion caught 6 passes for 134 yards, including a 76-yard touchdown run after pulling in a short pass. In the third quarter Bills' defensive end Mack Yoho trucked 15 yards with an interception (the Bills picked off 5 in the game) for a touchdown, and then Fowler scored from 19 yards, giving the Bills a 38-7 lead with fifteen minutes to play. After Fowler's jaunt, however, the bubble burst, mostly in the hands of Denver split end Lionel Taylor, who caught 3 touchdown passes within an eight minute span. All Buster Ramsey could do was watch as his defense was rendered defenseless against the Bronco aerial show that kept striking back and eventually earned a wild 38-38 tie. A home win over Boston, 38-14, and a final game loss in Houston closed the season.

Fullback Wray Carlton was the Bills' leading rusher with 533 yards followed by Fowler with 370. Tight end Tom Rychlec caught 45 balls for tops on the team, but Elbert Dubenion provided deep impact with his team-leading 752 yards on 42 catches, which found pay dirt seven times. The kicking game was another reason the offense failed to yield a knockout punch much of the season. Five different toes were employed by the Bills, the best belonging to Billy Atkins, who hit on 6 of 13 field goal attempts. All told, the Bills made only 12 of their 26 field goal attempts on the year. They finished third in the East with a 5-8-1 record, half a game ahead of Boston.

Leading passers	Attempts	Completions	Pct	TDs	Yards	Int
Johnny Green	228	89	39%	10	1267	10
Tommy O'Connell	145	65	44%	7	1033	13
Richie Lucas	49	23	46%	2	314	3
Bob Brodhead	25	7	28%	0	75	3

Leading rushers	Attempts	Yards gained	Average	TDs
Wray Carlton	137	533	3.9	7
Willmer Fowler	93	370	4.0	1
Joe Kulbacki	41	108	2.6	1
Elbert Dubenion	16	94	5.9	1

Remember the AFL

Leading receivers	Caught	Yards gained	Average	TDs		
Tom Rychlec	44	581	13.1	0		
Elbert Dubenion	42	752	17.9	7		
Wray Carlton	29	477	16.4	4		
Dan Chamberlain	17	279	16.4	4		
Monte Crockett	14	173	12.4	1		
Willmer Fowler	10	99	9.9	0		

Leading scorers	TDs	XPM	XPA	FGM	FGA	PTs
Wray Carlton	11					66
Elbert Dubenion	8					48
Billy Atkins		27	33	6	13	45

---

6. Attendance figures in the early years were not very authentic. One of the most notorious in reporting exaggerated numbers was Titans owner Harry Wismer, leading New York writers to describe the count of those phantoms watching Titan games at the Polo Grounds as fans that came disguised as what?

▪ NEW YORK TITANS ▪

WHERE THE NAME HARRY WISMER settles in the minds of AFL historians can range anywhere from that of clown prince to league savior. Both would be correct, for the principal owner of the New York Titans was not only a loose cannon from whom other owners came to expect the unexpected, but he was also a master salesman, the AFL's point man, and the only one able to successfully negotiate the league's first TV contract with the American Broadcasting Company (ABC). Harry was so tight with the dollar that he would refuse to turn on the stadium lights at the Polo Grounds on those dreary Sunday afternoons and also gained a reputation for counting in his attendance totals the fans who thought about coming to the game. His habitual padding of the figures prompted one New York writer to describe Titan games as performances in front of family, friends, and thousands of other fans who came disguised as empty seats. The New York Titans, for all of Wismer's antics, were not a team without talent. They had a bona fide NFL all-star at quarterback in Al Dorow, formerly of the Washington Redskins. Flanker Don Maynard played in the 1958 championship game for the New York Giants, and split end Art Powell had experience catching passes for the Philadelphia Eagles. To lead his team, Wismer, a former Redskins and Notre Dame announcer, hired legendary Redskin quarterback Slingin' Sammy Baugh as his head coach. He outfitted his Titans in uniforms that were virtually identical to those worn by his beloved Fighting Irish, except for the blue helmets with a gold stripe down the middle.

There was not a more active revolving door in the AFL than in the Titans' New Hampshire summer camp. Players came and

The Progress of the Seasons – 1960

went with the sunrise and sunset. By opening day only three drafted players remained on the thirty-three-man roster. With every cut by an NFL team came a new arrival to the Titans camp, hoping to show Sammy what he could do, making everyone on New York's present roster leery of meeting the Turk each evening.

The Titan backfield included Dick Jamieson, the first starting quarterback, and two relatively unknowns, except to coach Baugh, for whom both Dewey Bohling and Pete Hart played at Hardin-Simmons College in Texas. Others gaining starts on opening day were Don Maynard and Art Powell at flanker and split end and Thurlow Cooper at tight end. On the line were tackles Joe Katchik and Gene Cockrell, guards John McMullan and Bob Mishak, and center Mike Hudock. The defense listed Nick Mumley and Bob Reifsnyder at end with Tom Saidlock and Sid Youngelman at tackle. The linebackers were Eddie Bell, Bob Marques, and Larry Grantham with Fred Julian, Dick Felt, Corky Tharp, and Roger Donahoo in the secondary. For their home field, Wismer had contracted with the Polo Grounds, across the Harlem River from Yankee Stadium in an area known as Coogan's Bluff. The stadium had been the long-time home of the New York baseball Giants but had stood vacant since the team moved to San Francisco three years earlier. The stadium, now in decay, was not even considered good enough to be second rate. Nevertheless, for the Titans in 1960, it was home.

Bohling was the Titans' primary runner, leading the team with 431 yards on 123 carries. Their second-leading ball carrier was Bill Mathis, picked up from the Oilers. Mathis carried 92 times for 307 yards. First-game starter Pete Hart lasted for only 25 carries. Others to tote the pigskin in New York's first season included kicker/fullback Bill Shockley and scrambling quarterback Al Dorow. Dorow took command of the offense in the second quarter of the first game, relieving Jamieson, and captured the hearts of the fans by scoring 2 touchdowns, one on a 15-yard scramble. His 26 touchdown passes were a league high, and his 396 total passes were outdone by only two others. He also completed 50 percent of his aerials for 2,748 yards. Only Jack Kemp and Frank Tripucka threw for more. At the end of most of Dorow's completions were Don Maynard, who finished in a tie for second place in the league with 72, and Art Powell who caught 69. Powell's 14 TD receptions topped the league. The Titan passing attack finished second behind only Houston while their running game ranked fifth.

The Titans under Baugh started the season by beating Buffalo 27-3, but lost to Boston 28-24 in their second game. Against the Patriots the Titans led 24-21 with under one minute to play when punter Rick Sapienza fumbled a fourth down snap that was recovered by Boston safety Chuck Shonta after Pats defensive back Gino Cappelletti allegedly kicked the fumble forward 10 yards. Shonta returned his pick up 52 yards into the Titan end zone for the winning touchdown to make the final score 28-21. The next week the Titans trailed Denver 24-21 with fifteen seconds left to play when the Broncos were forced to punt from their own ten. An all-out effort by New York blocked the punt that was recovered by Titan safety Roger Donahoo who ran it into the end zone for the game-winning touchdown. The Titans won 28-24. Their first win streak was tallied the next week in Dallas as Al Dorow led the way with 4 touchdown passes in a 37-35 win. At 3-1 Baugh's boys flew to Houston tied with the Oilers. Houston was idle the previous week, and their rested troops proved to be too much for New York as the Titans lost 27-21. Jamieson and Dorow split the QB duties, with Jamieson throwing 2 TD's and Dorow adding another.

The AFL's first tragedy struck the Titans in Houston in a much more catastrophic way than just losing a football game. Reserve guard Howard Glenn, injured the previous week against Dallas, was pressed into action when starter Bob Mishak was injured during the game. Near the end of the first half Glenn was the lead blocker on a trap play up the middle when he was sandwiched between two Oiler defenders. After dropping to the ground he had to be assisted off the field. In these ragtag days of pro football there was no sideline medical staff, and Glenn was left to recover alone on the bench.

After the game he continued to feel the effects of the hit in the locker room and suddenly fell to the floor. His teammates came to his rescue and summoned the Oilers team doctor, who admitted Glenn to the hospital. But even before the Titan's plane back to New York left the ground, coach Baugh and his staff received word from the hospital that shortly after being admitted Glenn had passed away, the result of a broken neck.

After downing the Bills for the second time this season the Titans went on a four-game losing streak against the Oilers, Raiders, Chargers, and Patriots, knocking them back to 4-6 and into third place in the Eastern Division. With four games left on the schedule they trailed the first-place Oilers by three games. With Dorow at his offensive best, the Titans then took a 28-10 lead over Dallas as Maynard caught a 45-yard touchdown pass and Roger Donahoo scored his second touchdown of the season with a recovered fumble in the first quarter. Their defense struggled to hold off the Texans' offense the rest of the way but still managed to come away with a 41-35 victory, keeping their hopes of winning the division alive for another week. At 5-6 their only hope was for

The Progress of the Seasons – 1960

Houston to falter and drop them into a season-ending tie. But even though the Titans did their job by winning the next two games the Oilers refused to cooperate, posting a final 9-3 record by winning their remaining two games.

All that was left on the season's final day was to improve their record as the Titans, win or lose, would finish second in the East. Playing the L. A. Chargers, champions of the West, in the Coliseum, the Titans led 21-16 at halftime. The Chargers added 17 points in the third quarter but were countered by New York's 15. And that is where the Titan missile fizzled both offensively and defensively. L. A. duplicated their third quarter output in the final frame while Dorow could muster only one more touchdown. The Titans closed down their season losing 50-43 to post a 7-7 record. Guard Bob Mishak was the lone New York Titan to be placed on the all-league squad at season's end.

Leading passers	Attempts	Completions	Pct	TDs	Yards	Int
Al Dorow	396	201	50%	26	2748	28
Dick Jamieson	70	35	50%	6	586	2

Leading rushers	Attempts	Yards gained	Average	TDs
Dewey Bohling	123	431	3.5	2
Bill Mathis	92	307	3.3	2
Al Dorow	124	167	1.3	7
Bill Shockley	37	156	4.2	2
Leon Burton	16	119	7.4	1
Pete Hart	25	113	4.5	0

Leading receivers	Caught	Yards gained	Average	TDs
Don Maynard	72	1265	17.6	6
Art Powell	69	1167	16.9	14
Dewey Bohling	30	268	8.9	4
Bill Mathis	18	103	5.7	0
Dave Ross	10	122	12.2	1
Thurlow Cooper	9	161	17.9	3
Bill Shockley	8	69	8.6	2

Leading scorers	TDs	XPM	XPA	FGM	FGA	PTs
Bill Shockley	2	47	50	9	21	86
Art Powell	14					84

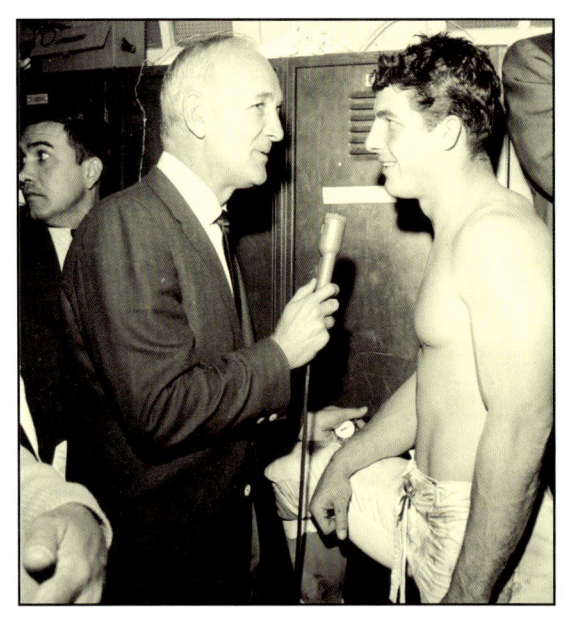

7. This former college All-American halfback was the first play-by-play announcer for the Los Angeles Chargers. Although he never played professional football he did produce in TV land. Both his son, a topnotch college quarterback, and his daughter realized successful acting careers in Hollywood. Who was he?

▪ LOS ANGELES CHARGERS ▪

THE LEGEND OF THE LIGHTNING BOLT was created by hotel heir Barron Hilton and brought to life on September 10, 1960, when the San Diego Chargers hosted the preseason favorite Dallas Texans in L. A.'s Memorial Coliseum. Led by former Rams head coach and offensive mastermind Sid Gillman, the Chargers were designed to be an explosive juggernaut defined by running back speed and long-range aerials. The offense featured ex-Pittsburgh Steeler and Giant quarterback Jack Kemp, All-American fullback Charlie Flowers from Mississippi, and a fleet of swift receivers that included Iowa All-American Don Norton, Ralph Anderson, Royce Womble, Dave Kocourek, and Howard Clark, in addition to mercurial halfback Paul Lowe. The Chargers, who won all four of their exhibition games, were thought to have a decided advantage over the rest of the original teams primarily because Sid Gillman was the lone AFL coach with championship game experience, and also for their illegal start of summer camp a week early, which earned them the AFL's first fine. Sid was considered to be the man with the magic wand among his coaching cohorts.

The Chargers quickly endeared themselves to fans coast-to-coast not only for their lightning-strike offensive arsenal but also for their uniform aesthetics that were unlike anything in the NFL. The Chargers wore white helmets with blue lightning bolts highlighted with a gold outline and the player's uniform number under the lightning bolts. Their jerseys were Pacific blue with white shoulder stripes accented with a blue lightning bolt in the middle of the stripe. Blue lightning bolts replaced the traditional stripe down the side of their

The Progress of the Seasons – 1960

white pants. The Barron's team was named, like many others of the day, through a fan contest, The winner was awarded a trip to Mexico. The winning name "Chargers," selected by Hilton, was a natural for several reasons, the most natural being that Hilton had just started a new charge card company known as Carte Blanche. The name fit perfectly. Another reason was that the name embodied the image of an electrifying, quick-strike team. Hilton also liked the idea of employing the services of a white charger, ridden by a knight in shining armor as his team's mascot. From the very beginning the Chargers had a Hollywood aura about them and were easily identified as the most glamorous team in the AFL.

Ironically, the main attraction in the first year was an employee of the Carte Blanche company. Paul Lowe was released by the San Francisco 49ers and found employment in the mail room of Carte Blanche in 1959. Remembering him from his collegiate days, Charger GM Don Klosterman invited Lowe to try out for the newly formed team. Lowe made the most of his invitation. He also made himself a piece of Charger history when he returned the opening kickoff of their first exhibition game against the Titans 105 yards for a touchdown in the Los Angeles Coliseum.

Lowe's career started inauspiciously with Los Angeles, where he was originally a fourth back, spelling former NFL backs Ron Waller and Howard Ferguson and rookie Charlie Flowers. After five games Lowe had a total of only 38 yards on 16 carries. In games two, three, and four Lowe touched the ball only one time in each. By week five the Chargers record was a disappointing 2-3. Then came week six in Denver. Waller had been cut loose and Lowe was now the starter at halfback alongside Howie Ferguson. The ex-Oregon Stater gained 72 yards on 11 carries, including touchdown runs of 12 and 44 yards. From then on it was the Paul Lowe Show in Southern California for Charger fans. His tally sheet the rest of the year had him gaining 817 yards on 120 carries in the last 9 games with three 100-yard-plus efforts. With his breakaway speed Lowe became the symbol of the big-play Charger offense, leading the league with a 6.3 yards-per-carry average. He finished second in the league in rushing, only 20 yards behind Dallas's Abner Haynes, who carried the ball 20 more times. Twice he gained over 135 yards in a game and twice he authored touchdown runs of over 60 yards. His crown-jewel performance came in the AFL Championship game when he almost single-handedly led the Chargers over Houston by gaining 174 yards on 21 carries. After

★ *Charger QB Jack Kemp and Coach Sid Gillman discuss strategy.* ★

Lowe was inserted into the starting lineup the Chargers won eight of their last nine games. Behind the running of Lowe and the radar-like passing of Jack Kemp, Gillman's legions became a high-scoring, fast-striking unit that was able to overwhelm opposing defenses. The Chargers put the ball in the air 441 times and ran it 437 times. While the NFL was running on three of every four downs the Chargers and most of the AFL's other teams were in the one-to-one range. This was a cause for ridicule by the established league and was described by NFL purists around the country as "basketball on cleats." But while being widely criticized by the established football media, the league was also appealing to a new generation of football viewers.

Through their first five games the Chargers looked unimpressive, and after suffering a humiliating 35-0 shutout at the hands of the Boston Patriots, Gillman knew that some changes would be needed to keep pace with the rest of the Western Division clubs. The Chargers were tied with Dallas at 2-3 as Kemp and company flew into Denver to meet the 3-1 Broncos in Bears Stadium. In the first quarter Paul Lowe was on the receiving end of a 56-yard pass play that took the Chargers to the Denver 12 yard line. On the next play he scored his first touchdown on a 12-yard

The Progress of the Seasons – 1960

sweep around left end. Kemp found him again in the second quarter with a 24-yard floater over the middle. The drive stalled, but forty-one-year-old kicker Ben Agajanian, then pro football's oldest player, put L. A. up 10-6 with an 11-yard field goal. Agajanian was one of those NFL castoffs who was given a second chance by the AFL. Released by the New York Giants, Agajanian was out of football for two years before signing with the Chargers. Somewhat of a marvel, big Ben was one of the best placekickers in pro football while kicking with a right foot that was missing four toes. After two more Agajanian field goals in the third quarter, Lowe again found pay dirt with another sweep around left end, this time for 45 yards and a 23-9 L. A. lead. The Chargers went on to gain a much needed 23-19 victory, lifting them to within a half game of the division-leading Broncos. After a week off the Chargers had their chance to avenge their previous loss to Boston. This time the result was significantly different, with L. A. taking a 28-0 lead into the locker room at the half way mark. The first half highlight was provided by cornerback Dickie Harris on a 42-yard interception return for a touchdown. Getting things started in the third quarter, Paul Lowe darted off tackle and went the distance on a 66-yard touchdown run. He later broke another run up the middle for 69 yards to the Patriot 10 before Agajanian kicked another 3-pointer. Kemp also hit Ralph Anderson for a 38-yard score in the Chargers 45-16 win, bringing their record to 4-3.

The next week, a 21-7 win over New York lifted the Chargers into first place in the West for the first time since opening day. Paul Lowe broke the game open for L. A. with another sprint up the middle from 62 yards away for a touchdown. Their win over the Titans was followed by a closely contested victory over Houston in which Jack Kemp passed to Ralph Anderson for 34-yard and 4-yard touchdowns in the first quarter on an L. A. Coliseum field that was covered with more sawdust than turf after a rain storm.

Paul Lowe continued to kick up his heels on the league as he took a pitch out around right end for 40 yards before scoring on a 3-yard run to the left. In beating the Oilers 24-21, L. A. had run off four wins in a row.

After a pasting by Buffalo the Chargers scored four consecutive wins starting with a 52-28 victory over the Raiders. Two touchdown passes by Kemp, one to Don Norton for 69 and another to Lowe for 63, put L. A. ahead to stay. A fourth quarter Doyle Nix touchdown with an interception put the icing on the day's victory cake in front of 15,075 in the Coliseum. The winning streak continued, again against Oakland on the first week of December in San Francisco's Candlestick Park where Lowe gained 90 yards rushing and was on the receiving end of a 49-yard scoring pass from Kemp. Linebacker Rommie Loudd scored on a 49-yard return of a Babe Parilli fumble to top off the Chargers point total. At 8-4 L. A. needed only one more win to clinch the West, which they got against Denver the next week in a 41-33 barn burner. Led by Paul Lowe's 106 yards rushing the Chargers jumped out ahead 24-23 by halftime, but Denver took the lead in the third quarter. With Jack Kemp throwing his third touchdown pass of the day, a 15-yarder to Don Norton in the fourth quarter, the Chargers sealed the game and the division title.

On January 1, 1961, the Chargers met the Houston Oilers in the first AFL Championship game, played in Houston's Jeppesen Stadium. The largest Houston crowd of the season, 32,183, filed in to see the two best teams joust for the AFL's first title trophy. Kemp and Houston's George Blanda filled the air with 72 passes, and Paul Lowe scampered for 174 yards in what was a closely contested, back-and-forth game. The Chargers held a 6-0 lead early before the Oilers scored 10 points of their own. Ben Agajanian's field goal right before halftime pulled L. A. to within one point at 10-9. Houston extended its lead to 8 with another touchdown, but Paul Lowe answered with a 4-yard score for the Chargers. Leading 17-16 as the fourth quarter began, the Oilers broke open the game with an 88-yard touchdown pass and run from Blanda to Billy Cannon. A last-gasp drive in the waning minutes brought the Chargers to the Houston 22 but that was as far as they would go. Their season ended with a 10-4 record and a proud showing in their 24-16 AFL Championship game loss.

For their efforts, Kemp, Lowe, and tackle Ron Mix along with DE Volney Peters and cornerback Dickie Harris were named to the AFL all-league team. Linebacker Paul Maguire led the league in punting with a 40.5 average and Kemp's 52 percent completion rate led all quarterbacks. While L. A.'s performance on the field was a resounding success, the performance at the gate was a cause of financial concern for Hilton. Charger crowds averaged only 15,768 with a low of 9,928. Hilton had lost nearly a million dollars in the Chargers, first year and was looking for greener, more profitable pastures in which to anchor his team. As the Chargers first season came to an end their outlook for a second year in Los Angeles was a cloudy one.

8. In 1961 Ben Agajanian set an AFL distance record with a 51-yard field goal for Dallas one week, then found himself kicking for the NFL Packers a week later. Somewhat of a kicking nomad, Ben kicked for his third AFL team in 1962, agreeing to play for nothing. What other AFL team did he kick for?

The Progress of the Seasons – 1960

Leading passers	Attempts	Completions	Pct	TDs	Yards	Int
Jack Kemp	406	211	52%	20	3018	25
Bob Clatterbuck	23	15	65%	1	112	1

Leading rushers	Attempts	Yards gained	Average	TDs
Paul Lowe	136	855	6.3	9
Howie Ferguson	126	438	3.5	4
Charlie Flowers	40	161	4.0	1
Fred Ford	20	154	7.7	2

Leading receivers	Caught	Yards gained	Average	TDs
Ralph Anderson	44	614	13.9	5
Dave Kocourek	40	662	16.5	1
Royce Womble	32	316	9.9	4
Howard Clark	27	431	15.9	0
Don Norton	25	414	16.6	5
Paul Lowe	23	377	16.4	2
Howie Ferguson	21	206	9.8	2

Leading scorers	TDs	XPM	XPA	FGM	FGA	PTs
Ben Agajanian		46	47	13	24	85
Paul Lowe	10					60

9. It wasn't quite like PT 109, nor could you mistake it for anything out of McHale's Navy, but these two AFL head coaches saw action together in the South Pacific during World War II as PT boat shipmates.
a. Mike Holovak and Wally Lemm
b. Hank Stram and Buster Ramsey
c. Lou Saban and Sid Gillman

■ HOUSTON OILERS ■

THE STORY OF THE HOUSTON OILERS begins with its owner, young oil tycoon K.S. "Bud" Adams. He and Lamar Hunt were the catalysts for the league's formation and its rivalry with the NFL. Adams also took on and beat the patriarchal monopoly headed by founding father George Halas when his well-conceived, in-your-face coup landed the signature of LSU All-American halfback Billy Cannon underneath the goal post after his final college game in the Sugar Bowl. Despite the fact that Cannon had already signed a contract with Pete Rozelle and the Los Angeles Rams, Adams defiantly contended that the NFL's signing was illegal and took matters into his own hands by legally signing Cannon after his college eligibility had expired and doubling the Rams $10,000 offer. The first AFL vs. NFL law suit ensued with the AFL winning the rights to Cannon and thus setting off years of sabotage and deceit that finally culminated in the merger. In Cannon

★ *The first training camp for the Houston Oilers, 1960.* ★

the league had their first nationally known player and first hint of credibility.

Three weeks prior to the Cannon signing, the Oilers had already started securing prospective players. On December 8, 1959, Oklahoma State All-American center Don Hitt and defensive back teammate Tony Banfield become the first players signed by the Houston franchise. Banfield would go on to become an all-league player but Hitt never made it to opening day. Among other early signings for the Oilers was one that Adams thought would be a perfect complement to Billy Cannon in the backfield. Ohio State All-American fullback Bob White had the distinction of running for the Buckeyes for three years without ever having lost a single yard. But after recovering from an early season knee injury, White played only sparingly at linebacker in 1960, and he retired after one year without ever running the football professionally. Also signed was the Washington Redskins leading receiver for the past four years, end Johnny Carson.

Adams believed that proven defensive backs would be in short supply in the AFL's first season and set out to build an offense that would depend on passing to give his Oilers the edge. Searching for a proven arm, Adams found disgruntled Chicago Bear quarterback and place kicker George Blanda. But Blanda was headed to Los Angeles and was set to sign with the Chargers for $17,000 a year. Not to be out done, the wealthy Texan quickly upped the ante and got Blanda's name on a contract for $3,000 more per year. Then came college teammates Charley Hennigan, a high school biology

The Progress of the Seasons – 1960

teacher who would go on to become one of the AFL's best flankers, and 5'6" fullback Charlie Tolar. After driving in for try-out camp together from Louisiana, both became cornerstones in the Oiler championship seasons and played together in Houston through 1966.

On October 31, 1959, Adams dubbed his new franchise "the Oilers" for obvious reasons, and dressed them in Columbia blue helmets with a single white stripe down the center, and a white oil well derrick on each side. Their shirts were also Columbia blue with white numbers accented with a red trim. Houston had a unique blend of youth and experience as the league became a reality in September of 1960. No less than four rookies laid claim to being college All-Americans the year before, led by TCU defensive end Don Floyd. His partner on the opposite side of the defensive line was Dalva Allen. The tackles were George Shirkey and Orville Trask. The opening day linebackers were Al Wichter, Dennit Morris, and Hugh Pitts with Chuck Kendall, Mark Johnston, Julian Spence, and Joe Majors in the secondary. On the offensive Johnny Carson and Hennigan lined up as wide ends. Al Jamison and Rich Michael were the tackles with Bob Talamini and Fred Walner the guards and George Belotti at center. The tight end was John White. Blanda, Cannon, and Dave Smith, out of Ripon Teachers College, made up the backfield.

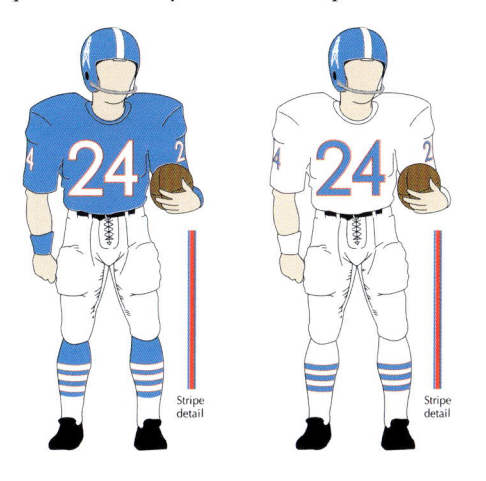

The Oilers were one of many teams that were having trouble finding a suitable stadium to call home. Unable to land Rice University, Adams turned to Jeppesen Stadium, a high school field, to play their home games. Adams even added 14,000 seats to the 22,000 seat venue, feeling that Cannon could fill the extra capacity, and for a mere thirty-eight dollars you could purchase a season ticket to all seven Oiler home games. Single game tickets sold for two dollars. It was the Oilers offense that initially triggered most of the wins in 1960 as they scored over 36 points in six games and 20 points or more in all but two of their fourteen starts. While the defense was tenacious, ranking them number two against the rush, the secondary was the AFL's worst.

Opening day found the Oilers in San Francisco's Kezar Stadium to play the Oakland Raiders on Sunday, September 11. With a disappointing crowd of only 12,703 on hand, George Blanda connected with Hennigan for 43 yards and the first official Houston touchdown. Little known Dave Smith ran 8 yards for the first Oiler rushing TD. Smith also became the Oilers first 100-yard ground gainer by carrying the ball for 109 yards on 19 carries against the Raiders in their 31-23 victory. Blanda spread the wealth in his first quarterbacking appearance in nearly two years by hitting Hennigan, Carson (twice) and Bill Groman for TD passes. In their home opener the following week Blanda scored three times on one-yard plunges, and Smith rambled 47 yards for his second TD in Houston's 38-28 win. Another home game the next week saw a rematch with Oakland come up short, 14-13, for Houston's first loss. A BYE week then gave coach Lou Rymkus an opportunity to regain the team's composure. Then they posted a 27-21 win over the Titans on October 9. At 3-1 the Oilers narrowly led New York (3-2) in the East.

Against Dallas in their third straight home game, the battle for Texas bragging rights went to Houston 20-10 and readied them for a showdown with the Titans the next week in the Polo Grounds. A reported 21,000 saw the Titans start the scoring in the first quarter. But Houston's Ken Hall returned the ensuing kickoff 104 yards to tie the score. Three first half touchdown passes to split end Bill Groman followed and gave Houston a 35-21 lead at the half. In the second half each team scored only once. The Oilers cruised to a 42-28 triumph. At War Memorial Stadium the next week Buffalo's Billy Atkins kicked two fourth quarter field goals to down the Oilers 25-24. Four more touchdown passes in Denver by Blanda in week nine and a 45-yard touchdown run by Dave Smith put Houston ahead by three games in the East as the Oilers stampeded over the Broncos 45-25.

The two divisional leaders, L. A. and Houston, faced off in the L. A. Coliseum on November 13. The Chargers, 5-3, were riding a three-game win streak while the Oilers, 6-2, were coming off their second loss. The Chargers led 24-14 in the fourth when Blanda found Billy Cannon in the end zone to make it close, but the final gun sounded with the Chargers on top 24-21. Blanda fired a season-high 55 passes, completing 31 for 366 yards in the loss. At 6-3 Houston still led the East by two games over the 4-5 Titans. At home a week later before 20,778 fans, Houston got back on track with a 20-10 win against Denver. Twenty-two-year-old rookie Jackie Lee subbed for an ailing George Blanda and quickly endeared himself to Oiler fans by hitting 3 of his 7 first half passes for pay dirt on gains of 78, 92, and 73 yards to Groman and Hennigan on Houston's rain soaked field. A win in Boston and a shut out loss in Dallas came next, but as the Oilers rode home with a 31-23 win over Buffalo on December 11, they had locked up their first division championship. They closed out the season with another defeat of Boston. At 10-4 the Oilers record was identical to that of their opponent, the Los Angeles Chargers, in the AFL's first championship game, played on January 1.

The game appeared on paper to be a toss up. Houston boasted one of the league's best running tandems in Billy Cannon (644 yards on 152 carries, 4.2 average) and Dave Smith (643 yards on 154 carries, 4.2 average). The two finished third and fourth respectively in the league,

The Progress of the Seasons – 1960

with the Oilers finishing third in rushing overall. L. A. had Paul Lowe, the league's second-best runner with the league's highest per carry average of 6.3. Signal callers Kemp and Blanda finished first and seventh in the rankings, but Houston posted the league's best passing attack while the Chargers settled in at fourth. The receivers for the Oilers were Bill Groman, the AFL's second-best pass catcher with 72 receptions (no one gained more than his 1,473 yards or averaged more per catch than his 20.5), Johnny Carson who caught 45 balls, and Hennigan who caught 44. Smith and Cannon caught 22 and 15 each. The Chargers leading receiver was Ralph Anderson, who had tragically passed away during the season, leaving the receiving corps in disarray. Dave Kocourek caught 40 passes with Royce Womble next with 32 catches. With an average attendance of 20,000 in the 36,000-seat capacity Jeppesen Stadium, the AFL elders decided for the good of the league to switch the game from its scheduled venue in the canyon-like L. A. Coliseum with a capacity of 100,000 seats, where the Chargers averaged little more than 15,000. Hilton and the Chargers agreed and instead of having to travel West, the Oilers now had the home field advantage. The turn-stiles clicked 32,183 times by game time on New Year's day, 1961 in Houston.

Charger kicker Ben Agajanian scored the first championship points for the rookie league with two first quarter field goals of 38 and 22 yards. Then George Blanda fired 8 straight passes to drive Houston over the goal line with the last pass covering 17 yards to fullback Dave Smith for the score, giving the Oilers a 7-6 lead. Field goals by both Blanda and Agajanian closed out the first half, keeping Blanda's team ahead 10-9. A TD pass to Bill Groman and a Paul Lowe short touchdown burst off left tackle took the game into the fourth quarter with Houston leading by the slimmest of margins, 17-16. Lowe gained 174 yards on the day for L. A. with Dave Smith and Billy Cannon each gaining 51 yards. As the game clock ticked down with the Oilers clinging to their 1-point lead early in the fourth quarter, George Blanda and company were faced with a third-and-nine situation on their own 12 yard line. Blanda then called for Cannon to run a short down-and-out route that would isolate him on a linebacker. As Blanda lofted his aerial Cannon had already beaten his coverage and took the reception 88 yards for the game's final and winning score. Needing a touchdown and a 2-point conversion to send the game to overtime the Chargers launched a drive to tie. A pass interference penalty on the Oilers then put L. A. deep into Houston territory at the 22 yard line, but on a last-chance fourth down try the Oilers defense held, and the Chargers final drive came to a halt. The Houston Oilers had won the first AFL Championship game 24-16. Billy Cannon, riding the crest of his touchdown reception, was the game's MVP. For their AFL championship each triumphant Oiler walked away with a winner's share of $1,016.42. And on January 2 each of the eight AFL franchises were finally able to sit back, smile, and breath a collective sigh of relief and accomplishment. The first successful season of the American Football League was now history!

Remember the AFL

Leading passers	Attempts	Completions	Pct	TDs	Yards	Int
George Blanda	362	168	46%	24	2413	22
Jacky Lee	77	41	53%	5	842	6

Leading rushers	Attempts	Yards gained	Average	TDs
Billy Cannon	152	644	4.2	1
Dave Smith	154	643	4.1	5
Charlie Tolar	54	179	3.3	3
Ken Hall	30	118	3.9	0
Doug Cline	37	105	2.8	2

Leading receivers	Caught	Yards gained	Average	TDs
Bill Groman	72	1473	20.5	12
Johnny Carson	45	604	13.5	4
Charley Hennigan	44	722	16.4	6
Dave Smith	22	216	9.8	2
Billy Cannon	15	187	12.5	5
Charlie Tolar	7	71	10.1	0

Leading scorers	TDs	XPM	XPA	FGM	FGA	PTs
George Blanda	4	46	47	15	33	115
Bill Groman	12					72

10. The league's leading punter in 1960 is one of only two AFLers to come from The Citadel, where he led the nation in pass receiving in 1959. He also lays claim to having worn those hideous vertically striped socks and gold and brown Denver uniforms. Who is this former Charger and Buffalo Bill?

1961

AMERICAN FOOTBALL LEAGUE - 1961 FINAL STANDINGS

EASTERN DIVISION

TEAM	GP	W	L	T	PF	PA	PCT.
HOUSTON OILERS	14	10	3	1	513	242	0.769
BOSTON PATRIOTS	14	9	4	1	413	313	0.679
NEW YORK TITANS	14	7	7	0	301	390	0.500
BUFFALO BILLS	14	6	8	0	294	342	0.429

WESTERN DIVISION

TEAM	GP	W	L	T	PF	PA	PCT.
SAN DIEGO CHARGERS	14	12	2	0	396	219	0.857
DALLAS TEXANS	14	6	8	0	334	343	0.571
DENVER BRONCOS	14	3	11	0	251	432	0.214
OAKLAND RAIDERS	14	2	12	0	237	458	0.143

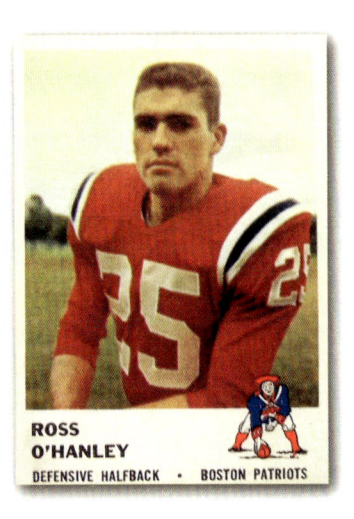

Ross O'Hanley was a local favorite out of Boston College when he joined the Patriots for their first season and gained all-league honors at safety. The 6', 175 lbs. defensive back intercepted 3 passes in 1960 as the cornerstone of Boston's pass defense. Ross missed part of the 1961 season as a National Guardsman and the entire 1966 season with an injury after being selected by the Miami Dolphins in the AFL's first expansion draft. A member of the Patriots and the AFL from 1960–1965, O'Hanley retired after the '66 season having helped write a chapter of AFL history as one of its originals.

■ BOSTON PATRIOTS ■

COMING OFF OF A SEASON THAT SAW them score fewer points than any other AFL team, the Boston Patriots were desperate for offensive firepower. Their hope was to find it in the person of Vito "Babe" Parilli, a veteran quarterback with NFL experience. Parilli was a backup to Tom Flores in Oakland in 1960 but his arm and play-calling savvy were assets Boston admired and needed. Sending their top two rushers, Alan Miller and Dick Christy, to the Raiders brought Parilli and Oakland's leading receiver, Billy Lott, to Boston. The trade paid immediate dividends for Boston as they scored 127 more points in 1961 and posted

The Progress of the Seasons – 1961

four more victories. Parilli and Butch Songin split the quarterbacking duties, combining for over 2,700 yards passing and 27 touchdowns against 18 interceptions. They ranked fifth and seventh among all AFL quarterbacks at the season's end. Besides a change at quarterback the 1961 Patriots also changed the logo on their helmets. Scrapped was their tri-cornered hat graphic; Pat the Patriot minuteman replaced it. The logo was submitted the year before by a *Boston Globe* writer.

Once again the Patriots opened the season on September 9. And with Parilli under center, Boston trailed New York 23-21 with only minutes to play and a chance to win the game as kicker Gino Cappelletti lined up a 32-yard field goal. But his attempt drifted wide and for the second year in a row Boston dropped their season opener. In his Patriot debut Parilli connected on 11 of 26 passes for 1 touchdown, to Cappelletti, Boston's kicking and new receiving threat. Cappy scored 14 of the Pats 20 points on a touchdown, 2 field goals, and 2 PAT's.

Butch Songin, the starting quarterback of a year ago, was the hero of game two as he relieved Babe and passed the Patriots to a 45-17 win over Denver. A 23-21 victory against Buffalo in week three pushed the Pats over .500 for the first time ever at 2-1. New York made it two in a row over Boston in week four, handing the Pats a 37-30 defeat. Cappelletti continued his offensive barrage, scoring 18 points and even threw a 27-yard touchdown pass to halfback Larry Garron on a fake field goal. With a loss to San Diego 38-27 at BU field in the fifth week of the season, owner Billy Sullivan was unhappy with his team's results and decided to make a bold move in hope of reviving the Pats. He handed coach Lou Saban his walking papers. The speculation for a large part of the firing was that Saban and the front office had a disagreement over Saban's desire to trade Sullivan's first franchise draft choice, Ron Burton. With Saban's departure, Sullivan turned to assistant coach Mike Holovak as his new leader. In his first game Holovak faced the defending champion Houston Oilers who were floundering with a 1-3 record and also experiencing some internal turmoil. With five seconds left in the game Houston's George Blanda booted a 24-yard field goal to salvage a 31-31 tie for Houston, sending Holovak home disappointed in his first game as head coach.

For the next several games Holovak, unable to determine who was the better choice, alternated both Parilli and Songin the way Cleveland Browns coach Paul Brown sent in plays using alternating messenger guards. A blowout over Buffalo 52-21 at BU the following week earned Holovak his first victory. The Patriots were suddenly hot, and home and away wins against Dallas had Holovak undefeated through his first four games. They took

65

a 5-3-1 record into Houston, who rode a five-game winning streak. With first place in the East at stake the Oilers extended their streak to six in a row with a 27-15 win over the disappointed Pats. Boston then ran the table in their last four games with wins over Oakland, Denver, Oakland again, and the Western Division champion Chargers, who they destroyed 41-0. Against the Raiders the Pats were down 17-13 with a little over two minutes to play when a Raider punt from their own end zone hit an upright (the goal posts were still on the goal line in the '60s) bounded back into the end zone, and was recovered for a Boston touchdown. The Pats won 20-17.

Under Holovak's leadership Boston went 7-1-1. Finishing behind only Houston in points scored and only San Diego and Houston in fewest points allowed, the turnaround was the most dramatic in the league. The defense also gave up fewer yards on the ground (only 3 yards per carry) than any other AFL team. The front four was anchored by Holy Cross standout Jim Hunt, who was released by the NFL Cardinals, Houston Antwine, released by the NFL Lions as well as the Oilers, and Boston College and Holy Cross alums Larry Eisenhauer and Bob Dee. The group sacked opposing quarterbacks 44 times. This front four would go on to be one of the most dominant and stable in AFL history. An all-league safety in 1960, Ross O'Hanley missed half of the season as he was called to duty by the National Guard and played only seven games.

At 9-4-1 Boston finished only one game out of first place, and while there were certainly a lot of highlights for the Patriots in 1961, including standout performances like Larry Garron's 85-yard touchdown run, his 88-yard kickoff return for a touchdown, and Ron Burton's 91-yard kickoff return for a touchdown, probably the most bizarre play in AFL history also occurred in New England that year and involved not only the Boston Patriots but also one of their frenzied fans. It happened on November 3 during the closing seconds of their Friday night game against the visiting Dallas Texans. The Patriots had a 28-21 lead on the Texans, who were driving toward the Boston end zone. The Boston faithful, anticipating a Patriot victory, were lining the field for the last play of the game. Having one last crack at the goal line from inside the Patriot ten-yard line, quarterback Cotton Davidson shot a pass over the middle intended for Chris Burford in the end zone. No one noticed that prior to the snap a fan in a gray coat ran onto the field and inconspicu-

The Progress of the Seasons – 1961

ously positioned himself behind Boston's middle linebacker. As Davidson threw in Burford's direction the fan reached his arm up and knocked the pass to the ground. As he immediately ran off, those fans who had lined the field stormed onto it, claiming victory. The Texans, realizing what had happened, protested vehemently to the officials who were oblivious to what had occurred. With instant replay still years away, they had no evidence that anything out of the ordinary had occurred. The Patriots victory went into the books as well as the folklore of the AFL.

Leading passers	Attempts	Completions	Pct	TDs	Yards	Int
Babe Parilli	198	104	52%	13	1314	9
Ed "Butch" Songin	212	98	46%	14	1429	9

Leading rushers	Attempts	Yards gained	Average	TDs
Billy Lott	100	461	4.7	5
Larry Garron	69	389	5.6	2
Ron Burton	82	260	3.3	2
Babe Parilli	38	183	4.8	5

Leading receivers	Caught	Yards gained	Average	TDs
Gino Cappelletti	45	768	17.1	8
Jim Colclough	42	757	18.0	9
Billy Lott	32	333	10.4	6
Larry Garron	24	341	14.2	3
Tom Stephens	19	186	9.8	2
Ron Burton	13	115	8.8	0

Leading scorers	TDs	XPM	XPA	FGM	FGA	PTs
Gino Cappelletti	8	48	50	17	32	147
Billy Lott	11					66

11. There are several theories about the origin of the New York franchise's name, the Titans. One is that principal owner Harry Wismer wanted to go one better on his crosstown competition, the NFL's New York Giants. So he needed a name that was bigger than a Giant. The U.S. Air Force had just unveiled its new Titan missile, and the suggestion that a Titan was bigger than a Giant appealed to Wismer, who approved it as the official name. Another is that Wismer was so cheap in running his team that he didn't want to spend money on a new marquee sign for the front of the Polo Grounds. So he used what was already there by mixing the letters left behind by the NY baseball Giants. He only needed to change one letter, from a G to a T to complete the name. In those early New York Titans days, Wismer even skimped on the team's office. Where did he set up his first team and ticket office?

■ OAKLAND RAIDERS ■

AS THE RAIDERS READIED FOR THEIR second season, the front office was in disarray. Owner infighting created chaos on the field, and the team could sign just six of their first thirty draft choices. It wasn't until commissioner Joe Foss stepped in to intervene that the rubble could be sorted out. With the flip of a coin the Oakland ownership was reduced from eight members to three in a prearranged buyout. Looking for more clout on the gridiron, Oakland then traded backup quarterback Babe Parilli and fullback Billy Lott to Boston for the Patriots' starting backfield mates Dick Christy and Alan Miller.

The Oakland faithful again had to put their tails between their legs and travel across the Bay Bridge to see their favorites. With Erdelatz realistically optimistic, the Raiders opened the new season with the Houston Oilers, just as they did in 1960, but this time it was on the road. The optimism quickly turned to gloom as the champion Oilers trampled Oakland 55-0. As if things could not have gotten worse, the Raiders traveled down the California coast to play the Western Division champion Chargers on week two. The Chargers, now relocated in San Diego and playing in ancient Balboa Stadium, with the impact of a heavyweight knockout punch, sent the Raiders to the canvas with a 44-0 loss. Two weeks into the new season Oakland found themselves with an 0-2 record, having lost by a combined score of 99-0. It was the ticket out of town for coach Eddie Erdelatz, who became the first AFL head coach to be fired. Line coach Marty Feldman assumed the top spot but faired no better. The Raiders went 2-10 the rest of the way but were close enough to win in at least five of them. Against Boston, the Raiders held a 17-13 lead with 2:40 left when Wayne Crow's punt from his own end zone hit an upright, bounced back into the end zone and was recovered for a Boston touchdown. The Raiders lost 20-17. While they led Denver 24-13 late in the fourth quarter, rookie halfback Charlie Fuller fumbled twice in the waning minutes, leading to 2 Bronco touchdowns and another last-minute Raider loss. They also lost by 5 points to Buffalo and by 7 to Dallas.

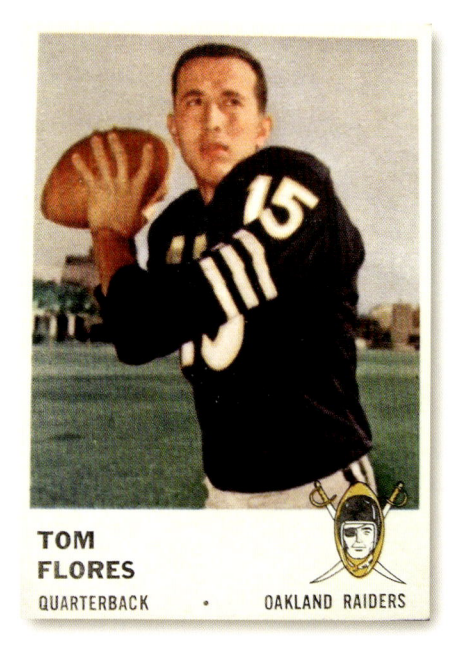

Finishing a dismal 2-12, the Raiders were led on the ground by Wayne Crow, who gained only 490 yards on 119 carries and Alan Miller, with 255 yards on 85 carries. Needing more punch and speed in the backfield, the Raiders also used Clem Daniels, who had been released by Dallas, on 31 carries. Daniels gained 154 yards for a team-high 4.9 average. Tight end Doug Asad was the leading pass catcher with 43, followed by Alan Miller, and rookie Bob Coolbaugh. Tom Flores had another good year and finished as the second-ranked thrower in the league behind George Blanda. As a team the Raiders were last in both rushing and passing. They also gave up more yardage than every other AFL defense, being outgained almost 2 to 1 on the ground. It was a giant step backward for the franchise that hoped to move to a legitimate home in Oakland for 1962, while Feldman planned to rebuild the worst team in the AFL.

Leading passers	Attempts	Completions	Pct	TDs	Yards	Int
Tom Flores	366	190	52%	15	2176	19
Nick Papac	44	13	29%	2	173	7

Leading rushers	Attempts	Yards gained	Average	TDs
Wayne Crow	119	490	4.1	2
Alan Miller	85	255	3.0	3
Clem Daniels	31	154	5.1	2
Charlie Fuller	38	134	3.5	0

Leading receivers	Caught	Yards gained	Average	TDs
Doug Asad	43	592	13.9	2
Alan Miller	36	315	8.8	4
Bob Coolbaugh	32	435	13.6	4
Charlie Hardy	24	337	14.0	4
Wayne Crow	23	196	8.5	0
Jerry Burch	18	235	13.1	1

Leading scorers	TDs	XPM	XPA	FGM	FGA	PTs
George Fleming	1	24	25	11	26	63
Alan Miller	7					42

▪ BUFFALO BILLS ▪

FOR THE BILLS, 1961 WAS A SHORT chorus of "second verse, same as the first!" Following up their 5-8-1 record in 1960, the Bills went 6-8 in their second season. Again the defense carried them with a front four comprised of all-league end Laverne Torczon, Mack Yoho, Chuck McMurtry, and Jim Sorey. The Bills were the third-best team against the run but the pass defense left a lot to be desired with defenders Richie McCabe (all-league in '60), Jim Wagstaff, Bill Johnson, Billy Atkins ranking next to last even though Atkins led the league with 10 interceptions. On offense the Bills struggled again, showing only an 8-point improvement from the previous season.

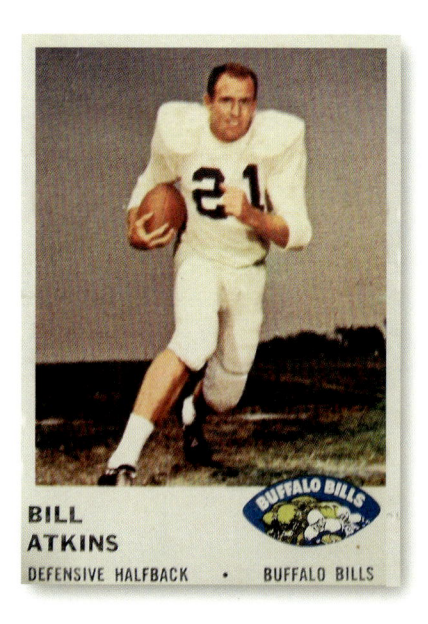

BILL ATKINS
DEFENSIVE HALFBACK • BUFFALO BILLS

Head coach Buster Ramsey was still unsettled at quarterback and just as in 1960, he chose to shuttle his signal callers. This time he employed five, one more than a year ago. Tommy O'Connell, the starter in 1960, played just one game and faded into retirement, faring better as a member of the coaching staff. The franchise's first-draft choice, Richie Lucas, saw work as a runner, pass catcher, and thrower, but played only eight games and threw only 50 passes before being lost to the Army. Holdover Johnny (Chuck) Green also played eight games and pitched 126 passes, completing only 56 of them. Two NFL castoffs also threw their helmets into the ring. Ex-Lion Warren Raab showed well in his nine games, completing 46 percent of his 74 attempts for 5 touchdowns, against only 2 interceptions. But the man who saw the most action at quarterback under Ramsey in '61 was former Washington Redskin M. C. Reynolds. Reynolds threw for a team high 1,004 yards and completed 83 of his 181 passes, but only 2 found the end zone, while 13 ended up in the clutches of opponents.

In an effort to spring flanker Elbert Dubenion from the double coverage he saw too often in 1960, Ramsey picked up rookie Glenn Bass, a former running back from Tennessee who had been cut by the Chargers. Bass ended up being a great acquisition as he led the Bills with 50 receptions for 755 yards. Tight end Tom Rychlec, the team recepton leader a year ago, caught 33, followed by Dubenion, who fell off to 31 catches, 6 for TD's, adding another 2 running flanker-around plays. To start the season Buffalo found themselves at home for seven of their first nine games, but the Bills failed to capitalize on their home field advantage and won only three of them. The youngest team in the league then hit the road and won only three more all season.

Life on the road originally looked like it was just what the doctor ordered as Buffalo won their first two in Dallas and Denver but then headed back home to drop a 21-14 decision to the Titans. Another trip out West had the Bills winning in Oakland 26-21 but losing on their first-ever trip to San Diego 28-10. The offensive output was a major cause for concern for Ramsey, as only once in their fourteen games did the Bills score more than 30 points, averaging 21 per game on the season while giving up an average of 24.

The ground game was another area where the Bills came up short. Their 1,608 yards was fifth out of eight, led by Syracuse rookie Art Baker with 498 yards for a low 3.3 yards per carry average. Wray Carlton's 311 yards gained put his average even lower at 3.1. Fleet-footed halfback Wilmer Fowler, Buffalo's second leading rusher in 1960, returned a kickoff 100 yards early in the season then went down for the rest of the year with a knee injury. Defensive tackle McMurtry and middle linebacker Archie Matsos were selected to the all-league team. For Matsos it was his second straight honor. At the end of the season the Bills two-year record of 11-16-1 under Ramsey was not good enough to bring him back for a third. Upon relieving him of his coaching duties, owner Ralph Wilson looked to former Patriots head coach Lou Saban to turn the Buffalo fortunes around.

Leading passers	Attempts	Completions	Pct	TDs	Yards	Int
M. C. Reynolds	181	83	46%	2	1004	13
Johnny Green	126	56	44%	6	903	5

Leading rushers	Attempts	Yards gained	Average	TDs
Art Baker	152	498	3.3	3
Wray Carlton	101	311	3.1	4
Fred Brown	53	192	3.6	1
Elbert Dubenion	17	173	10.2	2

Leading receivers	Caught	Yards gained	Average	TDs
Glenn Bass	50	765	15.3	3
Tom Rychlec	33	405	12.3	2
Elbert Dubenion	31	461	14.9	6
Monte Crockett	20	325	16.3	0
Perry Richards	19	285	15.0	3
Wray Carlton	17	193	11.4	0

Leading scorers	TDs	XPM	XPA	FGM	FGA	PTs
Elbert Dubenion	8					48
Billy Atkins		29	31	2	6	42

12. The first Buffalo football franchise in the 1940s was named the Bisons but later changed to the Bills so they could separate their identity from the city's baseball and hockey teams with the same name. What is the significance of their name Buffalo Bills?

• DENVER BRONCOS •

Frank Tripucka never intended to be quarterbacking the Broncos in 1960 let alone lead them into their second season. Tripucka signed on from the Canadian Football League to be a coach. But after every recruit paled in relation to the coach, he was pressed into duty, throwing more passes than any other AFL quarterback the first year. He was back chuckin' another 344 times in 1961. Along with backup George Herring, the Broncos in 1961 threw at a rate of almost a 2-to-1 to their running game. With only Ken Adamson at guard and Eldon Dannenhauer at tackle showing any semblance of professional blocking skills, the entire group of Denver running backs gained only 1,019 yards on the ground—only 143 yards more than the AFL's leading runner, Billy Cannon, gained by himself. With the absence of a running game Tripucka and Herring fired over 500 passes, averaging some 40 aerials every game. By contrast they handed off less than 25 times per game and averaged a mere 78 yards rushing, the worst in the league.

To simply survive, the Broncos had to put the ball in the air. Previously, Tripucka relied on his football knowledge to lead the offense, many times drawing up plays in the dirt in the huddle. In the offensive scheme of things, the Broncos had not evolved much past that practice. The game plan called mainly for the same strategy used on millions of playgrounds around the country, which was "everybody go out for a pass." Herring and Tripucka threw for more than 1,000 yards, but between them they were picked off forty-three times, a league high. Denver had the third-best passing attack behind only Houston and San Diego, both winners of their respective divisions again. With the abundance of balls put up for grabs, Lionel Taylor became the main beneficiary. His number was called more than any other, and as a result he pulled in more receptions (100) than any other receiver in the history of professional football. But for all his receptions, Taylor was able to crack the goal line only four times, drawing mostly double coverage inside the 20-yard line. Diminutive Al Frazier was Tripucka's other prime target, catching 47 balls including 6 for touchdowns. Tight end Gene Prebola grabbed 29 throws but caught only 1 for a touchdown.

On defense only the 2-12 Raiders allowed more points, with Denver being the only other club to allow over 400 points, for an average yield of 31 per game against their own scoring average of only 18. Defensive tackle Bud McFadin, a bonified jammer in the middle of the line, joined Taylor as the only Bronco selected to the all league squad. He and Austin Gonsoulin were also the only two defensive players from Denver picked to play for the West in the first AFL All-Star game. On offense, fullback Donnie Stone, who gained a team-high 505 yards, joined the record-setting Taylor for the game.

The Broncos kicked off their second season with a 22-10 win in Buffalo. The Bills still had not found a quarterback or an offense, and Denver was able to take advantage of the shortcoming. Taylor started the scoring in the first period with a 50-yard reception but it was from neither Tripucka nor Herring. Hitting on one of his four completions in nine season attempts, halfback Gene Mingo used an option play to find Taylor for 6 points. In the third quarter Mingo found Taylor in the end zone again, this time for 52 yards. Discounting these 2 scoring passes at the end of Mingo's halfback passes, Taylor caught only 2 of his other 98 catches in the end zone from Bronco quarterbacks. The defense was uncharacteristically strong in the opener and allowed only 1 touchdown all afternoon. The Bills only score of the second half came as George Herring ran out of the end zone in the fourth quarter with the game well in hand for Denver.

In Boston for a Saturday night game on September 16, Denver ran into an improved Patriot offense. The Patriots stayed close for a half and trailed 10-3, and then turned on their scoring machine to tally 35 points to Denver's 14 in the second half. Denver scored when Tripucka connected with Mingo for 69 yards and with Taylor for a 3-yarder. A third straight game on the east coast had the Broncos on the short end a second time. The New York Titans jumped ahead 14-0 then 28-7 at the midpoint. Denver made it a thriller with 3 rushing touchdowns in the third and fourth quarters, but the 35-28 result dropped them to 1-2 with still another road game to come before they could go home.

Traveling to San Francisco's Candlestick Park, the Broncos fell victim to one of Oakland's two 1961 victories, 33-19, in front of a skeleton crowd of only 8,361 fans. Finally playing at home, the Broncos entertained 14,500 onlookers and the Dallas Texans. Trailing 19-0 in the fourth quarter, Tripucka fired 2 TD passes, 1 to Frazier, and 1 to Taylor in the fourth quarter, but the result was the same as the previous three games, another loss, this time 19-12. Thankfully the next week brought the Oakland Raiders and their 1-3 record to Bears Stadium to play the 1-4 Broncos. It looked like the Raiders would walk off with their second win, but the Bronco defense forced 2 fourth-quarter fumbles, and kicker Jack Hill kicked 2 field goals in the last frame, sending the Denver fans home happy with a comeback 27-24 win. October 22 was the last happy day for Denverites, as the Broncos dropped New York 27-10 for their second straight win to raise their record to 3-4. The game's final touchdown had the look of another Frank Tripucka play drawn up in the huddle, except that it was George Herring leading the charge. After catching a quick pass, tight end Gene Prebola lateraled to Gene Mingo who galloped to an 18-yard touchdown and their last win of the season. A 37-0 loss to San Diego followed. Then a 55-14 drubbing at the hands of Houston.

What looked like a fourth Denver win in front of 7,859 at Bears Stadium started with an 87-yard bomb from Tripucka to Al Frazier, giving Denver a 9-0 lead over the Chargers in the fourth quarter. But win number four wasn't in the stars for the Broncos as San Diego pulled out a 19-16 win to stay undefeated. A 23-10 loss to Buffalo, a 45-14 loss to the Oilers, and a close 28-24 loss at the hands of Boston set up the season finale with Dallas. The result was no different, as Denver dropped their seventh in a row 49-21. Finishing 3-11, the Broncos took a step backward from their 4-9-1 record of 1960, spelling doom for coach Frank Filchock who would not return in 1962.

A season total of only 74,508 saw the Broncos in action at home in their second go-around. The average of 10,648 was nearly 12,000 a game less than the year before. Losing over $200,000, owner Bob Howsam and his team were in jeopardy, and their future in the western city had become uncertain.

Leading passers	Attempts	Completions	Pct	TDs	Yards	Int
Frank Tripucka	344	167	48%	10	1690	21
George Henning	211	93	44%	5	1160	22

Leading rushers	Attempts	Yards gained	Average	TDs
Donnie Stone	127	505	4.0	4
Steve Bukaty	76	187	2.5	5
Dave Ames	19	114	6.0	0
Al Frazier	23	110	4.8	0

Leading receivers	Caught	Yards gained	Average	TDs
Lionel Taylor	100	1176	11.7	4
Al Frazier	47	799	17.0	6
Donnie Stone	38	344	9.1	4
Gene Prebola	29	349	12.0	1
Steve Bukaty	14	96	6.7	0
Jim Stinnette	11	58	5.2	1

Leading scorers	TDs	XPM	XPA	FGM	FGA	PTs
Al Frazier	8	1 (run)				50
Donnie Stone	8					48
Gene Mingo	2	11	11	3	10	32
Jack Hill		16	16	5	15	31

13. Although it may be hard to believe, the New York Titans played an exhibition game on August 19, 1961, that had more fans in the seats than all of their 1960 home games combined, with 73,916 onlookers filling Philadelphia's Memorial Stadium (later renamed JFK). The game between the Titans and Patriots became known as the _____ Bowl because of the free tickets given away with a $10 purchase at the local Acme Markets.

■ NEW YORK TITANS ■

WHEN THE SEASON OPENED ON September 9 the Titans and Boston Patriots found themselves playing each other for the third time in a month. Thirteen new faces, including halfback Dick Christy, a former Boston runner, suited up for New York. In contrast, only ten Patriots were around to see last season's opening game. The Titans again featured a wide-open offense and a defense designed to log only enough minutes to give the offense a breather. The offensive line returned with Gene Cockrell and Jack Klotz at tackle, Mike Hudock at center, and John McMullen and all-league Bob Mischak at guard. Thurlow Cooper returned as the blocking end as did Art Powell at split end. Al Dorow, Don Maynard, Bill Mathis, and Dick Christy filled out the backfield. Mathis in 1961 carried the ball 202 times, more than any other AFL runner, and gained more yards (846) than all except Billy Cannon. Christy led the league in punt-return average. Al Dorow was not as fortunate. His 30 interceptions were more than every other AFL quarterback, and his 44.9 pass-completion percentage was the lowest among AFL starting quarterbacks. Dorow was forced to play under every condition due to the lack of an effective backup. Dick Jamieson, Dorow's backup last season, injured a disc in training camp and never took a snap in '61. The receivers were led by Powell's 71 catches, 5 for touchdowns, and Maynard who caught 43 passes. Both averaged less than 15 yards per catch. The Titan passing attack was only a shadow of the previous year and finished ahead of only Buffalo's musical-chair quarterbacks and the receiver-weak Raiders in the rankings. The running, on the other hand, finished third, with Mathis, Mel West, Christy, and Dorow providing the yardage.

The Titans, under second-year coach Sammy Baugh, were an exemplary AFL team, looking to score from anywhere on the gridiron and throwing (51 percent) more than running the football. But the top scoring team of a year ago had slipped, dropping 81 points on the scoreboard and scoring fewer points than four other teams.

The defense had an authentic front line of Mike Saidock, Sid Youngelman, Nick Mumley, and Dick Guesman, but the team that allowed more points (399) than any other team their first year tightened their belt by only 9 points in their second season. Suffering the loss of their best player to military service did not help the Titan cause either. Linebacker Larry Grantham did not play his first game

TOM SAIDOCK
DEFENSIVE TACKLE • NEW YORK TITANS

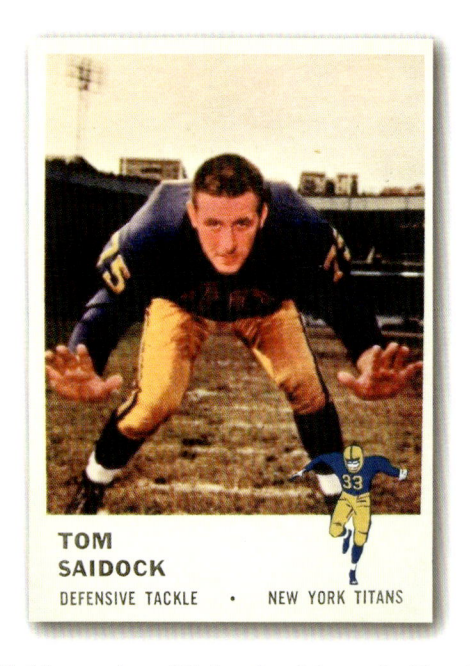

until November 23 in the Mayor's Trophy Game on Thanksgiving Day. The defense suffered further when his replacement, Jim Furey, was lost to injury. But for all of the points they allowed, the Titan defense specialized in take-aways. Forty-six times the New Yorkers stopped opponent drives with 25 interceptions and recovered 21 of the opposition's 36 fumbles. The secondary of Dick Felt, Lee Riley, Johnny Bookman, Don Flynn, and Dainard Paulson allowed quarterbacks only a 45.7 completion percentage, the league's third best. Linebackers Hubert Bobo, Pat Lamberti, along with Grantham and Furey, provided defensive run and pass support. The Titans also benefited from the coaching turmoil in Houston and the inconsistency of Boston to stay competitive, and even led the Eastern Division for six of the first seven weeks. They were not eliminated from contention until the season's fourteenth week.

Against Boston in the opener, the Titans' first touchdown was a repeat of last year, with Dorow scoring on a 2-yard sneak. The back-and-forth battle had New York up by 7 in the first quarter but in the second new Patriot quarterback Babe Parilli tied it with a sneak himself. Dorow countered with a 16-yard touchdown pass to tight-end Thurlow Cooper. Fending off a 17-14 deficit in the fourth quarter, Dorow fired his second touchdown pass of the day, this time to Don Maynard for 37 yards to take the lead again at 21-17. A Boston field goal with eight minutes left narrowed the lead to 1, and with four minutes to play, Boston had the ball on the Titan 38-yard line. On fourth down the Pats looked to take the lead with a field goal attempt, but the kick drifted wide, and Sammy Baugh had his first win of the second season.

In Buffalo on week two the offense lit up the scoreboard with 24 points in the first half. But the defense was having another ineffective day and made Richie Lucas, second in the 1959 Heisman voting, look like an all-star. They gave up 28 points to Buffalo in the first two periods. The scoring slowed in the last two frames, but in the end Buffalo had its first win of the season and New York its first loss 41-31.

The first-half fireworks continued against Denver in the Polo Grounds on September 24. A reported 14,381 watched Dick Christy return a Bronco punt 70 yards for New York's first 6 points and then witnessed an encore performance in the second quarter when he ran 64 yards with another punt for 6 points. Before the half was over Dorow, playing with an injured back, and Maynard, teamed up for a 39-yard touchdown giving the Titans a 28-7 halftime lead. The Broncos made a valiant effort to comeback as quarterbacks Tripucka and Herring desperately threw 32 times in the second half, but the home team prevailed with a 35-28 victory and a share of first place with Boston, their next opponent.

While Houston was losing to Dallas, the Titans took over sole possession of first place with a thrilling 37-30 win the following week against the Patriots in the Polo Grounds. The New York defense thwarted every touchdown threat the Patriots mustered in the first quarter and forced Boston to score their first 9 points on field goals. Dorow and new backup Bob Scrabis from Penn State had the Titans answering with 20 straight points in the second quarter and led at halftime. Tied in the fourth quarter, Dorow, who had to leave the game with a bruised neck in the first half returned to hit Don Maynard with a 13-yard pass that the flanker wrestled away from DB Fred Bruney in the end zone for the winning score. A fourth down interception by Lee Riley on Boston's last possession sealed the New York victory. A well-earned bye week followed and set up a match-up of first-place teams against San Diego at home on October 15. Wismer's figures showed 25,136 in attendance for the faceoff, but the anticipation of the feature even fared better than the game itself. New York lost 25-10, but stayed alone in first place by virtue of a tie between Boston and Houston, while lifting 3-3 Buffalo into second place. Traveling to Denver for their next game, the Titans were anxious to get back on the winning track. A 10-7 halftime lead had the Titans feeling confident even after they lost Don Maynard with an injured shoulder. The Broncos strategy against the Titans always seemed to be to wait until the mile-high altitude kicked in to make their move. It worked again, as they scored 17 points in the fourth quarter to overtake the New Yorkers 27-10. The Titans dropped to 3-3, but they remained in first place. Continuing West for their next game against Oakland the Titans used two Bill Mathis touchdown runs to score their 14 points and then watched the defense put in their finest effort so far by denying the Raiders a single touchdown. Winning 14-6, the Titans still sat in first place even though Houston and Boston both won their second game in a row. A trip south to San Diego on week nine was the beginning of the end for Sammy and his Titans. One week after the Titans best effort defensively, the Chargers exposed every weakness imaginable to score 42 points in the second half and won easily 48-13. With a record that now stood at 4-4, the Titans awoke Monday morning to find themselves in third place behind both Houston and Boston, who were now each riding three-game win streaks. Another win against the Raiders (23-12) kept the Titans close, but they were unable to put together another two wins in a row the rest of the way. And as the season wound down the residents of Coogan's Bluff checked into third place in the East with a 7-7 record for the second year in a row.

Bob Mischak and Bill Mathis made the all-league team for 1961 and joined Al Dorow,

Dick Felt, and Larry Grantham on the first Eastern Division all-star team. Owner Harry Wismer continued to be an embarrassment for the New Yorkers as he made it a practice of doubling the attendance reports to the press and also relished bringing more attention to himself than his team and players. And just as he was waging a one-man war on commissioner Joe Foss, calling for the dismissal, he would later turn around and solicit Foss' service to be the best man in his wedding. In another audacious move, Wismer asked Sammy Baugh to step down as head coach to become an assistant. Baugh requested to be fired, which would make him eligible to collect the remaining year's salary on his contract. When Wismer declined, Baugh became the most expensive assistant in the league before Wismer was forced to buy out the last year of Baugh's contract by best man and commissioner Joe Foss.

Leading passers	Attempts	Completions	Pct	TDs	Yards	Int
Al Dorow	438	197	45%	19	2651	30
Bob Scrabis	21	7	33%	1	82	2

Leading rushers	Attempts	Yards gained	Average	TDs
Bill Mathis	202	846	4.2	7
Mel West	46	232	5.0	3
Al Dorow	54	317	5.9	4
Dick Christy	81	180	2.2	2

Leading receivers	Caught	Yards gained	Average	TDs
Art Powell	71	881	12.4	5
Don Maynard	43	629	14.6	8
Dick Christy	29	521	17.9	1
Bob Renn	18	268	14.9	1
Thurlow Cooper	15	208	13.9	4

Leading scorers	TDs	XPM	XPA	FGM	FGA	PTs
Bill Mathis	8					48
Don Maynard	8					48
Dick Guesman		24	26	5	15	39

The Progress of the Seasons – 1961

■ DALLAS TEXANS ■

IN THEIR SECOND SEASON, THE TEXANS continued to be an enigma. They had one of the best owners, one of the best coaches, many top-notch players, the top running game, and an excellent defense. And yet, they weren't able to perform consistently. As the season opened, they felt confident they could compete with the Chargers for supremacy in the West. The Texans owned the best running game in the AFL with the tandem of league-leading rusher Abner Haynes and fullback Jack Spikes, along with reserves Johnny Robinson, Frank Jackson, and Bo Dickenson. Haynes also posed a formidable pass-catching threat with his speed and crafty moves. But Spikes, a better-than-average runner, was lost after six games in what was turning into an all-league season for him. With the Texans still on the Chargers' tail with a 3-3 record, Spikes had gained 334 yards on 39 carries, giving him a league-leading average of 8.6 yards per carry. After his loss, the Texans lost three games in a row.

The Dallas offensive line was often blamed for not protecting quarterback Cotton Davidson long enough to allow the QB to find his open receivers. Opposing scouts advised defenses to get to him early and cause him to rush his passes. Davidson threw 330 times in '61, completing 151 (45.8 percent) for 2,445 yards. His 23 interceptions were second most in the league. Seventeen of his completions were for touchdowns. Offensively, Dallas was statistically one of the best, finishing fourth in passing and first in rushing.

Just as in their first season, the Texans started with a game against the Chargers. The defending Western champions shut them out for three periods before Spikes kicked a field goal. Two fourth-quarter Charger touchdowns gave San Diego a 26-3 lead when Spikes broke off a 74-yard touchdown run to make the final score 26-10. For the game, Spikes carried 7 times, gaining 109 of the Texans' 209 running yards, but Davidson and second-stringer Randy Duncan could muster only 83 yards through the air. Dallas' receiving corps was another inconsistent area for the Texans. Stanford All-American Chris Burford drew raves around the

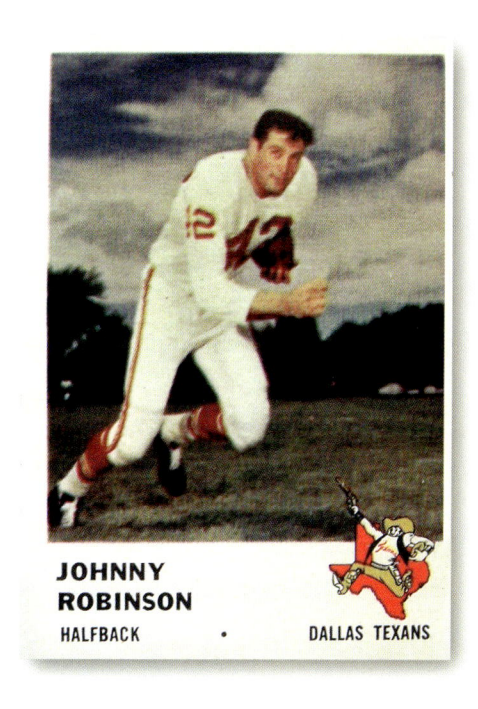

JOHNNY ROBINSON
HALFBACK • DALLAS TEXANS

league as a fast, gritty pass catcher who could block with the best of them. He caught 51 passes for the season, with 5 touchdowns. But the lack of other good receivers had Stram calling on his backs to take the pressure off Burford. Haynes was the best of the lot, but he would suffer a sub-par year plagued with multiple injuries. His 34 catches were good for third on the team. Halfback Johnny Robinson caught 35. Tight end Max Boydston caught less than 1 per game, as did split end Tony Romeo.

With their lack of striking power through the air, the Texans looked more like an NFL offense. Stram's offensive show had Davidson and Duncan putting the ball up 339 times and handing it off 439, the only team in the AFL that ran more than they passed. Finishing in the middle of the pack in passing and team defense, the Texans never got untracked, and after the first four weeks the optimism drifted to disappointment, as neither side of the line could take charge.

Defensive end Mel Branch, coming off of an all-league season, suffered all year with a nagging leg injury. Paul Rochester, Paul Miller, and rookie Jerry Mays were adequate line mates, but it was the group of linebackers that gave the defense its edge. Sherrill Headrick repeated as the all-league middle backer, and youngsters Smokey Stover and E.J. Holub had a lock on youth and toughness. In the secondary, Dave Webster joined Headrick on the all-league team and combined with Duane Wood, Dave Grayson, and Doyle Nix for 25 interceptions, but they failed to stop 50 percent of their opponent's passes.

A back-and-forth battle with Oakland brought Dallas its first taste of victory in '61. Randy Duncan and Davidson passed for 3 touchdowns between them, and Jack Spikes and Dick (Bo) Dickenson added two more on the ground. There were five lead changes before Dallas finally won 42-35. The high point of the season came on October 1 in the first of two games with the Oilers. The Cotton Bowl hosted 28,000 fans who watched in awe as Houston's Billy Cannon started the scoring in the first quarter with a 70-yard touchdown pass from George Blanda. Not to be denied, the Texans stormed back with 4 straight touchdowns, 3 by Spikes on runs of 31, 2, and 73 yards, 1 by Abner Haynes, a 24-yard jaunt. The Texans held off a late Oiler uprising to win 26-21, giving them a 2-1 record. Dumping the Broncos 19-12 gave them their third straight win to trail the Chargers by only a game. In Buffalo on October 15, it took more than three periods to get the Texans untracked. Losing 20-3, they struck with 2 Abner Haynes touchdowns to trail by 3 with plenty of time left. Buffalo's Richie Lucas then picked up a fumble and scored from the 19 yard line to increase the Bills lead to 10. Haynes brought the crowd to their feet on the ensuing kickoff by taking it 87 yards for a touchdown. But it was too little too late, and the beginning of a six-game losing streak had begun. Again the inconsistency of Dallas proved to be their own demise.

The play of the offensive line did give Stram some reason to smile. Although Krisher did not repeat as an all-leaguer, he and Marvin

The Progress of the Seasons – 1961

Terrell were as good as they come at leading a sweep. Tackles Jerry Cornelison and massive Jim Tyrer were both big and mobile, while center Jon Gilliam was a comer. With these five lineman driving holes in the defense, Dallas owned the best running game in the AFL. Another win over Oakland and season-ending victories over Denver and New York brought the 6-8 season to a close, a full six games behind division-winning San Diego. For a team that hoped to challenge, a two-year record of 14-14 was a Texas-sized disappointment, and both Lamar Hunt and Hank Stram knew that to win the hearts of Dallas fans and compete with the rival Cowboys, the victories would have to come more frequently. Changes were in store for the Texans in 1962, with upgrades at quarterback and on defense being the top priorities. For Texan fans, the best was yet to come.

Leading passers	Attempts	Completions	Pct	TDs	Yards	Int
Cotton Davidson	330	151	46%	17	2445	23
Randy Duncan	67	25	37%	1	361	3

Leading rushers	Attempts	Yards gained	Average	TDs
Abner Haynes	179	841	4.7	9
Frank Jackson	65	386	5.9	3
Jack Spikes	39	334	8.6	5
Bo Dickinson	71	263	3.7	3

Leading receivers	Caught	Yards gained	Average	TDs
Chris Burford	51	850	16.7	5
Johnny Robinson	35	601	17.2	5
Abner Haynes	34	558	16.4	3
Bo Dickinson	14	209	14.9	2
Frank Jackson	13	171	13.2	2
Max Boydson	12	167	14.0	1

Leading scorers	TDs	XPM	XPA	FGM	FGA	PTs
Abner Haynes	13					78
Jack Spikes	5	10	14	4	13	54

14. When Barron Hilton purchased the Los Angeles franchise he gave the task of naming his new team to the public in a team-naming contest. The winner won a vacation to Mexico with the name "Chargers." Which of the following is one of reasons the name made sense?
A. Hilton forced the league to accept Oakland into the league after Minnesota dropped out, thus "charging" the league into northern California.
B. Sid Gillman, the new head coach, had a "charging" style of offense, and the reference fit perfectly.
C. The team mascot had already been declared to be a white charger horse.

■ SAN DIEGO CHARGERS ■

WITH THEIR FIRST WESTERN DIVISION title in hand but a weak following in Los Angeles, Barron Hilton relocated his Chargers in San Diego, the self-described *City in Motion*. Recruited by San Diego sportswriter Jack Murphy and then mayor Charles L. Dale, the Chargers move became official on February 10, 1961. Mr. Hilton was pleased to find that within weeks of their announced move the new San Diego Chargers had sold over ten thousand season tickets for their new home, Balboa Stadium, which was being enlarged from twenty thousand seats to 34,500 to accommodate their new fans. To accentuate their split from L. A., the Chargers made a few enhancements to their already-attractive uniform by changing the lightning bolt on their helmets from blue outlined in gold, to gold outlined in blue. Likewise the bolts on their jerseys and pants also reversed their color scheme.

Their move completed, the Chargers set out to defend their crown with a hearty combination of experienced veterans from the previous season and a blue chip group of rookie draft choices. Kemp, Lowe, Kocourek, Mix, Ernie Wright, Dickie Harris, and Paul Maguire—last year's key players—welcomed draftees Keith Lincoln, Earl Faison, Ernie Ladd, Bob Scarpitto, Claude Gibson, Bud Whitehead, and Chuck Allen. All played significant roles in three more Charger division titles yet to come. Paul Lowe's breakaway brilliance, despite nagging injuries, continued to define the Chargers offense as he finished fourth in the league with 767 yards rushing and put his signature on the longest run from scrimmage in 1961 at 87 yards. He also had a league-high 9 rushing touchdowns. Jack Kemp fell off to third in the league after being the leading passer in 1960. His completion rate dropped from 52 percent to 45 percent, but his leadership and tenacity were still tops in the West. While Kemp's stats may have dipped, the team jumped to second in passing, moving up from fourth the year before. Some of Kemp's woes could be traced to the limited action of all-league tackle Ron Mix, who was deployed to the U.S. Army much of the season. The offense finished third in scoring, while the defense allowed a league-low 219 points and were one of only two teams to hold opponents under 300 points.

While most of the Charger fame and popularity resulted from their explosive offense, the defense was the team's real strength. Ranking as the league's best, the Chargers led in fewest total yards allowed and first in pass defense, allowing the fewest yards through the air and setting a pro football record with 49 interceptions, 929 yards returned with interceptions, and 9 interception returns for touchdowns. The best secondary in the AFL was made up of Charlie McNeil (9 interceptions, 2 TDs), Bob Zeman (8 interceptions), Dick Harris (7 interceptions, 3 TDs), and Claude Gibson (5 interceptions), aided by backups Bud Whitehead and George Blair. Also scoring on interception returns were linebackers Bob Laraba (2 TDs), Chuck Allen, and Bill Hudson.

But as good as the secondary was statistically, their success could be directly traced to the relentless penetration of the original fearsome foursome. This group of four massive specimens, put together by defensive coach Chuck Noll ranked second only to Boston in fewest yards allowed rushing. Averaging 6'6 ½" in height and 273 lbs. in weight, defensive ends Ron Nery and rookie-of-the-year Earl Faison and defensive tackles Ernie Ladd and Bill Hudson comprised the best front line in pro football. Linebackers Paul Maguire, Emil Karas, and all-league rookie Chuck Allen rounded out the defensive unit that drew comparison to those of the NFL and notoriety among the growing army of AFL followers. Faison, Allen, Harris, and McNeil were selected to the all-league team.

In winning the West the Chargers used their four straight exhibition game wins as momentum, then ran the table for eleven straight wins before succumbing to Houston on December 3 for their first loss of the season. Their opening day win before 24,500 Cotton Bowl fans began with Lowe sprinting 87 yards for the Chargers first touchdown of 1961. He also hit split end Don Norton with a 44-yard pass later in the game. As Dallas focused on stopping San Diego's game breaking halfback, the Chargers unveiled another world-class sprinter in the backfield. Olympian Bo Roberson took a Jack Kemp handoff around left end and crossed the goal line 59 yards later in his debut. With Lowe gaining 100 yards and the Chargers intercepting 4 Texan passes, San Diego surged to a 26-10 win.

The second week's scoring got started before an inaugural crowd of 20,216 in Balboa Stadium with Dick Harris racing 41 yards with an interception, compliments of Tom Flores. Roberson found the end zone two more times with runs of 31 and 17 yards, part of his 90 yards gained on the day as the Chargers gave their San Diego fans something to remember in their first game at their new home by trouncing Oakland 44-0. Wins over Houston 34-24 and Buffalo 19-11 had the Chargers riding the crest of the Western Division wave after their first month with a 4-0 record. Against the Bills, Dick Harris again started the scoring with a 56-yard interception return for a touchdown in the first quarter followed by Paul Lowe's 30-yard TD dash, part of his 128 yards on the day. In the October 7 victory over the Patriots at Boston University, Bob Zeman returned a blocked punt 65 yards for a touchdown, and Jack Kemp found Dave Kocourek with a 75-yard touchdown bomb as well as finding Don Norton with a 30-yarder en route to their 38-27 triumph.

After four straight road games the Chargers came home to 32,584 Balboa Stadium fans and showed them their defensive best, allowing the Broncos only 76 yards on the

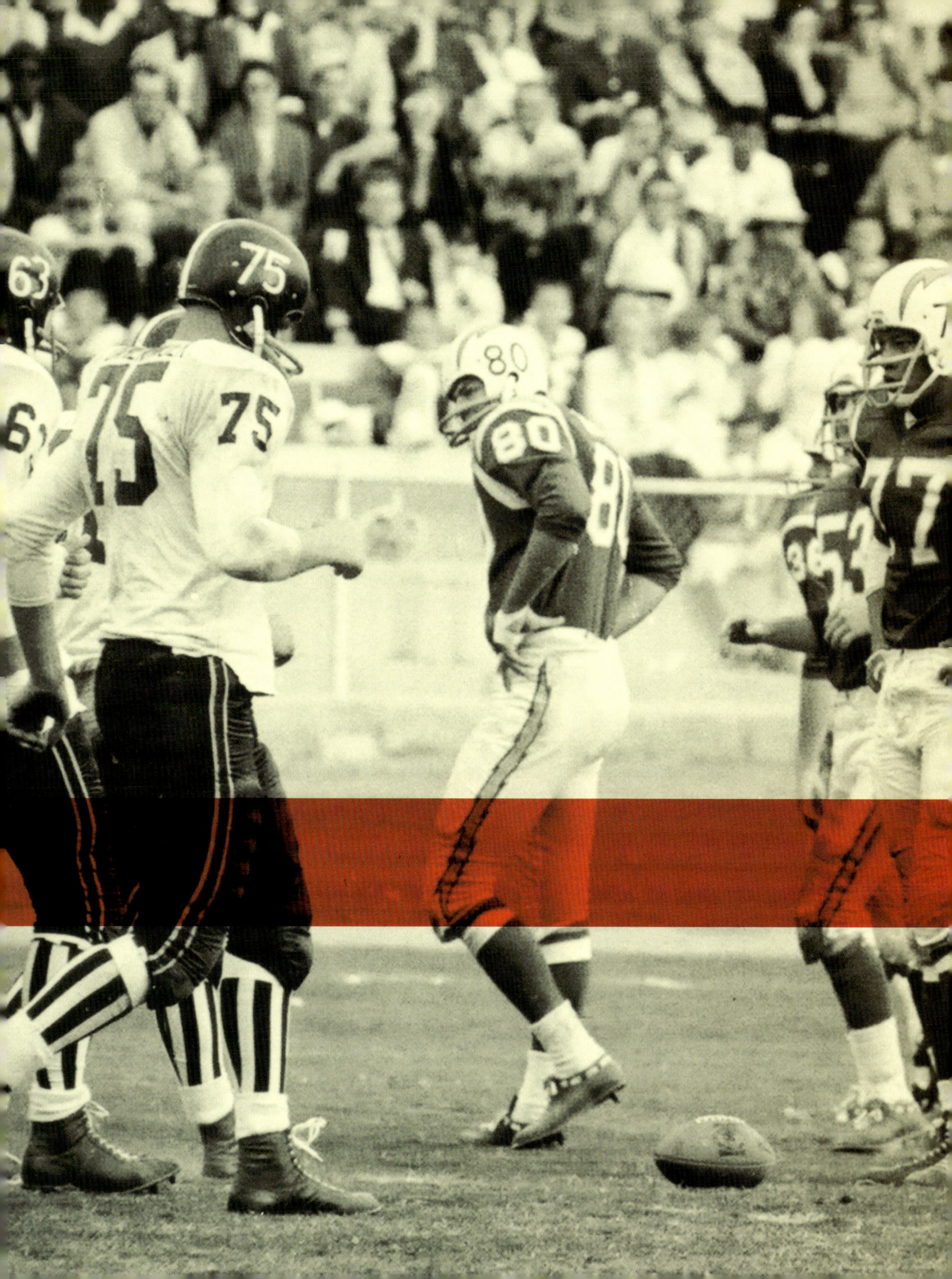

★ *San Diego's Fearsome Foursome: (left to right) Ron Nery, Ernie Ladd, Bill Hudson, and Earl Faison line up against the Denver Broncos.*

ground and harassing the Denver quarterbacks into 4 interceptions. Linebackers Bob Laraba and Chuck Allen returned 2 of them for touchdowns of 57 and 59 yards respectively. In shutting out Denver 37-0, the Chargers won their eighth straight and had a four-and-half game lead on second-place Dallas.

The Chargers found themselves at home for the second straight week against the Titans on November 5, and for the first time this season found themselves trailing at halftime. But in the third quarter Jack Kemp scored on a 1-yard sneak, followed by Paul Lowe's 67-yard run for another touchdown. Kemp then hit Don Norton for a 13-yard score and before the quarter closed Charlie McNeil ran an Al Dorow interception back 41 yards for still another score. As quick as lightning the Chargers scored 28 points in the first fifteen minutes of the second half, and the fearsome foursome shut down the Titans the rest of the way. San Diego had win number nine, 48-13 and with five games remaining had locked up at least a tie for Western Division title. Playing in front of their smallest crowd in two years, the Chargers withstood a potential upset in Denver by coming back from a 9-2 deficit at halftime to take a 12-9 lead into the fourth quarter. But crafty Frank Tripucka put Denver up 16-14 in the final stanza by finding flanker Al Frazier for an 87-yard strike. With time running out, Kemp hit rookie Bob Scarpitto with a game-winning 16-yard touchdown. The Chargers won their tenth in a row and fourteenth straight dating back to November 27, 1960. They clinched their second consecutive Western Division championship.

They set a pro football record the following weekend with their eleventh win in a row, a 24-14 victory over Dallas and fifteenth straight victory over two seasons, an AFL record. While the Texans defense was shutting down the Chargers running game (they gained only 3 yards for the day), Kemp had to use his rocket arm to launch the Chargers to victory. In the second quarter, a 61-yard missile to tight end Dave Kocourek and a 30-yard touchdown run with an interception by Bob Laraba put San Diego up 17-0 after two quarters. Kemp again launched one of his bombs in the fourth quarter and found rookie Bob Scarpitto on the receiving end of 53-yard strike. The Chargers were now 11-0 with the rest of the division having only eight wins between them.

The Chargers then dropped two of their last three outings, including their final game to Boston, before the championship game rematch on Christmas Eve against Houston in Balboa Stadium. A happy ending to the season was not waiting under the Christmas tree. Riding a nine-game win streak of their own, the Oilers led 3-0 at the half and 10-0 after three quarters. The game was a battle of defensive giants and bone-crunching tackles, as no less than thirteen players were assisted off the field. Oiler flanker Charlie Hennigan made 5 catches in the first twenty minutes but was knocked unconscious in the second quarter and did not return until late in the second half. Even the largest player on the field, defensive tackle Ernie Ladd, was carried off and unable to return. The Chargers finally got on the

The Progress of the Seasons – 1961

scoreboard when a tight end screen pass to Dave Kocourek took them to the Houston 12-yard line and led to George Blair's field goal thirty-nine seconds into the final period. The kick closed the Oiler lead to 7 points. The Chargers now could tie the game on their next possession. They needed one more opportunity to ignite a game-tying drive and got it when cornerback Bob Zeman came up with San Diego's fifth interception of the day. After making a diving over-the-shoulder catch at the San Diego 2-yard line, Zeman rolled into the end zone for a touchback. Or so he thought! The officials ruled him down at the spot of interception, leaving Kemp's offense with 98 long yards ahead of them to pull even. After another punt the Chargers got one final possession with less than two minutes left. A pass interference call against Houston suddenly had the Balboa Stadium crowd buzzing, and the Chargers miraculously knocking on the door at midfield. But Kemp's last-ditch effort ended up being his fourth interception of the day, and Houston won the championship for the second year in a row 10-3. The Chargers averaged 27,859 fans in their new San Diego home, an increase of more than 12,000 per game over 1960.

Leading passers	Attempts	Completions	Pct	TDs	Yards	Int
Jack Kemp	364	165	45%	15	2686	22
Hunter Enis	55	23	41%	2	365	3

Leading rushers	Attempts	Yards gained	Average	TDs
Paul Lowe	175	767	4.4	9
Bo Roberson	58	275	4.7	3
Charlie Flowers	51	177	3.5	3
Keith Lincoln	41	150	3.7	0

Leading receivers	Caught	Yards gained	Average	TDs
Dave Kocourek	55	1055	19.2	4
Don Norton	47	816	17.4	6
Paul Lowe	17	103	6.1	0
Charlie Flowers	16	175	10.9	0
Luther Hayes	14	280	20.0	3
Keith Lincoln	12	208	17.3	2

Leading scorers	TDs	XPM	XPA	FGM	FGA	PTs
George Blair		42	47	13	27	77
Paul Lowe	9					54

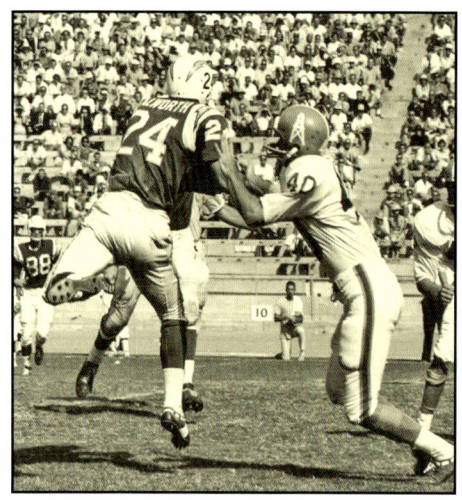

15. As a rookie out of Arkansas in 1962, San Diego's Lance Alworth wore the unfamiliar number 24 during his injury-shortened 1962 season. What Charger flanker preceded Lance in wearing number 24 for the Chargers in 1961?
A. Bob Scarpitto
B. Luther Hayes
C. Bo Roberson
D. Jacque MacKinnon

▪ HOUSTON OILERS ▪

THERE WAS TROUBLE IN PARADISE for the Oilers as their second season began—paradise being Hawaii, where owner Bud Adams took his AFL Champions for their preseason as a reward for winning it all in 1960. On August 5 the Oilers left Houston for Honolulu, and coach Lou Rymkus was not happy about his team starting their title defense in the middle of the Pacific Ocean. A stop in San Diego to play the Chargers was the first sign of things to come as they lost all-league fullback Dave Smith, who went down with a knee injury, limiting his season to only a few games. The Hawaiian trip then took another turn for the worse as the players seemed to be on a mission to spend all free time creating adventures and sustaining injuries. The Chargers flew over to play their second exhibition game against the Oilers and shell-shocked them by rolling up a 39-0 halftime lead. Houston was quick to realize that their week in paradise had actually become a disaster. Rymkus voiced his displeasure at having to take his team across the Pacific and at the same time put himself on the rocks with the Oilers management. The landslide of unpleasant events was just beginning. Rymkus was ornery and determined to defend his AFL title by running a hardnosed and contact-intense training camp that the players resented, and told him so. As camp broke, the players and their coach were clearly at odds, but everyone continued to have the same goal in mind for the team—to win. The Oilers were still stockpiling players as they prepared for their opening game with the key addition being tight end Willard Dewveall, the first player to jump leagues from the NFL to the AFL. Dewveall, one of the NFL's top four receivers, jumped from the Chicago Bears.

George Blanda was back at quarterback, as was Jacky Lee, the best backup in the AFL. And with the injury to Smith, Charlie Tolar

The Progress of the Seasons – 1961

became the starting fullback along side Billy Cannon, who was about to experience his breakout season. Houston made only a slight change in their uniforms for their second season by changing their numbers to a block format and the color of their away numbers from blue to red.

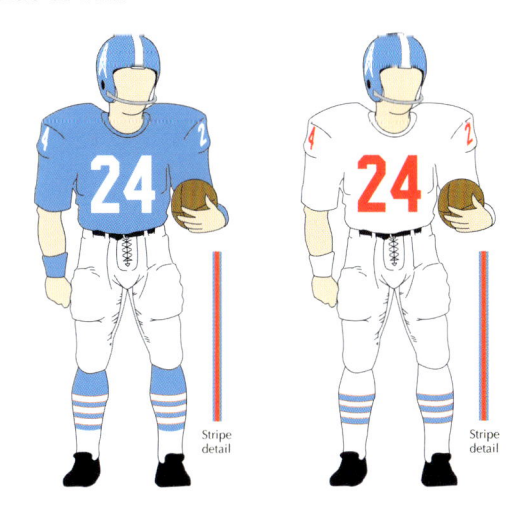

On September 9, the first game of the new season had the Oakland Raiders visiting Jeppesen Stadium just as Hurricane Carla and her driving wind and rain came calling. But the Oilers did more damage to Oakland than Carla, demolishing them 55-0. Blanda threw 3 touchdown passes, kicked 6 PATs, and had 2 field goals.

Despite the victory, Lou Rymkus contined to fall from favor with his players. Two straight losses after Oakland didn't help his standing with the front office either, and as they prepared for 1-2 Buffalo, Rymkus was threatening to shoot himself if his team came away with loss number three. After the Bills dominated with a 22-12 victory, everyone was now wondering if the Oilers were sabotaging their games to get rid of their despised coach. The loss now had the Oilers looking up at the three other teams in the East. Gloom and fog greeted them in Boston as they flew in for a Friday night game on October 13. Rymkus knew he was on shaky ground and was looking for a spark. That spark was Jacky Lee, who was inserted at quarterback in place of the ineffective Blanda. Lee responded with an AFL record 457 yards passing. And as the game wound down he engineered a masterful drive that took the Oilers 69 yards, settling the ball on Boston's 24 yard line. Blanda was now called upon to split the uprights with his team behind 31-28. Hitting it squarely would tie the game and perhaps gain Rymkus a temporary reprieve. A miss could possibly spell the end for the coach. As those thoughts ran through Blanda's mind, the kicker swung his right foot into the pigskin that flew through the uprights, giving his team a come-from-behind, 31-31 tie. But as they found out the next morning, Blanda's professionalism and heroics did not save Rymkus' job. Former assistant Wally Lemm, who had retired so he could devote more time to his sporting goods business, replaced him on October 16. Under the more relaxed atmosphere and coaching philosophy the Oilers flourished, running off nine straight victories to win the Eastern Division title and the AFL Championship a second straight time.

In his first game against Dallas, Lemm had Blanda back in the starting lineup. George used the vote of confidence to show his team why he was still not only the best quarterback in Texas, but in the entire American Football League. Before 23,228 fans Blanda eclipsed the

★ *Oilers quarterback and AFL legend George Blanda*

The Progress of the Seasons – 1961

passing record set by Lee the week before by throwing for a new record 464 yards, 7 more than Lee. He also threw 3 touchdown passes. Blanda hit for 4 more touchdowns a week later against Buffalo, alternating throws to Charley Hennigan (56 and 80 yards) and Bill Groman (32 and 68 yards) for a TD in each period. Winning 28-16 put them back in the Eastern Division race at 3-3-1, a game behind the Titans. The offensive barrage continued in Denver on November 5. For the second time in the season Houston put 55 points on the board, thanks in part to Bill Groman's three touchdown catches of 2, 14, and 80 yards. Wally Lemm had his third straight win, and the Oilers were hitting on all cylinders, trailing the new division leader Boston by only a half game with the Patriots next on the schedule. It was the start of a four-game home stand and four consecutive wins. The Oilers jumped ahead of the Patriots 20-0 on another catch in the end zone by Groman, two Blanda field goals, and a 12-yard fumble recovery for a score by linebacker Doug Cline. Jacky Lee again spelled Blanda late in the game and finished off the day's scoring with a fourth-quarter TD pass to Willard Dewveall. By virtue of their 27-15 victory Houston took over first place in the East with five games remaining.

On November 19 Blanda established himself as the quarterback nonpareil in the AFL by throwing seven touchdowns against New York, a pro football record. His record-setting performance had his seven strikes going to Hennigan (28 yards) and Billy Cannon (6, 78 yards) in the first quarter and Groman (66 yards) and Cannon again (6 yards) in the second. Groman, who was on a touchdown tear, caught two more scores for 46 and 11 yards in the second half. At game's end Houston had a 49-13 victory and a 6-3-1 record. Denver, with a 3-8 record, visited Jeppesen Stadium next. Denver came and went without a whimper thanks to the secondary's six interceptions of George Herring passes and a 62 yard punt return for a touchdown by Mark Johnston.

The Oiler passing game was running full throttle with Blanda and Lee again ruling the air lanes. On the year, Blanda tossed 36 touchdowns and was the top-ranked QB in the AFL. When he needed a lift, coach Lemm looked to the young Jacky Lee, who connected on 66 of his 127 passes, 12 of them registering six points. Both Blanda and Lee completed more than 50 percent of their passes, with Blanda also leading the league with 3,340 yards gained through the air, 700 more than his closest rival. As Blanda and Lee led the way, the two quarterbacks had Houston's passing game at the top of the AFL.

On the ground Billy Cannon was finally living up to his Heisman headlines. Carrying the ball an even 200 times, the LSU All-American was the best runner in the American Football League, gaining 948 yards for a 4.7 average. Fullback Charlie Tolar was also having an outstanding season filling in for 1960s All-League fullback Dave Smith. Tolar's bulldozing runs behind Bob Talamini, Rich Michael, and company put him fifth among the league's best runners with 577 yards. Coming back from injury, Smith registered 258 yards on 60 carries. Smith, Tolar and Cannon gave the

Oilers the league's second-best running game behind only the Dallas Texans.

The receiving corps was headed by twenty-seven-year-old flanker Charley Hennigan, who left his high school teaching position in Louisiana to give pro football a shot when Hunt and Adams decided to buck the status quo and start their new league. Along with Bill Groman they were the most dangerous receiving duo around, combining for 29 touchdowns and 136 catches. Hennigan (12 TDs) caught 82 balls and finished second behind Lionel Taylor, with Groman catching 50 passes for a league best 23.5 yards per catch as well as a league high 17 touchdowns. Billy Cannon chipped in for 43 catches and 9 touchdowns to go with his 6 running touchdowns.

In a rematch against the Chargers, George Blanda struck for 4 more touchdown passes, finding tight end Bob McLeod for 1 and Hennigan for 3. Winning 33-13 kept them ahead of Boston, who also continued to win, keeping the heat on the Oilers who were now 8-3-1. Away for the first time in a month Houston found themselves in the Polo Grounds on December 10 to play the 7-5 Titans. It would be a day Billy Cannon would remember more than his legendary "Halloween run" at LSU. Carrying the ball 25 times, Cannon gained a league-record 217 yards and scored 5 touchdowns, including runs for 61 and 52 yards. The end result of the Cannon-blast was a 48-21 Houston victory and Wally Lemm's eighth straight win. With one week left in the season the 9-3-1 Oilers led second place Boston (8-4-1) by one game.

For the season's final game the Oilers would travel to Oakland to play the 2-11 Raiders while the Patriots also headed West to play the division champion Chargers. Blanda's throwing hand was still on fire as he hit for touchdown passes number 33, 34, 35, and 36 in Candlestick Park for an easy 47-16 win, making it nine wins in a row for Wally Lemm and another Eastern Division crown for Houston. A Christmas Eve Championship game at Balboa Stadium against the Chargers awaited them.

The game figured to be a high-scoring affair with the top two passing teams filling the air with short strikes and long bombs all day. In contrast, what the 29,566 fans on hand saw was a fierce display of defensive brutality and vicious trench warfare. More than a dozen players had to leave the game with injuries, including the largest player on the field, San Diego rookie defensive tackle Ernie Ladd. Charley Hennigan left the game unconscious after snaring 5 passes in the first half. He would not catch another the rest of the day. Bill Groman also went down for a spell. In probably the most vicious hit of the day, Charger cornerback Dick Harris had to be taken off the field on a stretcher after being laid out by tackle Al Jamison on a down-field block after the play. The defensive contest packed enough pressure to record 10 interceptions, 5 by Blanda, 1 by Bill Groman and 4 by Jack Kemp.

Ahead 3-0 and on San Diego's 35-yard line in the third quarter Blanda, who was successful on 18 of his 40 passes, found Billy Cannon over the middle at the 17-yard line. Cannon chugged the rest of the way to score

The Progress of the Seasons – 1961

the game's only touchdown and gave the Oilers a 10-0 lead. Cannon and Tolar combined for 100 yards rushing, with Charley gaining 52 to Billy's 48. Each team tallied 256 yards on offense. Clinging to a 10-3 lead late in the fourth quarter Houston tried to control a final Charger drive. Jack Kemp managed the clock and the field expertly as San Diego drove toward a chance to at least tie the game. The clock was down to 1:40 when Charger receiver Dave Kocourek had safety Jim Norton beaten deep. Norton's only hope was to reach out and neutralize the tight end. The flags immediately flew and Kemp and his team had a first down at midfield. Calling on his leading receiver again, Kemp let one fly downfield for Kocourek on the next play, but safety Julian Spence, released by Rymkus earlier in the year, shot in front of the receiver to intercept the pass and drive the last nail into the Chargers' championship coffin. As the final minute clicked off the Balboa Stadium clock, Houston had won their second AFL Championship, 10-3. Billy Cannon's 48 yards rushing and 5 receptions, 1 for the game-winning touchdown, earned him his second championship MVP award.

Four Oilers—flanker Charlie Hennigan, tackle Al Jamison, quarterback George Blanda, and halfback Billy Cannon—were selected for the all-league offensive team, and defensive end Don Floyd and cornerback Tony Banfield, who played every minute the defense was on the field in 1961, made the all-league defensive team. Blanda also walked off with the AFL Player of the Year Award, while Wally Lemm was honored as the AFL's Coach of the Year.

Despite his success in Houston, Wally Lemm, yearning to be closer to his Illinois home, resigned as head coach in late February to sign on with the NFL's St. Louis Cardinals, requiring the two-time AFL Champions to find their third head coach in as many seasons.

Leading passers	Attempts	Completions	Pct	TDs	Yards	Int
George Blanda	362	187	52%	36	3330	22
Jacky Lee	127	66	52%	12	1205	6

Leading rushers	Attempts	Yards gained	Average	TDs
Billy Cannon	200	948	4.7	6
Charlie Tolar	157	577	3.7	4
Dave Smith	60	258	4.3	2
Claude King	12	50	4.2	2

Remember the AFL

Leading receivers	Caught	Yards gained	Average	TDs
Charley Hennigan	82	1746	21.3	12
Bill Groman	50	1175	23.5	17
Billy Cannon	43	586	13.6	9
Charlie Tolar	24	219	9.1	1
Bob McLeod	14	172	12.3	2
Jan White	13	238	18.3	1
Willard Dewveall	12	200	16.7	3

Leading scorers	TDs	XPM	XPA	FGM	FGA	PTs
George Blanda		64	65	16	26	111
Bill Groman	18					108

---

16. The San Diego Chargers' defense, built by coordinator Jack Faulkner, set a pro football record in 1962 by intercepting 49 passes, surpassing the previous record of 42 set by the Green Bay Packers. The San Diego linebackers and defensive backs earned what moniker for their history performance?
A. The Magnificent Seven
B. The Air Force
C. The Seven Pirates
D. The Air Traffic Controllers

★ ★ ★ ★ ★ ★ ★ ★ ★ ★ ★ ★

Two weeks after hosting the AFL championship game, Balboa Stadium also hosted the first AFL All-Star Game on January 7, won by the West 47-27 in front of 20,973. The East scored 5 points on a field goal and safety in the opening period. Leads flip-flopped in the second quarter on touchdown passes from Dallas' Cotton Davidson to Bronco Donnie Stone for the West, followed by Oilers George Blanda and teammate Billy Cannon hooking up for the East. The West countered with a TD run by Abner Haynes and added to their point total with a scoring pass to Charger Dave Kocourek, giving the West a 21-12 halftime lead. They increased the margin to 35-19 after three periods. The West pulled away in the fourth quarter on a 53-yard interception return by Fred Williamson and a final 6-pointer by Stone. In leading the winners to 47-27 victory, Cotton Davidson's 16 completions on 28 passes for 239 yards and 3 touchdowns earned him the first AFL All-Star Game MVP Award.

★ ★ ★ ★ ★ ★ ★ ★ ★ ★ ★ ★ ★

1962

AMERICAN FOOTBALL LEAGUE – 1962 FINAL STANDINGS

EASTERN DIVISION

TEAM	GP	W	L	T	PF	PA	PCT.
HOUSTON OILERS	14	11	3	0	387	270	0.786
BOSTON PATRIOTS	14	9	4	1	346	295	0.679
BUFFALO BILLS	14	7	6	1	309	272	0.536
NEW YORK TITANS	14	5	9	0	278	423	0.357

WESTERN DIVISION

TEAM	GP	W	L	T	PF	PA	PCT.
DALLAS TEXANS	14	11	3	0	389	233	0.786
DENVER BRONCOS	14	7	7	0	353	334	0.500
SAN DIEGO CHARGERS	14	4	10	0	314	392	0.286
OAKLAND RAIDERS	14	1	13	0	213	370	0.071

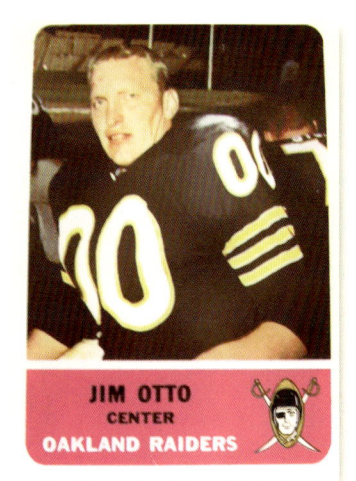

Originally the property of the Houston Oilers, **Jim Otto** was selected by Oakland in the restocking draft after Minnesota went to the NFL. They called him Mr. AFL, and no one represented the league with greater dignity and respect. Otto is one of only three players to play all 140 regular-season AFL games for his team—and the only non-kicker to do so. He made every all-league team in the AFL's existence and is the center on the All-Time AFL squad. He was truly the template for offensive centers. An undersized draft pick from the University of Miami, Otto's play established him as the giant of his trade. A throwback lineman, Jim refused to give up his two-bar face mask throughout his playing days.

■ OAKLAND RAIDERS ■

THERE WAS REASON FOR OPTIMISM IN 1962 as the Raiders finally had a home in Oakland. While plans emerged for a new, state-of-the-art stadium to be ready for the 1964 season, Oakland was able to play their 1962 home games in the newly constructed temporary stadium named Frank Youell Field, referred to as the erector set of stadiums. Named for city councilman Frank Youell, a local undertaker, it seemed appropriately named because the Raider franchise itself was close to death. Hoping to improve dramatically on their 2-12 record of 1961, the Raiders in their new home had but one way to go, or so they thought!

The Progress of the Seasons – 1962

★ *The 1962 Oakland Raiders* ★

With little talent to trade and even less success in convincing draft picks to come aboard Oakland's sinking ship, coach Feldman was looking under every rock imaginable for help. In what proved to be one of their worst moves ever, they traded their number two draft pick to San Diego for Olympic long jumper Bo Roberson and offensive line help. The traded pick turned out to be Lance Alworth, a future Hall of Famer. Then, before the season even began, they lost their best player, quarterback Tom Flores, for the season with a lung ailment. After soliciting the services of former NFL quarterback Don Heinrich, two years removed from the game, Oakland quickly learned they would need more help under center. After the first game of the season they found it in Dallas as they traded for recently displaced quarterback Cotton Davidson. As their number one man, Davidson would complete only 37 percent of his passes and throw a league-high 23 interceptions.

A string of thirteen consecutive losses followed the Raiders into the final week of the season against the Boston Patriots, who were challenging for the Eastern Division championship. Upon learning that the Oilers, the team Boston was chasing, had clinched the title in New York on the eve before their final game, the dejected Patriots became the Raiders only casualty of 1962. With a 20-0 victory Oakland had done what no other team in the AFL was able to do that season—shutout an opponent! The only uniform change the Raiders made for 1962 was to add a single white stripe to their helmet.

The Raiders finished last in total offense, defense, and points scored, and before midseason Marty Feldman became the second man to be a former Oakland head coach. At season's end even his replacement, Bill Conkright, was unemployed. After three seasons the Raiders had an AFL record of 9-33 and won only three of their last 38 games.

The first campaign with the team playing in Oakland kicked off on September 9 in Youell Field where 12,893 fans watched the Raiders' Jackie Simpson score the first professional football points inside of Oakland city limits with a 31-yard field goal in the second quarter against the Titans. In spite of the poor record, Oakland fans displayed loyalty and appreciation for finally having a hometown team by continuing to flock to their neighborhood stadium all year long, averaging over 10,000 for each contest. As the losses kept coming, both home and away, the Raiders also kept searching for way to become competitive. But nothing seemed to work. Through their first seven games the black and gold led opponents on only three occasions, and it wasn't until October 26 against the Patriots that they even had a halftime lead. Over their first eight games they had not yet taken a lead into the fourth quarter, which eventually happened against Houston on November 11 before giving up 21 unanswered points in the second half to lose their ninth in a row 28-20.

There were a few bright spots, however, for the Raiders in 1962. Clem Daniels continued to display his talent by running for 766 yards (fourth in the league) with a 4.8 yard rushing average while also catching 24 passes. But leading receiver Max Boydston's 30 catches, with none hitting paydirt, did not even crack the AFL's top twenty. One of Oakland's sources of pride was their defensive secondary which finished number one against the pass, but on the minus side, their front wall was the worst against the rush. While their three wins in two years represented the low watermark for the East Bay franchise, the Raiders of 1967 and '68 would turn that record around and would lose only 3 of 28 games over the course of those two seasons en route to three straight championship games. Although they did not know it at the time, there was a very bright and dominant future on the immediate Oakland horizon, but first there were some dramatic and lasting changes to be made.

Leading passers	Attempts	Completions	Pct	TDs	Yards	Int
Cotton Davidson	321	119	37%	7	1977	23
Hunter Enis	49	26	53%	1	217	1
Chon Gallegos	35	18	51%	2	298	3

Leading rushers	Attempts	Yards gained	Average	TDs
Clem Daniels	161	766	4.8	7
Bo Roberson	89	270	3.0	3
Alan Miller	65	182	2.8	1
Cotton Davidson	25	54	2.2	3

The Progress of the Seasons – 1962

Leading receivers	Caught	Yards gained	Average	TDs
Max Boydston	30	374	12.5	0
Bo Roberson	29	583	20.1	3
Dobie Craig	27	492	18.2	4
Clem Daniels	24	318	13.3	1
Dick Dorsey	21	344	16.4	2
Alan Miller	20	259	13.0	0

Leading scorers	TDs	XPM	XPA	FGM	FGA	PTs
Clem Daniels	8					48
Bo Roberson	7					42
Ben Agajanian		10	11	5	14	25

■ SAN DIEGO CHARGERS ■

THE SUMMER AND EARLY FALL SEASON for the Chargers progressed as advertised. All the preseason polls picked the Chargers to gallop to a third Western Division crown, and four exhibition wins, a 3-2 record, including a defeat of the Texans 32-28 on October 7, placed them one game out of first place in the West when their title train was derailed. And it wasn't until they had dropped a franchise-record six straight games that they were able to emerge with their fourth and final victory of 1962. But the biggest win of the season was a trade with the Oakland Raiders for a draft pick that turned out to be rookie flanker Lance Alworth. Needing to replenish their offensive line, the Raiders looked to the Chargers for help. Their need was filled with able bodies from San Diego that were already under contract, and Oakland guaranteed the Chargers future success with a Hall-of-Fame pass catcher.

But that is where the winning ended for the two-time Western Division champions. Injuries and front office blunders crippled the Chargers enormously as Sid Gillman's squad fell to a 4-10 record. The Charger decline was not because the rest of the league had caught up with the top defense and explosive offensive, but more because they had wounded them. Eleven key players, seven of them all-league selections, were lost for either all or half of the season. First it was All-Star halfback Paul Lowe, lost for the season with a fractured forearm. He never played a down in 1962. Then Jack Kemp threw only 45 passes in two games, completing a dreary 28 percent before he went down with an injury. Arguably the finest field general in the AFL, Kemp was a leading passer and scrambler, not to mention his superior intelligence on the field. He injured his finger in the season's second game and had to sit out for an extended period. As if losing Lowe were not enough to panic the Balboa Stadium contingent, what followed the injury to Kemp had all of Southern California in crisis. Whether through misinterpretation or an attempt at a master plan to manipulate the rules, head coach and GM Sid Gillman put Kemp on the league's injured-deferred list, which made him eligible to the highest AFL bidder at the bargain basement price of $100. It wasn't until after the quarterback-starved Buffalo Bills exercised their option and claimed Kemp that Gillman realized his blunder. Protests ensued, but to no avail. The injured Kemp was now the property of Buffalo, and the Chargers were faced with a major dilemma. Rookie John Hadl from Kansas University was their quarterback of the future, but two games into his first season was not future enough. Behind Hadl was only Dick Wood, summoned from Denver. Charlie McNeil, the all-league safety then went down with a bad knee, all-league middle linebacker Chuck Allen also went down to injury, as did all-league cornerback Dick Harris. Then all-league defensive end and rookie of the year Earl Faison went down with a knee injury and fearsome foursome sidekick Ernie Ladd was lost with a bad shoulder. As if plagued by an uncontrollable western epidemic, down, too, went starting rookie center Wayne Fraser (knee), spectacular flanker Lance Alworth (bruised thigh), second year halfback Keith Lincoln (leg), big-time college rookie Bert Coan (leg), and even Kemp's replacement John Hadl. Added to this infirmary list were twelve others who missed at least two games due to injuries. No one was spared from the injury plague.

With Kemp's departure John Hadl was given the "ready or not" S.O.S to call the plays. He was more 'not' than ready and fell prey to 24 interceptions. Forty-eight aerials went to veteran split end Don Norton, with help from tight end Dave Kocourek, who snagged 39. Kocourek and tackle Ron Mix were the only all-league selections for the Chargers after placing five on the prestigous unit in 1961. With injuries to key players, the Chargers' usually electric offense limped in at fifth in rushing and sixth in passing with the defense falling to sixth against the rush and fourth against the pass. With the loss of the front line's ferociousness came a decline in the secondary, causing a drop off from 49 to 29 interceptions and from 9 touchdowns via pickoffs to only 1. Using the disappointment of their injury-plagued 4-10 season as impetus, San Diego spent the rest of the winter planning their recovery. By July Sid Gillman and company had the answer that they felt would propel the Chargers back to the top of the West. It was called Rough Acres Ranch, and for those Chargers who gathered there for their summer training camp in 1963, it would become legendary!

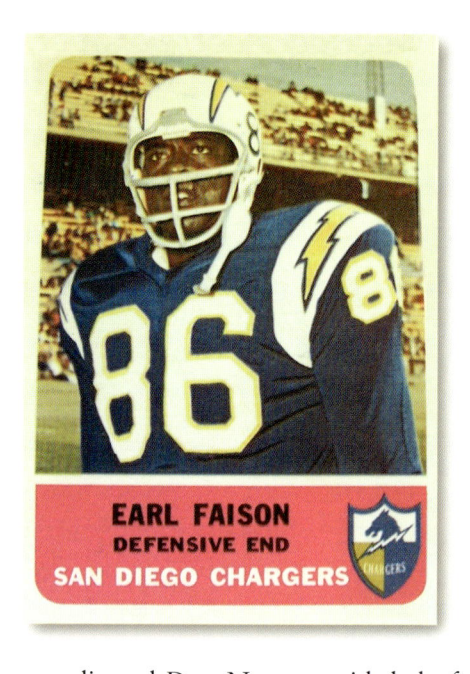

The Progress of the Seasons – 1962

Leading passers	Attempts	Completions	Pct	TDs	Yards	Int
John Hadl	260	107	41%	15	1632	24
Dick Wood	97	41	42%	4	655	7
Jack Kemp	45	13	29%	2	292	2

Leading rushers	Attempts	Yards gained	Average	TDs
Keith Lincoln	117	574	4.9	2
Bob Jackson	106	411	3.9	5
Jacque MacKinnon	59	240	4.1	0
Gerry McDougall	43	197	4.6	3

Leading receivers	Caught	Yards gained	Average	TDs
Don Norton	48	771	16.1	7
Dave Kocourek	39	688	17.6	4
Jerry Robinson	21	391	18.6	3
Keith Lincoln	16	214	13.4	1
Bob Jackson	13	136	10.5	2
Lance Alworth	10	226	22.6	3

Leading scorers	TDs	XPM	XPA	FGM	FGA	PTs
George Blair		31	34	17	20	82
Don Norton	7					42
Bob Jackson	7					42

17. The AFL had many characters, like Boston's Larry Eisenhauer, who is said to have once run around a snow-covered stadium wearing only his helmet, underwear, and spikes. There was also Denver linebacker Wahoo McDaniel and San Diego's Ernie Ladd, who were professional wrestlers in the off season. Another AFL player from the early years became known not only for his statistical prowess on the field (where he was a league leader) but also for his entrepreneurial spirit. It is said that this player, while playing for the Buffalo Bills, once sold Christmas trees outside of Buffalo's War Memorial Stadium. Who was this enterprising Buffalo Bill?

▪ NEW YORK TITANS ▪

IT HAS BEEN SAID OF THOSE WHO ARE falling, that it is not the fall itself that kills you, it's the sudden stop at the end that does you in. For Harry Wismer and his Jets, that sudden stop occurred on November 8, 1962, when the AFL commissioner's office took over the team's payroll and ultimately the management of the franchise before selling it at the end of the season. A constant source of embarrassment to the league, the charismatic Titan owner had become a bickering, attention-seeking malcontent who had piled up bills in excess of two million dollars, for which he could not make payment. His latest feat of shame centered on stripping head coach Sammy Baugh of his duties without the intent of releasing him. Instead, Baugh was relegated to coaching the kickers, while former Chicago

Bear great Clyde "Bulldog" Turner took over as leader of the New York club. The Titans, 14-14 through their first two seasons, stumbled, fell, and never picked themselves up in their third year. With a 5-9 record in 1962, there was more bounce to their paychecks than to their game. Never certain as to whether Wismer could make the payroll each week, the players were forced to organize a strike for their wages as the season progressed and at times suited up without having a game plan or a formal practice throughout the week.

Viewing the rest of the league from the seventh position both offensively and defensively, the Titans were now also playing a game of 'who will play quarterback this year,' constantly searching for someone to take over for former starter and team leader Al Dorow, since traded to Buffalo. It wasn't until less than a week before the team's opening game in Oakland that the Titans picked up wayward quarterback Lee Grosscup, who had been cut by both the New York Giants and Minnesota Vikings in the previous three weeks, to be their new man. He became an instant hero on his first official pass as a Titan, throwing an 80-yard bomb for a touchdown to Art Powell. His next pass was also a completion but was a bit shorter, only 19 yards, but had the same result, a touchdown, this time to halfback Dick Christy. He later fired another TD to Powell in the third period for 64 yards in New York's 28-17 victory. Grosscup's second game at the New York helm was not as successful on the scoreboard, but he did complete 20 of his 41 passing attempts for 216 yards and 2 more touchdowns to Powell. Another TD pass, this time to Thurlow Cooper in their win over Buffalo, had New York's record at 2-1. But Grosscup's season came to a screetching halt the following week with an injury against Denver. Giving up 19 unanswered points to the Broncos on week four gave the Jets their second loss as well as losing Grosscup's services for the rest of the season. Lost as well to injuries for much of the year was fullback Bill Mathis, the league's second-leading rusher in 1961. Mathis gained only 245 yards in 1962 and may be the biggest reason for the Titans' last-place finish in team rushing.

As in the previous two seasons, the New York offense banked heavily on its passing game, and had probably the best one-two receiving crew in the AFL. Art Powell and Don Maynard had established themselves as prominent deep threats and finished as the league's second- and fifth-leading pass catchers. Powell pulled down 64 and Maynard 56, with both receivers being the only AFL pass catchers to go over 1,000 yards gained for the year. Joining these two as an offensive threat was former All-American halfback Dick Christy, who finished as the league's third-best pass catcher with 62. Christy also led the AFL in punt returns, scoring twice in the process, and leading the team with 535 yards rushing.

Losses to Boston and Houston by a combined score of 99-31 were followed by a last-minute loss to Dallas by a field goal. It wasn't until October 28 that the Titans picked up their third win, behind 2 Don Maynard touchdowns and Dick Christy's 73-yard punt

The Progress of the Seasons – 1962

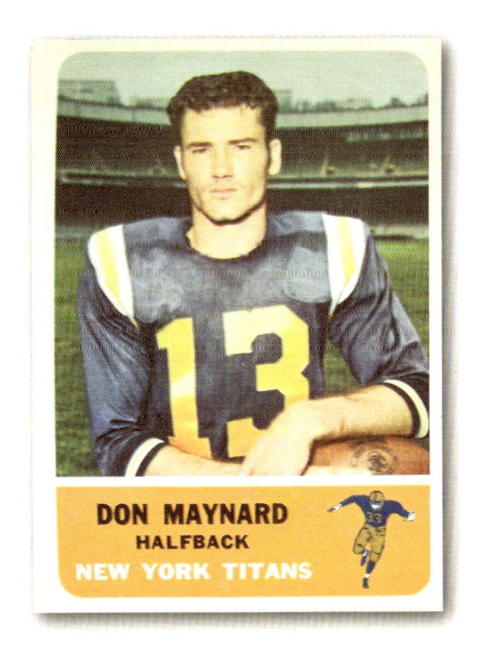

return for a score. Both Maynard and Powell topped 100 yards receiving passes from new QB Johnny Green. It took 28 second-half points to defeat Oakland on week ten to get win number four. Then, on Thanksgiving Day in Denver, the Titans gave a national audience a game for the ages. Leading by 17 points before Denver got on the scoreboard, New York took a comfortable 24-13 lead into the locker room at halftime. But two third-quarter touchdowns put the Broncos in the lead by one after the Titans scored on a safety. Don Maynard's 35-yard touchdown catch widened the lead to 32-27 as the game headed into its final fifteen minutes. After Lionel Taylor scored to give the Broncos the lead, safety Jim McMillin galloped 59 yards with an interception and Gene Mingo kicked a wind-assisted 49-yard field goal to widen the margin to 45-32 with only six minutes to play. But a confident Johnny Green brought the Titans back again with his fourth touchdown pass of the game, closing New York to within 6 points. Kicker Bill Shockley then booted deep to Denver, giving them the ball at the twenty. Needing a break for a chance to win, the Titans got their opportunity when halfback Al Frazier fumbled a handoff and safety Lee Riley recovered it. Green and the Titan offense built a drive culminating with a 3-yard touchdown pass from Green to Powell, and as Shockley kicked the conversion New York took a 46-45 lead and hoped to hang on against the league's best passing attack. One more time the Broncos offense was called upon to bring home a last-second victory as they drove into New York territory before they stalled. It was now up to kicker Gene Mingo to win it with a 52-yard field goal attempt. As he sent the ball flying through the Colorado sky it appeared as though it would split the uprights triumphantly, but it fell short, giving the Titans their fifth and most thrilling victory of an otherwise forgettable season. The only Titan receiving post-season recognition was third-year linebacker Larry Grantham who was selected to the first team all-league squad.

After the 1962 season the New York Titans became a memory, as Wismer was forced to sell his beloved franchise to a group headed by David "Sonny" Werblin, who renamed his new purchase the Jets. The brief but infamous days of padded game attendance figures, tightwad management, bouncing payroll checks, and inept leadership had finally come to an end. Ahead were brighter and more sophisticated horizons for the AFL in New York.

Leading passers	Attempts	Completions	Pct	TDs	Yards	Int
Johnny Green	258	128	50%	10	1741	18
Lee Grosscup	126	57	45%	8	855	8

Leading rushers	Attempts	Yards gained	Average	TDs
Dick Christy	114	585	4.7	3
Bill Mathis	71	245	3.5	3
Curley Johnson	26	114	4.4	0
Charlie Flowers	21	78	3.7	0
Jim Tiller	31	43	1.4	0

Leading receivers	Caught	Yards gained	Average	TDs
Art Powell	64	1130	17.7	8
Dick Christy	62	588	8.7	3
Don Maynard	56	1041	18.6	8
Curley Johnson	14	62	4.4	0
Jim Tiller	13	108	8.3	0
Thurlow Cooper	12	122	10.2	1

Leading scorers	TDs	XPM	XPA	FGM	FGA	PTs
Bill Shockley		29	30	13	26	68
Dick Christy	8					48
Don Maynard	8					48
Art Powell	8					48

▪ BUFFALO BILLS ▪

THERE WERE MORE CHANGES IN store for the Bills beyond the coaching staff in 1962. Gone were the Detroit Lions look-alike uniforms. For the new season the Bills would don white helmets with a red stripe down the center and a red buffalo, right off the flip side of a nickel, on the sides. The shirts were a darker blue with alternating white and red shoulder stripes. Finally the Bills had a uniform identity of their own with the look of a winner. Saban wasted no time making changes in personnel as well, with the biggest pick up in franchise history coming south of the Canadian border ready to lead the Bills to the promise land. His name was Carlton "Cookie" Gilchrist, and a better running back could not be found in the AFL. Originally courted by Paul Brown and the Browns, Gilchrist went right from high school to the CFL, where he quickly became a legend. A fast and punishing runner, Gilchrist was also an outstanding pass blocker, a capable pass

The Progress of the Seasons – 1962

★ *Buffalo's Cookie Gilchrist evades Ernie Ladd of San Diego.* ★

receiver and also doubled as a place kicker. Now it was time for him to make an impact in the American football arena, leaping across Niagara Falls from Toronto.

By opening day Saban had changed nearly half of the Bills' offensive unit that had shown little or nothing in the way of firepower and even less in consistency. Holdovers included center Al Bemiller, guard Billy Shaw, and tackle Harold Olsen on the offensive line. They were joined by 1961 defensive players Tom Day (defensive end) at guard and Stew Barber (linebacker) beside him at tackle and Ernie Warlick at tight end, replacing Tom Rychlec. Split end Glenn Bass and flanker Elbert Dubenion remained as receivers, as did Wray Carlton in the backfield. Along with newcomer Cookie Gilchrist in the Bills backfield came former Titan quarterback Al Dorow. But as the season got underway one could only wonder in what direction Saban was looking to go as the Bills lost their first five games. A 28-23 loss to Houston opened the season, due to a fourth-quarter pass from

Oiler halfback Billy Cannon to flanker Charlie Hennigan for a 20-yard touchdown, saving the day for the defending champions. After a 23-20 loss to Denver, the Bills took a 17-6 thumping from the Titans. In Dallas, halfback Abner Haynes took the first play from scrimmage 71 yards for a touchdown as the Texans spanked Buffalo 41-21. In Houston for game five, the Bills appeared to have their first win of the season in hand until George Blanda's fourth-quarter pass found Bill Groman in the end zone for a 17-14 Oiler win.

But the Bills' tale of two seasons was about to take a dramatic turn. Saban's legions suddenly turned the corner and posted a record of 7-1-1 in their final nine games. The new coach had painstakenly turned the Bills from pretenders into contenders, and it all started on October 13 against the San Diego Chargers, when the Bills' punter Wayne Crow boldly took off with the fake punt in the first period and rambled 49 yards to the San Diego twenty. Quarterback Warren Raab, who had taken over the reigns in game five, then threw a strike to Dubenion for the Bills' first score. Later in the second period he hit Glenn Bass for a 76-yard score followed by a 20-yard touchdown run by Gilchrist. The Bills had their first win under Saban, 35-10, and were not about to look back. In front of 21,000 Buffalo fans, the Bills made it two in a row against Oakland the next week by the score of 14-6, led by Gilchrist's 143 yards trudging through the driving rain and muck in War Memorial Stadium. The Bills were eating up big chunks of yardage on the ground and also controlling the ball in Saban's offensive system. And the re-tooled defense was on its way to yielding the third-lowest point total in the league while sporting three rookies in the secondary.

The young Bills then won their third in a row when they flew into Denver and came away with a thrilling, come-from-behind victory 45-38 after being behind 24-7 in the first half. Down 38-23 one minute into the fourth quarter, Warren Raab hit Dubenion for a 75-yard touchdown pass and on their next possession hit Glenn Bass for another 40 yards and a score. With time running out Raab then hit Gilchrist on a short 5-yard pass and watched as Cookie stampeded 76 yards to the Denver four. Rabb rolled out for the final 4 yards and the Bills were on a three-game winning streak.

The Patriots marched into Buffalo on November 3 and left with a 28-28 tie that looked like a fourth win in a row late in the fourth quarter. Archie Matsos intercepted an errant throw as Babe Parilli had three Buffalo defenders hanging on him. Matsos ran it back 50 yards for what he thought was a winning score, but the officials ruled that Parilli's forward motion had stopped just before he unleashed the ball. On week ten the Bills found themselves out in front of the Chargers 37-0 at halftime and won easily 40-20 for their fourth win of the season.

With the hope of pulling even at 5-5-1, the Bills found themselves in a taffy pull against Oakland the next week when Saban decided to go to the bullpen for Raab in the second half. Newly acquired quarterback Jack Kemp, who led the Chargers to two AFL championship games, was his reliever. Kemp had been picked up a few weeks earlier for a $100 waiver price when San Diego's GM/coach Sid Gillman either misunderstood the waiver rule or was caught trying to hide his starting play caller, who had injured his finger, on the injured reserve list. Kemp was now ready to be the savior. In his debut drive he first hit Ernie Warlick for 14 yards and followed it up with a 20-yard TD pass to Wayne Crow for the game's only touchdown. Later in the fourth quarter Kemp kept a critical drive alive by running out of the pocket for 28 yards and sealed a 10-6 win, lifting the Bills to an even record. Kemp started his first game for Buffalo on Friday night, November 23, in Boston. He completed 14 of 22 passes but also lost the services of Cookie Gilchrist in the third quarter. Cookie injured his ankle after gaining 22 yards on a pass from Kemp down the sideline. The loss of their fullback crippled the Bills offense as they came away with their first loss in seven weeks and fell to 5-6-1.

It took a career-best performance by Ernie Warlick to get the Bills back into the winning groove against the eventual AFL champion Dallas Texans on the second-to-last week of the season. Ernie caught 9 passes, 7 in the first half alone. Kemp started the Bills scoring with a short pitch to Tom Rychlec, then after linebacker Mike Stratton recovered a fumble on the Dallas sixteen, Kemp hit Warlick with a leaping 2-yard scoring pass in the left corner of the end zone. After Dallas scored 14 unanswered points in the fourth quarter it was time for Kemp to exert his panache just as he had with the Chargers. Buffalo had been without a real field general since their inception, and Kemp had the brains, grit, and talent to give them what they had sorely missed. Two quick completions to Cookie and Warlick put the Bills in position for Gilchrist to plow his way the final 2 yards for a score, one of Cookie's 15 on the year. Two fourth-quarter interceptions by Willie West, the final one in the end zone with under one minute to play, gave the Bills a 23-14 victory and a chance to register their first winning season.

A top quarterback and fullback had turned the Bills into one the AFL's elite teams. No longer could other teams take advantage of an inexperienced or ineffective quarterback. No more could teams sit and wait for Buffalo to scrap their inconsistent running game and take to the air where they could complete no better than 40 percent of their passes. Now they had their leader and a devastating advantage on the ground. As they headed into the Polo Grounds for the final game, Gilchrist was on the verge of becoming the first runner in the brief history of the AFL to eclipse 1,000 yards rushing. And he did it in fine style against the Titans as he first took off up the middle for 20 yards on a draw play. Then a jaunt off right tackle took him 43 more yards for a touchdown, putting him in the record books. In the fourth quarter he took off on another dash up the middle, this time for a 30-yard touchdown, and then kicked the extra point, giving the fullback 2 touchdowns, 2 field goals and 2 extra points, scoring all of the Bills' 20 points for the game. When the finale ended, Buffalo had a 20-3 win over New York and their very first winning season, posting a 7-6-1 record. Gilchrist led the AFL with 1,096 yards rushing with a 5.1 average and caught 24 passes to go with his 15 touchdowns, 14 extra points, and 8 field goals. He tied for second in the league in scoring with 128 points. With the right players finally in place, Buffalo had found an offense that could not only eat up yards, but also eat up time as well as score points. Their running game ranked first in the league, and although their passing finished on the bottom it should be remembered that Kemp saw action in only the final fourteen quarters of the season. The defense ranked third overall, behind only the two championship-game combatants, and led the league in interceptions with 36. After their spectacular turnaround in the second half of the season, all eyes in the East were now focused on Buffalo.

Leading passers	Attempts	Completions	Pct	TDs	Yards	Int
Warren Raab	177	67	38%	10	1196	14
Jack Kemp	94	51	54%	3	636	4
Al Dorow	75	30	40%	2	333	7

Leading rushers	Attempts	Yards gained	Average	TDs
Cookie Gilchrist	214	1096	5.1	13
Wayne Crow	110	589	5.4	1
Wray Carlton	94	530	5.6	2
Warren Raab	37	77	2.1	3

Leading receivers	Caught	Yards gained	Average	TDs
Ernie Warlick	35	482	13.8	2
Elbert Dubenion	33	571	17.3	5
Glenn Bass	32	555	17.3	4
Cookie Gilchrist	24	319	13.3	2

Leading scorers	TDs	XPM	XPA	FGM	FGA	PTs
Cookie Gilchrist	15	14	18	8	20	128
Elbert Dubenion	6					36

18. Buffalo ended the season with ex-Charger Jack Kemp in the driver's seat after he took over for Warren Raab, who took over for Al Dorow. All three had NFL experience prior to their AFL careers. What NFL teams did they each play for?

The Progress of the Seasons – 1962

▪ BOSTON PATRIOTS ▪

THE OUTLOOK FOR THE PATRIOTS IN 1962 was not so much about hope, as it was about expectations. Mike Holovak had infused the New England contingent after taking over five games into the season last year and now after a 9-4-1 finish a year ago the Pats hoped to rise to the top of the East. Instead of employing his rotating quarterback system of the previous year, Holovak was now putting all of his footballs into Babe Parilli's basket. With that commitment, Butch Songin was traded to the New York Titans for all-star defensive back Dick Felt in hopes of shoring up the weak pass coverage. Boston's defensive line play would be called upon to anchor the team. And the defensive unit answered the call by yielding the league's second fewest total yards gained on the ground. Larry Eisenhauer, Jim Hunt, Houston Antwine, Jess Richardson, and Bob Dee continued their reign of terror on offensive lines around the league and once again got outstanding play from linebacker Tom Addison. But once again the other AFL teams realized that they could not budge the immovable Pats front four on the ground so they took to the air in hope of finding pay dirt. And once again the Pats secondary accommodated, as they finished last in the league in guarding against the pass.

In Dallas to open the season, the Patriots stumbled and fell to the Texans 42-28 as the vaunted Boston defense could not contain Dallas halfback Abner Haynes, who scored 4 touchdowns in leading the Texans to victory in the Cotton Bowl. For Boston's home opener, this time playing in Harvard Stadium in front of 32,276 fans, the Pats pushed past the two-time defending AFL Champion Houston Oilers 34-21 and then hosted Denver with a 41-16 win for an early season 2-1 record. They improved to 3-1 with a win in the Polo Grounds against the Titans 43-14, as Babe Parilli threw 3 TD passes, and Gino Cappelletti scored 19 points before losing to Dallas the next week. But after successive victories over San Diego and Oakland, the Patriots record stood at 5-2 which set them on top of the Eastern Division. A visit to Buffalo's War Memorial Stadium followed, and left the Boston defense breathless after chasing hard-running fullback Cookie Gilchrist around the Rock Pile to the tune of 102 yards gained in a 28-28 tie. Their record improved to 6-2-1 after downing Denver, and then they headed to Houston for another first-place showdown, in which Boston not only lost the game 21-17, but also their quarterback and MVP Babe Parilli with a broken collar bone. Out for the season, Parilli was replaced by Tom Yewcic. Yewcic led Boston to victories in their next three games, taking them into the season's final weekend with a 9-3-1 record. It was the second time in as many years that the Patriots had a chance to win the division in their final game. A Saturday night loss by Houston would put their championship hopes on the line against winless Oakland on Sunday. But

Houston did not cooperate, clinching their third straight Eastern Division crown with a win over New York. With no hope of moving either up or down in the standings, Boston, sleep-walked through their final game, becoming the only team in the AFL to be shut out in 1962. Losing 20-0 gave Boston another 9-4-1 record as they caught their second bridal bouquet in three seasons.

The offense put up some impressive numbers again, led by Parilli's throwing accuracy. He threw only 8 interceptions in his 10 games and Boston College favorite Jim Colclough caught 10 touchdowns. Fullback Ron Burton caught 40 passes and also led the team in rushing with 538 yards for a 4.4 per carry average. It was Ron's best season to date. Gino Cappelletti and tight end Tony Romeo each caught 34 passes. Two standout rookies—linebacker Nick Buoniconti and guard Billy Neighbors—showed they were on their way to stardom, but the offensive line suffered from the absence of all-league guard Charlie Leo for half the season. For the first time in three years not one Patriot was selected for the all-league team.

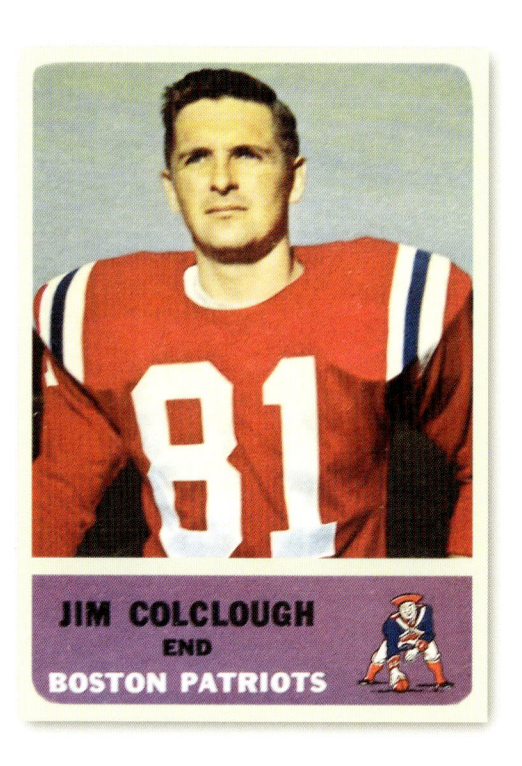

Leading passers	Attempts	Completions	Pct	TDs	Yards	Int
Babe Parilli	253	140	55%	18	1988	8
Tom Yewcic	126	54	43%	7	903	5

Leading rushers	Attempts	Yards gained	Average	TDs
Jim Crawford	139	459	3.3	2
Ron Burton	134	548	4.1	2
Larry Garron	67	392	5.9	2

Leading receivers	Caught	Yards gained	Average	TDs
Jim Colclough	40	868	21.7	10
Ron Burton	40	461	11.5	4
Tony Romeo	34	608	17.9	1
Gino Cappelletti	34	479	14.1	5
Jim Crawford	22	224	10.2	2
Larry Garron	18	236	13.1	3

The Progress of the Seasons – 1962

Leading scorers	TDs	XPM	XPA	FGM	FGA	PTs
Gino Cappelletti	5	38	40	20	37	128
Jim Colclough	10					60

■ DENVER BRONCOS ■

NEW OWNERSHIP, NEW LEADERSHIP, and a bonfire that destroyed all remnants of the awful memories of gold, brown, and those vertically striped socks marked a new beginning for the Broncos. Orange and blue were the colors of the day that brought a hint of respectability to the Colorado team. Solid orange socks replaced … well, you remember. The orange jerseys were supposed to resemble the Texas Longhorns but instead looked more like the Tennessee Volunteers. Nevertheless, no one east or west of the Rockies was complaining. The dramatic change in attire was done to lift the spirits and attitude of the Broncos, who were winners in only seven of their first twenty-eight games. The Broncos away jerseys were white with blue numbers with white pants and orange socks. Their helmets changed from the dark chocolate with plain white numbers, to orange, with a white stripe down the center and a white cartoon bronco on each side. Early in the year the bronco was a dark brown but displayed poorly from a distance and was changed to white after a few games. The players and fans both welcomed the change of colors and logo. In short, the Copper Bowl leftovers were finally and forever dead and buried.

The new day in Denver had arrived and with it came new and more winning ways. Denver is the only team in AFL history to never have finished a season over .500, and only once were they able to be even that good. But in 1962 the Broncos gave their fans many a thrill, and through the first half of the year there was no better team in the West than the 6-1 team from Denver. With Howsam looking to dump his albatross franchise, a group of businessmen from the southwest came looking to buy and move the team to San Antonio. Then in the spring of 1962, Cal Kunz Jr., a Denver businessman, began a spirited effort to keep the Broncos in Denver. Together with Gerald Phipps, Ben Stapleton Jr., and Ed Hirschfield, Kunz was able to gain ownership and a new lease on Denver's AFL life.

With the change in ownership a new head coach, Jack Faulkner, was hired. Faulkner had spent fourteen years assisting Sid Gillman on his staff at the University of Cincinnati and with the Chargers. Gillman was considered a master organizer as well as a devoted student of defense and an outright genius on offense. He had taught Faulkner every necessary detail in building a winning team from the bottom up. And that is how Faulkner set out to bring respectability to the floundering Broncos. There were changes in the front office as well as on the field. Faulkner insisted that if he were to take the reigns as head coach, he would have to gain complete control of the team's personnel. Permission was granted, and his first line of business was putting his 7-20-1 team into respectable uniforms. Hence, the purging of the duds that brought the team nothing but ridicule.

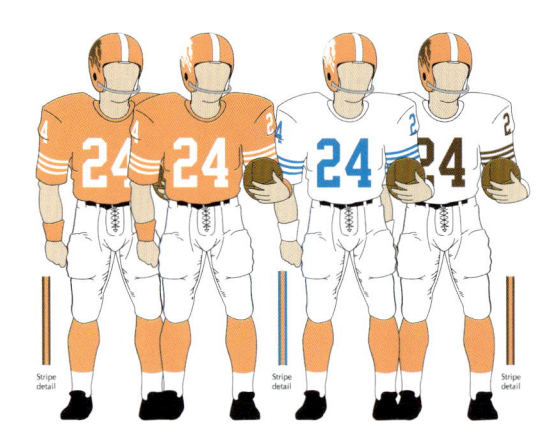

Faulkner inherited a roster of few stars and even fewer front-line performers. And as camp opened in July, no one had a lock on a starting position. His quarterback was again Frank Tripucka, back for his third season after expecting to retire long ago. Thirty-five years old and in his fifteenth pro season, the 'Tripper' set an AFL record by throwing 440 passes, while completing 240 of them for 2,902 yards. His favorite receiver, Lionel Taylor, was one of only two legitimate all-stars on offense, the other being offensive tackle Eldon Danenhauer. Banking on his positive relationship with his mentor in San Diego, Faulkner was able to acquire young Charger receivers Bob Scarpitto and Luther Hayes to help Taylor at flanker. Looking to upgrade his defensive secondary, Faulker struck gold by also bringing safety Bob Zeman to the Rockies from San Diego. Zeman was selected all-league in his first year in the Mile High city.

For the first time in franchise history the Broncos went into their opening game with a plan. Playing in Denver University Stadium the Broncos more than doubled their '61 average attendance with 24,928 seats filled to see them take on the two-time Western Division Champion Chargers. What they witnessed was something completely unexpected, as Denver upset San Diego 31-21 to register their third opening day victory in as many tries. Everyone in the near-capacity crowd was amazed and seemed to have the same question racing through their minds: Had the Chargers slipped that much or were their beloved Broncos suddenly that good? Gene Mingo's 5-yard run started the scoring and he added a field goal before the Chargers realized they were 10 points behind. Tripucka's 49-yard toss to former Charger Bob Scarpitto was good for another 6 points. Six more points were recorded when newly acquired Bo Dickenson latched on to another Tripucka TD pass for a halftime lead of 24-7. The finishing touches came in the second half on 2 field goals by Mingo, one for an AFL record 53 yards, which were enough to hold the Chargers off, 31-21.

Scoring twenty unanswered second-half points the next week was Denver's ticket to

The Progress of the Seasons – 1962

win number two in Buffalo by a score of 23-20, sparked by a 96-yard touchdown pass from Tripucka to speedy Al Frazier. But you don't go on an extended journey east without some kind of setback. For the Broncos, it came in Boston's Nickerson Field with a 41-16 loss. A trip to New York was next, where after the first three games the Titans found themselves in a three-way tie for first place with the Patriots and Oilers. Through three periods Denver clung to a 13-10 lead, then, thanks in part to Bob Zeman's 30-yard interception return for a touchdown, Denver went on to trample their host 32-10. With a 3-1 record the Broncos trailed only Western Division leader Dallas, who had yet to lose.

For Denver's second home game they took on the Oakland Raiders under the lights in front of 22,452 fans, the second consecutive game in which they doubled their previous year's attendance average. Gene Mingo's 82-yard run and two fourth-quarter interception returns for touchdowns by all-league safety Goose Gonsoulin and rookie John McGeever put Oakland away 44-7. The win regained the Western Division lead for Denver, who at 4-1 were now a half game up on 3-1 Dallas.

On successive weeks in October the Broncos and Raiders went at each other in a home and away series. And for the first time in franchise history the Broncos had a three-game winning streak. The defense was coming together, giving up a total of only 23 points during the streak. The story in the second game against Oakland was Gene Mingo, who kicked 3 field goals and scored on a 4-yard touchdown run, accounting for all of Denver's first 16 points. The 23-6 win marked Denver's best record ever at 5-1.

On October 21 the Broncos found themselves in an historic setting. Bear's Stadium was hosting a mid-season showdown pitting the Oilers, the best team in the East, against Denver, the best in the West. Again Denver used some fourth-quarter heroics. The teams traded field goals throughout the first half but Houston went ahead in the third when Billy Cannon pushed the ball over for a score from 2 yards out. In years past that would have been enough to deter the hapless Broncos. But this was 1962, the year of the orange jerseys and a game plan. Holding it together, Frank Tripucka engineered two drives that hit for 6 points both times. The second coming on a 20-yard gallop by fullback Donnie Stone. The 20-10 victory gave Denver a four-game win streak and a mid-year report card of 6 wins against only 1 loss, lifting them atop the Western Division.

The running game was still not a factor on offense even though they gained two hundred more yards than the year before. Injuries to top back Donnie Stone limited him to only 360 yards, with Gene Mingo gaining 287 yards for a 5.3 average. The multi-talented Mingo ran and kicked his way to a second scoring title (137 points) in three years and even set a pro football record by connecting on 27 field goals. Bo Dickenson, brought in from Dallas, had only a 3.3 rushing average but did finish fourth in the league in receiving with 60 catches. The running game also suf-

★ *Denver's Bob Zeman collars Charger tight end Dave Kocourek.* ★

fered from the absence of one of the league's top guards, Ken Adamson, who broke his jaw in game four and did not return. The ground game finished seventh, with only 1,298 yards.

It was the passing attack that again carried the Denver offense, placing three players in the league's top ten receivers, led by Taylor's 77 catches. Also cracking the group was tight end Gene Prebola, who grabbed 41. Adding an extra dimension was newly acquired flanker Bob Scarpitto. Scarpitto led the team in yards per catch, hauling in 35 balls for 19 yards per reception average and a team-high 6 touchdowns. The AFL's top passing team was riding the arm of a tiring Frank Tripucka right to the top of the division. Perhaps the biggest difference in the Broncos surge was the defense, led by all-league selections Bud McFadden, Austin Gonsoulin, and Bob Zeman. They were keeping the offense in games right up to the final gun and climbed two positions in fewest points allowed for the year as well as finishing fifth against both the pass and run. The offense checked in at number four, trailing Houston, Dallas, and Boston.

At the season's halfway mark the answer

The Progress of the Seasons – 1962

to all those questions about Denver being the real thing were about to be answered. And what appeared to be a stampede to a Western title would soon become little more than a bucking bronco being harnessed and saddled. It started against Buffalo on October 28. The same game a year ago produced one of the most exciting comebacks in the team's brief history when they fought back from being behind 30 points in the second half to earn a 38-38 tie. This would be another wild west show, but this time it was the Bills who would mount a last-period assault and overtake Denver. Behind 38-23 in the fourth quarter, Buffalo scored on a 75-yard pass, a 40-yard pass and a 4-yard run, scoring the final 22 points of the game and winning 45-38. With the loss the Broncos fell out of first place by a half game. Hoping to retake first place the next week, Faulkner's team found themselves losing 20-14 in the fourth quarter to San Diego until Donnie Stone scored his third touchdown of the game, catching a 14-yard pass from Tripucka. He previously ran for two scores from the one and five yard lines. The final 2 points came on a Charger punt snap that flew out of the end zone. The 23-20 win pushed their record to 7-2, sending Dallas, who lost to Houston, back into second place.

A loss to Boston, coupled with a Dallas win the next week, put the biggest game in franchise history on the horizon. The season's eleventh week brought Dallas, with a 7-2 record, to Denver to play the 7-3 Broncos. A 3-point lead in the first quarter had Denver's 23,523 crowd in mile-high spirits, but in the second period Chris Burford's 26-yard touchdown reception put Dallas ahead at halftime. Neither the Broncos nor Texans could mount any offense in the third period, and as the fourth quarter began, Dallas was hanging on to a 4-point lead. That's when the Texans took over the game, scoring 17 points and shutting down the Denver passing attack. The Broncos lost the game 24-3. Still, on November 22 with the Titans in town the Broncos were hoping that a win and a little luck would put them in a position to turn the tables on Dallas three weeks later. At first things did not look good as the Titans surged to a 17-0 lead. Things appeared to get even worse when they shot ahead 24-7. But the Bronco crowd came alive as their favorites scored 20 points in a row and finally, late in the fourth quarter, were in the driver's seat, leading 45-32 with less than six minutes to play. And then the season disappeared on them. Unable to contain Titan quarterback Johnny Green, who would throw 5 touchdown passes in the game, New York scored twice in the last four minutes to crush the dream of a title, eecking out a 46-45 win.

The Broncos would not win another game in 1962 and while some would see the fade from 6-1 to 7-7 as a lost season, their twelve week run at a title after only seven wins in their first two years energized Bronco followers about the future. With outstanding seasons under their belts, Taylor, Danenhauer, McFadin, Zeman, and Gonsoulin were all-leaguers. Denver had come a long way in Faulkner's first year, and set a solid foundation and the hope of a rising sun in the Western city.

Leading passers	Attempts	Completions	Pct	TDs	Yards	Int
Frank Tripucka	440	240	54.5%	17	2917	25
George Shaw	110	49	44.5%	4	783	14

Leading rushers	Attempts	Yards gained	Average	TDs
Donnie Stone	94	360	3.8	3
Gene Mingo	54	287	5.3	4
Bo Dickinson	73	247	3.4	0
Al Frazier	39	168	4.3	2
Johnny Olszewski	33	114	3.5	0

Leading receivers	Caught	Yards gained	Average	TDs
Lionel Taylor	77	908	11.8	4
Bo Dickinson	60	554	9.2	4
Gene Prebola	41	599	14.6	1
Bob Scarpitto	35	667	19.1	6
Donnie Stone	20	223	11.2	2
Gene Mingo	14	107	7.6	0

Leading scorers	TDs	XPM	XPA	FGM	FGA	PTs
Gene Mingo	4	32	34	27	39	137
Bob Scarpitto	6					36

19. Denver coach Jack Faulkner gained valuable knowledge about winning football from Sid Gillman, whom he assisted with both the Rams and Chargers. He was also on Gillman's staff at the University of Cincinnati. But the first introduction to his mentor came when he played linebacker for him at what university?
A. Miami of Ohio
B. University of Cincinnati
C. Ohio State

▪ HOUSTON OILERS ▪

ON MARCH 5 THE OILERS HIRED THEIR third head coach in as many years. Frank "Pop" Ivy, late of the same St. Louis Cardinals who had just employed resigned Oiler mentor Wally Lemm, filled the role. Ironically, both coaches left their former teams on their own terms, and what appeared as a coaching swap was nothing more than two teams hiring the best man available. Ivy was coming off a disappointing 5-7 season in St. Louis after turning the program around in the previous two years. A native of Oklahoma and a former player at the state's university, Ivy had also assisted legendary coach Bud Wilkinson for the Sooners. Impressed with the roster he inherited, Ivy planned to defend the Oilers second AFL title,

The Progress of the Seasons – 1962

which meant improving the running game that already boasted 1961 rushing champion Billy Cannon. The main benefactor of Ivy's reign was Charley Tolar, who became the first Oiler (and one of only three runners in 1962) to gain over 1,000 yards (1,012 on a league-high 244 carries). Ivy and Cannon feuded continually as Cannon's follow-up to his rushing title was plagued by a sore back and disagreements with his new coach, cutting his yardage to 474 yards, less than half of last year's total. The feud caused the Heisman Trophy winner to threaten an exodus if Ivy returned in 1963.

Split end Bill Groman limped through another season with injuries and shared his position with ex-Chicago Bear Willard Dewveall. The loss of Groman and his 20 yards per catch was a contributing factor to the average performances turned in by Charlie Hennigan and George Blanda. Dave Smith, who lost his all-league status and starting fullback spot in 1961 after injuries cut into his playing time was slowed again by a recurring leg injury.

All was well with Houston on September 9 as they began their second title defense in Buffalo. Charlie Tolar scored on a 19-yard run and Hennigan and Cannon chipped in with scores in the second quarter to post an early 21-3 lead. After Hennigan latched on to a 40-yard halfback pass from Cannon in the third quarter the defense held off a late Bills rush to win the opener 28-23. But a loss in Boston on the second week, despite two Hennigan touchdown catches of 78 and 40 yards, caused some concern for Ivy with a third game

on the road scheduled in San Diego the next week. On 3 Billy Cannon touchdowns (2 runs and a catch) the Oilers jumped out to a 28-10 halftime lead and won easily 42-17 after the Chargers were forced to play journeyman Dick Wood at quarterback in place of the injured Jack Kemp. Charley Tolar ran for 142 yards on 18 carries, Cannon added 70 more and Dave Smith chipped in with another 66. After a bye week, Ivy saw his new team overtake Buffalo in the fourth quarter, scoring 14 points on 2 touchdown passes from Blanda, 1 for 73 yards to flanker Charlie Frazier and another for three yards to Bill Groman, securing a 17-14 win. With two of their three wins looking less than glamorous, Ivy was hoping for a breakout game in their second home outing against New York.

The defense to this point, while not playing poorly, was still in need of a dominating performance. It came on October 14 against the Titans. After New York started the scoring with a 40-yard field goal, Blanda lit up the sky with 6 touchdown passes before allowing understudy Jacky Lee to toss a seventh. Groman and tight end Bob McLeod grabbed 2 each from Blanda. But it was the defense that created the brightest light, shutting down the New York offense as the Titans could muster only a punt return and a fumble recovery for touchdowns. Winning 56-17 gave Houston a 4-1 record and had Ivy feeling pretty confident about his chances. But two consecutive losses to Denver and Dallas put the Oilers behind Boston's 5-2 record. After a lackluster 4-3 record through the first

117

half of the season, the Oilers again put on a closing rush, winning their last seven games and finally overtaking the Patriots on November 18 for first place in the East.

The Oilers faced Dallas on November 4 in a home-and-away series that the AFL was fond of scheduling. The Texans were 6-1 and fighting to hold off Denver for the lead in the West. And it was time for the Oiler defense to show their mettle by locking newly acquired Dallas quarterback Len Dawson's offense out of the end zone. The 29,017 fans who filed into the Cotton Bowl saw a defensive tug-of-war with only three plays finding the end zone. Billy Cannon capped an Oiler drive in the second period with a 1-yard pass from Blanda and then cradled a 34-yarder in the end zone in the third. Led by big Ed Hussman's pressure, Houston was able to keep the Texans out of the end zone until Dawson found Chris Burford for 15 yards in the fourth quarter. Winning 14-6, the Oilers were able to stay a half game behind the Patriots and dropped Dallas a half game behind Western Division leader Denver. Traveling next to Frank Youell Field in Oakland to face the winless Raiders, Ivy's team found themselves behind 20-14 in the final frame. But Blanda and Tolar connected for a 35-yard touchdown pass, putting Houston on top 21-20. Gene Rabb scored the game's final touchdown by returning an interception 31 yards, handing Oakland their ninth straight loss of the season 28-20 and setting up the season's biggest game the next week against the 6-2-1 Patriots.

Bob McLeod snagged a 42-yard touchdown pass to give the Oilers a 14-7 lead, but before the half ended Gino Cappelletti kicked a 26-yard field goal. When Boston quarterback Babe Parilli was knocked out of action, punter and backup quarterback Tom Yewcic took over and directed the Pats to a third quarter score, but it was too little too late to overtake Houston. The 21-17 triumph gave the Oilers a 7-3 record and sent Boston out of town in second place at 6-3-1. With four games remaining, Ivy had his team in control of their own destiny with only 3-7 San Diego, 7-4 Denver, 0-10 Oakland, and 4-6 New York standing in their way.

The Oilers saw the Chargers jump out to a 14-0 lead the next week before Jacky Lee, subbing for Blanda, put himself into the record books with a 98-yard touchdown pass (longest in AFL history) to Willard Dewveall. Still trailing 27-19 in the fourth quarter, the Oilers scored the final 14 points on a touchdown, 2-point conversion and 2 field goals to withstand 5 interceptions and the Chargers scare, winning 33-27. Houston could muster only 47 yards rushing and Blanda connected on only 5 of his 18 passes before bowing to the assistance of Lee. The second stringer completed 7 of his 13 passes for 164 yards. With Boston beating Buffalo 21-10, the Oilers managed to cling to their slim lead in the East.

Blanda was back in favor on Sunday, December 2, and was able to find the end zone 3 times on passes to Cannon for 60 and 8 yards and Charlie Hennigan for 5. Defensive end Don Floyd then rumbled 28 yards with an interception, and Houston had a 34-

The Progress of the Seasons – 1962

17 victory over Denver. After keeping Oakland winless with a 32-17 win for their tenth victory, only the New York Titans stood in the way of another Eastern Division title. As Boston waited for their game with Oakland on Sunday, Houston lined up for the kick off in the Polo Grounds in front of only 8,167 fans on Saturday night, December 15, with a chance to lock up the division. Controlling their own fate on the last weekend of the season, the Oilers took control of the game after Titan defensive back Wayne Fontes put New York ahead in the first quarter with an 83-yard interception return for a touchdown. Then, for the second time in the season, the powerful Houston defense kept the Titan offense out of the end zone the rest of the way. Ranking only behind Dallas in team defense and points allowed, the Oilers used 3 touchdown passes by George Blanda and another by Jacky Lee to blow New York away 44-10 while simultaneously raising their third straight Eastern Division flag.

Eight days later they found things a bit more difficult in defending their AFL title against Dallas in the league championship game than they did defending their Eastern crown against their division rivals. Coming back from a 17-0 halftime deficit, only a blocked field goal with less than three minutes to play kept Houston from a third AFL championship. The back-and-forth battle had to be extended into a fifth and then a sixth period, becoming the longest game in pro football history, before the Oilers succumbed to Dallas 20-17.

Charlie Hennigan, with 54 receptions and eight touchdown catches, along with guard Bob Talamini, were selected first team all-leaguers. Defensive end Don Floyd and cornerback Tony Banfield were similarly rewarded on defense. The fourth-ranked Houston running game was led by Charley Tolar, whose 1,012 yards rushing were eclipsed by only Cookie Gilchrist and Abner Haynes. Finishing second behind Denver in team passing, the Oilers were the best team in the AFL in total offense, second in total defense and guarding against the pass. Rookie defensive back Bobby Jancik led the AFL in kickoff returns (30.2) and was second in punt returns with an 11.7 average.

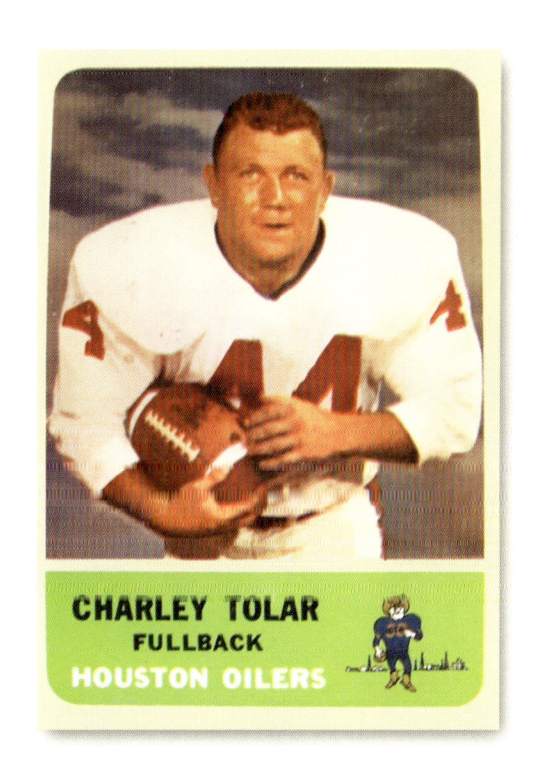

CHARLEY TOLAR
FULLBACK
HOUSTON OILERS

Remember the AFL

Leading passers	Attempts	Completions	Pct	TDs	Yards	Int
George Blanda	418	197	47.1%	27	2810	42
Jacky Lee	50	26	52%	4	433	5

Leading rushers	Attempts	Yards gained	Average	TDs
Charlie Tolar	244	1012	4.1	7
Billy Cannon	147	474	3.2	7
Dave Smith	56	249	4.4	1

Leading receivers	Caught	Yards gained	Average	TDs
Charley Hennigan	54	867	16.1	8
Bob McLeod	33	578	17.5	6
Willard Dewveall	33	576	17.5	5
Billy Cannon	32	451	14.1	6
Charlie Tolar	30	251	8.4	1
Bill Groman	21	328	15.6	3

Leading scorers	TDs	XPM	XPA	FGM	FGA	PTs
George Blanda		48	49	11	26	81
Billy Cannon	13	2				80

■ DALLAS TEXANS ■

MENTION THE 1962 TEXANS AND people immediately recall the Abner Haynes coin toss blunder or Tommy Brooker's sixth-period, sudden-death field goal that brought the AFL Championship to Dallas. The first recall is unfortunate, and the second an over dramatization that detracts observers from recognizing that this was a truly good football team. Dallas began turning the corner when Hank Stram lured his former Purdue pupil, All-American quarterback Len Dawson, to the AFL after he requested a release from the Cleveland Browns. Dissatisfied with Cotton Davidson, who posted good numbers but not enough wins in the first two years, Stram brought the former Steelers first-round draft pick to Texas—rusty arm, bruised ego, and all. Listed originally as the fourth quarterback, Dawson showed enough in the Texan exhibition games to earn the opening day start. One game into the season Davidson packed his bags for Oakland. Dawson led the franchise throughout the decade that included three championship games, two Super Bowls, two AFL and one AFL/NFL Championship.

In 1962 the Texans still featured Abner Haynes on offense and a linebacker-dominated defense of E.J. Holub, Sherrill Headrick, Smokey Stover, and Walt Corey. So good was the group of quad-backers that Stram occa-

The Progress of the Seasons – 1962

sionally used the four together with a front three. Defense was the Texan forte, and with the AFL's best running game, they continued to play more like an NFL team than part of the pass-happy AFL. Haynes was again teamed with Jack Spikes in the backfield, giving Dallas an especially strong and balanced offense. After Spikes went down to injury at mid-season, rookie Curtis McClinton (6'3", 230 lbs.) stepped in to carry the ball 111 times for 604 yards. He finished fifth in the league in rushing and walked off with the Rookie of the Year award. McClinton was also a reliable and punishing pass blocker, protecting Dawson and giving him time to find the steady Texan receivers. Frank Jackson led the team in yards per carry and proved to be the best second-string halfback in the league. His blazing speed led Stram to move him to flanker when Chris Burford was injured late in the season. Jackson's presence also allowed Johnny Robinson, a key third back for his first two years, to move to the other side of the line and shore up the defensive secondary.

Burford and newly acquired Bill Miller were the split end and flanker, although for much of the season Stram used a double tight end set with rookies Fred Arbanas and Tommy Brooker, both deft blockers, to enhance the running game. Burford was one of the best all-around receivers in the AFL and was widely acclaimed as the league's best third-down receiver. Haynes, too, often found himself split from the line in times of need. These skill-position players, however, relied on one of the biggest offensive lines in the AFL. The tackles were all-league Jim Tyrer and Jerry Cornelison with Marvin Terrell, Al Reynolds, and Sonny Bishop at guard, and Jon Gilliam at center. Tight end Arbanas was drafted in 1961, but sat out the entire season with a bad back. As a rookie in '62 he caught 29 passes for a 16.2 average and six touchdowns. He made the all-league second unit.

As the season began, Dawson's rusty arm had found some strength, and against the Patriots his leadership inspired captain Abner Haynes to award him his first game ball. A noble gesture from the halfback, in light of Abner's own 4-touchdown performance in the Texans' 42-28 triumph. Haynes ran in from 2 and 25 yards away in the second quarter, from 30 in the third and caught a 9-yard scoring pass in the fourth. It was Dawson's performance as well that prompted owner Lamar Hunt to make his first, and only, trade without his coach's knowledge or consent. Even with the league's decision to increase the rosters by three, to thirty-six players, Hunt did not see the need to carry more than two quarterbacks. The Oakland Raiders lost their top signal caller, Tom Flores, to illness and were in need of an experienced starter. Hunt had just the right medicine for what ailed them. In return for Davidson, the Texans received Oakland's first round draft pick, which turned out to be defensive tackle Buck Buchannan from Grambling. Not a bad deal for the owner turned GM for a day. With a roster that averaged little more than twenty-three years of age at the beginning of the season, Hunt and Stram were confident that

★ *Abner Haynes turns the corner with Oiler lineman Bill Wegener in hot pursuit.* ★

their new quarterback was the missing ingredient in the team's success recipe that had only managed to build a 14-14 record in their first two years. Davidson could well have saved the Raiders the price of a plane ticket enroute to the west coast as the Texans also traveled to Oakland for season's second game. His knowledge of the Dallas playbook did not seem to concern the Texans or Dawson. Lenny fired three touchdown passes to Chris Burford for 13, 27, and 21 yards to capture their second victory, 26-16.

As they hosted the Bills for their third game, the Texans cruised to a 41-21 win, in which Abner Haynes continued his touchdown barrage by scoring on runs for 71 and 13 yards in the first quarter. It was the first of four dances to the 1962 version of the "Texans three-step," referring to the team's pattern of winning this season. While they had a league best 11-3 record, matching the Houston Oilers, Dallas never won more than three games in a

The Progress of the Seasons – 1962

row throughout the season. Four times they strung together three wins in a row, starting with the season's first three games, which were followed by a loss—followed by three more wins, and a loss—and still another three wins, and another loss. Texans then filled their dance with wins in their final two regular season games and followed them up with a win in the AFL Championship game, giving them their third win in a row—as well as their first AFL Championship.

Offensively the Texans scored more points (389) than every other team, and defensively allowed the fewest points (233). Led by a confident and mobile quarterback, Stram's team was finally getting it done offensively. And at the end of the year Burford, Dawson, Haynes, and Tyrer were all-league first teamers. The all-league defensive team included E.J. Holub and Sherill Headrick, who joined second-time all-leaguer Mel Branch and first timer Jerry Mays. Defensive backs Duane Wood, Dave Grayson, and Bobby Hunt joined end Fred Arbanas on the all-league second unit. Interestingly, the only member of the secondary left off of both the first and second all-league teams was Johnny Robinson, in his first year at safety. Robinson would earn his due in the end, however, as he would be selected at his position for the AFL's All-Time Team at the end of the decade.

The team's first step backward came at the hands of the injury-riddled San Diego Chargers, who were now quarterbacked by rookie John Hadl after starter Jack Kemp injured his finger. Though suffering their first loss, 32-28, Haynes continued his torrid touchdown pace by adding two more notches to his belt. Looking for a less predictable formation with which to confuse defenses, coach Stram inserted a double tight end offense the next week against Boston's blitzkrieg defense. Using both Arbanas and Tommy Brooker as his blocking ends, Dallas ran away from the defensive-minded Pats 27-7. In the game Chris Burford caught a touchdown pass for the fifth week in a row, doing some blitzing of his own on Boston's safeties with 10 receptions. But not all was joyous in Dallas after the game, as fullback Jack Spikes was injured and lost for the second year in a row. His injury, however, created an opening for rookie Curtis McClinton.

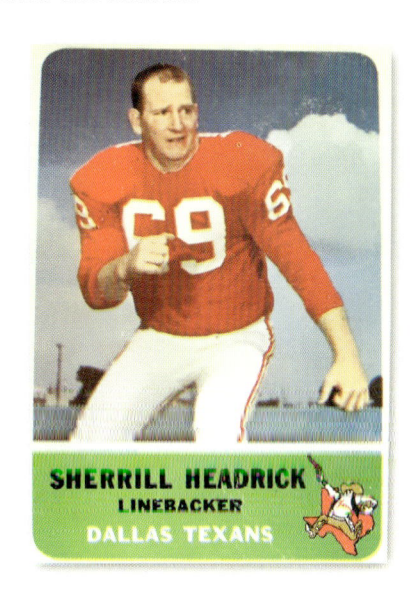

SHERRILL HEADRICK
LINEBACKER
DALLAS TEXANS

Against New York the Texans were victorious thanks to Tommy Brooker's game-winning field goal and two more Abner Haynes touchdowns, a 78-yard pass reception and a 1-yard plunge. In the battle against

Houston the next week, Haynes kept his streak alive again, leading his team to a 31-7 win and giving the Texans a 6-1 record. Back home against the same Oilers the next week, the Texas three-step missed a beat with a 14-6 loss that dropped them one-half game behind the 7-2 Broncos. But before a showdown in Denver's corral could take place, Dallas scored a season-high 52 points against the New York Titans. Abner Haynes recorded 3 more touchdowns with a 75-yard reception and runs of 1 and 9 yards. He also gained 107 against the Titans' weak front line. At 7-2, they now had a whispering lead on the 7-3 Broncos with a trip to Denver next.

A snow-covered Bears Stadium greeted Dallas on November 18, with 25,523 fans on hand for the fight for first place. With the defenses dictating the pace, scoring was limited to a Chris Burford touchdown catch and a Gene Mingo field goal. A scoreless third quarter followed. But in the final stanza the Texans proved their moxie without surrendering to Denver's twelfth man, the mile-high altitude. As the fourth quarter began, Dallas, still clinging to a 7-3 lead, upped the ante when Tommy Brooker connected with a 13-yard field goal. After Bronco punter Jim Fraser's punt caught a jet stream and landed on Dallas' three yard line, two runs up the gut got Dawson some playing room as he prepared for his third-and-five call—a play-action pass, faking McClinton up the middle. Lenny then fired a pass to Brooker at the Texans' 25 yard line and the tight end was off on a foot race and a 92-yard scoring play. It was Brooker's second touchdown reception of the season as well as only his second catch of the year. Fred Arbanas finished off the scoring with a 47-yard touchdown catch to give Dallas sole possession of first place in the West.

The offense and defense had reached the pinnacle, and Stram wanted to make sure they stayed there. Led by a renovated secondary of Robinson, Hunt, Wood, and Grayson, the backs were beaten for scores through the air only thirteen times in fourteen games. On offense, although Len Dawson, the AFL's Player of the Year, completed a league-leading 61 percent of his passes with 29 touchdown throws, Abner Haynes was the offensive catalyst, on his way to a pro record 19 touchdowns and finishing second in rushing with 1,049 yards while catching 39 passes.

By week twelve, Dallas needed only one more win to seal at least a tie for the division crown and faced the winless Raiders. Dawson made short order of this hapless brigade by handing Oakland their seventeenth loss in a row, 35-7. Haynes and McClinton were unstoppable as they piled up 112 and 109 yards rushing respectively, with Abner registering two more scores on runs of 31 and 19 yards. It was also only the second game of the year in which Chris Burford failed to snag a pass for 6 points. And for the third time that season Dallas had a three-game winning streak. But for the third time they took a step backward, losing on the following week. Still needing a win or a Denver loss to win the West, they traveled to War Memorial Stadium to take on the Bills, who won the game 23-14.

The Progress of the Seasons – 1962

But the Texans still clinched the Western Division title when the Broncos lost their third game in a row and their fifth of the year. As the defense tuned up its game, waiting to see who would emerge as the Eastern Division champion, Denver again failed to score an offensive touchdown on the league's best defense. In two games the Broncos managed 2 field goals and a fumble-recovery touchdown. Against Denver, Stram moved speedy Frank Jackson to the flank, while Burford nursed an injury. The move would foreshadow Stram's permanent switch of Jackson to flanker in 1963. The 17-10 victory over Denver included a 69-yard touchdown run by Curtis McClinton and a record-breaking nineteenth touchdown by Abner Haynes. All that remained was a victory over ailing San Diego in the season's last week before the first real "Battle for Texas" would take place in Houston's Jeppesen Stadium on December 23.

The day started with 37,981 onlookers jamming into the Jeppesen stands as the teams lined up for the opening kickoff. Seventy-seven minutes and fifty-four seconds of playing time later they were joined by millions of television viewers to witness Tommy Brooker's attempt at a 25-yard sudden death field goal. After the ball was snapped to holder Len Dawson, Brooker's square toe swung into the pigskin, which touched down in the end zone as the referee's arms stretched skyward, giving Dallas its first AFL Championship. The 20-17 sixth period victory was the longest game in professional football history. Without Chris Burford, sidelined for the final three games,

Dallas lined up Abner Haynes on the flank. With Jack Spikes returning to the team, McClinton joined him behind Dawson. The Oilers had the edge on experience with almost half their squad having either championship game or NFL experience. The Texans, by contrast, were infants to championship football. But it was the young and the restless who jumped out to a 17-0 lead at halftime.

Jeppesen Stadium had undergone a facelift in anticipation of the history-making game. The high school field had been overused, and the area between the 20 yard lines looked like a dust bowl. To remedy the lack of turf, a new carpet of grass ran down the middle of the field. And while the Oiler passing game would not be affected by the new turf, the footing for the Texan running game would be at a distinct disadvantage. Early in the game Dallas punter Jimmy Saxton shanked a 22-yard punt that gave Houston excellent field position. And Blanda immediately went for the kill. Runs by Billy Cannon and Charlie Tolar were linked to a Charley Hennigan reception, setting up a first-and-goal situation. Blanda went to the air on third down, and the first of his 5 interceptions on the day was returned 43 yards, shifting the momentum to Dallas. The Texans drove to the Houston 16 yard line but needed a Brooker field goal for the game's first score. Employing the double tight end set that Stram used successfully throughout the year, Dallas again drove down field in the second quarter, covering 80 yards on four plays. The final 28 yards culminated with Dawson hooking up with Haynes for a

125

touchdown pass, increasing the lead to 10-0.

Blanda again went to work through the air (he threw 46 passes on the day), but Dallas had another answer for the winged-T Houston offense with their second interception, this time by Duane Wood. Stram used four linebackers and a three-man line to neutralize the Houston backs on pass patterns, while the secondary that intercepted 32 passes on the year was busy holding Hennigan, Dewveall, and Bob McLeod to a combined 15 catches, frustrating Blanda all day. A two-yard dart by Haynes converted the interception into 7 more points, and as the thirty-minute mark approached, the two-time defending champion Oilers stared at a 17-0 deficit.

While the marching bands entertained the crowd and commissioner Joe Foss presented Curtis McClinton with the league's Rookie of the Year award, Pop Ivy and the Houston coaching staff devised plans for a grand comeback. Changing pace in the second half, Blanda marched the Oilers 67 yards for their first score of the afternoon on a 15-yard completion to Willard Dewveall. After stopping the Texans, Houston once again moved into scoring position when Johnny Robinson picked off Blanda's pass in the end zone. But the Dallas offense was unable to take advantage of the turnover. As the fourth quarter got under way, Blanda found Billy Cannon in the end zone from 31 yards away, but as the ball hit his fingertips, Cannon was broadsided by safety Duane Wood, jarring the ball loose for an incompletion. Blanda later completed the drive by connecting on a 31-yard field goal to draw Houston within a touchdown, at 17-10. After the ensuing kickoff, Houston again stymied Dawson, forcing another Dallas punt. After shanking a punt in the first quarter, Jimmy Saxton was replaced by reserve quarterback and backup punter Eddie Wilson. But Wilson could fare no better. His 6 punts in the game averaged only 32 yards, and on this crucial one in the fourth period he put Blanda's offense one yard inside Dallas territory. Behind by 7, Blanda immediately went back to the air, finding Cannon at the 33 yard line. As the drive continued, the veteran quarterback found Cannon again for a first down at the 10 and then rifled another throw to Hennigan at the one. With just under six minutes to play Charley Tolar busted over the right side of the Oiler line for the final yard. Blanda's conversion deadlocked the score at 17-17.

Since taking a 17-0 lead in the second quarter, Stram played a conservative offense, bringing Abner Haynes back to his setback position and calling only fourteen pass plays all afternoon. The result was a scoreless second half, and as Eddie Wilson flubbed another punt for only 23 yards, Blanda lined up at the Texan 41 yard line with under three minutes left to play, looking to bring home his third AFL title. But the drive stalled, and Blanda wiped off his kicking shoe on fourth down to try a game-winning field goal from 42 yards away. As the kick lifted off his toe, all-league middle linebacker Sherrill Headrick found a gap in the Houston line and got a hand on the ball, tipping it away. The score remained deadlocked. As regulation play ended, the two

The Progress of the Seasons – 1962

teams readied to make history by playing only the second championship sudden-death overtime period in pro football history

As the referees summoned the team captains to the center of the field for a second time, Stram gave his final instructions to Abner Haynes for the overtime coin toss. With the fifteen mph wind a factor, Stram instructed his captain, "If they win the toss and elect to receive, we want to kick to the clock." So as Haynes watched his call of "heads" turn up, he responded with the now famous line, "We will kick to the clock." Giving Houston both the ball and the wind at their backs. Field announcer Jack Buck, joining the ceremony at midfield with an open microphone, was stunned. And as Haynes rejoined his coach on the sideline, Stram, too, was shocked at the result of their winning coin flip.

Shrugging off the blunder, the Texans lined up to kick off. Both teams played cautiously in the fifth period, and neither was able to engineer into scoring position until Blanda brought the Oilers to midfield. Closing into field goal range he had the ball on the Texan 35 yard line, second down and eleven. With the wind at his back, he wanted to edge closer to the goal post and called for Hennigan to run a short down and out. But as he dropped back to pass, he did not see defensive end Bill Hull drop off the line and into Hennigan's path. As the ball left Blanda's hand, Hull swiped the pass out of the air and returned it to the 50 yard line. The game's fifth period came to a screeching halt for the Oilers, and as the sixth frame began, Dallas now had the ball and the wind to their backs. Dawson went right to work, determined to not give Blanda another opportunity to defend Houston's title. He started by tossing a completion to fullback Jack Spikes at the Oiler 38. Looking for another pass, the Oilers brought a blitz, hoping to catch Dawson for a loss. But the gamble ended up costing them dearly. As if anticipating the pressure, Dawson ran Spikes off left tackle for 19 yards to the Oiler 19. After a one-play try for the end zone, Stram decided to put the game's fate on the toe of rookie Tommy Brooker. Linebacker E.J. Holub was sent in as the designated long snapper, and as Dawson set up the ball at the 25, Brooker, head down and right leg swinging, lifted the ball over the outstretched hand of Houston's Ed Culpepper and over the crossbar for the game winner. The Texans, Lamar Hunt's team and one of the key teams of the league, were champions at last. Jack Spikes received the game's MVP award, having gained 77 yards on 11 carries, including the 19 yard gallop to set up Brooker's game-winning field goal.

Leading passers	Attempts	Completions	Pct	TDs	Yards	Int
Len Dawson	310	189	61%	26	2759	17
Eddie Wilson	11	6	55%	0	65	0

Remember the AFL

Leading rushers	Attempts	Yards gained	Average	TDs
Abner Haynes	221	1049	4.7	13
Curtis McClinton	111	604	5.4	2
Frank Jackson	47	251	5.3	3
Jack Spikes	57	232	4.1	0

Leading receivers	Caught	Yards gained	Average	TDs
Chris Burford	45	645	14.3	12
Abner Haynes	39	573	14.7	6
Fred Arbanas	29	469	16.2	6
Curtis McClinton	29	333	11.5	0
Bill Miller	23	277	12.0	0

Leading scorers	TDs	XPM	XPA	FGM	FGA	PTs
Abner Haynes	19					114
Tommy Brooker	3	33	33	12	22	87
Chris Burford	12					72

★ ★ ★ ★ ★ ★ ★ ★ ★ ★ ★

The second edition of the AFL All-Star game returned to Balboa Stadium on January 13, 1963, playing to a crowd of 27,641. From the start the game proved to be a close and entertaining battle as Dallas rookie-of-the-year Curtis McClinton took a handoff on the game's third play and ripped off a 64-yard touchdown jaunt. After a 14-0 halftime lead that looked like a repeat of last year's deluge by the West, the East mounted a comeback to deadlock the game at 14-14 in the fourth quarter, thanks to a Blanda-to-Hennigan pass and Larry Grantham's 29-yard touchdown return of an interception. Denver's Frank Tripucka entered the game to relieve Lenny Dawson at quarterback and navigated a game-winning, 89-yard drive in seven plays. Tripucka struck gold with his Bronco teammate Lionel Taylor for three passes on the drive, the last one a 20-yard touchdown pass to give the West their second All-Star game victory 21-14.

★ ★ ★ ★ ★ ★ ★ ★ ★ ★ ★

20. Although the season ended triumphantly for Dallas when rookie Tommy Brooker kicked a 25-yard, game-winning field goal, the tight end was not the number one kicker through the first four weeks of the season. Cotton Davidson finished the 1961 season as the top place kicker after Jack Spikes was injured. But Davidson had since been traded to Oakland. Who was the player who kicked thirteen extra points and two field goals for the Texans prior to Brooker taking over the duties?

1963

AMERICAN FOOTBALL LEAGUE – 1963 FINAL STANDINGS

EASTERN DIVISION

TEAM	GP	W	L	T	PF	PA	PCT.
BOSTON PATRIOTS	14	7	6	1	327	257	0.536
BUFFALO BILLS	14	7	6	1	304	291	0.536
HOUSTON OILERS	14	6	8	0	302	372	0.429
NEW YORK JETS	14	5	8	1	299	399	0.393

WESTERN DIVISION

TEAM	GP	W	L	T	PF	PA	PCT.
SAN DIEGO CHARGERS	14	11	3	0	399	256	0.857
OAKLAND RAIDERS	14	10	4	0	363	282	0.714
KANSAS CITY CHIEFS	14	5	7	2	347	263	0.429
DENVER BRONCOS	14	2	11	1	301	473	0.179

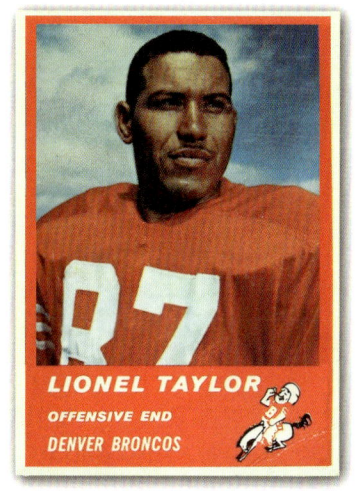

Lionel Taylor came to the Denver Broncos after the second week of 1960—and still led the league with 92 receptions! He also led the league in receiving in 1961, when he became the first player in pro football history to catch 100 passes in a season. He led the league again in '62, '63 and '65. Slowed by the wear and tear of his pass routes and double coverages, Taylor ended his career with Houston in 1968, catching only 9 passes in his farewell season. His 567 receptions put him ahead of all other AFL receivers in the league's ten-year history.

▪ OAKLAND RAIDERS ▪

CHANGE CAME TO OAKLAND IN A BIG way in 1963. Gone was the entire 1962 coaching staff. The new head coach was Al Davis, a brash and wealthy renegade from Brooklyn, recruited from Sid Gillman's staff. In laying his foundation, Davis purged the look of a loser—the nondescript black, gold, and white uniforms in favor of a simple but sophisticated look modeled after Army's black and gold. His silver-and-black colors became the backdrop of the franchise and the basis for his motto "a commitment to excellence." He demanded *pride and poise* under all circumstances and in all situations as he

The Progress of the Seasons – 1963

created his own earthquake in the Bay area.

His single-minded determination turned 1962's 1-13 team of misfits into an intimidating 10-4 offensive and defensive juggernaut that would eventually become the league's measuring stick. His leadership of the rejuvenated Raiders included employing a "strike from anywhere" game plan, enabling halfback Clem Daniels to erupt into the AFL's best runner. Daniels gained a league-leading and record-setting 1,099 yards even though he was sidelined for nearly four games. For his effort, Daniels received the 1963 Player of the Year award. The rookie head coach even welcomed disgruntled and difficult split end Art Powell from the Titans. Building a band of renegades, his prowess for handling players whom other teams viewed to be troublemakers brought Davis several more star performers over the rest of the decade and only enhanced what would become the Raider mystique. Powell finished second in the league in receptions, with 73, and first in the AFL in yards gained, with 1,304, and touchdowns caught, with 16.

Back from a year of recuperation, quarterback Tom Flores experienced a bit of a drop off from his previous campaigns and completed only 45 percent of his passes, in part because of the new "go deep at any time" philosophy. Flores, splitting the quarterbacking duties with '62 starter Cotton Davidson, threw for 20 touchdowns. Davidson threw a league-low 10 interceptions and was under center for both Raider wins over San Diego.

The Raiders started their new era in Houston with a surprising 24-19 win, scoring all 24 points after intermission and equaling their 1962 win production on opening day. Behind 6-0 at halftime, Flores replaced Davidson at quarterback and threw for 217 yards in the third and fourth quarters. His signature throw of the day was an 85-yard touchdown to new teammate Art Powell. The Raiders then shocked the Buffalo Bills at home a week later, 35-17. At 2-0, the Raiders were off to their best start ever, and including their season-ending win over Boston in 1961, had now run off three wins in a row. But four straight losses followed, which coincided with Daniels' injury. The Raiders then won their last eight games to finish a somewhat shocking 10-4. Even more shocking was their ability to challenge for the division crown right down to the wire. After scoring a team record 49 points in their win over the Titans, the Raiders took on and defeated the 5-1 Chargers, 34-33, in a classic AFL scoring deluge. Each team punched, then counter punched the ball over the goal line. Finally, after San Diego's Dick Harris scored on a 22-yard interception return, the Raiders needed to land one last knockout blow. First Cotton Davidson lofted a 39-yard touchdown pass to end Dobie Craig to get the Raiders to within 5 points, 28-33. Then with less than two minutes to play, Davidson fired a bullet to halfback Glenn Shaw for a game-winning touchdown from 9 yards away,

131

★ Al Davis huddles with his Raiders. ★

notching the first win in team history over the perennially strong Chargers, evening their record at 4-4.

Al's boys continued to match the Chargers step for step over the next four weeks until they met in another prize fight on December 8 at Youell Field. For the Raiders, it was the biggest game in team history. Davis had indeed worked a miracle with this band of misfits and a second win over San Diego would draw them to within one game of the leaders with two games still to play. The Raider defense held Charger breakaway threat Paul Lowe to only 5 yards on 6 carries and Keith Lincoln didn't do much better. Flores and Davidson split the play calling, with Flores throwing for 173 yards and Davidson tossing 2 touchdown passes and running 1 in himself. Daniels provided 90 yards running to frustrate the San Diego defense and keep the pressure off the quarterbacks. Oakland came away with a crucial 41-27 thumping of the Western leaders and had the Bay area buzzing at the possibility of postseason play. A 35-21 come-from-behind victory in Denver followed, keeping the Raiders within one game of the lead and setting up another must-win on the season's final weekend.

The Progress of the Seasons – 1963

The crown jewel of the Raiders turnaround came in the season finale, when they defeated the Houston Oilers 52-49. Needing a win and a San Diego loss to force a playoff, the Raiders were tied with the Oilers 35-35 at the half. Tom Flores threw 4 of his 6 touchdowns in the second quarter (he had 11 in the final two games), connecting with tight end Ken Herock (7 yards), halfback Clem Daniels (56 yards) and split end Art Powell (81 and 20 yards). For the game, Flores hit on 17 of 29 passing attempts for 407 yards. Powell was on the receiving end of scoring passes in the third and fourth quarters as well, for 45 and 23 yards, giving him 4 on the day. Place kicker Mike Mercer provided the game-winning, 39-yard field goal to temporarily prolong Oakland's playoff hope while San Diego was playing their final game farther down the coast against the 2-10-1 Broncos. The Chargers coasted 58-20, nosing out the resurgent Raiders by only a game for the division crown. But there was cause for celebration at the end of 1963 and a belief that the Davis way of playing football was indeed a winning one.

Standing out as some of the most valued pieces to Davis' commitment to excellence were the members of his overhauled offensive line, led by four-time all-league center Jim Otto. The tackles were now Proverb Jacobs and Dick Klein, the guards Wayne Hawkins and Sonny Bishop. Fred Williamson was the lone defensive all-league selection and although not chosen for all-league honors, defensive back Tom Morrow led the division with 9 interceptions (second in the AFL), contributing to the league's second-best pass defense. Rookie defensive tackle Dave Costa finished second in rookie-of-the-year voting and was one of only two rookies picked to play in the All-Star game. Spit end Art Powell, halfback Daniels, and center Otto were all-league offensive selections.

No longer the doormats of the AFL, the Raiders had turned the corner, and for Davis, who was honored with the AFL's Coach-of-the-Year Award, and the Pride and Poise Boys, the sky would be the limit in 1964!

Leading passers	Attempts	Completions	Pct	TDs	Yards	Int
Tom Flores	247	113	46%	20	2101	13
Cotton Davidson	194	77	40%	11	1276	11

Leading rushers	Attempts	Yards gained	Average	TDs
Clem Daniels	215	1099	5.1	3
Alan Miller	62	270	4.4	3
Cotton Davidson	26	115	4.4	4
Glenn Shaw	20	46	2.3	1

Leading receivers	Caught	Yards gained	Average	TDs
Art Powell	73	1304	17.9	16
Alan Miller	34	404	11.9	2
Clem Daniels	30	685	22.8	5
Bo Roberson	25	407	16.3	3
Ken Herock	15	269	17.9	2
Dobie Craig	7	205	29.3	2

Leading scorers	TDs	XPM	XPA	FGM	FGA	PTs
Art Powell	16					96
Mike Mercer		47	47	8	19	71

21. In 1963 Al Davis took over the 1-13 Raiders and immediately turned them into a 10-4 contender. In the AFL's first season, for what team was he an assistant coach?

▪ HOUSTON OILERS ▪

AFTER WINNING THREE DIVISION titles and two AFL championships in three years under three different head coaches, Oilers owner Bud Adams felt the team lacked stability in its leadership, so on Valentine's Day 1963, he bestowed upon Oiler coach Pop Ivy a new two-year contract and a vote of confidence by upgrading him to general manager to go along with his coaching duties. Adams hoped that his noble jesture would go a long way toward keeping his Oilers at the top of the Eastern Division. With their veteran players another year older, Houston was faced with defending their division title while attempting to rebuild on the fly as they signed six of their top college draft choices.

The Oilers were still the elite team in the East, employing more talent and experience than any of their Eastern rivals. Blanda was now thirty-six, but still the offensive catalyst. The backfield of Charley Tolar and Billy Cannon had few peers, and Charley Hennigan, Willard Dewveall, Bob McLeod, and young Charlie Frazier made up one of the finest receiving fleets in the AFL. All were back and healthy. The resurrected New York Jets did not figure to be a factor in the race this season but Buffalo, with Jack Kemp and Cookie Gilchrist, and Boston, with their superior defensive front seven and exceptional quarterback Babe Parilli, were expected to narrow the gap and give the Oilers a run for their money.

Sitting on a 5-3 record in late October the Oilers were back in their familiar first-place position, a half game in front of Boston and one and a half ahead of New York. Only in 1960, when they were 6-2 at the same point in the season, did they post a better record one game past midpoint. It looked like business as usual in Houston, although they were relying more and more on Blanda's throwing and less and less on what had been one of the league's better running attacks. This year the Oilers' usually multi-dimensional ground attack was taking a back seat to all but one other team in the league. Billy Cannon was still feuding with Ivy and was also nursing a sore back that reduced his production to only 13 carries and 5 receptions for the year. His replacement was reserve Bill Tobin, who gained 270 yards on 75 attempts, good for a 3.6 average. Without Cannon to balance the attack as the breakaway threat, defenses keyed on Tolar often enough to have his yardage plummet from 1012 to 659. Former starter Dave Smith was still having leg problems and managed only 50 carries, though his 4.0 yards-per-carry led the team.

As the season progressed into December the Oilers were setting the Eastern Division pace with a 6-5 record, maintaining a narrow half-game lead over Boston with New York and Buffalo lurking in the wings. With three games remaining, all four Eastern teams, as well as the top two in the West, were in a position to win their division titles. And Houston had to play three of the most powerful of the lot in their last three games. Boston, San Diego, and Oakland were also in must-win situations. With the season hanging in the balance, Houston prepared to hold off their challengers in search of their fourth straight championship game when the bottom of the oil well went dry. The Patriots surged to a dominating 46-28 win on December 8, dropping Houston a half game back. A week later the Chargers held Houston to 26 yards rushing, routing them 20-14 and ending the quest for another crown. At 6-7 Houston's season was as good as over, placing them behind both Boston and Buffalo, who were tied with 7-6-1 records. Another loss in their final game—52-49 to Oakland—gave the Oilers their first losing season. The disappointing season sparked a three-year rebuilding process, but Bud Adams promised they'd be back!

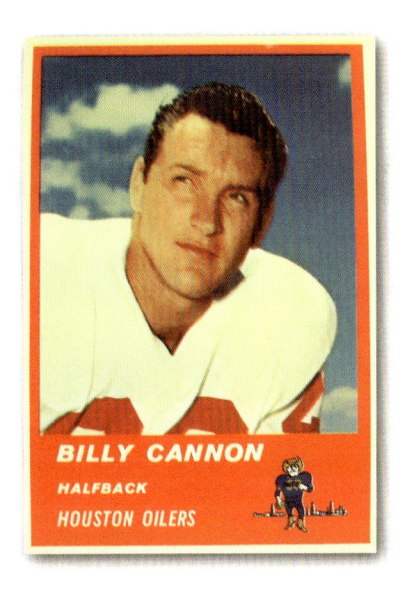

Despite the losing season, the Oilers found themselves on top of the league in passing. The combination of Blanda and Lee threw more passes (501) and more completions (261), for more yards (3210), and more interceptions (33) than all the rest. Blanda alone had 3,003 yards to go with his 52 percent completion rate. Charlie Hennigan finished seventh in receptions among AFL receivers with 61 catches, gaining 1,051 yards with 10 touchdowns. Willard Dewveall was next on the team with 58 catches followed by Tolar (41) and McLeod (33). But Houston's scoring had dropped to seventh (302 points) in the eight-team league, with the defense finishing sixth, allowing 372 points even though the secondary intercepted a league-high 36 passes. Safety Freddie Glick led the league with 12 interceptions, and only Glick and guard Bob Talamini made the all-league first team. For Houston, 1963 was a season of transition. They were now the league's sole occupants of Texas and were faced with starting a process of change that came sooner than they had expected. The AFL's first dynasty had suddenly come to an end, but Houston's unforgettable three-year reign as division and league champions was forever etched in the already rich and growing history of the AFL.

Leading passers	Attempts	Completions	Pct	TDs	Yards	Int
George Blanda	423	224	53%	24	3003	25
Jacky Lee	75	37	49%	2	475	8

Leading rushers	Attempts	Yards gained	Average	TDs
Charlie Tolar	194	659	3.4	3
Bill Tobin	75	270	3.6	4
Dave Smith	50	202	4.0	3
Billy Cannon	13	45	3.5	0

Leading receivers	Caught	Yards gained	Average	TDs
Charley Hennigan	61	1051	17.2	10
Willard Dewveall	58	752	13.0	7
Charlie Tolar	41	275	6.7	0
Bob McLeod	33	530	16.1	5
Dave Smith	24	270	11.3	2
Charlie Frazier	16	279	17.4	1

Leading scorers	TDs	XPM	XPA	FGM	FGA	PTs
George Blanda		39	39	9	22	64
Charley Hennigan	10					60

The Progress of the Seasons – 1963

▪ DENVER BRONCOS ▪

HEAD COACH JACK FAULKNER HAD TO wonder which team he would field after Denver's Jekyll-and-Hyde season in 1962. Leading the West with a 7-2 record, only to lose their last five games must have given Faulkner many sleepless spring and summer nights. For 1963, he had justifiable concerns. No less than fourteen rookies suited up for Denver's opening game, hosting the defending AFL Champions, who were now located in Kansas City. Included among the first-year players were fullback Billy Joe, kick return specialist Charlie Mitchell, and halfback Hewritt Dixon, along with quarterbacks Mickey Slaughter and Don Breaux and defensive backs Willie Brown and Tom Janik. The Broncos were also returning several veterans who had been around since their historic first victory. The AFL's most dangerous passing combination of Frank Tripucka and Lionel Taylor, which averaged more than 70 completions per year, also returned for a fourth season. To take away some of the defensive focus from Taylor, Faulkner traded for Houston's Bill Groman, an experienced split end with 143 receptions in the previous three years. Unfortunately, Groman was injured for much of the year and caught only 27 passes.

Tripucka fared no better. The veteran had thrown for more than 1,250 passes in three Denver campaigns, but he had been playing professional football since 1949 and appeared to be near the end. In Denver's first two games, both losses, he managed to complete only 7 of his 15 attempts for a paltry 33 yards with 5 interceptions. In both games he was relieved by rookie Mickey Slaughter. Following their second loss, a 20-14 defeat at Houston, Tripucka called it a career. His unexpected retirement suddenly forced Faulkner to scramble for a replacement at his most crucial position. With only rookies Slaughter and Don Breaux in reserve, he was forced to send out a distress signal for help. His S.O.S. was answered four days before their next game by former Minnesota Viking backup John McCormick, who was pressed into action against Boston with less than a week of practice. Knowing few names and even fewer plays, Johnny Mack miraculously led Denver to their first win of the season, 14-10. Behind 10-0 in the third quarter, he fired 2 touchdowns, including a 72-yard bomb to Taylor. With a full week to learn Denver's system, McCormick showed the Chargers some lightning of his own by leading his new team to a 50-34 upset victory, with 24 of those points coming in the final period before 18,428 at Bears Stadium. It was McCormick's and Denver's last grand moment of 1963.

The Broncos now stood at 2-2 and looked to get back into the Western Division race that was led by San Diego at 3-1, with 2-1-1 Kansas City close behind. A second match-up with Houston followed at home, and McCormick was primed for his third win in a row. But the Oilers linebackers and safeties blitzed at every opportunity, harassing the quarterback throughout the first half and finally stormed him under for a safety in the second quarter, injuring his knee and ending his season. Once again Faulkner put out an S.O.S. for a quarterback. He went to rookie Mickey Slaughter, whose 2 touchdown passes to flanker Bob Scarpitto were thrilling, but too little and too late. The Broncos lost 33-24, dropping two games behind the Chargers.

From that point, Faulkner and the Broncos failed to win any of their last ten games, sinking into the division basement with a 2-11-1 record. It was a season of almosts for the youngest team in the AFL, with five of their eleven losses coming by less than a touchdown. Slaughter and Don Breaux split the play-calling duties almost weekly, with both showing signs of talent and potential. Slaughter saw the bulk of the action, throwing 223 passes, completing 112 for 12 touchdowns and 14 interceptions. Breaux, too, hit on a shade more than 50 percent of his 138 attempts and found the end zone 7 times and opposing defenders 6 times. McCormick, the number-one man on the depth chart after coming over from the Vikings, managed only 72 throws prior to his season-ending injury. Even with four different quarterbacks firing passes to him, Lionel Taylor won his fourth straight pass receiving title, hauling in 78 balls, only 1 more than the year before with Tripucka and George Shaw. Once the most feared passing attack in the league, the Broncos air force now inhabited the bottom spot in the AFL. The running game was close behind. Fullback Don Stone was still the primary threat out of the backfield and showed his worth by running for 104 yards on 17 carries in their victory over the Chargers. But the new leading man in Denver was the young bull from Villanova. Rookie Billy Joe was a younger, faster version of Cookie Gilchrist, and in the years to come would be linked with him more than once. Joe was a bulldozer with enough speed to turn the corner, something that Denver fans had not witnessed in the team's earlier three years. And with Joe's power-packed running style he immediately became a fan favorite. By the end of the season he had gained 648 yards, more than any other runner in Denver to date, on 154 carries. For his efforts he walked off with the AFL's Rookie of the Year award. Stone was second on the team in yards gained with 382 for a 3.9 average, followed by oft-injured rookie Hewritt Dixon with 105 yards and Gene Mingo with 90. The Denver ground game fared better than only two others in the league. With the offense's inability to move the ball consistently, punter Jim Fraser, who never punted a ball in college, was fittingly the most active fourth down specialist among his peers. Seventy-eight times he ran onto the field to kick his mates out of trouble, punting for a league-best 46.1 yard average.

Having the worst passing game and the third-worst running game, Broncos fans had little reason to expect a surge on the scoreboard anytime soon. In fact their 301 points were more than only one other team. Their 473 points allowed was 74 more than the second-worst defense gave up. The defense

The Progress of the Seasons – 1963

obviously needed repair, especially in the porous secondary that picked off only 11 passes. Of the 5,081 yards allowed by the defense, 3,394 were from pass completions. Still there were some bright spots in the otherwise forgettable season for Denver. Austin Gonsoulin intercepted a team-leading 6 passes and was again named to the all league team at safety. Slaughter, Breaux, and McCormick all showed they were capable (if not spectacular) quarterbacks throwing touchdown passes in thirteen of their fourteen games.

Gene Mingo converted all 35 of his points after touchdowns. Rookie halfback Charlie Mitchell finished third in punt return average and fourth on kickoff returns. And then there was Billy Joe, already one of the best runners in the AFL.

After the success in 1962, hopes had soared over the Rockies in 1963, but after another bad season Faulkner realized the Broncos still had a long way to go before they could challenge the other heavily talented Western Division teams.

Leading passers	Attempts	Completions	Pct	TDs	Yards	Int
Mickey Slaughter	223	112	50%	12	1689	14
Don Breaux	138	70	50%	7	935	6
John McCormick	72	28	39%	4	417	3
Frank Tripucka	15	7	47%	0	31	5

Leading rushers	Attempts	Yards gained	Average	TDs
Billy Joe	154	649	4.2	4
Donnie Stone	96	382	4.0	3
Mickey Slaughter	32	124	3.9	1
Hewritt Dixon	23	105	4.6	2
Gene Mingo	24	90	3.8	0
Charlie Mitchell	23	45	2.0	0

Leading receivers	Caught	Yards gained	Average	TDs
Lionel Taylor	78	1104	14.2	10
Gene Prebola	30	471	15.7	2
Bill Groman	27	437	16.2	3
Donnie Stone	22	186	8.5	1
Bob Scarpitto	21	463	22.0	5
Billy Joe	15	90	6.0	1

Leading scorers	TDs	XPM	XPA	FGM	FGA	PTs
Gene Mingo		35	35	16	29	83
Lionel Taylor	10					60

■ KANSAS CITY CHIEFS ■

KANSAS CITY MAYOR H. ROE BARTLE, a.k.a. the Chief, is forever imbedded in the history of the Chiefs. The man for whom the transplanted Dallas Texans were in part named was the main recruiter of the franchise, selling the Midwest city to owner Lamar Hunt and convincing him that KC was ready to welcome the AFL. With an average attendance of 22,118 in 1962, Hunt saw the handwriting on the Cotton Bowl wall and knew his days in Dallas were numbered. After considering both New Orleans and Atlanta, Hunt conditionally committed to Bartle and Kansas City in February if they could sell 25,000 season tickets and agreed to expand Municipal Stadium. Although the ticket sales came up several thousand short of the goal, Hunt was impressed with the city's effort and in May made the move official. The Dallas Texans, defending AFL Champions, would play their 1963 season in Kansas City. To show his gratitude to Mayor Bartle for his tireless pursuit of the Texans to relocate, Hunt changed the name to Chiefs, which also acknowledged the Native American heritage of the region.

But as they prepared for the season, there was trouble on the new horizon. Nearly a third of the Chiefs' roster was made up of native Texans who were not happy about moving out of the Lone Star State. All-star defensive end Jerry Mays decided he would not play anywhere but Texas and retired but later joined the team in training camp. The fact that the team was moving without any of the players knowing about the decision created resentment that lasted through the season.

The new Chiefs uniform was the same as the one worn in Dallas, with the exception of a new insignia on the helmet, which was a white arrowhead with a red interlocking KC centered inside. For a brief and perhaps nostalgic moment, Hunt even considered keeping the name Texans in their new home, but thankfully his advisors talked him out of that misguided thought.

With another promising group of rookies, coach Hank Stram beamed at the possibility of repeating as AFL champs. That feeling changed in Wichita, Kansas, during the last exhibition game of the summer, when rookie flanker Stone Johnson from Grambling was carried from the field after jamming his helmet into an opponent's midsection on an attempted block on a kickoff return. Johnson had endeared himself to the squad not only through his talent but also through his demeanor and approach to the game. Originally thought to be a compound fracture of a vertebrae, the injury proved fatal. Johnson died a few days later. The sudden death of their teammate devastated many of the Chiefs, particularly Abner Haynes, whom it seemed to distract all year.

The Progress of the Seasons – 1963

★ *Abner Haynes breaks free of Charger Earl Faison.* ★

Their title defense began in the University of Denver's stadium on a rainy Saturday night on September 7. Len Dawson threw 4 touchdown passes in the 59-7 victory, and the champions never looked better or more dominant. The 59 points became an AFL record. Employing a new and innovative "I" formation and trick passes by left-handed fullback Curtis McClinton and by Haynes, Stram's boys stood poised to demolish the AFL en route to a second title. *Sports Illustrated* featured the Chiefs in its September 16 issue with a four-page article titled "Too Many Chiefs Made Too Many Touchdowns," questioning whether the Chiefs were too good for the young league. Little did they know that when the Chiefs beat Denver on December 8, it would be only their third victory of the season.

After their first four games, the Chiefs held steady at 2-1-1. But all they had to show in the win column after their initial victory in Denver was a 28-7 triumph over Houston on October 5. Even winning their last three games by scores of 52-21, 35-3, and 48-0, could not make their 5-7-2 record feel respectable. They had not only slipped below ny Robinson was better than most. The Chiefs defense came within one touchdown of leading the league in fewest points allowed. But it was a season of discontent for many of the other Chiefs, especially on offense, where they were outscored by half the league. The Chiefs even fell in attendance, averaging only 21,509 per game, a figure that was less than at the Cotton Bowl in 1962.

Haynes appeared to sleepwalk through most of the year's fourteen games, gaining a disappointing 352 yards on 99 carries to finish out of the top ten in rushing for the first time, while his touchdown production dropped from 19 to 6. He was so despondent that he even saw time on the bench, giving way to Jack Spikes. Curtis McClinton followed his rookie-of-the-year season as the Chiefs best ball carrier, gaining 598 yards and ranking eighth in the AFL. Steady Lenny Dawson led the league with 26 touchdown passes, and only four receivers in the league caught more passes than Chris Burford's 68. Frank Jackson enjoyed his first year at flanker with 50 receptions, while Fred Arbanas was again the league's best tight end with 34 catches and 6 touchdowns. Fred was joined on the all-league squad by tackle Jim Tyrer on offense and linebacker E.J. Holub and cornerback Dave Grayson on defense.

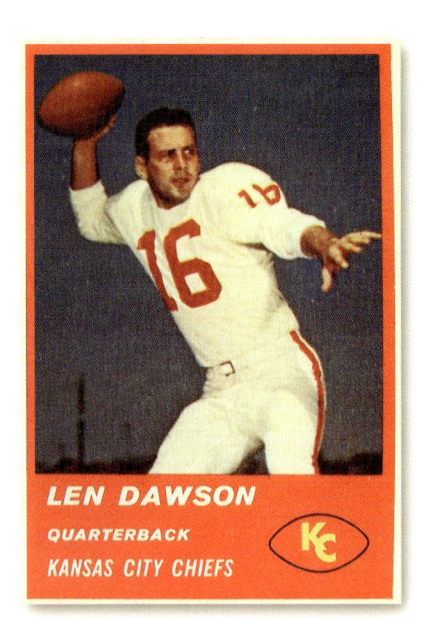

.500, they had done it with the same roster that had been successful the year before. In their defense it can be argued that the team did not get worse as much as the competition got better. San Diego and Oakland won a combined 16 more games than in 1962. San Diego, devastated by injuries the year before, was once again healthy, powerful, and at the top of the division, just as they had been in their first two years. And under the direction of a strong organizer and leader, the Raiders had turned their program around.

For all of Stram's disappointment in the season, he took pride in his daunting defense. His front line of Mel Branch, Buck Buchannan, Paul Rochester, and Jerry Mays was second to none, as was his linebacking trio of E.J. Holub, Sherrill Headrick, and rookie Bobby Bell, who spent time at defensive end as well as behind the front four. Even the secondary of Dave Grayson, Duane Wood, Bobby Hunt, and John-

With the franchise's relocation, the tragic death of Johnson, and the disappointment of their season behind them, Kansas City was ready to get back to the business of hunting, instead of being hunted. And with their wealth of talent, they felt they could return to the top of the AFL.

The Progress of the Seasons – 1963

Leading passers	Attempts	Completions	Pct	TDs	Yards	Int
Len Dawson	352	190	54%	26	2389	19
Eddie Wilson	82	39	48%	3	537	2

Leading rushers	Attempts	Yards gained	Average	TDs
Curtis McClinton	142	568	4.0	3
Abner Haynes	99	352	3.6	4
Len Dawson	37	272	7.4	2
Jack Spikes	84	257	3.1	2
Bert Coan	17	100	5.9	0

Leading receivers	Caught	Yards gained	Average	TDs
Chris Burford	68	824	12.1	9
Frank Jackson	50	785	15.7	8
Fred Arbanas	34	373	11.0	6
Abner Haynes	33	470	14.2	2
Curtis McClinton	27	301	11.1	3

Leading scorers	TDs	XPM	XPA	FGM	FGA	PTs
Tommy Brooker		20	20	6	14	38
Chris Burford	9	1				56
Frank Jackson	9					54
Jack Spikes	3	23	24	2	13	47

▪ NEW YORK JETS ▪

IT WAS FITTINGLY ON THE IDES OF March that the sale of the Titans to the five-man syndicate known as the Gotham Football Club for one million dollars was approved, with Gotham organizer David "Sonny" Werblin taking over the daily operation of New York's AFL franchise. Seeking to purge all memory of the earlier organization, Werblin renamed the team the Jets and changed the team colors to kelly green and white. Other than the new uniforms, the change was barely noticeable on the field, but it was very apparent in the professionalism with which the team did business. Under Werblin's watchful eye the season-ticket sales increased almost instantly, from five hundred to over four thousand, and over ten thousand *real live bodies* showed up for the first home game of 1963. At the end of the previous season, less than a thousand diehards witnessed the final game in Titans history. For the first time, the AFL had a truly professional

143

football franchise in New York.

The Jets wore green jerseys at home, perhaps because Werbin was born on St. Patrick's Day, with white sleeves and a single white shoulder and elbow stripe. Their helmets were white with a green stripe down the center and a green jet silhouetted on each side. On the fuselage, the name JETS was printed in white. Werblin also brought in a proven winner as his head coach. Wilber "Weeb" Ewbank, winner of two NFL championships in Baltimore, had become available, and Werblin wasted no time in luring him to the Gotham city. After seasons of ownership forgetting about or showing no interest in signing draft choices, one of Ewbank's initial missions was to organize a youth movement to complement his few productive veterans. Among them were all-leaguers Larry Grantham and Bill Mathis, along with flanker Don Maynard. Disgruntled split end Art Powell, one of the best receivers in the AFL, left for Oakland, opening the door for veteran Bake Turner. Turner quickly became a key target in the Jets offense, catching 71 passes, only 2 less than the departed Powell. He finished with the third highest total in the league and was also one of only five receivers to gain over 1,000 yards.

Quarterbacking was again a problem for New York. Injured Lee Grosscup was unable to play a single down, and Johnny Green, who replaced Grosscup in '62, threw only 6 passes in '63. To fill the void Ewbank signed Dick Wood, a vagabond with time logged with the Broncos and Chargers. Wood had never been the starter even in college. The book on Wood was, "strong arm with long-range accuracy but an inconsistent short game and inability to avoid the blitz." But Wood provided serviceable performance for the Jets, completing 18 passes for touchdowns with 45 percent of his attempts finding friendly receivers. He ranked sixth among the eight league starters. Bill Mathis, who supplied an outstanding sophomore season, was again banged up and carried the ball only 107 times for 268 yards and 1 touchdown. Sub-par also was Dick Christy, logging only 26 carries. Twenty-five-year-old Mark Smolinski filled the void. His 561 yards on 150 attempts led the team. Having only Smolinski as a real threat, the Jets running game floundered; they were the only AFL team to gain less than 1,000 yards on the ground. Offensively they scored fewer points (249) than all the rest. On defense their 399 points allowed was second-highest in the league. Place kicker Dick Guesman, who doubled as a tackle, made only 9 of his 24 field goal attempts for a league-worst 31 percent, although he did make all of his 30 conversion attempts.

The Progress of the Seasons – 1963

For the first month of the season, Ewbank had the Jets looking like the team to beat in the East, shooting out to a 3-1 start. But the ensuing five weeks failed to bring home a victory before they defeated Denver and shut out Kansas City for their fourth and fifth wins against five losses and a tie. In defeating the Chiefs 17-0, they earned their first shutout in the team's history and also saddled the Chiefs with their first scoreless game in fifty-four outings. Strangely enough, with three games left in the season the Jets were still in the divisional race, only a half game behind the Oilers, who were 6-5. With two games against last-place Buffalo and a season-ender against the struggling Chiefs, the team and their fans had their jet-propelled hopes soaring in December.

When the Patriots knocked off Houston on December 8, the Jets had their chance to move up, but a 45-14 pasting by the Bills dropped them to the bottom of the East with a 5-6-1 record. They faced Buffalo again the next week in the Polo Grounds and led 10-9 in the fourth quarter, only to give up a late touchdown and a safety to lose 19-10. The loss knocked them out of contention and lifted the Bills into a first-place tie with Boston. In the final game of the year, they suffered a humiliating 48-0 shutout at the hands of the Kansas City Chiefs, the team that failed to score a single point on them three weeks earlier. In their last three games, the Jets were outscored 112 to 24! For the first time in their four-year history the team failed to place a single player on the all-league first team.

While the gains made by the Jets in 1963 could not be immediately measured in the standings (5-8-1) or in the statistics, the new ownership had righted the sinking ship and patched the holes in the hull to get them sailing again. The next step in the master plan was to move into their brand new home at Shea Stadium, where the crowds would increase by thirty and forty thousand before signing their marquee quarterback and eventually winning their first AFL championship. Ewbank optimistically looked at a five-year plan, and Werblin provided the support, patience, and willingness to bankroll it. The two visionaries had more than just a pipe dream; they had a blueprint for a team that was destined to change the landscape of professional football.

Leading passers	Attempts	Completions	Pct	TDs	Yards	Int
Dick Wood	351	160	46%	18	2202	18
Galen Hall	118	45	38%	3	611	9

Leading rushers	Attempts	Yards gained	Average	TDs
Mark Smolinski	150	561	3.7	4
Bill Mathis	107	268	2.5	1
Dick Christy	26	88	3.4	1
Galen Hall	9	24	2.7	1

Leading receivers	Caught	Yards gained	Average	TDs
Bake Turner	71	1007	14.2	6
Don Maynard	38	780	20.5	9
Mark Smolinski	34	278	8.2	1
Dee Mackey	23	263	11.4	3
Bill Mathis	18	177	9.8	1

Leading scorers	TDs	XPM	XPA	FGM	FGA	PTs
Dick Guesman		30	30	9	24	57
Don Maynard	9					54

---

22. Lionel Taylor was easily the most dominant receiver in the American Football League for the first half of the decade. He led the league in receptions in the first four seasons, until relinquishing his crown to Charley Hennigan in 1964. But he won it back in 1965. Lance Alworth later won three pass-catching titles and was the only other player to win two in a row. Who was the only other AFL player to lead the league in pass receptions?

■ BUFFALO BILLS ■

THE COURSE OF THINGS TO COME for the new season was previewed in the last exhibition game against Denver in Winston-Salem, North Carolina. As Cookie Gilchrist rumbled for a 29-yard run he was tackled and not only tore a rib cartilage but also sprained an ankle. Other nagging injuries would prevent him from reaching full speed all season long, crippling the team's chances to dominate the division. With Cookie on the mend and running mate Wray Carlton limited to just 29 carries for the year, the Bills were forced to look to their rookies for an outside threat. All-time AFL safety-to-be George Saimes, split end Glenn Bass, versatile Ed Rutkowski, and Penn State standout Roger Kochman lent helping hands in an effort to balance the running game. Even Jack Kemp was called upon to run more than usual. For the first time in the Bills history they were starting the season with a bonified championship-caliber quarterback. In the three previous years only a trio of quarterbacks in the league could lay claim to playing in an AFL championship game. Kemp was one of them. And for the first time the Bills had a star-quality backup in Notre Dame rookie Daryle Lamonica. Throwing to Elbert Dubenion, newly acquired Bill Miller, Glenn Bass, and Ernie Warlick, the two quarterbacks elevated the passing attack to second in the league. And even with the ailing Gilchrist and his host of partners, the Bills ranked second in rushing. After three years of finishing in the bottom two in both departments, the Bills offense was now in the upper echelon of the AFL.

Gaining momentum from three straight exhibition victories, the Bills rolled into their season with high expectations. But for the fourth time in as many years, they stumbled out of the starting gate, losing not only their

The Progress of the Seasons – 1963

★ Buffalo quarterback Jack Kemp throws against the San Diego Chargers. ★

fourth straight opening-day game but also coming up winless in their first four outings. San Diego, Oakland, and Houston all victimized the Bills, with only a tie against Kansas City keeping them from an 0-4 record. As the season progressed, the Bills relied on Kemp throwing to Bill Miller (fourth in the league with 69 catches), Cookie stampeding up the middle, and rookie Roger Kochman slashing to the outside. Cookie rumbled for a league record 243 yards on the ground against the Jets on December 10 and scored 5 touchdowns in the process. Despite his ailments throughout the season, Cookie finished third in rushing with 979 yards for a 4.2 average and league-high 12 touchdowns.

Mired in fourth place in the East at 0-3-1, the Bills finally got untracked by tossing a 12-0 shutout at the Raiders in War Memorial Stadium. A Kemp-to-Miller scoring pass was the game's only touchdown. A week later in Kansas City, Kochman got things rolling with another breakaway run, this time for 48 yards. Kemp followed with a bootleg. After an interference call put the ball on the KC 1-yard line, Gilchrist bulled through for a score. Kemp also went deep to Kochman for a 63-yard score and to Duby for a 90-yard slant that also went all the way. Final score—Bills 35, KC 26! But they lost more than just another game in Houston the next weekend. Kochman got hit in the backfield and was taken off the field on a stretcher. He would never play another down. He had already gained 232 yards on 47 carries for a 4.9 average. What looked like a brilliant career in the making was suddenly over. The Bills found themselves behind 21-0 when Kemp hit Miller for 30 yards, followed it up with 22 more to Warlick, then rolled out to find Miller in the end zone for the final 4 yards and pay dirt. They made it close with a 55-yard TD toss to Warlick but lost for the fourth time, 28-14. At 2-4-1 the season was quickly slipping away and taking their playoff hopes with it.

It took a three-game win streak to restore their hopes, starting with a home win against Boston. Leading the Pats 14-7, Jack Kemp sneaked in for a touchdown to give the Bills a 21-7 lead in what was in the minds of Buffalo, a must-win game. But later in the period when Babe Parilli connected with split end Art Graham for a 77-yard score, the teams were deadlocked at 21. As his favorite receiver, Bill Miller, nursed an injury on the sidelines, Kemp found Charlie Ferguson for a 72-yard touchdown, sending the Bills home with a 28-21 victory. The next week in Denver, backup quarterback Daryle Lamonica, filling in for Kemp, fired 4 touchdown passes, and Gilchrst ran for 126 yards. But with the Bills leading 30-28 with two minutes left in the game, the usually reliable Gilchrist fumbled deep in Bills territory, and Denver had a chance to win it with a 28-yard field goal until, while trying to line up the ball for a straight line to the cross bar, Denver's Donnie Stone returned the favor with a fumble of his own, and the Bills walked away winners.

Denver then flew East. Kemp was back behind center and led the Bills to a 27-17 win. The next week, a record War Memorial Stadium crowd of 38,592 watched their Bills drop a close one to the Chargers 23-13. With two games remaining in the season, all four teams in the division remained alive. Boston stood on top with a 6-5-1 record, Houston was a breath behind at 6-6, and the Jets and Bills were looking up at the other two with 5-6-1 records. Home-and-away matches with New York awaited the Bills. Two wins by either, combined with a split by Boston, would force a playoff. Back-to-back wins by Houston could potentially put them in their fourth straight championship game. The Patriots won their next game 46-28 over Houston while Buffalo beat New York 45-14. The Pats were now 7-5-1, Houston 6-7, Buffalo 6-6-1, and New York eliminated at 5-7-1. Buffalo needed to win and hoped that Kansas City could knock off Boston to created a tie at the top of the East. They got their wish, but it took second-half heroics from Jack Kemp, this time relieving starter Lamonica to force a one-game playoff with Boston. A fourth-quarter drive gave the Bills a clutch 19-10 victory and 7-6-1 final record, the same as the Patriots.

The snow-covered field at War Memorial Stadium on December 28 was friendlier to the Patriots than to the Bills, as Buffalo fumbled the opening kickoff and Boston took advantage right away, going up 3-0. They increased their lead to 16-0 by halftime, a lead they would never relinquished as they rolled by Buffalo 26-8 to clinch their first division title in front of 33,044 frigid fans. Buffalo's most exciting season had come to a disappointing end, but the young Bills had their first taste of postseason play, a taste they would savor for the next three seasons.

The Progress of the Seasons – 1963

Leading passers	Attempts	Completions	Pct	TDs	Yards	Int
Jack Kemp	384	193	50%	13	2914	20
Daryle Lamonica	71	33	46%	3	437	4

Leading rushers	Attempts	Yards gained	Average	TDs
Cookie Gilchrist	232	979	4.2	12
Roger Kochman	47	232	4.9	1
Jack Kemp	52	226	4.3	0
Ed Rutkowski	48	144	3.0	0

Leading receivers	Caught	Yards gained	Average	TDs
Bill Miller	69	860	12.5	3
Elb Dubenion	55	974	17.7	4
Ernie Warlick	24	479	20.0	1
Cookie Gilchrist	24	211	8.8	2

Leading scorers	TDs	XPM	XPA	FGM	FGA	PTs
Cookie Gilchrist	14					84
Mack Yoho		32	35	10	24	62

■ BOSTON PATRIOTS ■

TWO 9-4-1 SECOND-PLACE FINISHES IN a row made Patriot fans wonder what it would take to dethrone the aging Houston Oilers in the East. Head coach Mike Holovak, 16-5-2 since taking over the Pats, looked no further for his answer than veteran quarterback Babe Parilli. Injured in the season's tenth game in 1962, Babe had Boston on the cusp of a title until the Oilers knocked him out for the season while taking over sole possession of first place. This time around the Babe would be there at the end. And in 1963, for the first time in their short history, the end extended beyond the regular season.

The Pats would have to play the new season without the services of leading rusher Ron Burton, who was out for the season with a back injury suffered in an exhibition game. Instead they relied on the combined running talents of Larry Garron and Jim Crawford. With the new season came a permanent home. After playing their first home game in BC Stadium the Pats moved to Fenway Park, their fourth venue in as many years, for the remainder of the season. As they split their first six games, they trailed Houston by a half game and took their 4-3 record into Buffalo to play the 2-4-1 Bills. On the ropes and losing 21-14 in the fourth quarter, Parilli hit rookie split end Art Graham with a 77-yard touchdown pass, tying the game at

21-21. But with only a half minute to play, the Bills found a hole in the Boston secondary for a 73-yard, game-winning touchdown pass, dropping the Pats to 4-4.

It was now déjà vu time, for just as in 1962 they had to play Houston, who stood at 5-3, needing a win to keep their title hopes alive. With memories of the Parilli injury and the demoralizing loss of a year ago as incentive, the Patriot defense took control, led by cornerback Bob Suci's 2 interceptions, 1 for a 98-yard Boston touchdown. As the Oilers continued to pound on the Boston door, both linebacker Tom Addison and safety Ross O'Hanley stopped crucial drives with interceptions in the end zone. Defensive tackle Jim Hunt also showed the Oilers some big-time speed when he out raced backs Billy Cannon and Charlie Tolar for 79 yards with still another interception return for a touchdown on a rain-soaked Fenway turf. The Patriots destroyed the Eastern leaders 45-3 and deadlocked the top of the division. Both teams now posted 5-4 records.

After a loss to the Chargers and a 24-24 tie with Kansas City, the Patriots hosted their second meeting of the year with Buffalo. Both teams sported 5-5-1 records as the Bills took a 7-0 lead into the locker room at halftime. Boston then came to life and went on to win 17-7 and take the division lead. With only two games remaining, Boston's title hopes would have to survive a visit to Jeppesen Stadium where the Oilers were camped at 6-5. A Boston win could seal the division, while a loss would find them in second place, a position they knew all too well. Fate would turn the Patriots in a different direction this day as they converted 2 Oiler fumbles into touchdowns en route to a colossal 46-28 victory, giving them sole possession of first place and a 7-5-1 record. In their two games against the three-time division champions the Patriots scored a total of 93 points. They now controlled their fate with only one game on the schedule. A win or a tie with Kansas City in the season's final game would clinch their first division crown.

But it wouldn't be easy. After getting off to an initial 3-0 lead, they surrendered 35 unanswered points in a disappointing 35-3 route. Boston's loss, coupled with Houston's loss and a Buffalo win over the Jets, had both the Pats and Bills sharing the top spot with identical 7-6-1 records. Both teams sat idle on the season's last weekend as Houston lost again. Boston and Buffalo now prepared for a one-game playoff that would determine the division's winner. The stage would be Buffalo's War Memorial Stadium on December 28.

The time had finally come for the Patriots to throw, rather than catch, the bridal bouquet. Facing their former head coach, Boston took the snow-covered field on December 28 and rolled over the Bills to the tune of 26-8. Leading 3-0 in the first period, Babe Parilli was able to loft a skate-and-go bomb to halfback Larry Garron that was good for a 59-yard touchdown, putting the Pats up 10-0. Two more Gino Cappelletti field goals in the second quarter gave Boston a 16-0 halftime lead. The Boston defense was spectacular in holding Cookie Gilchrist to a mere 7 yards

The Progress of the Seasons – 1963

on 8 carries. The blitzing defensive efforts of Larry Eisenhauer and company closed down the Bills ground attack and forced them to take to the air in an effort to get back into the game. With a 20-degree wind sweeping over the white field, the Patriot defenders held Jack Kemp and Daryle Lamonica in check, allowing only 19 of their 45 passing attempts to find Buffalo receivers while four of their tosses ended up in the hands of Boston defenders. The Pats were finally over the hump and headed to their first AFL Championship game, which would take place the following Sunday in San Diego's Balboa Stadium.

In their two previous meetings, the Chargers prevailed 17-13 and 7-6. On paper the matchup appeared even, matching San Diego's lightning-quick offense against Boston's strong, blitzing defense. However the victory over the Bills a week earlier would represent the apex for the 1963 Patriots. The Chargers, led by Keith Lincoln, exploited Boston's blitzing schemes with quick pitches and draw plays while moving the ball nearly at will and manhandling them 51-10.

Standout performers in Boston's season of success were Jim Colclough, the Pats leading pass catcher with 42 receptions, eleventh in the league, followed by Cappelletti with 34, tight end Tony Romeo with 31, and Larry Garron with 26. Rookie Art Graham caught 21 passes. Garron was also Boston's leading rusher with 750 yards, good enough to rank him fifth among AFL runners. Parilli, now thirty-four, fell to ninth among passers, throwing 24 interceptions with only 13 touchdowns. Gino Cappelletti won his second consecutive scoring title. Defensive standouts Larry Eisenhauer, Houston Antwine, and Tom Addison represented the Patriots on the all-league team and joined Bob Dee, Nick Buoniconti, and Ron Hall as division All-Stars. Defenders Ross O'Hanley, Ron Hall, Dick Felt, and Bob Suci combined for 30 interceptions and 3 touchdowns. With their first Eastern Division crown etched firmly in the team's history book the Boston Patriots were now a team setting their sights on repeating in 1964.

Leading passers	Attempts	Completions	Pct	TDs	Yards	Int
Babe Parilli	337	153	45%	13	2345	24
Tom Yewcic	70	29	41%	4	444	5

Leading rushers	Attempts	Yards gained	Average	TDs
Larry Garron	179	750	4.2	2
Jim Crawford	71	233	3.3	1
Tom Neumann	44	148	3.4	0
Harry Crump	49	120	2.4	5

Leading receivers	Caught	Yards gained	Average	TDs
Jim Colclough	42	793	18.9	3
Gino Cappelletti	34	493	14.5	2
Tony Romeo	32	418	13.1	3
Larry Garron	26	418	16.1	2
Art Graham	21	559	26.6	5

Leading scorers	TDs	XPM	XPA	FGM	FGA	PTs
Gino Cappelletti	2	35	36	22	28	113
Art Graham	5					30
Harry Crump						

■ SAN DIEGO CHARGERS ■

HAD THERE BEEN A SUPER BOWL IN 1963, the entire landscape of the NFL may look different today. At a time when the AFL was thirsting for recognition and respectability and the NFL was flaunting its supremacy, along came the 1963 Chargers. Arguably one of the best teams in AFL history, the team appeared to have more offensive firepower than anything that existed in the NFL. It also laid claim to a defense with a front four larger than Chicago's Monsters of the Midway and more larcenous than Green Bay's all-pro secondary. Coming off a season remembered more for its injury list than its accomplishment, coach Sid Gillman solicited the services of a strength coach named Alvin Roy to mentor his Chargers new weight-and-isometric exercise program. To get his troops into stronger and better shape than the rest of the league, Sid marched the Chargers to an isolated preseason camp at the Rough Acres Ranch in California, a place so remote that the players had no choice but to get strong and fit while growing together as a team. To this day the camp is a haunting legend for those who were there, with memories of a desert boot camp and pseudo prison compound. But in 1963 for the San Diego Chargers, the end justified the means, as their championship season led many writers and analysts to christen them,

The Progress of the Seasons — 1963

★ *Charger quarterback Tobin Rote under pressure from the Bronco rush.* ★

"professional football's best team in 1963."

The first step on the road to recovery for the Chargers was taken in mid-January when Gillman, Denver coach Jack Faulkner, and commissioner Joe Foss met in a San Diego hotel room to settle a player dilemma that could mean a championship for the Chargers. The player in question was Tobin Rote, the former 1957 championship quarterback for the Detroit Lions. Rote had been playing for the CFL Toronto Argonauts prior to becoming eligible to return to American football. As part of the AFL's agreement, Rote was the territorial property of the closest team to which he played in Canada, the Buffalo Bills. But the Bills now had a different kind of predicament. They didn't need a thirty-five-year-old quarterback on the down side of his career. They had Jack Kemp and were more than willing to trade the negotiating rights to Rote. Rote was a proven leader and legendary passer who had previously led both the NFL and CFL in passing. The Chargers were eager to acquire him. But so too were the Denver Broncos, whose starting quarterback was older than Rote. Foss, Gillman, and Faulkner agreed to the only fair and objective way of settling the matter—a coin flip. As the coin turned up in favor of the Chargers, they once again had a proven and experienced play caller to lead the most sophisticated offensive in pro football and immediately became the favorite to win the West.

153

Protecting Rote would be a strong and cohesive offensive line anchored by two of the best tackles in either league. Perennial all-leaguer Ron Mix and the equally efficient Ernie Wright were the rocks that flanked guards Sam Gruneisen, Sam DeLuca, and Pat Shea, all solid sweep leaders who efficiently sprang runners Keith Lincoln and Paul Lowe. Center Don Rogers took advantage of the vacancy created when Wayne Fraser went down with an injury the year before and was now one of the league's best. At flanker, sophomore Lance Alworth joined offensive mates Mix, Rote, Lincoln, and Faison on the all-league team. He led the Chargers with 61 receptions and the league with a 20-yards-per-catch average. Joining him as pass catchers were Don Norton and 1962 all-league tight end Dave Kocourek. As a unit they caught 17 touchdown passes.

Paul Lowe was the league's second-leading rusher in 1963, gaining 1,010 yards and backfield mate Keith Lincoln added another 826 to finish fourth. Their 5.7 and 6.4 yards per carry were the two best among the AFL runners. Player of the Year Tobin Rote was the league's top passer, giving him the trifecta of having led the NFL, CFL, and AFL, even though this time he threw less than any previous AFL leader. And with 399 points scored and 256 allowed, San Diego was the most efficient team on both sides of the football. The Chargers scoring machine simply could not be stopped. As the Chargers were solidifying their hold at the top of AFL, there was an interesting addition on the front of some of the helmets, a shield-like emblem representing a national award bestowed upon the city of San Diego, identifying it as an "All-American City."

On defense the Chargers still paraded their ferocious but retooled front four. Still in tow were big and powerful Earl Faison and even bigger and more powerful Ernie Ladd, both all-league selections at their position more than once. Joining them was end Bob Petrich and the rotating tackle tandem of George Gross and Henry Schmidt. In the linebacking corps, Chuck Allen was a red dog specialist, Emil Karas provided bone-jarring tackles, and newcomer Frank Buncom supplied the needed speed and agility on pass coverage. Assisting them off the bench were Penn State standout Bob Mitinger and veteran Paul Maquire. With the front seven once again creating pressure and chaos, the secondary returned to its 1961 record-setting brilliance against the pass. Defensive backs Dick Harris, Bud Whitehead, George Blair, and Charlie McNeil along with rookie-of-the-year runner-up Dick Westmoreland solidified the San Diego defense that was among pro football's finest. On the kicking end, Paul Maquire continued to be the fourth-down specialist, although with San Diego's offensive excellence he was called upon less than any other punter. Safety George Blair handled the place kicking and converted on 17 of his 27 field goal attempts. His .629 accuracy percentage was the league's best.

★ *Charger back Paul Lowe takes the handoff from Tobin Rote.* ★

Championship bound from the outset, the Chargers, who finished first in the West for the third time in four years with an 11-3 record, did not enjoy the luxury of running away from the pack in '63 as they did in '61. With Oakland now led by former Gillman assistant Al Davis, the Raiders were the barking dog on the Chargers' heels all year long. Oakland's resurgence may have kept Gillman's troops as sharp as they were for as long as they needed to be. Which was right up to the last game of the year, having to win to ward off their 10-4 neighbors from northern California.

The season kicked off on September 8 as Balboa Stadium played host to the Bills and Jack Kemp's first game against his former teammates. Also returning was halfback Paul Lowe, who missed all of 1962. Serving notice that he was completely healed, Lowe gained 96 yards on 10 carries against the daunting Bills defense, 48 of them on a third-quarter romp around right end for a touchdown. San

Diego won the defensive tug-of-war 14-10. In beating Boston 17-13 the next week, Lowe used his arm, firing a second-quarter, 29-yard touchdown pass to flanker Jerry Robinson, giving the Chargers a lead they did not relinquish. The Chargers next played host to the defending champion Kansas City Chiefs. Against KC, Rote was brilliant in his play calling and execution, completing 10 of his 16 passes for 3 touchdowns. The first went 20 yards to tight end Kocourek in the first quarter and the next to Kocourek again in the second for 35 yards. Keith Lincoln was on the receiving end of the third one after being set up by Lowe's 25-yard run. Stunned by the 21-3 halftime deficit, the Chiefs never recovered and managed only 10 points to San Diego's 24. Paul Lowe was spectacular in gaining 91 yards with Lincoln gaining another 59. The defense showed their mettle as well by closing down the powerful KC running game, holding them to just 27 yards and giving up only 164 total yards.

The Chargers then went on the road for the first time and came home with a 3-1 record as Denver ambushed them in the Rockies 50-34. Bronco kicker Gene Mingo kicked 5 field goals in the winning effort. Next up was the East's first-place New York Jets. San Diego painted an offensive masterpiece, mounting 510 yards total offense. Lowe accounted for 161 on the ground. The Jets drew first blood in the first quarter on a TD pass from ex-Charger Dick Wood to Bake Turner. After Tobin Rote (10-13 passing for the day) failed to lead the Chargers to a score, second-year quarterback John Hadl relieved the veteran and earned himself the Associated Press Player of the Week honor by completing 8 of 12 passes for one touchdown. The Chargers offense came to life when Hadl faked a handoff to Lowe and rolled out to pass but instead scampered 35 yards down the sideline. Aided by Lowe's 17-yard run, Hadl then split the defense with a 9-yard touchdown pass to Kocourek, tying the game at 10. A 40-yard pass-run to Lincoln then set up an 11-yard touchdown pass from halfback Jerry McDougall to a leaping Lance Alworth in the end zone. But 10 third-quarter points by the Jets had them ahead 20-17 in the final quarter. With 9:06 left in the game, Hadl used his slight of hand to fake a pitchout to Lincoln, then hand off to Lowe on a counterplay up the middle for the game-winning score. The Chargers won 24-20.

Their first visit to Kansas City was a tight-fisted match that found the Chargers behind by the score of 7-3 at the half. But with Rote hitting on 16 of 22 passes and Keith Lincoln running for 127 yards on 10 carries (76 of them on a fourth-quarter breakaway touchdown), the southern Californians scored 35 points in the second half to win 38-17. Sophomore flanker Lance Alworth had a stellar day, breaking tackles and outjumping the Chiefs secondary for four quarters. His best play of the afternoon came in the final period on a 72-yard touchdown reception. The young flanker ended the day with 9 catches for 232 yards. The game's final score came on another counterplay off a fake pitch. This time Lowe galloped 21 yards for his second touchdown of the game.

At 5-1, San Diego was still not in the clear, and the race for the Western crown tightened the next week with a 34-33 loss to the Raiders. The Chargers then went east for three games. Stopping first for their last visit to the cold, windy, and rainy Polo Grounds. Behind the masterful performance by Tobin Rote, the Chargers closed down the decrepit palace in superior fashion by piling up 528 yards of offense. Rote picked the Jet secondary to pieces, completing 21 of 29 passes for 369 yards and 3 touchdowns. And once again the fearsome foursome closed down the Jet running game, allowing only 39 yards. The bombing ended 53-7.

A .500 Boston team that appeared ready to hand the Chargers their second loss awaited them next in Fenway Park on November 10. San Diego needed a win to stay ahead of the dogged Raiders. Aided by lady luck in the first period, rookie Dick Westmoreland recovered Larry Garron's fumble to give the Chargers possession at the Patriot 23-yard line. Rote then faded back, gave a quick pump fake, and Lance Alworth was gone on a stop-and-go pattern for a 22 yard touchdown ... but it was called back. On the next play Rote called a number that they had not yet used in '63. He rolled left, then stopped and threw back to the right where a waiting Lance Alworth pulled in the screen pass, used blocks from Sam DeLuca and Dave Kocourek and finished off a 27-yard touchdown pass. Alworth tied an AFL record on the day with 13 catches against the porous Boston pass defense.

Faison, Ladd, and company were outstanding and kept the Pats out of the end zone. The Chargers had their seventh victory in nine starts, winning 7-6. The last game of the road trip was in Buffalo, where 38,592 saw Keith Lincoln run for a 46-yard touchdown and 101 total yards. Gillman's gang won 23-13.

Moving back to Balboa Stadium on December 1, the Chargers jumped out to a 20-0 lead at the half then finished Houston off with a 22-yard touchdown pass to Alworth as Rote threaded the needle, finding his flanker between both Mark Johnston and Jim Norton. The 27-0 win marked the first time in forty-five games that Houston had been shut out. San Diego now had a two-game lead on Oakland, but Davis's boys changed that by beating the Chargers for the second time on the second Sunday in December, 41-27. With both teams winning the following week the Chargers needed to beat Denver at home in their final game to win the West, and Paul Lowe was ready. Scoring on runs of 10 and 66 yards, Lowe totaled 183 yards rushing for the game. Leading 26-17 at the half, the Chargers went on to score 24 third quarter points, and with word from up the coast that Oakland had won their final game 52-49 over Houston, continued to roll up the points and earn their third division title in four years, defeating the Broncos by a whopping 58-20. For the sixth time on the season the San Diego defense held the opposition to less than 100 yards rushing. The Raiders, who turned their 1-13 record of 1962 into an incredible 10-4 mark, finished one game behind the 11-3 Chargers.

For the second time in four years Balboa Stadium played host to the AFL Championship game. The Boston Patriots had defeated the Bills in a tie-breaking playoff a week earlier to earn the right to face the Chargers. Prognosticators made San Diego a slight favorite by virtue of home-field advantage and because by the slimmest of margins, defeated Boston in both of their regular season meetings. Pitting their top-ranked offense against the AFL's best defense, Gillman sought to employ some new ideas he picked up on their last visit to Boston to counter the Patriot's blitzing defense. He put his backs in motion and ran traps, quick pitches, and draw plays to freeze and confuse the defense. The plan worked to perfection. On the opening series fullback Keith Lincoln took a handoff on a draw play and streaked 56 yards to the Boston 5. Two plays later Tobin Rote, hoping to be the only quarterback to win both an NFL and AFL championship, snuck the final 2 yards for the first score on the sun-drenched afternoon. After Chuck Allen and the San Diego defense stopped the Pats, Lincoln again showed why he was the AFL's all-league fullback, speeding 64 yards for the Chargers second touchdown in the game's first five minutes. On his first 2 carries Lincoln already had 110 yards rushing, and he was not nearly finished. A Boston score temporarily raised Boston's hopes, but on San Diego's next possession Keith Lincoln decoyed the defense one way while Paul Lowe took a pitchout from Rote the other and dashed 58 yards for a touchdown.

With the Chargers leading 31-10 at the half, the Balboa Stadium crowd cheered the offensive outburst. The San Diego defense smothered the Boston ground game, holding them under 100 yards and forcing Babe Parilli to take to air. But Earl Faison and Chuck Allen led the charge, and shut out Boston in the second half. Keith Lincoln and the Chargers, on the other hand, were just hitting stride. In the third quarter, Rote lofted a bomb to acrobatic flanker Lance Alworth who outjumped defender Bob Suci to pull down the ball for a 48-yard touchdown. Keith Lincoln piled up yardage, accounting for 206 yards on the ground while catching a game high 7 passes for an additional 123 yards. His last reception, a 25-yarder from John Hadl, ended up in the end zone. San Diego called it a day after Hadl engineered a 66-yard drive for the final score. The Chargers had just torched the AFL's best defense for over 600 yards and won in dominating style, 51-10. It was the Chargers first AFL Championship. Keith Lincoln was a unanimous choice for the game's MVP as he accounted for a record 329 yards running and receiving. In winning their first crown, the new champions each walked away with a winner's share of $2,498.89. An ensuing offer by Gllman to George Halas to play his NFL Champion Chicago Bears and initiate the first AFL/NFL championship game went unanswered.

The Progress of the Seasons – 1963

Leading passers	Attempts	Completions	Pct	TDs	Yards	Int
Tobin Rote	286	170	59%	20	2510	17
John Hadl	64	28	43%	6	502	6

Leading rushers	Attempts	Yards gained	Average	TDs
Paul Lowe	177	1010	5.7	8
Keith Lincoln	128	826	6.5	5
Gerry McDougall	38	199	5.2	1
Bob Jackson	18	64	3.6	1

Leading receivers	Caught	Yards gained	Average	TDs
Lance Alworth	61	1205	19.8	11
Paul Lowe	26	191	7.3	2
Keith Lincoln	24	325	13.5	3
Dave Kocourek	23	359	15.6	5
Don Norton	21	281	13.4	1
Jerry Robinson	18	315	17.5	2
Jacque MacKinnon	11	262	23.8	4

Leading scorers	TDs	XPM	XPA	FGM	FGA	PTs
George Blair		44	48	17	28	95
Lance Alworth	11					66
Paul Lowe	10					60

For the third year in a row Balboa Stadium was the site for the AFL's annual All-Star game on January 19. And for the third straight year the West defeated the East. But this time they had to come from behind to do it. The West, coached by Sid Gillman, put on a second-half uprising after trailing Mike Holovak's East team 24-3 at the start of the third quarter. Charger runners Keith Lincoln and Paul Lowe, scoring on runs of 64 and 5 yards, set the stage for another set of Western Division teammates to pull off their own game-winning heroics, just as Tripucka and Taylor did in last year's win. This time it was Oakland teammates Cotton Davidson, subbing for starter Tobin Rote, and Art Powell who pulled the slight of hand. With forty-three seconds left in the game, Davidson connected with his split end for a diving 25- yard touchdown pass, giving the West 24 unanswered points in the second half to nose out their third straight All-Star game win over the East, 27-24.

1964

AMERICAN FOOTBALL LEAGUE – 1964 FINAL STANDINGS

EASTERN DIVISION

TEAM	GP	W	L	T	PF	PA	PCT.
BUFFALO BILLS	14	12	2	0	400	242	0.857
BOSTON PATRIOTS	14	10	3	1	365	297	0.750
NEW YORK JETS	14	5	8	1	278	315	0.393
HOUSTON OILERS	14	4	10	0	310	355	0.286

WESTERN DIVISION

TEAM	GP	W	L	T	PF	PA	PCT.
SAN DIEGO CHARGERS	14	8	5	1	341	300	0.607
KANSAS CITY CHIEFS	14	7	7	0	366	306	0.500
OAKLAND RAIDERS	14	5	7	2	303	350	0.429
DENVER BRONCOS	14	2	11	1	240	438	0.179

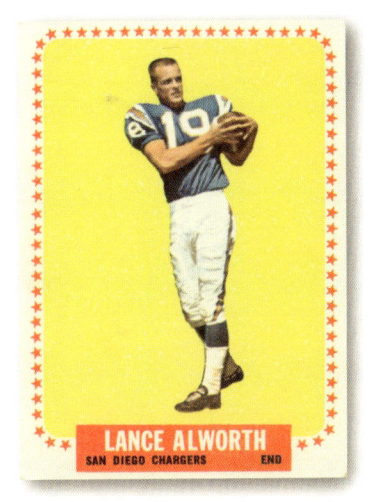

Lance Alworth, "Bambi," was an All-American halfback at Arkansas in 1961. Drafted by the Chargers with a pick they received from Oakland, he made an immediate impact in 1962 before being injured early in the season. He led the AFL in receiving three times, is tied for the most passes caught in one game (13), and when he retired was the all-time leader in most consecutive games catching a pass at 95. From 1963 to 1969 there was no better receiver in football and no more dangerous a deep threat. He was the first AFL player to be voted into the Pro Football Hall of Fame.

■ BOSTON PATRIOTS ■

WITH THE CHANGING OF THE GUARD in the East in 1963, the Patriots found themselves in unfamiliar territory at the beginning of the season. They were now the hunted, instead of the hunters. Although there may have been cause for concern in New England after the Pats dropped all of their exhibition games, they opened the season with four straight victories. Starting out on the West Coast, Boston pinned a 17-14 loss on the resurgent Oakland Raiders followed by a rematch of the '63 championship game in San Diego, this time with a different result, a 33-28 victory. Gino Cappelletti aided the win with 4 field goals. Then in knocking off New York in their home-away-from-home opener at Boston College 26-10, the defense picked off 3 New York passes and Gino kicked 4 more field goals. But Gino's best was yet to come. As Boston was pasting Denver 39-10 in Colorado, Cappelletti was setting an all-time pro football record by knocking 6 fields goals through the uprights in Bears Stadium. Hitting for 6 as well was the defense, as they tied a league record by intercepting 6 Denver passes. The Pats were off to their best start ever, yet it was only good enough to match Buffalo, also undefeated with four wins.

They came back to earth the next week at Fenway Park as Lance Alworth grabbed 7 of John Hadl's passes and the Chargers handled Boston 26-17. Next came Oakland. Things looked grim for the Pats as they trailed 34-14 before things started to click in the second half, leading to 21 unanswered points and a 35-34 lead with eight minutes left. In years past Oakland by now would have sunk into the bay, but these were not the Raiders of old, and a quick strike by quarterback Cotton Davidson to Art Powell put Oakland back on top, 40-35. Knowing the Patriots offense had heated up and not wanting a last-minute touchdown by Boston to be a winning one, Oakland decided to try a 2-point conversion to put them up by 7. It failed. Minutes later Oakland's fear became a reality when Babe Parilli found Larry Garron with a touchdown pass and a 41-40 lead. Now it was Mike Holovak's turn to roll the dice. The Pats' try for 2 was converted and Boston had a 43-40 lead with only forty-eight seconds left, as the Fenway crowd huddled close and held their breath. A valiant effort brought the Raiders to the Boston 31-yard line. With ten seconds to play, Oakland lined up for a 38-yard field goal attempt by Mike Mercer. As time clicked down, Mercer swung his toe into the kick and all eyes turned just in time to see the ball split the uprights and send the Pats and Raiders home with a heart-pounding 43-43 tie.

The next week Babe Parilli showed that being a thirty-four-year-old quarterback was as good as a fine wine that had aged gracefully. The Babe hit on 13 of 18 passes with 2 of them ending up in Jim Colclough's hands in the end zone. The Pats record at midseason stood at a powerful 5-1-1, but they were still chasing the undefeated Buffalo Bills.

For game eight Boston traveled to the new Shea Stadium home of the New York Jets

The Progress of the Seasons – 1964

on Halloween night and quickly learned that New York is not a safe place to play a game of trick-or-treat. A crowd of 41,910 fans saw Boston trail 21-0 at the half, largely on the throwing efforts of Jet quarterback Dick Wood. Wood was in the process of completing 11 passes in a row and 22 of 36 on the night. When the final gun sounded, the Jets showed 35 points to Boston's 14, dropping them to 5-2-1, while Buffalo continued to win. Back home at Fenway, Boston was in a must-win situation and things looked bleak when George Blanda's field goal gave Houston a 24-22 lead with thirty-two seconds left in the game. What the Fenway faithful saw in that last minute gave all of New England hope that this might be the Patriots' season after all. Two Babe Parilli pass completions to Tony Romeo and Gino Cappelletti put the Pats on their own 44 yard line with only eleven ticks left on the clock. On the next play, the Kentucky Babe was unable to find an open receiver and took off toward the end zone, but he knew he couldn't make it all the way so he ran toward the sideline and stepped out of bounds on the Oiler 36, stopping the clock with only one tick left. On marched the field goal unit. With the Babe holding, Gino hit the ball squarely, straight, and true to give Boston a spectacular 25-24 victory.

Cappelletti was having a tremendous season not only as the league's best kicker but also as the Patriots' leading receiver. He was averaging almost 18 yards a catch. Gino was also about to set a new scoring record for a season by rounding up 155 total points. The Patriots season was as heated as it could get with the year's most crucial game against the undefeated Buffalo Bills next. Heading into the showdown rushers Larry Garron and Ron Burton were each averaging a little more than 3 yards a carry, prompting the Boston offense to rely more and more on its miserly defense and the vintage arm of Babe Parilli to make things happen. Against Buffalo, Babe threw for 5 touchdown passes on the day, but deep into the third quarter the injury-riddled Bills held a 28-14 lead. Capitalizing on a Bill turnover when defensive end Larry Eisenhauer recovered Daryle Lamonica's fumble, Babe led the Pats into the end zone not once, not twice, but three more times, all on passes to Cappelletti. Thanks to Boston's 35-28 win, they had moved a step closer to the Bills.

Boston won their next three games while Buffalo lost only once, creating a showdown in the last game at icy Fenway Park between the 11-2 Bills and the 10-2-1 Patriots. For the fourth year in a row Boston's final weekend would determine whether they finished first or second in the East. Fenway was packed with 38,000 fans in the midst of a December New England snowstorm. The Bills started the scoring and went up 7-0, but Parilli answered with a 37-yard touchdown pass to Tony Romeo. Needing a win to overtake Buffalo, the Pats went for a 2-point conversion. Looking left and right for an open receiver, Babe found Cappy all alone in the end zone, but Gino's footing betrayed him on the frozen turf and the pass fell to the ground. Another Buffalo touchdown and field goal put the Patriots behind by 11 points at the half. But they could score no more, and their most successful season of 10-3-1 would fall

Remember the AFL

short of defending their Eastern Division title.

Larry Eisenhauer, Nick Buoniconti, Babe Parilli, and Tom Addison made the all-league team. Babe also led the league with 3,465 yards passing and 31 touchdown passes. Cappelletti set an AFL record on November 20 with a 51-yard field goal, the longest in league history, and was named the league's MVP. Mike Holovak was named the AFL's Coach of the Year. While they posted what would be their best record in their AFL years, once again the Patriots were bridesmaids.

Leading passers	Attempts	Completions	Pct	TDs	Yards	Int
Babe Parilli	473	228	48%	31	3465	27
Larry Garron	2	0	0%	0	0	0
Tom Yewcic	1	1	100%	0	2	0

Leading rushers	Attempts	Yards gained	Average	TDs
Larry Garron	183	585	3.2	2
Ron Burton	102	340	3.3	3
J.D. Garrett	56	259	4.6	2
Babe Parilli	34	168	4.9	2

Leading receivers	Caught	Yards gained	Average	TDs
Gino Cappelletti	49	865	17.7	7
Art Graham	45	720	16.0	6
Larry Garron	40	350	8.8	7
Jim Colclough	32	657	20.5	5
Ron Burton	27	306	11.3	2
Tony Romeo	26	445	17.1	4

Leading scorers	TDs	XPM	XPA	FGM	FGA	PTs
Gino Cappelletti	7	36	36	25	39	155
Larry Garron	9					54

24. On October 4, 1964, Gino Cappelletti set a record for the most field goals in one AFL game when he hit on every attempt against the Denver Broncos in Bears Stadium. How many field goals did Gino kick for the record?

25. In the 1964 AFL championship game, the Chargers bolted to a quick 7-0 lead on their first possession. Fullback Keith Lincoln darted up the middle for 38 yards on the first play from scrimmage, followed shortly by a 26-yard TD pass from Tobin Rote to Dave Kocourek. Lincoln had already gained 47 yards on 3 carries and caught 1 pass for 11 yards in the first quarter; then came the "hit heard around the world!" A short, floating pass from Rote to the left flat arrived just as the approaching Bills linebacker met Lincoln. "The hit" broke two of Lincoln's ribs and sidelined him for the rest of the game. Buffalo went on to win 20-7. After Lincoln left the game, who replaced him at fullback for the Chargers?

The Progress of the Seasons – 1964

■ OAKLAND RAIDERS ■

RIDING THE CREST OF AN EIGHT-GAME winning streak that closed out 1963, the Raiders believed they could contend again in 1964. But they no longer possessed the element of surprise, and the rest of the league would be ready this time around. Davis wanted to improve his running game since the loss of Clem Daniels in '63 for nearly four games played a significant role in their four consecutive losses, and so he jumped at the chance to grab another disgruntled star, trading for halfback Billy Cannon less than a week before the start of the season. Although Cannon needed time to learn the new system, he finished second on the team in both rushing and pass receiving among running backs.

Their first step toward contending was dimmed on September 13 when the Patriots beat them 17-14 victory at Frank Youell Field. A fumble at the Boston 4 yard line in the fourth quarter sealed the Raiders' doom. The second week fared no better, as the Raiders fell to Houston 42-28. Next it was Kansas City, and another loss. They then dropped a thriller in Buffalo 23-20 when their last drive to the Bills 35 yard line was stopped by the final gun. By the time the Raiders made it to week five, the light of hope for a crown in 1964 had been turned off. The team that drew accolades for their unexpected success in 1963 appeared to be looking for an identity.

Following their loss to the Bills, they needed a field goal from Mike Mercer with ten seconds left to earn a 43-43 tie in Boston. Then Oakland's pride and poise kicked in. Looking again like the team from '63, the Raiders drubbed Denver 40-7. Davis pulled his boys together in the second half of the season and finished with a 5-2-1 record after their disastrous 0-5-1 start. A tie with Denver and victories over the two championship game combatants, Buffalo and San Diego, in the final three weeks showed Davis the huge potential of his team but also brought the season to an end with a disappointing 5-7-2 record.

One particularly gratifying win was the 16-13 victory over Buffalo on the second last week of the season. Trailing 13-9 with ninety-five seconds left, the Raiders were on their own 15 yard line and looking for a miracle. With perhaps his best drive of the season, quarterback Tom Flores engineered a masterful drive that put Oakland on the Buffalo 1 yard line with only four seconds left. On the game's last play, Flores lofted an alley-oop pass into the end zone where the 6'3" Art Powell out jumped Buffalo's Butch Byrd for a game-winning touchdown and the Raiders fourth win of the season. They then beat rival San Diego 21-20 on the season's final day.

Cotton Davidson, ranking fifth among AFL passers, threw for 2,489 yards and 21 touchdowns. Fullback Clem Daniels carried the ground game and finished third in rushing, while Art Powell was again the star of the receiving corps and finished second in the AFL

★ *Raiders defensive stalwarts Ben Davidson (83) and Dan Birdwell (53).* ★

and also caught 11 touchdown passes. Flanker Bo Roberson led the league in kickoff returns and safety Claude Gibson was number two in punt returns. Offensive clout and scoring were not Oakland's problem during the season. The Raiders finished second in total offense and second in passing. The offensive line performed well, with Jim Otto gaining all-league status for the fifth straight time, joined by first-time all-league guard Wayne Hawkins. But the offensive heroics were not enough to place the Raiders among the AFL elite. Their weakness was in keeping opponents off the scoreboard. And while the defense was strong enough to hold Cookie Gilchrist, the league's leading rusher, to a mere 24 yards on 10 carries in one game, as a unit they finished sixth in total defense. Only Houston and Denver allowed more points. The master plan had hit a speed bump, but the confident Davis was not about to panic. With pride and poise he simply went back to the drawing board and readied for 1965.

The Progress of the Seasons – 1964

Leading passers	Attempts	Completions	Pct	TDs	Yards	Int
Cotton Davidson	320	155	48%	21	2497	19
Tom Flores	200	98	49%	7	1389	14

Leading rushers	Attempts	Yards gained	Average	TDs
Clem Daniels	173	824	4.8	2
Billy Cannon	80	338	3.8	3
Cotton Davidson	29	167	5.8	2
Tom Flores	11	64	5.8	0
Bob Jackson	15	53	3.5	0

Leading receivers	Caught	Yards gained	Average	TDs
Art Powell	76	1361	17.9	11
Bo Roberson	44	624	14.2	1
Clem Daniels	42	696	16.6	6
Billy Cannon	37	454	12.3	5
Ken Herock	23	360	15.7	2

Leading scorers	TDs	XPM	XPA	FGM	FGA	PTs
Mike Mercer		34	34	15	24	79
Art Powell	11					66

26. After three straight all-star games played in San Diego, the 1964 AFL game was scheduled to be played in Tulane Stadium in New Orleans on January 16, 1965. But after the African-American players complained to the league about the discriminatory treatment they received in the southern city, the players threatened to boycott the game unless the league made a stand. After much discussion and negotiation, AFL officials decided that the best move was to relocate the game. Where was the site to which the game was moved?

▪ DENVER BRONCOS ▪

HEADING INTO THEIR FOURTH campaign, Denver was well aware of the fact that they were one of only two AFL teams that had yet to post a winning season. And for the Broncos there was only one way to go after a stinging 2-11-1 season. As their July training camp opened in Ft. Collins, Colorado, the Broncos still suffered an identity crises at quarterback, having John McCormick and Mickey Slaughter fighting for the job. Then McCormick's season came to an abrupt end when he suffered a knee injury in an exhibition game. With only one quarterback, head coach John Faulkner went looking to find help yet again. He pulled off one of the most bizarre trades in sports history, bringing Houston's young backup Jacky Lee to Denver for all-league defensive tackle Bud McFadin, under the condition that Lee would be returned to Houston after two years, essentially becoming more of a loan than a trade.

Four games into the season Denver was still without a victory, losing by gaping margins of 24, 17, 21, and 29 points, resulting in Faulkner's dismissal. He was replaced by assistant coach Mac Speedie. Riding an eleven-game losing streak, Denver needed a change, which paid instant dividends in Speedie's first game on October 11 against Kansas City. Trailing 13-12 at halftime, Lee fired a third-quarter touchdown pass to Lionel Taylor to put Denver ahead 19-13. On their next possession, Lee lofted a screen pass to halfback Charlie Mitchell just before he was sacked by two Chiefs. Mitchell sped 58 yards for their third touchdown and increased the margin to 26-13. Then early in the fourth quarter Lee threw his third touchdown pass of the day, caught again by Taylor for 34 yards and a 33-13 spread. The crowd of 16,285 Denver fans then had to sit back and endure two quick KC scores, the second coming after a successful onside kick, to get the Chiefs to within 6 at 33-27. But the Broncos held on, coming away with their first win of the season. All-league safety Goose Gonsoulin was the defensive star of the game, picking off 3 Len Dawson passes.

As the season progressed, four more losses followed. The defense was on its way to allowing a league-high 438 points, the second year in a row they topped the AFL. With the league's worst defense came the most anemic offense, scoring 240 points and averaging just 17.1 while allowing 31.2. Denver also came in last in both rushing and passing. Though Lee and Slaughter each completed over 50 percent of their passes, they posted the bottom two yards-per-completion averages in the league.

The youthful tandem of Billy Joe and Charlie Mitchell in the backfield did show promise, but the holes closed too quickly on the sophomores, who gained 590 and 415 yards respectively. Joe was particularly disappointing in his second year, hampered by recurring foot problems. And with the absence of a strong passing game, the backs usually found nowhere to run. On the receiving end, Lionel Taylor relinquished his crown for the first time in five years, finishing tied for second with 76 catches. Second-year tight end Hewritt Dixon was next on the team with 38, followed closely by flanker Bob Scarpitto with 35. Taylor, who scored 7 times, led the dreadful Broncos in scoring with a meek 42 points, ranking him twenty-third in the league. Kickers Gene Mingo, and later Dick Guesman, left the Broncos severely wanting and caused the coaching staff to forego the 3-pointers to call plays on many fourth downs rather than

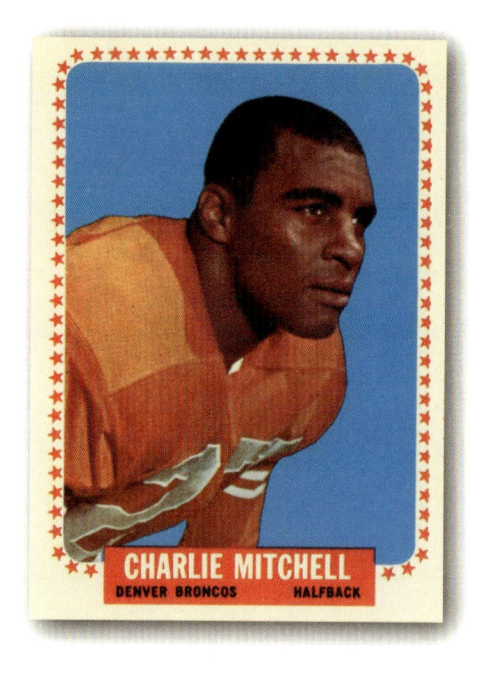

The Progress of the Seasons – 1964

attempting field goals. Guesman hit on a mere 6 of 22 tries and Mingo 8 of 12 prior to leaving for Oakland.

The second win of the season did not come until November 15, a 20-16 triumph over the Jets in the first and only game played in the snow in 1964. Billy Joe set the Denver single-game rushing record by gaining 108 yards, and on two consecutive plays in the first half he ran for 21 and 51 yards up the middle. With an ineffective kicking game, the Broncos scored their first touchdown on a fourth down from the New York 10, with Lionel Taylor making a leaping catch in the end zone. Odell Barry, the AFL's leading punt returner, then gave the Broncos the go-ahead touchdown on a 48-yard return. After the Jets scored to close the gap to 6 points, Mickey Slaughter took a snap on fourth down in the closing minute from his own 10 yard line and strategically ran out of the end zone for a safety, allowing valuable seconds to be run off the clock. The win was also the high point of the season for the defense, with the front four sacking Jet quarterbacks eight times in the game. Prior to the game, Jets throwers had been dropped only fourteen times all year. They also intercepted 6 New York passes, with Willie Brown grabbing four and even had a fifth nullified by a penalty. The all-league cornerback's last pick was a crucial one, coming with forty-one seconds left in the game to seal the victory. The season's second win was followed by four more weeks without a victory, the third such run of the year, condemning the Broncos to their second consecutive 2-11-1 season.

Along the way the Broncos did enjoy some exciting highlights, such as their hard-fought loss at Boston on November 20, when defensive end Leroy Moore set a Denver record for the longest return of an interception. Picking a Babe Parilli flair pass out of the air he juggled it for 8 yards and then rumbled 76 more to the Boston 11 yard line. The defense again was spectacular, allowing only one touchdown in the 12-7 defeat. Much of the praise on defense went to the outstanding play of the secondary that finished second in the league with 32 interceptions. Against the Patriots they intercepted 5, 4 in the last period, bringing the total to 11 in their last two games. Hosting Oakland on November 29, the Broncos came close to knocking off the Raiders on a fourth-down try. Needing only a field goal to win, Speedie called for Mickey Slaughter to roll left for 6 points on the last play of the game rather than put the game on the foot of his weak kicker. Slaughter was stopped on the one, ending the game in a 20-20 tie. The 1964 Denver season brought their five-year record to 18-49-3, the lowest four-year win total in the AFL.

Leading passers	Attempts	Completions	Pct	TDs	Yards	Int
Jacky Lee	265	133	50%	20	1611	11
Mickey Slaughter	189	97	51%	11	930	3

Leading rushers	Attempts	Yards gained	Average	TDs
Charlie Mitchell	177	590	3.3	5
Billy Joe	112	415	3.7	2
Jacky Lee	42	163	3.9	3
Mickey Slaughter	20	54	2.7	0
Donnie Stone	12	26	2.2	0

Leading receivers	Caught	Yards gained	Average	TDs
Lionel Taylor	76	873	11.5	7
Hewritt Dixon	38	585	15.4	1
Bob Scarpitto	35	375	10.7	4
Charlie Mitchell	33	225	6.8	1
Al Denson	25	383	15.3	1

Leading scorers	TDs	XPM	XPA	FGM	FGA	PTs
Lionel Taylor	7					42
Charlie Mitchell	6					36
Dick Guesman		13	15	6	22	31

KANSAS CITY CHIEFS

ONE YEAR REMOVED FROM THEIR championship season, the Chiefs wanted to return to the top of the West. And in their first game, Hank Stram's boys were shown just what it would take to make it back up the mountain. Thanks to 2 KC fumbles inside the 20 yard line and a pass interception deep inside Chief territory, the Buffalo Bills, out to make an impact of their own, struck for 31 points in the first quarter and prevailed 34-17. In many ways the 1964 season in Kansas City was similar to the one in San Diego in 1962. The Chiefs endured injury after injury and were never able to get their entire team on the field at the same time. No less than ten starters were injured and missed games, beginning with star fullback Curtis McClinton, who missed the first four games with a broken hand and never regained his bulldozing effectiveness. Standout split end Chris Burford was slow to heal from off-season knee surgery and missed six weeks, causing star halfback Abner Haynes to play out of position in his stead. All-league linebacker E.J. Holub missed the last five games and had now logged seven knee operations in his career. His backup, Walt Corey, also spent time on the trainer's table. Stalwart safety Johnny Robinson went down with a rib injury and halfback Bert Coan, hoping to make an impact in his third year, still could not rebound from a leg injury suffered in college. Fred Arbanas, the AFL's best tight end, was lost for the final two games. Then there was Len Dawson's shattered nose that caused him to miss part of three games, although he was

The Progress of the Seasons – 1964

still the league's best quarterback at the season's end, completing 56 percent of his passes for 2,879 yards and 30 touchdowns. When Lenny was unable to answer the bell, backups Eddie Wilson and rookie Pete Beathard moved in with little impact.

After an open date on the second week of the season, the Chiefs got back on track by beating both Oakland, 21-9, and Houston, 28-7. Their 2-1 record had them a half game up on San Diego, at 1-2-1. Even at 2-2, KC stood at the top of their division, but two more losses followed, dropping them two games behind the Chargers. From that point on they never moved either up or down in the standings, although they weren't really eliminated from winning the division until the season's twelfth week.

With McClinton sidelined early, Stram looked for a big, powerful replacement and out of the rough came a diamond—Mack Lee Hill, a ramrod of a runner who was every bit as bruising as the Count. Finishing ninth in the league, Hill, who gained 576 yards on 105 carries, had a league-high 5.5 yards per carry average. Teaming with a revived edition of Abner Haynes, the two combined for 1,255 yards on the ground. Haynes gained 697 yards for an even 5 yards per carry, giving the Chiefs the second-best running team in the AFL. The loss of Burford was somewhat mitigated by the emergence of Frank Jackson at flanker. A reserve halfback for Haynes the previous two years, Jackson posted the league's third-highest receiving total with 62, 9 of them for touchdowns and a 15.9 yards per catch average. For all his time away Burford, true to his form, caught 51 passes with 7 touchdowns. Arbanas added 34 receptions, 8 TDs and an incredible 20.2 yards per catch, tying him with Lance Alworth at the top of the league in that department. Haynes caught 38 passes.

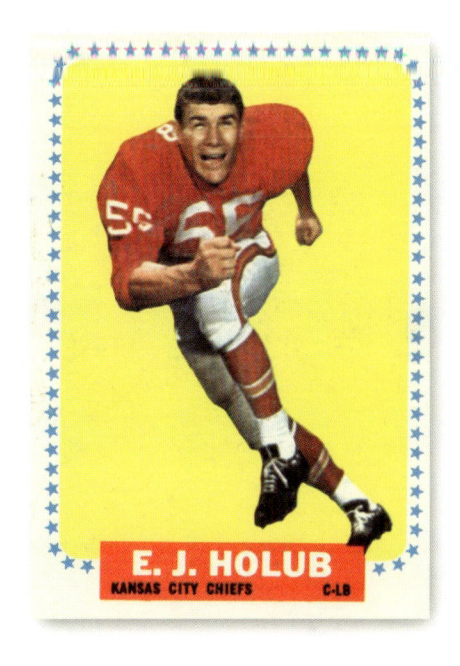

On November 15 the Chiefs were 4-4, behind the Chargers at 6-2-1. A home victory over San Diego on this day would close that margin to a game and a half with five contests remaining. Indicative of the KC season, the Chiefs fumbled 9 times on the afternoon and trailed the Chargers 28-0 in the second quarter. The 28-14 loss put the Chiefs three and a half games off the pace. In their rematch on December 13, with the title already in hand for the Chargers, the Chiefs scored 27 points in the fourth period in a 49-6 route. Dawson fired 4 touchdowns and completed 17 of his 28 passes, eight to flanker Frank Jackson. No

171

one ever argued that Kansas City lacked the talent to win, but at 7-7, they continued to frustrate the organization with their lack of consistency.

Offensively they outscored everyone but the AFL champion Bills. Their 306 points allowed was the league's fourth best, a touchdown behind the Chargers. Fred Arbanas, Jim Tyrer, Jerry Mays, and Dave Grayson were all-league selections.

Leading passers	Attempts	Completions	Pct	TDs	Yards	Int
Len Dawson	354	199	56.2%	30	2879	18
Eddie Wilson	47	25	53.2%	1	392	1

Leading rushers	Attempts	Yards gained	Average	TDs
Abner Haynes	139	697	5.0	4
Mack Lee Hill	105	576	5.5	4
Curtis McClinton	73	252	3.5	1
Jack Spikes	34	112	3.3	0

Leading receivers	Caught	Yards gained	Average	TDs
Frank Jackson	62	943	15.2	9
Chris Burford	51	675	13.2	7
Abner Haynes	38	562	14.8	3
Fred Arbanas	34	686	20.2	8
Mack Lee Hill	19	144	7.6	2
Curtis McClinton	13	221	17.0	2

Leading scorers	TDs	XPM	XPA	FGM	FGA	PTs
Tommy Brooker		46	46	8	17	70
Frank Jackson	9					54

• HOUSTON OILERS •

SIX WEEKS BEFORE THEIR SUMMER training camp opened, owner Bud Adams did the inevitable. He fired coach Pop Ivy, his third head coach in four years, and brought in fellow Texan Sammy Baugh to lead his Oilers. For the disenchanted football team it was a welcome change, especially for their prodigal son, Billy Cannon, who openly feuded with Ivy. As camp opened, Baugh, a Hall of Fame quarterback for the Washington Redskins, was thrilled to see the wealth of talent at his favorite position. Leading the group was thirty-seven-year-old George Blanda, entering his fifteenth season in professional football. His backup, Jacky Lee, was thought to be good enough to start for more than a few other teams. Rounding out the deep list of playcallers was rookie Don Trull, the nation's top thrower from Baylor.

The Progress of the Seasons – 1964

But the three did not share the spotlight for long. In fact, within one week of Baugh declaring he was not interested in trading any of his quarterbacks, he sent Lee to Denver for all league defensive tackle Bud McFadin and the Broncos' first round draft choice. To make the trade one of the most bizarre in professional sports, the deal called for Lee to be returned to Houston after two years with no strings attached. Commissioner Joe Foss approved the trade conditions, knowing that Denver was in need of a leader to solidify the perennially weak team and, with hope, to convince the Bronco owners to keep the franchise in Colorado. A week before their opening game, the Oilers also traded Billy Cannon, who had worn out his welcome with Baugh by breaking curfew more than once. Baugh deemed the oft-injured Cannon, limited to just 13 carries in '63, expendable due to the unexpectedly quick development of swift and elusive rookie halfback Sid Blanks. Shortly after the trade, Adams, in a show of support to his head coach, declared that the Oilers would dedicate 1964 to rebuilding the team into a championship contender.

For the new year, the Oilers added two red stripes to border the center white stripe on their helmet and replaced the red numbers on their away uniforms with blue ones. They also added three stripes at the bottom edge of their shirt sleeves.

Running out of the backfield with more power and speed than Cannon was able to provide over the past two years, Blanks would make the Houston fans forget the Heisman winner by turning in the fifth-best rushing total in the league and finishing a close second to Jet Matt Snell for Rookie of the Year honors. Blanks gained 756 yards and had a 5.2 rushing average. He also caught 55 passes, second most on the team. In one game against the New York Jets, he gained a season-high 179 yards on 21 carries, 91 coming on a touchdown run that also set a league record. Teaming with fullback Charlie Tolar, who finished tenth in the league with 526 yards, the two accounted for 87 percent of Houston's running plays. And although they were the league's second-weakest running team, their ranking was due to the fact that the Oilers ran a league-low 327 times. Houston made its yardage in the air. Blanda shattered Frank Tripucka's pass-attempt record by putting the ball up 505 times, more than any quarterback before him in either league. His 262 completions were also a record, giving old George a 52 percent completion mark. As expected, the Oilers led the league in passing. With that many passes filling the air, the Oilers needed able receivers to haul them in. And in 1964, there

173

★ Houston's Charley Hennigan hauls in one of his record-setting 101 receptions. ★

was none better than the reliable and sure hands of Charley Hennigan. Charley latched on to an all-time record 101 passes during the campaign, one more than the previous record set in 1961 by Denver's Lionel Taylor. Gaining a league-high 1,546 yards he was close to unstoppable and averaged a strong 15.4 yards per reception.

After losing to San Diego in their first game, Houston won two in a row, beating Oakland, 42-28, and Denver, 38-17. The promising start, however, quickly ended as they piled up nine straight losses and fell to 2-10. Wins over the Jets and Broncos in their final two games closed out their self-declared rebuilding season at 4-10. On Friday, December 18, two days before the end of the season, coach Baugh added still another bizarre page to Houston's lost season by resigning his position as head coach to become a backfield coach in 1965 ... for the Houston Oilers!

The Progress of the Seasons – 1964

Charley Hennigan and guard Bob Talamini, along with Bobby Jancik, the league leader in both interceptions and punt returns, were selected to the all-league team. With the reconstruction project a year into production, the Oilers needed a stronger defense and steadier blocking. The project appeared to have long way to go.

Leading passers	Attempts	Completions	Pct	TDs	Yards	Int
George Blanda	505	262	60%	17	3287	27
Don Trull	86	36	42%	1	439	2

Leading rushers	Attempts	Yards gained	Average	TDs
Sid Blanks	145	756	5.2	6
Charlie Tolar	139	515	3.7	4
Don Trull	12	42	3.5	0
Dave Smith	8	16	2.0	0

Leading receivers	Caught	Yards gained	Average	TDs
Charley Hennigan	101	1546	15.3	8
Sid Blanks	56	497	8.9	1
Willard Dewveall	38	552	14.5	4
Charlie Tolar	35	244	7.0	0
Charlie Frazier	31	423	13.6	2
Willie Frazier	9	208	10.1	2

Leading scorers	TDs	XPM	XPA	FGM	FGA	PTs
George Blanda		37	38	13	29	76
Charley Hennigan	8					48

■ NEW YORK JETS ■

FINALLY KISSING THE POLO GROUNDS good-bye, the Jets moved into their new home across the street from the New York World's Fair on September 12, 1964. Shea Stadium (named for attorney William Shea, who led the way in bringing National League baseball back to New York) was another piece of Sonny Werblin's rebuilding puzzle. An AFL record crowd of 44,967 poured into the Saturday night game for the first Shea Stadium kickoff against the Denver Broncos. They did not go home disappointed. The Jets mauled their opponent 30-6 with quarterback Dick Wood throwing 2 touchdown passes and rookie fullback Matt Snell grinding out 82 yards on 22 carries in his professional debut.

Prior to the season the Jets pulled off a nine-player trade with the Broncos that brought safety Bob Zeman, defensive tackle Gordy Holtz, linebacker Wahoo McDaniel, and tight end Gene Prebola to New York in exchange for defensive tackles Dick Guesman and Charley Jenerette, defensive end Ed Cooke, guard Sid Fournet, and linebacker Jim Price. The Jets also brought in guard Sam DeLuca from San Diego and DE Sid Youngleman from Buffalo. McDaniel turned out to be the jewel of the trade, bringing cheers of "WAHOO" every time he was involved in a tackle. McDaniel's popularity was due in part to his off-season job as a professional wrestler.

The team uniforms underwent only one change in '64. The Jet silhouetted on the helmet was replaced by a white oval outlined in green with JETS printed in green with a small green football underneath. Unless you were on the field, the sidelines, or within ten feet of the players, the new logo was difficult to distinguish.

After starting the season at home with a victory, the Jets lost at Boston and returned to New York for a 17-17 tie with the Chargers, in which McDaniel blocked two field goal attempts that would have sealed a victory for the visitors. With the legend and popularity of Wahoo growing and the fans packing their new home at an average of 40,000 a game (a far cry from the 13,000 in '63 in the ancient Polo Grounds), the Jets were playing their best football in years. Two more home games—on October 10 against the Raiders and October 17 against the Oilers—resulted in two more victories. In beating Oakland, New York scored 5 touchdowns before allowing Billy Cannon to score from 1 yard away. Even with Wood completing only 3 of 14 passes, the offense moved the ball, mostly because rookie fullback Matt Snell set a franchise record by rushing for 168 yards on 26 carries. The Jets won handily 35-13.

In their third home game on another Saturday night against Houston, Wood and Maynard teamed up on 24-yard and 49-yard scoring passes to ignite a 24-0 halftime lead. Eclipsing his own Jet record set a week earlier, Matt Snell became the hottest runner in the AFL by dashing through the porous Houston defense for 180 yards on 36 carries. The Jets walked off with a 24-21 win and a 3-1-1 record. The Buffalo Bills, however, were undefeated in six outings. The two faced each other the following week in Buffalo.

The Jets and Bills traded scores throughout the first half. Wood found Bake Turner and Don Maynard on short strikes in each period, giving the Jets a 14-10 lead. Another touchdown pass to Maynard and a Jim Turner field goal increased their lead to 24-10 with twenty-five minutes to go. But Buffalo handed the offense to Daryle Lamonica and the best backup quarterback in the league led the Bills to 24 points while the league's best defense held the Jets scoreless in the final frame, resulting in a 34-24 loss.

At 3-2-1 the news around the AFL was that the Jets, in the second installment of Ewbank's five-year plan, were for real. As teams began to key on Snell, Dick Wood threw

The Progress of the Seasons – 1964

more often, giving defenses more opportunities to blitz and pressure the slow-footed quarterback, who was not adept at scrambling. Bill Mathis, Snell's running mate, was again agonizing through another sub-par season in which he averaged less than 3 yards per carry. Even in reserve the Jets got little help for Snell as Mark Smolinski registered only 34 running attempts for the year, two less than Snell attempted against Houston in one game.

Another Saturday game at Shea on Halloween night had the Jets tricking the Patriots and treating the 45,000 in attendance to a 35-14 triumph. The trickery was largely dished out by Dick Wood, who enjoyed the best day of his career, completing 22 of 36 passes for 325 yards and 3 touchdowns. The biggest treat of the night may have been the first-quarter interception by McDaniel who returned it 38 yards for a touchdown. At 4-2-1 Weeb was feeling pretty good about his team's progress and hoped to put on another strong showing against the 8-0 Bills the next week in their first Sunday home game at Shea. The two teams traded bombs in the first half, Wood to Turner for 71 yards in the first quarter and the Bills' Lamonica to Elbert Dubenion for 80 yards in the second. At the final gun the Bills remained undefeated as the Jets bowed 20-7 in front of a new AFL record crowd of 60,300. Six losses in the next seven games parked the Jets at the East's third-place hanger with a 5-8-1 record.

The 1964 season was a transition year for the Jets, as number one draft choice Matt Snell walked off with the Rookie of the Year award and ended up only 33 yards behind leading rusher Cookie Gilchrist. The Jets finished in the middle of the pack in team rushing stats. Snell also showcased his versatility by catching 56 passes, finishing second on the team behind Bake Turner's 58 but ahead of Maynard's 46.

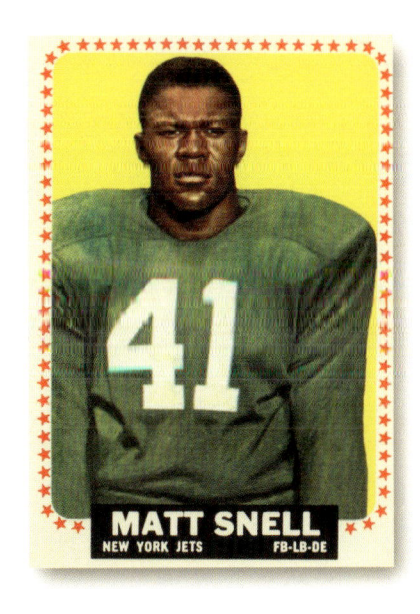

Wood shared quarterback duties later in the season with Mike Taliaferro and Pete Liske, giving the Jets a fifth-best scoring average of 22.5 points per game. On defense there was no better team at picking off passes than the New York secondary of Dainard Paulson, Bill Baird, Clyde Washington, Marshall Starks, Willie West, and Bill Rademacher. They combined for 34 interceptions, returning 4 for touchdowns. Paulson's 12 picks led the league with Baird not far behind with 8. Other standout performers on defense were linebacker Larry Grantham, who joined Paulson on the all-league defensive team, rookie Gerry

177

Philbin, and LaVerne Torczon at defensive end, and middle linebacker McDaniel. Perhaps the biggest indicator of the Jets being on the right track was the season's attendance that grew from 91,000 in 1963 to 298,000 with their move to Flushing Meadows. As New York embraced their Jets, the cloud with the silver lining was could be seen on the horizon.

Leading passers	Attempts	Completions	Pct	TDs	Yards	Int
Dick Wood	358	169	47%	17	2298	25
Mike Taliaferro	73	23	32%	2	341	5
Pete Liske	18	9	50%	0	55	2

Leading rushers	Attempts	Yards gained	Average	TDs
Matt Snell	215	948	4.4	5
Bill Mathis	105	305	2.9	4
Mark Smolinski	34	117	3.4	1
Mike Taliaferro	9	45	5.0	0

Leading receivers	Caught	Yards gained	Average	TDs
Bake Turner	58	974	16.8	9
Matt Snell	56	393	7.0	1
Don Maynard	46	847	18.4	8
Dee Mackey	14	213	15.2	0
Gene Heeter	13	153	11.8	1

Leading scorers	TDs	XPM	XPA	FGM	FGA	PTs
Jim Turner		33	33	13	27	72
Bake Turner	9					54

■ SAN DIEGO CHARGERS ■

RIDING THE CREST OF THEIR 51-10 AFL Championship victory over Boston, the Chargers were favored to win their fourth Western Division title in five years. And by virtue of a midseason, six-game win streak sandwiched between a 1-2-1 start and a 1-3 finish, they were able to march to the championship game with a modest 8-5-1 record.

There were few changes in the Chargers lineup in '64. The defense still showcased the huge front line of Earl Faison, Ernie Ladd, and sophomores George Gross and Bob Petrich. The linebackers still included Frank Buncom and Chuck Allen, and a secondary of Bud Whitehead, Jim Warren, and Dick Westmoreland welcomed rookies Leslie Duncan and Kenny Graham. George Blair, who doubled as the team's place kicker, was healthy for only four games and was easier to replace on defense than he was at the tee. Three place

★ Keith Lincoln breaks into the Raider secondary. ★

kickers shuffled through the system, including Keith Lincoln, Herb Travenio, and the grand old man, Ben Agajanian. Of the three, Gillman gave Lincoln the most attention, and the fullback responded by converting 5 of 12 field goal attempts and all but 1 of his 17 point after touchdowns.

The main issue, as in 1962, was health. The Chargers were hampered by injuries throughout the year. All-star flanker Lance Alworth missed seven of the season's first twelve quarters and defensive backs Charlie McNeil and Dickie Harris played in only six games. Bud Whitehead also sat out two. Quarterback Tobin Rote suffered nagging arm and shoulder pains. He alternated with backup John Hadl for much of the season.

Defeating the Oilers 27-21 got the Chargers off on the right foot. Rote completed 15 of his 26 passes for 235 yards and 3 TD throws, while Alworth caught 6 balls for 119 yards and 1 touchdown. But in their return to Balboa Stadium in week two, the Patriots avenged their championship game humiliation by cutting into the Chargers for 33 points while giving up 28. Rote, ineffective with his first 16 passes, gave way to Hadl who completed 11 of 19 attempts. At 1-1 the Chargers flew to Buffalo where they lost 30-3 while Paul Lowe sat out his second game in row with injuries. Their first visit to New York's Shea Stadium a week later ended in a 17-17 tie, giving the defending champions a 1-2-1 record one month into their defense.

Offensively San Diego was not clicking, though the lineup was virtually unchanged from the year before. Ron Mix and Ernie Wright were the best set of tackles in the league, and Walt Sweeney and Pat Shea at guard and Don Rogers at center were as good an any. All-stars Don Norton and Dave Kocourek entered their fifth year catching passes together for the Chargers. Backs Lincoln and Lowe were the best tandem in the business at running the ball. The difference seemed to be Rote, who was now completing only 45 percent of his passes compared to 59 percent a year earlier. The offense lacked a knockout punch, and late in the season when the Chargers should have been fine tuning things to meet the winner of the East, they lost to Buffalo 27-24, Kansas City 49-6, and Oakland 21-20. San Diego's 8-5-1 record represented the lowest winning percentage of any Western Division champion to date.

Heading into the Championship game on December 26 in Buffalo, the Chargers were still not at full strength and took the field without Lance Alworth, injured a week earlier against Oakland. Paul Lowe was also ailing. Looking for big-game experience for the title showdown, Gillman started his two-time championship quarterback Tobin Rote, damaged wing and all. On the first play from scrimmage, Rote called for a fullback draw that sent Keith Lincoln up the middle for 38 yards. Two plays later a touchdown pass to Dave Kocourek put the Chargers ahead 7-0. They could muster nothing else offensively for the rest of the day. Rote was relatively ineffective against the AFL's best defense and was able to complete only 10 of 26 passes and threw 2 interceptions. In relief, Hadl found his target on only 3 of his 10 passes. But the play that dictated outcome was Bills linebacker Mike Stratton's hit on Keith Lincoln as he leaped for a flare pass in the first quarter. The hit broke Lincoln's ribs and although he tried to convince Gillman to let him play the second half, his day and the Chargers chances to repeat were over. They lost their third AFL Championship game 20-7.

Leading passers	Attempts	Completions	Pct	TDs	Yards	Int
John Hadl	274	147	54%	18	2157	15
Tobin Rote	163	74	45%	9	1156	15

Leading rushers	Attempts	Yards gained	Average	TDs
Keith Lincoln	155	632	4.1	4
Paul Lowe	130	496	3.8	3
Jacque MacKinnon	24	124	5.2	2
Keith Kinderman	24	111	4.6	0

The Progress of the Seasons – 1964

Leading receivers	Caught	Yards gained	Average	TDs		
Lance Alworth	61	1235	20.2	13		
Don Norton	49	669	13.7	6		
Keith Lincoln	34	302	8.9	2		
Dave Kocourek	33	593	18.0	5		
Paul Lowe	14	182	12.0	2		

Leading scorers	TDs	XPM	XPA	FGM	FGA	PTs
Lance Alworth	15					90
Keith Lincoln	7	14	17	9	11	87

■ BUFFALO BILLS ■

IF THEY WERE EVER GOING TO seriously contend for the Eastern Division title, the Bills needed to turn their September walkabouts into winning voyages. Over the past two seasons under Lou Saban, the Bills were 0-for-September. In both years they had to mount late-season surges to muster 7-6-1 records. Winning the East would require winning before the ground froze in War Memorial Stadium. As it turned out, they would not lose in 1964, *until* the ground froze. Their nine straight wins led the East as they geared up to host the Boston Patriots on November 15. The Pats brought a 6-2-1 record into Buffalo needing a win while the Bills hoped to distance themselves from their closest challenger. For the third time in five years the Bills changed their uniforms, moving their shoulder stripes of the past two years further down their sleeves.

On opening day the Bills jumped out to a 31-0 first quarter lead over the Chiefs and rolled to a 34-17 win for their first 1-0 record ever. The Bills had put together the fiercest defense in the league, allowing only 65 yards per game on the ground and ranked at the top of the league in total defense. The front four of Tom Sestak, Tom Day, Jim Dunaway, and Ron McDole rivaled Boston's and San Diego's man for man. Defensive backs Booker Edgerson, George Saimes, Butch Byrd, Ray Abruzzese, and Hagood Clarke were also the AFL's stingiest unit, holding rival quarterbacks to a league-low completion percentage of 46 percent. With the dominating defense holding opponents to 17 points per game, lowest in the AFL, the

181

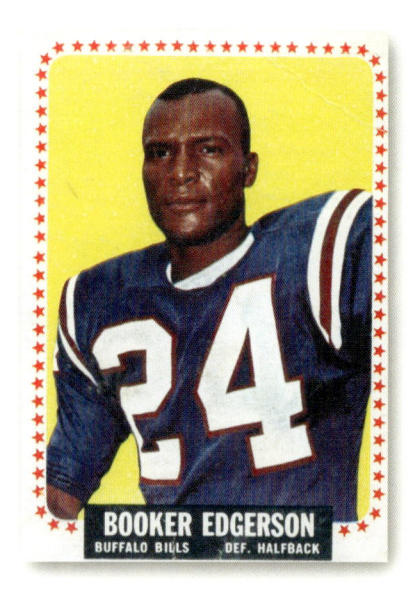

offense averaged a league-high 28 points per game. Kemp and Lamonica continued to share the load with Kemp using his field management and savvy to lead the team and Lamonica providing the necessary change of pace when they got bogged down. Lamonica also gave the Bills an extra dimension with his running prowess, and along with Cookie Gilchrist led the league with 6 rushing touchdowns. In seven of their first nine victories, Lamonica came off the bench to kickstart the Bills offense.

Cookie Gilchrist was again running full throttle, as he became the first AFL running back to win a second rushing title. With Wray Carlton suffering through another injury-riddled season and Glenn Bass shifted to flanker, the Bills turned to yet another rookie to complement their bone-crushing fullback. Bobby Smith from North Texas State provided outside speed. He averaged 4.9 yards per carry on 62 attempts. Cookie again led the league in rushing attempts en route to his 981 total yards, enabling the Bills to use a ball control offense that ran more often than any other team and topped the AFL in rushing. The passing game kept opposing defenses from concentrating solely on stopping the ground attack. They posted the league's third-best passing offense with a league-low 397 attempts that netted a league-high yards-per-catch average gain.

The hottest story of 1964 was Buffalo's young Hungarian kicker out of Cornell University. Pete Gogolak attacked the ball like no one had ever seen in American football. He used a soccer-style kick, throwing his instep into the ball after approaching from the side rather than hitting it with his toe in the conventional way. His unconventional style helped him kick field goals with more accuracy than anyone in the AFL. He connected on 19 of his 29 field goal attempts and missed only 1 of his 46 PATs. Gogo revolutionized the art of kicking a football, and two years later would be a catalyst for a merger between the AFL and NFL when he became the first AFL player to jump across the leagues to the New York Giants. In doing so he set off a player signing war that finally forced the leagues to combine. For now he was one of many offensive weapons in the Bills arsenal that had lifted them to their most successful season with five weeks remaining.

With the biggest game of the season in week ten against the Patriots, the Bills were ready to pull out all the stops to win the East. But the game almost spelled disaster for the

The Progress of the Seasons – 1964

Bills in more ways than in the standings. They jumped ahead 10-0, but Boston fought back and led 14-13 at halftime. The Bills came roaring back to lead 28-14 in the third quarter. After that, the Bills could simply not hold onto the ball. Three fumbles led to Patriot scores, and the Buffalo sidelines were showing signs of stress. Then Cookie Gilchrist refused to re-enter the game in the fourth quarter, outraging Saban and drawing not only a stiff fine, but also a suspension. Only the mediation skills of future U.S. Senator Jack Kemp saved Gilchrist and the Bills championship run. Boston went on to win 36-28 and draw themselves a game closer to the division leaders.

The Bills at 9-1 now led Boston with a 7-2-1 record by only a game and a half. When the Bills lost to the Raiders on December 6, the Patriots moved even closer and set up a final showdown, this time in Boston. Buffalo sported an 11-2 record, Boston was 10-2-1. A victory for the home team would give the Pats their second division title. On Sunday December 20, the two teams were greeted in Fenway Park by a New England snowstorm that covered the field. For the second year in a row the teams faced each other in the last game of the season for the right to meet the San Diego Chargers for the AFL championship. And again it was on a snow-covered field. This time the outcome would be different as Kemp led the way, hitting on 12 of 24 passes and giving the Bills their first division title with a 24-14 victory. They would host the AFL Championship game on the following Saturday.

It was a typical December day in Buffalo for their first title game—dark, dreary, and overcast with a muddy terrain. San Diego arrived wearing pristine white jerseys, white pants, and white helmets. The Bills wore their home blue. By the end of the game hardly a number was visible. The Chargers were without their top receiver, Lance Alworth, injured the previous week against the Raiders. Tobin Rote started at quarterback, just as he had a year ago against Boston, and commanded a high-powered offense. On the first play from scrimmage, fullback Keith Lincoln, the MVP of last year's Championship game, tore up the middle on a draw play and gained 38 yards. Two plays later Rote hit tight end Dave Kocourek in the end zone for a touchdown. San Diego led 7-0 with less than three minutes gone.

Buffalo's first drive stalled, and when the Chargers regained possession, Rote tried to hit Lincoln with a second-down flare pass in the left flat. Buffalo right side linebacker Mike

183

Stratton had keyed on Rote and anticipated the lofted pass. He arrived at the precise moment the ball landed in Lincoln's grasp, driving his right shoulder through the back's rib cage. The entire Buffalo crowd felt the impact and knew that the game's momentum had just shifted to their Bills. Lincoln didn't return that day, and the Bills defense tamed the Chargers' storm. With Gilchrist putting on a superb performance, gaining 122 yards on 16 carries, and Kemp completing 10 of his 20 passes, the Bills took a slim 6-point lead (13-7) into the fourth quarter. Kemp then hit Glenn Bass on a 15-yard slant that ended up on the San Diego 1 yard line. Two plays later the QB snuck it into the end zone for a 20-7 advantage. The Buffalo defense continued to lock up the Charger offense the rest of the way, even as John Hadl relieved Rote behind center. The Bills had overcome their heart-breaking playoff loss to Boston a year ago to finally arrive at the apex of the league. The Buffalo Bills were the 1964 AFL Champions!

At season's end tackle Stew Barber, guard Billy Shaw, fullback Cookie Gilchrist, and defensive players Tom Sestak, Mike Stratton, and George Saimes were selected to the all-league first team.

Leading passers	Attempts	Completions	Pct	TDs	Yards	Int
Jack Kemp	269	119	44.2%	13	2285	26
Daryle Lamonica	128	55	43%	6	1137	8

Leading rushers	Attempts	Yards gained	Average	TDs
Cookie Gilchrist	230	981	4.3	6
Bobby Smith	62	306	4.9	4
Joe Auer	63	191	3.0	2
Jack Kemp	37	124	3.4	5
Wray Carlton	39	114	2.9	1

Leading receivers	Caught	Yards gained	Average	TDs
Glenn Bass	43	897	20.9	7
Elbert Dubenion	42	1139	27.1	10
Cookie Gilchrist	30	345	11.5	0
Ernie Warlick	23	478	20.8	0
Ed Rutkowski	13	234	18.0	1
Joe Auer	11	166	15.1	0

Leading scorers	TDs	XPM	XPA	FGM	FGA	PTs
Pete Gogolak		45	46	19	29	102
Elbert Dubenion	10					60

27. The Jets played in their Flushing Meadows home for nineteen years, from 1964 through 1983. And quarterback Dick Wood christened the new stadium with a touchdown pass in the first quarter. Who was the New York tight end who caught the historic TD pass, which was his only TD reception of the year?

The Progress of the Seasons – 1964

The annual AFL All-Star game in 1964 was nearly never played. Lobbying the AFL for a possible expansion team, the city of New Orleans offered to host the annual event. But as the African-American players arrived, they experienced signs of discrimination and refusals to be served throughout the city. They threatened to boycott the game unless the league took a stand. With the threat of having no players to play the game, commissioner Joe Foss moved the venue on less than a week's notice to Houston's Jeppesen Stadium. On January 16, an impromtu crowd of 15,446 watched as Keith Lincoln (broken ribs and all) stormed through the East defense on the game's first play from scrimmage for a 73-yard touchdown dash. Lou Saban's East team then traded scores with Sid Gillman's West squad to trail by only 3 points at halftime. Then the West outscored the East 21-0, starting with another touchdown dash by Charger Keith Lincoln, this time for 80 yards on the West's first possession of the second half. Two touchdown passes by John Hadl followed, one going to Charger teammate Lance Alworth and the other to Raider Art Powell. The West coasted to a 38-14 thumping of the East. For the second year in a row Lincoln was voted the All-Star game MVP. The West, now undefeated in four tries against their rivals, appeared to be the dominant division. The result concerned the game committee, and leery of the possibility that fan interest for the game may be waning, commissioner Joe Foss and his staff came up with a change in format that they hoped would pique more interest in 1965.

1965

AMERICAN FOOTBALL LEAGUE – 1965 FINAL STANDINGS

EASTERN DIVISION

TEAM	GP	W	L	T	PF	PA	PCT.
BUFFALO BILLS	14	10	3	1	313	226	0.750
NEW YORK JETS	14	5	8	1	285	303	0.393
BOSTON PATRIOTS	14	5	8	2	244	302	0.357
HOUSTON OILERS	14	4	10	0	298	429	0.286

WESTERN DIVISION

TEAM	GP	W	L	T	PF	PA	PCT.
SAN DIEGO CHARGERS	14	9	2	3	340	227	0.750
OAKLAND RAIDERS	14	8	5	1	298	239	0.607
KANSAS CITY CHIEFS	14	7	5	2	322	285	0.571
DENVER BRONCOS	14	4	10	0	303	392	0.286

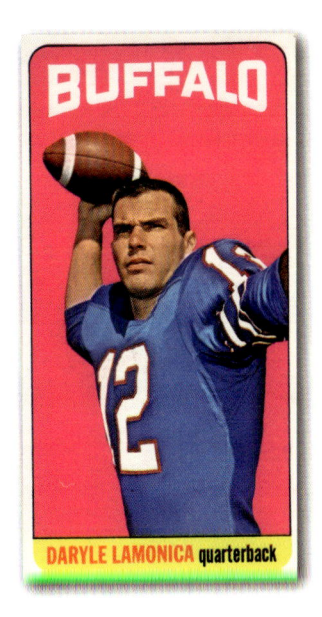

Not everyone remembers **Daryle Lamonica** as Jack Kemp's back-up with the Bills from 1963 through 1966, before being traded to Oakland and becoming "The Mad Bomber." A star at the University of Notre Dame, Lamonica spent his first four years in Buffalo before gaining fame as the AFL Player of the Year in 1967 and 1969, hitting the likes of Fred Biletnikoff, Warren Wells, and Billy Cannon with long bombs and leading the Raiders to three straight championship games in 1967, 1968, and 1969.

■ NEW YORK JETS ■

IT WASN'T SO MUCH ABOUT WINNING for the Jets in 1965 as it was about publicity, earning valuable experience, and the $400,000 quarterback. The arrival of Joe Willie Namath from Alabama to the AFL was the biggest story in sports, not only because Namath shunned the NFL, but because he earned so much money for doing it. Even Namath could not believe how much he was going to be paid. The public-

★ Joe Willie takes the field at Shea Stadium, 1965. ★

ity the AFL and the Jets attracted for the signing was worth millions. Forgotten in the hoopla over Namath were the players owner Sonny Werblin added along with Broadway Joe. The Jets also signed Notre Dame's Heisman Trophy-winning quarterback John Huarte for an equally unbelievable $200,000, Virginia Tech halfback Bob Schweickert, and Princeton fullback Cosmo Iacavazzi. Both inked contracts for a $100,000. Signing untried college players to such large contracts was unprecedented in pro football and sent a frightening message to the NFL that "the other league" was not going to fold its tent. Unfortunately for Huarte, he reported to camp three weeks later than the rest of the rookies after playing in the college All-Star game in July and spent the entire year on the taxi squad. A year later he was traded to Boston for flanker Jim Colclough. Princeton's Iacavazzi, who

The Progress of the Seasons – 1965

finished ninth in the Heisman voting, never made it as a pro.

Head coach Weeb Ewbank held to his plan of blending highly talented youngsters with dependable veterans on both offense and defense. Still looking for small successes, his Jets finished ahead of only Houston in their ability to stop the run in '65, giving up 1,551 yards on the ground with a front four featuring two defensive ends with only one year of experience between them. Gerry Philbin was considered the best defender on the squad but many felt he was too small for the position. At the end of the decade Philbin was voted to the All-Time AFL team. His partner was 6'4" rookie Verlon Biggs, who gave the Jets a strong and sinister presence. They also started a rookie defensive tackle, Jim Harris, and six-year veteran Paul Rochester. Larry Grantham and Wahoo McDaniel backed the line along with Ralph Baker. The secondary consisted of Dainard Paulson, Willie West, Bill Baird, and Clyde Washington. After the group led the AFL in pass interceptions in 1964, they suffered the dubious distinction of giving up the second highest number of touchdown passes, 22. They did manage to pull down 26 errant throws, with Paulson picking off 7 and West 6.

Joe Namath was clearly the story in New York in 1965, taking the field at camp wearing white shoes, attracting still more attention to himself. At first the veterans appeared to resent him, while many of the rookies admired him. But Joe dealt with his teammates directly. When he brought up the issue of his popularity among fans and the press and the resentment the attention caused, he gained volumes of credibility with the team, including Ewbank and his staff. Weeb's plan called for Namath to be weaned into his role as team savior. Third-year pro Mike Taliaferro, who completed only 31 percent of his passes in 1964, was named the starting quarterback. Namath pitched in when needed.

He was needed in every game for the first six weeks and finally took the starting job. To protect his rookie quarterback who already had delicate knees, Ewbank assembled an offensive line of large, immovable strongmen who allowed only seventeen sacks in fourteen games. At tackle was Sherman Plunkett, 6'2", 295 pounds, a veteran who won two NFL championships with Ewbank's Colts. At the other tackle was Winston Hill, considered one of the league's best at 6'4", 275 pounds. The guards, Sam DeLuca and Dave Herman, were both 6'2", 250 pounds and equally physical and quick. The two flanked center Mike Hudock, the rock in the middle since the Titan days.

Both the defense and

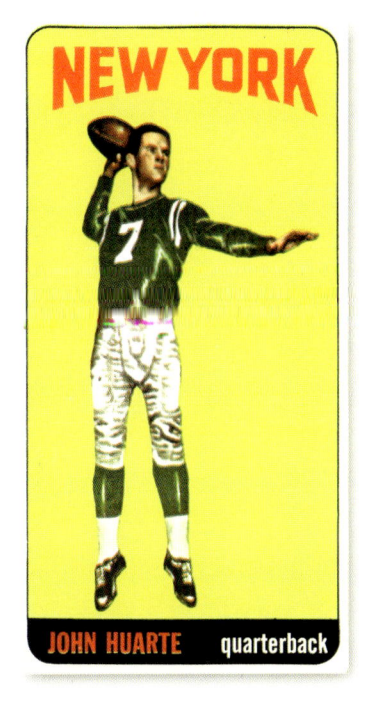

189

offense struggled early and failed to record a single victory through their first six games. Taliaferro and Namath alternated through the first half of the season with Taliaferro drawing the starts most of the time. Neither could spark the offense, averaging only 16 points per contest. It didn't help either that the Jets fumbled 27 times during the season. Through it all Ewbank remained optimistic, and on Halloween in a home game against the Broncos he sensed his team was ready to turn the corner. And turn it they did. The 55,572 onlookers watched the first victory of the Namath era, as the Jets thumped Denver 45-10. Taliaferro and Namath each threw touchdown passes, but by now everyone knew Joe was ready. Three more wins in a row under Namath's leadership brought the Jets out of the basement and into second place with a 4-5-1 record. The Jets knew they lacked the tools to overtake the Bills, who were 8-2, but they felt invigorated by their progress and looked for continued improvement.

The backfield of Matt Snell and Bill Mathis finished fourth and seventh in the league respectively. Mathis rebounded from a sub-par season and kept defenses from keying on Snell, who did not have to carry the burden of the entire running game on his sophomore shoulders. Mathis, an original Titan, ran for 604 yards, a 4.1 average, more than a yard per better than last season. He also had the second-longest run from scrimmage in 1965, a 79-yarder. In his second year out of Ohio State, Snell carried the ball almost 50 times less than in his rookie campaign, when he averaged 4.4 yards per carry. His 763 yards gave him a 4.5 average. For receiving targets, Namath relied on crafty veteran Don Maynard, who enjoyed one of his finest seasons, catching 68 passes for 1,218 yards for an 18-yard average and a league-leading 14 touchdowns. Snell caught 38 passes out of the backfield. The split-end position, once the domain of Art Powell and then inherited by Bake Turner, was now shared by Turner and second-year receiver George Sauer. And although they combined for 60 catches, neither struck fear into the hearts of opposing secondaries, which many times placed multi-player coverage on Maynard.

By November Namath had emerged as the team's starting quarterback. In October Taliaferro was throwing 35 times a game to Namath's 5. By December those numbers were reversed. Namath's finest hour of his Rookie of the Year campaign came on November 21 in Shea Stadium against Houston. In many respects it was a changing of the guard for AFL quarterbacks. Long the patriarch of AFL signal callers, George Blanda could not manage a score for three quarters, while Joe Willie in his white shoes threw four touchdowns to Bake Turner, George Sauer, Curley Johnson, and Don Maynard, leading the Jets to a 41-14 victory. Since Joe became the starter, New York had a 5-3 record. And all of New York took notice. Attendance at Jet games rose by 91,000 in 1965, the total number of people that attended all seven home games their last year in the Polo Grounds. Over 384,000 fans came to Shea Stadium to embrace their new Jets, almost

The Progress of the Seasons – 1965

★ All-league punter Curly Johnson gets one away against the Pats. ★

twice as many as most other AFL clubs drew. Namath completed a respectable 48 percent of his 340 passes for 2,220 yards, with 18 going for scores, ranking him as the third best quarterback in the league. His interception rate was also lower than veterans Hadl, Dawson, Parilli, Blanda, and Kemp.

The Jets saved the most encouraging game of the year for last. Hosting the defending and eventual AFL champion Buffalo Bills, the Jets toughed out an inspiring 14-12 victory, with Namath tossing 2 touchdown passes and the underestimated Jet defense giving up only a fourth-quarter touchdown to the league's third-highest scoring team. It was only the third loss of the season for Buffalo.

For the third year in a row the Jets finished with five wins. This year they all came in their last eight games. But this year had the look of good things to come. This one made everyone believe that the Jets were ready to emerge as challengers for a division title.

The all-league team for 1965 included a kicker and punter for the first time. The Jets Curley Johnson gained the latter honor to become the first punter ever selected. He booted 72 times for an average of 45.3 yards per punt.

Leading passers	Attempts	Completions	Pct	TDs	Yards	Int
Joe Namath	340	164	48%	18	2220	15
Mike Taliaferro	119	45	38%	3	531	7

Leading rushers	Attempts	Yards gained	Average	TDs
Matt Snell	169	763	4.5	4
Bill Mathis	147	604	4.1	5
Mark Smolinski	24	59	2.5	0
Kern Carson	7	25	3.6	2

Leading receivers	Caught	Yards gained	Average	TDs
Don Maynard	68	1218	17.9	14
Matt Snell	38	264	6.9	0
Bake Turner	31	402	13.0	2
George Sauer	29	301	10.4	2
Bill Mathis	17	242	14.2	1
Dee Mackey	16	255	15.9	1

Leading scorers	TDs	XPM	XPA	FGM	FGA	PTs
Jim Turner		31	31	20	34	91
Don Maynard	14					84

28. The AFL played the first three All-Star games in the San Diego sunshine at Balboa Stadium. The 1964 game was played in Houston as an alternative site after the New Orleans problem could not be resolved. What were the only other two cities in which the AFL All-Star game was played?

29. Joe Namath was the Jets' number-one draft pick out of the University of Alabama in 1965. Owner Sonny Werblin signed him to the now-famous $400,000 contract. What NFL team also made Namath their first draft choice?

▪ DENVER BRONCOS ▪

IN 1962, BUFFALO'S COOKIE GILCHRIST and Dallas' Abner Haynes were the AFL's top two rushers. In 1965 they both started in Denver's backfield. Haynes came from Kansas City in a trade for linebacker/punter Jim Fraser, and Gilchrist, banished from Buffalo for his unpredictable behavior, exchanged places with 1963 rookie of the year Billy Joe, who had suffered through the sophomore jinx and foot problems in '64. Upon his arrival, the controversial Gilchrist announced that the Broncos had just upgraded their running game and claimed he was a better fullback than the departed Joe. He even chose to wear number two on his jersey, one better than the number three worn by Joe during his two-year stay in Denver. Joe countered the move by wearing number thirty-

The Progress of the Seasons – 1965

three in Buffalo, one better than Gilchrist's thirty-four.

That the Broncos still played in Denver in 1965 was a welcomed surprise because the second group of owners, headed by Cal Kunz, wanted to move the franchise to Atlanta. The Phipps brothers, Allan and Gerald, came to the rescue. As minority stockholders, they refused to relinquish their voting shares in favor of moving the team. Instead, vowing to keep the team in Denver, they purchased the franchise on February 15 for 1.5 million dollars. To show their appreciation, the fans of Denver purchased a record 22,000 season tickets prior to the season, surpassing their largest one-game attendance in 1964 and giving the Broncos a division-record 31,398 average attendance in 1965. By remaining in Denver and upgrading the roster, the team doubled last year's win total. With the new ownership also came a new style of uniform for 1965. Still wearing a combination of orange, blue, and white, the Broncos accented their solid orange home jersey with blue sleeves and white stripes on the top and bottom.

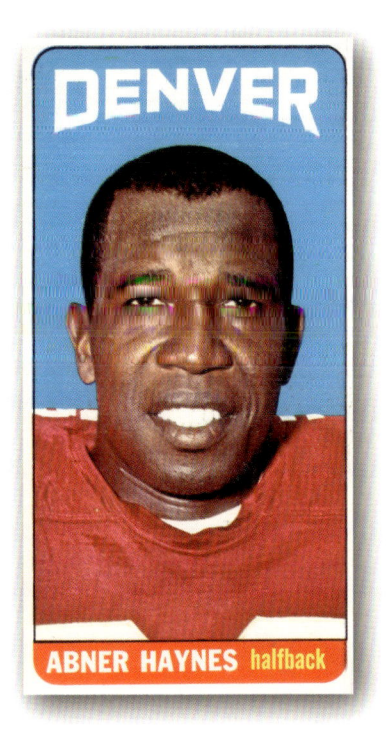

As training camp opened, the Broncos returned much of the previous year's squad. All-league veteran Eldon Danenhauer and Bob Breitenstein were again the offensive tackles with Jerry Sturm and Bob McCullough at guard. Ray Kubala was the center as well as the team's place kicker. In years past the Denver offense consisted primarily of passes to Lionel Taylor. The absence of a formidable running game naturally allowed defenses to focus on stopping Taylor and the other receivers. Now with Gilchrist, Haynes, and rookie Wendell Hayes tearing up the turf, the offense enjoyed its most balanced and productive season. Not even the loss of star halfback Charlie Mitchell, who missed the entire season with a leg injury, could curtail the Denver ground stampede, which sprang from dead last in 1964 to second best in 1965. Gilchrist finished second in the league with 954 yards for a 3.79 average, but Haynes found himself playing second fiddle to the young Hayes at halfback and saw more action

193

★ *Charger defenders surround Cookie Gilchrist.* ★

running pass patterns than running the football. He carried only 41 times for 166 yards but used his speed to burn secondaries for 26 pass receptions. He also led the league in kickoff returns with a 26.5 average and teamed with mercurial Odell Barry, last season's punt-return leader, to give Denver the AFL's fifth- and sixth-leading punt returners. The surprise of the season was Wendell Hayes, who gained 526 yards for a 4.05 average. For the first time Denver had two runners in the league's top ten, Gilchrist and Hayes.

But again the Bronco offense lacked a consistent quarterback. Mickey Slaughter started the season as the number-one play caller until John McCormick returned from injuries on September 24. Two heartbreakers—one to San Diego, 34-31, and a second, 30-15, at home against Buffalo—began the season. When McCormick returned for a Friday night game in Boston, the Broncos put on an awesome display of ball control by keeping possession for 45 plays in the second half, allowing the Patriots a mere 10 snaps. In winning their first game of the season, the Broncos so thoroughly dominated the game that they held the Boston offense to only two offensive plays in the third quarter.

The Progress of the Seasons – 1965

McCormick was at his best in that period as he led his team on a 91-yard drive that lasted ten minutes, stringing together 18 plays, 16 of them runs. The Broncos tallied 220 yards on the ground, a team record. On defense Denver was ecstatic with the play of rookie linebacker John Bramlett from Memphis State, a hard-nosed tackler who thrived on contact. At season's end Bramlett led all first-year defensive players in the rookie-of-the-year balloting. Only Joe Namath received more than votes for the honor than Johnny B.

On October 3 the Broncos hosted the New York Jets, led by Namath, in front of 34,988 fans, the largest crowd in team history, and earned a 16-13 triumph, highlighted by a 44-yard run on a fake punt by Bob Scarpitto that ignited a Bronco score. But in winning the game, they lost Mickey Slaughter for a month with an injured throwing arm. Despite renewing musical chairs at quarterback with McCormick, Slaughter, and Jacky Lee, the offense finished with the league's third-best passing game to go with their new running success, posting the fourth-highest point total with 303, a 63-point improvement over 1964.

The defense also began to take shape, allowing 46 fewer points in '65. Against the pass the Broncos fielded a fine group of ball hawks that included one of the best, Willie Brown, and rookie Nemiah Wilson on the corners. Wilson's 65-yard interception return for a touchdown was the league's fourth-longest return of the year. Goose Gonsoulin and John Griffin again held things together at safety.

November 14 was a particularly gratifying day for the Broncos, who had never beaten the powerful Oilers in Houston in five previous tries. But a flury of 17 points in the fourth quarter led to a 31-21 win-sparked by a 57-yard punt return for a touchdown by Abner Haynes and rookie John Bramlett's 71-yard interception return for a touchdown. The Bronco secondary intercepted 6 passes.

The win put their record at 4-6, behind San Diego's 6-2-2 and Oakland and the Chiefs who were both 5-4. In the final four weeks of the season the Broncos continued to put up a valiant effort against their opponents. On November 21 they took a 14-14 tie into the fourth quarter, but 2 long interception returns for touchdowns put the Raiders ahead. The Broncos came back with a touchdown pass from Lee to Taylor, but the effort fell short 28-20. Two weeks later after losing another one to Oakland 24-14 the Broncos went down to the wire against Boston. But even after scoring 14 points in the final quarter they lost again 28-20. On the final week of the season they spotted Kansas City 21 points in the first quarter and then took the Chiefs to the limit in a high-scoring, seesaw battle, falling short 45-35.

Many good things happened for Denver in 1965. Their offense found a groove and for the first time they had as formidable a running game as they did a lethal passing attack. Their balanced offense was one of the league's best. Cookie Gilchrist and Lionel Taylor, who again led the league with 85 pass receptions, and tackle Eldon Danenhauer represented Denver on the AFL all-league team. The defense also

195

showed signs of improvement and with a few more pieces hoped to take the next step toward respectability. The best aspect of the season, however, proved to be the renewed fan interest. Along with the commitment to keep the team in Denver, the Broncos were committed to improving enough to make a run at the three powerhouses they had to climb over to win the West.

Leading passers	Attempts	Completions	Pct	TDs	Yards	Int
John McCormick	253	103	41%	7	1292	14
Mickey Slaughter	147	75	51%	6	864	12
Jacky Lee	80	44	55%	5	692	3

Leading rushers	Attempts	Yards gained	Average	TDs
Cookie Gilchrist	252	954	3.8	6
Wendell Hayes	130	526	4.0	5
Abner Haynes	41	166	4.0	3
Bob Scarpitto	4	94	23.5	0

Leading receivers	Caught	Yards gained	Average	TDs
Lionel Taylor	85	1131	13.3	6
Bob Scarpitto	32	585	18.3	5
Abner Haynes	26	216	8.3	2
Hewritt Dixon	25	354	14.2	2
Wendell Hayes	24	294	12.3	2
Cookie Gilchrist	18	154	8.6	1

Leading scorers	TDs	XPM	XPA	FGM	FGA	PTs
Gary Kroner		32	32	13	29	71
Wendell Hayes	7	1				44
Cookie Gilchrist	7					42

30. In 1965 the AFL experimented with a new All-Star game format. What was different about this year's game?

■ HOUSTON OILERS ■

THE LEND-LEASE DEAL WITH DENVER, trading quarterback Jacky Lee for a two-year period and then returning him to Houston, continued to pay dividends for the Oilers. The deal brought Bud McFadin, one of the AFL's best run stoppers, and opened the backup QB spot to Baylor All-American Don Trull. Though he wasn't setting the league on fire, Lee gained valuable playing time he would not have gotten in Texas. The final payoff came

The Progress of the Seasons – 1965

when the Oilers used Denver's number-one draft pick that came along with the lease to secure Trull's All-American pass catching partner at Baylor, flanker Larry Elkins, the Southwest Conference's all-time leading receiver.

The Oilers headed into their sixth season with their fifth head coach, Hugh (Bones) Taylor. Taylor (a pass catching buddy of Baugh's while they were teammates with the Washington Redskins) was elevated to the position on December 22, 1964, four days after his boss, Sammy Baugh, stepped down. Baugh was now Taylor's backfield coach and after adding Lou Rymkus to oversee the offensive line, the Oilers had a coaching staff that included three of the five head coaches that walked the sidelines for Bud Adams. Taylor had his new team ready for opening day as the only AFL team to win all five of their exhibition games. But it was not without sacrifice. Lost for the season with injuries were rookie Larry Elkins and more critical, their 1964 rushing leader, Sid Blanks. George Blanda led the team, and at the age of thirty-eight continued to put up inspiring numbers like his league-high 442 aerials, 186 completions, 25 touchdown passes and longest strike of the year from scrimmage, a 95-yard TD to end Dick Compton. Blanda also led the AFL with 30 interceptions. Understudy Don Trull was used sparingly and struggled to find his form.

Houston continued to win through the first two weeks of 1965, including the inaugural game in their new home at Rice Stadium, a victory over the Jets, 27-21 which set an opening-day attendance record of 62,680 fans. Don Trull, relieving Blanda, threw 3 touchdown passes in the game. The next week it was Blanda's turn to connect for 3 scores with his new contingent of Oiler receivers in a 31-10 win over Boston. No longer was it Hennigan, Dewveall, and McLeod catching Blanda's throws. Flanker Charlie Frazier and third-year tight end Willie Frazier moved into the starring roles. The Willie half of the young Frazier combination was named to the all-league team. He had 38 receptions and set a new AFL record with 8 touchdown catches by a tight end. Charlie Hennigan came out of retirement before the season began, but knee problems limited him to 41 catches, a drop of 60 from his record-setting 101 of a year ago.

In the absence of Sid Blanks at halfback, Taylor inserted young Ode Burrell as fullback Charlie Tolar's running mate. Seizing the opportunity, the Mississippi State star became Houston's leading runner and pass receiver. He tallied 528 yards rushing and 55 receptions for 650 yards. Burrell was the only AFL player to crack the top ten in both running and

BUD McFADIN def. tackle

197

★ Charlie Tolar and George Blanda get instructions on the bench. ★

receiving in 1965.

After suffering three consecutive defeats to teams from the West, the Oilers got back on the winning track with a 38-36 heart-stopper against Kansas City. Blanda threw 5 touchdowns in the second half as the Oilers scored 28 points in the third quarter and 10 more in the fourth. The game-winning points came on

The Progress of the Seasons – 1965

an 18-yard field goal by former Chief Jack Spikes. They upset the defending champion Bills in similar fashion the next week, as Blanda made good on a game-winning 3-pointer from seven yards away, giving the Oilers another come-from-behind victory, 19-17. It was their last win of the season, finishing with a 4-10 record.

The defense gave up a league-high and team-record 429 points. More passes were thrown and completed against them than any other team, revealing their lack of both a respectable pass rush and effective pass coverage. Guard Bob Talamini joined tight end Willie Frazier as the only Houston players named to the all-league team.

Leading passers	Attempts	Completions	Pct	TDs	Yards	Int
George Blanda	442	186	41%	20	2542	30
Don Trull	107	38	36%	5	528	5

Leading rushers	Attempts	Yards gained	Average	TDs
Ode Burrell	130	528	4.1	3
Charlie Tolar	73	230	3.2	0
Jack Spikes	47	173	3.7	3
Don Trull	29	145	5.0	2

Leading receivers	Caught	Yards gained	Average	TDs
Ode Burrell	55	650	11.8	4
Charley Hennigan	41	578	14.1	4
Charlie Frazier	38	717	18.9	6
Willie Frazier	37	521	14.1	8
Charlie Tolar	25	138	5.5	0

Leading scorers	TDs	XPM	XPA	FGM	FGA	PTs
George Blanda		28	28	11	21	61
Willie Frazier	8					48

■ OAKLAND RAIDERS ■

AS THE RAIDERS PREPARED FOR THE new season, several rookies emerged as possible impact players. Cornerback Kent McCloughan from Nebraska played like a veteran on pass coverage, and flanker Fred Biletnikoff, the Florida State All-American, though lacking the speed of Olympian Bo Roberson, had a soft and sticky pair of hands that caught every ball that came his way. He started seven games after Roberson was traded to Buffalo and finished third on the team with 24 catches.

Head coach and general manager Al

Davis had Oakland primed to contend in his third season at the helm. An opening day win by 27 points over the Chiefs confirmed that the Raiders were a team to be taken seriously. But a second-week loss to the Chargers brought the Raiders quickly back to earth. The team evened their record with two closely contested games with differing results—a 21-17 win over Houston and a 17-13 loss to Buffalo. Then a 24-20 victory over Boston and a 24-24 tie with the Jets brought them to within a game and a half of the Chargers and a slim half game behind the Chiefs.

Halfback Clem Daniels again led the ground game, gaining 884 yards on 219 carries and again finished third in the league in rushing. Only Denver's Cookie Gilchrist carried the ball more often. Clem also caught 36 passes for second best on the team and his 7 catches for touchdowns gave him a total of 12 scores for the year. With his enormous talent and durability, he could run off tackle and around end, both left and right, as well as up the middle, averaging 4 yards per carry. Alan Miller, Roger Hagberg, and speedy Larry Todd alternated as his running mates and chipped in another 626 yards, making the Oakland running game the AFL's fourth best.

Another win over Boston put them in second place at 4-2-1, followed by a 14-7 loss to Kansas City, a 33-21 win over Houston, and another close loss, 17-14, to Buffalo. Through the first ten weeks the Raiders could not win two in a row, and their 5-4-1 record trailed division-leading San Diego. On week eleven the Raiders used 2 fourth-quarter interception returns for touchdowns—first by Gus Otto for 68 yards then by Dave Grayson for 42 yards—to break a 14-14 deadlock and overtake the Broncos 28-20. San Diego continued to set the pace with a 6-2-3 record; at 6-4-1 Oakland could still rise to the top of the division. After a bye week they finally put together back-to-back victories with another win over Denver on the season's second to last week. A 24-14 victory against the Jets moved them into second place with an 8-4-1 record.

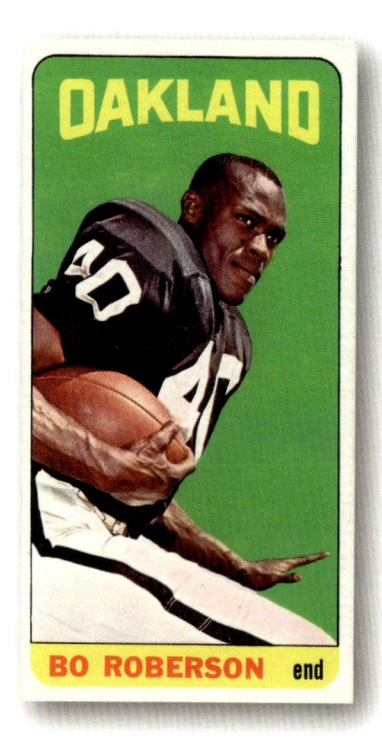

The Chargers also won on December 12, clinching the West, but the Raiders faced the champs in a season-ending home game. A win would seal the Raiders season at 9-4-1, but while a San Diego loss would end the Chargers season at 8-3-3, the Chargers would still win the West by percentage points. After the first thirty minutes the Raiders clung to a 14-7 lead, but the Chargers held them scoreless the rest of the way, winning the finale 24-14. The season ended for Oakland with an 8-5-1 record.

Split end Art Powell caught 52 passes

The Progress of the Seasons – 1965

(fifth best in the league) with 12 touchdowns (second best). A chronically sore back caused Billy Cannon to consider retirement, but he drew a new lease on his career with a move to tight end and also filled a team void, although he pulled down only seven passes. Cannon proved to be a deft run blocker and competent receiver despite being undersized for a blocking end. Rookie Fred Biletnikoff came along faster than anticipated and allowed Davis to trade starting flanker Bo Roberson to Buffalo at midseason, enabling Oakland to bolster their defense with tackle Tom Keating in return for the pass catcher. Tom Flores returned to his starting quarterback position and threw for 14 touchdowns and 1593 yards, but completed only 45.3 percent of his passes. His backup was Dick Wood, who added 8 touchdowns and completed 43 percent. The passing game finished at the bottom of the AFL statistically in '65 as Oakland continued to crave an impact passer.

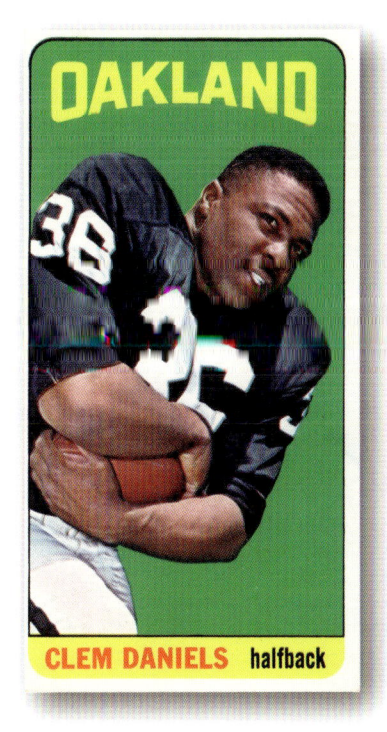

It was on defense that the Raiders began to demand attention. Emerging stars like Ben Davidson, Dan Conners, Gus Otto, and Dave Grayson supplied the framework for a unit that would become known in the years ahead as the "Eleven Angry Men." Ike Lassiter, Dave Costa, and Dan Birdwell were also part of the feared unit. The defense jumped from the bottom in 1964 in points allowed to third from the top, yielding 111 fewer points. Even the kicking game, long an Oakland weakness, improved with Mike Mercer booting 35 straight PATs and 9 of 15 field goals. He shared the kicking load after Bronco scoring champ Gene Mingo arrived. Mingo made good on 8 of his 19 field goal attempts. Art Powell, Jim Otto, and Dave Grayson earned spots on the all-league squad.

Leading passers	Attempts	Completions	Pct	TDs	Yards	Int
Tom Flores	269	122	45%	14	1593	11
Dick Wood	157	69	44%	8	1003	6

Leading rushers	Attempts	Yards gained	Average	TDs
Clem Daniels	219	884	4.0	5
Alan Miller	73	272	3.7	1
Larry Todd	32	183	5.7	0
Roger Hagberg	48	171	3.6	1

Remember the AFL

Leading receivers	Caught	Yards gained	Average	TDs		
Art Powell	52	800	15.4	12
Clem Daniels	36	568	15.8	7
Fred Biletnikoff	24	331	13.8	0
Alan Miller	21	208	9.9	3
Ken Herock	18	221	12.3	0
Bo Roberson	15	220	14.7	0

Leading scorers	TDs	XPM	XPA	FGM	FGA	PTs
Art Powell	12					72
Clem Daniels	12					72
Mike Mercer		35	35	9	15	62

---

31. The 1965 season marked a change in positions for Billy Cannon from halfback to tight end. Who was the Raider tight end he displaced as a starter?

■ KANSAS CITY CHIEFS ■

HANK STRAM WAS STEADILY BUILDING a team of goliaths, fielding offensive and defensive units that were bigger, stronger, and faster than anyone they played against. The offensive line consisted of guards Ed Budde, 6'5", 260 pounds, and Curt Merz 6'4", 250, tackles Dave Hill 6'5", 250, and Jim Tyrer 6'6", 292, and center Jon Gilliam, the little guy at 6'2", 245. On defense, the front four featured Buck Buchanan 6'7", 280 and Ed Lothamer 6'4", 250 at the tackles and ends Jerry Mays 6'4", 250 and Mel Branch 6'2", 250. Outside linebackers Bobby Bell and E.J. Holub both measured 6'4" and middleman Sherrill Headrick was 6'2". Add two and a half feet of raised arms on these pass rushers and it's easy to see why this group struck fear into the hearts of passers who stepped into the pocket.

The Chiefs started 1965 with an impressive 3-1-1 record, with the tie coming against the Chargers. With Abner Haynes now running in Denver, Stram relied on Mack Lee Hill, who filled the big shoes of injured Curtis McClinton last season. Now teamed with the Curtis, they made up the burliest backfield in the AFL. McClinton tipped the scale at 232 pounds and Hill at 225. Along with backup Bert Coan, they gave KC the best per-carry average in the league and rushed for third-best in yards. Finishing as the number five and six runners in the AFL, the "Mac Attack" was led by McClinton who picked up 661 yards followed by Hill who gained 627. Mack Lee's 5.02 yards per carry was the second best average in the AFL. Quarterback Len Dawson was again the most accurate AFL passer, completing 53 percent of this throws with a league-high 21 touchdowns. He was picked off only fourteen times all year. His favorite target this season, as in the past, was Chris

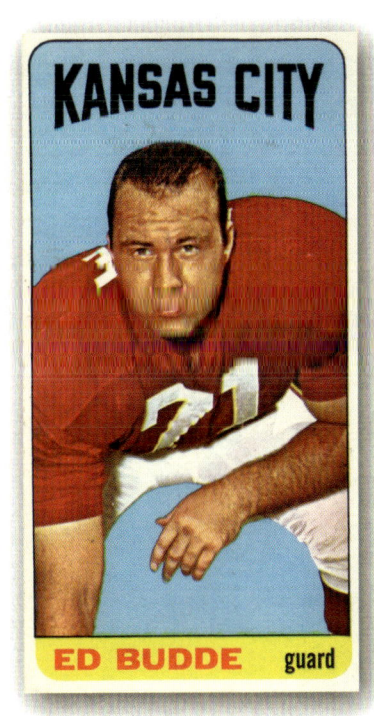

Burford, who caught 47 passes. Curtis McClinton was next highest on the team with 37 receptions but Frank Jackson dropped off from 62 catches in '64 to only 28. He shared his flanker spot with rookie Otis Taylor, who impressed people with his size, speed, and pass-catching ability. Taylor caught 26 passes for a team-high 17.2 yards per catch.

It was hard to imagine how the Chiefs offense, second only to San Diego in points scored with 322, was not able to light up every scoreboard on their schedule. But after their first three games they put up only 34 points combined against Oakland, New York, and the Chargers. Four more times during the season the Chiefs were unable to muster more than 2 touchdowns in a game. Yet, on five other occasions they topped the 30-point mark. Too often fumbles were the best defense against the Chiefs. They dropped the ball 24 times, losing 13 of them. In their second meeting with the Chargers, the Chiefs were in a must-win situation, and the defense provided the impetus to carry the team to victory, giving the high-octane San Diego offense only 7 points and leaving Dawson and his offense to do the rest. The 31-7 win put KC's record at 5-4-1 and handed the Chargers their second loss, dropping their mark to 6-2-2. In their two meetings against the AFL's best offense the Chief defense held San Diego to a total of 17 points. If Stram could somehow squeeze out wins in the final four games and the Chargers stumbled twice the Chiefs could capture to West. They were in a position to defeat Boston the next week if they could convert on a 30-yard field goal with less than a half minute to play. But Tommy Brooker's kick sailed wide, ending

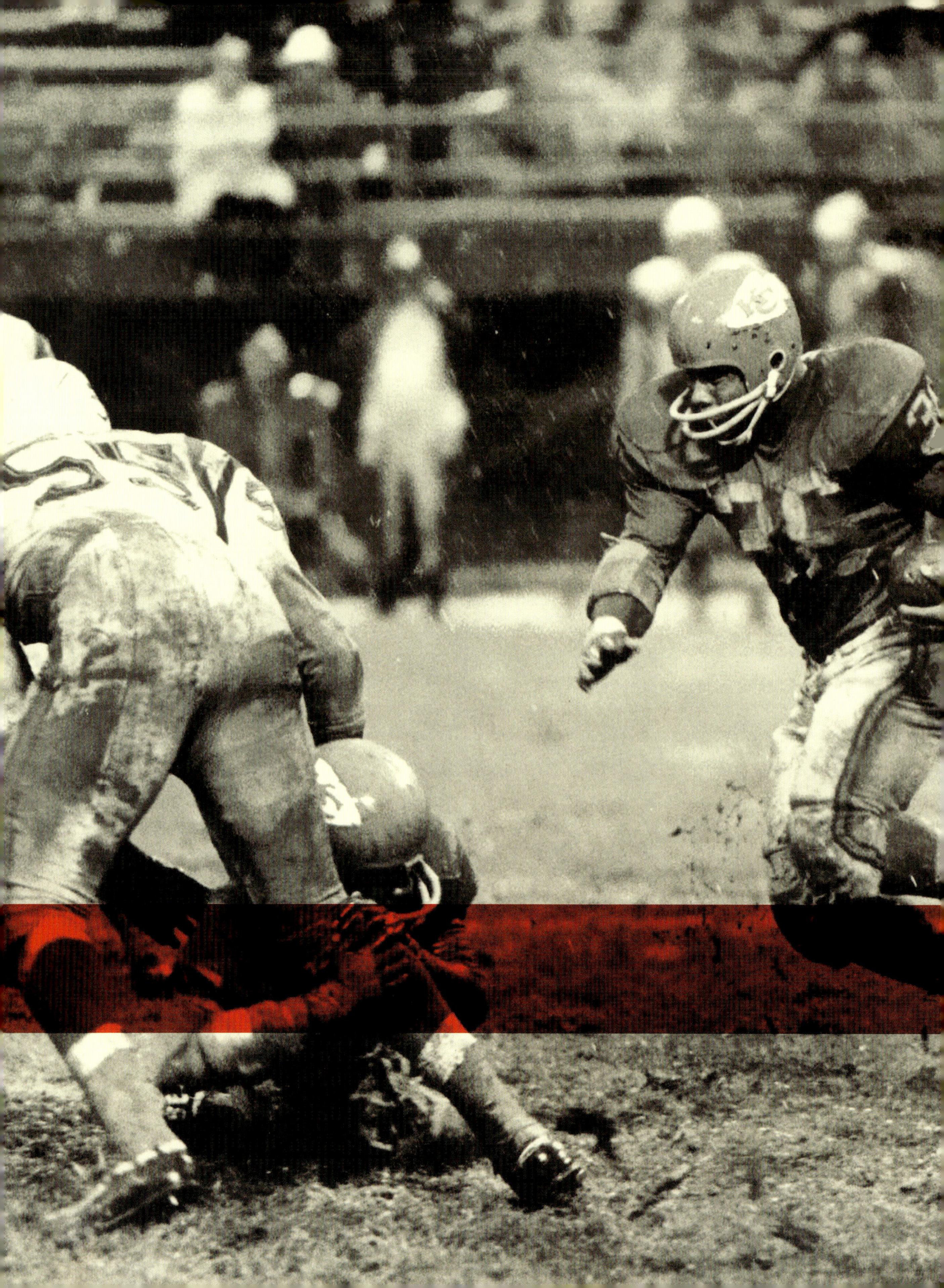

★ *The Chiefs' Mack Lee Hill in action against the Chargers.*

the game in a 10-10 tie and ending KC's hope for another division crown.

The defense was the league's second best in 1965, with a front seven second to none and an improving secondary. Fred Williamson came from Oakland to bolster the deep backs and team with Willie Mitchell, Bobby Hunt, and Johnny Robinson. The group intercepted 20 passes. KC was consistently inconsistent this year as they went through their schedule without ever winning or losing more than two games in a row, with both happening only once during the course of their fourteen games. They finished behind both San Diego and Oakland in the West for the second time in three years.

For the second time in four years they had to endure the death of a teammate when standout fullback Mack Lee Hill died from complications while undergoing knee surgery near the end of the season. The haunting episode took its toll on his devastated colleagues. Jim Tyrer, Bobby Bell, Jerry Mays, and Johnny Robinson were honored on the all-league first team at season's end.

Leading passers	Attempts	Completions	Pct	TDs	Yards	Int
Len Dawson	305	163	53%	21	2262	14
Pete Beathard	89	36	40%	1	632	6

Leading rushers	Attempts	Yards gained	Average	TDs
Curtis McClinton	175	661	3.8	6
Mack Lee Hill	125	627	5.0	2
Len Dawson	43	142	3.3	2
Bert Coan	45	137	3.0	1

Leading receivers	Caught	Yards gained	Average	TDs
Chris Burford	47	575	12.2	6
Curtis McClinton	37	590	15.9	3
Frank Jackson	28	440	15.7	1
Otis Taylor	26	446	17.2	5
Fred Arbanas	24	418	17.4	4
Mack Lee Hill	21	264	12.6	1

Leading scorers	TDs	XPM	XPA	FGM	FGA	PTs
Tommy Brooker		37	37	13	30	76
Curtis McClinton	9					54

32. In 1965 the Buffalo Bills won their division with a 10-3-1 record while the rest of the teams in East posted losing records. What is the only other year in which an AFL team won a division title while the rest of the teams in their division had losing records?

The Progress of the Seasons – 1965

• BOSTON PATRIOTS •

FOR FOUR CONSECUTIVE YEARS THE Patriots took championship hopes into the last weekend of the season. The strength of the squad was the strong, physical defense. The front four was led by all-league Larry Eisenhauer and all-star Bob Dee at end and all time AFL first-teamer Houston Antwine and Jim Hunt at tackle. Backing them up was an enviable group that included all-leaguers Tom Addison and Nick Buoniconti, assisted by Jack Rudolph. Together they yielded the second-fewest yards gained on the ground and kept the Patriots close nearly every week.

Babe Parilli, last year's top AFL quarterback, was protected by the top-notch line of Jon Morris at center, Billy Neighbors and Charlie Long at guard, with Tom Neville and Don Oakes at tackle. In 1965, Boston again had high hopes of bringing a title to Beantown, but both the offensive and defensive backfields needed up grades. The secondary of Ross O'Hanley, Ron Hall, Dick Felt, Don Webb, and Chuck Shonta gave up more passing yards than any other team last year, and the offensive duo of Larry Garron and Ron Burton was far from dynamic. To remedy their running woes, Boston drafted Jim Nance from Syracuse. Nance was a crushing, powerful fullback in the Cookie Gilchrist mold. Also on board and back from a four-year stint with the Navy was 1960 Heisman Trophy halfback Joe Bellino. Bellino was penciled in as a possible flanker while Nance's name was more indelibly etched as the battering-ram to drag would-be tacklers at least 3 yards every time he ran.

But the hope in New England soon turned to wonder and then fears, as the Pats lost to Buffalo, Houston, Denver, Kansas City, and Oakland in succession to start the season. The next week they managed to tie San Diego to post a record of 0-6-1. In their first seven games the Patriots failed to score more than 17 points on any afternoon. Their losing ways continued in Oakland before they were able to crack the win column on Halloween with a 22-6 victory over the previously unbeaten Chargers in San Diego. After losses to Buffalo and New York and a tie with Kansas City, the Pats stood at 1-8-2, by far the franchise's worst record to date. The running game, thought to be bolstered with Nance and Bellino, was still averaging less than 4 yards a carry. Nance battled his weight and consequently had quickness problems all year. While he

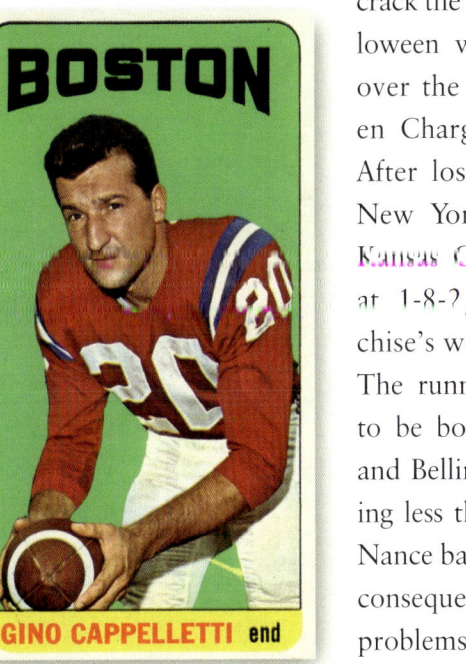

207

was the leading Boston rusher, he gained only 321 yards for a meager 2.9 per carry, the lowest average among AFL starting runners. Larry Garron was second on the team with 259 yards. Bellino failed to make an impact and carried the ball only 24 times for 49 yards and caught only 5 passes.

The defense, however, was still the most dominating in the league against the run, giving up less than 3 yards per carry. They also led the league with 37 quarterback sacks. The secondary, once the liability of the defense, mustered a league-low pass-completion percentage of 40.8 percent and ranked third in interceptions. The breakdown was clearly on offense. Babe Parilli sank to sixth in the league in passing and threw 26 interceptions to his 18 touchdowns. The only saving grace in the Patriots season was winning their final three games, highlighted by a game-winning field goal on November 28 in Shea Stadium by Gino Cappelletti. His game winner connected for a league-record 53 yards. The only uniform change that year was a single blue stripe added to the center of their helmet.

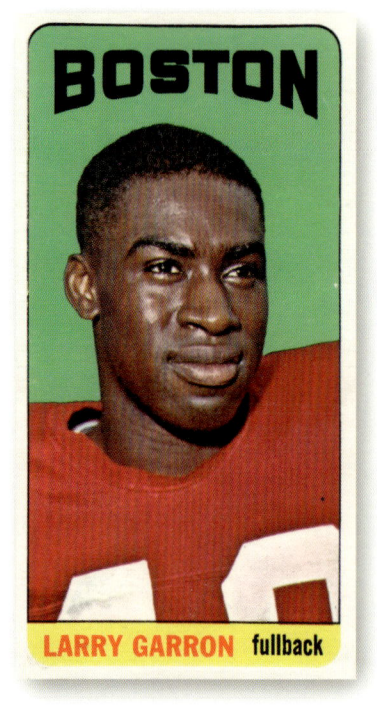

While their 1965 won-lost record was the worst in the team's history, bright spots did shine through. Nick Buoniconti was once again voted to the all-league team. Gino Cappelletti led the league in scoring for the third year in a row, and rookie Tommy Hennessey from Holy Cross was a standout in the secondary. Until suffering a knee injury in San Diego he was bringing raves about his play and talk of challenging for rookie-of-the-year honors. Another local rookie, tight end Jim Whalen out of Boston College, caught 22 passes and showed all-star potential. With the continued development of Nance and Whalen, the return from injury by Art Graham, and the ongoing dominance by the defensive unit there was reason for the Patriots to look forward, as they readied themselves to make a comeback in 1966.

Leading passers	Attempts	Completions	Pct	TDs	Yards	Int
Babe Parilli	426	173	41%	18	2597	26
Eddie Wilson	46	20	44%	1	257	3

Leading rushers	Attempts	Yards gained	Average	TDs
Jim Nance	111	321	2.9	5
Larry Garron	74	259	3.5	1
Babe Parilli	50	200	4.0	0
J.D. Garrett	42	147	3.5	1

The Progress of the Seasons – 1965

Leading receivers	Caught	Yards gained	Average	TDs
Jim Colclough	40	677	16.9	3
Gino Cappelletti	37	680	18.4	9
Art Graham	25	316	12.6	0
Jim Whalen	22	381	17.3	0
Tony Romeo	15	203	13.5	2
Larry Garron	15	222	14.8	1

Leading scorers	TDs	XPM	XPA	FGM	FGA	PTs
Gino Cappelletti	9	27	27	17	27	132
Jim Nance	5					30

■ SAN DIEGO CHARGERS ■

THE CHARGERS WERE NOT ONLY THE best offensive team in the AFL in 1965, they were also the best defensive team. They scored more points than everyone and gave up only one more than league-leader Buffalo. They had the best running game as well as the best passing game and also led the league in punt-return average, thanks to the fleet feet of Speedy Duncan, who averaged 15.5 yards per return and scored twice. Even new kicker Herb Travenio, a former U.S. postal worker, got into the act by hitting on 18 of his 30 field goal attempts for a 60 percent average. He also made good on all 40 of his PATs. Travenio was the league's third-highest scorer. On defense the Chargers big front four of Earl Faison, George Gross, Ernie Ladd, and Bob Petrich was one of tallest and widest in the AFL. The foursome picked up where they left off the year before, harassing passers into hurries and intimidating runners to head for the sidelines instead of turning up field. The linebackers were a steady group made up of former all-league middleman Chuck Allen, along with second team all-leaguer Frank Buncom, Emil Karas, and rookie Rick Redman. The secondary that posted the second-best interception total featured Dick Westmoreland and Jim Warren on the corners and the league's second-best pass intercepter, Bud Whitehead, and Kenny Graham at safety. This Charger eleven held the opposition to 14 or less points in eight of their fourteen games.

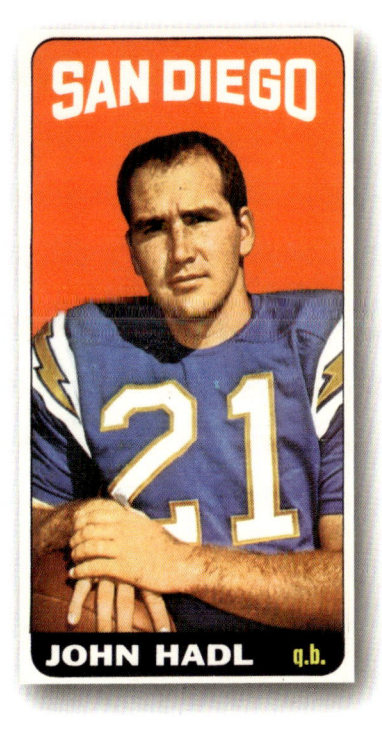

209

★ *Lance Alworth and Coach Sid Gillman on the Charger sideline* ★

But the Charger trademark has always been their lightning-bolt offense. And in 1965 it was never better, leading the league by averaging 24 points per game. The receiving corps that had been together for four years included Dave Kocourek with 28 receptions at tight end, Don Norton with 34 receptions at split end, and flanker Lance Alworth, the league's second-best pass catcher with 69. Alworth's 1,602 yards was the AFL's best, as were his 23.2 yards per catch and 14 touchdown receptions. Keith Lincoln was the team's best at coming out of the backfield with 23 catches. With the best set of pass receivers on hand for so many years it is easy to see why John Hadl settled into his position as the AFL's top passer. After being thrown to the wolves as a rookie in 1962, Hadl spent all of '63 and part of '64 being mentored by Tobin Rote. By 1965 Hadl was ready to take command. Hitting on 50 percent of his passes, he threw for a league-high 2,798 yards and 20 touchdowns. His 8.04 average gain was also the league best, as was his .816 quarterback rating. For the fifth time in six years and the third in a row the Chargers were masters of the Western Division. A credit to their GM and head coach, Sid Gillman.

With an opening day crowd of 27,022 at Balboa Stadium the Chargers needed every bit of offense they could muster to overtake the Denver Broncos, a team that always seemed to give San Diego fits. Paul Lowe, healthy again after a sub-par '64, shot to 122 yards on 18 carries. Keith Lincoln sat out with an injury

The Progress of the Seasons – 1965

while rookie Gene Foster teamed with Lowe for 49 yards. Hadl threw for 246 yards, and Lance Alworth caught 7 passes for an incredible 211 yards in the 34-31 barn-burner. Against Oakland in their second game, Gene Foster took the pressure off of Lowe by running for 104 yards. The Chargers won 17-6. A 10-10 tie with Kansas City was next, then a 31-14 win back in Balboa where Lowe ran for 157 yards on 20 tries. Alworth again eclipsed the century mark with 145 on only 4 receptions, catching two for 69- and 57-yard touchdowns. Hadl threw for 242 yards on the day.

Seeking revenge for their championship game loss to Buffalo, the Chargers returned to War Memorial Stadium and turned on the afterburners, winning 34-31. Hadl was outstanding while completing 18 of his 29 passes for 314 yards, with 168 of them going to Alworth and 107 to Don Norton. After tying Boston, they headed into Shea Stadium to play the Jets. While Paul Lowe went over 100 yards rushing for the third time in seven games (he also ran for 91 yards against Boston) and Alworth also eclipsed the century mark for the fifth time, the Charger defense held the Jets to three field goals.

After seven weeks the Chargers posted a 5-0-2 record. Their first loss came the next week against Boston, 22-6. Their only score came in the fourth quarter on a 1-yard run by Keith Lincoln. Another win against Denver was followed by the second loss of the season, this time at the hands of the Chiefs. In their win against Denver Hadl fired 3 touchdowns and Lowe again broke the century mark rushing. Against KC on November 14 the lightning offense lacked the necessary thunder to penetrate the Chiefs defense in a 31-7 drubbing. With four games left on the schedule, the Chargers led the West with a 6-2-2 record. Oakland and the Chiefs checked in at 5-4-1.

One of the main ingredients in the San Diego offense that year was the return of Paul Lowe to his high-stepping, breakaway form. Held to under 500 yards in 1964, mostly due to a sore leg, Lowe romped through the AFL at a record pace. As the leading rusher, Lowe set a new league mark with 1,121 yards gained and a league-best 5.05 yards per carry. His new record broke the previous high of 1,099 yards set in 1963 by Clem Daniels.

A tie on Thanksgiving Day with Buffalo, the destruction of New York (38-7), and a 37-26 win in a free-wheeling offensive display against the Oilers on December 12 gave the Chargers an 8-2-3 record (they finished 9-2-3 overall) and their third straight Western Division crown, setting up a rematch of the 1964 Championship game against Buffalo, to be played in San Diego the day after Christmas. It should have been the Chargers' second AFL Championship, as Buffalo was damaged severely, losing star receivers Elbert Dubenion and Glenn Bass early in the season and running without Cookie Gilchrist for the first time in four years. The Bills still had one of the league's strongest defenses, but the AFL's best offense and defense should have put the game away by the middle of the third quarter. Instead, what viewers saw from sunny southern California that day was a frustrated Charger team and a confused John Hadl. The Chargers could muster only 12 first downs and gained only 223 yards in the game. It was a Las Vegas bookmaker's dream, as the Chargers, heavy favorites before the game, were shutout 23-0 and lost their fourth AFL Championship game in five tries. It was the last time they would make it so far for the rest of their AFL years.

Leading passers	Attempts	Completions	Pct	TDs	Yards	Int
John Hadl	348	174	50%	20	2798	21
Don Breaux	43	22	51%	2	404	4

Leading rushers	Attempts	Yards gained	Average	TDs
Paul Lowe	222	1121	5.0	7
Gene Foster	121	469	3.9	2
Keith Lincoln	74	302	4.1	3
Jim Allison	29	100	3.4	0

Leading receivers	Caught	Yards gained	Average	TDs
Lance Alworth	69	1602	23.2	14
Don Norton	34	485	14.3	2
Dave Kocourek	28	363	13.0	2
Keith Lincoln	23	376	16.3	4
Paul Lowe	17	126	7.4	1
Gene Foster	17	199	11.7	0

Leading scorers	TDs	XPM	XPA	FGM	FGA	PTs
Herb Trevenio		40	40	18	30	94
Lance Alworth	14					84

---

33. In the AFL's six years the Chargers signed seven first-round draft choices. Which one of the following is NOT one of the seven?
1. Lance Alworth
2. John Hadl
3. Ron Mix
4. Keith Lincoln
5. Rufus Guthrie
6. Steve De Long
7. Earl Fasion
8. Walt Sweeney

The Progress of the Seasons – 1965

■ BUFFALO BILLS ■

COMING OFF OF THEIR FIRST AFL Championship season the Bills appeared ready to become just the second AFL team to repeat. But after three years of tolerating the eccentricities of all-star fullback Cookie Gilchrist, the honeymoon with Lou Saban was over. Miffed at Gilchrist's constant need to have a separate set of rules for himself, Saban sent him packing to Denver for 1963 Rookie of the Year fullback Billy Joe. Joe limped through a foot injury and a sophomore slump in '64 but lost twenty pounds and was raring to bolt through the huge holes the Buffalo line could open for him. With returning starters at every position, the Bills were now the standard for excellence in the AFL and had an offense and defense superior to many teams in the NFL.

Their hopes to repeat were dimmed when flanker Elbert Dubenion and split end Glenn Bass were both injured in the first four games and lost for the season. They were the second- and third-leading receivers in the league at the time, and Kemp was the league's number one passer. Only Charley Ferguson remained as a deep threat. Owner Ralph Wilson's favorable relationship with Oakland (he was a stockholder) may have enabled Buffalo to acquire flanker Bo Roberson to fill in for Duby and take some pressure away from Ferguson and rookie tight end Paul Costa. But the passing game that had been second best in '64 fell off to second last in '65. The injuries also affected the running game, which was already below Buffalo standards without Gilcrhist. The team that was second in rushing in '63 and first in '64 with Cookie, dropped to sixth without him. Although he had big-time potential, Joe still suffered from a sore foot and averaged only 3.1 yards per carry. Back from two injury-riddled seasons, Wray Carlton was the Bills most efficient runner, leading the team with 592 yards and also catching 24 passes. With adversity surrounding their offense, Kemp stepped up his game in every category. His passed more consistently and was relieved by Lamonica less and less, finishing the season ranked third among AFL quarterbacks. His leadership, play selection, and will to win earned him the AFL's Player of the Year award.

The Bills shot to the top of the East in the season's first week and were never challenged after that. Their 10-3-1 record far out distanced New York's 5-8-1 second-place record. They topped the league in fewest points allowed for the second straight year and posted more points than all but two others. Starting the season with four straight wins over Boston, Denver, New York, and Oakland, the Bills averaged 26 points per game while giving up less than 2 touchdowns per outing. In defeating Denver, the Bills held former teammate Gilchrist to 2.2 yards per carry. In round one of their grudge match, Joe walked off with the bragging rights.

Their first setback came on October 10

213

at the hands of the Chargers, 34-3. But they won 23-7 the following week in Kansas City. A 19-17 loss to Houston put their record at 6-2. But two more wins over Boston and Oakland and a tie in their rematch with San Diego kept them on top of the East with an 8-2-1 record. By November the Bills already had enough wins to clinch the division title. Boston, winless in their first seven games, was never a factor, and the Jets, winless in their first six, were busy grooming Broadway Joe for the future. Houston looked like they might challenge but fell to 4-6 and were in the process of losing their last seven games in a row. Even with the absence of Gilchrist and a formidable passing attack, the Bills ball-control offense and dominating defense gave them more than enough to run away from the rest of the East.

When the offense occasionally stalled, they always had their ace in the hole, soccer-style kicker Pete Gogolak, whose range far exceeded his counterparts throughout the league. The Bills called on him 46 times, and 28 times his kicks registered 3 points. He also converted on all of his PATs. Only Boston's Gino Cappelletti, by virtue of his 9 touchdown catches, outscored Gogo.

When the December 26 Championship game arrived, the Bills, with more than their share of injuries on both sides of the ball, limped into San Diego as the defending champions but also as underdogs to the Chargers. San Diego featured superstars at most of the skill positions and ranked first in both rushing and passing offense and total defense. The Bills boasted the second-best defense against the rush. It was a rematch of the 1964 Championship game, only this time the Bills were at less than full strength, just as the Chargers were the year before. Buffalo's lineup included all-league guard Billy Shaw and all-league defenders Tom Sestak, Mike Stratton, Butch Byrd, and George Saimes.

In contrast to the 1964 championship game that was played in freezing weather on a muddy field, the conditions in sunny San Diego in 1965 were nearly perfect—a dry and balmy 59 degrees. It didn't take long for Buffalo's gloomy fortunes to worsen as Billy Shaw was injured on the opening kickoff and lost for the game. Split end Charley Ferguson was also out, lost a week earlier in the final game against the Jets.

To stop the Chargers, Lou Saban set up a double-team coverage on all-league flanker Lance Alworth and assigned safety George Saimes more jamming duties in the middle of the defense. He also sent Saimes on well-concealed safety blitzes. On offense, with the absence of Ferguson, Saban installed a double tight end formation, giving Kemp a little more time to throw while bulking up the blocking for his ground game. Knowing they had to keep the San Diego offense off the scoreboard, the Bills planned to control the ball. Kemp threw only 19 times, completing 8 for 155 yards. The Bills ran 34 times, with Carlton and Joe handling it 18 and 16 times respectively, for a combined 98 yards.

Five minutes into the second quarter with the game still scoreless, Kemp spotted Ernie

The Progress of the Seasons – 1965

★ *Bills quarterback Jack Kemp hands the ball off to Bobby Smith.* ★

Warlick ahead of cornerback Leslie Duncan near the end zone and hit the tight end with an 18-yard touchdown pass. Warlick, who caught only 8 passes during the season, caught 3 passes on the day. The San Diego offense failed to mount a drive on their next possession, and punter John Hadl booted the ball to the Bills.

As Butch Byrd fielded the punt at the Buffalo 26, he got a quick block from Ed Rutkowski that sprung him down the right sideline and off he went for a 74-yard touchdown, giving Buffalo a 14-0 halftime lead.

The San Diego crowd, as well as most TV viewers, were stunned by the Chargers inability to crack the Bills defense. So daunting was the Buffalo unit that Hadl and company did not penetrate beyond the Buffalo 24 yard line for the entire game. The irresistible force was being stopped by the immovable object. San Diego's frustrations continued in the second half. Buffalo's three-man rush allowed them more pass coverage, and the blitzing Saimes kept Hadl on edge and added to his confusion in picking out his receivers. The rest of the day's scoring came compliments of Pete Gogolak. The Hungarian kicker booted field goals of 11, 39, and 32 yards and enabled the Bills to celebrate their second consecutive AFL Championship over the San Diego Chargers, 23-0.

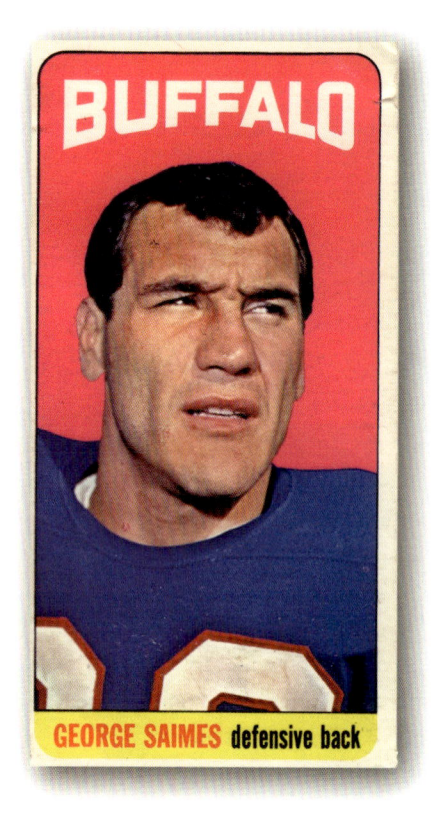

One week after the victory, the team was stunned when Lou Saban, the AFL's Coach of the Year for the second consecutive season, resigned to take the head coaching job at the University of Maryland. The Bills named their thirty-four-year-old defensive coordinator Joel Collier as Saban's successor. Then kicker Pete Gogolak decided to play out his option with the Bills and signed a contract with the NFL's New York Giants. By jumping to the rival league, Gogolak set off a raiding war on team rosters between the two leagues and proved to be the main catalyst that would eventually force a truce and ultimately a merger.

The Progress of the Seasons – 1965

Leading passers	Attempts	Completions	Pct	TDs	Yards	Int
Jack Kemp	391	179	46%	10	2368	18
Daryle Lamonica	70	29	41%	3	376	6

Leading rushers	Attempts	Yards gained	Average	TDs
Wray Carlton	156	592	3.8	6
Billy Joe	213	377	3.1	4
Bobby Smith	43	132	3.1	1
Donnie Stone	19	61	3.2	0

Leading receivers	Caught	Yards gained	Average	TDs
Bo Roberson	31	483	15.6	3
Billy Joe	27	271	10.0	2
Wray Carlton	24	196	8.2	1
Paul Costa	21	401	19.1	0
Charley Ferguson	21	262	12.5	2
Glenn Bass	18	299	16.6	1
Elbert Dubenion	18	281	15.6	1
Ed Rutkowski	18	247	13.7	1

Leading scorers	TDs	XPM	XPA	FGM	FGA	PTs
Pete Gogolak		31	31	28	46	115
Wray Carlton	7					42

★ ★ ★ ★ ★ ★ ★ ★ ★ ★ ★ ★

The All-Star Game was played in Houston's Rice Stadium on January 15, 1966, and matched the recently crowned AFL Champion Buffalo Bills against all-stars from the rest of the American Football League. The new format, predicated in part by the Western Division winning all four previous games, was a unique twist to the annual gala in hope of reviving interest in the game.

The Bills drew their sword first, when safety George Saimes ran 64 yards for a score after recovering a fumble in the first quarter. Both teams added a pair of field goals in the first thirty minutes as the Bills held a 13-6 half-time lead. The only rookie selected to the all-star team was New York Jet Joe Namath, who took over as quarterback in the third quarter and engineered 4 scoring drives, throwing 3 touchdown passes, 2 to Lance Alworth. The first-year phenom ran away with the game's MVP award by leading the All-Stars to a 30-19 win over the repeat champions.

By the end of 1965 the AFL had closed the gap to respectability by becoming more competitive in their pursuit of players coming out of college. But they continued to draw criticism from NFL followers. The writers who covered the senior league and fancied themselves football purists, staunchly held to the premise that football needed to be played in the trenches with players running the football over and through opponents, testing their grit and mettle. The pass was used largely to keep defenses honest or to mount a desperate comeback.

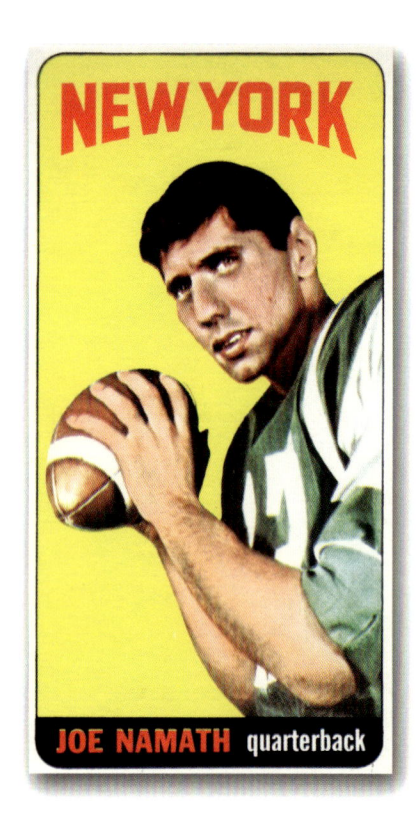

The AFL focused on passing in their maiden season, but despite the immediate criticism about too much passing, AFL teams were passing four times more after six years. In 1960 the league averaged 66 passes per game and 65.3 running plays. In all, there were 3,699 throws and 3,657 rushes. Every AFL team threw at least 400 passes, ranging from a high of 508 by Denver to a low of 435 by Dallas. Running plays ranged from a low of 402 by Boston to a high of 483 by Dallas. By comparison, in 1960 NFL games averaged 52.7 passes per game against 65.2 running plays, with six of the thirteen teams passing more often than they ran. Baltimore set the pace with 392 passes with Cleveland throwing a league-low 264 times. The St. Louis Cardinals ran a league-high 484 times while the first-year Dallas Cowboys ran a league-low 312 times for an average of 26 per game. No AFL team averaged less than 28 runs per game, and they did not pass less than 31 times per game.

In 1961 the number of passes per game in the AFL dropped slightly to 64.8 for a league total of 3,630 passes for the year compared to 1960's 3,699. The number of rushes per game fell to 57.4 with a league total of 3,218 running plays, a drop of 439 runs. The NFL in 1961 averaged 54 passes and 62.3 runs per game.

The Progress of the Seasons – 1965

With the arrival of Cookie Gilchrist from the CFL in 1962, but in the absence of Paul Lowe (injured for the entire season), the AFL found the number of passes drop to 3,456, averaging 61.7 per game while the number of running plays rose to 3,285 for an average of 58.6 per game. The NFL ran the ball 61.8 times per game against 54.6 passes. Even in 1963, the NFL maintained the status quo, averaging 62.3 runs and 55.2 passes per game. The 1963 AFL numbers were almost identical, but reversed, averaging 54.8 runs and 63.2 passing plays per game, with the eight AFL teams totaling nearly 100 more passes (3,540) in '63 over '62. Running attempts dropped off by over 200, to 3,074. The lowest total over the league's four years. Through the 1963 season the number of offensive plays per game dropped from 65.6 the first year, to fifty-nine offensive plays per game in the fourth year. In 1964 the league's total number of passing plays reached an all-time high of 3,750, an average of 66.9 throws per game, and the total number of rushing attempts rose also, increasing by 39 over last season to 3,113 but showing a drop of over 500 carries from the 1960 total. In their first season the AFL averaged 65 runs per game; the 1964 average dropped to 55.5 per contest. And for the first time ever, the '64 season saw two teams put up more than 500 passes, with Houston setting the league record of 592.

The arrival of Joe Namath to New York in 1965 did not have any significant impact on the league's passing statistics his first year. Teams passed 3,652 times, an average of 65.2 per game and ran the football 3,203 times, 90 more times than in '64 and averaging 57.1 runs per game. By contrast, the NFL in 1965 was still throwing only a scratch over 50 times while running plays still averaged in the low 60s—the same as six years earlier. The AFL was rapidly coming into its own and the $36 million, five-year television contract signed with NBC confirmed that the six-year-old league had truly arrived with the fans and could compete with the NFL for revenue, players, and—in the minds of most AFL believers—on the field. With football fans across the country tuning in to the AFL's Sunday doubleheader each week in record numbers, the voice of the fans was being heard. The AFL and its passion for passing was anything but second rate and was definitely here to stay!

★ ★ ★ ★ ★ ★ ★ ★ ★ ★

★ *Merger*

It was called a *merger*, but in fact it was more of a truce, and it called for the AFL to fork over $18 million for the privilege of joining the National Football League. As a result, both league's agreed to a cease-fire on raids of each other's rosters. The sudden interest by Dallas owner Tex Schramm and the other NFL owners was a direct result of the AFL's bullish new commissioner, Al Davis, declaring a war on the NFL and encouraging his AFL owners to sign as many players away from the NFL as possible.

The uproar began when the NFL's New York Giants broke an unwritten agreement between the leagues and signed Buffalo kicker **Pete Gogolak**. Davis immediately began contacting NFL players who were close to their option year, singing the praises of the AFL. The realization that many players could jump leagues for exorbitant amounts of money caused everyone (except the players) concern, but the situation was more unsettling to the tight-fisted NFL owners than to the new breed in the AFL. High-profile NFL names like Roman Gabriel and John Brodie were surfacing as possible renegades to jump to the AFL. All-NFL tight end Mike Ditka of the Bears planned to do the same. Each week brought more new names as potential transfer prospects, and before long the AFL had eight NFL quarterbacks under agreement to jump leagues. Seeing no end and no easy solution to these raids on their rosters, Schramm called AFL patriarch Lamar Hunt and scheduled a meeting to call a truce and talk about merging the two leagues.

The merger, signed on June 8, 1966, also specified that the two leagues would play a season-ending championship game against each other after the NFL and AFL Championships, starting in 1966. A common college draft would follow. The two leagues would then begin playing each other during the exhibition season in 1967. Regular season games against each other were scheduled to start in 1970 when the newly signed AFL television contract expired. His mission accomplished, Davis resigned as commissioner of the AFL after only four months in the position and moved back to Oakland. Milt Woodard headed the AFL until the NFL's Pete Rozelle would take command in 1970.

★ ★ ★ ★ ★ ★ ★

1966

AMERICAN FOOTBALL LEAGUE – 1966 FINAL STANDINGS

EASTERN DIVISION

TEAM	GP	W	L	T	PF	PA	PCT.
BUFFALO BILLS	14	9	4	1	358	255	0.679
BOSTON PATRIOTS	14	8	4	2	315	283	0.643
NEW YORK JETS	14	6	6	2	322	312	0.500
HOUSTON OILERS	14	3	11	0	335	396	0.214
MIAMI DOLPHINS	14	3	11	0	213	362	0.214

WESTERN DIVISION

TEAM	GP	W	L	T	PF	PA	PCT.
KANSAS CITY CHIEFS	14	11	2	1	448	276	0.821
OAKLAND RAIDERS	14	8	5	1	315	288	0.607
SAN DIEGO CHARGERS	14	7	6	1	335	284	0.536
DENVER BRONCOS	14	4	10	0	196	381	0.286

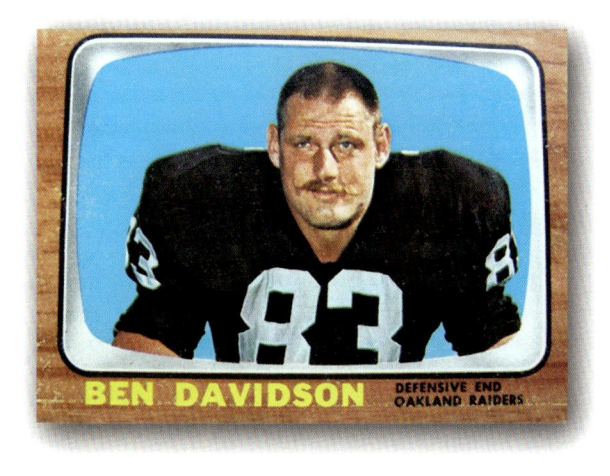

Ben Davidson was every team's nemesis. With his 6'8" frame and vulture-like wing span he epitomized the guts-and-glory, rough-and-tumble (and, some felt, occasionally dirty) style of play of the Oakland defense in the last few years of the AFL. Examples of his notorious style include a play in 1966 when he leap-frogged a standing pass blocker while rushing Denver quarterback Max Choboian, and the time in Oakland when he literally tore Joe Namath's helmet off his head with a vicious forearm hit. His sinister Snidely Whiplash handlebar mustache became as much a trademark to his persona as Namath's white shoes were to his Broadway Joe image. Both added to the identity and color of the league.

■ MIAMI DOLPHINS ■

THE FIRST EXPANSION TEAM IN THE American Football League joined in 1966 as the Miami Dolphins, owned by Minneapolis attorney Joe Robbie and entertainer Danny Thomas. The Dolphins played their home games in Miami's Orange Bowl, fully equipped with a swimming pool in one end zone that was occupied by a TV celebrity dolphin named Flipper, who retrieved and tossed out extra-point kicks and field goals that landed in his domain. Stocked with an interesting set of veterans and blue-chip rookies, the first-year fish were coached by former Detroit Lion head man George Wilson. Veteran and star names like Dick Westmoreland, Jim Warren, and Dave Kocourek, were curiously set free by the Chargers. Kansas City contributed Frank Jackson and aging all-star Mel Branch. Houston grudgingly parted with young guard Norm Evans, and the champion Buffalo Bills let fullback Billy Joe and flanker Bo Roberson move south. Other notable draft names found on the first Dolphins roster were Wahoo McDaniel from the Jets, Ed Cooke and Tom Nomina from Denver, and Dick Wood and Gene Mingo from Oakland, creating a pretty competent group of starters.

With youth also needing to be served, Miami filled many of their open slots with college stars like Howard Twilley, the all-time collegiate pass-receiving champ from Tulsa, lightning-fast flanker John Roderick from SMU, hard-hitting linebacker Frank Emanuel from Tennessee, and All-American quarterback Rick Norton from Kentucky. One intriguing name that popped up on the roster as well was punter/quarterback George Wilson Jr., the coach's son. The Dolphins, like many other new teams, were named through a contest that attracted several thousand entries. Settling on the name Dolphins, Miami players were outfitted in white helmets with aqua marine and orange stripes down the center. A dolphin diving through a hooped image of the sun appeared on each side of the helmet. Their home jerseys were aqua with alternating white and orange sleeve stripes with white pants and aqua socks. The newly formed Miami team exuded a tropical look from head to toe.

As if on cue on September 2, Miami's Joe Auer fielded the opening kickoff of their first regular season game against Oakland and took it coast to coast for a 95-yard touchdown. In the second, third, and fourth quarters Miami was not as fortunate, but turned some heads in their loss to the Raiders 23-14. To start the season, coach Wilson tapped Rick Norton to direct his offense, backed up by Dick Wood and then George Jr. All three saw plenty of snaps over the first several weeks. The steady play of halfback Joe Auer, their leading ball carrier with 416 yards, gave Miami a reliable runner and receiver, but

The Progress of the Seasons – 1966

throughout the year Wilson was never able to provide him with a capable backfield mate. First it was NFL castoff Rick Casares, then Billy Joe, rookies Sam Price and George Chesser followed, and finally that master of disaster himself, Carlton "Cookie" Gilchrist, the best running and blocking back in the AFL (when he wanted to be). In 1966, he didn't want to be. Their best receiver was tight end Dave Kocourek, an all-star from San Diego, although his team-leading 27 catches was nothing to write home about. Roberson, Auer, Jackson, Twilley, Gilchrist, Joe, and Roderick all caught a few and dropped a few, but when your leading quarterback completes only 36 percent of his passes, there are a lot of uncatchable balls being thrown.

The Dolphin defense was able to keep the opposition relatively close in most games, with their strength coming from a backfield of proven starters. Westmoreland and Warren were better than average, having started at cornerback on San Diego's divisional-champion team. Willie West (Jets), John McGeever (Broncos) and Pete Jaquess (Oilers) were equally strong at the safeties. The Dolphin ball hawks were the second-best group in the AFL at intercepting passes in year one, hauling down 31 and returning a league-high 4 of them for touchdowns. West, the team MVP, led the group with 8 interceptions. Though past their prime, defensive ends Mel Branch and Ed Cooke had the experience to keep the line competitive. The kicking game, as could be expected, finished last in the AFL, and although veteran Gene Mingo did make all 23 of his PATs, he hit only 10 of his 22 field goal tries. Punter George Wilson Jr. finished in the middle of the pack with a 42.1 average.

It wasn't until their sixth game, on October 16, that the Dolphins were able to feel their first taste of victory as a franchise. And who more fitting to be behind center when it happened than the coach's son? Against Denver, a first-quarter touchdown pass from George Jr. to Billy Joe and 2 second-half touchdown runs by Joe Auer put 24 points on the board for Miami. The defense did the rest, holding the Broncos to a single touchdown while giving the 23,393 Dolphin fans in attendance a taste of winning a professional football game for the first time. A week later they were able to duplicate the feat by knocking off the Houston Oilers in Texas by the score of 20-13. For their second victory, Rick Norton led the way, and one of those he led was the Dolphins' new fullback Cookie Gilchrist, purchased from Denver for whom he had refused to sign. Following the two victories, Miami endured six losses, until the season's last game, when they brought home their third win. To gain the 29-28 victory on the final week, the Dolphins had to score 2 touchdowns in the fourth quarter, the last one with only thirty-eight seconds left, to overtake the feisty Oilers. Were it not for a 2-point conversion after their touchdown in the second quarter, win number three may have escaped. Engineering their last win was the fourth and statistically the best quarterback to lead Miami in 1966. John Stofa completed 22 of 38 passes for 307 yards against the Oilers, with 4 touchdown passes.

In his short cameo, Stofa completed 50 percent of his 57 passes with all 4 touchdowns coming in the December 18 win against Houston. No other Miami QB was able to complete more than 41 percent of their passes. Finishing with a 3-11 record, the Dolphins produced an exciting season for an expansion team. With plenty of building yet to come, Miami was off and running, and proud to be part of the AFL's history as its first new addition.

Leading passers	Attempts	Completions	Pct	TDs	Yards	Int
Dick Wood	230	83	36%	4	993	14
George Wilson	112	46	41%	5	764	10
John Stofa	57	29	51%	4	425	2
Rick Norton	55	21	38%	3	192	6

Leading rushers	Attempts	Yards gained	Average	TDs
Joe Auer	121	416	3.4	4
Cookie Gilchrist	72	262	3.6	0
Billy Joe	71	232	3.3	0
George Wilson	27	137	5.1	0
Rick Casares	43	135	3.1	0
Sam Price	31	107	3.5	0

Leading receivers	Caught	Yards gained	Average	TDs
Dave Kocourek	27	320	11.9	2
Bo Roberson	26	519	20.0	3
Joe Auer	22	263	12.0	4
Karl Noonan	17	224	13.2	1
Frank Jackson	16	317	19.8	2
Cookie Gilchrist	13	110	8.5	1
Billy Joe	13	116	8.9	1

Leading scorers	TDs	XPM	XPA	FGM	FGA	PTs
Joe Auer	9					54
Gene Mingo		23	23	10	22	53

■ SAN DIEGO CHARGERS ■

THE CHARGERS ENTERED 1966 WITH the same offensive firepower that won the previous 3 Western Division titles. And with names like Hadl, Alworth, Lincoln, Lowe, Mix, and Sweeney, there was no reason to think a changing of the guard would happen this season. Sid Gillman made a few changes to shake up the troops, causing some folks to question letting two offensive and three defensive starters relocate in Miami through expansion. He also let another defensive stalwart play out his option. Along with tight end Dave Kocourek and guard Ernie Park, cornerbacks Dick Westmoreland and Jim Warren went to Miami. Later in the year, all-star defensive end Earl Faison joined them. Gone, too, was moody but menacing defensive tackle Ernie Ladd, who no longer played with the intensity that once made him the most feared defensive lineman in the AFL. After Ladd played out his option and signed with Houston, all-league tight end Willie Frazier was awarded to the Chargers as compensation. A change also came to the Chargers uniform in 1966. The lightning bolt on their helmet switched from gold, back to navy blue, and their pants were now gold instead of white. The lightning stripe on their pants was dropped for a plain alternating blue-white-blue stripe.

Gillman hoped he could replace at least one of his two former all-league behemoths on the front four with Outland Trophy winner Steve DeLong from Tennessee. George Gross and Bob Petrich were hold-over defensive line starters with second-year Howard Kindig filling the other end spot with moderate success. Kick return specialist Leslie Duncan and partner Miller Farr, who came from Denver, took over the vacated cornerback positions to team with all-league strong safety Kenny Graham and free safety Bud Whitehead. Duncan was also the AFL's best punt returner with a 13.2 average. The kicking was another area of change in San Diego. After stints with Ben Agajanian, George Blair, Keith Lincoln and Herb Travenio over the years, a new toe came to town. Dick Van Raaphorst handled all of San Diego's place kicking, making 39 of 40 conversion attempts and 16 of his 31 field goal tries. His 87 points placed him sixth among the league scoring leaders.

Before the opening game against the Bills, San Diego went through the pregame workout in Balboa Stadium when long-time split end Don Norton pulled up lame, forcing the Chargers to insert San Diego State rookie Gary Garrison in his place. Not only did the Chargers avenge their shutout loss to the Bills 27-7, they also discovered a new offensive star. Using the opportunity of his unexpected debut, Garrison caught 2 passes for 47 yards, and John Hadl picked up where he left off (as the AFL's top-rated passer in '65), completing 14 of 18 passes for 169 yards. Speedy Duncan closed out the San Diego scoring when he returned a Paul Maquire punt for an 81-yard touchdown in the fourth quarter. Hadl went on to have another strong season, finishing second in the league in passing and completing 53 percent of his throws for 23 touchdowns against only 14 interceptions. After upsetting Buffalo, they played host to the Patriots and

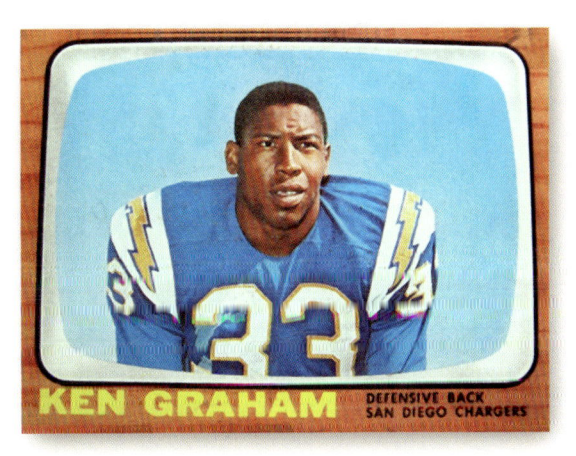

★ John Hadl commands the Charger huddle. ★

shut them out 24-0. Although the game was statistically even, 4 Babe Parilli interceptions proved catastrophic for Boston. Strong safety Kenny Graham returned one of them 32 yards for a touchdown in the second quarter.

On September 25 the Chargers made their first visit to Oakland-Alameda County Coliseum, the new home of the Raiders, and whipped their upstate rivals 29-20, building a 3-0 record. A fourth straight victory, against the upstart Dolphins in Balboa Stadium, placed them at the top of the West. The victory was led by second-year quarterback Steve Tensi, who relieved a temporarily ineffective Hadl in the second half after trailing 10-6. Tensi completed 9 of his 12 passes for 223 yards and 4 touchdowns, 3 coming in the fourth quarter. The revamped defense dug in for the final thirty minutes, shutting down Miami and prevailing 44-10.

It looked like business as usual for San Diego through their first four games. Against the Jets in New York on October 8, however, the Chargers started a streak that would spell their downfall for the rest of the season. A missed 21-yard field goal on the game's last play led to a 17-16 loss. That was followed by a 17-17 tie with the Bills and a 35-17 loss in Boston, even as Hadl threw for 289 yards and Alworth caught 6 passes for 177 yards. The losses sparked concern in Southern California about the lack of explosiveness on offense and the inability to stop the run on defense. The loss of Faison (after three games) and Ladd was taking its toll. In the past, the big front line kept pressure on the passer, which kept pressure off the rest of the defense, but the biggest difference was against the run, where the Chargers were giving up an average of 171 yards per game. Opponents piled up over 2,400 yards for the year and scored 19 touchdowns on the ground.

Getting back on track against Denver with a 24-17 triumph kept the Chargers close to the top, but the Chiefs looked stronger each week and sat at 6-2. A visit to Municipal Stadium to play the division leaders on November 6 ended with San Diego's 24-14 defeat, and when they lost their fourth game in five weeks to the Raiders, 41-19, the Chargers found themselves looking up in the standings at both KC and Oakland. The fall continued after a bye week with a loss to the Broncos 20-17, dropping them to .500 with a 5-5-1 record, three games behind the Chiefs with three to play. The once dynamic duo of Paul Lowe and Keith Lincoln rarely posed a threat anymore. Injured early in the year, Lincoln grew irritated with his diminished role in the offensive game plan. Lowe's performance varied week to week. The once balanced attack took to the air, becoming more and more unbalanced. Hadl and Tensi threw 434 times in 1966, while calling only 361 runs. The Chargers scored 29 touchdowns through the air and only 9 on the ground.

Receivers Garrison, Alworth, Jacque MacKinnon, and Willie Frazier established themselves as the best group in the league.

Alworth led the league in catches (73), yards gained (1,383), and touchdowns (13). Rookie Garrison's 46 receptions were the most by any first-year receiver, and tight end McKinnon, with fullback Gene Foster, each pocketed 26. Ex-Oiler tight end Willie Frazier wound up in Gillman's doghouse early in the year and never broke free of the leash. He caught only 9 passes after pulling in 37 for Houston in '65.

A 2-1 finish in the final weeks gave the Chargers a 7-6-1 record at the end of the year, narrowly avoiding their second non-winning season. They finished with the third-best record in the West and fifth-best in the AFL. The disappointing season started a four-year run of frustrating third-place finishes. The first half of the decade belonged to the Chargers, as they appeared in four of the league's first five championship games, winning it all in 1963. They had been the prototype franchise for offensive firepower and one of the most feared on defense. But now the Chiefs and Raiders began separating themselves from the rest of the league. The best running and passing offense in 1965 dropped to fourth in rushing behind Kansas City, Boston and Buffalo, while the Jets and Raiders surpassed them in the air. Still one of the premier franchises in the AFL, the Chargers had the misfortune in the second half of the decade of playing in the same division as the two most dominating teams in the league, often finding themselves as either the third- or fourth-best team in the AFL. Once the measuring stick for offensive and defensive excellence, the Chargers had almost overnight become also rans.

Remember the AFL

Leading passers	Attempts	Completions	Pct	TDs	Yards	Int
John Hadl	375	200	53%	23	2846	14
Steve Tensi	52	21	40%	5	405	1

Leading rushers	Attempts	Yards gained	Average	TDs
Paul Lowe	146	643	4.4	3
Gene Foster	81	352	4.3	1
Keith Lincoln	58	214	3.7	1
Jim Allison	31	213	6.9	2

Leading receivers	Caught	Yards gained	Average	TDs
Lance Alworth	73	1383	18.9	13
Gary Garrison	46	642	14.0	4
Jacque MacKinnon	26	477	18.3	6
Gene Foster	26	260	10.0	2
Keith Lincoln	14	264	18.9	2

Leading scorers	TDs	XPM	XPA	FGM	FGA	PTs
Dick Van Raaphorst		39	40	16	31	87
Lance Alworth	13					78

34. After coming close a few times, San Diego's Lance Alworth won his first receiving title with 73 catches in 1966. How many more times did Alworth lead the league?

A. 1
B. 2
C. 3
D. 0

230

The Progress of the Seasons – 1966

■ BOSTON PATRIOTS ■

THE 1966 SEASON WOULD FIND THE Patriots in a familiar position at the end of the season—sitting in second place, only a half game from winning the division. Fullback Jim Nance powered the turnaround from the disappointing previous season, showing up for training camp twenty pounds lighter and lightyears quicker. The result was a 4.88 rushing average and a league-leading 1,458 yards, a new AFL record. Nance's closest competitor for the rushing title finished 600 yards and 150 carries behind. For his renewed effort, Nance was selected the AFL Player of the Year. On October 30, against the Oakland Raiders, he rumbled 208 yards on a whopping 38 carries. No other AFL runner had ever carried the ball that many times in one game.

In the first game of the season, the Patriots appeared primed to repeat their '65 performance. Traveling to San Diego, they took a 24-0 thumping. But on the following week, Nance and the Pats served notice that they were on their way back. Nance took over the game in the second half and ended up rushing for 126 yards, putting him at the top of the league in rushing, where he stayed for the rest of the year. In Fenway for their home opener, they faced the Chiefs. Len Dawson picked the Patriots secondary to pieces with 5 touchdown passes, 3 to Chris Burford, in the Chiefs 43-24 victory. The inconsistent Pats came away without a "W" again the following week, when they settled for a 24-24 tie against the Jets. Ahead 24-7 in the fourth quarter, Boston suddenly fell under the spell of Broadway Joe, who completed 14 fourth-quarter passes, including 2 touchdowns. After a last-minute New York field goal, the Pats felt more like losers than a team that had fought to a draw.

In the middle of the pack with a 1-2-1 record, the Pats went on a tear that saw them lose only once in the next nine games, putting them in the driver's seat heading into the last weekend of the season. For the fifth time in six years, Boston, with an 8-3-2 record, could win the division in the season finale, this time against the Jets. In 1961 they crushed the Chargers 41-0 in their last game, only to finish second by one game, as Houston also won their season ender. In 1962 the Oilers again got the drop on Boston with a season-ending win, sending the Pats home one game behind. A 35-3 loss to Kansas City then dropped them into a tie with Buffalo in their last game of 1963, forcing a playoff that the Pats won. The next year, in a heart-wrenching loss on the final day to Buffalo, the Bills pushed past the first-place Pats to give Boston yet another second-place finish. Now in 1966, as Yogi Berra once said, "It was déjà vu all over again!"

Just how close the Pats came to winning the East is best exemplified by one play on November 6 against the Broncos. With the score tied at 10-10 and sixteen seconds to play, Broncos quarterback Max Choboian lofted a go-for-broke pass to the left sideline. Boston safety Chuck Shonta, who was double-covering tight end Al Denson, zeroed in on the ball and had a game-ending interception in his grasp. But the ball caromed off his chest high into the air where Denson plucked it and bolted 30 yards into the end zone, and Denver had a 17-10 win. Boston's record dropped to 4-2-1 and into a tie with the Jets for the East's top spot.

The 5-6-2 Jets could only be spoilers. Buffalo, sitting on an 8-4-1 record, could only watch and wait to see what their fate would be in the final game. For Boston, several key players either stepped up their play or were heading toward break-out seasons. Offensive leader Babe Parilli put together a good year that earned him the league's comeback player award. Split end Art Graham, also back from injury, caught 51 passes to rank seventh in the AFL. Cappelletti, Garron, and Whalen also were among Babe's favorite targets. The front line defense, as always, ranked in the top two, but no other secondary in the league gave up more yards or a higher pass completion percentage than Boston.

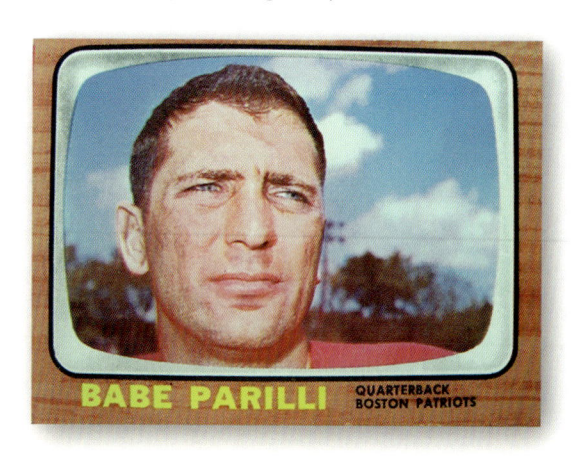

And so the team that threw the most passes and gained the most yards through the air, the New York Jets, faced the most pourous pass defense in the league. The Pats defensive backs clearly needed a big game to keep their hopes of playing in the first Super Bowl alive. But in that final game, the secondary was not the problem. Two weeks after holding Buffalo's third-ranked running game to only 40 yards, the Jets running backs ran wild. Matt Snell and running mate Emerson Boozer both eclipsed the century mark, piling up 241 yards, 160 yards more than Boston's average allowance. It was a see-saw battle, and for every bit of magic Babe Parilli displayed, Joe Namath had an answer. Parilli completed 21 passes for 378 yards, and Boston put up 28 points. But Namath and the Jets countered with 38 of their own.

After their loss to the Jets on Saturday, the Patriots had one last hope. If the Broncos could beat or tie Buffalo on Sunday, their season would still be alive. But Buffalo won 38-21, and even though the Patriots beat the Bills twice during the season, 20-10 and 14-3, the Bills had their third straight Eastern Division title and the chance to play in Super Bowl I. Once more, and for the final time as members of the AFL, the Patriots had an outstanding season with nothing but memories to show for it. For all of the excitement they created during the 1966 season, the Patriots were anointed by their devoted and appreciative fans as the "Champions Without a Crown." For the team that always seemed to be scratching until the end, 1966 was in many ways Boston's most exciting and successful season. It would prove to be their last AFL hurrah.

The Progress of the Seasons – 1966

Leading passers	Attempts	Completions	Pct	TDs	Yards	Int
Babe Parilli	382	181	47%	20	2721	20
John Huarte	11	5	46%	0	63	1

Leading rushers	Attempts	Yards gained	Average	TDs
Jim Nance	299	1458	4.9	11
Larry Garron	101	319	3.2	4
Bob Cappadona	22	88	4.0	1
Babe Parilli	28	42	1.5	1

Leading receivers	Caught	Yards gained	Average	TDs
Art Graham	51	673	13.2	4
Gino Cappelletti	43	676	15.7	6
Larry Garron	30	416	13.9	5
Jim Whalen	29	502	17.3	4
Jim Colclough	16	284	17.8	0
Jim Nance	8	103	12.9	0

Leading scorers	TDs	XPM	XPA	FGM	FGA	PTs
Gino Cappelletti	6	35	36	16	32	119
Jim Nance	11					66

▪ DENVER BRONCOS ▪

THE HOPE IN DENVER WAS TO START fresh in 1966, with 17 rookies making the 40-man roster. But of the 23 veterans who suited up to start the season, one was conspicuously absent. Star fullback Cookie Gilchrist had reported to camp on time for the first time, giving Mac Speedie a reason to believe the Broncos would build on one of the league's best offensive teams in '65 and be a factor in the West. But when Cookie's best friend, Willie Ross, was cut by the Buffalo Bills, Gilchrist requested that Speedie give him a tryout. Speedie was not interested, and when he declined the request Cookie left camp never to return. This event was the second time Ross brought havoc to Gilchrist's career. Cookie had sent in Ross as his replacement in Buffalo in 1964, sparking Cookie's suspension and ultimately the trade to Denver. Gilchrist sat out for nearly the first half of the season to spite Speedie's decision, and when he did not return six games into the schedule, he was traded to the Miami Dolphins for two draft choices.

The tell-tale performance of Denver's season occurred in their opening game and set the stage for the rest of the year with a 45-7 loss to the Houston Oilers, who were not considered one of the league's top teams. The

★ *Rookie Bronco quarterback Max Choboian hurls one downfield.* ★

Broncos set an AFL record by failing to get even one first down for the entire game. They extended their string one more quarter in their next game, which ended as a 24-10 loss to Boston. Not anticipating the loss of Gilchrist, the Broncos used two halfbacks in the backfield. Abner Haynes and Wendell Hayes were lightweights and together totaled only 721 yards rushing for the season. Hayes averaged 3.9 yards per carry and Haynes a career low 2.3. Charlie Mitchell, the running back surprise in 1964 who sat out all of 1965 with

The Progress of the Seasons – 1966

cartilage deposits in his leg, carried 70 times for 199 yards. The league's second-best ground game of a year ago with 1829 yards rushing had fallen to their familiar last place in 1966, accumulating only 1,173 yards.

The poor start caused Mac Speedie to resign, and he was replaced by assistant coach Ray Malavasi. A 16-7 loss to the Jets put Denver at 0-3 before the Oilers came West on October 2 for their second meeting of the season. The Broncos appeared poised to crack the win column, holding on to a 23-17 halftime lead thanks in part to rookie Goldie Sellers' second kickoff return for a touchdown against Houston (he also scored a TD in the season opener vs. Houston). This time he went the full length of the field from goal line to goal line. Houston took their first lead 31-30 in the third quarter but had to retake it again late in the fourth, 38-37. Finally, with thirty-seven seconds left to play, Bronco center/kicker Gary Kroner connected on a 46-yard field goal to end Denver's losing streak in dramatic style.

The Broncos were 1-7 before registering another win, again needing a miracle to do it. Played on a mud puddle in Boston's Fenway Park, the game appeared to be stalled in a 10-10 deadlock until rookie quarterback Max Choboian earned the player-of-the-week award with a 65-yard bomb that bounced off a Boston defender and into the hands of tight end Al Denson for a touchdown with only sixteen seconds remaining. Choboian was a breath of fresh Colorado air for Denver fans. At 6'4" and 205 pounds he appeared to have all the tools to be the quarterback a team could rally around. Sharing the spot with the oft-injured John McCormick and Mickey Slaughter with stints from un-retired Tobin Rote and rookie Scotty Glacken, Max was the leading thrower, completing 50 percent of his 163 passes. McCormick managed to complete only 35 percent.

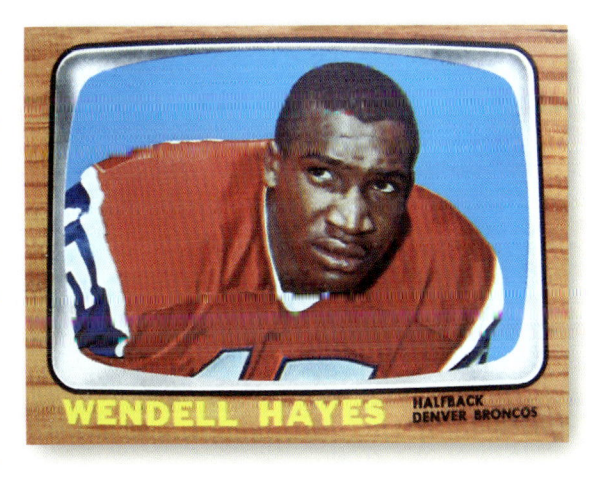

For receivers, 1965 was a year of transition in the Mile High city as well. After leading the league in receptions for five of its first six years, Lionel Taylor was not even the leading receiver on the team. Catching a career-low 35 passes with only 1 touchdown, Taylor finished third on the team behind Al Denson and Abner Haynes, who caught 36 and 46 respectively.

After a loss to the Raiders, the Broncs had their finest hour, knocking off San Diego 20-17 with 2 outstanding touchdowns in the final period. The first came as linebacker John Bramlett blocked a Charger field goal attempt and ran it back 72 yards. The second was a zig-zagging 56-yard touchdown run by Abner Haynes. A week later Denver won its second game in a row for the first time that season by

WENDELL HAYES — HALFBACK, DENVER BRONCOS

235

beating Miami 17-7 in their last home game. It was their fourth and final win of the year. Losses to Oakland, 28-10, and Buffalo, 38-21, closed out another dismal and disappointing season in the Rockies with a 4-10 record. In the past four years the Broncos posted records of 4-10, 4-10, 2-11-1, and 2-11-1 making them the AFL's poster team for futility. And if not for the devoted loyalty of their fans, the team would have packed its bags and moved on.

Rookie Goldie Sellers led the league in kickoff returns, and Bob Scarpitto, even though he had not punted since 1960 at Notre Dame, led the AFL with a 45.8 average. Though the team's fortunes did not change in 1966, the uniforms did slightly—a blue stripe was added down the center of the helmet with white stripes on either side.

For some, the biggest victory of 1966 came on December 19, the day after the regular season ended, when team president Allan Phipps signed former AFL coach of the year Lou Saban to lead the Broncos for the next ten years. Saban had led the Bills to two straight AFL championships before resigning to take a job at the University of Maryland. After one year, he was coming back to take on perhaps his biggest challenge. He inherited an offense that scored an anemic 18 offensive touchdowns, only 6 on the ground, and a defense that finished last in almost every category and was unable to stop anyone from doing anything. The secondary intercepted a woeful 13 passes, only three more than league leaders Johnny Robinson and Bobby Hunt of Kansas City each had by themselves. The new hope in Denver was now firmly placed on Saban's broad shoulders to fix a franchise without much direction and even less success.

Leading passers	Attempts	Completions	Pct	TDs	Yards	Int
John McCormick	193	68	35%	6	993	15
Max Choboian	163	82	50%	4	1110	12
Mickey Slaughter	25	7	28%	1	124	0
Scotty Glacken	11	6	55%	1	84	0

Leading rushers	Attempts	Yards gained	Average	TDs
Abner Haynes	129	304	2.4	2
Wendell Hayes	105	417	4.0	1
Charlie Mitchell	70	199	2.8	0
Bob Scarpitto	4	110	27.5	1
Darrell Lester	34	84	2.5	0

Leading receivers	Caught	Yards gained	Average	TDs
Abner Haynes	46	480	10.4	1
Al Denson	36	725	20.1	3
Lionel Taylor	35	448	12.8	1
Bob Scarpitto	21	335	16.0	4
Charlie Mitchell	14	239	17.1	2

The Progress of the Seasons – 1966

Leading scorers	TDs	XPM	XPA	FGM	FGA	PTs
Gary Kroner		20	20	14	25	62
Bob Scarpitto	5	1				32

35. Unlike the rival NFL, the American Football League set out to find the best players, not just the best players from the biggest and best football schools. As a result, many AFL stars came from smaller, less known colleges. Match the players below with the small colleges they played for:

A. Elbert Dubenion _____ Villanova
B. Lionel Taylor _____ San Fernando St.
C. Charlie Hennigan _____ McNeese St.
D. Abner Haynes _____ Bluffton
E. Tom Sestak _____ NE Louisiana St.
F. Otis Taylor _____ North Texas St.
G. Max Choboian _____ Prairie View
H. Billy Joe _____ Lincoln
I. Zeke Moore _____ New Mexico Highlands
J. Dudley Meredith _____ Lamar Tech

■ NEW YORK JETS ■

THE NAMATH ERA HAD OFFICIALLY begun in New York. With his quick-release passes setting the tone, Broadway Joe led his Jets to a 4-0-1 record. Living up to everyone's expectations, Namath enjoyed his breakout season in 1966. After a brief internship as a rookie in '65, he was handed control of the offense in his seventh game and never looked back. In 1966 Broadway Joe threw more passes and more completions for more yardage than any other AFL quarterback. Nineteen of his completions were for touchdowns. As could be expected from a sophomore quarterback still emerging as a pro, he had a bit too much confidence in his gun-slinger release and rocket-armed delivery, causing him to throw into coverage at times rather than throw a few away. The result was a league-high 27 interceptions.

Other pieces of coach Weeb Ewbank's five-year plan settled into place. Rookie halfback Emerson Boozer gave the Jets their first legitimate outside threat. With Snell and Mathis grinding out yardage between the tackles, Boozer supplied a breakaway threat, averaging 4.6 yards per carry, gaining 455 yards on

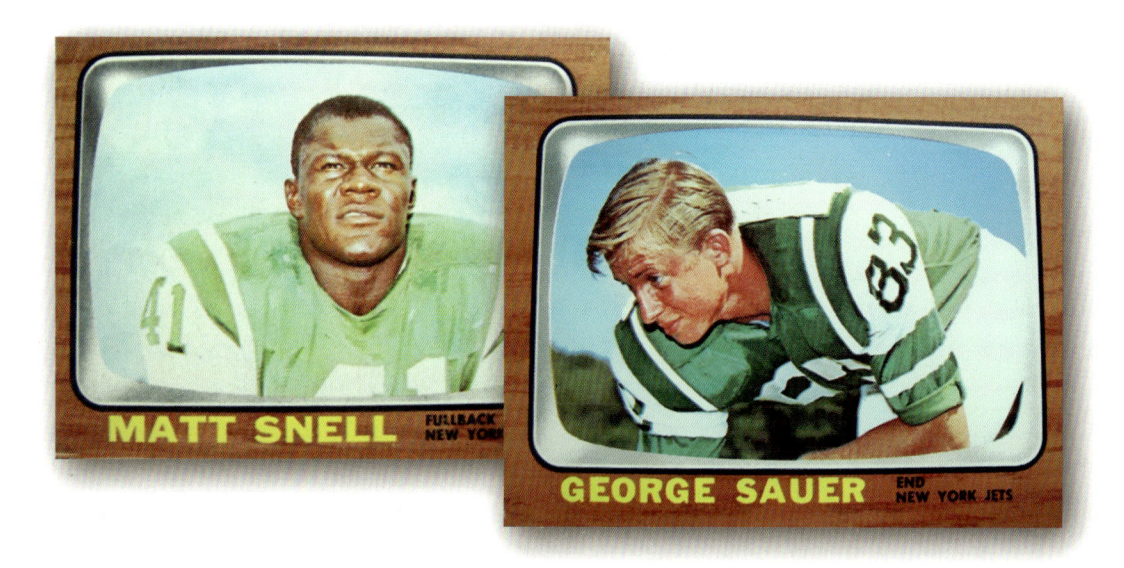

97 carries for tenth-best in the league. Of his 4 touchdowns, two were for 39 and 47 yards, with his longest run of the year coming on a 54-yard sprint. Another rookie, Pete Lammons, a big tight end from Texas, gave the Jets their best inside blocker at that position in seven years, and gave Namath sure hands and massive size to target in traffic over the middle. With center Mike Hudock gone to Miami in the expansion draft, Hofstra snapper John Schmitt stepped into the middle of the line. Surrounding him were Winston Hill, Sam DeLuca, Dave Herman, and Sherman Plunkett, the only Jet to make the all-league team.

After a season-opening win against the Dolphins, in which an injured Namath came off the bench, the Jets came home to play in front of 54,681 fans, who watched Namath pass through the Houston defense to register 38 points and 5 touchdown passes in three quarters. He sat out the fourth period, allowing Mike Taliaferro to throw a sixth TD over the Oilers secondary, hitting Curly Johnson and giving New York a lopsided, 52-13 win. Namath's 5 6-pointers were for 67 yards to George Sauer, 25 yards to Matt Snell, 13 to Lammons, and 55 and 37 yards to Don Maynard. Rookie Emerson Boozer added a 39-yard touchdown run.

In Denver the next week, kicker Jim Turner kicked 3 field goals in a 16-7 triumph. Against the Patriots, the Jets looked beaten after three quarters with the score 24-7 in Boston's favor. With the wind swirling around Fenway Park, it took Namath three quarters to figure out the defensive schemes and jet streams, but in the fourth quarter he showed his moxie by completing 14 of 23 passes (he threw 56 times on the day) for 205 yards. With touchdown throws to Snell and Lammons and a game-tying, 17-yard field goal by Turner, the Jets pulled out a confidence-boosting 24-24 tie in the closing minutes.

The defense showed great improvement, especially on the front line where Verlon Biggs, Jim Harris, Paul Rochester, and Gerry

The Progress of the Seasons – 1966

Philbin were coming together as a unit. Larry Grantham and Al Atkinson were the pluggers behind the line, but Oklahoma All-American Carl McAdams, slated to be the third linebacker, broke his ankle, opening the job for Ralph Baker to solidify himself on the left side. Cornerback Johnny Sample, joining the Jets from the Redskins, led the squad with 8 interceptions and added depth to the secondary of Bill Baird, Ray Abruzzese, and Jim Hudson. Willie West, a starter in 1965, was picked up by Miami along with Hudock.

A stirring 17-16 victory over San Diego kept the Jets undefeated after five games. Emerson Boozer, eluding tacklers on an 8-yard run, scored the game winner with the Jets behind 16-10 in the fourth quarter. Then it was time for a reality check. When Namath's game was on, he could carry a team, but he still had to learn that he could not shoot the wings off a mosquito from 50 yards away every time he wanted to. In suffering their first defeat, a 24-0 loss to Houston, Joe threw 4 interceptions to the same Houston defenders who weeks earlier allowed him to hit his receivers for pay dirt five times.

The Jets lost again the next week, this time to Oakland 24-21, when fullback Hewritt Dixon plunged over the goal line on fourth down with two seconds remaining. Then 5 more Namath interceptions against Buffalo gave the Jets a third straight loss, 33-23, as Namath took to the air 53 times.

Following a bye week, the Jets played the Bills again, losing 13-3. The game which pitted the 5-3-1 Bills against the 4-3-1 Jets was scoreless at the half, with only a field goal separating the two teams as the game moved into its final quarter. When Jim Turner attempted to draw New York even in the 6-3 contest, Buffalo defensive tackle Jim Dunaway got a hand on Turner's field goal try. Scooping it up, he returned it 72 yards for a touchdown, sealing Buffalo's sixth win, 13-3. New York, once an undefeated 4-0-1 team four weeks ago, now dropped their fourth straight game.

The Jets needed a solid game after failing to win their last four outings and found it at home on November 20 against Miami, with a strong 30-13 win. Emerson Boozer, now starting at halfback, scored 2 touchdowns, one from a yard out and another on a 96-yard kickoff return, to start the second half. Powerful Kansas City dropped them back to .500 the next week before they tied Oakland 28-28. A clutch 47-yard touchdown dash by Boozer and a 2-point conversion from Namath to George Sauer in the fourth quarter salvaged the tie.

The Jets took a 5-6-2 record into the season's final weekend against Boston, with the Patriots in a must-win situation. A Boston win would clinch the East for the New England team. A loss, coupled with a Buffalo win, would eliminate the Pats. The Jets were determined to crack the six-win plateau for the first time in five years and wanted to make their mark in the East as spoilers. This time it was not Joe's arm alone that led to victory, although he did throw 3 touchdown passes. With the help of a dominating performance from the offensive line, Snell and Boozer became the first set of backs in franchise history to go over 100 yards rushing in the same game. Namath threw only 21 times, completing 14 for 287 yards in leading the Jets to a 38-28 upset and a team record of 528 yards total offense. The win brought the Jets to 6-6-2, and although the franchise had yet to record a winning record, Ewbank knew after four seasons in New York that his blueprint for success was only a year away. Second-year split end George Sauer, who left the University of Texas a year early, was sensational, and led the Jets with 63 receptions (second in the league) while being called a faster version of NFL legend Raymond Berry. Fellow Texan Don Maynard caught 48 passes, and rookie Pete Lammons pulled down 41. Matt Snell had another fine year with 644 yards rushing (sixth in the league). His 48 receptions tied him for ninth with Maynard.

Leading passers	Attempts	Completions	Pct	TDs	Yards	Int
Joe Namath	471	232	49%	19	3379	27
Mike Taliaferro	41	19	46%	2	177	2

Leading rushers	Attempts	Yards gained	Average	TDs
Matt Snell	178	644	3.6	4
Emerson Boozer	97	455	4.7	5
Bill Mathis	72	208	2.9	2
Mark Smolinski	21	69	3.3	2

Leading receivers	Caught	Yards gained	Average	TDs
George Sauer	63	1079	17.1	5
Don Maynard	48	840	17.5	5
Matt Snell	48	346	7.2	4
Pete Lammons	41	565	13.8	4
Bill Mathis	22	379	17.2	1
Emerson Boozer	8	133	16.6	0

Leading scorers	TDs	XPM	XPA	FGM	FGA	PTs
Jim Turner		34	35	18	35	88
Matt Snell	8					48

▪ OAKLAND RAIDERS ▪

IN APRIL OF 1966, RAIDER FORTUNES took a slight detour. Needing a competent and forceful commissioner who could take on the cold war with the NFL, AFL owners summoned head coach Al Davis to take the lead. Davis handed the team's leadership to top assistant John Rauch. No one knew that Al's bullish leadership approach and declaration of war on

The Progress of the Seasons – 1966

the senior league would speed a merger with the NFL. With his job completed by July, he returned to the Raiders organization, this time as its principal owner and managing partner.

Looking for running help for Clem Daniels, Davis traded for Denver tight end Hewritt Dixon in hopes of converting him into a fullback. Like the year before, when Billy Cannon was converted from the backfield to tight end, Dixon made an easy transition. Also coming to Oakland was hard-nosed middle linebacker Archie Matsos from Buffalo. The beginning of 1966 also marked the opening of Oakland's new Oakland-Alameda County Coliseum. There would be no more memories made at the portable erector set known as Frank Youell Field.

The Raiders stumbled out of the gate in their first season under Rauch as they lost three of their first four games. They beat the expansion Miami Dolphins on opening day but were then shutout by Houston. In front of almost 51,000 fans, the Raiders christened their Coliseum by getting hammered by Kansas City 32-10. They lost at home again the next week against San Diego, 29-20. But a visit by Miami stopped the three-game skid and earned the silver and black their first win in their new home. After an inconsistent start with Cotton Davidson at quarterback, Tom Flores took over behind center against the Dolphins and threw for 261 yards and 3 touchdowns.

The Raiders followed the Miami victory with a 34-13 win over the Chiefs in which Flores threw 3 touchdowns in the second quarter, 1 to Billy Cannon for 75 yards and 2 to Hewritt Dixon for 10 and 76 yards. Dixon added a 1-yard plunge in the period as the Raiders exploded for 28 unanswered points in the period to bust the game wide open. The Raider defense kept the Chiefs out of the end zone all afternoon. The winning momentum continued into New York on October 23 as 58,000 fans came to see if Joe Namath could dazzle the Raiders. Instead, Tom Flores did the dazzling. He drove the Raiders 82 yards in the final two minutes before Dixon, on the last play of the game, plowed over the goal line for the winning touchdown in a 24-21 thriller. The Raiders were becoming one of the premier teams in the AFL, and Clem Daniels, Art Powell, and Tom Flores led the way.

A 24-21 loss to Boston dropped their record to 4-4. It was the last time in AFL history that they would not have a winning record. Following the loss to the Patriots, Oakland rebounded against Houston, winning 38-23, thanks in part to a 78-yard touchdown reception by second-year receiver Fred Biletnikoff to get the scoring started in the first period. Oakland hoped to run the table as they traveled to San Diego on November 13. The Raiders turned up another big win, lighting up the scoreboard for 41 points to the Chargers 19, on a big day for the Raider ground game. Led by the outstanding line play of center Jim Otto, guards Wayne Hawkins and Jim Harvey, and tackles Harry Schuh and Bob Svihus, the backfield of Clem Daniels, Hewritt Dixon, and Roger Hagberg had their finest day, combining for 219 yards rushing.

A Thanksgiving Day victory in Denver

★ *Raider running back Clem Daniels splashes for a touchdown against the Oilers.*

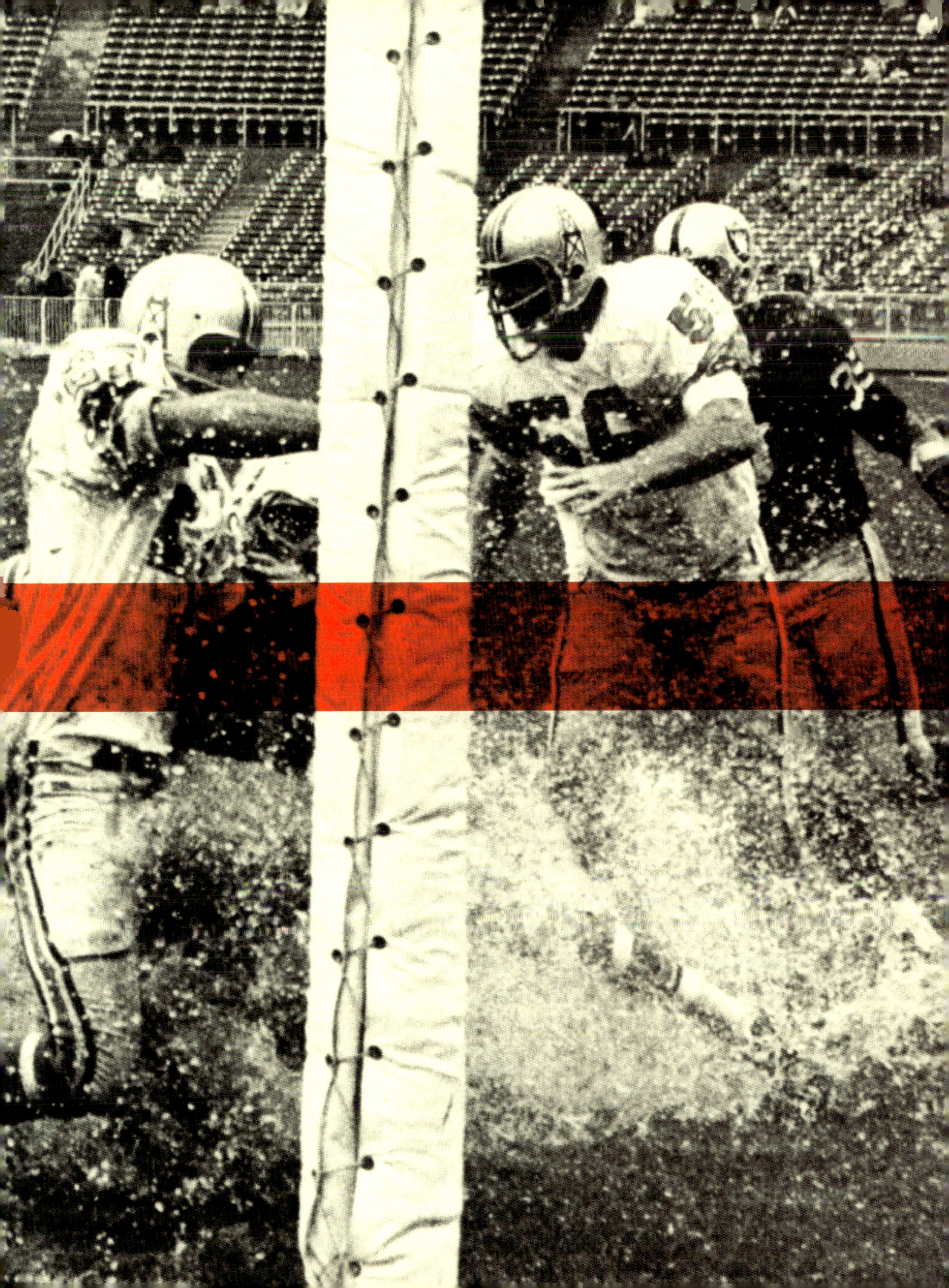

and the season's last loss to Buffalo the following week put the Raiders' record at 7-5 with two weeks left in the season. The Chargers at this point were 6-6 with Kansas City ahead by two games and in the Western Division driver's seat at 9-3. A visit by the Jets in a rare Thursday night game on December 3 would be the most crucial game of the season. The Raiders needed to win to stay in contention, but the Jets were looking to avenge their last-second loss six weeks earlier. The teams traded leads five times before the Raiders took control in the fourth quarter and posted a 28-20 lead, but Joe Namath brought his New Yorkers back, capped by Emerson Boozer sprinting 47 yards for a touchdown. Needing a 2-point conversion to tie the game, Namath found George Sauer in the end zone to earn a 28-28 tie. A 28-10 win over Denver closed the Raiders season with an 8-5-1 record, and for the third time in four years they settled into second place in the West.

It was a huge year for the Oakland defense, as no team in the league allowed fewer yards per game. They were led up front by newly acquired defensive tackle Tom Keating, big Ben Davidson, Dan Birdwell, and Ike Lassiter, while all-AFL cornerback Dave Grayson and partner Kent McCloughan became the best defenders in the league. On offense, Hewritt Dixon gained 277 yards to

★ *Ben Davidson clobbers Joe Namath!* ★

become a punishing complement to Daniels. The latter finished third in the league for the third year in a row with 801 yards. Roger Hagberg teamed with Dixon at fullback for an additional 282 yards and averaged 4.5 yards a carry. The passing game ranked behind only New York, led by Art Powell's 53 catches. Clem Daniels pulled down 40, and Dixon took in 29 throws while tight end Tom Mitchell caught 23. As Al Davis and the rest of the organization knew, at 8-5-1 there was still plenty of room for improvement on both sides of the line, and Davis would work tirelessly to make sure the 1967 Raiders would rise to the top of the West.

Leading passers	Attempts	Completions	Pct	TDs	Yards	Int
Tom Flores	306	151	49%	24	2638	14
Cotton Davidson	139	59	42%	2	770	11

The Progress of the Seasons – 1966

Leading rushers	Attempts	Yards gained	Average	TDs
Clem Daniels	204	801	3.9	7
Roger Hagberg	62	282	4.5	0
Hewritt Dixon	68	277	4.1	5

Leading receivers	Caught	Yards gained	Average	TDs
Art Powell	53	1026	19.4	11
Clem Daniels	40	652	16.3	3
Hewritt Dixon	29	345	11.9	4
Tom Mitchell	23	301	13.1	1
Roger Hagberg	21	248	11.8	1
Fred Biletnikoff	17	272	16.0	3
Billy Cannon	14	436	31.1	2
Larry Todd	14	134	9.6	1

Leading scorers	TDs	XPM	XPA	FGM	FGA	PTs
Mike Eischeid		37	37	11	26	70
Art Powell	11					66

■ HOUSTON OILERS ■

THE BIG NEWS IN HOUSTON WAS the return of Wally Lemm as the Oilers head coach. He wasn't exactly new, but he was the sixth head coach in the latest round of musical coaching chairs. The hero who saved the 1961 season from disaster was back in the saddle to work his magic once again. There were other changes as well in Houston, like the addition of Ernie Ladd, who was in camp after playing out his option with the Chargers. With the Oilers finishing 1965 with the lowest-ranked defense, they welcomed the addition of giant Ernie, who drew further attention to himself by donning a uniform number that had never been seen before, ninety-nine instead of his usual seventy-seven. Three years after Bud Adams declared that his rebuilding program had begun, the lineup showed improvement and some significantly different looks, and yet some noticeably similar ones on both sides of the ball.

The offensive line was made up of veteran all stars and all-stars in the making. Former all-leaguer Rich Michael was still at tackle but gave way to rookie Glenn Ray Hines midway through the year. Young Walt Suggs manned the opposite tackle position. All-league bulldog Bob Talamini and an improving Sonny Bishop, who came to Houston from Oakland in the Billy Cannon trade, played guard. Converted linebacker Bobby Maples took over at center when John Frongillo suffered an injury. Bob McLeod returned to the starting lineup when all-league tight end Willie Frazier went to San Diego as compensation for the Ladd signing. Sinewy Charlie Frazier came back at flanker for his second year to lead the team with 57 receptions and 12 touchdowns while averaging just under 20 yards per catch.

Ode Burrell continued to be the team's leading rusher in '66, just as he was in '65, Charlie Tolar returned to the fullback position he had held since 1961. But now twenty-eight, Tolar carried the ball only 46 times for a 2.28 average and showed signs of seven years of wear. Another old pro looking to bolster the running attack behind Tolar was thirty-five-year-old John Henry Johnson, who had a few yards left in his legs after several outstanding years in Detroit and Pittsburgh. He carried 70 times for 226 yards and 3 touchdowns. By the end of the season, rookie fullback Hoyle Granger took most of the snaps. He ran with authority and enough speed to rank right behind Burrell as the league's fourteenth-best ground gainer. Though he carried the ball only 56 times, his 388 yards gained gave him a 6.9 per carry average.

Wally Lemm chose George Blanda to be the quarterback, but the writers and fans called for Baylor star Don Trull, and by midseason Lemm handed the reigns to the backup. When he finally got his chance to start, Trull turned in some fairly good numbers, completing 84 of his 172 passes for 48 percent and 1,200 yards. He also threw 10 touchdown passes with only 5 interceptions to rank him sixth among AFL passers. Blanda completed only 45 percent of his passes with 17 touchdowns and 21 interceptions. He ended up eighth in the rankings. Jacky Lee, back after

The Progress of the Seasons – 1966

two years in Denver, suffered an injury in his first game and threw only 8 passes all season.

The combination of old and new meshed beautifully early in the season, when the team won its first two games by a combined score of 76-7. In their first game, against Denver, the previous year's weakest defense set an AFL record by not allowing the Broncos a single first down. Denver's 7 points came via Goldie Sellers' kickoff return for 88 yards after Houston went up 7-0. The next week the defense held the Raiders offense scoreless and won 31-0. The Oilers not only had some new looks in the lineup, they also had a new look in their attire, changing their familiar Columbia blue helmets to silver, with their traditional oil well derricks now blue instead of white. Their white pants became silver/gray as well. Their jerseys and socks, still tradional blue, featured red trim.

In the first two games the defense relied on Don Floyd, who was off to a fine start in his seventh season at defensive end, and Gary Cutsinger who was equally outstanding on the opposite side. Cutsinger made such an impact that he was named the team's MVP. Pat Holmes, back in Houston after a four-year hiatus in Canada, joined Ernie Ladd at the tackles. On paper the front four looked as good as any in the league, but on the field they lacked intensity on the pass rush and Ladd became a huge disappointment. Floyd went down with a season-ending injury in game three, and young Scott Appleton replaced him. Seven-year veteran Doug Cline manned the middle, flanked by Johnny Baker and Dan Brabham. Brabham lasted only two games before being lost for the season to injury. The secondary also started well but ended as a liability. All-league safety Freddy Glick, another of the Houston walking wounded, pulled a hamstring and played only five games, and former all-league defensive back Tony Banfield never regained his form, leaving Jim Norton and W.K. Hicks to chase receivers for ungodly lengths of time as a result of the ineffective pass rush and inadequate coverage.

The Oilers hadn't been a factor in the East for four years, and just as their first 4-10 finish in 1964 seemed to be better than their 4-10 performance in '65, their 3-11 record in 1966 appeared to be an improvement. The Oilers may have been the best 3-11 team in football history. In their third game Joe Namath picked apart the defense for 5 touchdowns and backup Mike Taliaferro threw a sixth. The Jets stormed to a 52-13 win. Yet Lemm was still optimistic and even had the Oilers in position to earn a gritty comeback tie with the champion Bills the next week when Blanda hit his stride and looked like the George of old, instead of just old George. Behind 20-6, he pulled his team even in the fourth quarter and had them driving toward a possible win when Hagood Clarke intercepted a pass on the Bills 44 yard line. He returned it all the way for the winning touchdown.

In Denver a week later, Blanda played the hero again, hitting Bob McLeod with a go-ahead 9-yard touchdown pass late in the fourth quarter. Leading 38-37 with thirty-eight seconds left, the Oilers fell again, as Denver's Gary Kroner kicked a 46-yard field goal. With a little luck the Oilers easily could have been 3-1-1 rather than 2-3. After a week off the defense gained revenge on New York by shutting down Joe Namath and his Jets 24-0, drawing their record even at 3-3. But a string of eight straight losses followed. Of their eleven losses, six were by a touchdown or less, with four of them happening in the last minute of play, including a 29-28 loss to Miami in their final game of the season.

A few less miscues and a few more breaks would have turned around the season. Oft-injured Sid Blanks showed signs of regaining his form and finished as the team's third-best runner. Second-year flanker Larry Elkins, who sat out all of 1965 with an injury, returned to catch 21 passes for 3 touchdowns and appeared ready to step into Charlie Hennigan's role. The young offensive line, along with Burrell and Granger, brought the Oiler running game out of the basement and back into the league's top five. And Don Trull, who finally got his long-awaited chance, had the passing game back among the league's top four again. Only Buffalo and Kansas City scored more points than Houston's 335 in 1966. Lemm now needed to shore up the shaky defense so that they would not give up more points than the rest of the league for a third straight year in 1967.

Leading passers	Attempts	Completions	Pct	TDs	Yards	Int
George Blanda	271	122	45%	17	1764	21
Don Trull	172	84	49%	10	1200	5
Buddy Humphrey	32	15	47%	2	168	1
Jacky Lee	8	4	50%	0	27	1

Leading rushers	Attempts	Yards gained	Average	TDs
Ode Burrell	122	406	3.3	0
Hoyle Granger	56	388	6.9	1
Sid Blanks	71	235	3.3	0
John Henry Johnson	70	226	3.2	3
Don Trull	38	139	3.7	7
Charlie Tolar	46	105	2.3	0

The Progress of the Seasons – 1966

Leading receivers	Caught	Yards gained	Average	TDs
Charlie Frazer	57	1129	19.8	12
Ode Burrell	33	400	12.1	5
Charley Hennigan	27	313	11.6	3
Bob McLeod	23	339	14.7	3
Larry Elkins	21	283	13.5	3
Sid Blanks	19	234	12.3	2

Leading scorers	TDs	XPM	XPA	FGM	FGA	PTs
George Blanda		39	40	16	30	87
Charlie Frazier	12					72

---

36. Tiny Prairie View A&M in Texas produced many players who starred in the AFL. Which one of the following all-stars was not from Prairie View?
A. Alvin Reed
B. Otis Taylor
C. Clem Daniels
D. Ken Houston
E. Dave Grayson
F. Jim Hunt
G. Jim Kearney

▪ BUFFALO BILLS ▪

NO TEAM IN PROFESSIONAL FOOTBALL has ever won three consecutive league titles, so Buffalo's rookie head coach Joel Collier faced not only the challenge of becoming the first team to win a triple, but also to become the first AFL representative in the Super Bowl. With the abrupt departure of Lou Saban, Collier became the youngest head coach in professional football, and his task of keeping the Bills title run intact was a tall order. Gone in the expansion draft to the Miami Dolphins from the starting lineup were fullback Billy Joe and flanker Bo Roberson. Replacing them would be keys to a successful season. Glenn Bass and Elbert Dubenion were returning from injuries, so replacing Roberson would not be a problem, and Arkansas rookie Bobby Crockett filled in as a pass-catching reserve.

Replacing Billy Joe would be far more critical as the Bills had become more and more reliant on their power running game. To his surprise, Collier got more than he had ever expected when he inserted rookie Bobby Burnett, an Arkansas teammate of Crockett's and a standout runner in his own right, into the Bills backfield. Burnett became the primary offensive weapon in 1966, not only because of his speed, quickness, and power, but also for his sure hands as a receiver out of the backfield. Jack Kemp returned behind center, but he brought along his chronically sore arm, described in the '60s as tennis elbow. Daryle Lamonica came back for his fourth year, giving the Bills the best backup quarterback in the league. Due to his constant arm pain, Kemp amassed the lowest completion

★ Bobby Burnett breaks off a long run against the Pats. ★

percentage (42 percent) of his career, and for the eighth year in a row he threw more interceptions than touchdown passes. But his value could not be measured by his arm alone. His grit and drive, his intelligent play-calling, and his unparalleled leadership more than off set his lack of throwing accuracy. Knowing his arm was at less than full strength, Kemp threw more short passes and scrambled more often.

Beginning the season in a championship game rematch with San Diego, the Bills completed only 9 passes and were held scoreless until late in the game. The Chargers cruised to a 27-7 win. Their home opener against Kansas City proved no better. The game pitted USC's Heisman Trophy-winning rookie Mike Garrett against the Bills' own rookie sensation, Burnett. The Chiefs' prize showcased himself first with a 79-yard punt return for a touchdown, and for only the fourth time in Bills history, the team gave up more than 40 points, the third time at the hands of the Chiefs. Again the passing game could not carry its weight on offense, with only 11 completions, and the Chiefs won 42-20. The Bills did, however, counter Garrett's punt-return touchdown with one of their own when Ed Rutkowski took one back 73 yards for a score.

The expansion Miami Dolphins made their introductory visit to the Rock Pile on week three, and the Bills looked forward to notching their first win of the season, though the Dolphins posed a formidable threat to opponents, losing their first games by a combined total of only 14 points. Early in the first quarter with the Bills leading 7-0, all-league cornerback Butch Byrd picked off a pass by rookie quarterback Rick Norton and returned it 60 yards for a touchdown. Moments later Byrd registered an encore by returning a punt 72 yards for another score. Linebacker Mike Stratton also snagged an interception of his own that he returned to the Miami one yard line, from which halfback Bobby Burnett plunged for another touchdown. Burnett scored again later in the period to give Buffalo a halftime lead of 48-10. The Bills showed no mercy on their way to their first victory of the season, scoring a team-record 58 points, only one less than the league record set in 1963 by Kansas City.

Looking to even their record, the Bills hosted Houston on September 25 and surged to a 20-6 lead at the half. But as the Bills defense knew, as long as George Blanda quarterbacked the Oilers, no lead was safe. Sure enough, Blanda worked his magic in the third and fourth quarters and tied the game at 20 with less than a minute to play. As the history of the AFL will attest, there are times when he who lives through the air will die by the air. The killing blow came on Houston's last possession. Blanda fired a pass to tight end Bob McLeod, but safety Hagood Clarke stepped in front of McLeod for an interception at the Houston 44 and sprinted down the sideline for the winning score. The Bills had their second win of the season. A week later they turned the tables on the Chiefs in their rematch by shutting out the KC offense for the final three periods and winning 29-14. They then lost to the 1-3 Patriots on October 8 to drop to 3-3.

Upon the defection of Pete Gogolak from western to eastern New York, fans figured the Buffalo kicking game would fall into oblivion, but new kicker Booth Lusteg posted numbers every bit as good as Gogolak's and replaced him not only on the field but also as the league's second-highest scorer. Lusteg hit on 19 of his 38 field goal attempts and made all but one of his 42 PATs.

The defense often carried the team in 1966, but the combination of fullback Wray Carlton and running mate Bobby Burnett gave Buffalo one of the most efficient backfields in the league. After six weeks Carlton ranked second in the league and Burnett followed close behind. On the year, only Kansas City and Boston gained more yards on the ground, and no one scored more rushing touchdowns than the Bills' 19. After tying San Diego, the Bills traveled to New York to take on the first-place Jets in front of 61,552, their largest audience of the year. In a record-setting sidelight to the game, the Bills linebacking trio of John Tracey, Mike Stratton, and Harry Jacobs set a pro football record by playing in their sixty-second straight game together. The three linebackers rushed Joe Namath into throwing 5 interceptions on the afternoon. Defensive tackle Jim Dunaway even picked up a fumble and rumbled 75 yards for a touchdown. Kick returner Charley Warner went the distance in returning a kickoff 95 yards for another score. The Bills knocked off the Jets 33-23 to earn a share of first place with a 4-3-1 record.

The victory launched a five-game winning streak that took Collier's men into the second last week the season with a 8-3-1 record and in need of a win over 7-3-2 Boston, their annual nemesis, to stay in first place. With stars Burnett and Kemp sidelined with injuries, the Bills managed only a field goal, and Boston took sole possession of first place with a 14-3 victory. With only one game remaining in the season, the Bills no longer controlled their destiny. To have a chance at a third straight title they needed the Jets, who had won only once in their last eight games, to beat the Patriots. A Boston win in their Saturday game would eliminate the Bills, who were hosting Denver on Sunday.

Divine intervention, or at least Joe Namath and the running game, came to the rescue as New York shocked the Pats with a 38-28 victory, and suddenly the Bills regained control of their post-season plans. Denver, 4-9, was facing Buffalo for the first time this season, since the addition of Miami no longer allowed the original eight to play their traditional home-and-away series. A Bills victory would put them in their third straight AFL championship game against Kansas City, the newly crowned winners of the West. Jack Kemp returned from injury to lead the offense, while the defense remained strong, setting the pace for fewest points allowed. On the game's key play, all-league safety George Saimes blitzed quarterback John McCormick and forced a fumble on Denver's 24 yard line that Mike Stratton scooped up and ran into the end zone. It was then business as usual the rest of the way, as the Bills captured their third straight division crown with a 38-21 win.

The Buffalo running game, as in the past, formed the backbone of the offense. Bobby Burnett and Wray Carlton finished as the league's fourth- and fifth-best rushers. Burnett also finished second on the team in receptions and won the AFL Rookie of the Year award. Elbert Dubenion caught 50 passes to lead the team, but Glenn Bass had trouble coming back from injury, catching only 10 passes. Rookie Bobby Crockett caught 31, followed by second-year tight end Paul Costa with 27. Kicker Booth Lusteg's 98 points were good enough to place him behind only perennial scoring champion Gino Cappelletti. Offensively, only Kansas City scored more points than the Bills, but the real story in Buffalo was again the defense that allowed a league-low 3.06 yards per carry and a league-low pass completion percentage of 44 percent.

With their third division title in hand, the Bills hosted the 1966 Championship game at War Memorial Stadium and found the Kansas City Chiefs a more formidable foe than in their past two title attempts. Buffalo miscues in the first half gave KC a 21-7 lead at the half, and even with a valiant effort to mount a second-half comeback, the two-time AFL champions could not overtake the powerful Chiefs, who won the right to represent the AFL in Super Bowl I with a 31-7 victory.

Leading passers	Attempts	Completions	Pct	TDs	Yards	Int
Jake Kemp	389	166	43%	11	2451	16
Daryle Lamonica	84	33	39%	4	549	5

Leading rushers	Attempts	Yards gained	Average	TDs
Bobby Burnett	187	766	4.1	4
Wray Carlton	156	696	4.5	6
Allen Smith	31	148	4.8	0
Jack Kemp	40	130	3.3	5
Jack Spikes	28	119	4.3	3

Leading receivers	Caught	Yards gained	Average	TDs
Elbert Dubenion	50	747	14.9	2
Bobby Burnett	34	419	12.3	4
Bobby Crockett	31	533	17.2	3
Paul Costa	27	400	14.8	3
Wray Carlton	21	280	13.3	0
Charley Ferguson	16	293	18.3	1

Leading scorers	TDs	XPM	XPA	FGM	FGA	PTs
Booth Lusteg		41	42	19	38	98
Bobby Burnett	8					42

• KANSAS CITY CHIEFS •

SINCE THE MOVE TO KANSAS CITY, the Chiefs started every season as one of the top two contenders to win the Western Division. But in only one of those years did they wind up on top. In 1966 Hank Stram's club again featured a strong set lineup with as much talent as any in the AFL. On offense the Chiefs had only two new starters to begin the season. Bert Coan inherited the halfback position vacated by the death of Mack Lee Hill and teamed with Curtis McClinton at fullback. USC halfback Mike Garrett alternated with Coan and ended the season as the league's second-best ground gainer with 801 yards, even though he did not become a starter until the eleventh game. Garrett's quickness and speed gave the Chiefs the outside threat they'd lacked since Abner Haynes left, and his ability to change directions added an extra dimension to his running repertoire. Garrett led the league with a 5.45 yard per carry average. The second change on offense was at flanker, where Otis Taylor took over the job he shared in 1965 with Frank Jackson, who had since moved to Miami in the expansion draft.

On defense, Chuck Hurston and Aaron Brown split time at end, replacing Mel Branch, another expansion draftee. The starters at the other ten spots returned. Jerry Mays, Buck Buchanan, and Ed Lothamer completed the line, while E.J. Holub, Bobby Bell, and Sherrill Headrick backed the front four. Fred Williamson and Willie Mitchell manned the corners, and Bobby Hunt and Johnny Robinson were the safeties. The secondary led the AFL with 33 interceptions. The stiffest competition for a starting job during training camp came at quarterback. Dawson, the incumbent, had been rock solid since he was recruited from the Cleveland Browns in 1962. But he was now being pressed by third-year thrower Pete Beathard. During the exhibition season, Beathard impressed the coaching staff with his ability to get his team into the end zone as well as with his knack for hitting receivers in stride 60 yards downfield. In the end, Dawson's experience put him in control of the offense as the Chiefs took the field in War Memorial Stadium for their first game of the year. But Beathard saw action in every game until KC played San Diego for first place at home in the season's ninth game.

For receivers, Dawson and Beathard paid particular attention to Chris Burford and Taylor. Both caught 58 passes, tying them for third in the league. Burford, a seven-year veteran, was his old reliable self, but Taylor also was turning the heads of defenders as well as coaches, writers, and fans. Bigger and stronger than the other flankers, Taylor, at 6'2" and 211 pounds, had the size and toughness of Art Powell and the speed and agility of Lance Alworth. His 89-yard touchdown catch against Miami was the longest reception in the league in 1966. Taylor also caught touchdowns for 71, 74, and 77 yards during the

The Progress of the Seasons – 1966

season. Gaining 22.4 yards per catch, the second-year man out of Prairie View produced the best average in the AFL, and muscled his way into the league's fraternity of elite pass receivers. Both Taylor and Burford caught 8 touchdown passes on the year. Fred Arbanas caught 22 balls, with McClinton, Coan, and Garrett pulling down 12 among them. McClinton, Coan, and Garrett also made KC the first AFL team to place three runners among the league's top ten. Along with Garrett, who had the year's longest run from scrimmage, a 77-yard touchdown, big Mac's 540 yards placed him eighth in the league and Coan's 521 put him ninth. Only league-leader Jim Nance scored more touchdowns on the ground than Coan's 7.

After drawing a free-pass on the season's first week, the Chiefs thumped the defending champion Bills 42-20 in the opening game. In his new starting role, Bert Coan gained 101 yards and scored the Chiefs' first 2 touchdowns, while Mike Garrett flashed his Heisman talent by returning a punt 79 yards for a touchdown, establishing a franchise record. Taking their juggernaut to Oakland the following week, the Chiefs flexed their muscles again. Len Dawson riddled the home team for 3 touchdowns, leading to a 32-10 victory. Dawson was even better at Fenway Park on Sept 25. He found Chris Burford for 11 passes, 3 of them for touchdowns. Lenny also hit Curtis McClinton for a TD in the third period and Mike Garrett for another in the fourth, giving him 5 for the game and 10 in three weeks. Johnny Robinson scored KC's sixth touchdown when he returned a Babe Parilli pass 29 yards in the first quarter.

A loss in a rematch with the Bills dropped the Chiefs into second place behind San Diego. Also lost in the game was place kicker Tommy Brooker, leaving coach Stram to find a replacement before their next game. In typical Stram fashion he landed the best. Luring Oakland's Mike Mercer, he never imagined his new acquisition would turn into the best kicker in the AFL for the remainder of the year. Mercer kicked 35 of 38 extra points, and he made 21 of 30 field goals attempts, giving him a league-best percentage of 70 percent. His 98 points tied him for second in scoring with Buffalo's Booth Lusteg.

As with most championship teams, the Chiefs did not take losing in stride and prepared to avenge their first loss with a return to winning ways the next week. The defense turned in its best performance of the year against Denver on October 8, giving up only 3 points. Denver's only touchdown came in the fourth quarter when Nemiah Wilson returned a kickoff 100 yards following Mike Garrett's 61-yard touchdown jaunt. The Chiefs won 37-10 to extend their record to 4-1.

Their last loss of the year came on October 16 to Oakland. The rest of the way Kansas City could not be stopped. They tamed the Broncos in Denver behind Bert Coan's 111 yards and 4 touchdowns, 56-10. They drilled the Oilers 48-23, with Mike Garrett turning in a 77-yard touchdown run and Beathard and Dawson each throwing for 2 touchdowns. At 6-2 the Chiefs then faced the Chargers, who were 5-2-1, and won in front of 41,000 fans, 24-14. Only Gino Cappeletti's game-tying field goal with eighteen seconds to play blemished KC in their final four games. With an 11-2-1 record, the Chiefs had finally put together a season that everyone expected of their talent. The success on the field drew 259,071 to the seven home games, setting a new Western Division record.

For the first time in the AFL's existence, the league championship game would not end the season. The merger agreement called for the champion of the NFL and the champion of the AFL to meet to determine an ultimate winner of the professional football crown. KC owner Lamar Hunt dubbed the game "The Super Bowl." In order to play in the inaugural edition, the Chiefs would have to beat the defending champs, the Buffalo Bills, on New Year's Day. In their two meetings during the season, each team earned victories on the road. So as the Chiefs traveled to Buffalo's War Memorial Stadium for the second time in 1966, they were 3-point favorites. The Chiefs, the AFL's leader in points scored (448), averaged 32 points per game, with the next closest team 90 points behind. Eight times during the season the Chiefs scored more than 30 points and four times scored more than 40. They were the AFL's best running team with 2,274 yards on 439 carries. They passed 377 times, with Dawson throwing 284 of them, completing 56 percent. He also threw a league-high 26 touchdown passes and a league-low 10 interceptions.

Defensively, KC finished second to Buffalo in points allowed, giving up less than 20 per contest. As they prepared for their second AFL Championship game in seven years, the Chiefs appeared ready.

As the nation rung in 1967, War Memorial Stadium hosted their second Championship game in three years, and 42,080 frozen fans huddled together hoping to go home with their Bills having one more game to play. But the Chiefs caught a break when they recovered a Buffalo fumble on the opening kickoff on the 29 yard line. Then, just as the Chargers did in the last AFL Championship game played at the Rock Pile, the Chiefs struck for 6 points three plays later on a touchdown pass to their tight end. This time it was Fred Arbanas, just as Tobin Rote had hit Dave Kocourek on the game's third play two years earlier for San Diego. The Bills quickly tied the game at 7-7. On their first possession, a 69-yard bomb from Jack Kemp to Elbert Dubenion brought the Bills right back.

Then, just as quickly, the game turned into a series of missed opportunities for the hosts. Right after an errant Len Dawson pass sailed through the hands of Buffalo's Tom Janik, Otis Taylor put KC ahead 14-7 with a 10-yard touchdown reception in the second quarter. Not to be denied, Kemp marched his team down the field to KC's 10 yard line right before halftime. Kemp found an open receiver in the end zone, and he fired what seemed to be a touchdown pass, but at the last second free safety Johnny Robinson snared the ball and raced all the way back to the Buffalo 28. The clock showed only three seconds left in the half, and Mike Mercer ran onto the field

The Progress of the Seasons – 1966

to attempt a field goal. Mercer split the uprights with a 32-yard field goal and instead of taking a 14-14 deadlock into the locker room, the Chiefs now led 17-7.

JOHNNY ROBINSON — DEFENSIVE BACK, KANSAS CITY CHIEFS

The teams played scoreless football in the third quarter, with both defenses stiffening, the Chiefs front seven applying ferocious pressure on Kemp. As the game moved into the last period, the Chiefs took possession at their 37, and Dawson put on his best drive of the afternoon, maneuvering 63 yards on seven plays, ending with a 1-yard plunge for a touchdown by Mike Garrett on a fourth and goal. With a little under nine minutes to play, Kansas City took a 24-7 lead. As their hopes dwindled, the Bills mounted a drive, but KC safety Bobby Hunt recovered a fumbled pass reception and ran it back to the Buffalo 21 yard line. Another missed opportunity for the Bills. Three plays later, Mike Garrett took a handoff at the 18 yard line and looked for an opening around left end. As the hole quickly closed, Garrett reversed his field and sprinted back to the right where he found that side of the field clogged with approaching linebackers as well. After a second's hesitation, he reversed his field again, and now found nothing but daylight in front of him. Garrett's second touchdown of the fourth quarter gave the Chiefs an insurmountable 31-7 lead. Kemp and the Bills valiantly tried to find the end zone, but each time they were stopped by the Chiefs, ending their last attempt with under two minutes left when defensive back Emmitt Thomas intercepted Kemp's last pass of the day. The Kansas City Chiefs won the AFL Championship and with it the right to play the Green Bay Packers in the first NFL/AFL Championship game—Super Bowl I!

Surrounded by more media hoopla and hype than ever seen in pro football, the ground-breaking game took place at the Los Angeles Coliseum on January 15 with a less than sellout crowd of 63,036 on hand. The NFL's CBS and the AFL's ABC broadcast the game using the same cameras, but each used its own announcers. The Chiefs fell behind first when the Packers reserve split end Max McGee, who was pressed into emergency action after an early injury to Boyd Dowler, reached back with one arm for a pass that was behind him. He seemed as surprised as anyone when the ball stuck to his right hand, and he ran into the end zone for a 37-yard touchdown.

The Chiefs, dressed in their white uniforms, tied the game in the second quarter with a 7-yard pass from Dawson to McClinton. But shortly after the Chiefs scored, Packer fullback Jim Taylor followed guards Jerry Kramer and Fuzzy Thurston around left end for a 14-yard touchdown that put Green Bay back in front by a touchdown. Before the half ended, KC's Mike Mercer kicked a 31-yard field goal to close the gap to 14-10.

Being behind by only four points at the intermission gave the Chiefs and their AFL boosters high hopes. Dawson called plays with confidence against the NFL powerhouse until the Chiefs started a downward spiral toward disaster on a third-down pass in the third quarter. Stepping in front of Fred Arbanas, Packer safety Willie Wood intercepted a pass and returned it to Kansas City's 5 yard line. It took the Packers only one play to put 6 more points on the board, extending the lead to 21-10. Two more Packer touchdowns followed, giving Green Bay their winning edge of 35-10.

Statistically, the game looked closer than it was. The Packers gained 130 yards on the ground to KC's 72. In the air, Green Bay gained 250 yards to the Chiefs 228. Each team intercepted 1 pass and was assessed four penalties. For one half of play, the Chiefs stayed with the NFL's best, and while some described the game as a humiliation for the league, proving the superiority of the NFL, the AFL learned lessons from the event that would help carry them to the next level. Equality for the two leagues, in their minds, was not far away, and the Kansas City Chiefs still had a big role to play in the AFL getting there.

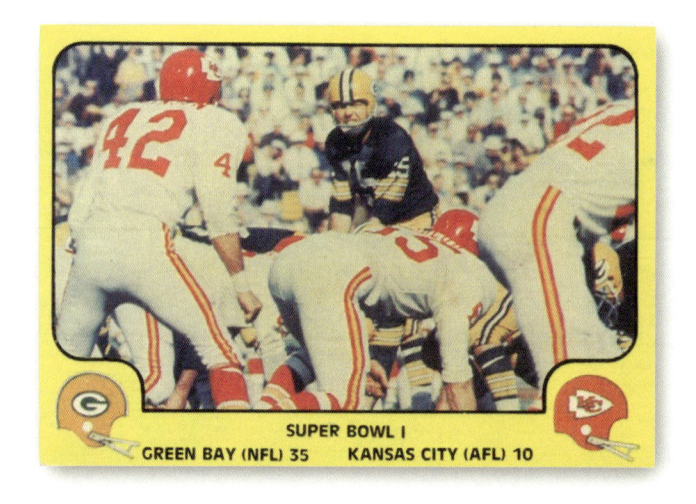

SUPER BOWL I
GREEN BAY (NFL) 35   KANSAS CITY (AFL) 10

Leading passers	Attempts	Completions	Pct	TDs	Yards	Int
Len Dawson	284	159	56%	26	2527	10
Pete Beathard	90	39	43%	4	578	4

Leading rushers	Attempts	Yards gained	Average	TDs
Mike Garrett	147	801	5.4	6
Curtis McClinton	140	540	3.9	4
Bert Coan	96	521	5.4	7
Len Dawson	24	167	7.0	0

The Progress of the Seasons – 1966

Leading receivers	Caught	Yards gained	Average	TDs
Otis Taylor	58	1297	22.4	8
Chris Burford	58	758	13.1	8
Fred Arbanas	22	305	13.9	4
Curtis McClinton	19	285	15.0	5
Bert Coan	18	131	7.3	2
Mike Garrett	15	175	11.7	1

Leading scorers	TDs	XPM	XPA	FGM	FGA	PTs
Mike Mercer		33	35	20	26	93
Bert Coan	9					54
Curtis McClinton	9					54

★ ★ ★ ★ ★ ★ ★ ★ ★ ★

On January 21, 1967, the sixth AFL All-Star game was played in Oakland-Alameda County Coliseum. The experimental Champs vs. League All-Stars format was scrapped after one year, and the contest returned to the traditional East vs. West rivalry. The East hoped to change their luck in the annual game, but the West took a quick 16-0 lead and then extended it to 23-2 in the third quarter. Played in a driving rainstorm in the East Bay, the game featured players sloshing through ankle-deep water retained on the Coliseum turf, which was below sea level. The weather kept the crowd under 19,000.

The scoring started after a fumble recovery by the West's E.J. Holub. Taking advantage of the turnover, Len Dawson hooked up with teammate Curtis McClinton for a 31-yard scoring pass. A slippery ball that flew out of the end zone on a fourth-down center snap accounted for the West's second score and a 9-0 margin. In the second quarter, Tom Flores hit Raider teammate Hewritt Dixon for a 17-yard touchdown, giving the West a 16-0 lead.

The East finally scored by sacking Dawson in his own end zone for a safety. The West then struck again with another score when Buck Buchannan raced 39 yards with a recovered fumble to give his side what seemed to be a big enough lead at 23-2. But Jets defensive end Verlon Biggs intercepted a pass and returned it 50 yards for the East's first touchdown, and when Babe Parilli relieved Jack Kemp the momentum changed dramatically. Parilli tossed 2 touchdown passes, and the Bills' Bobby Burnett ran in another after the East recovered a fumble. The second of Parilli's two scoring passes proved to be the game winner as he hit Oiler Charley Frazier for 17 yards. The East surged to scored 28 unanswered points in the last two periods and ended the West's four-game winning streak by gaining their first All-Star game victory 30-23.

★ ★ ★ ★ ★ ★ ★ ★ ★ ★ ★ ★

1967

AMERICAN FOOTBALL LEAGUE – 1967 FINAL STANDINGS

EASTERN DIVISION

TEAM	GP	W	L	T	PF	PA	PCT.
HOUSTON OILERS	14	9	4	1	258	199	0.679
NEW YORK JETS	14	8	5	1	371	329	0.607
BUFFALO BILLS	14	4	10	0	237	285	0.286
MIAMI DOLPHINS	14	4	10	0	219	407	0.286
BOSTON PATRIOTS	14	3	10	1	280	389	0.250

WESTERN DIVISION

TEAM	GP	W	L	T	PF	PA	PCT.
OAKLAND RAIDERS	14	13	1	0	468	233	0.929
KANSAS CITY CHIEFS	14	9	5	0	408	254	0.643
SAN DIEGO CHARGERS	14	8	5	1	360	352	0.607
DENVER BRONCOS	14	3	11	0	256	409	0.214

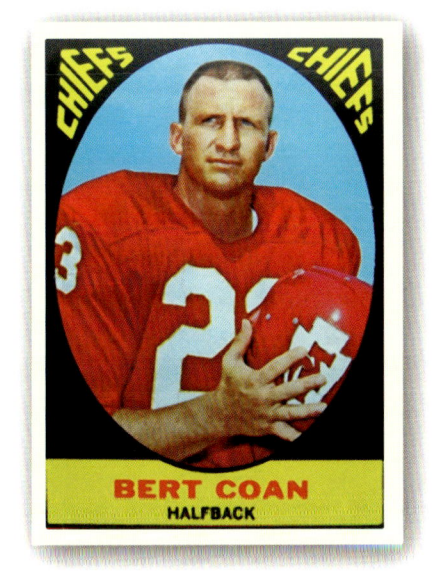

Bert Coan was a highly touted halfback out of the University of Kansas in 1962. At 6'4", 225 lbs. with 9.6 speed, Coan was said to have the potential to be a faster version of Jim Brown. Drafted by the Chargers, Coan played only briefly his first year, running the ball only twelve times in four games, having suffered a broken leg. After he recovered he was never quite the same, lacking the speed and explosion he once possessed. He went on to play six productive years with Kansas City, first as a backup to Abner Haynes, then as a starter in 1966, gaining 521 yards on 96 carries for a handsome 5.4 yards per carry before returning to the sidelines as Mike Garrett's backup. Elroy Bert Coan III retired after the 1968 season with 1,259 yards gained and 19 touchdowns after appearing in seventy-two American Football League games.

▪ BUFFALO BILLS ▪

AFTER FOUR STRAIGHT POST-SEASON appearances, including three league Championship games and two AFL titles, the Bills had begun to show signs that time, and the rest of the Eastern Division, were catching up with them. Built in the blueprint style of an NFL team, the Bills relied on a steady diet of overpowering defense and a bulldozing running game. The offensive line, one of the most stable in the league, supplied one of the main ingredients in the Buffalo success formula. Al Bemiller, Dave Behrman, Billy Shaw, Dick Hudson, and Stew Barber led the way for Buffalo runners who consistently finished at the top of the AFL in rushing. With the formidable front five opening holes for them, Bills runners enjoyed a decided advantage. Year after year the line formed the foundation of the ball-control offense, and as one runner moved on or got hurt, another moved in. It started with the arrival of Cookie Gilchrist, who captured two AFL rushing titles and one second-place finish. Then came rookie Roger Kochman, who was on the cusp of unquestionable greatness until he fell victim to a career-ending injury. When Gilchrist became disenchanted and was let go, along came Billy Joe, who teamed with the always reliable and underrated Wray Carlton to keep the Bills among the league's elite running games. Then came surprising Bobby Burnett, who bolted to Rookie-of-the-Year status, all of the backs enjoying success behind the five earth movers that defined the Buffalo offense.

The defense fielded the same group of destroyers against whom other teams tried to measure themselves. Tom Day, Ron McDole, Jim Dunaway, and perennial All-AFL tackle Tom Sestak anchored the front four. And always there was Harry Jacobs, Mike Stratton, and John Tracey backing them up. As the last line of defense, the secondary stuck like glue and hit like steamrollers. Tom Janik led the league with 10 interceptions in 1967 and teamed with Booker Edgerson, Hagood Clarke, Butch Byrd, and George Saimes, who were as good as any the NFL had to offer, keeping quarterbacks around the league talking to themselves and coaching staffs lying awake at night wondering how to infiltrate them. From 1963 to 1966 the Bills defense had few rivals. But things were about to change.

After their 31-7 loss to Kansas City in the 1966 Championship game, the Bills traded backup quarterback Daryle Lamonica and defensive end Tom Day. Lamonica was relieving Kemp with less frequency, while his pass completion percentage dropped in each of his four years, settling at 39.2 percent in 1966. Collier felt that packaging him and disappointing split end Glenn Bass in a deal for Oakland starters Tom Flores and former all-league end Art Powell would significantly upgrade both his quarterbacking and receiving. Day went to San Diego in exchange for triple-threat halfback Keith Lincoln. In the two deals, Collier picked up two all-star offensive weapons and a quarterback with starting ability, while giving up only one starter, Day, and two backups. But over the next three seasons Lamonica outlasted and out-produced all three offensive players the Bills received. Lincoln did lead the team in receiving and rushing in '67 with 601 yards on the ground to finish sixth in the league, but Powell, injured for half the season, caught only 20 passes and Flores completed only 34 percent of his 64 throws without a touchdown.

The usually powerful running game finished second from the bottom, and the top three rushers in the league each out-gained Lincoln's and Wray Carlton's combined total.

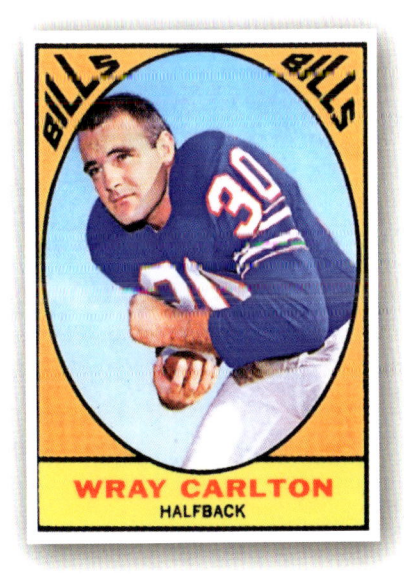

The passing attack plummeted to the bottom of the league. Injuries and age both played significant roles in Buffalo's fall from the Eastern pedestal. All-league guard Billy Shaw missed half the season, and receivers Charley Ferguson and Bobby Crockett never played a down. Kemp and Flores both saw time on the injured list, as did starters Wray Carlton, Hagood Clarke, and Harry Jacobs. And in the most devastating loss to the offense, halfback Bobby Burnett, last year's catalyst, injured his knee so severely that he carried the ball only 45 times and was left unprotected in the 1968 expansion draft, where he was selected by the Cincinnati Bengals.

As the Bills readied themselves for a run at their fourth consecutive Eastern Division title, it appeared to be status quo in Buffalo on opening day. Many around the league felt that Buffalo's biggest challenge in the East would come from the team they would host in the season opener, the improved and maturing New York Jets. The New Yorkers took a 17-0 lead into the fourth quarter while the Bills were showing little, if any, signs of life offensively until Jack Kemp finally connected with Powell for 2 touchdown passes on consecutive possessions. The defense then shut down the Jet offense. After New York was forced to punt, the Bills advanced to mid-field, where newly acquired kicker Mike Mercer nailed a 51-yard field goal to tie the game with less than three minutes left. With help again from the defense, the Bills got the ball back and began a final drive as valuable seconds ticked off the scoreboard clock. Finally, Mike Mercer again split the uprights from 43 yards away to push the Bills past a stunned team of New Yorkers. Both Powell and Lincoln played key roles in Buffalo's first win, Powell with his 2 touchdown receptions and Lincoln with 81 yards on the ground.

Remember the AFL

The dramatic win sent a strong message to the rest of the East that the Bills were still able to take on all comers—until all the comers heard the message and started to come. Hosting Houston and Boston in their next two games, the Bills could not mount any offense, and the once impenatrable defense could not hold off an opposing charge, leading to losses by a combined score of 43-3. After a third straight loss at home to San Diego, the Bills welcomed the road trip to Denver for a match against their former head coach Lou Saban. Winning 17-16 for their second victory only teased the Buffalo fans, as they knew these were not the same Bills that had rolled through the league for the past three seasons. The next seven weeks produced only one more win before the Patriots became their fourth and final victim of the season. The 4-10 season finally came to a merciful end on Christmas Eve with a 28-21 loss to Western Division Champion Oakland Raiders, led by none other than league-leading passer and AFL Player of the Year, Daryle Lamonica.

Arm pain nagged Kemp again throughout the season, and again he threw more interceptions (26) than touchdowns (14). It appeared as if his best days were behind him. Without Bobby Burnett the offense lacked speed in the backfield, leaving Lincoln and Carlton (467 yards) without any depth behind them. Lincoln became the primary weapon on the ground as well as in the air, leading the team in both departments. His 41 catches were 2 more than tight end Paul Costa pulled in. Elbert Dubenion and Powell, once two of the most prolific deep threats in the league, combined for only 45 catches. Dubenion was even shut out of the end zone for the first time in his career. The Bills had fallen on hard times in 1967, and although their 4-10 record was the worst in franchise history and five fewer than the previous year's division-leading total, things were about to take an even sharper turn for the worse!

Leading passers	Attempts	Completions	Pct	TDs	Yards	Int
Jack Kemp	369	161	44%	14	2503	26
Tom Flores	64	22	34%	0	260	8

Leading rushers	Attempts	Yards gained	Average	TDs
Keith Lincoln	159	601	3.8	4
Wray Carlton	107	467	4.4	3
Bobby Burnett	45	96	2.1	0
Jack Kemp	36	58	1.6	2
Charlie Bivens	15	58	3.9	0

The Progress of the Seasons – 1967

Leading receivers	Caught	Yards gained	Average	TDs		
Keith Lincoln	41	558	13.6	5		
Paul Costa	39	726	18.6	2		
Elbert Dubenion	25	384	15.4	0		
Billy Masters	20	274	13.7	2		
Art Powell	20	346	17.3	4		
Bobby Burnett	11	114	10.4	0		

Leading scorers	TDs	XPM	XPA	FGM	FGA	PTs
Mike Mercer		25	25	16	27	73
Keith Lincoln	9					54

---

37. The 1967 season was the first year in which the AFL and NFL faced each other in preseason games. In the first game ever played between the two leagues, outside of the championship arena, the Detroit Lions lost 13-7 to this AFL team.

38. On Saturday, September 9, 1967, the Patriots lost 28-14 to the Chargers in San Diego. On Saturday, October 7, 1967, Boston again played the Chargers in San Diego, tying them 31-31. Why did the Patriots play the Chargers twice in San Diego that year?

■ BOSTON PATRIOTS ■

AS NEW ENGLANDERS SPENT MOST OF the fall in a frenzy over the Red Sox in an autumn pennant race for the first time since 1949, the Patriots readied themselves for their eighth AFL season. With most of the focus on record-setting fullback Jim Nance, the team's aging but able quarterback and the defense that consistently ranked as one of the most difficult to score on became easy to overlook, not to mention the men who opened the holes for Nance. Center Jon Morris, guards Charley Long and Len St. Jean, and tackles Tom Neville and Don Oakes were the backbone of the offense. They provided Nance with the lanes to run through, and their fortress-like protection kept thirty-seven-year-old Vito "Babe" Parilli out of harm's way. And though the Pats fell to their worst record in team history (3-10-1), fingers didn't point at the offensive line as the cause.

DON OAKES — TACKLE

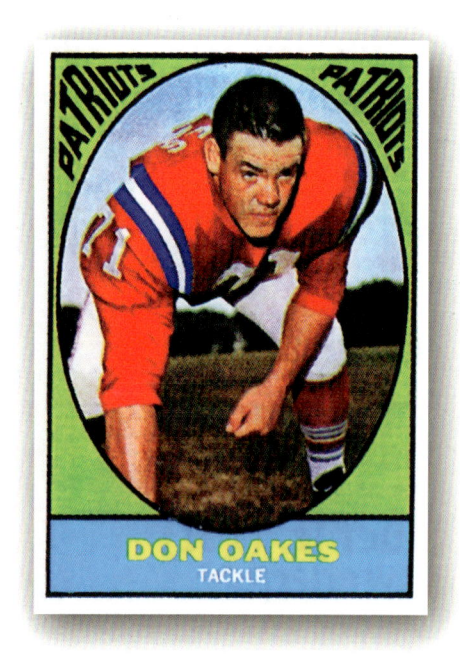

In an effort to shore up his perennially weak pass defense, Mike Holovak inserted rookies John Charles and Leroy Mitchell at the corners, and while the pair showed enormous potential, they also made rookie mistakes that subjected them to scrutiny from the rest of the AFL. As in seasons past, the Patriots allowed the highest percentage of pass completions in the league and the third highest total yards. All-star defensive end Larry Eisenhauer missed six games, and sidekick Bob Dee was showing signs of wear and tear from playing seven years without missing a single game. All-league middle linebacker Nick Buoniconti also missed several games early in the season with a kidney injury. Yet, through the efforts of defensive tackles Jim Hunt and Houston Antwine, the Patriots still posted the second-best defense against the run.

The season started in Denver, where Boston dropped a 26-21 gunfight, with the Broncos winning score coming via a 29-yard interception return by Goldie Sellers in the fourth quarter. They then traveled to San Diego and another loss 28-24, after the Chargers scored the game's last 21 points. Again the final score was the result of an interception return for a touchdown. A trip to Oakland brought the same losing result, and again after a first quarter 7-7 tie, the Raiders rung up 28 straight points in the last three periods while holding Boston scoreless. It took a return cross-country flight to Buffalo and a shutout to record the first victory of 1967.

After starting the season with four games on the road, it was finally time to kick off in Fenway Park. Scheduled for their home opener on October 7, the Patriots were forced to travel back to San Diego for a home (away from home) game since Fenway's owners, the Boston Red Sox, were playing in the World Series. Not until October 15 were the Patriots (1-3-1) able to host a home game. In desperate need of a win, Boston proved that there was no place like home with their second victory, a 41-10 thumping of Miami ignited by 5 Babe Parilli touchdown passes. Losses to Oakland and the Jets followed, and after defeating Houston in their ninth outing, Boston lost their last five games against the Chiefs, Jets, Oilers, Bills, and Dolphins, dropping them to dead last in the East for the first time since 1960 with a franchise-worst 3-10-1 record. The lone Boston highlight in 1967 was Jim Nance, who won his second consecutive rushing title to become the first AFL runner to

The Progress of the Seasons – 1967

crack 1,000 yards in two consecutive years. Their second-leading rusher, Larry Garron, carried the ball only 46 times and gained only 163 yards. Art Graham (41 catches) and Jim Whalen (39) were the Pats most successful receivers. Boston's Champions Without a Crown in 1966 had fallen into the league's basement. Many questions needed answers before they would find a way out.

Leading passers	Attempts	Completions	Pct	TDs	Yards	Int
Babe Parilli	344	161	47%	19	2317	24
Don Trull	81	27	33%	1	442	7
John Huarte	9	3	33%	0	25	1

Leading rushers	Attempts	Yards gained	Average	TDs
Jim Nance	269	1216	4.5	7
Larry Garron	46	163	3.5	0
Bob Cappadona	28	100	3.6	0
Babe Parilli	14	61	4.4	0

Leading receivers	Caught	Yards gained	Average	TDs
Art Graham	41	606	14.8	4
Jim Whalen	39	651	16.7	5
Gino Cappelletti	35	397	11.3	3
Larry Garron	30	507	16.9	5
Jim Nance	22	196	8.9	1
Jim Colclough	14	263	18.8	0

Leading scorers	TDs	XPM	XPA	FGM	FGA	PTs
Gino Cappelletti	3	29	30	16	31	95
Jim Nance	8					48

39. Yearning to save face after their 35-10 loss in Super Bowl I, the Kansas City Chiefs played their first inter-league preseason game against the Chicago Bears. The Chiefs destroyed the Monsters of the Midway ___ to 24. How many points did the Chiefs run up against the Bears?

▪ DENVER BRONCOS ▪

WITH HIS TEN-YEAR CONTRACT IN hand, Lou Saban and his Broncos became heroes to all AFL players and fans on August 5, when they became the first American Football League team to defeat an NFL team. They did it in an exhibition game in the Mile High city against the Detroit Lions 13-7, and then put another hurt on the NFL's Minnesota Vikings the very next week! Of the three pre-games that AFL teams won against their NFL rivals in 1967, Denver authored two of them. The overall record between the two leagues in the first year of head-to-head, inter-league pre-season play was NFL 12–AFL 3. As one NFL representative said, "The leagues are still that far apart."

The Broncos changed uniforms and helmets again in 1967, and for the fourth time in eight years started the season with new attire. Their helmets went from being orange with a white bronco on the sides to blue with a white stripe down the center. Significant by its absence was the bucking bronco on either side of the helmet and, curiously, Denver's new helmet had no logo, caricature, or any other marking on either side, making them one of only two teams in both the NFL and AFL to not sport any type of helmet graphic (the Cleveland Browns being the other). Gone, too, were the contrasting sleeves of blue at home and orange on their road jerseys. New this year were traditional alternating blue and white stripes on the sleeves of their orange home shirts and blue, orange and blue on the white away shirts.

For most of the Broncos' season the story could be summed up in three names: Al Denson, Floyd Little, and Eric Crabtree. With legendary split end Lionel Taylor traded to Oakland, Lou Saban moved tight end Denson to split end where he had such a spectacular season that at the end of the year he found himself on the AFL's all-league team. He corralled 46 passes and had a league-high 11 touchdowns. His wide receiver partner Eric Crabtree also caught 46 passes, giving Denver two quality receivers. Rookie halfback Floyd Little, the latest in the long line of outstanding running backs from Syracuse, brought crowds to their feet with his exciting punt and kick-off returns and also gave the Broncos a star-quality halfback. Little dashed and dazzled his way to a league-leading 16.9-yard average on punt returns and a 26.9 average on kick returns. He also led the team with 381 yards rushing, and with 130 carries.

In an effort to balance his ground game, Saban spent most of the year looking for a compatible running mate for his rookie sensation. He tried Charlie Mitchell, who was still looking for his rookie-year magic, as well as another rookie, Bo Hickey. Even his old nemesis Cookie Gilchrist returned from Miami for a shot but lasted only 10 carries into the first game when he suffered a career-ending leg injury. Then came former starter Wendell Hayes, but no one was able to fill the bill with any consistency or reliability to take the defensive heat off Little.

Saban also put an end to the annual quarterback scramble by trading two first-round draft picks to San Diego for backup Steve Tensi, a durable 6'5" thrower from Florida State. Tensi had caddied for John Hadl the past two years and was thought to be a star needing an opportunity. He started slowly,

The Progress of the Seasons – 1967

gained momentum, and by the last third of the season looked like the player Saban hoped he would be. He started and finished all fourteen games and completed 40 percent of his 325 passes for 16 touchdowns.

The Broncos under Saban had their best preseason showing in team history, winning their final three games. And when the season started on September 3, the momentum kept them on the winning track with a 26-21 win over Boston, thanks in part to a fourth-quarter interception return for a touchdown by safety Goldie Sellers. After what looked like a bright beginning to the Saban era, they hit the wall—and nine straight losses followed, starting with a 51-0 embarrassment in Oakland. Their next win didn't come until November 19, a 21-20 win in Buffalo. Their third and last win of the season consequently knocked the wind out of the Eastern Division-leading Jets, as the Broncos converted 4 second-quarter interceptions and Floyd Little's 72-yard punt-return touchdown into 26 points to upset New York 33-24. The Jet loss would keep their hope of postseason play on hold for another season as they lost to the division-champion Oilers by one game. Playing spoiler to New York was Denver's proudest moment in an otherwise nondescript season. The season ended much the same as every other, this time with a 3-11 record.

Although Saban had made progress, and Tensi, Denson, Little, and Crabtree offered glimmers of hope, it was the same old story in the old West—too few points scored, too many points scored upon. Saban's first year in Denver was not a good one for the coach who was used to winning. His last stint in the pro ranks garnered back-to-back AFL titles and banked on a superior defense and a ball-control offense. In 1967, Denver had neither. Their passing finished seventh, their running ninth, and their defense left no one doubting why they gave up a league-high 409 points.

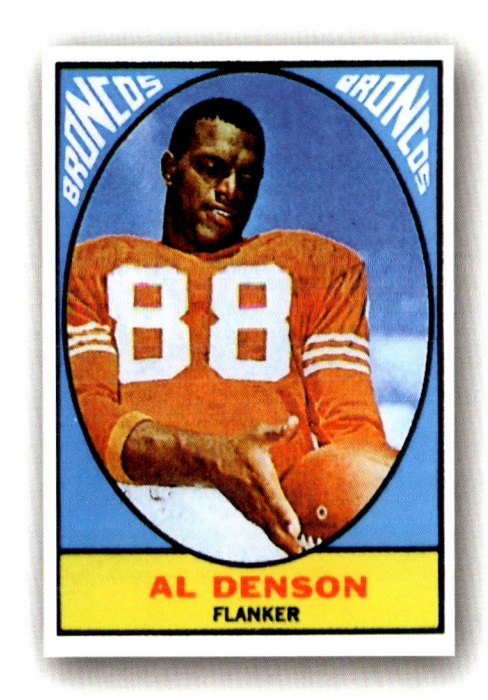

Remember the AFL

The team needed a blueprint for success similar to the one used in Houston. There was much more to do in Denver, and Saban had nine more years to do it. In spite of their long string of losing seasons, the Broncos were the AFL's equivalent of baseball's New York Mets. Their fans loved them, come rain, snow, sleet, or hail. Win (which wasn't often) or lose (which happened far too often), the Denver faithful came out to cheer their team. The Broncos drew a record 231,801 fans to Bears Stadium that year, and with a stadium expansion project scheduled in the off-season, 50,000 more seats were available for next year.

Leading passers	Attempts	Completions	Pct	TDs	Yards	Int
Steve Tensi	325	131	40%	16	1915	17
Jim LeClair	45	19	42%	1	275	1

Leading rushers	Attempts	Yards gained	Average	TDs
Floyd Little	130	381	2.9	1
Charlie Mitchell	82	308	3.8	0
Bo Hickey	73	263	3.6	4
Wendell Hayes	85	255	3.0	4

Leading receivers	Caught	Yards gained	Average	TDs
Al Denson	46	899	19.5	11
Eric Crabtree	46	716	15.6	5
Wendell Hayes	13	125	9.6	0
Tom Beer	11	155	14.1	0

Leading scorers	TDs	XPM	XPA	FGM	FGA	PTs
Al Denson	11					66
Bob Humphreys		18	19	7	15	39

▪ MIAMI DOLPHINS ▪

LOOKING TO THE FUTURE AND BUILDing their second-year franchise through the college draft, the Dolphins understood they were still a few years away from contention. After using four ineffective quarterbacks their first year, the Dolphins chose Purdue's Bob Griese as their franchise player. The coach's son was traded, and Rick Norton hoped to recover from a series of unfortunate injuries. John Stofa, who directed the Dolphins to a last-minute victory in the season's last game a year ago, became the starting play caller. But after scoring on an 8-yard run against Denver in the first quarter of the first game, Stofa fractured his ankle and missed the rest of the season. The Dolphins turned sooner than

GEORGE WILSON, JR.
QUARTERBACK

RICK NORTON
QUARTERBACK

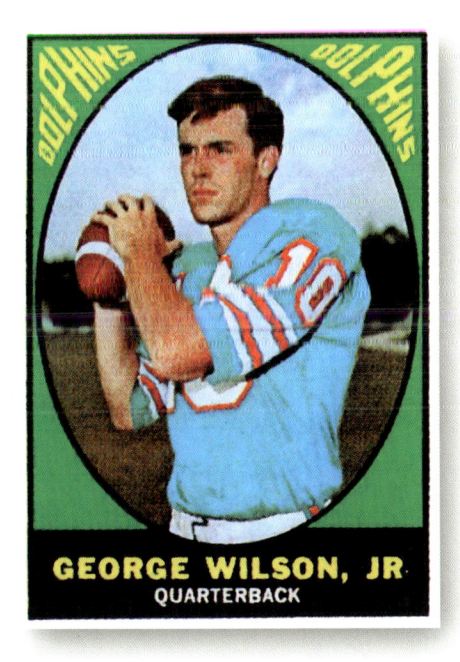

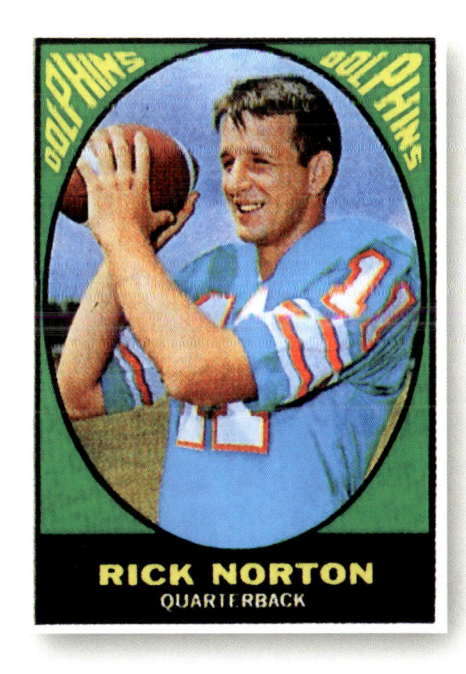

planned to Griese. In his first game, he dazzled the crowd by completing 12 of 19 passes, and newly acquired halfback Abner Haynes ran for 151 yards to lift Miami over the Broncos 35-21. Griese was the only rookie to start at quarterback in the AFL in '67, and he led his team to a respectable 4-10 record in only their second year. He threw 331 passes, completing 166 (50 percent) for 2,004 yards and 15 touchdowns to rank fifth best among AFL quarterbacks. He adjusted quickly to the pro game, and in one stretch threw 122 passes without an interception. He threw 18 for the year but gained invaluable experience that would pay off down the road.

Griese's receivers were young, fast, and talented, with the best of the lot also cutting his teeth as a rookie. Michigan's Jack Clancy pulled in a rookie-record 67 passes for the league's third-highest total behind only George Sauer and Don Maynard. Sophomore Doug Moreau, another quick study, unseated Dave Kocourek as the Dolphin tight end, catching 34 passes for a 12-yard average. Howard Twilley, another second-year receiver, caught 24 balls, while Karl Noonan, still another member of this great sophomore class, gave the starters a speedy backup.

Griese also benefited from an offensive line that featured some notable starters. Center Tom Goode and tackle Norm Evans, both snatched from Houston, protected the prize rookie, as did former Boston starter Billy Neighbors at guard. A lack of depth on the line and in the backfield, however, kept the running game from making the strides that coach Wilson hoped to see, making it difficult to establish a balanced attack. Ranking sixth out of the nine AFL teams, Miami's ground game toiled in anonymity. Big-name backs allowing 29 points per game.

After their opening-day win in the Orange Bowl, the growing pains for Miami continued. For the next eight games the Dolphins never lost by less than 19 points and allowed more than 30 in five of them. But in the last part of the season, they started to show signs of improvement by winning three of their final five contests. A 31-yard touchdown pass from Griese to Twilley with 1:01 left in the last quarter gave the Dolphins a come-from-behind win against the Bills, 17-14, on November 26. In their twelfth game they scored more than 17 points for only the second time all year, putting up a season-high 41 points against the 8-3 Chargers in their 41-24 win. The defense also came through with 5 interceptions in the game and held San Diego under 100 yards rushing. On December 17, the Orange Bowl hosted a game that could have been billed as "the battle to escape the Eastern Division basement" against the Boston Patriots. Miami was 3-9 and Boston was at 3-9-1. The Dolphins won with touchdown passes to Harper and Mitchell and 2 interception returns for touchdowns by cornerbacks Jim Warren and Dick Westmoreland. Kicker Booth Lusteg added 2 second-half field goals, and for the second week in a row they scored 41 points. The blend of age and youth kept the Dolphins competitive and enthusiastic all season, and while the growing pains continued, so did the improvements in nearly every department. The Dolphins were on the right track and excited about the future.

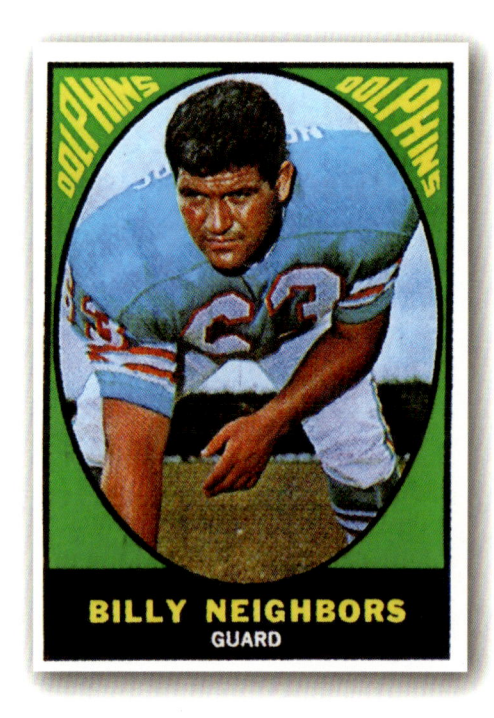

like Cookie Gilchrist and Billy Joe left for Denver and New York, and by mid-season leading rusher Abner Haynes also went to the Jets. Stan Mitchell, ranked eighteenth in the league, led the runners, picking up a scant 269 yards on 83 tries for a 3.2 average. His partners, Jack Harper (4.8-yard average) and Sam Price (3.9 average), each carried the ball less than 50 times with neither gaining 200 yards.

The Dolphins not only couldn't run, they couldn't stop the run either, allowing more yardage (2,145) on the ground than every other team. In the secondary, cornerback Dick Westmoreland tied for the league lead with 10 interceptions, but overall the corps was ineffective, allowing the opposition a 54 percent completion rate, a league high. As expected, the Dolphins also had trouble keeping their opponents out of the end zone,

The Progress of the Seasons – 1967

Leading passers	Attempts	Completions	Pct	TDs	Yards	Int
Bob Griese	331	166	50%	15	2005	18
Rick Norton	133	53	40%	1	596	9

Leading rushers	Attempts	Yards gained	Average	TDs
Abner Haynes	56	274	4.9	2
Stan Mitchell	83	269	3.2	3
Jack Harper	41	197	4.8	1
Sam Price	46	179	3.9	1

Leading receivers	Caught	Yards gained	Average	TDs
Jack Clancy	67	868	12.0	2
Doug Moreau	34	410	12.1	3
Howard Twilley	24	314	13.1	2
Stan Mitchell	18	133	7.4	1
Joe Auer	18	218	12.1	2
Abner Haynes	16	100	6.3	0

Leading scorers	TDs	XPM	XPA	FGM	FGA	PTs
Booth Lusteg		18	18	7	12	39
Jack Harper	4					24
Stan Mitchell	4					24

▪ NEW YORK JETS ▪

FROM THE FOURTH WEEK OF THE season through the fifteenth, the New York Jets either led or were tied for the lead in the Eastern Division. At 8-5-1 they finished one game behind the Oilers, and for the first time in franchise history won more games than they lost. Considering that the starting backfield of Matt Snell and Emerson Boozer appeared in only one game together, and the Jets had to rely almost exclusively on the arm of Joe Namath, they were arguably the East's best team. Snell, who carried only 61 times for 207 yards without a touchdown, suffered a knee injury in the opening game and had to sit out the next eight weeks. Although Bill Mathis, Billy Joe, and Mark Smolinski lent their able bodies, losing the threat of Snell—not to mention his running, blocking, and receiving skills—left a big void in the New York offense.

Emerson Boozer, perhaps the best halfback in the East through the first eight weeks, gained 442 yards on 119 carries to help fill the void. He was on his way to breaking the single-season touchdown mark, punching across the goal line for a league-leading 10 rushing and 3 receiving touchdowns in the first half of the season. But just as Snell was ready to rejoin him and make a push to win the division,

GERRY PHILBIN — DEFENSIVE END

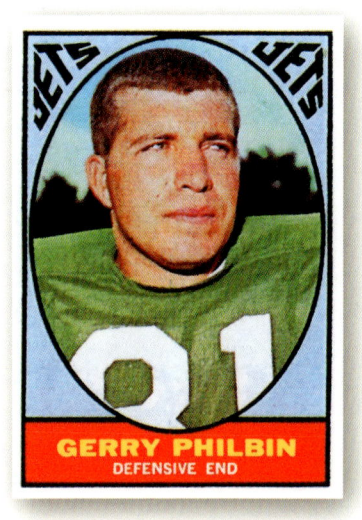

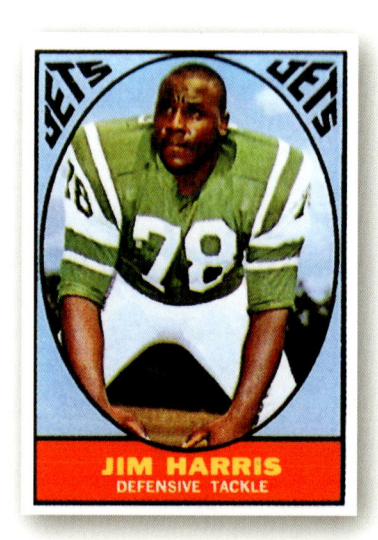

LARRY GRANTHAM — LINEBACKER

JIM HARRIS — DEFENSIVE TACKLE

Boozer got hurt and missed the last six games. With their new star back lost for the rest of the season, the Jets needed someone who could supply speed around the corners. They looked no further than their division mates in Florida and picked up aging star Abner Haynes from Miami, hoping that the AFL's first Rookie of the Year still had some magic left.

But Joe Namath remained the catalyst for the offense. When he was on, he was the most dangerous passer in the AFL. When he was off, his unrelenting confidence became his worst enemy. Many times he rushed his throws and often threw into heavy coverage. Sometimes he put the ball up for grabs in hope that his superior receivers would pull down his errant throws. Now in his third professional season, Namath threw more passes (491), for more completions (258) and more yards (4,007) than anyone in the AFL for the second year in a row. He also became the first quarterback in pro football history to pass for 4,000 yards in a season. He also threw more interceptions (28) than anyone else, and in one game against Houston set a record by throwing 6.

As Namath went in 1967, so went the Jets. As a result, New York led the AFL not only in passing offense, but also in total offense, eclipsing the champion Oakland Raiders by almost 600 yards through the air. And for the first and only time in the AFL's history, two receivers from the same team finished as the top two pass catchers. George Sauer led the AFL in receptions with 75 catches for a 16-yard average. Don Maynard caught 71 balls for a league-leading 1,434 yards and 10 touchdowns. Tight end Pete Lammons finished eleventh with 45 receptions. To provide protection for Namath and his gimpy knees, Weeb Ewbank built an outstanding line made up of tackles Sherman Plunkett and Winston Hill, guards Dave Herman and rookie Randy Rasmussen, who unseated veteran Sam DeLuca, and center John Schmitt.

New York's gallant run at the division title this year proved they were on the verge of greatness. They were young and dangerous on offense and within a piece or two on defense of getting to the next level. By getting to within one game of the division crown with their star runners hurt, the Jets knew they had unlimited potential.

In the opener against the mighty Bills, the Jets led 17-0 after three quarters, only to see their chance for an upset slipping away when kicker Mike Mercer tied it on a 51-yard field goal with 2:27 left in the game. He then won it with four seconds remaining with a walk-off 43-yard field goal to give Buffalo a 20-17 win. It was a wake-up call for the defense, a character builder for the entire team, and a taste of what it would take to beat the best. Three straight victories followed, including wins over Denver and Miami that acted as warm-ups to their highlight victory of the season, handing Oakland their only loss.

Led by Boozer's 8 touchdowns, they met for first place on October 15 against the revitalized Houston Oilers. Again the Jets jumped out to a 17-0 lead and tried to add to it in the closing seconds of the second quarter when Houston defensive end Pat Holmes got a hand on Jim Turner's field goal attempt. Houston rookie Ken Houston picked up the loose ball and returned it 71 yards for an Oiler touchdown. Shocked and disappointed, the Jets had difficulty finding their way in the second half. Namath tried in vain to will a New York victory, but 6 second-half interceptions brought Houston back to tie the game at 28-28 late in the fourth quarter. With five seconds to play, Namath, confident that he could pull a win out of his hat, challenged the Oiler secondary one last time. As he fired his last pass of the day down the middle of the field, cornerback W.K. Hicks picked it off and returned it to the Jet 35 yard line in the middle of the field where he was stopped. But before he went down, Hicks lateraled the ball to safety Ken Houston. Houston ran a few yards before getting hit, and just before he fell he lateraled to Larry Carwell, who headed down the right sideline toward the goal line. Dodging tackler after tackler, Carwell nearly broke free until Namath threw himself in front of the blocking escort at the 3 yard line, saving the tie for New York and allowing the entire Shea Stadium crowd to exhale.

On November 19 the Jets were 7-2-1 and ahead of second-place Houston by two games. But after a bye week, during which Houston won, the Jets took the Shea Stadium field against the 2-10 Denver Broncos with only a one-game lead. After a slow and scoreless start by both teams, the Broncos turned 4 Namath interceptions into 26 second-quarter points to knock off New York 33-25. With Houston winning again, the Jets now had to share first place with the surging Oilers. A second loss in a row, this time to Kansas City, coupled with an Oiler loss to Oakland, kept the two teams deadlocked with only two games left on the schedule. Houston had to play 8-3-1 San Diego at home and 3-9 Miami on the road, while the Jets had two games away with 11-1 Oakland and the Chargers.

The pressure enveloped the defense. Without a single member of the New York defense making the all-league team since 1964, the Jets needed an identity and a leader. The front four performed inconsistently. While Gerry Philbin continued to improve, his partner, Verlon Biggs, had yet to duplicate his strong rookie performance of 1965. Paul Rochester provided a veteran tower of strength at tackle, but Jim Harris dropped off and felt pressed by young John Elliott. Linebackers Larry Grantham, a former all-league selection, and middle man Al Atkinson led the Jets with 5 interceptions. Cornerbacks Randy Beverly and Johnny Sample, along with safety Jim Hudson, each intercepted 4. Bill Baird, the other safety, added three to the team's 27 total.

With visions of a championship dancing in their heads, the Jets now faced two of the league's most difficult opponents, starting on December 17 in Oakland. Since the earlier game between the teams, the Raiders had not lost, running off eight straight victories over the next two months. By the end of the day, they won nine. Losing to the Raiders 38-29, coupled with Houston defeating San Diego, dropped the Jets out of first place for the first time since September 24. On the season's final weekend, the Jets took on the Chargers while Houston needed only to knock off Miami to claim the Eastern crown. The Jets finished the season on a high note with a 42-31 victory in San Diego. Namath finished with a flurry of passes to Maynard, the team's MVP, and Sauer, both of whom went over 100 yards in the game. Namath completed 18 of 26 passes for 343 yards. But a one-sided victory by Houston over Miami sealed the East for the Oilers and sent the Jets into the off-season looking toward the future.

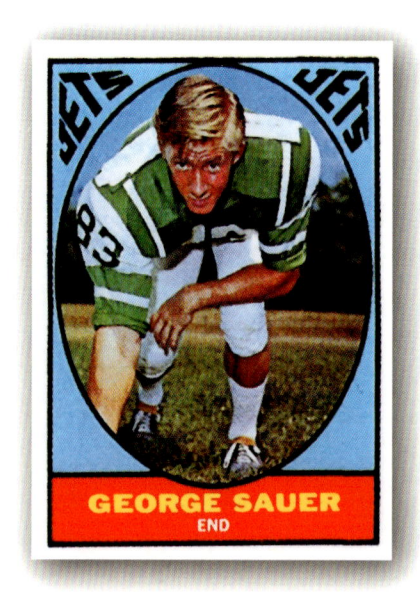

The Jets knew they had relied too heavily on Namath's arm to offset their hobbled running game. They'd also blown two 17-point leads that led to a loss to Buffalo and a tie with Houston. But the power structure in the East had changed in 1967, as perennial powerhouses Buffalo and Boston had dipped below .500 and the Oilers, who had just suffered through four straight losing seasons, leaped to the top of the division with a defense that seemed to score nearly as often as their offense. To many, the Jets were the best and most balanced team in the East. But it would take much more consistency on defense and more maturity from Namath before anyone saw them as more than just the best team on paper. The old Brooklyn battle cry "Wait 'til next year" swirled through the off-season winds of Flushing Meadows. And the New York Jets finally believed they were a team on the threshold of greatness.

The Progress of the Seasons – 1967

Leading passers	Attempts	Completions	Pct	TDs	Yards	Int
Joe Namath	491	258	53%	26	4007	28
Mike Taliaferro	20	11	55%	1	96	1

Leading rushers	Attempts	Yards gained	Average	TDs
Emerson Boozer	119	442	3.7	10
Bill Mathis	78	243	3.1	4
Matt Snell	61	207	3.4	0
Billy Joe	37	154	4.2	2
Mark Smolinski	64	139	2.2	1
Abner Haynes	16	72	4.5	0

Leading receivers	Caught	Yards gained	Average	TDs
George Sauer	75	1189	15.9	6
Don Maynard	71	1434	20.2	10
Pete Lammons	45	515	11.4	2
Bill Mathis	25	429	17.2	3
Mark Smolinski	21	177	8.4	3
Emerson Boozer	12	205	17.1	3

Leading scorers	TDs	XPM	XPA	FGM	FGA	PTs
Jim Turner		36	39	17	32	87
Emerson Boozer	13					78

■ KANSAS CITY CHIEFS ■

THE CHIEFS WERE PRIMED FOR THE biggest game of the year, and it was still only August! Since January 15, they wanted to show the NFL that they were a better team than they showed in their 35-10 loss to Green Bay in Super Bowl I. To atone for their humiliation, the Chiefs planned to take their frustration out on George Halas and his Chicago Bears. It was Super Bowl I-A. They had already rolled over three of their top AFL foes, including a 48-0 romp over Oakland as tune-ups for their only home exhibition game. The red and white reeled off a team-record 66 points against one of the NFL's premier teams, whose very owner and head coach had played a major role in the creation of the AFL with a staunch refusal to allow Lamar Hunt membership to his elite league. The best running team in the AFL piled up 182 yards rushing, with second-year back Mike Garrett, who scouts said was too small for the NFL, scoring four times. Len Dawson also enjoyed a big game, firing 4 touchdown passes. The defense, exploited by the Packers seven months ago, chilled the Bear ground game by holding the NFL's best runner, Gale Sayers, to 35 yards.

Sayers had been KC's top draft pick in 1965 but chose to go to the NFL with Papa Bear in the Windy City. With the Super Bowl finally behind them, the Chiefs set out to defend their AFL title.

In their first regular season game, against Houston, Len Dawson set a pro football record by completing 15 straight passes, and rookie kicker Jan Stenerud, a Norwegian ski jumper from Montana State, nailed a 54-yard field goal to get the Chiefs started with a 25-20 win. Stram was especially thrilled with the play of the six rookies who made the squad, including linebacker Jim Lynch from Notre Dame, the Maxwell Trophy winner, and Willie Lanier, also a linebacker and Little All-American. Stenerud, a long-range soccer-style kicker, regularly sent kickoffs 70 yards deep and had a field goal range that was nearly as far. Gloster Richardson was a willowy flanker, while speedy Nolan Smith, a 5'6" 154-pound kick returner, was so quick and elusive that Stram immediately dubbed him the "super gnat." All of the blue-chip rookies would be around to see action in Super Bowl IV for the Chiefs in 1969.

A 2-point loss to Oakland after shutting out Miami gave KC a 2-1 record in September. Then in the home opener, the Chiefs shut out Miami again, 41-0, intercepting 5 passes in the game. In their second meeting against Houston, the Chiefs dominated in every category expect the final score. They doubled Houston's offensive output and held former teammate Pete Beathard to only 3 pass completions and 7 first downs, but lost the game 24-19. A Houston kickoff return for a touchdown and an interception return for another touchdown were the downfalls.

The big defensive front four in Kansas City took on another dimension as the season progressed. Trading Beathard to Houston brought in massive defensive tackle Ernie Ladd, who played alongside Buck Buchannan, giving the Chiefs two inside pass rushers over 6'7" and 300 pounds. With Jerry Mays playing up to his all-league caliber for another year, the pass rush and run defense was without equal. Willie Lanier filled in for long-time middle linebacker Sherrill Headrick, who suffered several injuries. Lanier also experienced some self-imposed trouble as his crushing tackles caused him chronic headaches before he began wearing a specially designed helmet with an extra exterior cushion. E.J. Holub even saw action in the middle on certain coverages, but his damaged knees limited him to only a half season. Jim Lynch became a force on the outside with Bobby Bell, one of the best linebackers in the game, a deterant on the other side of the defense. Fred Williamson and Willie Mitchell, who Green Bay targeted and exploited in the Super Bowl, experienced the same treatment from AFL teams, causing Stram to insert Fletcher Smith, the team leader with 6 interceptions, and Jim Kearney on the wings more frequently. Johnny Robinson and Bobby Hunt continued to play well as the safeties.

The Chiefs stood at 3-3 when they made a three-game surge both offensively and defensively. Denver took a 52-9 shellacking. Dealing out much of the torment was Mike Garrett,

BOBBY BELL
LINEBACKER

JOHNNY ROBINSON
DEFENSIVE HALFBACK

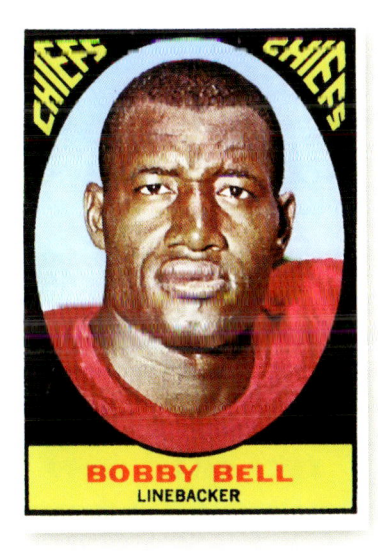

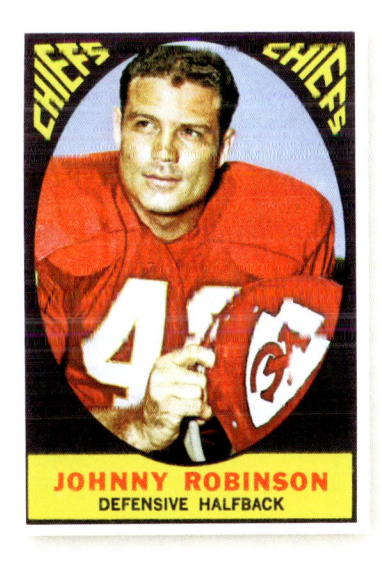

who rushed for more than 100 yards for the second time in the season, and Len Dawson, who struck for three touchdown passes. KC then pounded the Jets 42-18. Leading by only 13-10 at the half, the Chiefs got rolling in the third quarter thanks in part to Mike Garrett's team-record 192 yards rushing for the game. Boston felt the same hurt a week later as the Chiefs pushed their record to 6-3 with a 33-10 win over the Pats.

Kansas City was on a roll, but still needed a win the next week against San Diego to stay in contention. With twenty-three seconds left and the Chiefs behind 17-16, reliable rookie Jan Stenerud uncharacteristically missed a 23-yard field goal, which pinned all their hope of defending the 1966 crown on their next game, a Thanksgiving Day contest against the Raiders in Municipal Stadium. On that gray, overcast afternoon, hope turned to dismay as the Chiefs lost again to Oakland, 44-22. With a record of 6-5 the Chiefs dropped four games behind the Raiders, who sported an insurmountable 10-1 record with only three games remaining.

In their final game, a win over Denver, Kansas City set two team records when Nolan Smith ran back a kickoff 106 yards for a touchdown and Mike Garrett became the first KC runner to go over 1,000 yards rushing. He gained 169 yards against the Broncos to end the season as the league's third-best runner with 1,087 yards for a 4.9 average and 9 touchdowns. Garrett's 236 carries nearly tripled those of Curtis McClinton, who carried the ball 97 times for 392 yards. But as coach Stram noted, much of Garrett's success with the ball could be attributed to McClinton's deft blocking. Reserve Bert Coan ran the ball 63 times for 275 yards.

Winning their last three games raised the Chiefs to 9-5, the AFL's second-best record. Stram noted that their failure to defend their title was more a matter of the Raiders flat out taking it. Only three teams in all of pro football posted more wins in 1967 than the Chiefs, who were second in scoring and third in fewest points allowed in the AFL.

The defense led the AFL in interceptions with 31, returning 4 of them for touchdowns. Len Dawson, the league's second-best passer, completed an incredible 57.7 percent of his throws with 24 touchdowns and 2,651 yards. Emerging superstar Otis Taylor pulled down 59 receptions (fourth in the league) for a 16.2 average and a league-high 11 touchdowns. Mike Garrett caught 46 passes, with McClinton and Chris Burford grabbing 26 and 25 respectively. Rookie sensations Nolan Smith and Jan Stenerud provided still more reason to cheer the team. Smith returned more kickoffs (41) and gained more yards (1148) than any other returner, and Stenerud, the league's number-two scorer, was perfect on 45 extra point tries while hitting on 21 of 36 field goal attempts, for 108 points. The Chiefs were now established as one pro football's most powerful teams, and they set a new Western Division attendance record that included a franchise record 33,118 season ticket sales. Only the New York Jets drew more fans. The rivalry with the Raiders became the hallmark of the league in its final years. The two goliaths would meet an unprecedented six more times, in what would be the most classic confrontations the league had ever known.

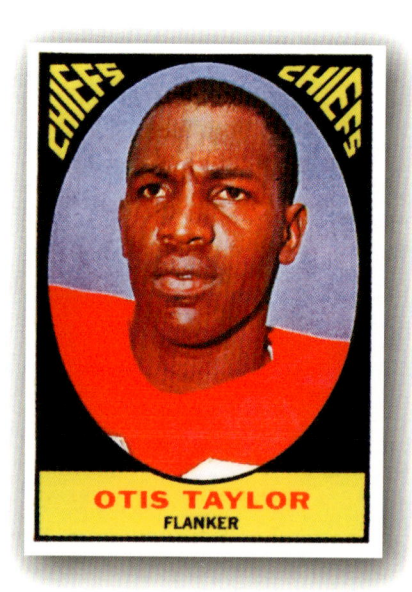

Leading passers	Attempts	Completions	Pct	TDs	Yards	Int
Len Dawson	357	206	58%	24	2651	17
Jacky Lee	19	6	32%	1	105	2

Leading rushers	Attempts	Yards gained	Average	TDs
Mike Garrett	236	1087	4.6	9
Curtis McClinton	97	392	4.0	2
Bert Coan	63	275	4.4	4
Gene Thomas	35	133	3.8	1

Leading receivers	Caught	Yards gained	Average	TDs
Otis Taylor	59	958	16.2	11
Mike Garrett	46	261	5.7	1
Curtis McClinton	26	219	8.4	1
Chris Burford	25	389	15.6	3
Fred Arbanas	20	295	14.8	5
Gene Thomas	13	99	7.6	2

The Progress of the Seasons – 1967

Leading scorers	TDs	XPM	XPA	FGM	FGA	PTs
Jan Stenerud		45	45	21	36	108
Otis Taylor	12					72

---

40. E. J. Holub was a stellar player for the Dallas Texans and Kansas City Chiefs for nine years at linebacker and center. The J. in his name stood for Joe, but what did the E. stand for?
A. Emil
B. Elijah
C. Estes
D. Earl

■ SAN DIEGO CHARGERS ■

THREE YEARS AFTER THE NEW YORK Jets became the envy of the league with Shea Stadium, and one year after the Oakland Raiders christened their state-of-the-art facility in Alameda County, the San Diego Chargers cut the ribbon on a brand new venue, the 50,000-seat San Diego Stadium. And after the first three preseason games in their new home, all losses to NFL opponents, the Chargers had to wonder what their fate away from cozy Balboa Stadium would bring when the regular season began.

With the new stadium came new uniforms, or rather a return to the old ones. They reverted to the gold lightning bolts on their helmet and also brought back the bolt stripes on their gold pants. It looked like old times as the season kicked off with fullback Gene Foster and halfback Paul Lowe in the backfield for the first two games. But injuries to both players created opportunities for two rookies. Dickie Post and Brad Hubbert became the new star tandem that rivaled the memory of Lincoln and Lowe in their heyday. While injuries opened the door, it was the brilliant offensive line that drove the rookies to finish fourth and fifth among AFL rushers, even though they did not become starters until the season's third game. Ernie Wright, Ron Mix, Walt Sweeney, Gary Kirner, and Sam Gruneisen not only opened holes for the league's fourth-best running attack, they also held off pass rushers with better protection than any AFL team in history, allowing only 11 quarterback sacks all year. More than a dozen times they sprang runners and receivers for gains of over 60 yards, and twenty times for gains of more than 50 yards. Without a doubt the offensive line earned the team MVP.

Prognosticators tapped San Diego to finish third and even as low as fourth in the West, mostly due to the improving Chiefs and

Raiders. While the offense still ranked among the best, the defense lacked the intimidating forces of the past. Though talented, the front four lacked experience. Tom Day, who came from Buffalo in a trade for Keith Lincoln, was an established player, but he did not perform nearly as well as he did for the Bills. He was replaced during the year by 6'7" rookie Ron Billingsley, a physically imposing pass rusher in need of development. The best defensive lineman was Steve DeLong, who shuffled between end and tackle with Scott Appleton and Houston Ridge. Linebackers Chuck Allen, Rick Redman, Frank Buncom, and rookie Jeff Staggs were average at best. The secondary of Joe Beauchamp, Jim Tolbert, Ken Graham, Speedy Duncan, and Bud Whitehead intercepted a league-low 13 passes, although Graham did take one 68 yards for a touchdown and Duncan went 100 yards with another. Opposing quarterbacks completed half their passes against the Charger defense, with AFL teams averaging 25 points per game against them.

Despite these shortcomings, when San Diego prepared to play the 9-1 Oakland Raiders on December 3, they held an 8-1-1 record. After winning their first two games against Boston and Houston, coach Gillman inserted Post and Hubbert in the same backfield for the first time against the Bills. They responded with 178 yards rushing, with Post accounting for 121 of them. The rookie runners led the Chargers to their third straight win over their two-time championship game foe with a 37-17 victory. Through their first three games the defense ranked among the league's best, allowing only 34 total points.

The schedule next called for the Chargers to face the Patriots at Fenway Park, but because the Red Sox needed the field for the World Series, the game took place in San Diego. The Chargers played poorly against a mediocre Boston team and needed two fourth-quarter touchdown passes to pull out a 31-31 tie. On October 15, the Chargers scored more points on the Kansas City Chiefs than anyone before them, ignited by Speedy Duncan's 35-yard touchdown on a fumble recovery in the first quarter and a 100-yard interception return for another touchdown in the second period. Dickie Post went over 100 yards rushing for the second time in three starts with 116. The Chargers surged to a 45-31 victory and kept their unblemished record of 4-0-1 at the top of the division.

Against Denver, John Hadl passed for 3 touchdowns, extending the Chargers (5-0-1) undefeated season before the showdown with

The Progress of the Seasons – 1967

FRANK BUNCOM — LINEBACKER

STEVE DeLONG — DEFENSIVE END

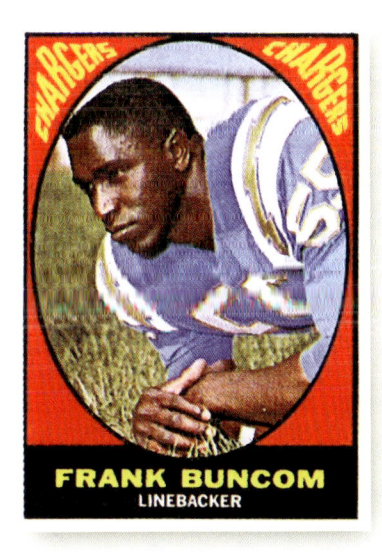

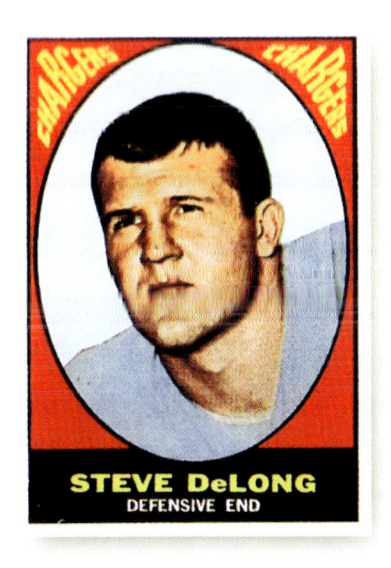

the Raiders (5-1) in front of a packed house of 53,474 in their new home. The Raiders exposed some glaring weaknesses in San Diego's defense. Though Hadl threw for more than 300 yards, the Raiders stormed to 35 straight points in the second half and handed the Chargers (5-1-1) their first loss, 51-10, and dropped them a half game behind the Raiders, who were now 6-1. After shutting out Miami a week later, the Chargers squeaked out a 17-16 win in Kansas City, turning in their best defensive effort of the year by stopping the Chiefs eleven times inside the 10 yard line. Chief halfback Mike Garrett dove, burrowed, sprinted, and crashed into the Chargers' line from inside the 1 yard line seven times without reaching the end zone. Dickie Post starred again as he gained over 100 yards on the ground. The next week, in front of a national audience on Thanksgiving Day, the Chargers put on a fourth-quarter surge, again ignited by a Speedy Duncan 72-yard touchdown run after he picked up a blocked field goal attempt, to whip the Broncos 24-10, setting up another meeting for first place with the Raiders next week.

John Hadl produced one of his finest seasons as a pro in 1967, despite his tenuous relationship with coach Sid Gillman. He completed 51 percent of his passes for 3,365 yards and 24 touchdowns, throwing to one of the best threesomes in the AFL. Lance Alworth, still the league's marquee receiver, caught 52 passes and went over 1,000 yards for the fifth straight year despite missing three games. Gary Garrison, in his second year, caught 44 passes and established himself among the best. After spending most of 1966 in Gillman's dog house, tight end Willie Frazier enjoyed an all-league season, leading the Chargers with 57 catches and 10 touchdowns. Post caught 32 passes, including a 66-yard touchdown to go with his 663 yards gained rushing. Rookie running mate Brad Hubbert ran for 643 yards

★ *Gary Garrison streaks down the sideline with Willie Mitchell in pursuit.* ★

and had the best per carry average in the AFL at 5.5. Russ Smith, another rookie runner, gained 115 yards for a 5.2 average on only 22 carries. The entire right side of the Chargers offensive line—Willie Frazier, Ron Mix, and Walt Sweeney—made the all-league team. The Chargers finished the year as the league's third-best passing team. But on the defensive side, only three teams gave up more points.

The second meeting with Oakland marked the beginning of the end for San Diego. Clearly the best team in the West, the Raiders sprinted to a 31-21 halftime lead and shut out the big-play Charger offense the rest of the day while amassing nearly 500 yards on offense. In both games against the powerful Raiders, the Chargers failed to register a point in the second half. It was the first of four straight losses for the Chargers, who ended what had appeared to be one of their most outstanding seasons with a respectable but disappointing third-place finish and an 8-5-1 record.

In many ways, Gillman had never

coached better. No one expected the Chargers to be anywhere near the top of the division, let alone competing for the crown ten games into the season. But the Legend of the Lightning Bolt still lit up the Western Division skies, and they remained in the title hunt right up to the second last week of the season.

Leading passers	Attempts	Completions	Pct	TDs	Yards	Int
John Hadl	427	217	51%	24	3365	22
Kay Stephenson	20	11	42%	0	117	2

Leading rushers	Attempts	Yards gained	Average	TDs
Dickie Post	161	663	4.1	7
Brad Hubbert	116	643	5.5	2
Russ Smith	22	115	5.2	1
John Hadl	37	107	2.9	3
Gene Foster	38	78	2.1	0

Leading receivers	Caught	Yards gained	Average	TDs
Willie Frazier	57	922	16.2	10
Lance Alworth	52	1010	19.4	9
Gary Garrison	44	772	17.5	2
Dickie Post	32	278	8.7	1
Brad Hubbert	19	214	11.3	2

Leading scorers	TDs	XPM	XPA	FGM	FGA	PTs
Dick Van Raaphorst		45	45	15	30	90
Willie Frazier	10					60

▪ HOUSTON OILERS ▪

WHEN WALLY LEMM TOOK OVER THE Oilers for the second time in 1966, he inherited a team that had grown old and out of shape. And after four consecutive losing seasons, Lemm understood the task he faced. He also knew that the legends of the past were not going to lead the Oilers to another division title. Talent waited in the wings, and it was time to give them their shot. Quarterback Jacky Lee, an original Oiler, had become a career backup for George Blanda. And after three seasons on the clipboard, Don Trull feared that he would suffer the same fate. A move had to be made. After seven years of calling plays for the Oilers, forty-year-old George Blanda was unceremoniously released. He quickly found a job as the backup signal caller and kicker in Oakland, where he led the league in scoring.

It was the end of an era in Houston, as

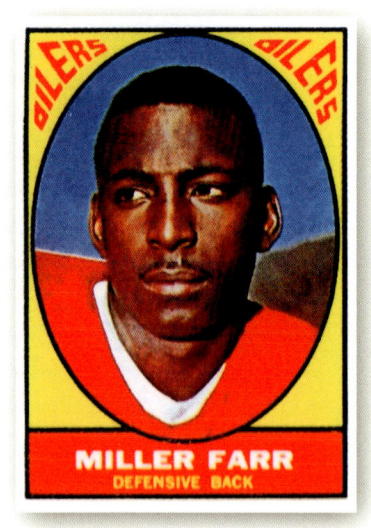

several other players from the early glory days also moved on, including Charlie Tolar, Freddy Glick, Rich Michael, and Doug Cline. All either retired or were released. Charlie Hennigan, Johnny Baker, and Scott Appleton were traded to San Diego for cornerback Miller Farr and draft picks, and Gary Cutzinger sat out the season with an injured back. After the housecleaning, only four original Oilers remained on the roster: Don Floyd, Jim Norton, Bob Talamini, and Lee. Suddenly the Oilers sported a new look and a new approach, featuring fourteen rookies on the forty-man roster in 1967, four of them starters.

In 1966 Houston's defense finished again at the bottom of the league, having given up more points than every other AFL club in the past two seasons. Of the eleven starters on that unit, only cornerback W.K. Hicks found himself back at the same position. The defensive ends were Pat Holmes, moved over from tackle, and Don Floyd, who was later replaced by Dick Marshall. After four games, tackle Ernie Ladd headed for Kansas City, and Willie Parker joined George Rice in the middle. The pair quickly became terrors. The gem of the draft, All-American George Webster from Michigan State, took the spot at left-side linebacker and won the AFL's Rookie of the Year award, only the second defensive player to win it. Of all the new starters, if there was one person to be singled out who made the greatest impact on the success of the Oilers that year, it was Webster, who was voted to the AFL's All-Time team in 1969.

Garland Boyette, a defensive end the year before, stepped in at middle linebacker and teamed with Olen Underwood to make up a superior group behind the line. But the cornerstone of the Houston defense was a revamped secondary. The Oilers gave up 50 touchdowns in 1966, with 35 of them coming through the air. This time around, starters Miller Farr and W.K. Hicks on the corners and Jim Norton and Ken Houston at safety, along with reserves Larry Carwell, Zeke

Moore, and Bobby Jancik, established a new AFL standard for most yards gained running back interceptions (676), and also for returning interceptions for touchdowns (6). They allowed only 10 touchdowns through the air, helping the defense drop the number of touchdowns scored to 18. All-league cornerback Miller Farr led the league with 10 interceptions and scored touchdowns on 3 of them, recording an AFL record number of return yards while surrendering only 1 touchdown. Ninth-round pick Ken Houston, the 214th player picked in the first AFL/NFL combined draft, scored touchdowns on 2 interceptions and ran back a blocked field goal 71 yards for another score.

With their amazing turn around, the Oilers became the first team in professional football history to go from last place to first place in one year. And the defense sparked the improvement. They went from being the worst unit in 1965 and 1966, to the AFL's all-time best in 1967. They also were the first AFL team to hold their opponents under 200 points, a drop from 396 to 199. In addition to setting the record for the fewest points allowed, they also set marks for fewest touchdowns allowed and fewest touchdowns passing allowed.

The year didn't begin well, as the Oilers dropped all their exhibition games and stood at 2-2 after their first four games. While giving up only 47 points in those four games, they scored only 53, and Lemm needed a quarterback who could get the Oilers into the end zone. He had given Trull and then Lee their chance, but neither could move the offense. He even tried Bob Davis, a rookie from Virginia, but he did no better. In games three and four—a loss to San Diego 13-3 and a win over Denver 10-6—the Oilers failed to score a single offensive touchdown. If not for Miller Farr's 39 yard interception return for a touchdown in the third quarter at Denver, Houston would have sat in the cellar of the Eastern Division.

With a third of the season gone, Houston gambled by trading ineffective defensive tackle Ernie Ladd, Jacky Lee, and a number-one draft choice to the Chiefs for Len Dawson's backup, Pete Beathard. Don Trull was packaged to Boston to make way for Beathard, who jumped right into the line of fire when he started against the Jets in New York only days after his arrival. His receivers—Charlie Frazier, Ode Burrell, and Larry Elkins—were either banged up or unable to get open, while rookie tight end Alvin Reed was still a project under development. The receiving corps did include old pros Glenn Bass and the AFL's all-time leading receiver, Lionel Taylor, both of whom Lemm lured out of retirement to lend experience to his offense, which relied heavily on fullback Hoyle Granger and halfback Woody Campbell. Along with reserve Sid Blanks, the trio gained a league-best 2,122 yards and scored 12 times.

On October 15 at Shea Stadium, with 62,729 fans watching, the Oilers (2-2) and Jets (3-1) put on one of the AFL's best shows ever. The Oilers trailed 17-0 near the end of the first half, when the Jets tried a field goal from

★ *Oiler quarterback Pete Beathard readies to fire downfield as Hoyle Granger sets up to block.*

the twenty-nine yard line. Defensive end Pat Holmes broke through and swatted the ball, rookie safety Ken Houston picked it up and raced 71 yards for Houston's first score, taking a 17-7 deficit into the locker room rather than 20-0. In the third quarter, the Oilers continued to hurry Joe Namath into errors—an AFL record 6 interceptions, with 2 returned for touchdowns. Houston pulled within 3 points, 17-14, when Miller Farr took an interception down the sideline for a 51-yards touchdown. After the Jets kicked a field goal to lead 20-14, Farr intercepted his second pass of the day and returned it 67 yards to the Jet 20 yard line. Beathard then put together a short drive that ended with him rolling right and hitting Monte Ledbetter in the end zone for his first Houston touchdown pass, giving the Oilers a 21-20 lead. Namath brought back the Jets with sharp passes, but when he tried to thread the needle to tight end Pete Lammons over the middle near the end of the quarter, Ken Houston stepped in and intercepted, running it back 43 yards for the Oilers third defensive touchdown of the day. As Jon Wittenborn kicked the extra point, the Oilers took a 28-20 lead into the last quarter. Namath again forged a drive, ending with Emerson Boozer's 4-yard touchdown run. Trying for a 2-point conversion to tie the game at 28, Namath worked his magic again, hitting Don Maynard in the corner of the end zone with defensive back Larry Carwell hanging all over him. The Oilers offense sputtered throughout the last quarter, and when the Jets took over for one last charge, Namath went for the win.

With five seconds left, he fired a desperation bomb over the middle for Lammons, but into the hands of W.K. Hicks for Houston's sixth interception. Hicks returned the ball almost 20 yards, helping to set a single-game record for most yards returned with interceptions, as the clock clicked to :00. By then Hicks was trapped in Jet territory. With nowhere to run and no time left, Hicks lateraled to Ken Houston, but Houston could advance only 5 more yards before he too was boxed in by a host of Jet tacklers. He tossed the ball to Larry Carwell who took off to the right with linebacker Boyette as an escort. A miracle score with time expired would give the Oilers a share of first place, and as Carwell reached the 7 yard line only Joe Namath stood in his way. As Boyette plowed Namath toward the sideline, Joe hit the turf in a heap and Carwell fell over him at the 3, bringing to a close one of the most thrilling endings to a game in AFL history.

The 28-28 tie kept Houston a half game behind the Jets in the East. After tying New York, every week presented a must-win situation. A rematch with Kansas City had the Chiefs ahead 3-0 after Jan Stenerud's 40-yard field goal until the ensuing kickoff, which rookie Zeke Moore returned 92 yards for a touchdown. Of the last 5 Oiler touchdowns, the offense generated only 1. Two resulted from interception returns, 1 from a blocked field goal, and now Moore's kickoff return. Moore went on to lead the AFL in kick returns with a 28.9 average. After Jon Wittenborn kicked a 45-yard field goal and Sid Blanks scored on a 23-yard pass from Pete Beathard, the defense scored again. Safety Jim Norton returned an interception 23 yards for Houston's last touchdown. For Norton it was the first one of his eight-year career. The Oilers beat KC 24-19.

The coaching staff proclaimed the 1967 squad the youngest and fastest team the franchise ever had. Needing another win against Buffalo, the defense allowed only a first-quarter field goal, and the offense did just enough to win, 10-3. By December, only the Jets challenged the Oilers for the division flag, with New York at 7-2-1 and Houston at 6-3-1. The Dolphins had beaten the Oilers in their previous two meetings, but Houston's defense had yet to establish itself as one of the best in the league. Houston led 10-7 in the fourth quarter when Beathard gambled on fourth and three at the Miami 5 yard line. As he rolled right he was stopped at the 3 until tackle Walt Suggs cleared out the would-be tacklers, springing Beathard and enabling him to fall forward at the 2 yard line for a first and goal. Woody Campbell took the ball over from the 1 yard line to give Houston the victory 17-14. With the Jets losing to Denver, the Oilers had a piece of first place for the first time.

Both teams lost the next week to set up do-or-die games on December 16, the second-last weekend of the year. In rainy Rice Stadium, Houston played San Diego, a team they had not beaten since 1962, while the Jets traveled to Oakland. At the end of the day, the Oilers stood alone at the top of the East with one game left against the 4-9 Dolphins in Miami.

The year before in Miami in the last game of the season, Houston suffered an embarrassing loss in the final thirty-eight seconds. This time Hoyle Granger came to the rescue. In an outstanding season, Granger had bulldozed his way through opponents and often out-ran them. In seven of his fourteen games, Granger exceeded 100 yards rushing. Often he would dart through the line and race for long runs, like his 67-yarder against Boston. In Miami he found a seam up the middle and dashed 64 yards to set up Woody Campbell's 14-yard touchdown run, giving Houston a 14-0 lead. Holding their fate in their hands, the Oilers ran up their highest point total of the season and beat the Dolphins 41-10 to win their fourth Eastern Division Championship. Granger, the second-leading rusher in the AFL, set a Houston record by gaining 1,194 yards with an exceptional 5.1 yards per carry.

It was an incredible comeback season for Houston, a team that won with defense and just enough offense, carried by the league's best running attack. Besides Granger's total, Woody Campbell gained 511 yards for a 4.6 average, and Sid Blanks, the starter before Campbell took over, gained another 206 yards. The running game carried the Houston offense.

Granger also led the team in receiving with 31 catches while Charlie Frazier was second with 23. Lionel Taylor caught 18 in his eight games, with Campbell one behind. Pete Beathard's forte with the Oilers was his leadership and play-calling ability. He completed only 40 percent of his passes, finishing ninth in the quarterback rankings and threw for 9

The Progress of the Seasons – 1967

touchdowns. In Houston's Cinderella season, Beathard fit the glass slipper. But the stroke of midnight was about to chime for the team from Texas. Without a strong passing game to keep the 13-1 Raiders occupied, Oakland concentrated on stopping Granger and Campbell in the AFL Championship on New Year's Eve in Oakland. The Raiders were just too powerful and too balanced for Houston to make a game of it. Granger was held to just 19 yards on 14 carries and the offense gained only 180 yards for the entire game, 38 of them on the ground. Oakland moved on to Super Bowl II. Cinderella's carriage turned back into a pumpkin as Houston rang in 1968, but they will always remember what a great time they had at the ball, turning a last-place team into the champions of the Eastern Division!

Leading passers	Attempts	Completions	Pct	TDs	Yards	Int
Pete Beathard	231	94	41%	9	1181	16
Jacky Lee	70	36	51%	2	242	2
Bob Davis	19	9	47%	0	71	2
Don Trull	11	4	36%	0	38	0

Leading rushers	Attempts	Yards gained	Average	TDs
Hoyle Granger	236	1194	5.1	6
Woody Campbell	110	511	4.6	4
Sid Blanks	66	206	3.1	1
Roy Hopkins	13	42	3.2	0

Leading receivers	Caught	Yards gained	Average	TDs
Hoyle Granger	31	300	9.7	3
Charlie Frazier	23	253	11.0	1
Lionel Taylor	18	233	12.9	1
Woody Campbell	17	136	8.0	2
Ode Burrell	12	193	16.1	0
Alvin Reed	11	144	13.1	1
Sid Blanks	11	93	8.5	1

Leading scorers	TDs	XPM	XPA	FGM	FGA	PTs
John Wittenborn		30	30	14	28	72
Hoyle Granger	9					54

41. In 1967, for the second year in a row, at least five teams had winning records. But there were three years when as few as three AFL teams had better than .500 records. Which three years were they?

OAKLAND RAIDERS

At the start of the 1967 season, the Oakland Raiders were not yet the best team in the league, but principle owner Al Davis knew what it would take to get to the next level and he would not rest until he got there. The missing link was a quarterback who could throw deep as well as he could throw short, and had enough mobility to elude the blitz, the stability to withstand the entire season, and the ability to reach the end zone from anywhere on the field. Davis had coveted Buffalo backup Daryle Lamonica for years, while his split end Art Powell wanted to move back East. Davis put together a deal that sent Powell and quarterback Tom Flores to the Bills for Lamonica and wide receiver Glenn Bass. With the final piece to the championship puzzle in place, the Raiders headed for the top.

They also added one of the best defensive backs in the league by acquiring Denver's Willie Brown for offensive tackle Rex Mirich and a draft choice. And in what could be considered the icing on the cake, Davis signed veteran kicker and renowned quarterback George Blanda, who was recently released by Houston. Bringing Blanda on board the pirate ship upgraded the kicking game significantly, as he replaced the limited Mike Eischeid, and provided an invaluable mentor and backup for Lamonica. With Clem Daniels and Hewritt Dixon churning up the yards behind all-league linemen Harry Schuh, Jim Otto, and rookie Gene Upshaw, the Raiders posted a league-record 13 wins against only 1 loss, and won their first AFL Championship going away. They had stockpiled the best talent in the AFL and were more dangerous offensively and more dominating defensively than the 1963 Chargers. They also scored more points than any other team and finished second in fewest points allowed. Houston's "washed up" quarterback/kicker George Blanda, playing his eighteenth year of professional football, led the league in scoring with 56 extra points and 20 field goals in 30 tries.

After four years of relief work in Buffalo, Lamonica had a breakout season. He led the AFL in passing, threw 30 touchdowns and was named AFL Player of the Year while earning the moniker "The Mad Bomber" for his long-distance strikes. Lamonica put the league on notice in the season opener when the Raiders trounced the Broncos 51-0. Even George Blanda got into the act by throwing a 50-yard touchdown pass in the fourth quarter. The Raider defense held Denver to minus 53 yards passing and minus 5 yards of total offense. A visit by Boston brought a similar result, with Lamonica throwing 3 touchdowns in a 35-7 pasting of the Patriots. The hated Chiefs were next. A fourth-quarter touchdown pass from Lamonica to Billy Cannon put Oakland up 23-14, and they held on to win 23-21, earning a piece of first place in the West with the unbeaten Chargers. The Raiders and Chargers both lost the next week, while

Raider quarterback Daryle "The Mad Bomber" Lamonica

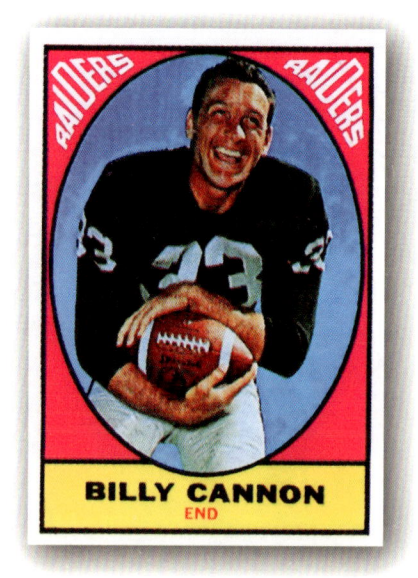

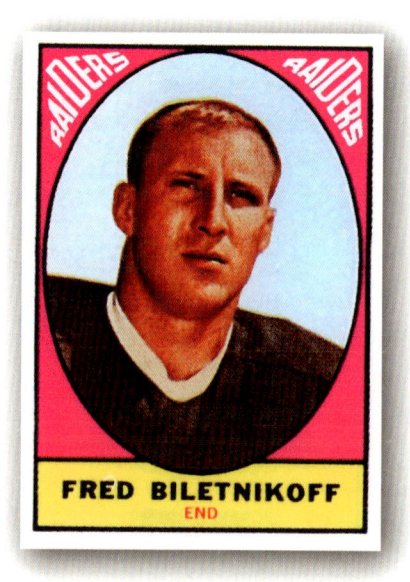

Kansas City posted their third victory, giving all three teams a 3-1 record one month into the season.

After losing to the Jets, 23-14, for their only loss of the season, the Raiders ran off ten straight victories, including a 51-10 win over the Chargers, who were tied for first place in the West at the time. Dave Grayson, subbing for injured Willie Brown on the corner, intercepted 3 John Hadl passes to earn a defensive game ball. But all was not rosy after the win, as all-star halfback Clem Daniels, who had gained 575 yards through nine games, was lost for the season. Pete Banaszak took over the next week and gained 81 yards in a 44-22 victory over the Chiefs. Banaszak went on to average 5.5 yards per carry on the year. With their victory in KC, Oakland sat on top of the West at 9-1, but led San Diego (8-1-1) by only a half game. Exploding into San Diego Stadium, the Raiders took the Chargers 41-21 to clinch the division, shutting them out in the second half for the second time that year. Lamonica threw four touchdown passes, to Biletnikoff, Cannon, Bill Miller, and Cannon again, completing 21 passes for 349 yards.

The Raiders closed out the season with victories over Houston, New York, and Buffalo, then readied themselves to play the Oilers for the AFL Championship. They dominated the league so completely that they led in all but thirteen quarters during the year and averaged 33 points per game while giving up only 17. With Daniels missing the last five games, Hewitt Dixon emerged as the lead runner. He finished the season with 559 yards rushing and also caught a team-high 59 passes. Fred Biletnikoff followed with 40, and split end Bill Miller had 38. Tight end Billy Cannon had 32 catches and was named the all-league tight end. Although Clem Daniels did not finish the 1967 season, he became the first AFL rusher to gain over 5,000 yards for a career. In his stead Pete Banaszak gained 376.

The Progress of the Seasons – 1967

The Raiders of 1967 were a team unlike any the AFL had ever seen. They had a fast and powerful running game, finishing third in the league. Their backs could also catch both short and long passes for the AFL's top passing team. Biletnikoff established himself as one of the best receivers at running precision patterns, especially Oakland's favorite cornerback-to-the-sideline route. But the man who made the difference was AFL Player of the Year Daryle Lamonica. "The Mad Bomber" started slowly during the exhibition season, but once he was told to "air it out" he became the most talked about quarterback in the league. He completed a career-high 51.8 percent of his passes for 3,228 yards and 30 touchdowns. Clearly he put them over the top. Harry Schuh, Otto, Upshaw, Lamonica, Cannon, and Dixon reaped all-league honors on offense.

In the Championship game, Oakland's number-one offense met Houston's number-one defense. The Raider defense ranked second behind only Houston, but they were every bit as good and probably more disruptive. The front four of Ben Davidson, Tom Keating, Dan Birdwell, and Ike Lassiter sacked quarterbacks 67 times, 24 more than the next best team and almost triple that of Houston's top-ranked defensive eleven. Hard-hitting linebackers Bill Laskey, Dan Conners, and Gus Otto stopped both the pass and the run. The cornerbacks also matched Houston's group man for man. Willie Brown and Kent McCloughan, and safeties Warren Powers and Dave Grayson, had few peers. They intercepted 30 passes and returned four for touchdowns. Former starters Roger Bird and Howie Williams backed up in the secondary. Davidson, Keating, Conners, and McCloughan received all-league notice at the end of the season.

Oddsmakers favored the Raiders to win the Championship game quite handily. In the end, it was not even that close. The Raiders demolished Houston 40-7, mainly because the fierce Raider defense held the league's best running attack to just 38 yards on 22 carries. Oakland's runners, Hewritt Dixon and Pete Banaszak, both ground out over 100 yards. The Raiders dominated in every department. Perhaps the most crushing blow of the afternoon for the Oilers came with just eighteen seconds left in the first half, with the Raiders leading 10-0. Oakland lined up to kick a 24-yard field goal, but holder Daryle Lamonica suddenly came up throwing and receiver Dave Kocourek was wide open. The backup tight end ran untouched for a 17-yard touchdown, embarrassing the Oilers and taking a 17-0 lead into the locker room. The Raiders put up 23 more points in the second half, completing the most successful and dominating season by an AFL team and giving the league reason for optimism as they headed into Miami for Super Bowl II.

Two weeks after destroying Houston, the Raiders trailed Green Bay by only a touchdown at halftime in the Orange Bowl before falling 33-14 in Super Bowl II. With 1962's 1-13 representing the lowest point in Oakland Raider history, 1967's 13-1 record became their brightest achievement, and perched them proudly at the top of the American Football League.

Remember the AFL

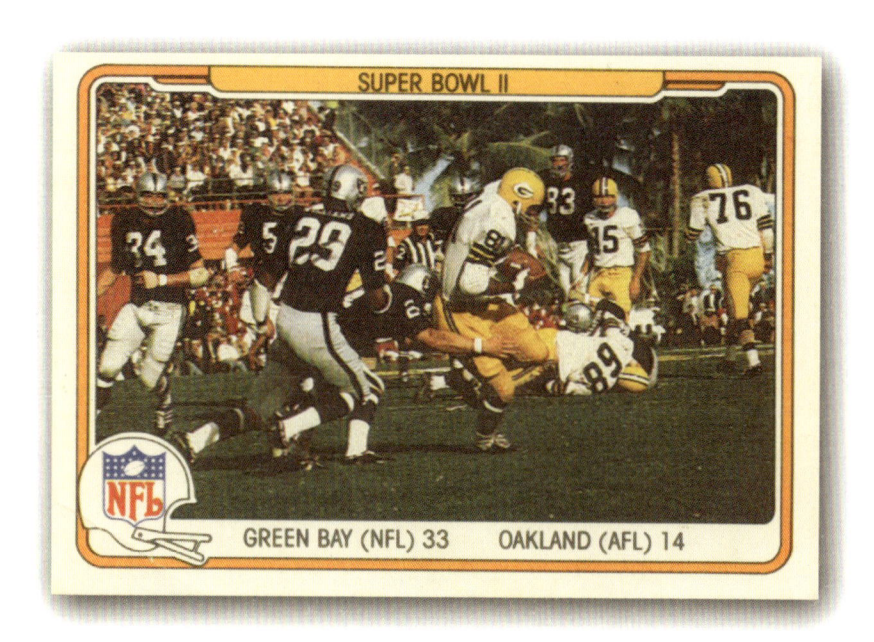

SUPER BOWL II

GREEN BAY (NFL) 33   OAKLAND (AFL) 14

Leading passers	Attempts	Completions	Pct	TDs	Yards	Int
Daryle Lamonica	425	220	52%	30	3228	20
George Blanda	38	15	40%	3	285	3

Leading rushers	Attempts	Yards gained	Average	TDs
Clem Daniels	130	575	4.4	4
Hewritt Dixon	153	559	3.7	5
Pete Banaszak	68	376	5.5	1
Roger Hagberg	44	146	3.3	2

Leading receivers	Caught	Yards gained	Average	TDs
Hewritt Dixon	59	563	9.5	2
Fred Biletnikoff	40	876	21.9	5
Bill Miller	38	537	14.1	6
Billy Cannon	32	629	19.7	10
Clem Daniels	16	222	13.9	2
Pete Banaszak	16	192	12.0	1

Leading scorers	TDs	XPM	XPA	FGM	FGA	PTs
George Blanda		56	57	20	30	116
Billy Cannon	10					60

The Progress of the Seasons – 1967

The AFL All-Star game, played on January 21, 1968, in Jacksonville, Florida, was another topsy-turvy, come-from-behind victory for the East squad. After losing the first four post-season showcases to the West, the East showed its teeth with fourth-quarter comebacks. Buffalo kicker Mike Mercer started the scoring for the East with a 10-yard field goal in the first quarter. But on the ensuing kickoff San Diego's Speedy Duncan scored on a 90-yard return to put the West in front. By halftime the West increased their spread to 21-13. After a scoreless third period the West jumped further ahead on a George Blanda field goal, giving them an 11-point lead. Then the record crowd of 40,103 in the Gator Bowl watched the magic of Joe Namath as he connected with Jet teammate Don Maynard for a 24-yard touchdown.

With his team now behind 24-19, Namath tried but failed on a 2-point conversion. But time remained for another heroic comeback by the East. After snuffing another West possession, the East took the ball back with two minutes left. After a pass and two runs they stood on the 1 yard line with fifty-eight seconds remaining. With Hoyle Granger and Larry Garron lined up behind Namath, the defense dug in to stop whichever of the backs tried to plunge for the winning score. But Namath pulled off the ultimate deception play as he called his own number and snuck the ball over for 6 points and a 25-24 East lead.

Hoping to widen the spread to 3, the East tried but failed again on a 2-point conversion. The battle was not yet over. The "Mad Bomber" from Oakland, Daryle Lamonica, re-entered the game and brought the West to within field goal range. Their hope for victory now rode on the toe of the AFL's scoring leader George Blanda from 35 yards away. The center snapped the ball to the holder who put it in place and Blanda booted it skyward toward the goal post—only to sail inches wide of another win for the West. For the second year in a row the East put together a comeback All-Star game victory.

1968

AMERICAN FOOTBALL LEAGUE – 1968 FINAL STANDINGS

EASTERN DIVISION

TEAM	GP	W	L	T	PF	PA	PCT.
NEW YORK JETS	14	11	3	0	419	280	0.786
HOUSTON OILERS	14	7	7	0	303	248	0.500
MIAMI DOLPHINS	14	5	8	1	276	355	0.393
BOSTON PATRIOTS	14	4	10	0	229	406	0.286
BUFFALO BILLS	14	1	12	1	199	367	0.107

WESTERN DIVISION

TEAM	GP	W	L	T	PF	PA	PCT
OAKLAND RAIDERS	14	12	2	0	453	233	0.857
KANSAS CITY CHIEFS	14	12	2	0	371	170	0.857
SAN DIEGO CHARGERS	14	9	5	0	382	310	0.643
DENVER BRONCOS	14	5	9	0	255	404	0.357
CINCINNATI BENGALS	14	3	11	0	215	329	0.214

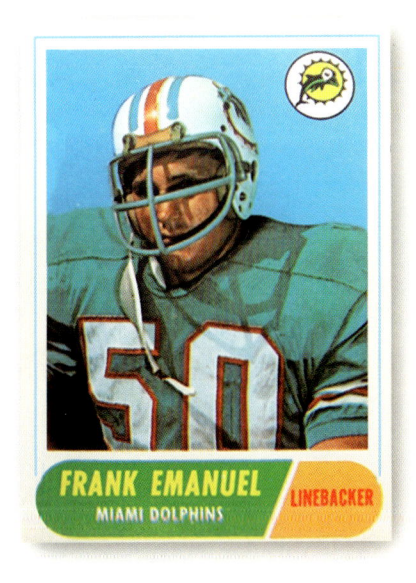

Frank Emanuel was an All-American linebacker from Tennessee when the Dolphins selected him in 1966. He was the first Miami Dolphin to grace the cover of *Sports Illustrated* (only the fifth time the AFL was highlighted) when he appeared as a rookie in August of 1966. Frank played in every one of the Dolphins 56 AFL games and in 2000 was inducted into the College Football Hall of Fame.

▪ CINCINNATI BENGALS ▪

THE AFL MOVED FORWARD WITH ITS second expansion team in 1968, awarding a franchise to Cincinnati and a group that included 59-year-old Hall of Fame coach Paul Brown, who gained fame with the Cleveland Browns of the old All-American Football Conference and the NFL. In seventeen professional seasons he took his teams to eleven championship games. The Bengals took their name from the city's football team that played in the original AFL back in the 1930s. Their black and orange colors, it is said, were influenced by two Princeton alums on Brown's staff who were charged with coming up with the name and colors.

Like all expansion teams, the Bengals lineup was a mixture of cast-off veterans and college draftees. Brown specialized in building a strong offensive line, and used his linemen as a messenger system to send in plays to his quarterbacks. Bob Johnson, Tennessee's All-American center and Cincinnati's first draft pick, anchored the line that included Ernie Wright, a first-class veteran from San Diego and rookie Howard Fest at tackle. Sophomore Dave Middendorf manned one guard spot while Brown's messengers, Pat Matson and Pete Perreault, took the other.

The skill players were mostly small and quick, starting with flanker Warren McVea, a 5'9", 175 pound All-American from the University of Houston. McVea became the punt and kick return specialist and was used for end-around and reverse plays. On one of his nine carries, McVea sped 80 yards around right end for a touchdown. S.T. Staffold and Rod Sherman shared the split end role and 6'5" Bob Trumpy, the team leader with 37 catches, worked both at tight end and wide receiver. Coached by an old-school leader, the Bengal offense was a hybrid of opportunistic passing, unconventional sleight-of-hand flea-flickers and precision running that stretched the defenses both vertically and horizontally.

In the first year, the running game made the offense click, focused primarily on one of Paul Brown's genius draft choices. Paul Robinson was a track star at Arizona when the Bengals made him one of their three third-round picks, the 82nd player chosen overall. He certified himself as the best runner in the AFL, running away with the Rookie of the Year award as only the second rookie in pro football history to gain 1,000 yards. The sleeper pick of the 1968 draft gained league highs in yardage (1,023), touchdowns rushed (8), longest run from scrimmage (87 yards) and carries (238). Robinson led the Bengals to the league's third-best running offense. He also caught 24 passes. His supporting cast in the backfield consisted of rookies Tom Smiley, a prototype fullback who was lost after eight games to the military, and quick and nimble Essex Johnson, who had a team-high 6.8 yards rushing on 26 carries. Estes Banks and Ron Lamb also saw limited action running the ball.

Throughout the year a trio of interchangeable signal callers took the field. The top man, John Stofa, taken from the Dolphins, was injured early in the season and gave way to

The Progress of the Seasons – 1968

Dewey Warren. After Warren went down with a concussion, Sam Wyche came off of the taxi squad to complete 64 percent of his 55 passes. Wyche, too, got hurt (ankle) after three games behind the line. Warren, nicknamed "The Swamp Rat," returned to complete 59 percent of his throws in seven games. With two years experience, Stofa was the veteran, and he came back and led the Bengals for ten games with 85 completions in 177 passing attempts and the league's lowest interception percentage, throwing only 5. They collectively produced the fifth-best passing offense in the AFL.

If the offense suffered occasional lapses with rookie mistakes and injuries, the defense played like a team on a search-and-destroy mission, giving up fewer points than four of the other established AFL teams. A mixture of talented veterans and highly regarded rookies, they synchronized into a deadly pack of gang tacklers that hurried, harassed, and frustrated opponents, gaining the respect of the nine other teams. The front four blended rookies Harry Gunner and Bill Staley with San Diego's Jim Griffin and New York's Dennis Randall. The linebackers combined the skills of veterans Sherrill Headrick, the defensive captain and former all-league middle man from Kansas City, with another all-star, Frank Buncom from San Diego, and big-time rookie Al Beauchamp from Southern University. The trio played better than expected for a first-year expansion team and were equally adept at plugging holes, as they were on pass coverage and blitzing, where they helped drop passers 32 times. The black and orange secondary featured cornerbacks Charlie King from the Bills and Fletcher Smith from the Chiefs, a punishing twosome, along with safeties Bobby Hunt (KC) and rookie Jess Phillips.

After winning their last two exhibitions games against the Jets and Steelers, the Bengals met the San Diego Chargers on September 5 to kick off the AFL's ninth year in a nationally televised game. In true Paul Brown style, the Bengals marched straight down the field on their first possession and scored a touchdown on a 2-yard run around left end by Robinson. To everyone's surprise, the first-year team took the Chargers, still one of the top four AFL teams, into halftime tied at 10 before running out of gas and coming up short in their first game. But the Chargers win did not come without a struggle, serving notice to the rest of the AFL that this was not just any expansion team to be taken lightly.

Cincinnati won its first franchise victory in the first home game at Nippert Stadium on September 15, whipping Denver 24-10. The Broncos were without their starting quarterback, and the hungry Bengals took advantage of substitute Jim LeClair's inexperience. After a scoreless first half, the Bengals jumped ahead with a 49-yard field goal by Dale Livingston and then a 58-yard touchdown pass from Stofa to Bob Trumpy.

Remember the AFL

★ Bengal quarterback Sam Wyche escapes the grasp of Jeff Staggs. ★

But they needed a comeback after Denver tied the game at 10-10 in the fourth quarter. Stofa connected with Warren McVea on 54-yard touchdown pass to move ahead, and later in the game Essex Johnson snuck through an opening in the center of the line and ran for a 35-yard score. In celebration of their historic first win, the game ball was sent to the Hall of Fame.

For the second game at Nippert, Cincinnati hosted the Bills, who were on their way down the AFL ladder after years of success. Again the Bengals took advantage of an inexperienced quarterback to surge to victory. They chased Bills rookie Dan Darragh all over the field and hurried him into erratic throws that led to 2 interception returns for touchdowns in the second half. The 2 interceptions provided the margin of difference in the 34-23 win. A long distance touchdown run by Warren McVea put Cincy ahead 10-0. The rookie showcased his blistering speed on an end-around play for 80 yards in the first quarter. Cornerback Charlie King returned an interception 32 yards in the third quarter and linebacker Al Beauchamp added another interception return in the fourth for a 17-yard score to make the Bengals the first expansion team in history to win two games in a row. They lost their next two games, but the defense made the victors struggle for every

The Progress of the Seasons – 1968

inch and every point, giving up only 1 touchdown each in losses to Denver and Kansas City. The Denver loss was particularly disappointing since the Bengals held a 7-3 lead with less than two minutes to play when the Broncos recovered a fumble on the 35 yard line and drove in for a game winning score. Against the Chiefs, the Bengal offense stalled twice inside the KC 10 yard line and fell short 13-3. They then fell short of tying Miami at home on October 20 when they failed on a 2-point conversion attempt in the fourth quarter, producing a third straight loss, 24-22.

The Bengals third and last win of their first year came on November 17 in Miami. They struck for 21 unanswered points in the fourth quarter to take the game 38-21, piling up 422 yards offensively, led by Paul Robinson's 134 yards and 3 touchdowns. As their first season drew to a close, Cincinnati's strong showing gave the chief architect, Paul Brown, a strong foundation on which to build future Bengal successes.

Leading passers	Attempts	Completions	Pct	TDs	Yards	Int
John Stofa	177	85	48%	5	896	5
Dewey Warren	80	47	59%	1	506	4
Sam Wyche	55	35	64%	2	494	2

Leading rushers	Attempts	Yards gained	Average	TDs
Paul Robinson	238	1023	4.3	8
Essex Johnson	26	178	6.8	3
Tom Smiley	63	146	2.3	1
Warren McVea	9	133	14.8	1
Estes Banks	34	131	3.9	0

Leading receivers	Caught	Yards gained	Average	TDs
Bob Trumpy	37	638	17.3	3
Paul Robinson	24	128	5.3	1
Warren McVea	21	264	12.6	2
Tom Smiley	19	86	4.5	0
Saint Saffold	16	172	10.8	0

Leading scorers	TDs	XPM	XPA	FGM	FGA	PTs
Dale Livingston		20	20	13	26	59
Paul Robinson	9					54

42. Bengals coach Paul Brown employed an unusual offensive system that used players rotating into the game from the sidelines as messengers, bringing in plays that Brown called. What position did Brown use as messengers?

43. After Pete Gogolak introduced pro football to soccer-style kicking, the AFL added a second side winder in 1967 and then another in 1968. Who was the league's third soccer-style kicker after Gogo and Jan Stenerud?

DENVER BRONCOS

THE BRONCOS FOUND THEMSELVES in another difficult predicament. The team anticipated success with the offensive combination of quarterback Steve Tensi, wide receiver Al Denson, and halfback Floyd Little, but after the first seven weeks of the season, the three had yet to take the field at the same time. Tensi missed seven games after separating his collar bone two times. Given that Denver played in the Western Division with three of the AFL's top four teams, they faced a difficult challenge. Even by doubling their number of victories from last season, the Broncos would still not be a .500 team.

Though they couldn't change their place in the standings, they did change their helmets switching from the no-frills blue head gear with only white and orange stripes down the center, to a new one displaying an over-sized D with a snorting bronco inside. The center stripe was reversed—an orange stripe between two white ones. On the road the Broncos wore orange pants, a change from the previous white. The home uniform remained the same.

Defense played a major role in the success of the 5-9 Broncos in 1968, just as it had in Buffalo under Saban. The improvement centered on all-league end Rich "Tombstone" Jackson, who was especially adept on the pass rush that led to 33 quarterback sacks. A one-man wrecking crew, Jackson knocked down 15 passes. The dogged defense created disruption by committee, featuring an interchangable mix of Jackson, Paul Smith, and Pete Duranko at the ends and Dave Costa, Rex Mirich, and Jerry Inman rotating on the inside to give the Broncos their best front wall in team history. Against the rush, this group was better than six other AFL clubs. Linebackers Carl Cunningham, John Huard, and Fred Forsberg played adequately, but needed outside help on sweeps and covering backs on pass routes. The secondary needed assistance and stability, as it broke down frequently after the line jammed up the running game and forced offenses to go to the air. The quintet of Charley Greer, Drake Garrett, Gus Hollomon, Pete Jacquess, and Tom Oberg fended off less than 50 percent of the passes thrown against them and gave up a league-high 3,419 yards through the air. Denver's 404 points allowed was more than all but one other AFL team.

The offense had the tools and the talent to put points on the scoreboard, but too often the tools were not in the tool box when they were needed. Tensi's first injury occurred prior to the season, forcing Saban to use second-year quarterback Jim LeClair to open against Cincinnati, with rookie Marlin Briscoe in

The Progress of the Seasons – 1968

reserve. Both teams started slowly in a scoreless first half. In the third quarter the Bengals, already playing their second game, scored the first 10 points, but a field goal by Bronco kicker Bob Humphrey and a fourth-quarter strike from LeClair to flanker Eric Crabtree tied the game. Offensive mistakes and ineffectiveness followed, however, and the Broncos etched themselves in the history books as the first team to lose to the expansion Bengals, 24-10.

In another poor showing in their second game, the Bronco offense could not muster a single point in Kansas City. The defense managed a safety, tackling Chief's punter Eddie Wilson in the end zone in the opening period. Needing a lift and a change of pace, Saban handed the quarterback reigns to rookie Marlin Briscoe the next week against the Patriots, making him the first African-American quarterback to start a regular season pro football game. He ignited the offense to a first-half touchdown that tied the game. He then scrambled for 12 yards in the fourth quarter and capped an 80-yard drive to get the Broncos to within 3 points of a tie. But the man who would be referred to as "Marlin the Magician" for his ability to pull a big play out his helmet fell short in his first magic show, 20-17.

Finally, on October 5, the Broncos notched their first win with a repaired Steve Tensi coming off the bench in the second half to throw the game-winning touchdown pass with less than five minutes left to beat Cincinnati, 10-7. For most of their first six games Denver endured the absence of their best passer and best runner. Floyd Little missed three of the first six games, and Tensi did not play the first 14 quarters of the season. Al Denson played in the season opener, but then went on the injury list, leaving the receiving burden in the hands of a capable but over-matched Eric Crabtree. Eric's only help on the outside was Billy VanHeusen, whose 19 catches placed far down the list in the league's receiver rankings. Tight end Tom Beer helped a little with 20 receptions, but for much of the season Crabtree remained the lone receiving threat. His 35 catches led the team. Upon his return, Denson continued his all-league performance of a year ago, and in eight games pulled down 34 passes and tied Crabtree for the team lead with 5 touchdowns. Without Little to dance through the middle of the line and skirt the ends, Denver relied on Fran Lynch (221 yards on 66 carries), Garrett Ford (186 yards on 41 carries), and Brendan McCarthy (86 yards on 28 tries).

None of those backs kept opposing defenses awake at night, but Marlin Briscoe did. He was the talk of the league after his debut

305

Remember the AFL

★ *Denver quarterback Steve Tensi gets the pass away just in time.* ★

performance, scrambling and gambling his way through the AFL. At 5'10" 178 pounds, the diminutive rookie from Omaha gave defenders nighmares with the threat of running or passing every time he took a snap. He was Denver's second-leading rusher with 308 yards on 41 carries, for a 7.5 average. Clearly the most versatile quarterback in the league, Briscoe was at his magical best against the Miami Dolphins on October 27, when he pulled 21 points out of his hat, to bring the Broncos back from a 14-0 deficit in the fourth quarter. The Magician scored twice in the comeback, running into the end zone on a 10-yard quarterback sneak up the middle for the game-winning touchdown. Floyd Little helped keep the pressure off of Briscoe by running for 126 yards in the game.

After Steve Tensi led them to their first win against the Bengals in game four, he started the next week against the Jets, and in front of more than 62,000 fans, he out-played Joe Namath, handing the eventual Super Bowl Champions the second of only three losses that year. Namath led a 60-yard drive on the first possession, but the Broncos intercepted 5 passes and held the Jets to only 2 Jim Turner field goals the rest of the day. Two short touchdowns by Fran Lynch and a 72-yard pass from Tensi to Crabtree gave Denver a 21-13 upset win. In all, the Broncos won five of Tensi's seven appearances in 1968.

Saban showed progress in turning the Broncos into a respectable team, impressing everyone with his resurrected defense. The offense finally came together against the Patriots in the eighth game of the season, the first

The Progress of the Seasons – 1968

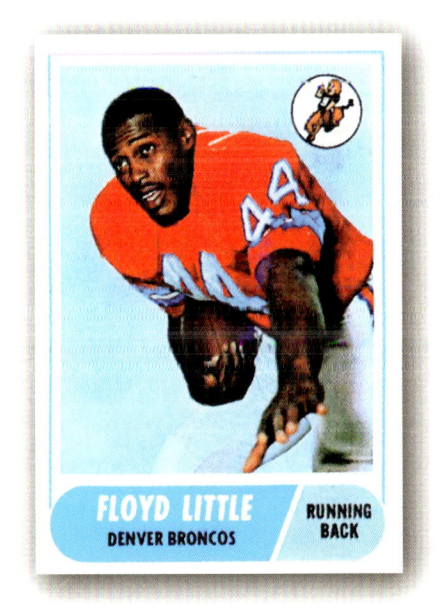

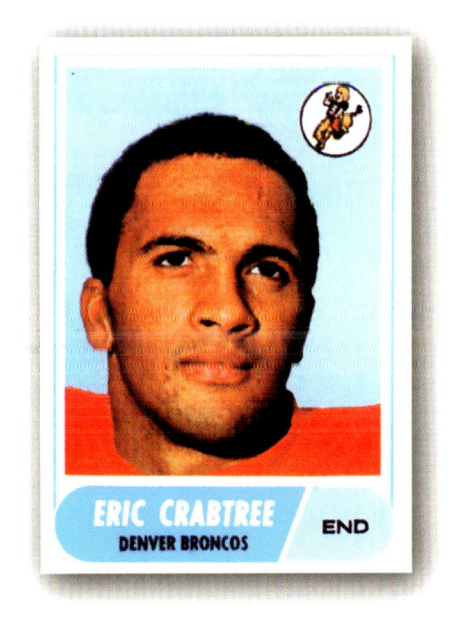

one featuring Denson, Tensi, and Little in the lineup at the same time. The result was a 35-14 Bronco stampede. Tensi completed 11 of 17 passes for 206 yards and 2 touchdowns, and Floyd Little ran for a team-record 147 yards. Losses to Oakland and Houston on November 10 and 17 set up a return performance by Marlin the Magician, leading Denver to its fifth and final win of the season against Buffalo. Briscoe threw 3 first-half touchdown passes—to McCarthy for 40 yards, Crabtree for 15, and Little for 66—to build a 21-7 lead at halftime. But the Bills fought back and took the lead 32-31 with only forty-two seconds left in the game. Briscoe pulled out his wand for the last time, dropping back and firing a desperation pass into Floyd Little's arms 50 yards downfield with just enough time on the clock for Bobby Howfield to kick a 12-yard field goal and win the game, 34-32.

Briscoe ended the season as the Broncos' top quarterback, finishing seventh in the league, completing 93 of his 224 passes for 14 touchdowns. Little led the team in rushing with 584 yards on 158 carries despite missing three games with an ankle injury. He also ranked second on kickoff returns and fourth in punt returns with one of his 24 covering 67 yards for a touchdown. Flanker Billy VanHeusen doubled as the team's punter and finished second behind league leader Kansas City's Jerrell Wilson. English kicker Bobby Howfield, the AFL's third soccer-style kicker, made half of his 18 field goal tries.

The Broncos' 5-9 record in 1968 was second best in their nine-year history and showed a marked improvement over the team Saban took on two years ago. The defense was a strong and developing unit, and the offense proved that when healthy, they could score with the best of them. There was also improvement in the fan base, as home attendance averaged over 40,000 a game for the first time to establish a new record.

Leading passers	Attempts	Completions	Pct	TDs	Yards	Int
Marlin Briscoe	224	93	42%	14	1589	13
Steve Tensi	119	48	40%	5	709	8
Jim LeClair	54	27	50%	1	401	5
John McCormick	19	8	50%	0	89	1

Leading rushers	Attempts	Yards gained	Average	TDs
Floyd Little	158	584	3.7	3
Marlin Briscoe	41	308	7.5	3
Fran Lynch	66	221	3.3	4
Garrett Ford	41	186	4.5	1
Brendan McCarthy	28	89	3.2	0
Terry Erwin	24	76	3.2	0

Leading receivers	Caught	Yards gained	Average	TDs
Eric Crabtree	35	601	17.2	5
Al Denson	34	586	17.2	5
Tom Beer	20	276	13.8	1
Billy VanHeusen	19	353	18.6	3
Floyd Little	19	331	17.4	1
Jimmy Jones	13	190	14.6	2
Mike Haffner	12	232	19.3	1

Leading scorers	TDs	XPM	XPA	FGM	FGA	PTs
Bobby Howfield		30	30	9	18	57
Eric Crabtree	5					30
Al Denson	5					30

44. After a sensational rookie season, Paul Robinson, the Bengals' league-leading ground gainer and AFL Rookie of the Year, was only second on the team in 1969. Who was the 1968 Bengal defensive starter that led Cincinnati in rushing in their second year?

MIAMI DOLPHINS

FOR THE THIRD YEAR IN A ROW THE Dolphins improved their number of victories by one. In 1968 they also reduced their losses by two and moved up another place in the standings, to third in the East, with a 5-8-1 record. Fourth in passing and sixth in rushing, the young Miami team was still teething on the AFL schedule, but little by little they were leaving their imprint. Bob Griese became the hottest young quarterback this side of Joe Namath, and their two rookie runners already formed the backbone of the offense that five years later led an undefeated Super Bowl Champion team. Jim Kiick from Wyoming and Larry Csonka from Syracuse developed into Mr. Inside and Mr. Outside, balancing

The Progress of the Seasons – 1968

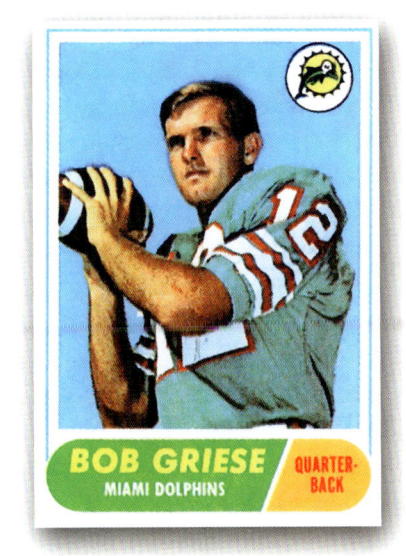

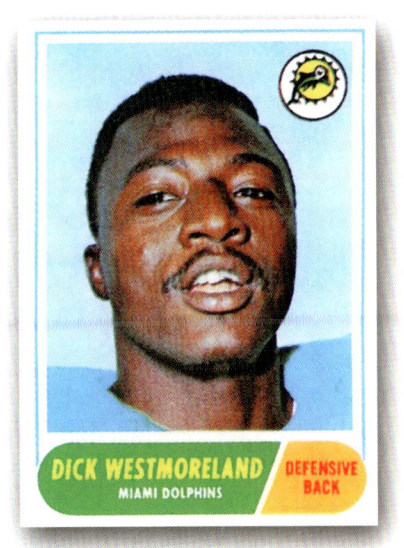

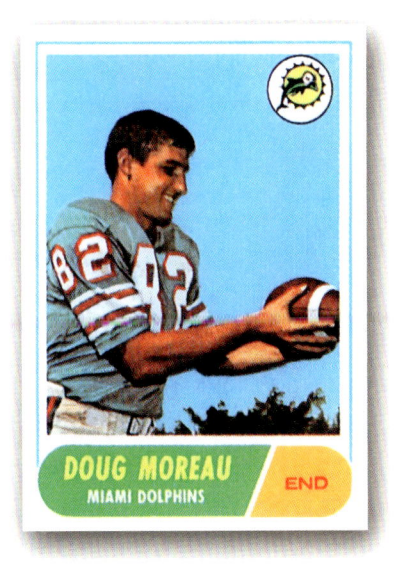

Griese's pinpoint marksmanship and uncanny knack for picking apart a defense. Griese, who had taken over for starter John Stofa in the first game of 1967, was now the number-one man. Miami had so much confidence in him that they traded Stofa to Cincinnati for a draft pick that turned into starting tackle Doug Crusan. Griese was an efficient and mobile field leader who, despite Miami suffering a league-leading 53 sacks, completed 52 percent of his 355 passes for 2,473 yards and 21 touchdowns without his best receiver. Jack Clancy, who set a rookie record of 67 receptions the year before, was injured in the second-last preseason game and lost for the season. One of only four AFL passers to fire more touchdowns than interceptions in 1968, Griese ranked fourth in the league and threw all but 67 of the Dolphins 423 passes. Former first pick Rick Norton and Florida State rookie Kim Hammond backed him up but each saw action in only three games.

Csonka and Kiick drew attention around the league, and the offensive line found new energy. Norm Evans emerged as an above-average tackle and first-rounder Doug Crusan was not far behind. Guards Billy Neighbors and Max Williams and center Tom Goode provided steady performance. An occasional letdown by the line and periodic scrambling by Griese made him the team's third-leading rusher. When he had time to pick apart the defense, Griese spread the wealth to an excellent corps of receivers who filled Clancy's void without missing a beat, or a pass. A free agent two years earlier, Karl Noonan caught 58 passes, fourth highest in the AFL. His 11 touchdown catches shared the league lead with Oakland's Warren Wells. Behind Noonan was the AFL's only player to finish among the top 10 in both rushing and receiving—Jim Kiick, who pulled in 44 passes and also ran for 621 yards and 4 touchdowns. Howard Twilley increased his productivity

309

by 15 catches to 39 and led the team with a 15.5 average gain per catch. Tight end Doug Moreau, who also saw some action as a place kicker, pitched in with 27 receptions.

Now in their third season, the Dolphins reached the point at which some of the better veterans from the 1966 expansion draft neared the end of their careers. Defensive back Dick Westmoreland, an all-star who led the league in interceptions in '67 was slowed by injuries and fell off to only 1 interception in '68. Jim Warren, his partner since their days with the Chargers, dropped off to only 2 interceptions. Rookie Dick Anderson emerged as the new leader with his hard hitting and range. He, too, would be around to enjoy Miami's undefeated 1972 season. Willie West returned at safety after sitting out much of the previous year with an injury. The secondary allowed opponents to complete a league-high 52.3 percent of passes against them, due in part to the absence of a strong front four. Mel Branch, Ray Jacobs, Tom Nomina, and Manny Fernandez not only produced a league-low 21 sacks, they also allowed more yards on the ground (4.9 yards per carry average) than every other team. With a weak pass rush and over-worked secondary Miami gave up an eighth-ranked 2,904 yards through the air. Linebackers Randy Edmunds, John Bramlett, and Frank Emanuel were experienced but mostly ineffective.

Having to play the AFL's three strongest teams in their first four games gave the Dolphins a difficult challenge to start the season. After losses to Houston, Oakland, and Kansas City on consecutive weeks, Griese and company traveled to the Astrodome for a rematch with Houston. The Oilers jumped out to a 7-point lead before Miami's offense finally broke out of their doldrums for 24 unanswered points on the defending Eastern Champs. Jim Kiick, in his first start of the season, ran for 102 yards and established himself as one of the futures stars. Fullback Larry Csonka plowed his way for 82 of his season total of 540, as the Dolphins drilled the Oilers 24-7. Csonka had been inconsistent through the first four games until a specially made helmet helped reduce the concussions he was experiencing from using his head as a battering ram.

After tying Buffalo, the Dolphins won the first "AFL Expansion Bowl" by knocking off the Bengals 22-20 behind Griese's 3 touchdown passes and Kiick's 97 yards rushing. Miami's best showing of 1968 came as the Buffalo Bills looked like they would run away with a 17-0 halftime lead. With Kiick again running for over 100 yards and Griese taking a giant step toward maturity, the Dolphins came back to score 21 points in the second half and defeat the Bills 21-17. The final month of the season had the Dolphins pitted in home-and-away matchups with the Patriots and Jets. Two wins against the Patriots, 34-10 and 38-7, balanced two losses to the Jets. In the first loss, New York backup Babe Parilli piled up the final 21 points on touchdown passes to Don Maynard twice and a 40-yard game winner to Bake Tuner.

The Dolphins finished with a record of 5-8-1, good enough for third place in the East.

The Progress of the Seasons – 1968

They continued to build with the future in mind as they inched closer to the division's top teams. Over the winter the acquisition of middle linebacker Nick Buoniconti would be the first step in the process of putting together a defense that could keep opponent points off the board. And with Griese and his youthful offense now a balanced running and passing unit, they demanded respect from everywhere on the field. Now with the concentrated plan for improving on defense, Miami looked to take another step up the ladder in 1969.

Leading passers	Attempts	Completions	Pct	TDs	Yards	Int
Bob Griese	355	186	52%	21	2473	16
Rick Norton	41	17	42%	0	254	4
Kim Hammond	26	13	50%	0	116	2

Leading rushers	Attempts	Yards gained	Average	TDs
Jim Kiick	165	621	3.8	4
Larry Csonka	138	540	3.9	6
Bob Griese	42	230	5.5	1
Stan Mitchell	54	176	3.3	1

Leading receivers	Caught	Yards gained	Average	TDs
Karl Noonan	58	760	13.1	11
Jim Kiick	44	422	9.6	0
Howard Twilley	39	604	15.5	1
Doug Moreau	27	47	13.5	3

Leading scorers	TDs	XPM	XPA	FGM	FGA	PTs
Karl Noonan	11					66
Jimmy Keyes		30	30	7	16	51

45. Olympic Gold Medalist Frank Budd of Villanova, winner of the 100 yard dash in Tokyo at the 1960 games, had a brief pro football career with the Philadelphia Eagles and Washington Redskins in 1962 and 1963 as a wide receiver. Bob Hayes from Florida A&M, the 1964 Gold Medalist in the same event, made a much stronger showing as one of the NFL's best receivers with the Dallas Cowboys starting in 1965. Who was the Texas Southern 100 yard dash Gold Medalist in the 1968 Olympics, and a sixth-round draft pick for Miami, to become the third "World's Fastest Human" to try his hand at pro football with a preseason tryout as a flanker for the Dolphins, and then making the team the following year in 1969?

BOSTON PATRIOTS

AFTER POSTING A 3-10-1 RECORD IN 1967 with many of the names that brought football glory to New England, the Patriots knew they needed to make some changes. The biggest of those names was Babe Parilli, the starting quarterback for the past seven years, who was traded to New York to become Joe Namath's backup in 1968. Don Trull, Parilli's backup, returned to Houston after one year. Gone, too, but only through injury, was Bob Dee, who had not missed an AFL game since its beginning. Dee couldn't play a single game. Defensive backs Ron Hall and Chuck Shonta were also among the missing. Additional losses in personnel included all-stars Larry Eisenhauer and Nick Buoniconti who played in only eight games, and Jim Nance, who missed the start with a weak ankle, causing him to play at less than 100 percent for eight games. For the season, Nance carried the ball nearly one hundred times less than the previous two campaigns when he led the league, gaining less than half of the previous year's 1,293 yards. Art Graham, the team leader in receptions for the last two seasons with 92, also got hurt and caught only 16 passes.

New names arrived to replace the old. From New York came Mike Taliaferro to play quarterback, and rookie Tom Sherman from Penn State, to be his caddie. Looking to take pressure off of Nance, Holovak brought in speedy halfbacks Gene Thomas and R.C. Gamble to take over for Larry Garron. Saved from a last-place finish in the East only by a disastrous 1-12-1 Buffalo season, Boston, at 4-10, limped through the season without much to cheer about.

An opening day win over Buffalo and a win in their third game against Denver got the season off to a decieving 2-1 start, but only a second victory over Buffalo and a win against the first-year Bengals brightened the dismal season. For the second year in a row the Patriots had to move their home opener to a venue in another state, facing the New York Jets in Birmingham, Alabama, on the season's second week. Without a healthy Jim Nance, the offense continually stalled, and neither Taliaferro nor Sherman, who took over as the starter at midseason, was able to complete over 40 percent of their passes. One Boston bright spot, however, was the emergence of tight end Jim Whalen, named to the all-league team with 47 catches. But the next best Patriot receiver, rookie flanker Aaron Marsh, caught only 19. Gino Cappelletti, succumbing to his age, saw less time on offense and caught only 13 passes, though he did become the first AFL player to score 1,000 points on November 17 with his first touchdown catch of the season against the Chargers.

Without a capable offense the Patriots found themselves scoring more points than only Buffalo and Cincinnati. And without Eisenhauer and Dee around to complement tackles Jim Hunt and All-AFL Houston Antwine, the Patriot defense fell to only the fifth-best unit against the run. It was the first

The Progress of the Seasons – 1968

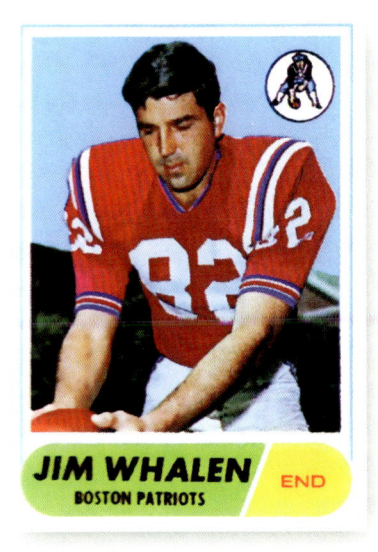

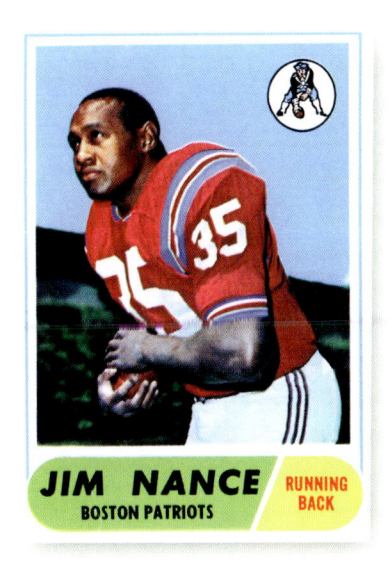

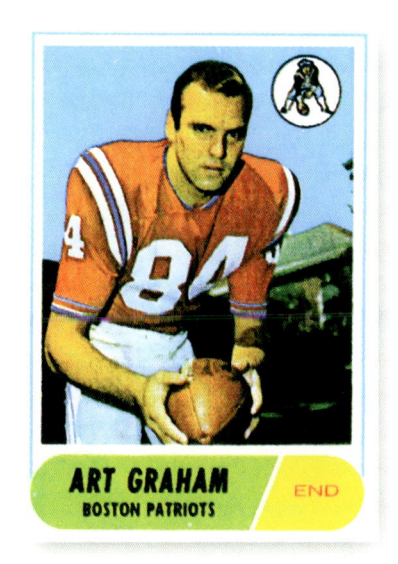

time Boston posted back-to-back losing seasons, and fans in Beantown believed a third loomed on the horizon.

The last loss of the 1968 season occurred after the season ended. Long-time coach and general manager Mike Holovak, always a player favorite, was relieved of his duties, taking with him a 52-46-9 record, one Eastern Division title, four title chases that went down to the wire, and the admiration of dozens of players who had the opportunity to play for such a classy and dignified coach.

Leading passers	Attempts	Completions	Pct	TDs	Yards	Int
Tom Sherman	226	90	40%	12	1199	16
Mike Taliaferro	176	67	38%	4	889	15
King Corcoran	7	3	43%	0	33	2

Leading rushers	Attempts	Yards gained	Average	TDs
Jim Nance	177	593	3.4	4
R.C. Gamble	78	311	4.0	1
Gene Thomas	88	215	2.4	2
Larry Garron	36	97	2.7	1

Leading receivers	Caught	Yards gained	Average	TDs
Jim Whalen	47	718	15.3	7
Aaron Marsh	19	331	17.4	4
Bill Murphy	18	268	14.9	0
Art Graham	16	242	15.1	1
Jim Nance	14	51	3.6	0
Gino Cappelletti	13	182	14.0	2

313

Remember the AFL

Leading scorers	TDs	XPM	XPA	FGM	FGA	PTs
Gino Cappelletti	2	26	26	15	27	83
Jim Whalen	7					42

---

46. In Super Bowl III the Jets intercepted 4 passes. Which of these New York defensive backs did NOT pick off a Baltimore Colt pass?
A. Johnny Sample
B. Randy Beverly
C. Bill Baird
D. Jim Hudson

• BUFFALO BILLS •

THE SEASON BEGAN FOR THE BILLS innocently enough. As training camp opened they still had veteran Jack Kemp at quarterback, with Tom Flores, a dependable starter in Oakland for years, backing him up, and a young rookie signal caller from William & Mary named Dan Darragh backing the two veterans. Leading rusher and receiver Keith Lincoln and dependable Wray Carlton returned at running back, and young Bobby Crockett joined former all-leaguer Art Powell as receivers. The offensive line, consistently one of the best blocking crews for years, was still stocked with a solid front five.

But before their opening kickoff, Murphy's Law 1A came true—who ever could get injured, got injured. Kemp injured his knee in training camp and then Flores hurt his shoulder. Lincoln, Crockett, and offensive line starters Joe O'Donnell and Dick Hudson filled the injured list before the end of training camp. To make matter worse, Carlton and Powell were released. How quickly things change!

Faced with only Dan Darragh, the untested rookie, as his quarterback, third-year head coach Joel Collier brought in Kay Stevenson from the Chargers as insurance. Stevenson, too, was lost in his second game, breaking his collar bone. The injury list grew longer when Darragh became the fourth quarterback to get hurt, giving Collier no choice but to turn to versatile Ed Rutkowski, who had not taken a snap since his Notre Dame days eight years ago. Rutkowski had become the jack-of-all-trades with the Bills, running back punts and kickoffs as well as lining up at halfback and flanker. Now he became the AFL's version of Tom Matte, the Baltimore Colt halfback who was pressed into action as a quarterback when Johnny Unitas and backup Gary Cuozzo were injured in 1965. Called upon to salvage what was left of the second-worst season record in AFL history, Rutkowski tried nobly to fill the void by completing 41 of his 100 passing attempts and gaining 96 yards on 20 carries, mostly scrambles.

As they lined up for their first game on

The Progress of the Seasons – 1968

September 8, the Bills starting backfield had been completely changed from the preseason depth chart. All four starters were rookies. Joining Darragh behind the line were Ben Gregory at fullback, 5'8" Mini Max Anderson at halfback, and top draft pick Haven Moses at flanker. Wide receiver Richard Trapp from Florida was also a rookie. With the offense spending most of the season learning on the job, Buffalo finished ninth in both running and passing. Darragh completed 43 percent of his 215 passes as the highest-ranking quarterback in the lot. Mini Max, the best of the young Bill runners, gained 545 yards, twelfth in the league, for a 3.6 average. Anderson was also the only kick returner to score a touchdown in 1968, taking one back 100 yards against Cincinnati. Ben Gregory finished second on the team in rushing, accounting for 283 yards and a team-high 5.4 yards per carry. Bob Cappadona and Gary McDermott also saw stints in the Buffalo backfield, as did Keith Lincoln, who carried 26 times for 84 yards before being traded back to San Diego. Moses caught 42 aerials, but the next best receiving totals dropped off to Richard Trapp's 24 and Anderson's 22. Tight ends Paul Costa and Billy Masters caught 22 between them.

Despite the dreary, injury-riddled offense, the defense played as well as any in the league. Buffalo had gained a reputation as being one of the AFL's best at handcuffing opposing offenses, and this year was no exception. Ranking in the middle of the heap, the Bills held most teams in check with little scoring help. The offense scored a league-low 199 points, while the defense gave up 367.

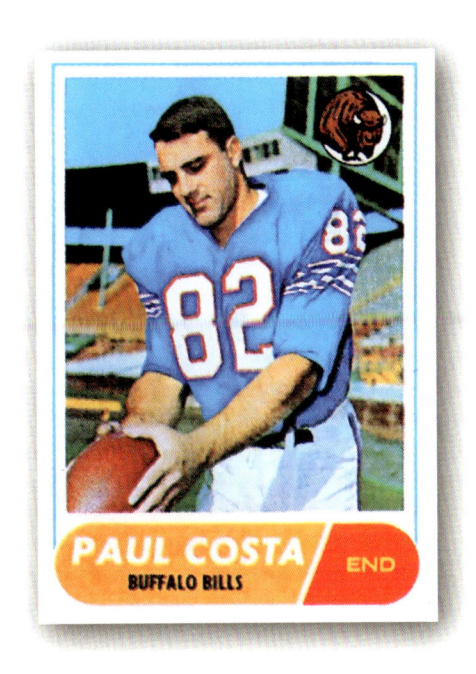

Even with a 1-12-1 record, the Bills were never patsies and played some of their best games against the league's top three powerhouses. They took Western leaders Kansas City and Oakland to the limit before losing 18-7 and 13-10. They also registered their only 1968 victory against the 1968 Super Bowl Champion New York Jets, 37-35. In their September 28 win over the Jets, the Buffalo defense helped Joe Namath throw 7 touchdown passes, giving up 4 and scoring 3 for themselves, an AFL record for returning interceptions for touchdowns in a game. Butch Byrd took one of his two picks 53 yards for a score, and Booker Edgerson added 6 more points by returning his intercepton 45 yards. Safety Tom Janik, who caught 2 of Namath's 5 interceptions, set another league record by returning one of them 100 yards for a touchdown.

315

Remember the AFL

In their second meeting against the Jets, the Bills came up only 4 points short of another victory, fallling 25-21. In seven of their twelve losses and one tie, the Bills had the opportunity to pull the game out at the end. An opening-day loss to Boston ended only 9 points shy, with Cincinnati winning by less than 2 touchdowns two weeks later. The three losses against Kansas City, Oakland, and New York could have been won with a more consistent offense. Against Miami, one game ended in a tie while in the loss Buffalo led for 58 minutes. After leading in Denver for 59 minutes and 53 seconds, the Bills fell victim to Bobby Howfield's 12-yard field goal with seven seconds left for still another fist-pounding loss, 34-32. In all, seven more victories were within reach despite a 14 points per game scoring average.

One can only wonder what impact the injured offensive starters would have had on those outcomes. There were many exciting and frustrating moments for the young and wounded Bills in 1968. And although they brought home only one victory in fourteen games, the Bills did something that not even the powerful NFL Champion Baltimore Colts could do in Super Bowl III—they beat the New York Jets!

Leading passers	Attempts	Completions	Pct	TDs	Yards	Int
Dan Darragh	215	92	43%	3	917	14
Ed Rutkowski	100	41	41%	0	380	6
Kay Stephenson	79	29	37%	4	364	7
Tom Flores	5	3	60%	0	15	1

Leading rushers	Attempts	Yards gained	Average	TDs
Max Anderson	147	525	3.6	2
Ben Gregory	52	283	5.4	1
Bob Cappadona	73	272	3.7	1
Gary McDermott	47	102	2.2	3
Ed Rutkowski	20	96	4.8	1
Keith Lincoln	26	84	3.2	0

Leading receivers	Caught	Yards gained	Average	TDs
Haven Moses	42	633	15.1	2
Richard Trapp	24	235	9.8	0
Max Anderson	22	140	6.4	0
Gary McDermott	20	115	5.8	1
Bob Cappadona	18	92	5.1	2
Paul Costa	15	172	11.5	1

Leading scorers	TDs	XPM	XPA	FGM	FGA	PTs
Bruce Alford		15	15	14	24	57
Gary McDermott	4	1				26

The Progress of the Seasons – 1968

47. This former leading receiver for the Jets was a backup to Don Maynard and George Sauer in 1968 and the fourth New York pass catcher to have played for a Texas university (Texas Tech). Who was he?

▪ HOUSTON OILERS ▪

THE HOUSTON ASTRODOME, HOME to the Astros, also became the home of the Houston Oilers in 1968 after a long running feud between Bud Adams and Houston Sports Association president Judge Roy Hofheinz. The Oilers were the Eastern Division's defending champs for the fourth time and still depending on their outstanding defense to set the tone. Coach Wally Lemm, knowing that to stay on top he would need to rev up his anemic passing attack, drafted wide receivers Mac Haik and Jim Beirne with his second (their first pick went to KC in the Beathard deal) and fourth picks. The two quickly joined the starting lineup after being fazed in behind Charlie Frazier and Lionel Taylor.

On the AFL's best defensive unit from the previous year, only rookie Elvin Bethea at end was new, replacing injured veteran Gary Cutzinger who was lost for the season. Willie Parker and George Rice provided solid play at tackle, backed up by rookie Tom Domres. The group held AFL runners to 3.7 yards per carry, third best in the league. End Pat Holmes, linebacker George Webster, and cornerback Miller Farr formed arguably the best left side trio in pro football. A preseason bout with hepatitis slowed Farr early in the year, but he remained an all-league performer for the second year in a row. He only intercepted 3 passes all season, but his pass coverage was so deadly that teams just stopped challenging him. Of the 3 interceptions Farr did make, he returned 2 for touchdowns of 52 and 40 yards. Webster earned his second straight all-league selection, and in his second year he ranked as one of pro football's best. In the defensive secondary, sophomore strong safety Ken Houston led the team with 5 interceptions, returning 2 for touchdowns. Larry Carwell also returned 1 of his 4 interceptions for a touchdown, adding to Houston's league-leading 5 for the season. With assistance from Zeke Moore and W.K. Hicks, the Oilers secondary allowed opposing passers to complete only 44 percent of their attempts and gave up a league-low 13 touchdown passes. Opponents scored only 248 points against Houston, the league's third fewest. They also came within 36 inches of yielding the fewest average total yards per game, at 241. In four of their 14 games, Houston allowed less than 10 points and in only one did they give up more than 26.

The league's best running offense of a year ago fell to fourth best, but they maintained one of the best blocking lines with veterans Walt Suggs, Sonny Bishop, and Bobby Maples teaming with youngsters Tom Regner and Glen Ray Hines. Fullback Hoyle Granger, nursing a sore back much of the year, finished fourth in rushing, with 848 yards and 26 receptions. His backfield mate, Woody Campbell, ran for 436

317

yards despite spending his week days with the Army. (Most of Campbell's 1969 season would be spent in Vietnam.) Sid Blanks, once the team's best runner, gained 169 yards as a backup. His longest run from scrimmage was only 10 yards, while his 2.7 yards per carry average was his most telling statistic. For the unveiling of the Astrodome, the Oilers also made a subtle change in their uniforms, adding more red trim to their jerseys.

In their home opener against Kansas City, the first pro football game played indoors, quarterback Pete Beathard showed why he earned All-American honors at USC. Throwing for over 400 yards, he brought his team back from a 26-7 deficit with 2 touchdown passes to rookie Mac Haik in the fourth quarter and was driving toward a game-winning score when, with under two minutes left to play, KC cornerback Emmitt Thomas intercepted a pass at the 10 yard line. The defense dug in and used their three time outs to get the ball back with less than a minute to play. A long completion to Ode Burrell from midfield settled the ball at the 12 yard line, and on fourth down with twenty-one seconds remaining, Beathard attempted to connect with Sid Blanks in the end zone. But the pass fell harmlessly to the ground for a 26-21 Kansas City victory.

The first win of the new season came a week later against Miami, assisted by Ken Houston's 66-yard interception return for a touchdown. It was one of the secondary's 3 interceptions on Bob Griese. The only team to score 30 points on Houston handed the Oilers their second loss in San Diego when John Hadl put 21 fourth quarter points on the board to defeat them, 30-14. After a 24-15 loss to Oakland, the 1-3 Oilers needed a quarterback. Pete Beathard underwent an emergency appendectomy three days before facing the Dolphins and missed the next five weeks. Lemm tapped second-year quarterback Bob Davis for emergency service. His first start in Miami pushed the defending champs further behind the Eastern Division eight ball with a 24-7 loss and a 1-4 record. In his second start, Davis put his team back in the winner's circle with a 16-0 win over Boston. His 7-yard run accounted for the game's only touchdown.

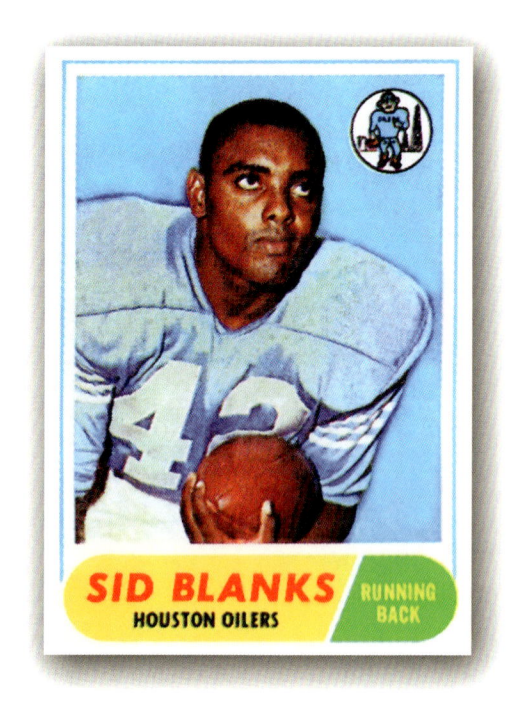

After giving up on long-time backup Don Trull the year before, the Oilers re-signed the Baylor star when the Patriots no longer wanted him. Trull came off the bench in the second half against the Jets and put his team in

The Progress of the Seasons – 1968

the lead 14-13 with four minutes to play. But in 1968 the Jets did little wrong, and Joe Namath pulled this one out in the last minute, 20-14. As Trull took command, the Oilers went on to win five of their last seven games. Even when Beathard returned three weeks later, Lemm looked more to Trull in a pinch. Wins over Denver 38-10, Buffalo 35-6, and Boston 45-17, landed Houston solidly in second place with a 7-7 record, four games behind New York and two ahead of Miami. Of their seven losses, six were against the AFL's elite—Oakland, Kansas City, New York, and San Diego—establishing the Oilers as merely the best of the rest.

An exciting trio of young receivers brought Houston's passing game to the next level. Both Mac Haik and Jim Beirne gave Beathard and Trull able receivers. Haik, with 32 catches, and Beirne, with 31, finished second and third on the team behind all-star tight end Alvin Reed, who in his second year became one the best in the AFL. His 46 catches placed him ninth in the league. Kickoff specialists Zeke Moore and Larry Carwell gave Houston the AFL's best average of 23.3. One area in need of improvement was the kicking game, which made just 12 of 29 field goals. Jon Wittenborn made 4 of his 13 attempts and was replaced by Wayne Walker at midseason. Walker connected on 7 of his 9 attempts inside the 40.

Out of pure necessity, the AFL had developed a superior group of young linebackers and defensive backs that now rivaled the NFL. The offenses continued to become more complex and less predictable, and linemen became bigger and faster, as the entire league was now running more often. Over the years the ratio of running to passing plays had steadily narrowed. In 1964 teams threw over 600 more passes than running plays. That dropped to 400 in 1965, then to 300 in 1966. And 1967, AFL teams passed only 160 more times than they ran. In 1968, for the first time in the league's existence, there were more running plays than passes. The pattern paralleled the increase in the quality of overall play by the AFL teams. Winners of only 3 of 12 interleague games the first year, AFL teams won 13 of 23 games in 1968. Over the years, young college recruits had regularly chosen the opportunity to play right away in the AFL over waiting their turn in the NFL. The dividends were starting to show, and if there *was* still a gap between the leagues in 1968, the ten American Football League teams didn't notice.

Leading passers	Attempts	Completions	Pct	TDs	Yards	Int
Pete Beathard	223	105	47%	7	1559	16
Don Trull	105	53	51%	10	864	3
Bob Davis	86	33	38%	0	441	6

Leading rushers	Attempts	Yards gained	Average	TDs
Hoyle Granger	202	848	4.2	7
Woody Campbell	115	436	3.8	6
Sid Blanks	63	169	2.7	0
Roy Hopkins	31	104	3.4	0

Leading receivers	Caught	Yards gained	Average	TDs
Alvin Reed	46	747	16.2	5
Mac Haik	32	584	18.3	8
Jim Beirne	31	474	15.3	4
Hoyle Granger	26	361	13.9	0
Woody Campbell	21	234	11.1	0
Sid Blanks	13	184	14.2	0

Leading scorers	TDs	XPM	XPA	FGM	FGA	PTs
Wayne Walker		26	26	8	16	50
Mac Haik	8					48

---

48. The Baltimore Colts' Super Bowl III roster included the first former AFL player to play for the NFL against his former league in the championship. Who was this back up tight end who caught 14 passes in 1966 for the Oakland Raiders before joining the Colts in 1968?

• SAN DIEGO CHARGERS •

THROUGH THE FIRST TEN GAMES OF 1968 the Chargers fell 10 points short of being undefeated. At 8-2 they had the second best record in the AFL, were tied with the Raiders for second place in the West, and sat only a half game behind the 9-2 Chiefs. Only a 3-point loss to the Jets and a 7-point loss to the Chiefs kept them from an unblemished record. And with only four games remaining on their schedule, Sid Gillman's troops marched into the final month to battle for another championship. John Hadl enjoyed an MVP season, throwing for 3,473 yards with 208 completions on 440 attempts with 27 touchdowns, all league highs. On five occasions he passed for over 300 yards. On the down side, he threw 32 interceptions, 13 in the final four weeks. As usual, Lance Alworth led the receivers on the way to his sixth straight season of gaining 1,000 yards receiving and his second pass catching title with 68 receptions and 10 touchdowns. His partner, Gary Garrison, caught 10 of his 52 receptions for touchdowns and his 1,103 yards receiving made the Chargers one of three AFL teams (along with New York and Oakland) to have two receivers with more than 1,000 yards. Jacque MacKinnon and Willie Frazier continued to spell each other at tight end with 33 and 16 catches respectively. All assisted in making the Chargers the league's most productive passing team. Combined with a fifth-ranked rushing attack,

The Progress of the Seasons — 1968

★ *Lance Alworth clears a path through Bengal defenders for Dickie Post.* ★

they finished with the second-best total offensive production in the AFL. Only New York and Oakland scored more points.

Protected by one of the AFL's best front walls, Hadl was dropped for losses only 10 times all year. Tackle Ron Mix and guard Walt Sweeney anchored one of the best right sides of the line in all of pro football. Sam Gruneisen was highly regarded at center, with the left side guarded by Gary Kirner and Terry Owens. Under Hadl's direction, the offense struck for 45 touchdowns, 15 of them covering more than 35 yards, with 29 of them coming through the air. The Chargers also registered more first downs than any other AFL team. Clearly the offense did not concern Gillman as he readied for the home stretch.

The defense was another story. Only Cincinnati yielded more first downs, and only the Bengals and Broncos allowed more yards per play. The San Diego pass rush, made up of ends Houston Ridge and Steve DeLong, along with tackles Scott Appleton and Russ Washington, proved somewhat less than formidable. Their 24 sacks put them ahead of only Miami. And while the Chargers surrendered an average rush of only 3.7 yards, opposing quarterbacks completed more than 50 percent through the air, though Speedy Duncan, Bobby Howard, Joe Beauchamp, and Ken Graham were all experienced pass defenders.

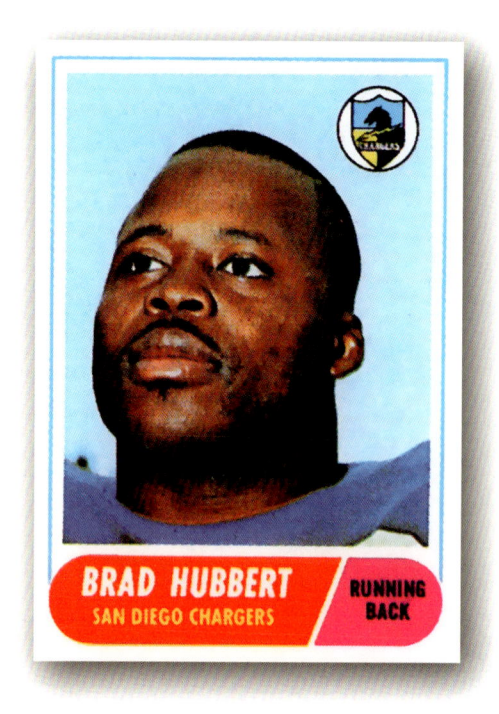

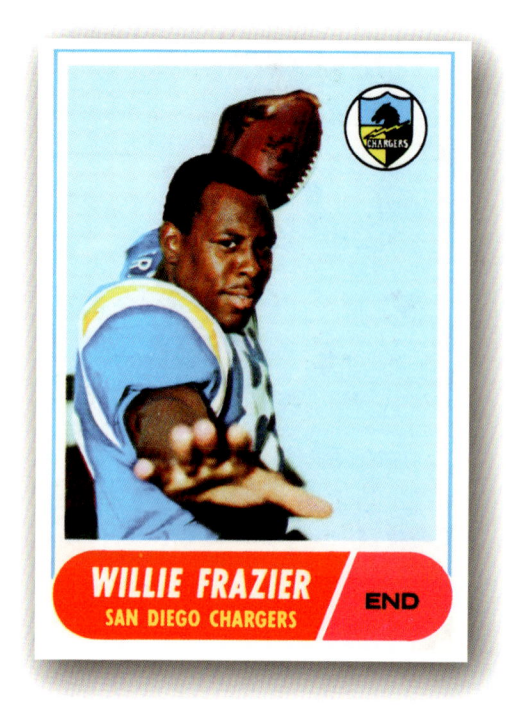

As the countdown began, losses to New York, Kansas City, and Oakland sandwiched a lone win over Denver. The final month proved they were still several steps behind their two formidable foes in the West, and they finished in third place again with a 9-5 final record.

In the crucial last four games, and in spite of their defensive short comings, the offense kept charging on. One pleasant addition that year was multi-dimensional kicker Dennis Partee from SMU. The Chargers had never employed a kicker who did both the punting and place kicking until Partee joined the team. As the league's fourth-highest scorer, he made 18 of 24 field goal attempts inside the 40, with 12 of his 14 splitting the uprights from inside the 30. He even made good on 4 of 7 attempts between the 40 and 50 yard line and converted on 40 PATs on 43 tries.

The Chargers running game also performed well. Although fullback Brad Hubbert injured his knee in the second game and missed the rest of the season, Dickie Post again ran through and around most defenses that were designed to stop him. He averaged a league-best 5.0 yards per carry for a fifth-best 758 yards. Two of his 3 rushing touchdowns went for 62 and 48 yards. Without Hubbert powering through the line, Gillman relied on Gene Foster, along with second-year back Russ Smith. Foster had been a starter for several years and continued to be a valuable asset by running for 394 yards and catching 23 passes. He had never been one of the glamour players on the San Diego marquee, but around the league he was known for his strong running and consistent blocking. Smith, out of Miami, carried 88 times and notched 426 yards for an impressive 4.8 yards per carry. For two years in a row, the Chargers challenged for the division title through November, only to see their title hopes fade in December, making Gillman all too aware that if his team was going to step over Oakland and Kansas City in 1969, he was going to have to build a defense that could hold them.

Leading passers	Attempts	Completions	Pct	TDs	Yards	Int
John Hadl	440	208	47%	27	3473	32
Jon Britenum	17	9	53%	1	125	1

Leading rushers	Attempts	Yards gained	Average	TDs
Dickie Post	151	758	5.0	3
Russ Smith	88	426	4.8	4
Gene Foster	109	394	3.6	1
Brad Hubbert	28	119	4.3	2

Leading receivers	Caught	Yards gained	Average	TDs
Lance Alworth	68	1312	19.3	10
Gary Garrison	52	1103	21.2	10
Jacque MacKinnon	33	646	19.6	6
Gene Foster	23	224	9.7	0
Dickie Post	18	165	9.2	0
Willie Frazier	16	237	14.8	3

Leading scorers	TDs	XPM	XPA	FGM	FGA	PTs
Dennis Partee		40	43	22	32	106
Lance Alworth	10	1				62
Gary Garrison	10					60

49. Before Super Bowl III Joe Namath declared that Earl Morrall, the Colts' starting quarterback, would only be third string on the Jets. Who was New York's second-string QB, previously a starter with two other AFL teams, who was supposedly better than Morrall?

▪ KANSAS CITY CHIEFS ▪

NO TEAM IN THE AFL WON MORE games during the regular season than the Kansas City Chiefs. Posting a 12-2 record was a high water mark in wins for the Chiefs and Hank Stram, who had five new starters in a lineup that led the league in total offense, punting, and punt returns. The defense was more tenacious than ever, allowing only 170 points for the year, breaking the record of 199 set the year before by Houston. Except for one game with Oakland, the Chiefs allowed only 14 touchdowns in the other thirteen games.

The league had never seen such a dominant defensive team. In five games, opponents failed to score a single touchdown, and in four other games they managed only one 6 pointer. Over the entire season they gave up only 19 touchdowns.

On opening day, Houston crossed the goal line three times, and in a game against Oakland the Chiefs gave up five scores. They smothered every other AFL team. During one streak, the defensive unit went 10 quarters without allowing a touchdown and in one four-game stretch gave up less than 8 points in each. Incredibly, the Chiefs allowed more than two touchdowns in only two of their fourteen games. And Stram had called this a rebuilding year! Always the innovator, Stram confounded the other teams on offense as well. He incorporated a moving pocket for Len Dawson to give him more time against heavy rushes. His tight end regularly set up in the backfield before going in motion to take his position on either side of the line to confuse the opposition. In one game against the Raiders, Stram even set pro football back fifteen years by using three running backs in the backfield for the entire game, calling the full house backfield his "Model T." Injuries to the entire KC wide receiver contingent necessitated the move. It was another stroke of genius, as Stram's boys handed Oakland one of its two losses by running the ball 60 times and passing it a league-record three times. The 24-10 win was so unorthodox that guard Ed Budde was named the AFL's player of the week for enabling Mike Garrett, rookie Robert Holmes, and Wendell Hayes to amass 293 yards on the ground. It was the first time a lineman had ever won the award. E.J. Holub, once an all-league linebacker, had given in to his worn-out knees and moved to the offensive side to play center. He was surrounded by Jim Tyrer and Dave Hill at tackle, with Budde and rookie Mo Moorman at guard. Fred Arbanas continued his yeoman work at tight end.

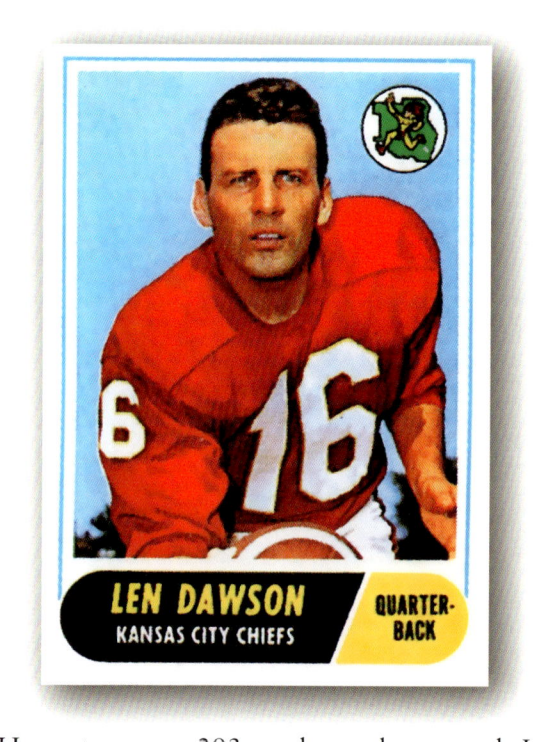

Behind this immovable offensive line, Dawson enjoyed better protection. Only Joe Namath and John Hadl were sacked less often, in part due to the moving pocket and also because the stellar running backs diverted attention from him. Mike Garrett gave his featured-back billing to Holmes and became the Chiefs' top receiver. Holmes in turn exploded through the league with a style that earned the nickname "The Tank." He compiled the second-best yard total in the league and was the runner-up in rookie of the year balloting. He gained 866 yards on 174 carries and also caught 19 passes. Wendell Hayes, late of the Denver Broncos, reliable veterans Bert Coan and Curtis McClinton, all averaged more than 4 yards a carry splitting time with the regulars.

On the passing front, flanker Otis Taylor pulled a groin muscle in the first game and missed most of the season, but his absence did not hinder KC's ability to move the ball through the air. Gloster Richardson and Frank Pitts filled in for Taylor with flying colors, with Pitts catching 30 passes on the season and Richardson catching 22, a pair more than Taylor. Dawson completed 58.5 percent of his passes, clicking for 17 touchdowns against only 9 interceptions and ranking first among AFL's quarterbacks for the fourth time in seven years.

The Chiefs won their first game of the year over the defending Eastern Division Champion Houston Oilers 26-23, then lost a nail-biter to the Jets 20-19 before they ripped off six wins in a row. They didn't lose again until November 3, when Oakland avenged the earlier loss. Five more victories in a row gave them more wins in a season (12) than they had ever won before. But having the best record in franchise history, or even in the AFL, was not good enough this year. This year their 12-2 record was only good enough to tie the defending Western Division Champion Raiders, who marched through their season by winning their last eight games. The identical records created a need for the second post-season division playoff game in league history, to be played on December 22 in Oakland.

By the time they met for their third battle of the season, the Raiders had figured out more ways to stop the Chiefs than the Chiefs did to stop the Raiders. And after playing with so much power and authority through the season, Kansas City was forced to take an alternate route to their third AFL championship game and another Super Bowl. One that would delay them for one more year.

Leading passers	Attempts	Completions	Pct	TDs	Yards	Int
Len Dawson	224	131	59%	17	2109	9
Jacky Lee	45	25	56%	3	383	1

Leading rushers	Attempts	Yards gained	Average	TDs
Robert Holmes	174	866	5.0	7
Mike Garrett	164	564	3.4	3
Wendell Hayes	85	340	4.0	4
Bert Coan	40	160	4.0	1
Curtis McClinton	24	107	4.5	0

Leading receivers	Caught	Yards gained	Average	TDs
Mike Garrett	33	359	10.9	3
Frank Pitts	30	655	21.8	6
Gloster Richardson	22	494	22.5	6
Otis Taylor	20	420	21.0	4
Robert Holmes	19	201	10.6	0
Wendell Hayes	12	108	9.0	1
Fred Arbanas	11	189	17.2	0

Leading scorers	TDs	XPM	XPA	FGM	FGA	PTs
Jan Stenerud		39	40	30	40	129
Robert Holmes	7					42

• OAKLAND RAIDERS •

HOW COULD THE RAIDERS IMPROVE on a season that brought them 13 wins and an AFL Championship? For Al Davis and head coach John Rauch, it wasn't even a question. It was a mission! And that mission focused first and foremost on backfield and wide receiver speed. Enter second-year flanker Warren Wells and multi-dimensional rookie halfback Charlie Smith. The Raiders set out to prove they could make it back to the Super Bowl and win under any circumstance. Even with Davis's passion for a vertical offense, the cornerstone of the team had shifted to the defensive side of the line. And although the "Eleven Angry Men" lost three starters from the '67 unit (linebacker Bill Laskey, all-league defensive tackle Tom Keating, and for most of the year, all-league cornerback Kent McCloughan), the Raider defense never missed a beat. Instead, they found free-spirited USC linebacker Chip Oliver to move in for Laskey, the enormous Carlton Oates for Keating, and sensational rookie George "Butch" Atkinson for McCloughan.

Another key change in the defensive backfield that proved noteworthy was moving Willie Brown to the corner, switching positions with Dave Grayson who was now at safety.

The offensive line of Jim Otto, Gene Upshaw, Jim Harvey, oft-injured Wayne Hawkins, Harry Schuh, and Bob Svihus remained rock solid and enabled Daryle Lamonica enough time to toss 25 TD passes, 11 to deep threat Warren Wells. Wells caught 53 passes on the season and averaged 21.5 yards per catch. Fred Biletnikoff finished third in the league with 61 catches. Rounding out the passing attack was Hewritt Dixon, who had another superb season with 38 receptions, tight end Billy Cannon with 23 receptions, and rookie Charlie Smith with 22. The Raiders 453 points was the benchmark for scoring, and the defense ranked second to only Kansas City in fewest points allowed.

On their way to a 12-2 record, which tied them for division honors with Kansas City, Oakland players also authored several

★ *Raider wide receiver Fred Biletnikoff*

team and league records. Dave Grayson tied former Raider Tom Morrow with 10 interceptions, place kicker George Blanda broke his own league scoring record of 116 points by one, and Daryle Lamonica broke his own team single-season passing yardage record set in 1967 by throwing for 3,245 yards. Rookie George Atkinson led the league in kickoff returns and was second in punt returns, running 2 back for TDs.

In their first game of the year, the defense so dominated the Bills that Buffalo's final passing stats showed a minus 19 yards for the day. The Raiders scored 48 points in the opener, including Atkinson scoring on an 86-yard punt return the first time he touched the ball as a pro. He also set an AFL single-game record by returning 5 punts for 205 yards in his first game. Through their first four straight victories, the Raiders tallied 160 points against Buffalo, Miami, Boston, and defensive-minded Houston. Until San Diego defeated them 23-14 in week six, the Raiders had a league-high 14-game winning streak, only one shy of tying the league record dating back to 1961, set by the Chargers. The next week, the Raiders were bushwhacked by Kansas City, 24-10, when the Chiefs employed an unconventional ball-control, full-house backfield, necessitated by several injuries to the KC wide receivers. It was the first time since September 18, 1966, that Oakland lost two in a row.

Heading into the season's ninth week, the Raiders trailed the Chiefs by one game and needed to knock them off to gain a share of the Western Division lead. Striking for 24 points in the second quarter, the Raiders took a 31-7 halftime lead. After increasing the lead by 7 points in the third quarter they withstood 2 KC touchdowns in the final period to walk away with a 38-21 win and a first-place tie. Neither team lost over the next six weeks, as the Raiders ran off eight in a row after the loss to Kansas City, closing the regular season by shutting out the Bengals 34-0, holding off Buffalo 13-10 without an offensive touchdown, and whipping Denver 33-27 and San Diego 34-27 to set the stage for their playoff grudge match with their arch-enemy, the Chiefs.

In the second divisional playoff game in AFL history, the favored Raiders demolished the Chiefs 41-6 to set up the sixth and last time an AFL team would have a chance to defend its title—in a championship game in New York against the Jets. But the game we still remember between the Raiders and Jets in that year took place in week eleven, on Sunday, November 17, and took its place in sports history as "the Heidi game." Two Jet field goals of 44 and 18 yards started the scoring in the first quarter before Lamonica connected with both Warren Wells and Biletnikoff for touchdowns of 9 and 48 yards in Oakland-Alameda Coliseum. Joe Namath brought New York back before the half with a 1-yard run, but his pass for a 2-point conversion failed, giving Oakland a 14-12 lead at the intermission. When Bill Mathis ran the ball in from 4 yards away the Jets took the lead 19-14. The Raiders answered with a 3-yard run by Charlie Smith to retake the lead, 20-19, later in the third quarter and converted on their 2-point attempt. The intensity level jumped a notch as Namath kept anwering the Oakland attack. The Jets recaptured the lead when Namath hit Don Maynard for 47 and then 50 yards, with the second completion ending in the Oakland end zone.

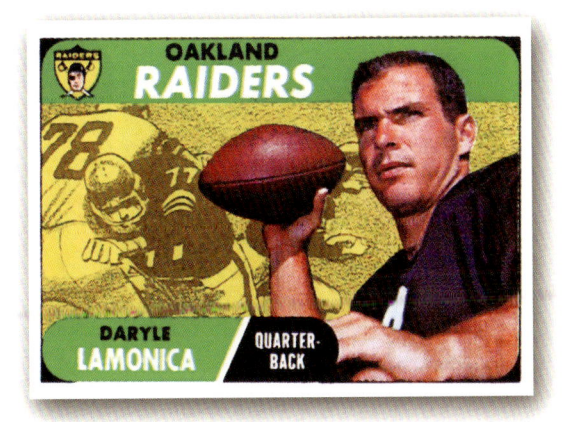

The drama and scoring continued and with only 1:05 left to play, the Raiders trailed 32-29 after Jim Turner's 26-yard field goal broke the tie. At seven o'clock Eastern time, as the Raiders took the ensuing kickoff and Daryle Lamonica went into his hurry-up offense, NBC-TV cut away to their regularly scheduled national broadcast of the children's classic *Heidi*. Within seconds of NBC breaking away, Lamonica took Oakland the length of the field, aided by a 15-yard, face mask penalty after Smith took a screen pass 20 yards downfield. From the Jet 43 yard line Lamonica sent Fred Biletnikoff on a deep down-and-out pattern to the left and Warren Wells longer down the middle to the end zone. Lamonica then found halfback Charlie Smith all alone with a 20-yard hook pass. Smith sprinted the final 23 yards to the goal line, retaking the lead for the Raiders, 36-32, with under a minute left to play. The Jets needed another touchdown, and Joe Namath was capable of getting them one in a hurry. As irate fans flooded the switchboards at NBC, what happened next would engrave the name Preston Ridlehuber in the annals of AFL history forever. After fielding the squib kickoff, Jet kick returner Earl Christy ran upfield until one of his blockers brushed him from the blind side, causing Christy to fumble. Raider Howie Williams slammed into Christy while little-known Preston Ridlehuber, charging down field full tilt, scooped up the loose football and tumbled into the end zone for another Raider touchdown. Fourteen points in nine seconds! Raiders 43-Jets 32, game over!

AFL fans east of the Rockies believed that the Jet defense had held off the Raiders in the last minute to give them a hard-fought 32-29 victory. But as the Monday morning quarterbacks awoke the next day and read the newspaper, they learned that the Jets had done the incomprehensible—THEY LOST THE GAME. The decision makers at NBC-TV were left with a huge breakfast egg on their faces.

Six weeks later, the Jets avenged the loss on a cold December day in Shea Stadium with a 27-23 victory in the AFL Championship game. Although the pride-and-poise boys failed to defend their AFL crown in 1968, twenty-five wins in two years established that the Oakland Raiders were one of the best teams in all of pro football.

Remember the AFL

★ *Raider defenders scramble to recover a fumble in "the Heidi game."* ★

Leading passers	Attempts	Completions	Pct	TDs	Yards	Int
Daryle Lamonica	416	206	50%	25	3245	15
George Blanda	49	30	61%	6	522	2

Leading rushers	Attempts	Yards gained	Average	TDs
Hewritt Dixon	206	865	4.2	2
Charlie Smith	95	504	5.3	5
Pete Banaszak	91	362	4.0	4
Roger Hagberg	39	164	4.2	1

Leading receivers	Caught	Yards gained	Average	TDs
Fred Biletnikoff	61	1037	17.0	6
Warren Wells	53	1137	21.5	11
Hewritt Dixon	38	360	9.5	2
Billy Cannon	23	360	15.7	6
Charlie Smith	22	321	14.6	2
Pete Banaszak	15	182	12.1	1

Leading scorers	TDs	XPM	XPA	FGM	FGA	PTs
George Blanda		54	54	21	34	117
Warren Wells	12					72

The Progress of the Seasons – 1968

50. The Buffalo Bills earned the rights to the NFL/AFL combined draft's #1 choice with their 1-12-1 record in 1968. The pick was USC All-American and Heisman Trophy winner O.J. Simpson. NFL teams had the #2, 3 & 4 picks. Who was the second player picked by an AFL team (at #5), who received more Rookie of the Year votes in 1969 than Simpson?

▪ NEW YORK JETS ▪

THEY CALLED IT THE GAME THAT changed pro football, and the biggest upset in the sport's history. There is no denying that the New York Jets changed the minds of millions of football fans on January 12, 1969, when they made good on Joe Namath's guarantee to win, and beat the heavily favored Baltimore Colts in Super Bowl III, 16-7. The Colts had demolished the Cleveland Browns 34-0 in the NFL Championship game and were said to be the best team in the NFL in more than a decade. They breezed through the regular season with a 13-1 record and were favored over the Jets by more than two touchdowns. Writers around the country facetiously solicited the NFL to institute a "mercy rule" for the game to emphasize the mismatch. But they failed to understand the confidence Namath and head coach Weeb Ewbank had in themselves and in their team.

The game plan called for Namath to use the running lanes and expose the right side of the Baltimore defensive line in order to set up the passing attack. Namath knew the blitzing power of the Colts and had studied their tendencies endlessly to pick up their patterns. He knew he could frustrate them by checking off plays at the line of scrimmage and confuse their ability to jam up his offense. On their first possession the Jets ran at the Colts to no avail and after a three-minute drive, called on Curly Johnson for the game's first punt. The Colts immediately began moving at will, first on a 19-yard pass to tight end John Mackey. Then runners Tom Matte and Jerry Hill powered into Jet territory before Earl Morrall fired a pass to backup tight end Tom Mitchell at the Jets 19. The Jets seemed to be scrambling for answers. Three more plays failed to move the Colts closer, and kicker Lou Michaels attempted a 27-yard field goal that sailed wide.

A relieved Jet offense charged back onto the field, but still couldn't move against the Colt defense. The first quarter ended when Colt linebacker Don Shinnick recovered a Jet fumble on the New York 12 yard line, and Baltimore readied for the certain score. As Morrall dropped back to drill the first nail into the Jets' coffin, his touchdown pass to Tom Mitchell caromed high in the air off the tight end's shoulder pad and into the waiting arms of Jet cornerback Randy Beverly. The second Colt drive that should have put points on the board had failed, and again gave the Jets new life.

This time Namath would not be denied. He marched his team down the field, running Matt Snell left on 3 plays to near midfield, then took to the air with 4 straight completions to Bill Mathis, George Sauer, and Snell

★ *Jet backs Emerson Boozer and Matt Snell* ★

that settled them at the Colt 9 yard line. Throughout the drive, Namath seemed to have a telepathic sense for what plays to call, fooling the Baltimore defense time and again. Snell ran the ball to the 4, and then followed his blockers in textbook fashion around the left side, tumbling into the end zone for the game's first touchdown and a 7-0 lead.

The Colts again proceeded to move the football at will between the 20s, but inside the red zone the Jets dug in. From the Jet 15 yard line, Morrall faded back and spotted flanker Willie Richardson slanting across the field. As he rifled the ball in hope of splitting the defense, Jets cornerback Johnny Sample intercepted the pass at the 1 yard line. The Jet defense had held off a Baltimore scoring drive for the third time, and the second one inside the 20 yard line. After stopping the ensuing Jet drive, the Colts, with one final first-half charge, tried to catch the Jet defense off guard with a flea-flicker that had worked for a touchdown a few weeks earlier against the Atlanta Falcons. A handoff to Matte moving

The Progress of the Seasons – 1968

to his right called for him to stop short of turning it upfield and throw the ball back to Morrall, who would then find an open receiver downfield for a long gain. It worked to perfection until Morrall failed to identify split end Jimmy Orr waving his arms frantically near the goal line. Instead, he forced a pass down the middle of the field that ended up becoming the Jets' third interception of the half, this time by safety Jim Hudson with twenty-five seconds left. As the clock ran out, a stunned audience saw Namath lead his Jets into the locker room with a 7-0 lead.

Things got even better for the Jets on the first play of the second half when Tom Matte fumbled and Jim Turner turned it into 3 more New York points and a 10-0 margin. Namath continued to confound the Baltimore defense with audibles at the line, and by out maneuvering the blitz schemes with quick look-in and short out patterns to Sauer and Maynard. His mastery kept the ball in New York's hands for twelve of the third quarter's fifteen minutes.

As the fourth quarter got underway, the Jets culminated their latest drive with Jim Turner's third field goal of the day to take a 16-0 lead. Desperate for a change of pace, Colt head coach Don Shula turned to legendary quarterback John Unitas to come off the bench and ignite the offense. Ten years earlier Unitas brought these same Colts back from certain defeat to force the first overtime championship period against the New York Giants and won. Now he was asked to perform another miracle against a different New York team. Unitas had some initial success, but as the Colts desperately drove into New York territory, he threw long for flanker Jimmy Orr, and Randy Beverly grabbed his second interception of the day. As the clock wound down under three minutes, the Colts finally scored a touchdown, but they still needed 2 more scores. Everyone in the Orange Bowl's capacity crowd not to mention the millions watching on television—knew the Colts would try an onside kick.

Though the Jets were not fooled, the Colts managed to recover the kick, giving them, and the NFL, a glimmer of hope. The Jets went into a prevent defense, wanting only to protect against a deep strike as Unitas picked his way downfield with passes underneath and to the outside of the secondary to stop the clock. With twenty-three seconds left, he faced a fourth down inside Jet territory. One last pass for glory, one final attempt to avoid a crushing defeat to the American Football League, one closing play to the greatest upset in sports history remained left. Unitas threw a pass that sailed too long, and the New York Jets were the World Champions of professional football. The unimaginable had happened—the AFL had defeated the NFL in Super Bowl III, sending the sports world into a frenzy.

Joe Namath, the AFL's Player of the Year, could now add the game's MVP Award to his trophy case. He had backed up his guarantee to win by playing the game of his life, as did his teammates. Statistically, the game was incredibly close, with the teams rushing for 143 and 142 yards and passing for 181 and

195 yards, giving the Jets an offensive advantage of only 13 total yards. But had it not been for two key plays two weeks earlier, the Jets trip to Miami may never have happened.

On Sunday, December 29, the Jets and Oakland Raiders met in the AFL's ninth Championship game in frigid temperatures and a swirling wind in Shea Stadium. The Jets drew their sword first on their intial possession with a touchdown pass to Don Maynard in the front corner of the end zone, then took a 10-0 lead later in the first quarter on a Jim Turner field goal of 33 yards. In true Raider fashion, Daryle Lamonica brought his team right back with a 29-yard touchdown strike to Fred Biletnikoff, who escaped Johnny Sample's attempt to decapitate him at the 10 yard line before running it in. Turner and George Blanda then traded fields goals for a 13-10 New York advantage at the half.

In the third quarter Blanda connected on another field goal to tie the game at 13-13, but Namath countered with a 20-yard touchdown pass to tight end Pete Lammons. The wind played havoc on both teams' passing throughout the day. Lamonica completed 20 of his 47 attempts, while Namath hit on only 19 of his 49. The Jets defense, which was one of the best in the AFL against the run, held Oakland to 50 yards on the ground, forcing Lamonica to take to the air. But the unforgiving wind of Shea Stadium frustrated even the best of quarterbacks, and the Jets held a 20-13 lead as the fourth quarter began.

As the New York defense dug in time and again, the first of those key plays occurred when the Jets goal line defense stopped the Raiders. George Blanda's third field goal narrowed the lead to 4 points, but also saved the Jets 4 points, thanks to the goal line stand. Namath tried to increase New York's lead midway through the fourth quarter, but the wind kept a pass up long enough for rookie George Atkinson to sprint in front of the receiver, pick the ball out of the air, and race down the sideline until the last player in his path, Joe Namath, knocked him out of bounds at the Jet 5 yard line. With six minutes left, halfback Pete Banaszak gave Oakland their first lead of the game with a 5-yard run and a 23-20 advantage.

Weeks earlier in sunny California against these same Raiders, Namath took his team 97 yards on back-to-back passes covering 47 and 50 yards to Don Maynard for a touchdown. Now it was time for Joe to strike again. He sent Maynard deep on Atkinson again on what amounted to a skid-and-go over the frozen baseball infield part of the gridiron. As Namath sent a bomb into the biting wind from his 37 yard line, Maynard got a step on the rookie defender and made a beautiful over-the-shoulder catch, then ran it to the Raider 6 yard line. On the next play, Namath looked left to find George Sauer in the end zone, but the Raiders had him covered. He looked down the middle for Lammons, but found no one. Then he looked to the right, where Maynard again had beaten his coverage. Namath fired a bullet right on his numbers and Maynard cradled it for the score. The Jets took the lead again 27-23, and Oakland needed a touchdown to win.

The Raiders pushed down the field all the way to the Jet 12 yard line after a pass completion to Warren Wells was supplemented by a 15-yard piling-on penalty. Needing to score, Lamonica thought he had fooled the defense on a swing pass to halfback Charlie Smith in the right flat. It was the second key play that lifted the Jets into the Super Bowl. Lamonica threw the pass from the 20 yard line, but it was a bit behind Smith and fell incomplete at the 22. Unknown to Smith, the pass was ruled a lateral, making it a live ball. Jet linebacker Ralph Baker raced in front of Smith to grab it and head upfield before the Raiders realized what happened. What had come so close to becoming a heartbreaking defeat, had miraculously turned into a heart-stopping finish for the new AFL Champion New York Jets.

It was that kind season for Ewbank and the team. An 8-6 record in 1967 had given them a vision of how far they could go and also gave them the incentive to take the next giant step up the Eastern Division ladder. In 1968 Joe Namath made the transition from being just a hard-throwing quarterback into the team leader and mature play caller. In the season opener at Kansas City, Namath showed his new maturity by running out the last six minutes of the game with a brilliant drive that kept the Chiefs 1 point short of victory. Playing in Birmingham against the Patriots, who were forced to move their home game, Namath lit up the scoreboard for 47 points and gave the Jets their second win. But against Buffalo the next week, he gave the Bills 3 touchdowns off 5 interceptions in the Jet first loss, 37-35. Perhaps a bit gun shy in their first home game on October 5 against the undefeated Chargers, Namath called for runs on the first eleven plays before he went to the air. As an AFL record crowd of 63,786 looked on, the Jets edged San Diego with one minute left to play when Emerson Boozer punched the ball over the goal from 1 yard away to give the Jets a come-from-behind win, 23-20. The victory, described in *Sports Illustrated* as "Winning With a Loser's Look," exemplified the team's ability to rise above any circumstance.

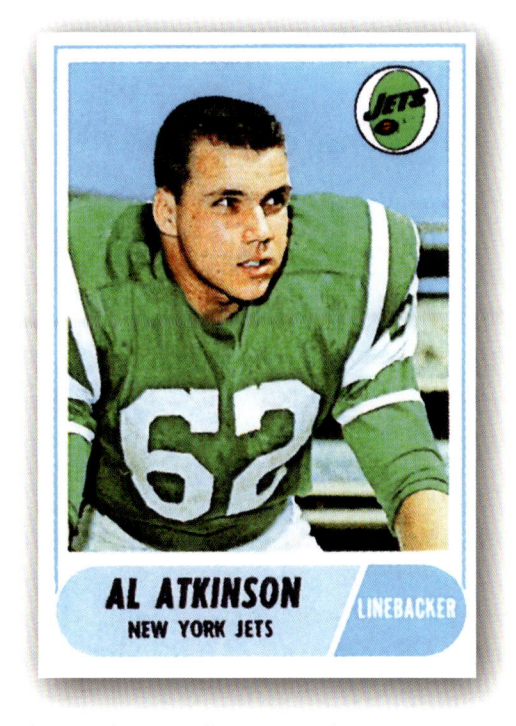

Having Snell and Boozer together for the entire season allowed the Jets to combine their dangerous passing attack with a ball-control offense for the first time in Namath's four-year career. The pair led the Jet running game that scored more touchdowns (22) on the ground than any other team. In fact, with the running of Snell and Boozer at full tilt, Namath did not have to throw a touchdown pass for six straight weeks. On five of those weeks, New York came away victoriously. Backing them up was Bill Mathis, a New York original, along with a revised edition of Billy Joe and handy Mark Smolinski. Starters Snell and Boozer gained 747 and 441 yards respectively and combined for 11 of the 22 rushing touchdowns. Mathis added 208 yards and 5 touchdowns, and Billy Joe picked up 186 yards, punching across the goal line 3 times. The New York line that opened the holes for the Jet runners was equally as effective warding off would-be attackers for Namath. The Jets tied for the league lead with San Diego by allowing only 18 quarterback sacks during the season. With Winston Hill and Dave Herman at tackle, Randy Rasmussen and Bob Talamini at guard, and John Schmitt at center, the Jets had one of the best lines in AFL history.

Another delay in Namath's maturing process occurred eight days after their thrilling defeat of the Chargers. Coming to town with a 1-3 record, the Denver Broncos used 5 more Namath interceptions to score 21 points and hand the Jets their second loss in five games. But Joe made amends in his first trip to the Astrodome after the Oilers scored 14 fourth-quarter points to take a 14-13 lead with only four minutes remaining. Joe took the Jets the length of the field, and with under a minute to play, handed the ball to Matt Snell from the 2 yard line for the winning touchdown. It was clear sailing from there, as the next week the Jets intercepted 5 passes against Boston, and led the Patriots at one point 44-0 before allowing 2 fourth-quarter scores. A record-tying, 6 field goals by Jim Turner was the margin of victory over Buffalo, assisted by Johnny Sample's 36-yard touchdown with an interception in the next game, bringing the Jets record to 6-2. Only the last-minute Heidi game loss in Oakland blemished the Jets record in their final six games, giving them a franchise-best 11-3 finish in the East, four games ahead of the 7-7 Oilers.

While one of the best lines in football led a rugged group of runners and a ball-control offense, it was the Jet receivers who Namath looked to when he needed to ignite his high-powered team. Don Maynard, on his way to a Hall of Fame career, finished among the top ten receivers every year. Over his ten AFL seasons he teamed first with Art Powell, then Bake Turner, and finally George Sauer. He caught passes from Al Dorow, Al Jamieson, Lee Grosscup, Dick Wood, Mike Taliaferro, Babe Parilli and the best of all, Joe Namath. In 1968 Maynard pulled down 57 passes for 1,297 yards, for a league-best 22.8 average and was one of only three AFL receivers to catch 10 touchdown passes. Sauer finished second in the league with 66 receptions for 1,141 yards, and Pete Lammons hauled in 32 passes. Namath, who completed 49.2 percent of his throws, struck for 15 touchdowns and did not rely as heavily on his arm as he did his savvy and football intelligence. In

The Progress of the Seasons – 1968

1968 Namath became a quarterback.

When the Jets offense stalled, it relied on the accurate toe of Jim Turner, who led the AFL in scoring with 145 points on 43 PATs and 34 field goals in 46 attempts. He made 29 of 36 inside the 40 yard line, including 23 of 26 tries from inside the 30. His 34 field goals set a new pro football record.

There were times in the past when as quickly as Namath's offense would ring up points, the defense would give them away. Twice they finished sixth and once fifth in points allowed. But for the first time in team history, the Jets defense held opponents under 300 points, making them the fourth-toughest defense in the league to score on. They ranked first against the rush and second against the pass and also allowed a league-low 178 first downs. Gerry Philbin, the All-Time AFL defensive end, teamed with Verlon Biggs, Paul Rochester, John Elliott, and sub Carl McAdams up front. Their ferocious pass rush and hole-plugging tackles allowed linebackers Larry Grantham, Al Atkinson, and Ralph Baker to drop deeper into the pass coverage to help Sample, Beverly, Cornell Gordon, Dick Hudson, and Bill Baird stop 55 percent of their opponent's passes and intercept 28 of them (second best in the league).

Sports writers and NFL fans laughed when the AFL started play in 1960, and continued to laugh through Super Bowls I and II, claiming the AFL was far inferior and years away from equality with the senior league. But because of a brazen and confident quarterback named Joe Namath and his Champion New York Jets, after January 12, 1969, they laughed no more.

SUPER BOWL III
NEW YORK (AFL) 16   BALTIMORE (NFL) 7

SUPER BOWL III
NEW YORK (AFL) 16   BALTIMORE (NFL) 7

Remember the AFL

Leading passers	Attempts	Completions	Pct	TDs	Yards	Int
Joe Namath	380	187	49%	15	3147	17
Babe Parilli	55	29	53%	5	401	2

Leading rushers	Attempts	Yards gained	Average	TDs
Matt Snell	179	747	4.2	6
Emerson Boozer	143	441	3.1	5
Bill Mathis	74	208	2.8	5
Billy Joe	42	186	4.4	3

Leading receivers	Caught	Yards gained	Average	TDs
George Sauer	66	1141	17.3	3
Don Maynard	57	1297	22.8	10
Pete Lammons	32	400	12.5	3
Matt Snell	16	105	6.6	1
Emerson Boozer	12	101	8.4	0
Bake Turner	10	241	24.1	2

Leading scorers	TDs	XPM	XPA	FGM	FGA	PTs
Jim Turner		43	43	34	46	145
Don Maynard	10					60

★ ★ ★ ★ ★ ★ ★ ★ ★ ★

The All-Star game in Jacksonville on January 19 was more than just a season-ending showcase for the players. It was more of a gala with every player on both the East and West squads beaming from ear to ear. One week earlier the Jets did not just bring the NFL to its knees by winning Super Bowl III for the team and city of New York, they won it for every player, coach, and owner that had ever been part of the American Football League.

The game started with Joe Namath and San Diego's John Hadl behind center, with the only scoring in the opening quarter coming from Jim Turner and Jan Stenerud, who traded field goals. Turner connected for field goals two, three, and four in the second frame, adding nine more points to Miami halfback Jim Kiick's 2-yard touchdown to give them a 19-3 lead heading into the third quarter.

The Progress of the Seasons – 1968

A new set of quaterbacks piloted the teams as the second half began. As Kansas City's Len Dawson led the West to 10 third-quarter points, Miami's Bob Griese drove the East team into field goal range for Jim Turner's fifth 3-pointer of the afternoon—and a 22-13 advantage. A sixth Turner field goal then lifted the East to a seemingly insurmountable 24-13 lead before the Western Division's deluge. Raider fullback Hewritt Dixon blasted into the end zone from 1 yard away after being set up by Floyd Little's 81-yard dash with a pass from Dawson. An onside kick then caught the East napping, and the West had the ball again. Bengal runner Paul Robinson then scored the first of his two fourth-quarter touchdowns before Stenerud put the cherry on top with a 32-yard field goal. After watching the East dance off the field with victories in the last two years, the West scored 25 fourth-quarter points to win their fifth of the seven meetings and again took bragging rights with a scintillating 38-25 victory.

★ ★ ★ ★ ★ ★ ★ ★ ★ ★

1969

AMERICAN FOOTBALL LEAGUE – 1969 FINAL STANDINGS

EASTERN DIVISION

TEAM	GP	W	L	T	PF	PA	PCT.
NEW YORK JETS	14	10	4	0	353	269	0.714
HOUSTON OILERS	14	6	6	2	278	279	0.500
BOSTON PATRIOTS	14	4	10	0	266	316	0.286
BUFFALO BILLS	14	4	10	0	230	359	0.286
MIAMI DOLPHINS	14	3	10	1	233	332	0.250

WESTERN DIVISION

TEAM	GP	W	L	T	PF	PA	PCT.
OAKLAND RAIDERS	14	12	1	1	377	242	0.857
KANSAS CITY CHIEFS	14	11	3	0	359	177	0.857
SAN DIEGO CHARGERS	14	8	6	0	288	276	0.643
DENVER BRONCOS	14	5	8	1	297	344	0.357
CINCINNATI BENGALS	14	4	9	1	280	367	0.214

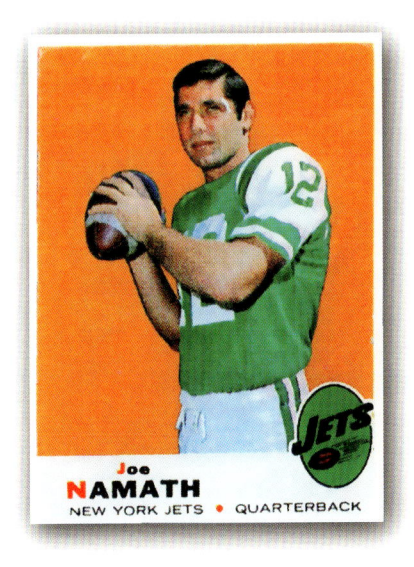

Broadway Joe Namath is credited with saving the AFL with his high-profile signing for $400,000 by the Jets in 1965 and his guaranteeing a Super Bowl III victory. Backing up his words made him an AFL folk hero. Then in June, 1969, his ownership of a Manhattan nightclub caused a brief retirement, rather than obey commissioner Pete Rozelle's edict to sell his interest because it was said to be frequented by well-known bookies and gamblers. Namath was back in uniform with the Jets before the preseason began.

▪ SAN DIEGO CHARGERS ▪

IN THE THREE YEARS SINCE THE SAN Diego Chargers won their last Western Division title, they continued to be a very good team with one of the league's most respected offenses. They just weren't good enough. In both 1967 and 1968, Sid Gillman's gang was within a half game of the division lead after ten games, only to lose four in a row in '67 and three of their last four in '68, finishing third both years. The mission in 1969 was to change all that. And change it they did. Instead of losing three or four games in the

★ John Hadl and Lance Alworth ★

last month, they strung together four straight wins at end of the season. In the preceding years they would have overtaken both the Chiefs and Raiders, but in 1969 the preceding ten games put the Chargers well behind the two powers of the West and out of any hope for a playoff spot. Their 8-6 record put them in third place for the fourth year in a row, still several first downs from challenging for the division leadership.

In 1969, Gillman, the only head coach the Chargers had ever known, voluntarily stepped out of his position after nine games due to declining health. Assistant coach Charlie Waller inherited the lead role for the last five games of the year and led them to wins in their last four to salvage a derailed season. Gillman's defense still could not stop the top offensive teams week after week. They showed improvement, giving up the fourth fewest points, yielding fewer than even the defensive specialists in Houston. But two consecutive losses—27-9 to Kansas City and 34-20 to Cincinnati—to open the season put them in a hole from which they couldn't escape. They did run off a sharp series of wins against the Jets, Bengals, Dolphins, and Patriots, but a return to their own division saw them on the short end in games against Oakland, Denver, Kansas City, and Oakland again to seal their doom for the season.

Especially perplexing was the inconsistent performance of the once-terrifying offense that for five weeks in a row failed to score more than 1 touchdown in a game, including three weeks in a row without a single 6-pointer. Even with Dickie Post leading the league in rushing and the second-best

The Progress of the Seasons – 1969

ground game in the league, San Diego did not look like the long-range scoring machine that defined the organization over the years. The passing attack dropped to an unprecedented seventh place, even though John Hadl had a decent year, completing 49 percent of his 324 passes and throwing a career-low 11 interceptions. But he also managed only 10 touchdown passes, the fewest of his career as a starter and 17 less than the year before. He felt pressure from the bench, where Columbia's Marty Domres waited for a chance to throw to the Chargers group of premier receivers. When Domres did get onto the field he completed 47 of 112 attempts, 2 for touchdowns with 10 interceptions.

The Chargers once again featured wide receivers Lance Alworth and Gary Garrison. Since 1966 the pair finished among the best in receptions and yards gained, and this year was no different. Alworth brought home his third receiving title with 64 catches and gained over 1,000 receiving for the seventh straight year. He also set a pro football record by catching at least 1 pass in 96 straight games. Garrison was nearly as dangerous from the other side of the field, although injuries limited him to ten games and 40 receptions with 7 touchdowns. Tight ends Willie Frazier and Jacque Mackinnon spelled each other, depending on the receiving or blocking situation. Few teams could match their versatility.

In the years since Lincoln and Lowe formed the backfield, there was never a time that the team could match the offensive balance of 1969. Only Kansas City gained more yards on the ground than the Chargers, and no one moved the chains on first downs more often. In gaining his league-leading 873 yards, Post gained over 100 yards four times. He also caught 24 passes for 235 yards. After sitting out all but two games in 1968, Brad Hubbert returned to Post's side to grind out 333 yards. Gene Foster and Russ Smith chipped in with 236 and 211 yards. Both finishing right behind Hubbert in the league's rushing statistics.

When the offense needed help, they called on the league's best punter, Dennis Partee, who paced the AFL with a 44.6 yard average. One of a dying breed, he also kicked field goals.

Though the defense sometimes failed, the secondary remained strong. Their 31 interceptions were one short of leading the league, and their 3 returned for touchdowns led all teams except Oakland. Veterans Speedy Duncan and Ken Graham led the group. Duncan returned one of his 6 interceptions all the way, and was also the AFL's second-best punt returner and third-best kick returner. Graham put his signature in the end zone on 2 of his 4 interceptions. Youngsters Bobby Howard equaled Duncan's interception total, with free safety Jimmy Hill leading the team with 7.

Two losses, four wins, four losses, four wins! That is how the Chargers season went in 1969 and pretty much mirrored their last four years in the AFL. Oakland and Kansas City had separated themselves from the rest of the Western Division, and San Diego had become just another American Football League team,

★ *Guard Walt Sweeney leads the sweep for Dickie Post.* ★

but also a team with a proud history. The star-studded Chargers remained among the classiest teams in the league, from their first owner Barron Hilton, to GM/coach Sid Gillman and his fleet of all-stars like Paul Lowe, Keith Lincoln, Lance Alworth, John Hadl, Earl Faison, and Ernie Ladd. Together they seemed to invent the term *vertical offense* and also were the first to coin the phrase *fearsome foursome*.

For eight of the AFL's ten seasons the Chargers contended for the Western Division crown, and in five of those seasons won it. Many experts believe the 1963 Championship team was the best in pro football that year and one of the best in AFL history. Five times in the league's first six years Sid Gillman's team appeared in the AFL Championship game. In 1960 they fell short by 8 points and in 1961, the margin of defeat was only 7. After an injury-marred 1962, they returned to the Championship game in 1963 and set an AFL standard with a 51-10 win over Boston. They came back again the next two years but could not win the title. The San Diego offensive juggernaut for many years provided the measuring stick for the rest of the AFL.

More than anyone else, Lance Alworth, the man called "Bambi," characterized the San Diego Chargers and the American Football League. With his lightning speed and acrobatic catches, he was the best pass receiver in pro

The Progress of the Seasons – 1969

football during his time in the league. Seven times he was named to the all-league team and three times won the league's pass receiving title. For seven straight years he caught passes for over 1,000 yards, and in eight years caught a total of 458 passes for an all-time AFL best 19.6 yards per reception. He holds the pro football record for catching passes in 96 consecutive games, was named to the AFL's All-Time team, and upon his retirement became the first American Football League player to be voted into the Pro Football Hall of Fame.

Leading passers	Attempts	Completions	Pct	TDs	Yards	Int
John Hadl	324	158	49%	10	2253	11
Marty Domres	112	47	42%	2	631	10

Leading rushers	Attempts	Yards gained	Average	TDs
Dickie Post	182	873	4.8	6
Brad Hubbert	94	333	3.5	4
Gene Foster	64	236	3.7	0
Russ Smith	51	211	4.1	2

Leading receivers	Caught	Yards gained	Average	TDs
Lance Alworth	64	1003	15.7	4
Gary Garrison	40	804	20.1	7
Dickie Post	24	235	9.8	0
Willie Frazier	17	205	12.1	0
Gene Foster	14	83	5.9	1
Brad Hubbert	11	43	3.9	0
Russ Smith	10	144	14.4	0

Leading scorers	TDs	XPM	XPA	FGM	FGA	PTs
Dennis Partee		33	33	15	28	78
Gary Garrison	7					42

51. What was the name of the New York nightclub that Namath partly owned in 1969?

52. The 1969 AFL season was run under a different postseason format than in previous years. What was different about the 1969 postseason and championship game?

• MIAMI DOLPHINS •

WITH A ROSTER OF TALENTED AND tenacious young stars ready to bloom and some outstanding veterans arriving via brilliant trades, the Dolphins were a team on the rise. Though still a few years away from maturity and still hampered by the cast of expansion picks, the team had progressed faster than anyone expected. The backfield of Griese, Kiick, and Csonka showed growth, and the core group of receivers developed as well. But in 1969 the Dolphins suffered one of those injury-plagued seasons that sets teams back and slows their progress. Team leader Bob Griese missed the final five games with an injured knee. Flanker Jack Clancy, who as a rookie caught 67 passes only to sit out all of 1968, went down again and played only seven games. Howard Twilley, another talented wide receiver, appeared in just four games, and starting tight end Doug Moreau saw action in only five. On the defensive side, cornerbacks Jim Warren and Dick Westmoreland both saw time on the injured list.

The injuries caused a drop to the bottom of the Eastern Division with a 3-10-1 record. Kiick and Csonka put together solid seasons, with Kiick gaining 575 on 180 attempts and scoring a league-high 9 touchdowns, and Csonka running 131 times for 566 yards and a 4.3 average. Rookie Eugene "Mercury" Morris emerged as a new threat, averaging 4.8 yards per carry on 23 rushes. He also authored the season's longest kickoff return, running 105 yards for a touchdown. The surprise of the offensive, however, was tight end/punter Larry Seiple. With injuries claiming most of the front liners, Seiple showcased his ability by hauling in 41 receptions, 5 for touchdowns. Kiick added 29 receptions, and Karl Noonan, the leading receiver in 1968 but slowed by injury, pulled in 29.

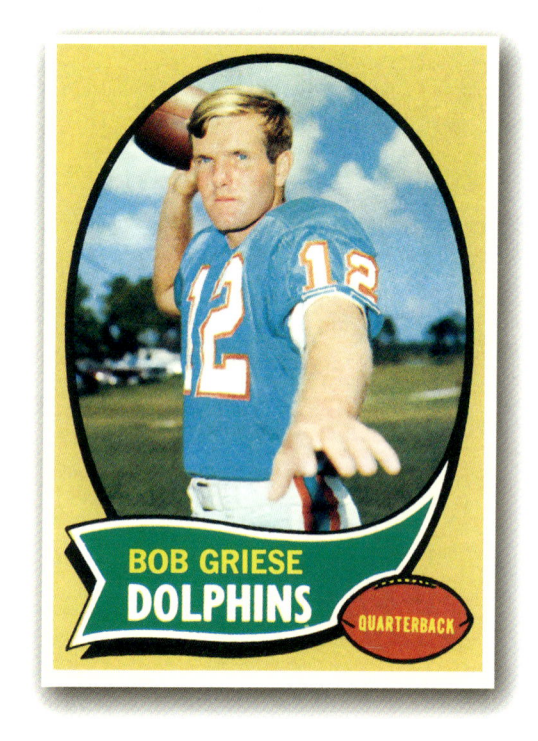

Defensively the Dolphins showed signs of growth, equaling the Super Bowl Champion Chiefs with a league-leading 3.5 yards allowed per carry. Opposing quarterbacks completed only 48 percent of their passes against them. The Dolphins picked off 18 passes and ran 2 back for scores, both by rookie defensive end Bill Stanfill. The secondary

★ *Dolphin all-purpose running back Jim Kiick*

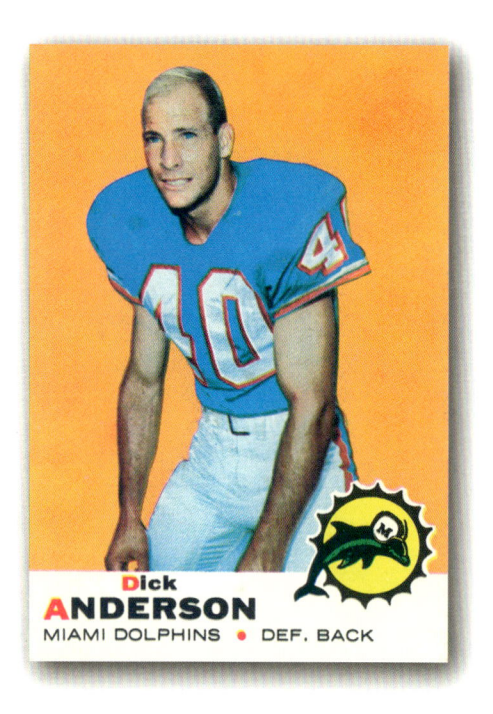

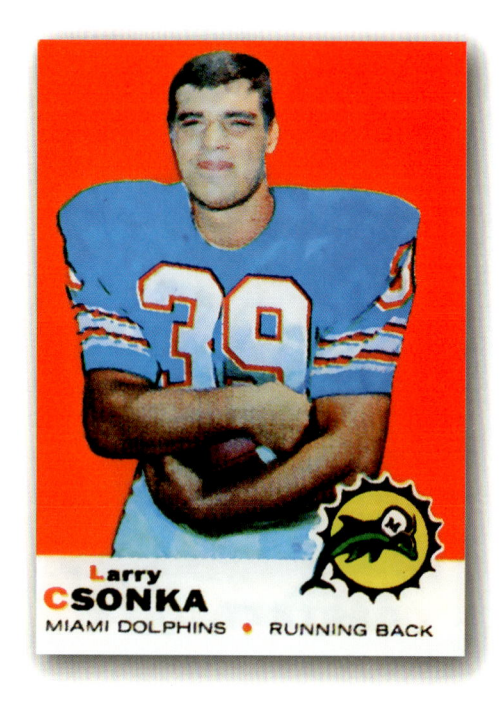

consisted of all-star Dick Anderson, leading intercepter Lloyd Mumford, along with Bob Petrella and Tom Beier. All-league Nick Buoniconti, Frank Emanuel, and Randy Emmunds played linebacker, while the tough front four was led by ends Stanfill and Manny Fernandez.

After rising to the middle of the East in 1968, the Dolphins planned to move higher in '69. But the season started inauspiciously, and it wasn't until game seven that they recorded their first win with a 24-6 triumph over Buffalo. Although they finished the season with 10 losses, 5 of their first 6 were by margins of a touchdown or less, and in the four games against league powerhouses, including three of the four AFL playoff teams, they played well. They lost by the narrow margin of 34-31 to Super Bowl III champions New York, gave Oakland all they could handle in a 20-17 loss and a 20-20 tie, and then pushed Kansas City to the limit in a 17-10 loss. The multitude of injuries to skill players simply undermined the possibility of greater success.

Despite the disappointment of their 3-10-1 season, Miami planned to build on positive experiences like tying Oakland Raiders, playing the Jets and Chiefs nearly even, holding Heisman Trophy rookie O.J. Simpson to 12 yards on 10 carries, having Larry Csonka power his way for 121 yards in a win over Boston, and stopping a late charge by Denver in a 27-24 win. After four years in the league the Dolphins were still a work in progress and still learning how to win with adversity, but they were young enough to rebound with passion, and hungry enough to get back on

The Progress of the Seasons – 1969

their upward climb to the division's top rung. In 1970, under new head coach Don Shula, the Dolphins would take a giant step toward their quest for the Super Bowl by turning their 3-10-1 mark of 1969 into a playoff-bound 10-4 record.

Leading passers	Attempts	Completions	Pct	TDs	Yards	Int
Bob Griese	252	121	48%	10	1695	16
Rick Norton	148	65	42%	2	709	11
John Stofa	23	14	61%	0	146	2

Leading rushers	Attempts	Yards gained	Average	TDs
Jim Kiick	180	575	3.2	9
Larry Csonka	131	566	4.3	2
Mercury Morris	23	110	4.8	1
Bob Griese	21	102	4.9	0
Stan Mitchell	23	80	2.9	0

Leading receivers	Caught	Yards gained	Average	TDs
Larry Seiple	41	577	14.1	5
Karl Noonan	29	307	10.6	3
Jim Kiick	29	443	15.3	1
Larry Csonka	21	183	8.7	1
Jack Clancy	21	289	13.6	1

Leading scorers	TDs	XPM	XPA	FGM	FGA	PTs
Karl Kremser		26	27	13	22	65
Jim Kiick	10					60

53. For Super Bowl IV, the last between true AFL and NFL teams, the Chiefs added something extra to their uniform. What was it?

▪ BOSTON PATRIOTS ▪

TWO WEEKS AFTER THE NEW YORK Jets won Super Bowl III, the Patriots named a Jets assistant, Clive Rush, as their new head coach. Taking over a team that won just seven games over the last two years, Rush knew he had a lot of work ahead of him. No team gave up more points in 1968 than the Patriots, and only the quarterback-deficient Buffalo Bills gained fewer yards. Rush had to decide which dismal situation to fix first. He chose the offense, and he never recovered from that mistake. One of his first moves was to trade perennial all-league middle linebacker Nick Buoniconti to the Miami Dolphins for second-year quarterback Kim Hammond and hard-hitting linebacker John Bramlett. Buoniconti would again be

Remember the AFL

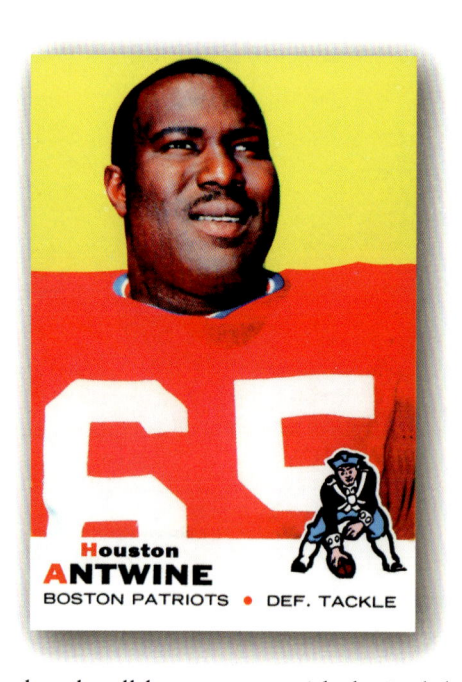

named to the all-league team with the Dolphins that year, while Hammond would throw just 6 passes for Boston. Before the end of his second year, Hammond was gone, while Buoniconti went on to lead Miami to three Super Bowls and an undefeated season in 1972.

The Patriots came up with pretty good young talent in the draft, bringing in Hammond's fellow Florida State alum, All-American Ron Sellers, the best receiver available. Desperate for running help, they took Carl Garrett from New Mexico Highlands in round three. Garrett would have a spectacular rookie season, gaining 691 yards for a 5.0 yard per carry average, for which he was awarded *The Sporting News* AFL Rookie of the Year award. He was the first Patriot to receive the honor. Jim Nance rebounded from his ankle problem of a year ago and carried 193 times for 750 yards. Nance and Garrett tied for the team lead with 29 pass receptions. The highly touted Sellers caught 27.

With Rush at the helm, quarterback Mike Taliaferro became more confident and completed 48 percent of his passes for 19 touchdowns. But those stats ranked eleventh among AFL throwers. Tom Sherman, who finished 1968 as the top man under center, saw action in only four games and did not throw a single pass. The Patriot offense finished dead last in rushing yards, dead last in passing yards, and dead last in points scored.

To make matters worse, only the second-year Bengals gave up more points. In their heyday, the Boston defense always ranked among the league leaders in stopping the run. In 1969, they gave up more rushing yardage than every other team. And no one allowed a higher pass completion percentage.

The season started with seven straight defeats until a 24-0 shutout over Houston in the Astrodome became Rush's first victory as a head coach. Then after a 1-point loss to Miami, the Pats ran off three wins in a row. Losses in the final two games brought the team's most dreadful season to a merciful end with their second straight 4-10 record, and their third straight losing season. The Patriots were back on the bottom with no solution in sight.

Throughout the '60s the Boston franchise epitomized the hard work and fighting nature of the league. In five of their first seven seasons they went into the final weekend with a chance of becoming the division champion. They called four different fields their home, and even played two home games in other

The Progress of the Seasons – 1969

states. Their defensive front seven was consistently a benchmark for the rest of the league and always seemed to place a representative on the all-league team. In a poetic touch, flanker Gino Cappelletti, who caught his first and only pass of 1960 on the season's last day, finished the AFL's last season with again only 1 reception. But what he did in between will live forever in the AFL record books. Gino led the league in scoring a record five times, he holds the two highest single-season point totals, and his 1,100 career AFL points is the league's best. He led the league in field goals three times and attempted more (318), and made more (170) field goals than any other AFL player. On October 4, 1964, he also kicked a record 6 field goals in 6 attempts against Denver. He is also the Patriots all-time leading receiver for the AFL's decade. Throughout the history of the league, Cappy was also one of only three players to see action in every game. With their 27-23 loss to the Houston Oilers on December 14, the Boston Patriots ended their AFL experience with a ten-year record of 63-68-9, with one division championship. Bravo for Boston's red, white, and blue—one of the AFL's original eight!

Leading passers	Attempts	Completions	Pct	TDs	Yards	Int
Mike Taliaferro	331	160	48%	19	2160	18
Kim Hammond	2	6	33%	0	31	0

Leading rushers	Attempts	Yards gained	Average	TDs
Jim Nance	193	750	3.9	6
Carl Garrett	122	566	4.6	5
R.C. Gamble	16	35	2.2	0
Sid Blanks	7	30	4.3	0

Leading receivers	Caught	Yards gained	Average	TDs
Jim Nance	29	168	5.8	0
Carl Garrett	29	267	9.2	2
Ron Sellers	27	705	26.1	6
Charlie Frazier	19	306	16.1	7
Bill Rademacher	17	217	12.8	3
Jim Whalen	16	235	14.7	1

Leading scorers	TDs	XPM	XPA	FGM	FGA	PTs
Gino Cappelletti		26	27	14	34	68
Charlie Frazier	7					42
Carl Garrett	7					42

54. O.J. Simpson was the first draft choice selected by the AFL in the combined draft. Although he finished sixth in the league in rushing, he was not selected the league's Rookie of the Year, even though he gained more yards than the award winner. How many yards rushing did O.J. gain his rookie year?
A. 774 B. 926 C. 697 D. 573 E. 801

CINCINNATI BENGALS

Three games into the 1969 season, the Bengals were undefeated and looking like a Super Bowl contender. Armed with their number-one draft choice at quarterback and a bolstered passing attack, the second-year team knocked off Miami, San Diego, and Kansas City. Playing on the same field (Nippert Stadium) where he gained fame in college, rookie quarterback Greg Cook had taken the AFL by storm, throwing two touchdown passes in his professional debut, a 27-21 victory over the Dolphins. In his second week against the Chargers, he played even better, throwing for 327 yards on 14 completions and 3 more touchdown passes. He also ran 9 yards for another score. Cook showed his prowess as a razor sharp passer and also showed he could scramble, taking off three times for 33 yards.

Paul Brown had wanted to improve the passing attack that finished in the middle of the AFL in the first season, and knew he needed a leader behind center. He also upgraded the Bengals kicking game by trading one of his best deep receivers, Warren McVea, to Kansas City for German soccer-style kicker Horst Muhlmann, and traded starting flanker Rod Sherman to Oakland for some defensive help. To replace McVea and Sherman, Brown then traded fullback Tom Smiley to Denver for spindly flanker Eric Crabtree. And then he replaced the departed Smiley by moving starting safety Jess Phillips across the line to the backfield with Paul Robinson.

The three moves made Brown look like a genius, as Crabtree led the Bengals in receiving with 40 receptions and 7 touchdown, Phillips unseated Robinson as the leading rusher by gaining 578 for a 4.9 average, and Muhlmann, the league's fourth soccer-style kicker, finished fourth in scoring and made a phenomenal 15 of 18 field goals from under 50 yards. Rookie Speedy Thomas (33 receptions for 481 yards) filled the other wide spot vacated by Sherman, and Bob Trumpy (37 catches and 9 touchdowns) lined up at tight end. Trumpy became the first Bengal to make the all-league team. Paul Robinson, the league leader last year, drew attention from defenses in his second season and dropped off to 489 yards after breaking the 1,000 marker as a rookie.

Rarely does a rookie quarterback move into a starting role and have a significant impact, but Cook defied the norm. He elevated the second-year team to the league's best passing offensive and finished the season as the AFL's top-ranked passer. The tough offensive line of Ernie Wright, Ernie Park, Bob Johnson, Howard Fest, and messenger guards Pat Matson and Guy Dennis protected the young star. With Phillips and Robinson following their lead, the running attack ranked seventh but lacked depth. Still, the Bengals put more points on the board than every team in the East except the Jets. The problem was that Cincinnati played in the West.

The Progress of the Seasons – 1969

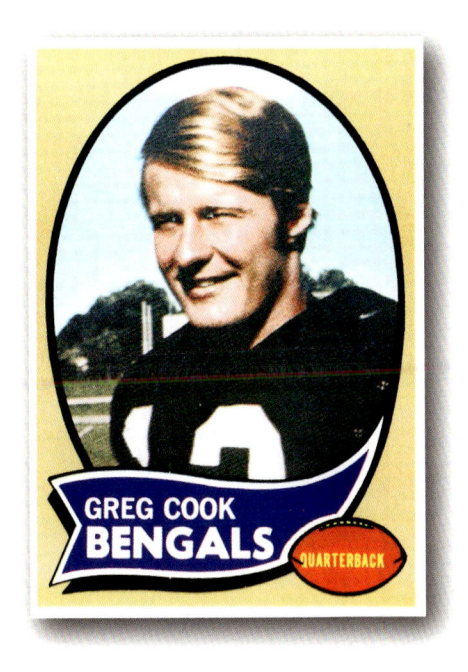

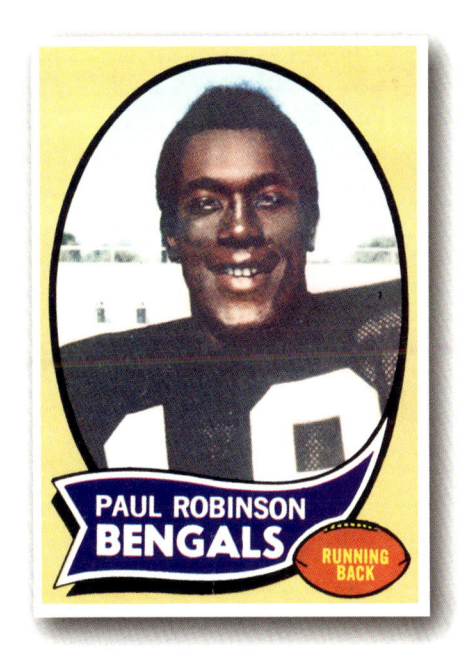

The defense changed a lot from the first year, but in the end they were still the weakest team at stopping the rush and sacking passers. Ends Royce Berry and Steve Chomyzek and tackles Andy Rice and Bill Staley got to the quarterback only 16 times and yielded a league-high 2,651 yards on the ground. The linebackers were a young but potentially outstanding group, led by outside backer Al Beauchamp and rookie middleman Bill Bergey, the defensive Rookie of the Year. Bill Peterson completed the group. The rebuilt secondary featured new comers Al Coleman and Ken Riley joining Bobby Hunt and Fletcher Smith. The latter three each intercepted four passes.

For their third straight home game on September 28, the Bengals put their unblemished record on the line against one of the AFL's strongest teams. In their first two games of 1968, the Kansas City Chiefs had outscored the Chargers and Patriots 58-9, and brought their own 2-0 record to Nippert Stadium, looking to add the Bengals to a growing list of casualties. The Bengal casualty was their quarterback prodigy who had to leave the game with an injured shoulder after connecting with Eric Crabtree in the first quarter on a 17-yard scoring pass. Coming off the bench in relief, Sam Wyche led Cincinnati to two fourth-quarter touchdowns and an upset victory over the eventual Super Bowl champs, 24-19. At 3-0, the Bengals stood at the top of the Western division with the mighty Oakland Raiders.

Without their star rookie, the Bengals lost their next four games to San Diego, New York, Denver, and the Chiefs, before returning home on November 2 to play the undefeated (6-0-1) Raiders. Cook returned to throw two second-quarter touchdown passes to receiver Chip Myers and had the Bengals leading the

Silver and Black 24-0 at the half. At one point in the fourth quarter the Bengals led 31-3. It was Cincinnati's fourth win of the season but regrettably their last. As the only AFL team to defeat both the Chiefs and Raiders that year, the Bengals went on to tie the Houston Oilers 31-31 a week after handcuffing Oakland behind four Greg Cook touchdown passes to give them an even record of 4-4-1. They then finished the season on the short end of their final five games.

Cincinnati's 4-9-1 record put them in last place in the division, but seventh best overall in the AFL. And though Brown hoped for better, the team's success earned him the AFL's Coach of the Year award. In his first season, Cook completed 54 percent of his 197 passes for 1,854 yards and 15 touchdowns, with only 11 interceptions. Unfortunately, the recurring shoulder problem that sidelined him for four games in 1969 would require off-season surgery that would keep one of the best quarterback prospects the AFL had ever seen out of action for the next three years. After a final comeback attempt in 1973, Cook called it quits.

Paul Brown planned to build upon the strong 4-3 record at home. And in their third year the Cincinnati Bengals would post an 8-6 record to win their merger-revised AFC Division and qualify for the playoffs.

Leading passers	Attempts	Completions	Pct	TDs	Yards	Int
Greg Cook	197	106	54%	15	1854	11
Sam Wyche	108	54	50%	7	838	4

Leading rushers	Attempts	Yards gained	Average	TDs
Jess Phillips	118	578	4.9	3
Paul Robinson	160	489	3.1	4
Greg Cook	25	148	5.9	1
Sam Wyche	12	107	8.9	1
Cecil Turner	23	105	4.6	0

Leading receivers	Caught	Yards gained	Average	TDs
Eric Crabtree	40	855	21.4	7
Bob Trumpy	37	835	22.6	9
Louis Thomas	33	481	14.6	3
Paul Robinson	20	104	5.2	0
Jess Phillips	13	128	9.8	0
Chip Myers	10	205	20.5	2

Leading scorers	TDs	XPM	XPA	FGM	FGA	PTs
Horst Muhlman		32	33	16	24	80
Bob Trumpy	9					54

55. In the AFL decade only five stadiums hosted an AFL Championship game. Name them.

The Progress of the Seasons – 1969

■ BUFFALO BILLS ■

THE BUFFALO BILLS' JOURNEY THROUGH the AFL was a perfect bell curve. They started near the bottom, gradually rising in the first three years until they sat at the top for four seasons, only to retreat back to the bottom in the league's final three campaigns. Over the course of their journey they established themselves as a bruising defensive team, a ball-controlling offensive force, and a team that took advantage of opportunities. For the Bills, 1969 represented the beginning of the road back from a 1-12-1 record, and they used the combined NFL/AFL draft's first pick to select two-time USC All-American halfback and college football legend Orenthal James "O.J." Simpson.

Under new head coach John Rauch, who bolted from the ever-present stare of Al Davis in Oakland, the Bills banked on a roster that included twenty-three players with either one or no years of pro football experience. For the second year in a row Buffalo started the season with two rookie running backs. Last year it was Max Anderson and Wayne Patrick, this year they presented the ball to Simpson and Bill "Earthquake" Enyart. In Rauch's offensive system, Simpson carried 181 times for 679 yards, sixth best in the league. The other four Buffalo runners carried the ball a combined 147 times for 651 yards. Running behind a line whose nucleus of Billy Shaw, Stew Barber, Al Bemiller, and Joe O'Donnell had been all or partially together since 1963, Simpson averaged 3.9 yards per carry. The offense, for the most part, underutilized his game-breaking talents.

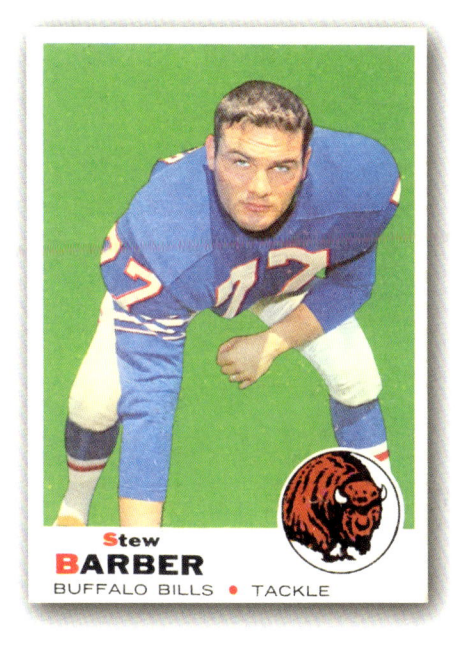

Jack Kemp called the plays in his last season, returning from a year of recuperation. He saw action in all fourteen games and threw 344 times, completing 49.4 percent with 13 touchdowns and 22 interceptions. Also, briefly taking snaps were Tom Flores in two games, and Dan Darragh, last year's rookie starter, seeing action in three games before heading to the injury list again. Rookie James Harris played against four opponents, and Boston castoff Tom Sherman and last year's heralded Bronco quarterback Marlin Briscoe saw action. The offense featured a young group of pass catchers headed by second-year flanker Haven Moses, who led the team with 39 receptions and a 19.3 average. Converted quarterback Marlin

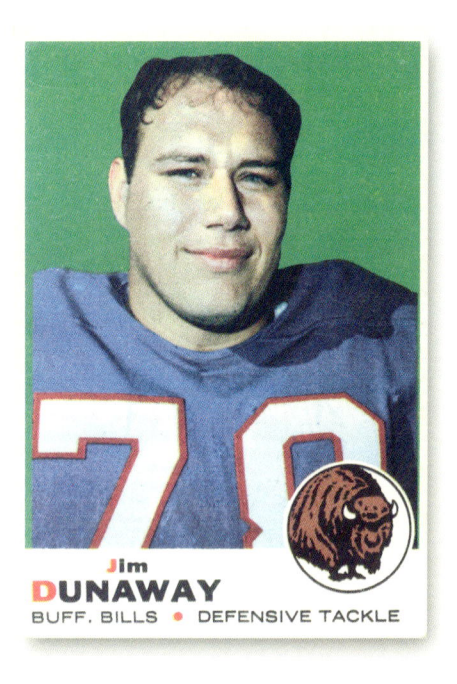

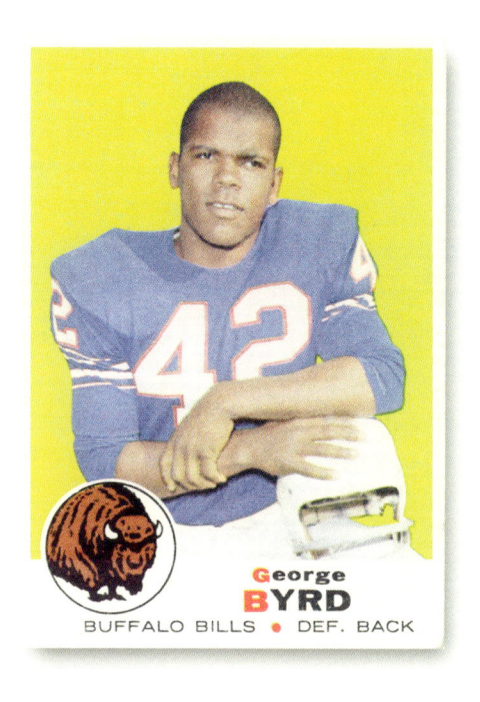

Briscoe caught 32 passes, and rookie Bubba Thornton caught 14. Paul Costa, once one of the best blocking tight ends in the league, moved one spot over on the line to help open more holes for Simpson, handing the tight end position to Billy Masters, who grabbed 33 passes. Fullback Wayne Patrick was the most active back in the pass attack with 35 receptions, with O.J. snaring 30. O.J. and Thornton shared the kick-return duties for the Bills, with both averaging 25 yards per return.

In the first game the Bills faced their in-state rival New York Jets, who squandared a 19-3 lead and found themselves tied in the fourth quarter. But the New Yorkers managed to walk away winners, 33-19. Houston arrived in town next and handed the Bills a second loss, 19-3. The first of the Bills four wins came against Denver in their third straight home game by the score of 41-28, their best offensive performance in '69. A second win came against the Patriots two weeks later, 23-16, ignited by a game-winning touchdown pass from halfback Preston Ridlehuber to Haven Moses that covered 45 yards. Halfback Max Anderson, starting for the injured Simpson, was lost for the season against Boston and necessitated the use of Ridlehuber, who was added to the roster only the day before. A loss the next week to Oakland then claimed rookie James Harris for the season, calling Dan Darragh to duty upon his release from the Army. After three appearances, he too was lost.

On defense the Bills made key changes. Gone was All-Time AFL defensive tackle Tom Sestak and defensive end Tom Day, who both retired. Jim Dunaway and Ron McDole remained in the front four, and were joined by Mick McMahon and Bob Tartek. Butch Byrd, the Bills leading intercepter with 7, was assisted by Booker Edgerson and George Saimes in the secondary. Pete Richardson replaced the injured Saimes during the season. Robert James and John Pitts also played in the defensive backfield.

Buffalo was 2-7 when they registered a big 28-3 win at home against Miami with O.J. scoring 2 touchdowns on passes from Kemp. The third win of the season put them within a game of matching their number of wins in 1967 with four games still to play. The equalizer could have happened in Boston the next week, but after taking a 21-21 tie into the fourth period, the Patriots added 14 more points to take it away from the Bills. Another chance unfolded on the snow-covered War Memorial Stadium turf on Thanksgiving Day (for the first time the AFL scheduled three games on the holiday), where 3 Bruce Alford field goals and Booker Edgerson's pick-pocket touchdown, with a ball he snatched out of the hands of the Bengals quarterback, put 16 points on the board against Cincinnati's 13 and gained them their fourth and final win of the year.

Throughout the season the Bills staff looked for small improvements and signs that they were on the road back to contention. One of those signs surfaced in Kansas City on December 7 in a back-and-forth battle against the Chiefs. The Bills were ahead 3-0, then behind 13-3. Alford and Stenerud traded field goals in the third quarter, and then flanker Marlin Briscoe beat the Chief defenders on a 17-yard touchdown reception, making the score 16-13 heading into the final 15 minutes. Stenerud's fourth field goal increased the Chiefs lead to 19-13, but the Bills answered the challenge when O.J. raced 32 yards for a game-tying touchdown. A botched snap from center on the 2-point conversion attempt kept the game deadlocked at 19-19 with 1:59 remaining—enough time for the Chiefs to navigate down the field and set up a game-winning, 25-yard field goal. Despite the final score, the Bills proved they could play with the best teams in the AFL.

It had been a long, hard journey for the Buffalo Bills through the AFL's decade. From Buster Ramsey's rugged defense and his search for offensive help in the early years, to Cookie Gilchrist plowing his way to two rushing titles and Elbert Dubenion catching long touchdown passes from Jack Kemp and Daryle Lamonica. After a disappointing play-off loss in '63, the Bills lifted themselves up to win two AFL Championships enroute to three straight title games appearances in the middle years. As the decade drew to a close, a host of key injuries limited them to only nine wins in their last three seasons. The road back had begun in an exciting way. They had the best young runner in pro football and were showing signs that the future held much more excitement.

Leading passers	Attempts	Completions	Pct	TDs	Yards	Int
Jack Kemp	344	170	49%	13	1981	22
Dan Darragh	52	24	46%	1	365	6
James Harris	36	15	42%	1	270	1

Leading rushers	Attempts	Yards gained	Average	TDs
O.J. Simpson	181	697	3.9	2
Wayne Patrick	83	361	4.3	3
Bill Enyart	47	191	4.1	1
Jack Kemp	37	124	3.4	0

Leading receivers	Caught	Yards gained	Average	TDs
Haven Moses	39	752	19.3	5
Wayne Patrick	35	229	6.5	0
Billy Masters	33	387	11.7	1
Marlin Briscoe	32	532	16.6	5
O.J. Simpson	30	343	11.4	3
Bill Enyart	19	186	9.8	2

Leading scorers	TDs	XPM	XPA	FGM	FGA	PTs
Bruce Alford		23	25	17	26	74
Marlin Briscoe	5					30
Haven Moses	5					30
O.J. Simpson	5					30

56. This enterprising AFL defensive back was one of Joe Namath's teammates, as well as one of his ownership partners in their infamous New York nightclub.

■ DENVER BRONCOS ■

LOU SABAN BROUGHT STABILITY AND focus to the struggling Broncos in 1967, and three years later, his efforts paid off. He inherited a defense that habitually finished at the bottom of the standings and turned it into one of the best units at stopping the run. The aggressive, pass-rushing front line sacked quarterbacks 45 times. Only Oakland and Kansas City had more. All-league defensive end Rich Jackson had established himself as one of the most feared pass rushers in the AFL, and linemates Dave Costa, Paul Smith, and Pete Duranko gave the Broncos one of the top front fours in the league. Saban next needed to reinforce his second line of defense. Linebackers Carl Cunningham, John Huard, and Chip Myrtle were only average pass defenders and run stuffers, and a below-par trio on the blitz. The secondary that included rookie Billy Thompson, Grady Caveness, Pete Jacquess, and Charlie Greer was below average, allowing opponents to complete 51 percent of their

The Progress of the Seasons – 1969

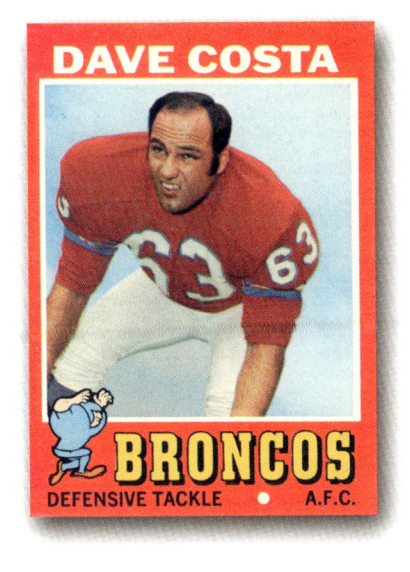

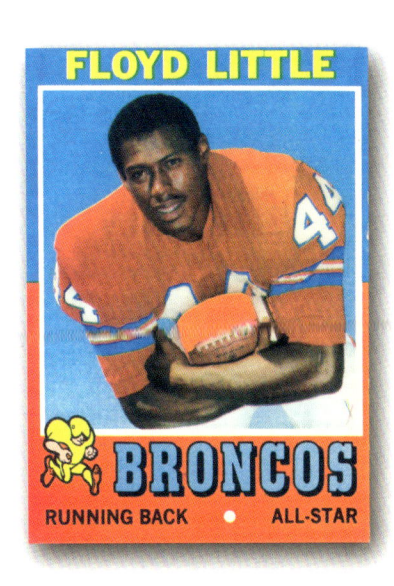

passes, while the entire defensive picked off only 14 passes led by Thompson, who was high man with 3. Thompson's value to the team in his first year with Denver was as the league's best punt- and kickoff-return specialist. He became the first player to lead the AFL in both return catagories. In spite of having a superior pass-rush and run-stopping unit up front, the defense experienced meltdowns to the tune of 344 points scored against them. They gave up 15 touchdowns on the ground and 19 through the air. Only Cincinnati gave up more 6 pointers.

After the first two weeks of the season, the Broncos found themselves on top of the West with a 2-0 record. Against Boston in their opener, Steve Tensi, completely mended from his two shoulder separations, threw 3 touchdown passes, and Floyd Little ran for 105 yards on 21 carries to hand the Patriots a 35-7 defeat. The defense stepped up their pass defense as well for this game, intercepting Mike Taliaferro 4 times. The victory against the Jets in game two was ignited by backup quarterback Pete Liske, who threw 2 touchdowns to Mike Haffner and Al Denson after Tensi was forced to the sidelines with a knee injury. Little ran for over 100 yards for the second week in a row. Beating the Super Bowl Champions 21-19 gave the Broncos a huge psychological lift that Saban hoped would carry them to new heights. But losses to Buffalo, Kansas City, and Oakland followed in succession. Righting themselves again, the Broncos got back on the winning trail with a 30-23 victory over the Bengals, led by Little's 166 yards rushing and the defense's 10 quarterback sacks.

With Tensi finally able to play a full season without prolonged injuries, the offense took on a new dimension to complement the renovated defense. Their 297 points scored led all teams except the Raiders, Chiefs, and

Jets. And with Little running better than ever, the Denver rushing offense finished sixth, with the passing attack rising to fifth in the AFL. Little was selected as the all-league halfback in 1969, even though he missed five games with injuries. He averaged 5.0 yards a carry, gained 729 yards on 146 carries and caught 19 passes. Besides Floyd, the Bronco runners included Fran Lynch, the team's second-leading ball carrier with 407 yards, Frank Quayle, who gained 183 yards, and Tom Smiley, who came to Denver from Cincinnati in a trade for Eric Crabtree. Smiley, a punishing run-and-pass blocker, gained 166 yards on 56 tries.

    The success of the running game resulted from Saban putting together a powerful offensive line. Sam Brunelli and Mike Current were the tackles, George Goeddeke and Bob Young the guards, and Larry Kaminski played center. Al Denson again led the Bronco receivers, finishing as the league's third best with 53 catches and 10 touchdowns. Mike Haffner took over for Crabtree at flanker until he was lost against Oakland. He caught 35 passes with 5 touchdowns. John Embree, another young pass catcher, caught 5 balls in the end zone as part of his 29 receptions, and tight ends Tom Beer and Dave Pivec each caught 9 passes without scoring. At quarterback, Steve Tensi put together his finest season, throwing 286 passes for 1,990 yards and 14 touchdowns. He completed 46 percent of his passes and was intercepted only 12 times in thirteen games. His backup, Pete Liske, competed 53 percent of his 115 passes, tossing 9 for touchdowns. Another offensive catalyst was place kicker Bobby Howfield, who finished eighth in the league in scoring, making 36 of his 37 extra points and 12 of 29 field goal attempts, a 45 percent success rate. He hit 8 of 13 attempts from inside the 30 yard line, but between the 30 and 49 only 4 of 13 went through the uprights.

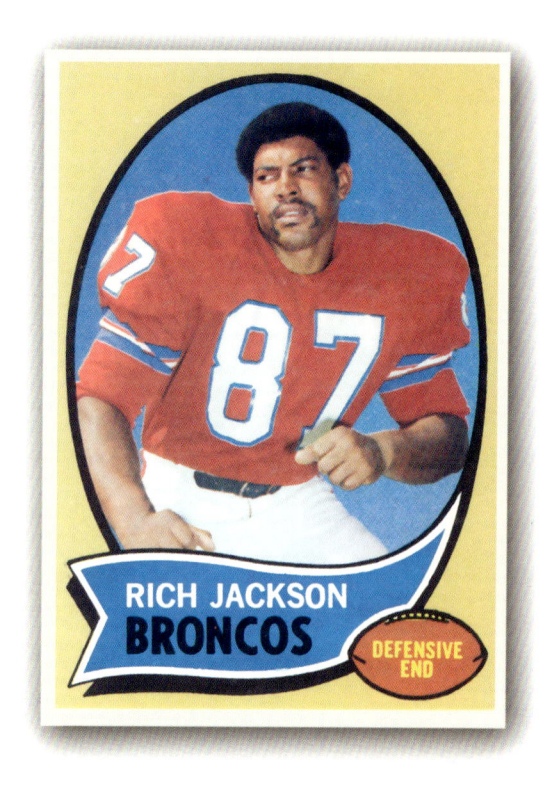

    Following their win in Cincinnati, the Broncos came up short in the Astrodome against the Oilers, 24-21, but returned to Mile High Stadium the next week to pitch the first shutout in franchise history against the Chargers, 13-0, scoring both their touchdowns in the third quarter—a 2-yard pass from Tensi to Denson and a 2-yard run by Little. The win lifted Denver's record to 4-4. In their ninth game, a loss to Oakland, the Broncos also lost wide receivers Mike Haffner and Billy Van Huesen for the year, after losing Floyd Little for five games the week before against San Diego.

In the absence of their best runner, the Broncos won one, lost three, and tied another. Particularly frustrating was their 20-20 tie with Houston after leading 20-10 three minutes into the fourth quarter. Only a Roy Gerela field goal with no time left on the clock stood in the way of another victory. Upon Little's return, Denver lost by 3 to Miami before closing out the year with a 27-16 win at home over the Bengals. They closed their season with a somewhat respectable 5-8-1 record, 4 points and one second short of a .500 record.

The Bronco squad under Saban was headed in the right direction after spending the first half of the decade paralyzed by a stingy budget and disinterested management. Many times they were the team that on any given week could bring you to your knees, but more often resembled a team without a plan or even a course to follow. It was good to see the loyal Denver fans and the young talented Bronco players finally getting their due!

Leading passers	Attempts	Completions	Pct	TDs	Yards	Int
Steve Tensi	286	131	46%	14	1990	12
Pete Liske	115	61	53%	8	845	11

Leading rushers	Attempts	Yards gained	Average	TDs
Floyd Little	146	729	5.0	6
Fran Lynch	96	407	4.2	2
Frank Quayle	57	183	3.2	0
Tom Smiley	56	166	3.0	3

Leading receivers	Caught	Yards gained	Average	TDs
Al Denson	53	809	15.3	10
Mike Haffner	35	563	16.1	5
John Embree	29	469	16.2	5
Floyd Little	19	218	11.5	1
Frank Quayle	11	167	15.2	0

Leading scorers	TDs	XPM	XPA	FGM	FGA	PTs
Bobby Howfield		36	37	13	29	75
Al Denson	10					60

HOUSTON OILERS

WITH THE BALANCE OF POWER IN THE West, and the change in the league's playoff structure that now qualified the top two teams from each division, the Oilers, who finished 6-6-2, were in the Super Bowl IV hunt as the Eastern Division's runner-up team. The addition of SMU flanker Jerry Levias gave the Oilers another quick and elusive receiver, joining second-year pass catchers Jim Beirne and Mac Haik. But the running game missed double-threat halfback Woody Campbell, deployed with the Army in Vietnam almost the entire season. Roy Hopkins partnered with Hoyle Granger until Campbell's return. Granger rumbled to a third-best finish in the AFL with 740 yards on 186 carries (4.0 average). Hopkins picking up 473 on 131 carries (3.1 average). Ode Burrell, once the team's rushing leader, filled in as the first back off the bench with 147 yards. Upon his return from the Army, Campbell carried 28 times for 98 yards. The entourage gave Houston the fifth-best rushing attack in the league.

Pete Beathard was again the starting quarterback, throwing 370 passes and completing 48.6 percent of them. But his 10 touchdown passes were too few, and his 21 interceptions too many. Don Trull and Bob Davis helped off the bench, but the passing game was still not on par with the AFL's elite. Rookie Levias caught 42 passes, as did Beirne, with Mac Haik catching 27 passes, as did Granger. Roy Hopkins showed soft hands and latched on to 29. The best of the Houston receivers was tight end Alvin Reed, surging to the fourth-highest spot in the league. Reed snared an AFL tight end record 51 passes for a 13 yard average. The offensive line once again performed well as one of the league's best. Together for the third year in a row, tackles Walt Suggs and Glen Ray Hines, guards Tom Regner and Sonny Bishop, and center Bobby Maples provided big holes and deft pass protection for Granger, Beathard, and company.

The biggest and brightest change in Houston was in its kicking game. Canadian Roy Gerela took over the duties as both the kicker and punter. The league now boasted five soccer-style kickers, and the latest, Gerela, was a booming kickoff specialist, giving the

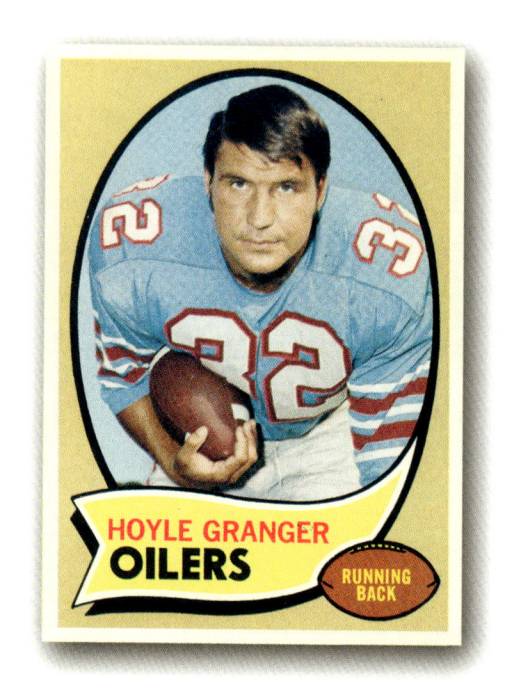

The Progress of the Seasons – 1969

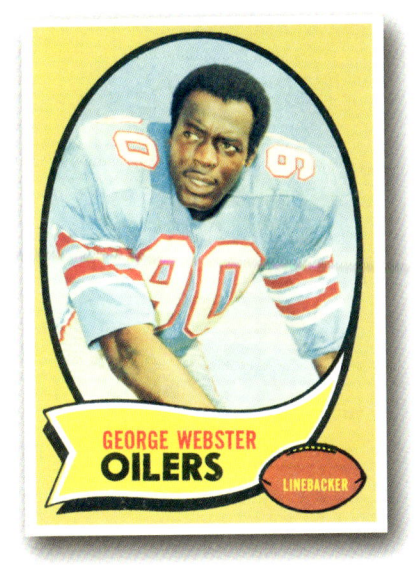

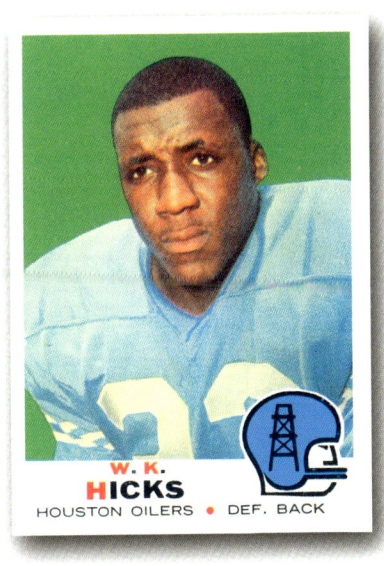

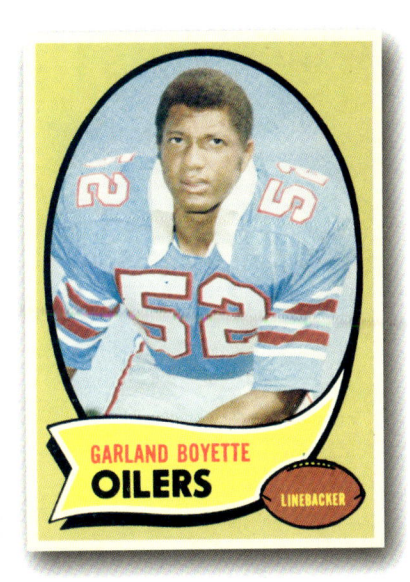

Oilers their best field goal kicker since George Blanda. He made 14 of his 15 attempts from inside the 30 yard line, but for all of his boom on kickoffs, his accuracy from 30 to 40 yards was weak, as he converted on only 3 of 12 tries. His 48 percent accuracy was a bit deceiving, however, because Lemm called on him from beyond 40 yards 14 times. He was able to split the uprights twice. His punting average was an adequate 40.4 yards.

Houston jumped into their 1969 schedule against an Oakland Raider team that had lost only three times in the previous two years and had one of the best offensive and defensive units the AFL had even seen. Relying on their outstanding defense, led by all-league linebacker George Webster, the Oilers held Oakland's offense in check most of the afternoon and led 17-14 in the final period when the Raiders found a seam in the secondary for a 64-yard touchdown, sending the Oilers home with a 21-17 loss. The next three weeks brought wins over Buffalo, Miami, and Buffalo again (for the sixth straight time), to post a division-best 3-1 record.

Consecutive losses to Kansas City and New York followed to even their record at 3-3. Roy Hopkins enjoyed his biggest day as a pro on October 16 against Denver, gaining 104 yards on the ground and helping his team get back on the winning track with two touchdowns, highlighted by a 43-yard jaunt in a 10-point fourth quarter to beat the Broncos 24-21. And with a shutout loss to Boston and ties with Cincinnati and Broncos on the ensuing weeks, the Oilers stood with a .500 record of 4-4-2.

They split their last four games, losing to San Diego and the Jets, surrounded by wins over Miami, and their season finale over Boston to finish in second place behind the Jets in the East and qualifying for the playoffs. As the second-place team, they faced the winner of the West, the 12-1-1 Raiders, to determine who would move on to the AFL Championship game. Hoping for the best, the Oilers flew to Oakland for their playoff showdown. It was a day the Oilers and owner Bud Adams would undoubtedly like to purge from team history. Totally overmatched on both sides of the line, the Oilers mounted little offense and the defense surrendered six first-half touchdown passes on the way to losing 56-7.

For their first three years, the Houston Oilers provided the AFL's mark of excellence, winning the first two championships and nearly capturing a third. And when they finally fell on hard times, they resurrected themselves and return to the top of the division five years later. They were a proud team owned by a proud owner, whose unwavering approach to building his team and the league were directly responsible for the overwhelming success of both.

Leading passers	Attempts	Completions	Pct	TDs	Yards	Int
Pete Beathard	370	180	49%	10	2455	21
Don Trull	75	34	45%	3	469	6
Bob Davis	42	25	60%	2	223	4

Leading rushers	Attempts	Yards gained	Average	TDs
Hoyle Granger	186	740	4.0	3
Roy Hopkins	131	473	3.6	4
Ode Burrell	41	147	3.6	0
Woody Campbell	28	98	3.5	1

Leading receivers	Caught	Yards gained	Average	TDs
Alvin Reed	51	664	13.0	2
Jerry Levias	42	696	16.6	5
Jim Beirne	42	540	12.9	4
Roy Hopkins	29	338	11.7	1
Mac Haik	27	375	13.9	1
Hoyle Granger	27	330	12.2	1

Leading scorers	TDs	XPM	XPA	FGM	FGA	PTs
Roy Gerela		29	29	19	40	86
Jerry Levias	5					30
Roy Hopkins	5					30

The Progress of the Seasons – 1969

▪ NEW YORK JETS ▪

THE DEFENDING CHAMPIONS OF PROfessional football started the season by defeating the Buffalo Bills 33-19 in War Memorial Stadium, where they had not won since 1962. They were the favored to run away from the other teams in the East, and in fact, won every game they played against their division foes. Their four losses in 1969 were dealt to them by the four original Western Division teams.

The offense returned every Super Bowl starter except guard Bob Talamini, where Sam Walton and Roger Finnie replaced the six time all-leaguer. Randy Rasmussen, Dave Herman, Winston Hill, and John Schmitt came back to their places, along with Snell, Boozer, Maynard, Sauer, Lammons, and Joe Namath. The defense saw changes at the left corner, where Cornell Gordon replaced Johnny Sample, and at safety, where John Dockery and USC rookie Mike Battle stepped in when Jim Hudson was injured. Steve Thompson also saw action on the front four with all-league teammates Gerry Philbin and John Elliott. Verlon Biggs completed the strong front line that was second best in the league against the rush and dropped quarterbacks 42 times. Linebackers Al Atkinson, Larry Grantham, and Ralph Baker were all back behind the line with help from Paul Crane.

For the fourth year in a row the mighty Jet duo of George Sauer and Don Maynard were the AFL's answer to Army's legendary Mr. Inside and Mr. Outside, as Mssrs. Short and Long. The two gave Namath a perfect balance of first-down finesse and long-bomb flair. Along with Pete Lammons, who specialized in opening up the middle passing lane, the three amigos keyed the New York offense. Maynard and Sauer finished sixth and seventh in receiving with 47 and 45 catches. Lammons followed them up with 33. Snell (22 receptions), Boozer (20), and Bill Mathis (18) diversified the passing game with circle and flare routes when defenses focused too strongly on the ends.

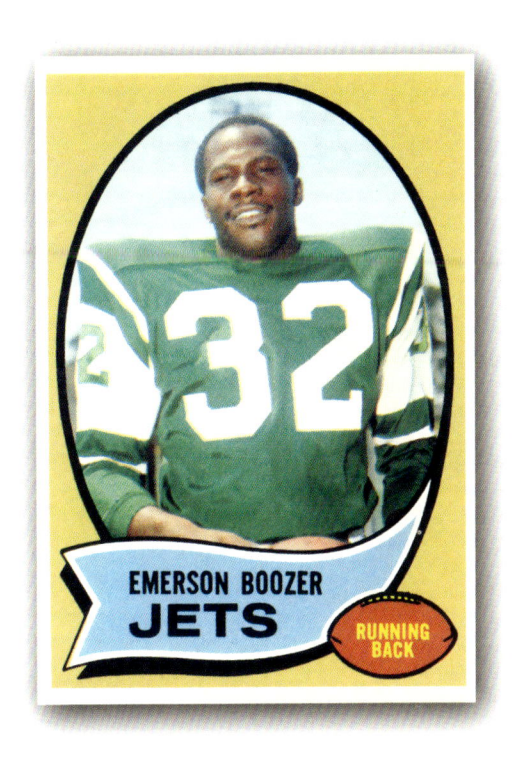

A case of a Mile High Stadium dizziness in week two knocked the Jets from the undefeated ranks when they blew a 13-0 first quarter lead and lost, 21-19. But new Jet kicker Steve O'Neal gave coach Weeb Ewbank a brief moment of relief when he set a pro football record by booting a 98-yard punt through the bright sky from his own end zone. The kick seemed to catch a Jet stream as it crossed midfield and just kept rolling. Another loss, this time to San Diego, suddenly had the Super Bowl champs under .500 for the first time since September 9, 1967.

Finally hitting their stride, the team took off on a six-game win streak that started on October 4 against Boston. The Jets ran the table against the rest of East with Cincinnati mixed in and didn't come back to earth until a November 16, 34-16 loss to the Chiefs. With the league now maintaining ten teams, the days of playing each AFL team twice was a thing of the past. The schedule called for teams to play home and away games against their division rivals and teams from the other division only once, with the exception of one team, which they would face twice. In 1969, the only Western Division team the Jets had to face more than once was the second-year Bengals. They handled them easily both times, 21-7 and 40-7.

Matt Snell and Emerson Boozer again started in the backfield, with both playing all fourteen games. Bill Mathis was coaxed out of retirement to back them up, making him one of only nineteen players to go the distance through all ten AFL seasons. Snell led the team with 695 yards on 191 carries, followed by Boozer's 604 on 130 tries. Behind Mathis, rookie Lee White, a 6'4" bruiser, was being groomed for a starting spot. Namath, who developed into the league's premier quarterback, had another superb season. As the Jets maintained a more balanced offense, his passing attempts dropped to 361, while his completion percentage rose to 51 percent. He finished behind only league-leader Greg Cook in the QB ratings.

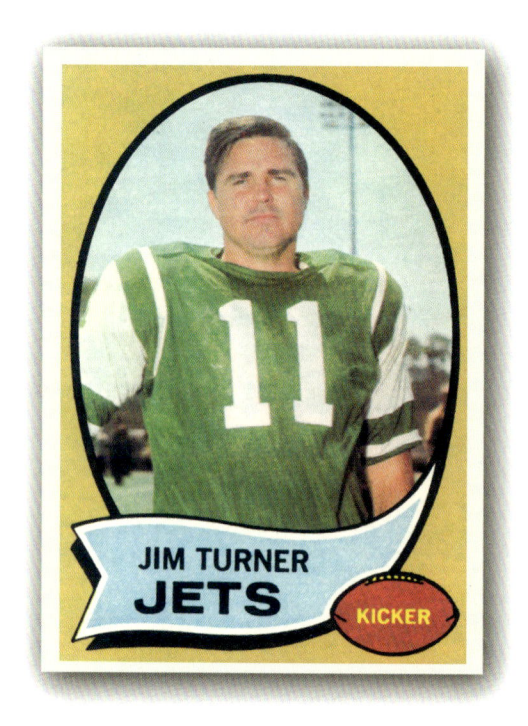

Two strong wins in the last two games gave the Jets a 10-4 record, giving them another first-place finish and a home-field advantage in the first round home of the playoffs against the 11-3 Kansas City Chiefs. On one of the coldest days in memory, the Jets prepared to defend their title on Saturday, December 20. A blustery arctic wind greeted them in Shea Stadium and had both teams contemplating a sustained ground game to increase their chances of moving on. But the need to dent the frigid conditions, the swirling, gusting wind, and the opposition's defense, had both the Chiefs and

Jets taking chances through the air more than anticipated. Dawson threw 27 times, completing 12 for 201 yards, but Namath, going against the number-one run and pass defense, put the ball in the air 40 times, completing only 14, with 3 interceptions. Through the first three periods the teams managed only mid-range field goals, one by Jim Turner (27 yards) and two by Jan Stenerud (23 and 25 yards).

The key series came in the fourth quarter with the Jets trailing 6-3. After a defensive pass interference call, the Jets had first and goal at the KC 1 yard line. Twice the Jets tried to bust over the goal line without success, and when Namath threw an incompletion on third down, Jim Turner was called on and tied the game at 6-6 with a 7-yard field goal. On their ensuing possession, KC threw their knockout punch that ended the Jets' title defense. The Chiefs completed a 59-yard pass to Otis Taylor that set up the decisive next play, a 19-yard scoring pass to Gloster Richardson for the game's only touchdown. The Chiefs went on to win 13-6.

After two glorious seasons with a combined record of 21-7, the Jets had built themselves into one of the top three teams in the AFL and were a far cry from the rag-tag days of Harry Wismer, the Titans, and the fans that came disguised as empty seats.

Leading passers	Attempts	Completions	Pct	TDs	Yards	Int
Joe Namath	361	185	51%	19	2734	17
Babe Parilli	24	14	58%	3	138	1

Leading rushers	Attempts	Yards gained	Average	TDs
Matt Snell	191	695	3.6	4
Emerson Boozer	130	604	4.6	4
Bill Mathis	96	355	3.7	4
Lee White	28	88	3.1	0

Leading receivers	Caught	Yards gained	Average	TDs
Don Maynard	47	938	20.0	6
George Sauer	45	745	16.6	8
Pete Lammons	33	400	12.1	3
Matt Snell	22	187	8.5	1
Emerson Boozer	20	222	11.1	0
Bill Mathis	18	183	10.2	1

Leading scorers	TDs	XPM	XPA	FGM	FGA	PTs
Jim Turner		33	33	32	47	129
George Sauer	8					48

OAKLAND RAIDERS

THE RAIDERS STORMED INTO THE 1969 season with an incredible record of 25-3 over the previous two years. With their offensive and defensive nucleus unchanged, and the return from season-ending injuries of defensive stars Bill Laskey, Tom Keating, and Kent McCloughan, the team had reason to believe they would once again roll through the AFL. Head coach John Rauch had moved East to coach the downtrodden Buffalo Bills, perhaps rationalizing that coaching a 1-12-1 team was still better than returning to Al Davis looking over his shoulder day and night. Taking over the Raider helm was John Madden, who at 32 was the youngest head coach in the league. Again Lamonica led the offensive assault with the helpful wisdom of his ageless backup, George Blanda.

The season got off to a torrid beginning defensively when Dave Grayson's 2 pass interceptions set up 2 quick scores by Charlie Smith against Houston in the first quarter of the year. Unable to mount any offensive consistency over the next two periods they watched their 14-10 lead with six minutes to play disappear when Houston jumped ahead 17-14. But late-game deficits never seemed to shake this confident group, who knew they could come up with a big play almost at will. As if on cue, Daryle Lamonica went vertical and found Warren Wells at the end of a 64-yard bomb that finished off Houston, 21-17.

Miami was next, and with fifteen seconds left on the clock, the scoreboard showed a 17-17 tie. Again the Raiders needed divine intervention, and for the second straight week their prayers were answered, this time with a 46-yard George Blanda field goal. Though 2-0, Oakland's record could easily have been reversed. Next they faced a Boston team that had won just 9 of their last 32 games. Again the Raiders started in a sleep walk, letting the Patriots jump out to a 13-0 lead in front of their home crowd at Boston College's Alumni Field. A Gus Otto interception and a sack of quarterback Mike Taliaferro by Ike Lassiter finally brought the Oakland offense to life. Lamonica unleashed 4 touchdown passes to Wells, Biletnikoff, Wells again, and finally Hewritt Dixon for a 38-23 triumph.

Three wins at the start of the season put the Raiders sky high as they then strutted into Miami. But after a hard-fought sixty minutes, they left shaking their heads in wonder. The Dolphins, for the second time in three weeks, played the Raiders as if *they* were the Super Bowl contenders. It took everything in the Raider arsenal to salvage a 20-20 tie. Blanda kicked 2 field goals into the Flipper tank and set an AFL record by scoring in his forty-sixth consecutive game. The Raiders then went to snow-covered Mile High Stadium, where a blocked Denver punt and 3 Lamonica touchdown passes paved the way to a 24-14 win. Finding their stride, Oakland then manhandled Buffalo behind 6 Lamonica touchdowns

The Progress of the Seasons – 1969

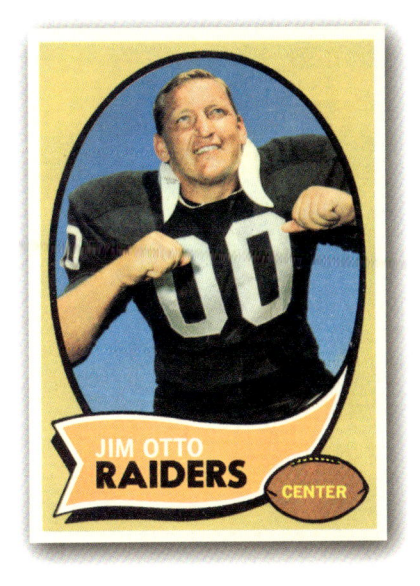

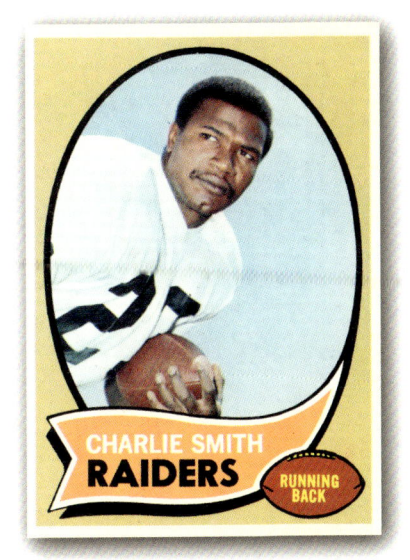

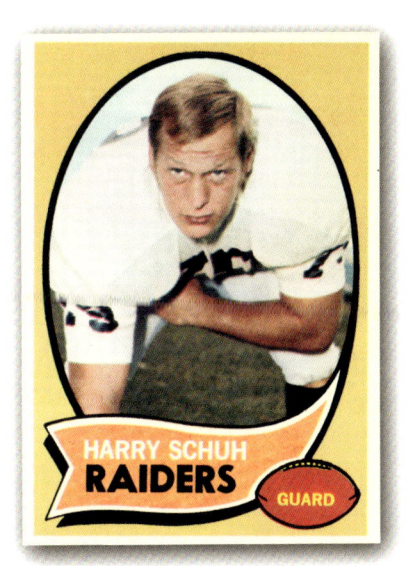

passes in the first half. The result was a merciless 50-21 win.

At 5-0-1, the Raiders threatened to tie San Diego's record for consecutive games without a loss. In forcing their way into the record book, the Raiders dominated the Chargers en route to a 24-12 win. Behind 3-0 early, Lamonica was knocked out of the game by a massive San Diego pass rush, but in true Raider fashion, he came back on the next play to fire a 48-yard touchdown pass to Larry Todd. The Pride and Poise Boys never looked back. Led by Dave Grayson's 3 interceptions, Oakland's victory put them into the record books. Their visit to Nippert Stadium, home of the Bengals, on November 2 was not as favorable, and served as another wake-up call. The Bengals, coming off a four-game losing streak and celebrating the return of rookie sensation Greg Cook, vaulted to a 24-0 halftime lead and were never challenged, handing Oakland their first loss, 31-17. It was the last winless week for the Raiders until the AFL championship game in January.

Finishing the season 12-1-1, which included two victories over arch-enemy Kansas City, culminated in an unprecedented three-year record of 37-4-1. In a cake walk over Houston, 56-7, in the AFL's revised playoff format, Lamonica threw 6 touchdown passes for the second time that year and provided the Raiders with little more than a warm up for the impending encounter with Kansas City. It would be their last battle as AFL combatants, and a fitting end to the historic decade. Three championship game appearances in three consecutive years tied the league mark shared by Houston ('60, '61, '62), San Diego ('63, '64, '65), and Buffalo ('64, '65, '66). Kansas City was also in their third AFL Championship game ('62, '66, '69).

For the second time in three seasons,

Daryle Lamonica was named the AFL's Player of the Year. His 34 touchdown passes led the league, giving him a three-year total of 89, while his favorite target continued to be sticky-fingered Fred Biletnikoff, whose 54 catches trailed only Lance Alworth. Flanker Warren Wells raised the bar for long-range strikes, torching AFL defensive backs for an incredible 26.8 yards per catch on his 47 receptions. He also led the league with 1,260 yards and 14 touchdowns. Again the Raiders were the most prolific scoring machine in the AFL, and once again, the second stingiest. And still again, they were the most penalized, which was equally important to their fans.

On January 4, 1970, the Kansas City Chiefs and the Oakland Raiders, the two AFL giants, faced off for the third time, playing for league bragging rights and AFL representation in Super Bowl IV. The sixty-minute tug-of-war that ensued was an AFL classic, with neither team giving in to the other's demands. The Chiefs tried first to throw, then to run, both to no avail, as the Oakland front four of Ben Davidson, Ike Lassiter, Tom Keating, and Carleton Oates locked in a jousting match with the huge Kansas City line. The Raiders scored first on a 4-yard run by Charlie Smith, but Kansas City tied it before the half. In the third quarter the Chiefs put together their most controversial drive of the year, traveling 98 yards on two plays. From their own 2 yard line, Len Dawson went deep down the right side line to Otis Taylor, who appeared to catch the ball out of bounds. But it was ruled a completion. Then Dawson went deep again, but this time overthrowing Taylor at the Oakland 2. And then a flag appeared. Oakland's Nemiah Wilson was called for interference, and the Chiefs had a first and goal. Fullback Robert Holmes ended the drive with a 2-yard sweep around left end, giving the Chiefs a 14-7 lead that they never relinquished. Three times in the fourth quarter the Chiefs turned the ball over to the Raiders. And each time, Oakland handed it right back. The Raiders came up short in their final championship bid for another trip to the Super Bowl, bowing to Kansas City 17-7 and ending their decade of war with Chiefs dead even, with 11 wins and 11 loses.

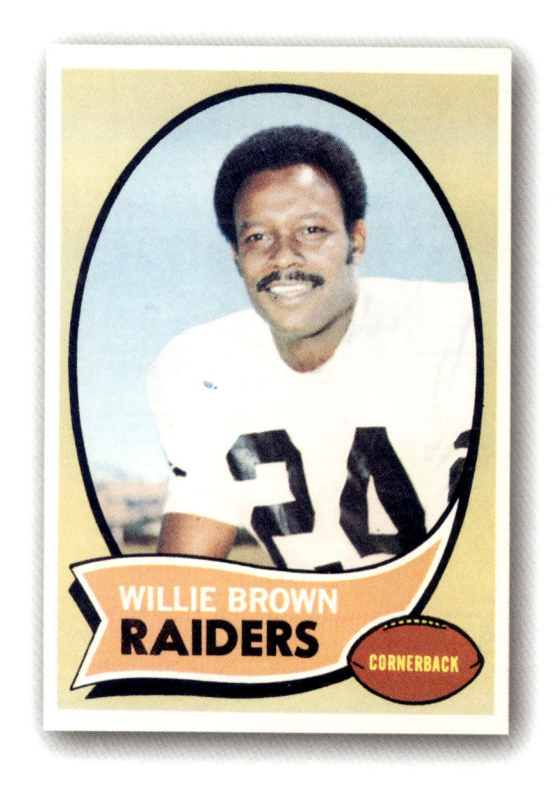

Seven Raiders, including Jim Otto, Fred Biletnikoff, Harry Schuh, Gene Upshaw, and Lamonica on offense, and defensive backs

The Progress of the Seasons – 1969

Willie Brown and Dave Grayson gained all-league honors. For the Raiders the 1969 season marked the end of a remarkable decade that began without a roster, with the wrong name, and on the wrong side of the bay. It culminated with them being the winningest team in the AFL over its last seven years. No other team in professional football history had ever won 12 games in two consecutive seasons. Oakland did it in each of their final three! They led the league in total offense and points scored for the last three years as well. The Oakland Raiders were Al Davis at his best. And the Silver and Black's commitment to excellence had made the Pride and Poise Boys one of the two most dominant teams in AFL history.

Leading passers	Attempts	Completions	Pct	TDs	Yards	Int
Daryle Lamonica	426	221	52%	34	3302	25
George Blanda	13	6	46%	2	73	1

Leading rushers	Attempts	Yards gained	Average	TDs
Charlie Smith	177	600	3.4	2
Hewritt Dixon	107	398	3.7	0
Pete Banaszak	88	377	4.3	0
Larry Todd	47	198	4.2	1
Marv Hubbard	21	119	5.7	0

Leading receivers	Caught	Yards gained	Average	TDs
Fred Biletnikoff	54	837	15.5	12
Warren Wells	47	1260	26.8	14
Hewritt Dixon	33	275	8.3	1
Charlie Smith	30	322	10.7	2
Billy Cannon	21	262	12.5	2
Pete Banaszak	17	119	7.0	3
Larry Todd	16	149	9.3	1

Leading scorers	TDs	XPM	XPA	FGM	FGA	PTs
George Blanda		45	45	20	37	105
Warren Wells	14					84

Remember the AFL

■ KANSAS CITY CHIEFS ■

IN WINNING SUPER BOWL IV 23-7, the Chiefs out played the Minnesota Vikings because they were better coached. Hank Stram espoused the philosophy that "if we cannot find a way, we will make one!" Minnesota brought superior defense and discipline to New Orleans, complemented by an offense that bombarded fourteen NFL opponents. As great a team as the 1968 Baltimore Colts were, the 1969 Vikings were greater. This was the team that the NFL earmarked to prove that Super Bowl III was nothing more than a one-day charade.

Hank Stram knew better. He had fostered a team so dedicated and loyal to the cause that no team on January 11, 1970, would be able to run onto the Tulane Stadium field against his boys and walk off with a victory. The Chiefs were ready for battle against the NFL's best, for the honor of the American Football League! With their triple-stack defense and multiple offensive sets that included a tight end, a moving pocket, and a flanker slotted between a guard and tackle split, the Chiefs confounded the vaunted Purple People Eaters for sixty minutes. The hulking KC defense allowed only 67 yards rushing and paralyzed quarterback Joe Kapp's passing game. And after defensive end Aaron Brown thumped him in the fourth quarter, Kapp retired to the bench for game's final six minutes.

Kansas City's defense was without weakness, and for the second year in a row allowed less than 200 points. The 177 points scored on them was only a single touchdown more than their 1968 AFL record. They also allowed the fewest yards per game rushing (77.9) and the least number of yards per game passing (148), to go with their league-leading 32 interceptions, which they returned for an AFL best 595 yards. The front four boasted Jerry Mays and Aaron Brown on the ends, with Buck Buchanan and former NCAA wrestling champion Curley Culp in the middle. They recorded a league-high 48 quarterback sacks. Their linebackers, always a Kansas City strength, were the best trio in the AFL and maybe in all of pro football. Bobby Bell was without rival on one side, with Jim Lynch on the opposite flank. Willie Lanier was in the middle. Lanier, at 245 pounds, became an even more ferocious tackler after starting to wear the specially constructed helmet that put more padding on the top to reduce the headaches he suffered early in his career.

The secondary featured rookie Jim Marsalis and veteran Emmitt Thomas, the AFL's leading intercepter, on the corners and Jim Kearney and Johnny Robinson at safety. Opponents completed only 47 percent of their passes against them. Besides their dominance on defense, the Chiefs also had the best offensive line in the AFL, with Jim Tyrer and Ed Budde making up perhaps the best left side in football. E.J. Holub and his eight knee operations gave KC outstanding play at center and

The Progress of the Seasons – 1969

★ *Kansas City coach Hank Stram with owner Lamar Hunt* ★

had Mo Moorman and Dave Hill at right guard and tackle. Fred Arbanas still performed better than most at tight end.

The Chiefs were on a mission after tying Oakland for the West in 1968 and then being overwhelmed by them in a playoff game for the division crown. With his insightful knack for evaluating and then motivating talent, Stram had assembled a team that neared perfection. Besides his defense that was beyond compare and a prototype offensive line, he added the final ingredient to his winning formula by bringing in 5'9" sprinter Warren McVea from the Bengals to give him another breakaway threat. For the past few seasons, KC had been missing a speed burner who could leave defenders in his dust. Carrying the ball 106 times, mostly to the outside, he gained an even 500 yards, for a 4.7 average and led the team with 7 rushing touchdowns. McVea was also the leader on kickoff returns, although with the KC defense he didn't see much action. Mike Garrett, another 5'9" halfback, still jitter-bugged his way through defenses as the team rushing and receiving leader, recording 732 yards on the ground to complement his 43 receptions. No other running back in the league caught more

★ *Chiefs middle linebacker Willie Lanier* ★

passes. Robert "The Tank" Holmes, the third 5'9" "Smurf," returned as the fullback. He was the Chiefs second-leading ball carrier, gaining 612 yards. Wendell Hayes was back as well, gaining 208 yards, spelling Holmes with 62 carries.

Flanker Otis Taylor remained one of the game's top receiving threats with 41 receptions, a 17-yard average, and 7 touchdowns. Split end Frank Pitts caught 31 passes, backed up by Gloster Richardson, who caught 23. Excellent deep threats, Pitts and Richardson kept defenses from smothering Taylor. Blending all of these weapons together was the most accurate passer in AFL history. Len Dawson just kept getting better, finding receivers at all distances. But he excelled at the midrange throw. Strained knee ligaments limited him to only nine games, after missing only three in the previous seven years, but his 59 percent completion rate was second to none. After Lenny was sidelined against Cincinnati, Jacky Lee took control of the offense, but he was sidelined in his first start. With Dawson still on the mend, the Chiefs turned to second-year quarterback Mike Livingston, who played only five downs in 1968 as a rookie. The unexpected injuries prompted Stram to look around the league for help, bringing in veterans John Huarte and Tom Flores. But Haurte never saw action for KC, and Flores threw only 1 pass on a muffed field goal try. He completed it for a 33-yard touchdown. Livingston's first start came in the season's fourth game, against the Broncos. For the season, he played in nine games and threw only five fewer passes than Dawson, completing 52 percent of his 161 throws.

Even Kansas City's kickers were incomperable. Jan Stenerud made all of his 38 extra points and 27 of his 35 field goal tries for a league best 77 percent. He hit on 19 of 23 attempts from inside the 40 yard line and finished second in scoring. Jerrell Wilson punted 68 times for a 44.4 average, only .2 yards per punt behind the league leader.

With all these weapons Kansas City took a 6-0 preseason record into San Diego to begin their tenth and final AFL season. With the KC defense tormenting John Hadl into 4 interceptions and Dawson throwing 2 touchdown passes to Otis Taylor, the Chiefs won 27-9. They then flew east, where they beat the Patriots into submission, 31-0, with a stop in Cincinnati on their third week's itinerary. It was in this game against the Bengals that Lee broke his ankle and was lost for the season. After taking early leads of 6-0, then 13-7, the Bengals seized their opportunity with both Dawson and Lee out of action, to score 14 points in the final period and defeat the Chiefs 24-19.

Livingston's first pro start came in Denver on October 5, with Kansas City sitting in an unfamiliar position of being behind undefeated Cincinnati and Oakland and tied with the Broncos. They needed to keep pace, and used four Stenerud field goals, a 12 yard run by Warren McVea, and a 60-yard interception return for a touchdown by Jim Kearney to thwart the Broncos 26-13 and raise their record to 3-1. Livingston's second start, KC's home opener, seemed more like a comedy of errors than a professional football game. Hosting the Oilers in a torrential downpour, the Chiefs fumbled 10 times and scored all their points in the first half. Houston also had trouble holding onto the wet pigskin, and after rookie punter Roy Gerela dropped one of the Oilers's 4 fumbles at the 5 yard line, George Daney picked it up and ran it in for the Chief's second score, giving them a 14-0 lead. Their final score came at the end of a mishandled field goal attempt. Holder Tom Flores could not control the placement and was forced to find someone to throw to. Robert Holmes came to his rescue 33 yards away for a touchdown, and KC won their fourth game of the year 24-0. It was also their second shutout of the season.

Against Miami, Livingston enjoyed his best day. He threw for 300 yards and connected with Otis Taylor on the AFL's longest play from scrimmage in 1969, a 93-yard pass, run, and lateral to Holmes, for a touchdown. The 17-10 victory extended Livingston's win streak as a starter to three. Against Cincinnati the next week, he extended it to four by throwing 3 touchdown passes and received assistance in the fourth quarter from Warren McVea's 80-yard touchdown run and safety Goldie Sellers' 21-yard fumble recovery for a touchdown. The Chiefs stood at 6-1 at midseason but trailed the 6-0-1 Raiders for the division lead. Livingston continued in his starter role the next two weeks, both victories, over Buffalo (29-7) and the Chargers (27-3), running his personal win streak to six before Len Dawson returned to lineup against the Jets in New York, on November 16.

After seven years as a pillar of stability, making a comeback from injury was new for Dawson, but he wasted no time establishing that he was still the team leader. In the first quarter he threw an 18-yard touchdown pass to Otis Taylor, then found him in the end zone two more times before the day ended. The Chiefs walked off with their ninth win (9-1) of the season, 34-16, and suddenly had a half game lead over the Raiders, who were now 8-1-1. The showdown with Oakland awaited them the next week. It was the twentieth time the two titans had clashed over the ten years. The Raiders started the scoring with a field goal, but the Chiefs used a short run by McVea to take the lead. One of the pivital plays in this 27-14 Chief loss happened in the second period with KC ahead 14-3. Dawson had just connected on a pass to Fred Arbanas at the 20 yard line, but as the tight end was bringing the ball in, Oakland safety George Atkinson ripped it away and ran for a touchdown. Raider linebacker Dan Conners returned another interception 75 yards for a score in the third quarter. The loss flipped the two in the standings, and now the Chiefs trailed the Raiders by a half game.

In the Thanksgiving Day win over Denver, the alert Bobby Bell lined up on the front line of the kick return squad anticipating an onside kick attempt by the Broncos, who had suddenly pulled to within a touchdown of tying the game with forty-eight seconds remaining. Bell fielded the squibbed attempt and returned it 53 yards for a score. A week later, Jan Stenerud kicked 5 field goals for the second time on the season to lead the Chiefs over Buffalo, 22-19.

On the final regular season weekend in AFL history, the Chiefs faced their arch rivals, the dreaded Oakland Raiders. The Chiefs had lost six of their last seven games against Oakland and were putting their 11-2 record on the line for the last time, against the 11-1-1 Raiders. Both teams had already won a playoff spot, but this game determined the Western Division title, home field advantage in the playoffs, and above all bragging rights. It was a game for ages, as the Chiefs again reverted to basic power football, running the ball 48 times against only 6 passes. Oakland again drew first blood with a 10-yard field goal in the second quarter. Both teams failed to change the scoreboard until the Raiders extended the lead to 10-0 in the fourth period when Charlie Smith caught an 8-yard touchdown pass. Then KC fought back, with Wendell Hayes punching across the goal late in the game to close the

The Progress of the Seasons – 1969

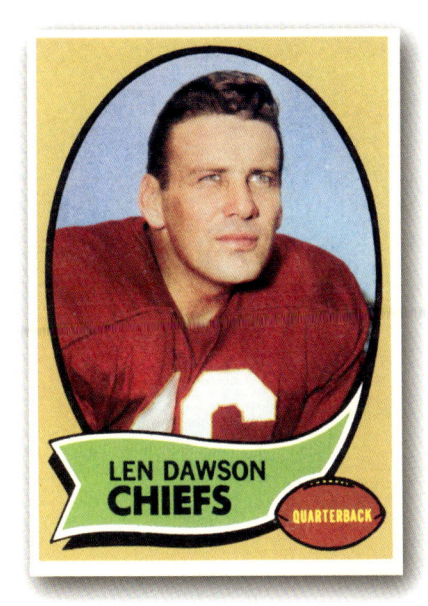

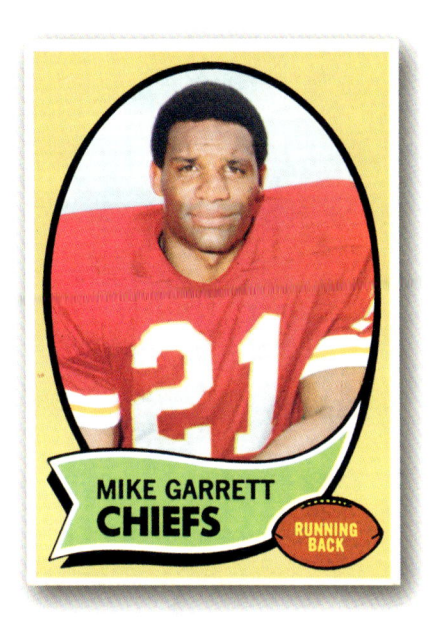

gap. But an attempt for a 2-point conversion failed and settled the score at 10-6. When time ran out KC's struggle to knock the Raiders from first place came up short. The runner-up Chiefs would have to visit the Eastern Division champions in New York on December 20 in the postseason.

Over 62,900 fans poured into Shea Stadium to witness the close of the AFL's decade. No matter who won, the Jets' next game at home would be played in the NFL's American Football Conference. Amid freezing temperatures and gusting winds, the Jets and Chiefs each managed only a field goal in the first half. Both Jan Stenerud and later Jim Turner, duplicated their 3 pointers in the second half, and in the final period the scoreboard showed a 6-6 score. After the kickoff following Turner's field goal sailed out of the end zone, the Chiefs stood 80 yards from victory and heading into a biting wind. If anything was going to happen, it would have to be now. Dawson went to the air and found a jet stream tunnel to throw in, completing a 61-yard pass to Otis Taylor on first down. With the ball on the Jet 19 yard line, Dawson went to the air again on first down and found Gloster Richardson for the game's only touchdown. Lenny-the-Cool had taken the Chiefs 80 yards on two plays and had not only pinned a 13-6 defeat on the defending champion Jets, he also set his team on a collision course with the Oakland Raiders for the twenty-second, and last time ever in the AFL. What could be a more fitting end to the glorious history of the American Football League than a Championship game between the Chiefs and Raiders?

On January 4, 1970, the Oakland-Alameda County Coliseum hosted the last official AFL Championship game. The favored Raiders had beaten the Chiefs for the seventh time in eight meetings two weeks earlier and for

377

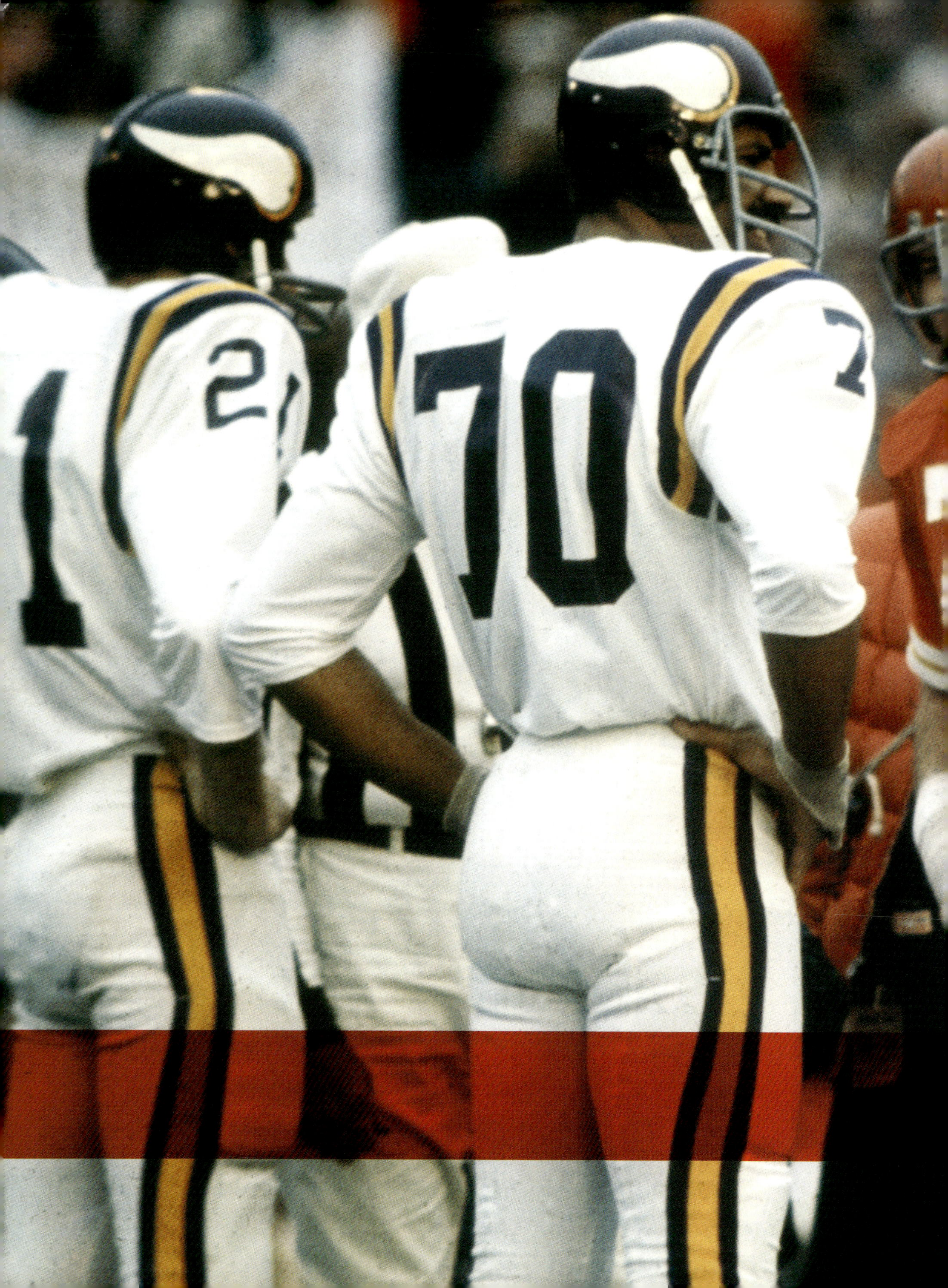
70

★ *The team captains of Minnesota and Kansas City meet at midfield before Super Bowl IV.*

the second time in the last five weeks. Around the league, people felt that perhaps the Raiders had KC's number. The game proved to be another in the long series of classic encounters, with both teams scoring only 1 touchdown in the first half and the Chiefs having the last say in the third quarter as they literally drove the length of the field, 98 yards, to take a 14-7 lead into the final fifteen minutes.

The game was dominated by the defenses, as neither team was able to gain more than 86 yards on the ground, or 154 yards in the air. Dawson tried 17 passes, completing 7. In contrast, Lamonica relied on his throwing arm 39 times, connecting on 15. The AFL was down to its final quarter, with the game's winner heading to New Orleans to play the Minnesota Vikings in Super Bowl IV. Three times in the last period it looked as if the Chiefs were going to put the game away, only to fumble all three times they penetrated the Oakland 30 yard line. Each time the Raiders were handed a game-tying opportunity, the Chiefs defense intercepted Lamonica. Jim Kearney picked one off at the KC 20, then rookie Jim Marsalis, and finally veteran Emmett Thomas, who returned his steal 62 yards to set up Jan Stenerud's 22-yard, game-sealing field goal. The epic battle ended the history of the AFL with the final score, Kansas City 17 - Oakland 7. The Chiefs were Champions of the AFL for a record third time (1962, 1966, 1969) and were now the first AFL team to head back to the Super Bowl.

Their final date with destiny as an AFL team awaited them on January 11, 1970, in New Orleans. A record Super Bowl crowd of 80,897 witnessed a shocker for the second year in a row. The Chiefs were fresh from two playoff wins in which their defense gave up only 13 points to the two best offenses in the AFL. But like the year before, the AFL team came in as a two touchdown underdog. Minnesota featured a blue-collar offense that depended on the running of rough Bill Brown and tough Dave Osborn. Joe Kapp was an unpolished quarterback who did nothing well, except win. Which he did twelve straight times in 1969 after an opening day loss to the New York Giants. Their defensive front four was one of the best in the business and the team's backbone comprised of Carl Eller, Jim Marshall, Gary Larson, and Alan Page. The NFL's best defensive unit allowed only 133 points in 1969, 44 less than Kansas City, the AFL leader.

On the game's opening drive the Vikings resembled the Colts in Super Bowl III, rolling downfield with little resistance. But once inside Kansas City territory their drive stalled at the Chiefs' 39, and with the wind in their face, they punted. The Chiefs first possession took them inside Minnesota territory. But they had the wind to their backs, and Jan Stenerud split the uprights from 48 yards away for the day's first score and the first quarter's only points. The KC defense matched the Vikings blow for blow. Time and again Kapp tried to beat the Chiefs into submission with his powerful running game. And on each drive the KC eleven held bulldogs Brown and Osborn to a total of 22 yards and no first downs rushing

The Progress of the Seasons – 1969

throughout the first half. Two more Stenerud field goals and the famous "65-toss-power-trap" 5-yard touchdown dash by Mike Garrett, called from the sidelines by coach Stram, gave the Chiefs a 16-0 lead after two quarters.

Just as the Jets had done a year earlier, the AFL Chiefs had shutout the NFL's best for the first thirty minutes of the Super Bowl. Within the first ten minutes of the third quarter the Vikings made their move, mixing passes and short runs on a drive that culminated with Dave Osborn scoring on a 4-yard run, narrowing the Chiefs' lead to 16-7. But Dawson and the Chiefs kept the pressure on. A well-concealed end-around play by Frank Pitts surprised the Vikings defense and netted KC a first down. On the next play a personal foul call gave the Chiefs the ball at the Minnesota 46. The Chiefs then sealed the Vikings doom with a quick hitch pass to Otis Taylor, who after grabbing the short 6 yarder, broke away from defensive back Earsell Mackbee's tackle and sprinted the last 40 yards all alone to give the Chiefs a 23-7 lead. The Vikings never got closer. For the Chiefs, the humiliation of Super Bowl I was vindicated. Now they were the Super Bowl Champions! As the leagues prepared to merge, both had two Super Bowl victories.

A Hollywood script writer could not have penned a better finish to the American Football League. Its founder and Kansas City owner Lamar Hunt placed his team in the last AFL vs. NFL Super Bowl—just as he had in the first one. Once again taking on the establishment that ten years earlier had turned down his request to join their league and who had mocked the AFL after his team was embarrassed in Super Bowl I. Now as the AFL lowered its curtain, his Chiefs took on the NFL's most powerful representative and the best Minnesota team ever, the same team that shunned the AFL for the NFL in 1960 after signing on as one of the original eight franchises. Again Hunt was the underdog. With his team wearing a commemorative ten-year patch on their jerseys to pay tribute to all the American Football League players who were part of its history, the Chiefs dominated the NFL's best, just as the Jets had done the year before.

After January 17, 1970, the AFL was no more. But in its ten short years, the dreaming and persevering of hundreds of believers enabled the AFL to reach the pinnacle of their existence. They reached equality with the NFL and had come in from the cold. As the AFL and NFL became one combined league, the memory of the American Football League, from 1960 through 1969, was left to live on forever. It was definitely a league for the ages and, without a doubt, one worth remembering!

Remember the AFL

SUPER BOWL IV
KANSAS CITY (AFL) 23, MINNESOTA (NFL) 7

Leading passers	Attempts	Completions	Pct	TDs	Yards	Int
Len Dawson	166	98	59%	9	1323	13
Mike Livingston	161	84	52%	4	1123	6
Jacky Lee	20	12	60%	1	109	1

Leading rushers	Attempts	Yards gained	Average	TDs
Mike Garrett	168	732	4.4	6
Robert Holmes	150	612	4.1	2
Warren McVea	106	500	4.7	7
Wendell Hayes	62	208	3.4	4
Mike Livingston	15	102	6.8	0
Paul Lowe	10	33	3.3	0

Leading receivers	Caught	Yards gained	Average	TDs
Mike Garrett	43	432	10.0	2
Otis Taylor	41	696	17.0	7
Frank Pitts	31	470	15.2	2
Robert Holmes	26	266	10.2	3
Gloster Richardson	23	381	16.6	2
Fred Arbanas	16	258	16.1	0

Leading scorers	TDs	XPM	XPA	FGM	FGA	PTs
Jan Stenerud		38	38	27	35	119
Mike Garrett	8					48

The Progress of the Seasons – 1969

★ ★ ★ ★ ★ ★ ★ ★ ★ ★ ★

In the final paragraph of the American Football League's story, the last AFL All-Star game was held in the Houston Astrodome on January 17, 1970. The record showed the West leading the classic with five wins to two for the East, with one victory for the All-League Stars against the 1965 Champion Bills. Five of the previous seven encounters resulted in comeback wins in the fourth quarter, beginning with the West overtaking the East to break a 14-14 tie in the second annual game following the 1962 season. The next year the West waited to score their game winner with only forty-three seconds remaining. Turning the tables on the West, the East came back to win the 1966 season's game with two last-period touchdowns to win for the first time, 30-23. They recorded their second win when Joe Namath led them to a last-minute go-ahead touchdown, then had to wait until George Blanda missed a field goal attempt to celebrate their 25-24 victory. The West then took control again after coming back from a 19-3 halftime deficit to defeat the East 38-25. This last hurrah wasn't even close, and established for the last time that the West was indeed the more dominant division.

The West took control right from the start with 2 touchdowns in the opening quarter, with the San Diego Chargers having the upper hand in each. Dickie Post, the league's leading rusher, scored on a 1-yard plunge, and John Hadl teamed with Lance Alworth for a 21-scoring pass. Jan Stenerud and Jim Turner, two names that always seem linked to All-Star game field goals then came to the aid of their teams in the third quarter. Stenerud connected again in the final period to give the West a 19-3 lead. Another touchdown by the West wrote the final sentence to the game and the league. The final, final score in AFL history was West 26 - East 3, giving the West their sixth victory in eight meetings against the East.

★ ★ ★ ★ ★ ★ ★ ★ ★ ★ ★ ★

Part 2

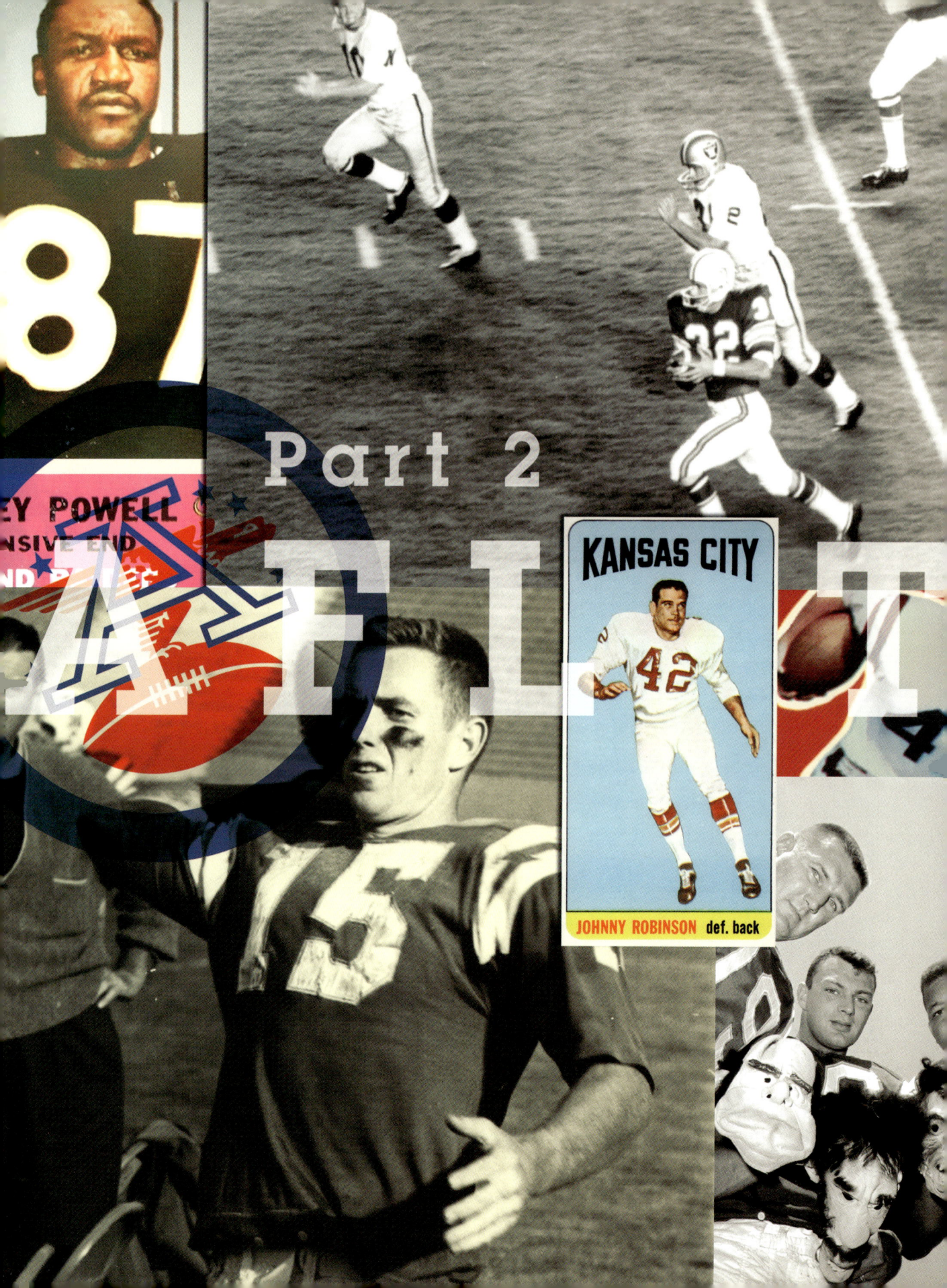

AFL II

BABE PARILLI
BOSTON PATRIOTS QUARTERBACK

TRIVIA

BOB JOHNSON
BENGALS AFC CENTER

Headgear Quiz

In what year did each helmet make its debut?

1. _____ 
2. _____ 
3. _____ 
4. _____

5. _____ 
6. _____ 
7. _____ 
8. _____

9. _____ 
10. _____ 
11. _____ 
12. _____

13. _____
14. _____ 
15. _____ 
16. _____

17.  _____ 18.  _____ 19.  _____ 20. _____

21.  _____ 22.  _____ 23.  _____ 24. _____

25.  _____ 26.  _____ 27. _____

387

In the Trenches

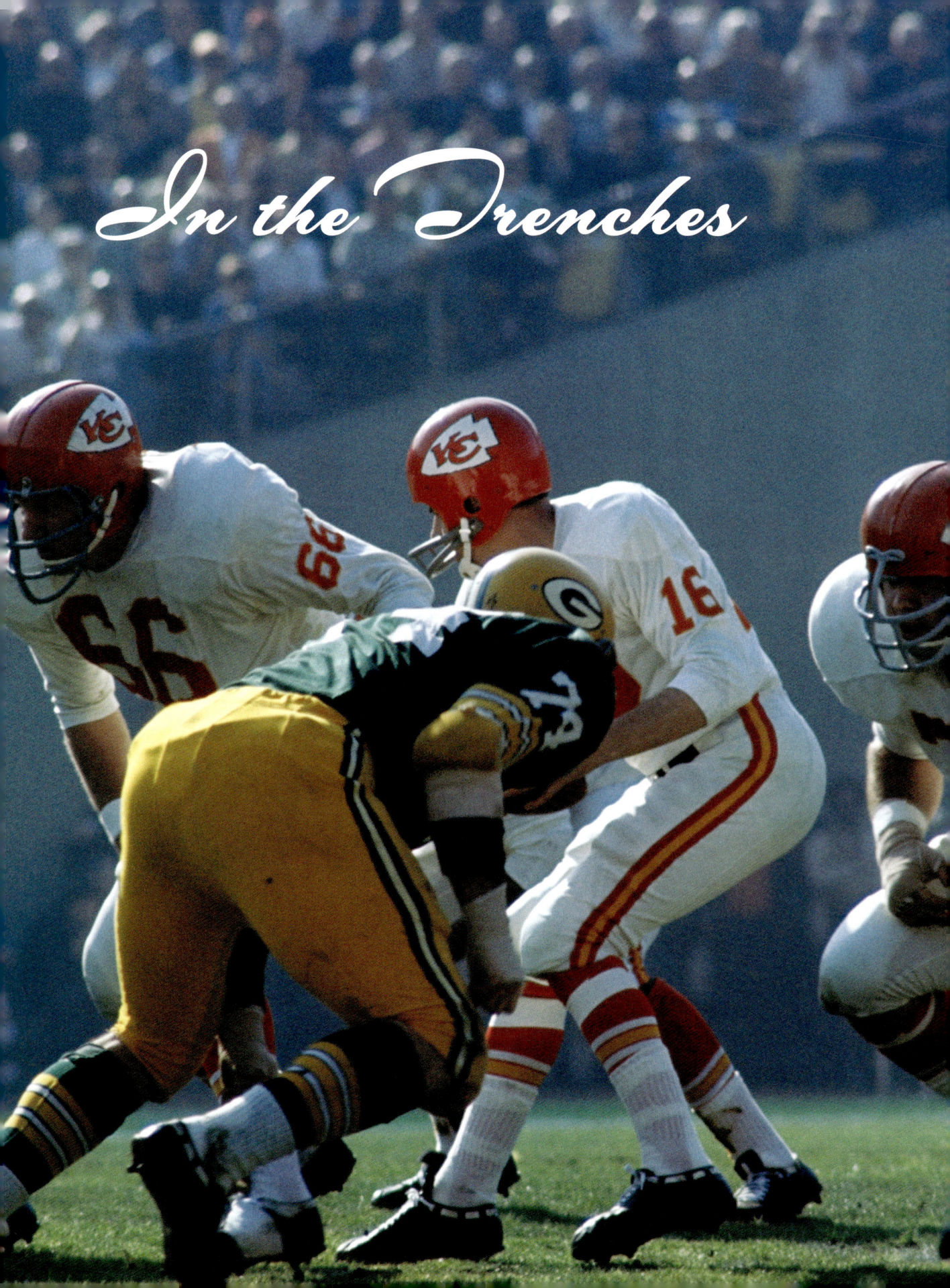

The list of players and events that carved the history of the American Football League is long, varied, and auspicious. From the opening kickoff in Boston on Friday, September 9, 1960, to the final whistle of the ninth annual All-Star Game on January 17, 1970, there were many battles. First for acceptance, then for players, and finally for respect. There were wars that had to be settled in court, and wars in the front office. There were territorial battles and above all, the wars with the check book. Through it all, the owners and players were unyielding and relentless.

When it was finally time to enter the arena and take the field of play, the AFLers also fought each other long and hard for bragging rights in the new league. At times it was an "all for one and one for all" approach. And at times it became a battle to see who would rise to be king of the hill. In the beginning it was the Oiler and Charger offenses breaking from the pack. Then Dallas found a quarterback and became a challenger, as did Boston and Buffalo. Eventually the Jets and Raiders also found field generals and joined the battle. In the later years, Houston, Oakland, and Kansas City developed immovable defenses that dominated the once-superior offenses.

What transpired through the ten AFL years was sometimes graceful, occasionally bizarre, and on occasion spectacular. All created by a most memorable cast of characters who fought the punishing hand-to-hand combat known as the war in the trenches.

---

1. Lamar Hunt, founder of the AFL, was a fourth string end for which Texas university? _____
2. What was the only original AFL team to not have a Rookie of the Year winner? _____
3. Only three players played every week of the AFL's history, all 140 games. Who are they?
   1. _____ 2. _____ 3. _____
4. The only player to win two AFL Player of the Year awards is _____
5. The last original Houston Oiler to retire from the team was also the first to have his number (43) retired. Who was he? _____
6. List the 10 AFL Rookie of the Year winners.
   1960 _____ 1965 _____
   1961 _____ 1966 _____
   1962 _____ 1967 _____
   1963 _____ 1968 _____
   1964 _____ 1969 _____
7. What player played in the most AFL championship games (7), missing only in '62, '66, and '69?
   _____

Remember the AFL

8. Three other players played in six AFL championship games, (two were teammates for the same two teams). Who are they?
   1. _____ 2. _____ 3. _____

9. Denver defensive back Goose Gonsoulin led the AFL in interceptions in 1960. What is Goose's given first name? _____

10. This actor was part owner of the expansion Miami Dolphins. _____

11. Field goal kickers aimed for this TV celebrity in one end of the Dolphins' Orange Bowl. _____

12. This team hit bottom when it lost its first two games of the 1961 season by a combined score of 99-0. _____

13. The NFL had 1960 Olympic gold medalist Bob Hayes, while the AFL had this '60 Olympic long jump silver medalist. _____

14. Barron Hilton loved the contest-winning name "Chargers" for his Los Angeles franchise because it could help promote his credit card business. What credit card did Hilton start? _____

15. One of the two best trades made by Miami GM Joe Thomas was with Boston for linebacker Nick Buoniconti. What young Florida State quarterback was traded for him from Miami? _____

16. Which team played an entire season with only one color jersey, used for both home and away games? _____

17. Much was made about Pete Gogolak being the first soccer-style kicker in professional football for the AFL Bills. Who was the second soccer-style kicker to play in the AFL? _____

18. Sid Gillman coached the Chargers every season of the AFL's existence, stepping down in November 1969 due to health problems. Who replaced him? _____

19. What was New York Jet owner Sonny Werblin's given first name? _____

20. A member of the Foolish Club, New York Titans owner Harry Wismer was the play-by-play announcer for this NFL team prior to owning the Titans. _____

21. The Denver Broncos bought their original uniforms from the defunct college all-star game known as the Copper Bowl. Where was the Copper Bowl played? City _____ or state _____

22. The 1960 version of the Boston Patriots helmet featured what image as a logo? _____

23. This player from Ripon College was the AFL's first all-league fullback. _____

24. In 1965 this Houston Oilers assistant coach was promoted to head coach when the current head coach stepped down to become an assistant for the same team. _____

25. Who was the Houston head coach in 1965 who voluntarily stepped down to be an assistant for the same team, something he did previously with another AFL team, although not voluntarily? _____

26. Which three stadiums simultaneously housed an AFL and an NFL team?
    1. _____ 2. _____ 3. _____

In the Trenches

27. The All-Time AFL team tight end, this standout receiver lost the sight in one eye after being jumped outside of a nightclub. _____

28. What college football team did Oakland's Al Davis model the Raiders' uniforms after when he took over as the team's head coach in 1963? _____

29. The first two players to catch 100 passes in pro football history were from the AFL. Who are they, and what years did they do it? 1. _____ 2. _____

30. Before deciding upon the name Raiders, what name did the principal owner of the Oakland franchise pick as the winner of the team's naming contest?

31. The original team colors of the Denver Broncos were _____ and _____

32. The original team colors of the Oakland Raiders were _____ and _____

33. He succeeded Joe Foss as the second commissioner of the AFL. _____

34. This quarterback lost his starting position to Len Dawson in 1962 and found himself starting for another team that same year. _____

35. The first eight cities to receive AFL franchises included Dallas, Houston, Buffalo, Boston, New York, Los Angeles, Denver, and _____

36. This defensive tackle was part of the 1960 NFL Champion Philadelphia Eagles. As a Boston Patriot, he was the last player to play pro football without a face mask. _____

37. He was the first quarterback without NFL experience to win an AFL championship. _____

38. These two head coaches (one from the NFL and one from the AFL) exchanged teams in 1962. The AFL coach went from Houston to St. Louis, and the NFL coach went from St. Louis to Houston. Who were they? _____ and _____

39. The first head coach of the Miami Dolphins was _____

40. Which team owns the longest losing streak in AFL history at 19? _____

41. This one-time Dallas Texan and Buffalo Bill preceded Warren Wells as a wide receiver (with Fred Biletnikoff) for the Raiders and also caught 2 touchdown passes in Super Bowl II. _____

42. The original uniform colors of the Buffalo Bills were _____ shirts and _____ helmets.

43. Who led the Los Angeles Chargers in receiving in 1960 before succumbing to diabetes in November of that first season? _____

44. In 1967 he became the first player in pro football history to throw for 4,000 yards. _____

45. This KC running back was the team rookie of the year and rushing leader in 1964. He died at the end of the 1965 season of complications from a knee operation. _____

46. He led the AFL in passing his rookie season but only completed one more pass in his career after that. _____

47. He was the first NFL player to play out his option and sign with an AFL team. He also was listed on his college football team's depth chart ahead of Lamar Hunt. _____

Remember the AFL

48. Who was the first AFL player to be signed by an NFL team after his option ran out, sparking a chain reaction and a war on signing players from the opposing league. _____

49. As a result of the player referenced in Question 48, these two NFL starting quarterbacks were rumored to have signed with AFL teams, giving impetus to the AFL/NFL merger. _____ and _____

50. Billy Joe, the 1963 Rookie of the Year for Denver, played college football for a Philadelphia university better known for its basketball program. _____

51. Who was the starting quarterback for the losing team in the 1967 AFL Championship game? _____

52. These two quarterbacks started the season for Houston in 1967 but failed to ignite the team-leading management to trade for a new starter from Kansas City. _____ and _____

53. After winning the Heisman Trophy for the Naval Academy in 1960, this player went on to run the football for the Boston Patriots. _____

54. From 1959 to 1969 AFL teams signed five of the ten Heisman Trophy winners—who were they?
    1. _____
    2. _____
    3. _____
    4. _____
    5. _____

55. In 1965 the New York Jets signed Joe Namath from Alabama for $400,000 and John Huarte from Notre Dame for $200,000. What other two collegiate running backs signed with the Jets the same year for $100,000? _____ and _____

56. These two teams played in the first AFL playoff game to break a tie for the division title. _____ and _____

57. He is the all-time leading ground gainer in AFL history. _____

58. The first coach to be fired in the AFL was _____

59. These three Titan originals also played for the Jets in Super Bowl III. _____ _____ _____

60. Who kicked the winning field goal in the second overtime period of the 1962 AFL Championship game? _____

61. Who was the first African-American player in both NFL and AFL history to be a regular starting quarterback? _____

62. This NFL city verbally agreed to join the AFL in 1966 but quickly backed out when the NFL offered it membership, leading the way for Miami to be the first expansion team to join the AFL. _____

63. What AFL franchise was the first to relocate to another city? _____

In the Trenches

64. The 1969 Super Bowl Champion Kansas City Chiefs had five quarterbacks on their roster. Four of them saw action during the season—name the five.

    1. _____
    2. _____
    3. _____
    4. _____
    5. _____

65. Clem Daniels made a name for himself with the Oakland Raiders, but what AFL team did he start out with in 1960? _____

66. This quarterback moved from one team, Houston, to the next, Denver, via what amounted to a lend-lease agreement that would return him to Houston after two years. _____

67. Once a fierce NFL fullback for the Bears, this player came out of a one-year retirement from the NFL to become the Dolphins' first fullback in 1966. _____

68. He ignited the crowd by returning a kickoff 95 yards for a touchdown for the Dolphins on the first play in Miami's history. _____

69. When Lou Saban resigned after winning the AFL title in 1965, this assistant replaced him as head coach of the Buffalo Bills. _____

70. Charger halfback Paul Lowe is the second-leading ground gainer in AFL history. With what team did he finish his career in 1969? _____

71. He was the head coach for three of the original AFL teams. Name him and the teams he coached.
    _____ coached the _____, _____, and the _____.

72. This African-American place kicker is the first winner of the AFL scoring title. _____

73. They were the Eastern-most Western Division team in the AFL. _____

74. Who is the only non-kicker in the top five all-time scorers in AFL history. _____

75. The top eight receivers in AFL history each played for an original AFL franchise, where they caught most of their passes. Write the name of the player next to the team.

    Boston _____ Buffalo _____ Denver _____
    Houston _____ Kansas City/Dallas _____
    New York _____ Oakland _____ San Diego _____

76. This college All-American lineman was the first draft choice of the expansion Bengals. What was his name, position, and college? _____ played _____ for _____

77. He was the first rookie in AFL history to gain 1,000 yards rushing. _____

78. This Buffalo Bill was the only AFL (or NFL) casualty of the Vietnam war. _____

79. A starting defensive back for the Bengals in 1968, this player was the Sporting News All-AFL fullback in 1969. _____

Remember the AFL

80. This USC wide receiver was the starting split end and second-leading receiver for the Bengals in their first season. He also filled in as the place kicker when the starter was drafted into the service. _____

81. He was the starting kicker and punter for the Bengals in their first season. _____

82. This Tennessee quarterback was one of the Bengals starters during their first season. _____

83. These two running backs, once traded for each other, ended up in the 1966 Miami Dolphin backfield. _____ and _____

84. This little All-American was the Bengals second draft pick in 1969. He later became known as a poor man's Dick Butkus and an all-pro at his middle linebacker position, and played in the 1980 Super Bowl. _____

85. In a role reversal in 1967, this team started a tight end who once led the AFL in rushing, and a running back who was a starting tight end the previous year. Who are the players? _____ and _____

86. Buffalo Bills owner Ralph Wilson prevented this franchise from failing by contributing $400,000 to its survival. In return he was given 25 percent of the team ownership—thereby having ownership of two AFL teams simultaneously. _____

87. He was the only player to start a game for both the expansion Dolphins and expansion Bengals in their maiden seasons. _____

88. In 1964 the San Diego Chargers used four field goal kickers. Select the four from this list: Herb Trevenio, George Blair, John Hadl, Bud Whitehead, Keith Lincoln, Ben Agajanian, Mike Mercer. _____, _____, _____, and _____

89. Who was the AFL Coach of the Year in 1962 for taking his team to a 7-7 record. _____

90. This was the last AFL team to NOT wear a logo, mascot, or name on their helmet. Name the team and year. _____ in _____

91. The 1968 Bills were 1-12-1. What team did they beat 37-35, thanks to five interceptions, three of which were returned for touchdowns? _____

92. Match the man with the team he coached:

    Charlie Waller _____   A. Oakland
    Clive Rush _____   B. Buffalo
    Ray Malavasi _____   C. Boston
    Harvey Johnson _____   D. Denver
    Marty Feldman _____   E. San Diego

93. The 1967-1969 Raiders defense was known by this nickname. _____

94. An All-American at Texas, he played five years with the Rams before retiring due to a gunshot accident. After a year in retirement he joined the Broncos and was all-league from 1960-1962. _____

In the Trenches

95. This AFL quarterback won a national championship with Notre Dame in the 40's, played for the Detroit Lions and Chicago Cardinals in the NFL, and last played for a Canadian team in 1959. _____

96. In 1964 Commissioner Joe Foss had to intervene on the league's and Denver's behalf to orchestrate what become known as the lend-lease trade, in which a quarterback was traded from Houston to the Broncos but would be returned to the Oilers in 1966. What two quarterbacks shared the lead role for Denver the previous year? _____ and _____

97. They became known as the "Salt and Pepper" linebackers for the Chiefs. Who are they? _____ and _____

98. This former NCAA wrestling champion started his pro career by wrestling AFL running backs to the ground. _____

99. He was the "Tom Matte" of the AFL, filling in as an emergency quarterback while three of his QB teammates were injured in 1968. _____

100. He was a high school All-American in football and basketball. While playing only six games as a sophomore in college, he led his fighting Illini team in receiving. Two years later as a senior he led the University of Utah in receiving. Drafted in round twelve, he played in the AFL All-Star game as a rookie and made All-Pro four times. When he retired he was the Bengals' all-time leading receiver. _____

101. In 1967 Oakland's Willie Brown and Kent McCloughan broke new ground by using the bump-and-run style of pass coverage. Brown learned this method from his former coach, Jack Faulkner in Denver. What basketball great, drafted by the LA Rams where Faulkner was an assistant, is credited with creating this basketball style of coverage while he was trying out for the Rams, prior to playing for the Boston Celtics in the NBA? _____

102. Who replaced Sammy Baugh as head coach of the Titans when owner Harry Wismer demoted Baugh to kicking coach? _____

103. Tragedy hit the AFL on October 9, 1960, when this player, a New York Titan guard, died as a result of a broken neck suffered in the Titans vs Oilers game. _____

104. In 1963 this Kansas City Chief was the second player in the league's short history to die from injuries suffered on the playing field, after he was hit in the chest on a kickoff return. _____

105. What significance does former Kansas City mayor H. Roe Bartle have in the Chiefs' history? _____

106. In January 1961 the Raiders' ownership tangled in an irresolvable dispute. Joe Foss, the AFL commissioner, intervened, and the owners agreed to flip a coin to determine which faction would sell out to the other. The result caused this owner, for whom the team was originally named, to relinquish his share of the team. _____

107. He is the only player in AFL history to win both an NFL and AFL title as a starting quarterback. _____

Remember the AFL

108. At the conclusion of the 1961 AFL season, only two of the original eight coaches were invited back for the 1962 season with their same team. Who were they? _____ and _____

109. Which two players played in all ten AFL seasons and also won a football National Championship as college teammates? _____ and _____

110. Among the more prominent of the 4,500 entries to the name-the-team contest for this team, were the Bullets, Nickels, and Blue Devils. This team finally settled on a wild west cowboy for its name. _____

111. In this franchise's team-naming contest in 1960, the winner was awarded an all-expenses-paid trip to Mexico. _____

112. This team was one of three original franchises to share a city with an NFL opponent. It was the second to relocate. _____

113. This team offered as a team-naming prize two lifetime passes to the team's games. While several hundred people submitted the same name, a tie-breaker was used to declare the winner. The tie-breaker was to correctly pick the winner and final score of that year's Notre Dame vs. Miami game. The game ended in a scoreless tie! _____

114. This is the only team to change its team name while staying in the same city for the AFL's ten years. _____

115. This team was named by a group of sportswriters whose choice paid tribute to the local history and regional holiday. _____

116. The winner of this team's naming contest won the prize, but management later rejected the name and chose a new one. _____

117. The Raiders' first real home stadium actually located in Oakland was Frank Youell Field. Who was Frank Youell? _____

118. What other two stadiums did the Raiders call home prior to playing in Youell Field? _____ and _____

119. What was the name of the Bengals' first home stadium? _____

120. What stadiums hosted the four Super Bowls?

    Super Bowl I _____   Super Bowl III _____
    Super Bowl II _____   Super Bowl IV _____

121. What two television networks broadcast Super Bowl I? _____ and _____

122. He was the coach's son and also one of the starting quarterbacks for the 1966 first-year Miami Dolphins. _____

123. Name the three other starting quarterbacks Miami used in 1966. _____, _____, and _____

124. The Cincinnati Bengals also started quarterbacks by committee their first year. Name the three who saw starting time in the Queen City. _____, _____, and _____

396

In the Trenches

125. What player scored the first touchdown for an AFL team in a Super Bowl? _____

126. In 1967 the Chargers did not have either Paul Lowe or Keith Lincoln in the starting backfield for the first time in their history. The two rookies who did not disappoint the Southern California faithful both finished among the top five AFL rushers. Who are they? _____ and _____

127. Who was the first AFL passing leader to not have NFL experience—and what year was it? _____

128. Who was the first AFL scoring champion to not score a touchdown? _____

129. This former AFL Player of the Year started five AFL championship games for two different teams. He played the second one after he was picked up on waivers for $100. _____

130. Who replaced John Rauch as head coach of the Raiders after he left for the Bills? _____

131. Match the Oakland Raider coaches with the years (1960-69) they led the team. (Some years may be used more than once.)

    John Madden _____
    Bill Conkright _____
    Marty Feldman _____, _____
    Al Davis _____, _____, _____
    Eddie Erdelatz _____, _____
    John Rauch _____, _____, _____

132. After starting the 1961 season 2-3, this coach was the second AFL head man to be fired. But later he came back to win two AFL titles. _____

133. Who replaced the coach in Question 132 as head coach for the team that fired him? _____

134. The Houston Oilers had five head coaches. Match them with the years they led the team. (Some years may be used more than once.)

    Frank (Pop) Ivy _____, _____
    Wally Lemm _____, _____
    Lou Rymkus _____, _____
    Sammy Baugh _____
    Hugh "Bones" Taylor _____

135. What two runners were the only ones to win an AFL rushing title twice? _____ and _____

136. Except for in 1960, this steady quarterback won the passing title in all of the even numbered AFL years. _____

137. In 1962 and again in 1967 the AFL boasted three 1,000 yard rushers. In '62 the Texans had _____, the Oilers had _____ and the Bills had _____ and in '67 the Patriots had _____, the Chiefs had _____ and the Oilers had _____.

Remember the AFL

138. These two runners were the only two to gain 1,000 yards more than once. _____ did it in 1963 and 1965 and _____ did it in 1966 and 1967.

139. In 1969, Kansas City's Johnny Robinson and Oakland's Dave Grayson both had 8 interceptions to tie for second in the AFL. What Kansas City DB led the league with 9? _____

140. Who was the third and final commissioner of the AFL? _____

141. Three of these quarterbacks did not throw a pass for the Denver Broncos in 1966. Who are they?
A. Scott Glacken, B. Dick Wood, C. Tobin Rote, D. Max Choboian, E. Mickey Slaughter, F. Jacky Lee, G. Steve Tensi, or H. John McCormick
1. _____ 2. _____ 3. _____

142. In one of the biggest trades in AFL history, the Raiders and Bills swapped quarterbacks and receivers. Oakland moved to the top of the AFL with Daryle "The Mad Bomber" Lamonica coming over with end Glenn Bass. What former Raiders starting quarterback and former all-league end went from Oakland to Buffalo? _____ and _____

143. In what year was the only AFL Championship game shutout played? _____

144. What stadium hosted the most AFL Championship games? _____

145. This journeyman proved his worth as a special-teamer by recovering a fumble for a touchdown seconds after his Raiders team went ahead of the Jets in the final minute of "The Heidi Game" on November 17, 1968. _____

146. Only four AFL teams played all their home games in one stadium. Who were they?
_____, _____, _____, _____

147. Only four runners in AFL history have gained over 200 yards in one game. Match the runner with the yardage he gained.
A. Billy Cannon _____   1. 208 vs. Oakland, 1966
B. Clem Daniels _____   2. 243 vs. New York, 1963
C. Cookie Gilchrist _____   3. 216 vs. New York, 1961
D. Jim Nance _____   4. 200 vs. New York, 1963

148. What two members of the AFL's All-Time team played in both Super Bowl I and IV?
_____ and _____

149. From 1965 through 1968 the AFL rushing champion gained over 1,000. What two runners won the titles the year before and the year after with less than 1,000 yards gained?
_____ and _____

150. In 1962, this quarterback was traded from the NY Giants, cut by the Vikings and Broncos, and found himself on Frank Youell Field on opening day throwing his first two passes for 80- and 19-yard touchdowns for the Titans. _____

151-169. Throughout the AFL's ten-year history, only nineteen players made it from the start of the league in 1960 to its end in 1969. Identify "The 19 Originals" from the following alphabetical list of thirty

In the Trenches

candidates: Lance Alworth, Fred Arbanas, George Blanda, Billy Cannon, Gino Cappelletti, Clem Daniels, Larry Eisenhower, Tom Flores, Larry Grantham, Wayne Hawkins, Abner Haynes, Jim Hunt, Harry Jacobs, Jack Kemp, Ernie Ladd, Paul Lowe, Jacky Lee, Bill Mathis, Paul Maguire, Don Maynard, Jerry Mays, Ron Mix, Jim Otto, Babe Parilli, Johnny Robinson, Paul Rochester, Charlie Tolar, Lionel Taylor, Jerrel Wilson, Ernie Wright.

151. _____
152. _____
153. _____
154. _____
155. _____
156. _____
157. _____
158. _____
159. _____
160. _____
161. _____
162. _____
163. _____
164. _____
165. _____
166. _____
167. _____
168. _____
169. _____

170-178. Of the nineteen players on the list above, nine played for only one franchise throughout their AFL career. Who were the nine?

170. _____
171. _____
172. _____
173. _____
174. _____
175. _____
176. _____
177. _____
178. _____

179. Who are the only four men to maintain ownership of their AFL franchise for all ten years?
_____, _____, _____, and _____

180. Who scored the last touchdown as a player for an AFL team? _____

Faces of the Game

In the 616 games played in the American Football League, approximately 1,500 players donned AFL uniforms. Some long and proud, some short and maybe not so sweet, but every one of them was significant and meaningful to the success of the league.

Kansas City quarterback Len Dawson, on the losing end in Super Bowl I but on the winning end in Super Bowl IV, said it best when the New York Jets won Super Bowl III and brought long-awaited respectability to the AFL, declaring that the 16-7 victory over the NFL powerhouse Colts was a win for the entire AFL. Dawson said, "We beat them, not just the Jets." Every player who ever wore an AFL uniform had a part of that Super Bowl III victory celebration.

At the start, team rosters were filled with NFL castoffs, undrafted and untried rookies, former players looking for a second chance, and others just looking for any chance to play professional football. They were from Notre Dame and USC, from Abilene Christian and Iowa, Penn State, Ripon State, and West Texas State. Some were from the Canadian Football League and others from the sandlots of America. They all came with the same hopes and dreams. A decade later, everyone who came was able to revel in the fulfillment and the knowledge that they had done what no other football league before them was able to do—survive and force a merger with the NFL!

On the following pages are some of the men who helped forge the success and memories of the AFL.

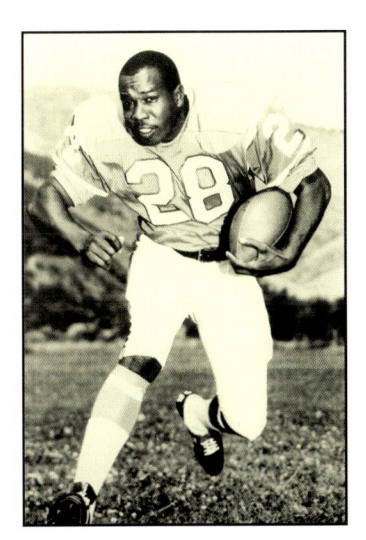

---

1. I was the first AFL Rookie of the Year and led the league in rushing in 1960. In 1961, I scored 5 touchdowns in a game against Oakland.

2. In the days of double duty, I played both linebacker and punter for Los Angeles and Buffalo. I led the league in punting in 1960 with a 40.5-yard average. Today I am a well-known TV football announcer.

Remember the AFL

3. I played for five different AFL teams and led the Jets in passing the year before Broadway Joe arrived.

_____

4. I played in the AFL from 1963 through 1969 and led the league with 10 interceptions in 1967 while with the Dolphins.

_____

5. An original Oakland Raider as a halfback/punter, I led the team in rushing in 1961. But I also had the dubious occasion to have one of my punts hit the goalpost and be recovered by a defender in my own end zone for a game-winning touchdown.

_____

6. As an original New York Titan defensive back, I once recovered a blocked punt with fifteen seconds left in the game and ran it back for a game-winning touchdown against Denver.

_____

7. A master of the fine art of punting a football, I am the punter on the All-Time AFL team, having led the league in 1965 and 1967.

_____

8. From 1961 to 1969 this is what opposing quarterbacks saw when I rushed them. I was an all-league defensive end in 1963, '64, and '66.

_____

9. I was only the second running back in Chargers history to wear number 22. As a rookie in '67 I was fourth in the league in rushing, in '68 I was fifth, and in '69 I led the league.

_____

Faces of the Game

10. In 1965, Buffalo's two best receivers were injured early in the season. Who are these two pass catchers shown on the sidelines in wheelchairs?

_____
_____

11. I played quarterback at Baylor and for Houston and Boston in the AFL from 1964-1969. I was also the first AFL player to grace the cover of *Sports Illustrated* by myself.

_____

12. I was an All-American running back from Ole Miss and played for the Chargers and Titans. But my claim to fame is that I gave Lance Alworth the nickname "Bambi."

_____

13. I was a starter in two of the first four Super Bowls, one on defense as a linebacker and the other on offense as a center.

_____

14. I coached and won the two biggest games in pro football history—the 1958 NFL overtime Championship game and Super Bowl III. What is my real first name?

_____

15. As a San Diego rookie in 1967, I was the fifth-leading rusher in the AFL and topped the league with 5.5 yards per carry.

_____

403

Remember the AFL

16. As a member of the Jets in 1964, I led the AFL in interceptions with 12. No AFL player ever intercepted more in one season.

_____

17. A member of the College Football Hall of Fame, I was the first player in the AFL from the Naval Academy. I was also a member of the original New York Titans as a defensive tackle.

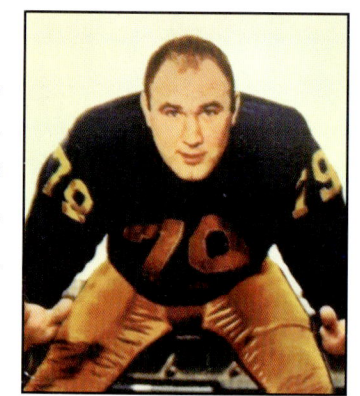

_____

18. I was a teammate with the Titans of the Midshipman in question seventeen and played across the line from him in the Army-Navy game. I made the first two AFL all-league teams as a guard.

_____

19. I was a college All-American, a Heisman Trophy winner, an AFL rushing champ, AFL Championship game MVP twice, and the Raiders second-best runner in 1964.

_____

20. I was a professional wrestler in the off season and the only player the AFL allowed to wear my first name on the back of my jersey.

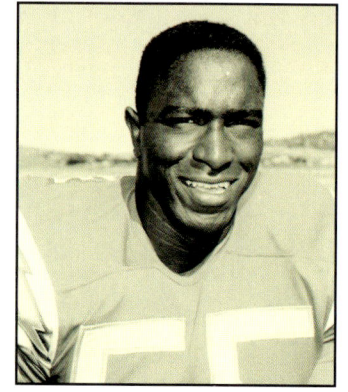

_____

21. I played quarterback in the NFL All-Star game in 1956 for the Redskins and also led the Titans in passing in 1960 and 1961. I threw a touchdown pass in 19 straight AFL games.

_____

22. An all-star linebacker with the Chargers, I succumbed to a pulmonary embolism while playing for Cincinnati in 1969.

_____

23. I was an offensive lineman for the Titans, Chargers, and Broncos from 1960 to 1964 but retired to pursue a career as an artist. Upon seeing my work you might agree that my unique style is as identifiable as that of Leroy Nieman.

_____

Faces of the Game

24. I was the split end on the first AFL all-league team and had more yards receiving than any other pass catcher that year. I also played for the Broncos and Bills.

_____

25. When the AFL started, I quit my high school teaching job to try out. No one caught more passes in one season (101) than I did in 1964.

_____

26. I was only 5'6" but packed a huge wallop in my 200 pounds, running the ball for the Oilers from 1960 through 1966 and gaining over 1,000 yds. in 1962.

_____

27. I was the runner-up for the 1965 Heisman Trophy, then caught passes for the Miami Dolphins in the pros.

_____

28. In 1969 I threw only 1 pass, but caught 32 for the Buffalo Bills. The previous season I led another AFL team in passing.

_____

29. I anchored the Denver Broncos line at tackle from 1960 to 1965—making the all-league team in both '62 and '65. My brother and I were the only AFL players from Emporia College.

_____

30. I was the first and only offensive lineman to be named AFL Player of the Week.

_____

31. From Boston College to the Boston Patriots, I was the starting tight end from 1965 through the rest of the AFL years. I caught 22, 29, 39, 47, and 16 balls from Babe Parilli, Tom Sherman, and Mike Taliaferro.

_____

Remember the AFL

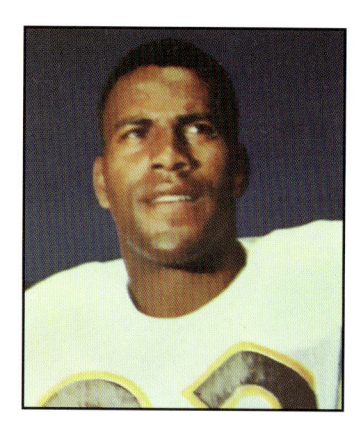

32. I was an all-league defensive back in 1962 and 1963 with Oakland and played in Super Bowl I with KC—where I got knocked out making a tackle. I'm "The Hammer!"

33. Everyone said I was too slow to play split end. But I caught touchdown passes for 82, 73, and 78 yards in one season and totaled 196 receptions in my five AFL years.

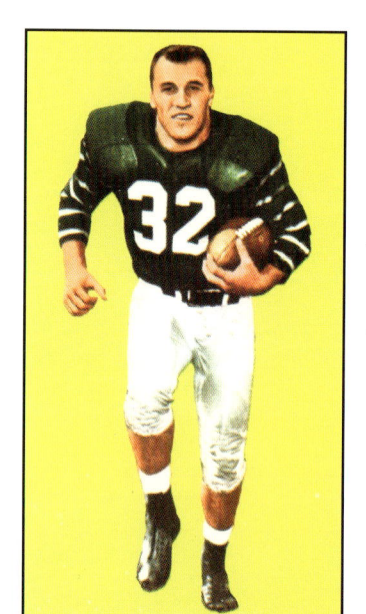

34. I was the only Princeton player to make it to the AFL. I signed for $100,000 to play fullback for the Jets the same year Joe Namath signed the big contract. I was inducted into the College Football Hall of Fame in 2002.

35. I was one of a handful of players to play in the AFL without any college experience. As a defensive end in 1960 and '61, I played against my New York Titan brother (see question 36).

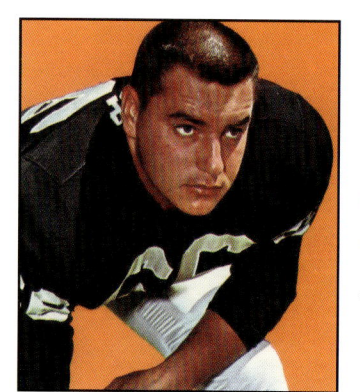

36. I played for the Eagles in the NFL and the Titans, Raiders, and Bills in the AFL. I also played against my brother in '60 and '61 and was an all-league split end from '63 through '66.

37. Fans were skeptical of my ability when I was traded for a Heisman Trophy winner, but I earned my keep as an outstanding lineman for six years with Houston. I was the only Sioux Indian to play in the AFL.

Faces of the Game

38. I was one of two Houston rookie receivers in 1968 and ranked third on the team in catches and caught 4 touchdowns. I played college ball at Purdue.

_____

39. By gaining 77 yards on 11 carries, including a 19-yard romp on the game-winning drive in the second overtime, I was named MVP of the 1962 AFL Championship game.

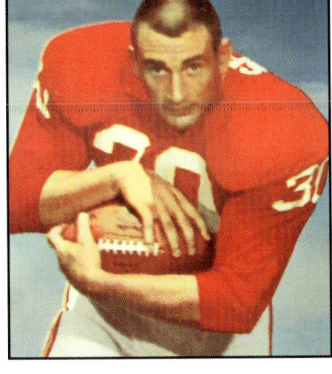

_____

40. The other tackle on my team may have gotten more notoriety and All-Time AFL team status. But I was one of only 19 players to participate in all 10 years of the league's existence, and played in all but one of the AFL's 140 league games.

_____

41. I was the AFL's answer to Paul Hornung as its "Glamour Boy" and was the 1963 AFL Championship game MVP for gaining 206 yards rushing and another 123 yards catching 7 passes.

_____

42. In the pass-happy AFL, I was the least known of the Titan receivers. Playing tight end from 1960 to 1963, I caught a total of 35 passes for 8 touchdowns.

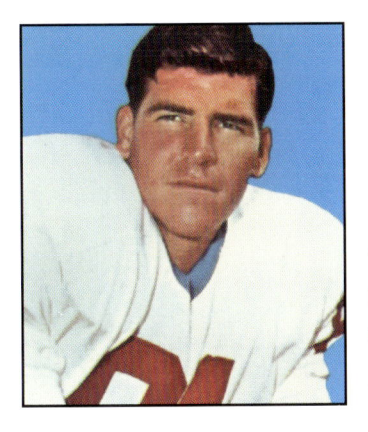

_____

43. I hold the record for most successful field goals in one season at 34— and did it twice. I also have the record for kicking field goals in the most consecutive games (18) and most field goals in one game (6).

_____

44. Although I played for the Houston Oilers from 1961 to 1966 I was probably the least known of their pass catchers. I caught 5 passes in the famous 1962 double-overtime Championship game.

_____

407

Remember the AFL

45. I played in the first AFL game, kicked an extra point, and also returned a punt 76 yards for a touchdown. I led the league in scoring twice, and once kicked a 53-yard field goal. As a triple threat, I could kick, run, and catch passes.

_____

46. I was a double-duty kicker for San Diego in 1968 and 1969, punting and kicking field goals. My 44.9 yards per punt led the league in 1969.

_____

47. I am the fourth-leading rusher in AFL history and also one of only two backs to lead the league in rushing twice and one of only four runners to gain over 200 yards in an AFL game.

_____

48. I was one of a long line of outstanding runners to come out of Syracuse—following Jim Brown, Ernie Davis, Jim Nance, and preceding Larry Csonka.

_____

49. The AFL had many like me—one-year wonders. In my year I played with the 1-12-1 Bills. But I got cut in '69, probably so O.J. Simpson, the rookie, could have his favorite number that was already mine when he arrived.

_____

50. In 1955 I played defensive back for the San Francisco 49ers and am the only player to ever pinch-hit for Hall-of-Fame baseball hero Ted Williams. I also pinch-hit for Red Sox legend Carl Yastremski and for Roger Maris. After retiring from major league baseball in 1965, I was an assistant GM for the Broncos in 1966.

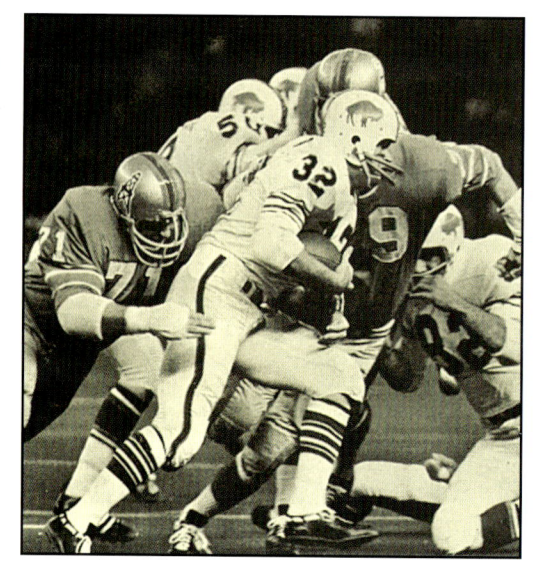

_____

Faces of the Game

51. This card had to be included somehow just because it is such a unique pose. It is of Gene Cockrell, a tackle from Hardin-Simmons University and the 1960 NY Titans. Who was his Hardin-Simmons teammate that led the Titans in rushing in their first season?

_____

From 1966 through 1969 Joe Namath had three standout receivers, "The Texas Trio," all of whom hailed from and played college football in Texas,

52. The tight end was from the University of Texas:

_____

53. The flanker was from Texas Southern:

_____

54. The split end was from the University of Texas:

_____

55. A member of the 1966 National Champion Notre Dame team as a defensive tackle, I was drafted by the Broncos in 1967 and had immediate impact as a defensive starter.

_____

56. As Shakespeare's favorite pass receiver, I caught 110 passes for the Patriots from 1962 through 1967.

_____

57. I led the league in interceptions with 11 in 1962, but more people know my younger brother for coaching the NBA Lakers and coining the phrase "3-peat."

_____

58. From 1960-1967, I was the backfield partner for the Bills with Cookie, Billy Joe, and Bobby Burnett.

409

Remember the AFL

59. I wrote *Confessions of a Dirty Ballplayer* about my career with the NFL Colts, Steelers, Redskins, and the AFL Jets. I intercepted a pass in Super Bowl III when we beat my former NFL team.

_____

60. I was a linebacker for the Chargers in 1960 and the Patriots in 1961 and '62. In 1966, I became the first African-American to be hired as a coach in the AFL when Mike Holovak appointed me linebacker coach.

_____

61. As a rookie in 1968 I was seventh in rushing and tenth in pass receiving, the only player to crack the top ten in both categories. In 1969, I scored more rushing touchdowns (9) than anyone else.

_____

62. Although I was there from beginning to end, I sat out the entire 1962 season with tuberculosis, disqualifying me as one of the "19 Originals" who played every year of the AFL. I threw touchdown passes with Oakland, Buffalo, and Kansas City.

_____

Hugh "Bones" Taylor was an outstanding NFL split end in the late forties and early fifties with the Washington Redskins. He is shown here with six of his star Houston Oiler receivers in 1965. From left to right, bottom to top, can you name them?

63. (#20, bottom left)
_____

64. (#28, bottom right)
_____

65. (#83, top left)
_____

66. (#26, top, second from left)
_____

67. (#81, top, third from left)
_____

68. (#87, top, far right)
_____

Faces of the Game

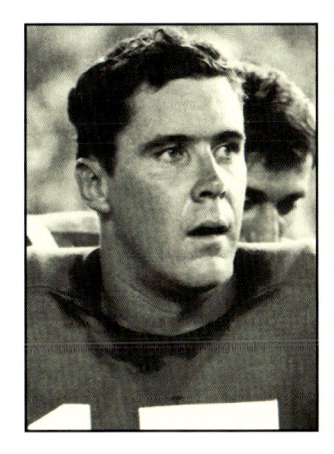

69. I got my fifteen minutes of fame when I was named the 1965 starting quarterback for the Jets but was replaced later in the year by rookie Joe Namath. Later in my career I was a starter for the Boston Patriots after I was traded for Babe Parilli.

_____

70. In 1967 I was the best first-year receiver in the AFL, catching a rookie-record 67 passes and finishing third in the league in pass receiving.

_____

After the Chargers won their first and only AFL Championship in 1963, these seven all-stars took a break for some cameo photos. Who are these seven AFL champs?

71. (#83) _____
72. (#74) _____
73. (#56) _____
74. (#86) _____
75. (#88) _____
76. (#22) _____
77. (#77) _____

During the AFL's last three years there was no fiercer rivalry than the one between the Kansas City Chiefs and Oakland Raiders. They met on the gridiron twenty-two times over ten years, with each team winning eleven of them. The following pages present some of the players who made the rivalry so great.

411

Remember the AFL

78. As a rookie in 1968 I led the league in kick returns and was second in punt returns, scoring touchdowns on two of them.

_____

79. One of two Raiders to make the All-Time AFL team at cornerback, I was the first bump-and-run pass defender.

_____

80. As a fullback I was one of the best at catching passes out of the backfield or just blasting for four yards off tackle.

_____

81 After Super Bowl II, the Raiders knew they needed more speed in the backfield. In 1968 they picked me off the University of Utah campus in the college draft.

_____

82. In 1967, I was named an all-league guard as a rookie. I was selected again in 1968 and 1969.

_____

83. If you were a Kansas City fan, my face stood for everything sinister. Called El Grande Gringo by some, I was the Snidley Whiplash of the AFL and probably the most hated Oakland Raider east of the Bay area. But if you were a Raider supporter, you loved me for those very same reasons.

_____

412

Faces of the Game

84. My given name is Junias, and I played college football at Grambling. I anchored the middle of a vaunted defensive front four and was an all-league tackle from 1966 to 1969.

_____

Known for our quickness, hard-hitting style, and versatility, our trio was arguably the best linebacking group in league history. Two of us were affectionately dubbed the "Salt and Pepper" linebackers. The other was just plain great!

Left to right:

85. _____

86. _____

87. _____

88. A Texan from SMU, I am an All-Time AFL defensive end and was an all-league selection in 1962, '64, '65, and '66.

_____

89. It was war in the Chiefs vs. Raiders trenches. My job on the KC line was to hold off big Ben Davidson.

_____

90. A member of the AFL All-Time Team, I anchored the KC line that protected Len Dawson in the pocket and opened holes for Mike Garrett, Robert Holmes, and company.

_____

413

2

36

12

50

52-54

28

BOSTON

23

56

82

26

42

11

HOUSTON

61

18

19

JACOBS **linebacker**

SAM GRUNIESEN
SAN DIEGO CHARGERS GUARD

By the Numbers

As the new kid on the football block, the AFL tried to win fans by giving them something different. Pass-dominated offenses, 2-point conversions, and player names on the backs of jerseys are innovations brought about by the American Football League.

With television reporters free to roam the sidelines, fans became familiar with the players up close like never before. The Fleer gum company produced the first set of AFL trading cards in 1960 and continued production until 1964 when Topps took over the AFL rights. From the beginning, the league had a youthful appeal and young fans collected AFL cards with a passion.

As they became more familiar, players numbers also became their calling cards. There was Paul Lowe's 23 speeding down the sidelines on a breakaway run and Lance Alworth's 19 leaping above a defender to catch a touchdown pass. Jim Otto's trademark was his 00, and Ernie Ladd's 99 took jersey numbers to the limit in Kansas City. There was Charlie Tolar's 44 plowing up the middle for a first down, Buck Buchanan's 86 smothering a quarterback, and there was no other 12 that mattered besides the one on Joe Willie's shirt.

The players' numbers and profiles were part of the AFL's persona. And as the quality of their game grew each week in every season, so did the legend of the American Football League.

WHICH AFL PLAYER WORE THE NUMBER OF EACH QUESTION?

00. He is Mr. AFL—and made every all-league team for his ten AFL years. _____

1. They called this KC kick return specialist "Super Gnat" for his diminutive size. He has the longest kickoff return in AFL history, 106 yards. _____

2. He chose this number when he was traded to Denver in 1965 because he said he was going to be "one better" than the player he was traded for, who wore number 3. _____

3. The Norwegian skier whose soccer-style kicking made him a sure thing from almost anywhere on his side of midfield. _____

5. He had a peculiar first name, but he was second in scoring in 1966 by hitting on 41 of 42 extra points and 19 of 38 field goal attempts for Buffalo in the post-Gogolak year. In '67 for Miami, he made 18 of 18 extra points and 7 of 12 field goal attempts. Then he was gone. _____

6. This speedster from the University of Houston was the second-leading receiver for the expansion Bengals in '68 but got his number 6 in Kansas City in '69 after being traded for kicker Horst Muhlmann. _____

7. His Heisman-winning career at Notre Dame out shone his AFL career that saw him on several AFL rosters after signing with the Jets for $200,000 in 1965. _____

Remember the AFL

9. The two-time All-Star game MVP wore this number on his second go around with the Chargers in 1968 because his old number belonged to someone else. _____

10. While he did not start Super Bowl IV at quarterback, he did throw half of Kansas City's passes in 1969. _____

11. This USC stalwart saw little action as a KC quarterback prior to leading the Oilers out of the basement and into the championship game in 1967. _____

12. This playboy was Suzie Storm's boyfriend and advertised pantyhose on TV. _____

13. In college he threw passes to Fred Biletnikoff for Florida State, and in the AFL he threw to Lance Alworth and then to Floyd Little. _____

14. He has one more major league baseball at bat and two more innings played than Moonlight Graham, catching in one game for the Detroit Tigers in 1957. He then punted for the Patriots from 1961-1966 while also throwing 12 touchdown passes. _____

15. He is one of many who rode the Denver quarterback merry-go-round. His last name is Choboian. What is his first name? _____

16. An uneventful career in Pittsburgh and Cleveland led him to ask for his release from the NFL so he could quarterback in Dallas. _____

17. In 1965 he was the Jets starting quarterback until a rookie replaced him. He later moved to Boston where he became starter again and played in the last AFL All-Star game. _____

18. This Arizona swifty played on the expansion Bengals and gained Rookie of the Year honors for his outstanding running. _____

19. This is the first AFLer to make the Pro Football Hall of Fame _____

20. An outstanding cornerback for Houston, he led the league in interceptions in 1967, returning 3 of them for touchdowns. _____

21. An All-American quarterback out of Kansas, he led the AFL in passing in 1965 and played in the 1963, '64, and '65 championship games. _____

22. A rookie in 1968, he lead the Bills in rushing despite being "Mini." _____

23. The 49ers didn't want him so he moved down the coast and led the AFL in rushing in 1965. He is the second-leading ground gainer in AFL history. _____

24. A starter for the Titans in 1960 and '61, this BYU safety played for Boston from 1962 to 1966 after being traded for backup quarterback Butch Songin. _____

25. The best wide receiver in Kansas City not named Otis Taylor from 1966 to 1969, he caught 3 passes in Super Bowl IV. _____

26. A college All-American on offense from Michigan State, he made the All-Time AFL team as a strong safety for the Bills. He was all-league in 1965, '66, and '67. _____

By the Numbers

27. He got an unexpected start in the opening game of 1966 when split end Don Norton was injured in the pregame warmup. Nicknamed "The Ghost" because defenders couldn't find him, he never relinquished his spot after that start. _____

28. The first leading rusher in AFL history, he is better known for his "We will kick to the clock" decision upon winning the coin toss to start the first overtime period in the 1962 championship game. _____

29. He intercepted passes for the team that had his sir name. _____

30. In 1962, '63, and '64, this Bill's last name and his running mate's first name were the same. _____

31. He ran the ball for Al Dorow, Lee Grosscup, Dick Wood, Mike Taliaferro, and Joe Namath as a member of the AFL New York franchise from start to finish. _____

32. This battering-ram running back teamed with Mack Lee Hill to make up the "baby elephant" backfield for KC in 1964. He was the AFL's Rookie of the Year in 1962. _____

33. From 1964 to 1969, W.K. Hicks played defensive back for Houston. What did W.K. stand for? _____

34. As a Boston rookie in 1969, this split end from Florida State caught 6 touchdowns and averaged 26.1 yards per catch, the second-best average in the AFL. _____

35. He averaged over 4 yards a carry for his four AFL years, leading the league in rushing in two of them. _____

36. Cut by the Texans after the 1960 season, he surfaced with Oakland and became the all-time leading rusher in AFL history. _____

37. A very competent second fiddle, he was Boston's second-leading rusher in 1960 and then also number two for Oakland in '61 and '63. Out of action in 1964, he closed out his AFL career with the Raiders in '65. _____

38. He started in Denver, then moved to KC where he was the third back behind Mike Garrett and Robert Holmes as well as being the third back in Hank Stram's "Model T" backfield. _____

39. Another power runner out of Syracuse, he teamed with Jim Kiick in the Miami backfield in '68 and '69. _____

40. An all-league safety in 1964, he also led the league in interceptions that year with 12. He played for the Titans/Jets from 1961 to 1966. _____

41. Rookie of the Year in 1964, he scored Super Bowl III's only Jets touchdown. _____

42. This Buffalo Bill was all-league in 1965, '66, and '69 as a cornerback. His 74-yard punt return for a touchdown in the 1965 AFL Championship game gave the Bills a 14-0 lead. _____

Remember the AFL

43. He was dangerous whenever he touched the ball on kick returns, punts, and especially when he intercepted a pass. His interception in the 1968 championship would have gone all the way had Joe Namath not stopped him at the 5 yard line. _____

44. They called this Bills receiver "Golden Wheels" for his spectacular speed. _____

45. Always among the league leaders in kickoff and punt returns, this Charger was also a deft cornerback and safety. He led the league in punt returns in 1965 and '66 and returned a kickoff 90 yards for a touchdown in the 1967 All-Star game. He is the all-time AFL leader in most punts returned and most punt return yards, and his 95-yard return is the longest in AFL history. Known as "Speedy," what was his real first name? _____

46. A safety out of Prairie View, this Chief played in the AFL from 1967 to 1969, teaming with Johnny Robinson, Emmitt Thomas, and Jim Marsalis to give Kansas City unparalleled pass coverage. _____

47. An all-league cornerback in 1967, he was co-author of the "bump-and-run" style of pass defense with Willie Brown in Oakland. _____

48. He joined the Jets in 1965 out of North Carolina A&T and specialized as an extra defensive back for New York. While Randy Beverly, Johnny Sample, and Dick Hudson were intercepting Baltimore passes in Super Bowl III, Bill Baird and this player were also hawking Colt receivers. _____

49. While teaming with Dick Westmoreland in Miami as he did in San Diego, this defensive back led the AFL in interception yards returned in Miami's first season with 198 yards on 5 interceptions, 70 of them on a return for a touchdown. _____

MATCH THE PLAYER WITH HIS 50s NUMBER

50. _____	An all-league middle linebacker as a rookie in '61	A.	Tom Addison
51. _____	Was the salt part of the "Salt and Pepper" linebackers	B.	Frank Buncom
52. _____	Oilers linebacker from Grambling	C.	Bob Johnson
53. _____	'60, '63, '64 all-league outside linebacker	D.	Chuck Allen
54. _____	First player drafted in the 1968 AFL draft	E.	Hubert Bobo
55. _____	USC All-American passed away in 1969 while playing with Cincinnati	F.	Emil Karas
		G.	Larry Kaminski
56. _____	All-star linebacker starter for the West from 1962 to 1964	H.	Jim Lynch
57. _____	Fullback at Ohio State/linebacker for Chargers and Titans	I.	Garland Boyette
58. _____	Starting outside linebacker for expansion Bengals	J.	Al Beauchamp
59. _____	Denver center from 1966 to 1969		

By the Numbers

MATCH THE PLAYER WITH HIS 60s NUMBER

60. _____	Stand-out guard for Patriots from 1964 to 1969	A. Billy Neighbors
61. _____	All-league guard 1962 thru 1967, played in Super Bowl III	B. Bob Talamin
62. _____	Super Bowl III middle linebacker for Jets	C. Sherrill Headrick
63. _____	Played eight years as a starting guard in Boston and Miami	D. Billy Shaw
64. _____	One third of a linebacking trio that set a longevity record	E. Len St. Jean
65. _____	The center on the line with Ron Mix and Walt Sweeney	F. Harry Jacobs
66. _____	Stand-out Bill is all-time AFL guard and four-time all-league	G. Dave Herman
67. _____	Played between Randy Rasmussen and Pete Lammons in 1968	H. Al Atkinson
68. _____	Special teamer and defensive tackle in San Diego in 1968-'69	I. Sam Gruneisen
69. _____	All-league linebacker 1960-'62, played 1968 with Cincinnati	J. Bob Briggs

WHICH OF THESE AFL PLAYERS DID NOT WEAR THE 70s NUMBER LISTED IN FRONT OF HIS NAME?

70. Al Jamison, Houston; Tom Sestak, Buffalo; Glen Ray Hines, Houston; Gene Cockrell, New York; Scott Appleton, Houston

71. Sherman Plunkett, New York; Ed Budde, Kansas City; Harry Schuh, Oakland; Don Oakes, Boston; Mack Yoho, Buffalo

72. Larry Eisenhower, Boston; Jerry Sturm, Denver; Ron McDole, Buffalo; Paul Rochester, New York; Dudley Meredith, Buffalo

73. Manny Fernandez, Miami; Billy Neighbors, Boston; Dave Hill, Kansas City; Norm Evans, Miami; Pat Matson, Cincinnati

74. Mike Reid, Cincinnati; Ron Mix, San Diego; Nick Mumley, New York; Winston Hill, New York; Tom Keating, Oakland

75. Don Floyd, Houston; Bob Svihus, Oakland; Jerry Mays, Kansas City; Ernie Wright, San Diego; Eldon Danenhauer, Denver

76. Mo Moorman, Kansas City; Dan Birdwell, Oakland; Walt Suggs, Houston; Jim Griffin, Cincinnati; Charlie Long, Boston

77. Jim Tyrer, Kansas City; Ernie Ladd, San Diego; Rich Michael, Houston; Stew Barber, Buffalo; Gordy Holz, Denver

78. Pat Holmes, Houston; Bobby Bell, Kansas City; Jim Dunaway, Buffalo; Walt Sweeney, San Diego; Art Shell, Oakland

79. Orville Trask, Houston; Jim Hunt, Boston; George Gross, San Diego; Pete Duranko, Denver; Bob Reisnyder, New York

Remember the AFL

BY THE BIG NUMBERS

80. This big man was the least known of the Super Bowl-winning Jets' front four. _____

81. He was the vertical threat of Oakland's "strike from anywhere" offense and helped gain Daryle Lamonica his "Mad Bomber" moniker. _____

82. A rookie tight end from Notre Dame in 1965, he caught 102 passes through 1968. Then in 1969 he was moved to offensive tackle to block for O.J. Simpson. _____

83. This big guy was all-league at defensive end in 1967, and he earned himself a bit part on a short-lived TV sitcom based on Jim Bouton's book *Ball Four*. His handlebar mustache was like a second AFL trademark. _____

84. This KC tight end is on the AFL All-Time team and was all-league in 1963, '64, and '66. _____

85. This middle linebacker for Boston and Miami is on the AFL All-Time team. _____

86. He was the AFL Rookie of the Year in 1961 and an all-league defensive end in 1961, '63, '64, and '65, but he was left unprotected by his team when the league expanded and was chosen by the Dolphins for the 1966 season, his last. _____

87. He is the all-time leading AFL receiver. _____

88. He led the Chargers in catches in '62 with 48 and had a '60-'62 total of 120. A Charger from 1960 to 1966, he caught a touchdown pass in the first AFL All-Star game. _____

89. The Boston Patriots consistently had one the best front fours in either league. Houston Antwine made the AFL All-Time team as a defensive tackle, and Jim "Pickles" Hunt was as strong as a bull at the other tackle. Larry Eisenhower made all-league at defensive end in '63, '64, and '66. The fourth member of the line was this 6'4" defensive end from Holy Cross who was a perennial Eastern Division all-star. _____

90. An All-American from Michigan State, he was an outstanding outside linebacker and one of only two Rookie of the Year winners to play defense. He is on the AFL All-Time team. _____

99. He was the first to push the envelope and venture beyond the 80s in jersey numbers. After outstanding years in San Diego, he played for Houston and Kansas City. In the off season he was a feared professional wrestler. _____

For the Record

The AFL's struggle for exposure, to a large extent, was satisfied by ABC-TV and later NBC's weekly game coverage. In most cases, the AFL had a Sunday double header, which allowed viewers who had just finished watching their local NFL game to extend their weekend of football by tuning in to the AFL's second game—usually from San Diego, Oakland, or Denver. But gaining respect and acceptance, and even coverage in the newspapers and magazines was difficult. In the early years, the preseason magazines that covered the pros and created interest always put the high-profile NFL players and teams on their covers.

Sports Illustrated, the icon of sports magazines, covered the AFL, but only sporadically on the inside, and then only in black and white, not the featured color layouts the NFL received. The magazine did not recognize the AFL on its cover for most of the first four years of the league's play. It wasn't until December of 1963 that San Diego quarterback Tobin Rote and halfback Paul Lowe broke the ice and appeared on the cover that predicted "A Coming World Series AFL vs. NFL." By that time, the NFL had been on the cover seventeen times since the American Football League began.

In 1964 the first solo AFL player to grace the cover appeared—young Houston quarterback Don Trull. In 1965 the Broadway Joe cover turned many an inquisitive head toward the league. Later that year, San Diego flanker Lance Alworth appeared on the cover, diving to catch a pass. It is one of the best covers in the magazine's history. With every *Sports Illustrated* cover came more exposure, more followers, more of an audience, especially young ones.

The expansion Dolphins rookie linebacker Frank Emanuel hit the *SI* cover on a Miami beach in full uniform during the summer of 1966. And then Namath appeared for a second time the same year. The next-to-last issue of '66 featured the AFL's third appearance of the year—Boston fullback Jim Nance busting through the Buffalo Bills defensive line.

Then *SI* threw a cover shutout at the league in 1967, and it wasn't until the first issue of 1968 that an AFL team was back on the front. Oakland's Hewritt Dixon split the cover with Packer Chuck Mercein, creating interest for Super Bowl II. Legendary coach Paul Brown of the expansion Cincinnati Bengals also appeared on a cover in the summer of 1968.

Sports Illustrated

A COMING WORLD SERIES AFL vs. NFL

SAN DIEGO'S ROTE HANDS OFF TO LOWE

For the Record

On December 9, 1968, Joe Namath appeared for his third *SI* cover, which included a most incredible story titled "A Champagne Party for Joe and Weeb," by Edwin Shrake. In his story, Shrake, writing a letter to a mythical friend overseas, describes how the Jets beat the Raiders in the AFL Championship game and then won the Super Bowl over the Colts. The story appeared more than a month before the game—and weeks before the playoff picture was even complete. On January 20, 1969, with Namath's guarantee and Shrake's prediction come true, the cover of Super Bowl III's victory appeared with Namath on it again.

The next time the AFL appeared on the front of *Sports Illustrated*, Joe took the spot again—this time weeping on the June 16, 1969, cover as he announced his retirement from football rather than give in to Commissioner Pete Rozelle's order to sell his interest in a New York nightclub that was allegedly frequented by gamblers. Eight weeks later, the unretired Namath again claimed the *SI* cover, throwing a pass in the traditional college all-star game from Chicago.

Heisman Trophy-winning rookie O.J. Simpson was the next AFLer to make the *SI* cover. It was the first look at O.J. in a Bills uniform and had him wearing an unfamiliar number 36 in a preseason game against the Lions. Four weeks later, Jets kicker Jim Turner presented proof positive that the AFL had arrived in the heart and mind of *Sports Illustrated* when he showed up on the cover of the annual Pro Football Preview issue—the first time the AFL was given that distinction.

The last two AFL/*SI* covers were both graced by Len Dawson and the Kansas City Chiefs. First on November 24, 1969, showing the Kansas City huddle as they "Painted New York Red" in a playoff game at Shea Stadium and for the last time on January 19, 1970, following their 23-7 win over the Minnesota Vikings in Super Bowl IV. In all, the AFL appeared on the front of *Sports Illustrated* seventeen times in the AFL's ten years. Joe Namath accounted for six.

For the record—the final *SI* cover score over the AFL's historic decade reads: NFL 55, AFL 17! On the following pages, you'll find questions about AFL records that were established between 1960-1969.

------

1. What Houston Oilers quarterback holds the record for longest TD pass (98 yards)? _____
2. Who caught the longest touchdown pass in AFL history (98 yards)? _____
3. Don Maynard caught the most touchdown passes in AFL history. How many did he catch? _____
   A. 90   B. 84   C. 75   D. 66   E. 57
4. In 1969, New York punter Steve O'Neal booted one into the thin air of Denver's Mile High Stadium that set an AFL record. How far did it travel? _____
   A. 98yds.   B. 95yds.   C. 87 yds.   D. 84 yds.
5. The two biggest days passing in AFL history (464 and 457 yards) both occurred in 1961 and both by different Houston Oilers quarterbacks. Who were they? _____ and _____

Remember the AFL

6. George Blanda kicked the longest field goal in AFL history. How long was it? _____

7. Three players in AFL history caught double-digit passes for over 200 yards twice. Who were they? _____, _____ and _____

8. He is the all-time leading pass interceptor in AFL history, playing for two AFL teams from the Western Division. _____

9. This San Diego and Buffalo fullback holds the single-season record for yards gained per carry (with a minimum number of carries to qualify) at 6.45. _____

10. As a kicker and flanker for ten years, he is the only AFL player to score 1,000 points for his AFL career. _____

11. The record for most receptions in one game is 13, held by four players. What Houston halfback is the only non flanker or split end of the four? _____

12. In 1963, this fullback set an AFL record for yards gained in one game with 243. _____

13. The most rushing touchdowns in one season is 13 held by these two AFL rushing champions. Both accomplished this feat in 1962. _____ and _____

14. Which three runners had the highest lifetime yards-per-carry average in the AFL at 4.87, 4.50, 4.46?
    1. _____ 2. _____ 3. _____
    A. Billy Cannon   B. Cookie Gilchrist   C. Paul Lowe   D. Clem Daniels   E. Jim Nance
    F. Keith Lincoln   G. Paul Robinson

15. Who threw more passes (3,055) than any other AFL quarterback? _____
    A. Jack Kemp   B. George Blanda   C. John Hadl   D. Len Dawson

16. In 1967 three players tied for the league lead in interceptions. Which of the following was not part of that threesome? _____
    A. Willie Brown   B. Miller Farr   C. Tom Janik   D. Dick Westmorland

17. Denver, Kansas City, Boston, and Cincinnati all share the record for fewest passes completed by a team in one game. How many did they complete? _____
    A. 10   B. 7   C. 5   D. 2

18. The Houston Oilers hold the AFL record (set in 1964) for the most passes completed in one game. How many did they complete? _____
    A. 46   B. 42   C. 37   D. 35

19. Only four players led the AFL in receiving through the ten years. Which of the following did not. _____
    A. Lance Alworth   B. Don Maynard   C. Lionel Taylor   D. Charlie Hennigan   E. George Sauer

For the Record

20. The AFL's aerial circus of the early years changed drastically over the final three seasons. During that time, defense began playing a bigger part in the outcome of games. Which two teams were the only ones to hold their opponents to less than 200 points from 1967 to 1969?
    _____ and _____
    A. Houston Oilers   B. Oakland Raiders   C. Kansas City Chiefs   D. New York Jets

21. The AFL record for yards gained rushing for a season is 1,458 set by this runner. _____
    A. Jim Nance   B. Clem Daniels   C. Cookie Gilchrist   D. Paul Lowe

22. Who holds the AFL's record for longest run from scrimmage—91 yards for a touchdown? _____
    A. Larry Garron   B. Paul Lowe   C. Paul Robinson   D. Sid Blanks   E. Warren McVea   F. Charlie Smith

23. Which two of the following records does George Blanda not hold? _____
    A. Most passing attempts for a season (505)
    B. Most passing attempts for a game (68)
    C. Most consecutive pass completions (15)
    D. Most touchdowns in a game (7)
    E. Most touchdowns in a season (36)
    F. Most touchdowns lifetime (182)

24. Who holds the AFL record for most consecutive games catching a pass (96)? _____
    A. Lance Alworth   B. Don Maynard   C. Lionel Taylor   D. Charlie Hennigan

25. Two players share the AFL record for longest return of an intercepted pass (100 yards) for a touchdown. Who are they? _____
    A. George Atkinson   D. Butch Byrd   B. Speedy Duncan   E. Goldie Sellers   C. Miller Farr   F. Tom Janik

26. The longest punt return in AFL history was a 95-yard touchdown and occurred on November 24, 1968. Who was the returner? _____
    A. Nolan Smith   B. Warren McVea   C. Speedy Duncan   D. George Atkinson   E. Zeke Moore

27. What kicker holds the AFL accuracy record for highest percentage lifetime (70.3)? _____
    A. Gino Cappelletti   B. Pete Gogolak   C. Jim Turner   D. Jan Stenerud

28. Which two teams hold the record for longest streak without losing a game in AFL history at 15?
    _____ and _____
    A. Boston   B. Buffalo   C. Cincinnati   D. Houston   E. Denver   F. Dallas/Kansas City
    G. Oakland   H. LA/San Diego   I. New York   J. Miami

29. What team holds the AFL record for points scored in one game (59)? _____
    A. Boston   B. Cincinnati   C. Denver   D. New York   E. Dallas/Kansas City   F. Oakland   G. Houston
    H. Los Angeles/San Diego   I. Miami   J. Buffalo

30. What team holds the AFL record for most interceptions in a season (49)? _____
    A. Boston   B. Cincinnati   C. Dallas/Kansas City   D. Oakland   E. Buffalo   F. Denver
    G. Miami   H. Los Angeles/San Diego   I. New York   J. Houston

Remember the AFL

MATCH EACH PLAYER WITH THE PLAYER(S) HE WAS TRADED FOR

31. Babe Parilli (QB) traded from Boston to the Jets for _____ in 1968.

32. Keith Lincoln (FB) traded from San Diego to Buffalo for _____ in 1967.

33. Pete Beathard (QB) traded from Kansas City to Houston for _____ in 1967.

34. Willie Brown (DB) traded from Denver to Oakland for _____ in 1967.

35. Ron Burton (FB) traded from Boston to Kansas City for _____ in 1966.

36. Ernie Ladd (DT) left San Diego to sign with Houston. In 1966, the compensation from Houston was _____

37. Bo Roberson (FL) traded from Oakland to Buffalo for _____ in 1966.

38. Daryle Lamonica (QB) traded from Buffalo to Oakland for _____ in 1967.

39. Miller Farr (DB) traded from San Diego to Houston for _____ in 1967.

40. Warren McVea (FL) traded from Cincinnati to Kansas City for _____ in 1969.

41. Cookie Gilchrist (FB) traded from Miami to Denver for _____ in 1967.

42. Jacky Lee (QB) was leased to Denver by Houston for _____ in 1964.

43. Billy Cannon (FB) traded from Houston to Oakland for _____ in 1964.

44. Arch Matsos (LB) traded from Oakland to Denver for _____ in 1966.

45. Cookie Gilchrist (FB) traded from Buffalo to Denver for _____ in 1965.

46. Lionel Taylor (SE) traded from Denver to Oakland for _____ in 1967.

A. Tom Day (DE)

B. Tom Keating (DT)

C. Horst Muhlman (K)

D. Bud McFadin (DT)

E. Billy Joe (FB)

F. Rich "Tombstone" Jackson (DE)

G. Sonny Bishop (G) and Bobby Jackson (FB)

H. Jim Colclough (FL)

I. Ernie Ladd (DT) and Jacky Lee (QB)

J. Willie Frazier (TE)

K. Mike Taliaferro (QB)

L. Art Powell (SE) and Tom Flores (QB)

M. Hewritt Dixon (TE)

N. Jim Fraser (LB/P)

O. Scott Appleton (DT)

P. Sid Blanks (HB) and Larry Carwell (DB) and Charlie Frazier (FL)

47. Leroy Mitchell (DB) traded from Boston to Houston for _____ _____ in 1969.

48. Tobin Rote's (QB) draft rights from Buffalo to San Diego for _____ in 1963.

49. Babe Parilli (QB) and Ronnie Lott (HB) traded from Oakland to Boston for _____ in 1961.

50. John Huarte (QB) traded from the Jets to Boston for _____ in 1966.

Q. Dick Hudson (G)

R. Mickey Slaughter (QB) and Rex Mirich (DT)

S. Dick Christy (HB) and Alan Miller (FB)

T. Abner Haynes (HB)

TRUE OF FALSE

51. T___ or F___ The original colors of the Houston Oilers were going to be brown and red until Bud Adams' wife suggested her favorite color, Columbia blue, be used.

52. T___ or F___ Sid Gillman was forced to step down as head coach of the Chargers midway through the 1969 season due to health problems. A few years later he re-entered the coaching ranks as the head coach of the Houston Oilers.

53. T___ or F___ San Diego flanker Lance Alworth's last career reception was a touchdown pass in the Super Bowl.

54. T___ or F___ San Diego star Paul Lowe ended his career with the Kansas City Chiefs.

55. T___ or F___ Raider DE Ben Davidson played for the Washington Redskins prior to joining the Raiders in the AFL.

56. T___ or F___ After his second go around with the Denver Broncos ended with an injury in the first game of 1967, Cookie Gilchrist went back to Canada to become part owner of the CFL's Ottawa Rough Riders.

57. T___ or F___ Clem Daniels, the AFL's all-time leading rusher, last carried the ball for the San Francisco 49ers in 1968.

58. T___ or F___ Houston Oiler and Oakland Raider quarterback/kicker George Blanda once played for the Baltimore Colts.

59. T___ or F___ Bobby Burnett, the 1967 AFL Rookie of the Year, played for the Broncos in 1969.

60. T___ or F___ Oiler/Raider halfback and tight end Billy Cannon finished his career by catching passes for the Kansas City Chiefs.

Remember the AFL

It's a Wrap

Match the wrapper with the year AFL cards appeared in them.

A

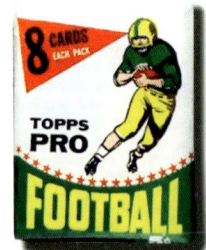

B

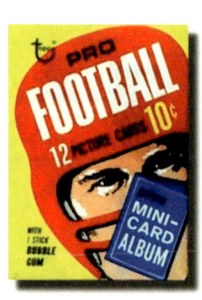

C

D

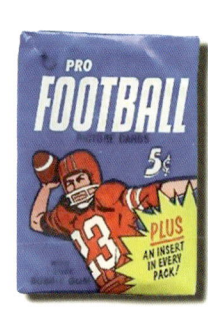

E

F

G

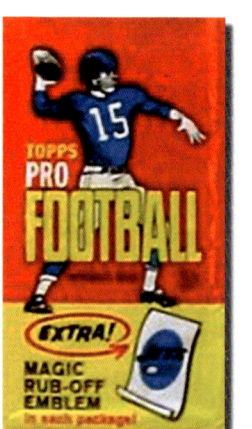

H

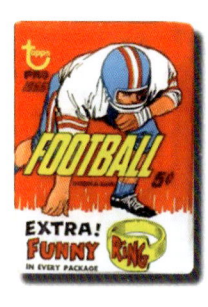

I

J

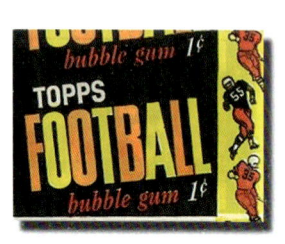

61. 1960 Fleer _____
62. 1961 Fleer _____
63. 1963 Fleer _____
64. 1961 Topps _____
65. 1964 Topps _____

66. 1965 Topps _____
67. 1966 Topps _____
68. 1967 Topps _____
69. 1968 Topps _____
70. 1969 Topps _____

430

Lists to Debate

The games are over, the lights have been dimmed, and the fans have made their way to the exits. Now all that remains of the AFL decade is on-going discussion and debate about our favorites and our not so favorites. We all have our feelings and opinions about certain players and teams, some based on numbers in history books, others formed mostly by our hearts. The lists that appear in this section represent the thoughts, feelings, and knowledge of the author about the late, great American Football League and the players who played the games. They are meant to kinder your spirit and ignite your own passion to create, debate, and discuss lists of your own.

BEST AFL TEAMS

1. **1969 Kansas City Chiefs**
   (11-3, Super Bowl IV Champs)
2. 1967 Oakland Raiders
   (13-1, AFL Champs)
3. 1963 San Diego Chargers
   (15 straight wins, AFL Champs)
4. 1968 New York Jets
   (11-3, Super Bowl III Champs)
5. 1968 Oakland Raiders
   (12-2, West Division Champs)
6. 1968 Kansas City Chiefs
   (12-2, tied for West Division)
7. 1969 Oakland Raiders
   (12-1-1, AFL runner up)
8. 1961 Houston Oilers
   (10-3-1, AFL Champions)
9. 1961 San Diego Chargers
   (12-2, AFL runner up)
10. 1965 San Diego Chargers
    (9-3-2, AFL runner up)

WORST AFL TEAMS

1. 1962 Oakland Raiders
   (1-13, 19 straight losses)
2. 1961 Denver Broncos
   (3-11)
3. 1962 New York Titans
   (5-9, terrible team management)
4. 1963 Denver Broncos
   (2-11-1)
5. 1966 Houston Oilers
   (3-11)
6. 1968 Buffalo Bills
   (2-12-1)
7. 1966 Denver Broncos
   (4-10)
8. 1968 Boston Patriots
   (4-10)
9. 1961 Oakland Raiders
   (2-12)
10. 1964 Denver Broncos
    (2-11-1)

Remember the AFL

HEROES
1. **Lance Alworth**
   (wasn't he everybody's?)
2. **Billy Cannon**
   (the first AFL glamour boy)
3. **Keith Lincoln**
   (the second AFL glamour boy)
4. **Kent McCloughan**
   (loved that bump-and-run defense)
5. **George Blanda**
   (the first big name player)
6. **Charley Hennigan**
   (101 catches in 1964)
7. **Miller Farr**
   (covered receivers like paint on a wall)
8. **Dick Post**
   (every run was an adventure)
9. **Fred Biletnikoff**
   (slow but gutty, "Mr. Glue Fingers")
10. **Joe Namath**
    (the white shoes, the fu Manchu . . . awesome!)

VILLIANS
1. **Fred Williamson**
   (no respect for this cheap-shot artist)
2. **Pete Gogolak**
   (he left us for the NFL)
3. **Ben Davidson**
   (the guy you loved to hate)
4. **Johnny Sample**
   (the mouth that roared, much too often)
5. **Lou Rymkus**
   (tyrant with a temper)
6. **Fletcher Smith**
   (Hammer must have been his hero)
7. **George Atkinson**
   (he was just too good to cheer for)
8. **Buck Buchanan**
   (the Wilt Chamberlain of the AFL)
9. **Art Powell**
   (should have been all world)
10. **Otis Taylor**
    (he always killed you in the clutch)

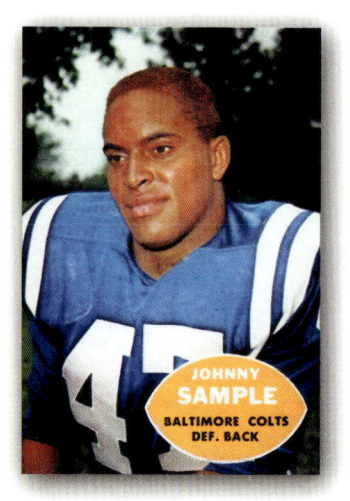

PLAYERS YOU DIDN'T WANT PLAYING AGAINST YOU WHEN THE GAME WAS ON THE LINE (because they were that good!)

1. **Daryle Lamonica**
   ("The Mad Bomber" knew how to do it)
2. **Nolan Smith**
   (don't kick to him, he'll be gone in a flash)
3. **Fred Biletnikoff**
   (crafty patterns and best hands, always seemed to make a clutch catch)
4. **Lance Alworth**
   (a deadly deep threat)
5. **Willie Brown**
   (refused to be beaten, ditto Miller Farr)
6. **Jan Stenerud**
   (could hit from 60 yards away)
7. **Charley Tolar**
   (could knock down castle gates)

432

Lists to Debate

8. **Otis Taylor**
   (had all the tools and could run you over after making a reception)
9. **Bobby Bell**
   (smart, fast, and fierce, simply the best)
10. **George Webster**
    (nearly as good as Bell, and bigger)

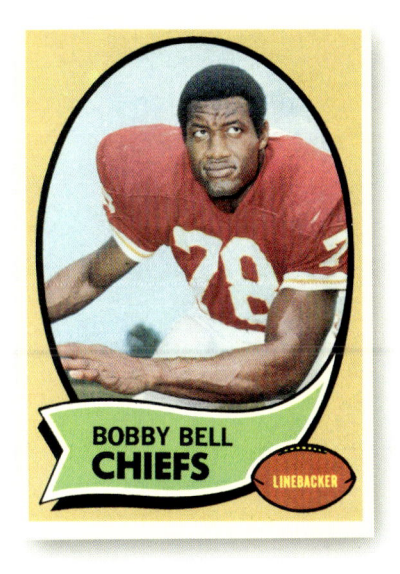

PLAYERS YOU DIDN'T MIND PLAYING AGAINST WHEN THE GAME WAS ON THE LINE (because they rarely hurt you)

1. **Anyone from the Boston Patriot secondary through 1967**
2. **Ed Rutkowski**
   (Bills quarterback in 1968, but in his defense, he was a fourth-string emergency)
3. **The Denver Bronco defense, 1963 and 1966**
4. **Steve Tensi**
   (Broncos quarterback)
5. **George Wilson Jr., Rick Norton, Dick Wood**
   (1966 Dolphin quarterbacks)
6. **The Oakland Raider defense, 1961**
7. **Joe Bellino**
   (Boston Patriots running back)
8. **Don Trull**
   (Oilers/Patriots quarterback)
9. **Tom Sherman**
   (Boston Patriots quarterback)
10. **The Denver Bronco runners 1960-1962**

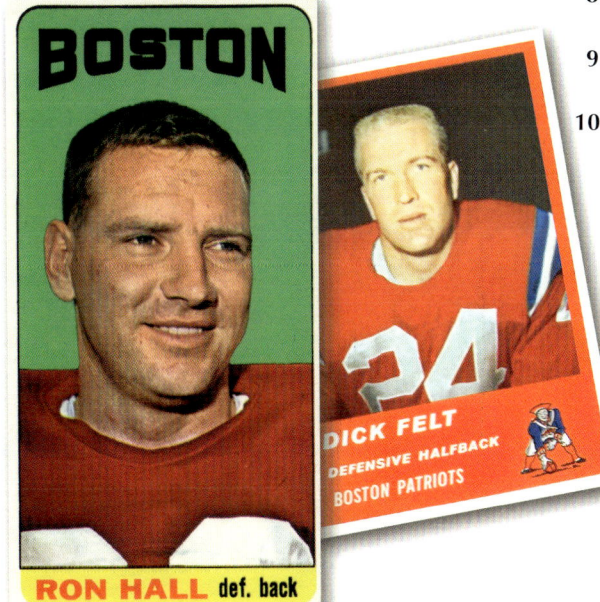

433

Remember the AFL

TOP AFL COACHES

1. **Hank Stram: Dallas Texans/Kansas City Chiefs**
   A master innovator, he won three AFL titles and one of two Super Bowls.
2. **Al Davis: Oakland Raiders**
   He turned the 4-10 Raiders into a 10-4 team and ultimately into a dynasty.
3. **Sid Gillman: San Diego Chargers**
   He was the best offensive coaching mind in the league.
4. **Paul Brown: Cincinnati Bengals** 
   A master organizer, he had the infant Bengals in the playoffs in their third year.
5. **Weeb Ewbank: New York Jets**
   He helped build the Jets into the winner of Super Bowl III.

BOTTOM AFL COACHES

1. **Eddie Erdelatz: Oakland Raiders**
   He lost the first two games of 1961 by scores of 55-0 and 44-0.
2. **Marty Feldman: Oakland Raiders**
   He finished 1-13 in 1962.
3. **Bill Conkright: Oakland Raiders**
   He couldn't right the Raiders' wrongs.
4. **Clive Rush: Boston Patriots**
   He was the AFL's answer to Phil Bengston.
5. **Frank Filchock: Denver Broncos** 
   He was not the man to introduce the wild west to pro football.

BEST UNIFORMS

1. **San Diego Chargers, 1963**
   (bright, colorful, and imaginative) 
2. **Oakland Raiders, 1967-69**
   (exude pride and poise)
3. **Denver Broncos, 1965**
   (colorful and unique)
4. **Kansas City Chiefs, 1969**
   (classic red and white, the red pants highlighted an already timeless uniform)
5. **Houston Oilers, 1967**
   (silver and blue was an exciting change, and the red trim made the '66 version even better)

WORST UNIFORMS

1. **Denver Broncos, 1960**
   (Worst. Pro uniform. Ever)
2. **Buffalo Bills, 1960**
   (a copy of the NFL Lions was an insult to the new league)
3. **Oakland Raiders, 1960**
   (the bland and black)
4. **Denver Broncos, 1967**
   (looked like high school hand-me-downs)
5. **Cincinnati Bengals, 1968**
   (totally unimaginative)

Lists to Debate

BEST HELMETS
1. San Diego Chargers, 1963
2. Houston Oilers, 1967-69
3. Miami Dolphins, 1967-69
4. Oakland Raiders, 1967-69
5. Kansas City Chiefs, 1966-69

WORST HELMETS
1. Buffalo Bills, 1960-61
2. New York Titans, 1960-62
3. Oakland Raiders, 1960-61
4. Denver Broncos, 1960-61
5. Denver Broncos, 1967

UNDERRATED
1. **Dickie Post**
   Halfback, San Diego Chargers
2. **Miller Farr**
   Cornerback, Houston Oilers
3. **Dave Hill**
   Tackle, Kansas City Chiefs
4. **Al Atkinson**
   Linebacker, New York Jets
5. **Wray Carlton**
   Fullback, Buffalo Bills
6. **Dick Christy**
   Halfback, New York Titans
7. **Pat Holmes**
   Defensive tackle, Houston Oilers
8. **Frank Pitts**
   Split end, Kansas City Chiefs
9. **Ernie Wright**
   Tackle, San Diego Chargers
10. **Curtis McClinton**
    Fullback, Dallas Texans

OVERRATED
1. **O.J. Simpson**
   Halfback, Buffalo Bills
2. **Verlon Biggs**
   Defensive end, New York Jets
3. **Don Trull**
   Quarterback, Houston Oilers/Boston Patriots
4. **Frank Emanuel**
   Linebacker, Miami Dolphins
5. **Steve Tensi**
   Quarterback, Denver Broncos
6. **Ernie Ladd**
   Defensive tackle (with the Oilers and Chiefs only)
7. **Jerry Levias**
   Flanker, Houston Oilers
8. **Ron Sellers**
   Flanker, Boston Patriots
9. **Johnny Sample**
   Cornerback, New York Jets
10. **Dewey Warren**
    Quarterback, Cincinnati Bengals

BEST ALL-TIME SPLIT END/FLANKER PAIRINGS
1. **George Sauer**, 75 catches and **Don Maynard**, 71 catches, 2,623 yds. – New York Jets, 1967
2. **Charley Hennigan**, 82 catches and **Bill Groman**, 50 catches, 2,921 yds., 29 TDs – Houston Oilers, 1961
3. **Lance Alworth**, 68 catches and **Gary Garrison**, 50 catches, 2,415 yds., 20 TDs – San Diego Chargers, 1968
4. **Don Maynard**, 72 catches and **Art Powell**, 69 catches, 2,432 yds., 20 TDs – New York Titans, 1960
5. **Fred Biletnikoff**, 61 catches and **Warren Wells**, 53 catches, 2,174 yds. – Oakland Raiders, 1968
6. **George Sauer**, 66 catches and **Don Maynard**, 57 catches, 2,438 yds. – New York Jets, 1968
7. **Otis Taylor**, 58 catches and **Chris Burford**, 58 catches, 2,055 yds., 16 TDs – Kansas City Chiefs, 1966
8. **Art Powell**, 64 catches, and **Don Maynard**, 56 catches, 2,171 yds. – New York Titans, 1962
9. **Lionel Taylor**, 100 catches, and **Al Frazier**, 47 catches – Denver Broncos, 1961
10. **Fred Biletnikoff**, 54 catches, and **Warren Wells**, 47 catches, 26 TDs – Oakland Raiders, 1969

Remember the AFL

BEST ALL-TIME RUNNING BACK TANDEMS
 1. **Paul Lowe**, 1,010 yds., 5.7 avg. and **Keith Lincoln**, 826 yds., 6.4 avg. – San Diego Chargers, 1963
 2. **Cookie Gilchrist**, 1,096 yds., 5.1 avg. and **Wayne Crow**, 589 yds., 5.4 avg. – Buffalo Bills, 1962
 3. **Abner Haynes**, 697 yds., 5.0 avg. and **Mack Lee Hill**, 576 yds. 5.0 avg. – Kansas City Chiefs, 1964
 4. **Dickie Post**, 663 yds., 4.1 avg. and **Brad Hubbert**, 643 yds., 5.5 avg. – San Diego Chargers, 1967
 5. **Abner Haynes**, 1,049 yds., 4.7 avg. and **Curtis McClinton**, 604 yds., 5.4 avg. – Dallas Texans, 1962
 6. **Billy Cannon**, 644 yds., 4.2 avg. and **Dave Smith**, 643 yds., 4.1 avg. – Houston Oilers, 1960
 7. **Bobby Burnett**, 766 yds., 4.1 avg. and **Wray Carlton**, 646 yds., 4.4 avg. – Buffalo Bills, 1966
 8. **Matt Snell**, 763 yds., 4.5 avg. and **Bill Mathis**, 604 yds., 4.1 avg. – New York Jets, 1965
 9. **Mike Garrett**, 732 yds., 4.4 avg. and **Robert Holmes**, 612 yds., 4.1 avg. – Kansas City Chiefs, 1969
 10. **Hoyle Granger** 1,194 yds. 5.1 avg. and **Woody Campbell**, 511 yds., 4.6 avg. – Houston Oilers, 1968

BEST ALL-TIME UNITS
FRONT FOUR
 1. **Larry Eisenhauer, Jim Hunt, Houston Antwine, Bob Dee** – Boston Patriots
 2. **Tom Day, Jim Dunaway, Tom Sestak, Ron McDole** – Buffalo Bills
 3. **Earl Faison, Dick Hudson, Ernie Ladd, Ron Nery** – San Diego Chargers

LINEBACKERS
 1. **Jim Lynch, Willie Lanier, Bobby Bell** – Kansas City Chiefs
 2. **E.J. Holub, Sherrill Headrick, Smokey Stover** – Kansas City Chiefs
 3. **John Tracey, Harry Jacobs, Mike Stratton** – Buffalo Bills

SECONDARY
 1. **Jim Norton, W.K. Hicks, Miller Farr, Ken Houston** – Houston Oilers
 2. **Willie Brown, Kent McCloughan, Roger Bird, Dave Grayson** – Oakland Raiders
 3. **Charlie McNeil, Bob Zeman, George Blair, Dick Harris** – San Diego Chargers

CORNERBACK COMBO
 1. **Willie Brown** and **Kent McCloughan** – Oakland Raiders
 2. **Dick Westmoreland** and **Jim Warren** – Miami Dolphins
 3. **Miller Farr** and **W.K. Hicks** – Houston Oilers

SAFETY COMBO
 1. **Bobby Hunt** and **Johnny Robinson** – Kansas City Chiefs
 2. **Goose Gonsoulin** and **Bob Zeman** – Denver Broncos
 3. **Jim Hudson** and **Bill Baird** – New York Jets

OFFENSIVE LINE
 1. **Jim Tyrer, Mo Moorman, E.J. Holub, Ed Budde, Dave Hill** – Kansas City Chiefs
 2. **Ernie Wright, Gary Kirner, Sam Grunniesen, Walt Sweeney, Ron Mix** – San Diego Chargers
 3. **Winston Hill, Randy Rasmussen, John Schmitt, Bob Talamini, Dave Herman** – New York Jets
 4. **Bob Svihus, Gene Upshaw, Jim Otto, Wayne Hawkins, Harry Schuh** – Oakland Raiders

KICKOFF and PUNT RETURN TANDEM
 1. **Bobby Jancik** and **Freddie Glick** – Houston Oilers
 2. **Goldie Sellers** and **Nemiah Wilson** – Denver Broncos
 3. **Speedy Duncan** and **Kenny Graham** – San Diego Chargers

Lists to Debate

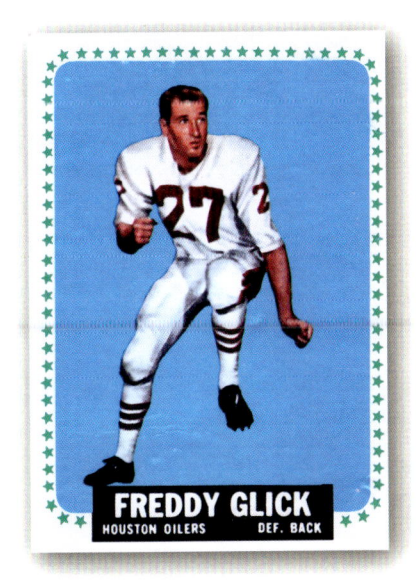

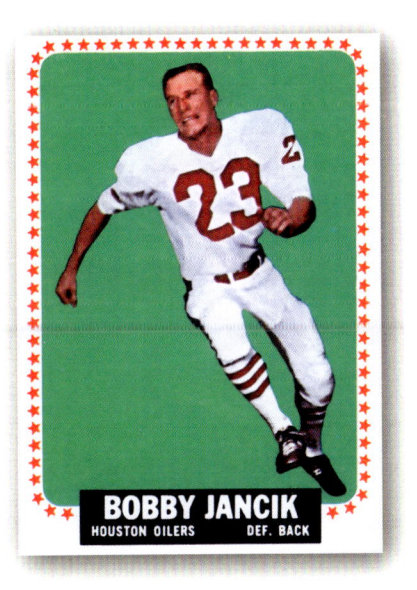

SNAPPER/HOLDER/KICKER
1. **John Schmitt, Babe Parilli, Jim Turner** – New York Jets
2. **E.J. Holub, Len Dawson, Jan Stenerud** – Kansas City Chiefs
3. **Jon Gilliam, Babe Parilli, Gino Cappelletti** – Boston Patriots
4. **Jim Otto, Daryle Lamonica, George Blanda** – Oakland Raiders

ANNOUNCER TEAM
There is only one: Charlie Jones and whomever he worked with. He was the best!

BEST STADIUMS
1. San Diego Stadium
2. Shea Stadium
3. The Orange Bowl
4. Oakland-Alameda County Stadium
5. Rice Stadium

WORST STADIUMS
1. War Memorial Stadium
2. Polo Grounds
3. Kezar Stadium
4. Harvard Stadium
5. Frank Youell Field

BEST SIDELINE/END ZONE MASCOT
1. **The New York Mini-Jet**
   (the green-and-white jet car was driven around the Shea Stadium sideline.)
2. **Flipper**
   (the celebrated dolphin swam around the tank in the Orange Bowl waiting to toss back field goals and extra points kicked into it.)
3. **Kansas City's War Paint—the pony and its rider**
   (the chief would take his touchdown rides with no hands on the reins.)
4. **The Charger Stallion and Knight**
   (it had to be hot in that armor.)
5. **Titans' owner Harry Wismer**
   (he was annoyingly always there, usually paging himself or antagonizing officials.)

Remember the AFL

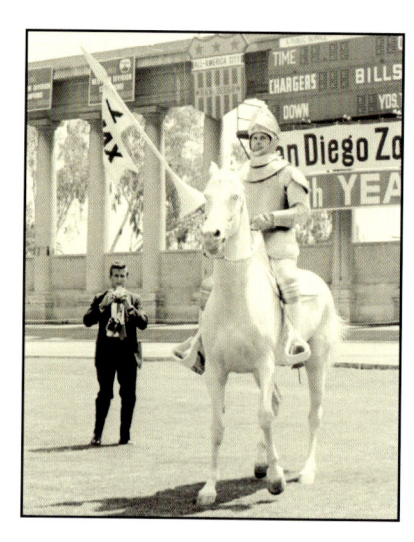

ALL-NAME TEAM
Representing the best and most unique AFL names at each position.

OFFENSE
Remi Prudhomme (Center, Buffalo/Kansas City)
Hogan Wharton (Guard, Houston Oilers)
Leon Dombrowski (Guard, New York Titans)
Sherman Plunkett (Tackle, San Diego Chargers/New York Jets)
Eldon Danenhauer (Tackle, Denver Broncos)
Willard Dewveall (Tight End, Houston Oilers)
Olie Cordill (Split End, San Diego Chargers)
Monte Ledbetter (Flanker, Houston Oilers/Buffalo Bills)
Hoyle Granger (Fullback, Houston Oilers)
Cosmo Iacavazzi (Halfback, New York Jets)
Max Choboian (Quarterback, Denver Broncos)
Americo Sapienza (Punter, New York Titans)

DEFENSE
Mack Yoho (Defensive End, Buffalo Bills)
Hatch Rosdahl (Defensive End, Buffalo Bills/Kansas City Chiefs)
Proverb Jacobs (Defensive Tackle, New York Titans/Oakland Raiders)
Hansen Churchwell (Defensive Tackle, Oakland Raiders)
Hubert Bobo (Linebacker, Los Angeles Chargers/New York Titans)
Wahoo McDaniel (Linebacker, Houston Oilers/Denver Broncos/New York Jets/Miami Dolphins)
Garland Boyette (Linebacker, Houston Oilers)
Ceasar Belser (Defensive Back, Kansas City Chiefs)
Carroll Zaruba (Defensive Back, Dallas Texans)
Booker Edgerson (Defensive Back, Buffalo Bills)
Dainard Paulson (Defensive Back, New York Titans/Jets)
Booth Lusteg (Kicker, Buffalo Bills/Miami Dolphins)
Preston Ridlehuber (Special teams player, Oakland Raiders/Boston Patriots)

HOYLE GRANGER
OILERS

WAHOO McDANIEL
LINEBACKER

DAINARD PAULSON
DEFENSIVE HALFBACK
NEW YORK JETS

DON DANENHAUER tackle

GARLAND BOYETT
OILERS

BOOKER EDGERSON

WILLARD DEWVEAL
HOUSTON OILERS

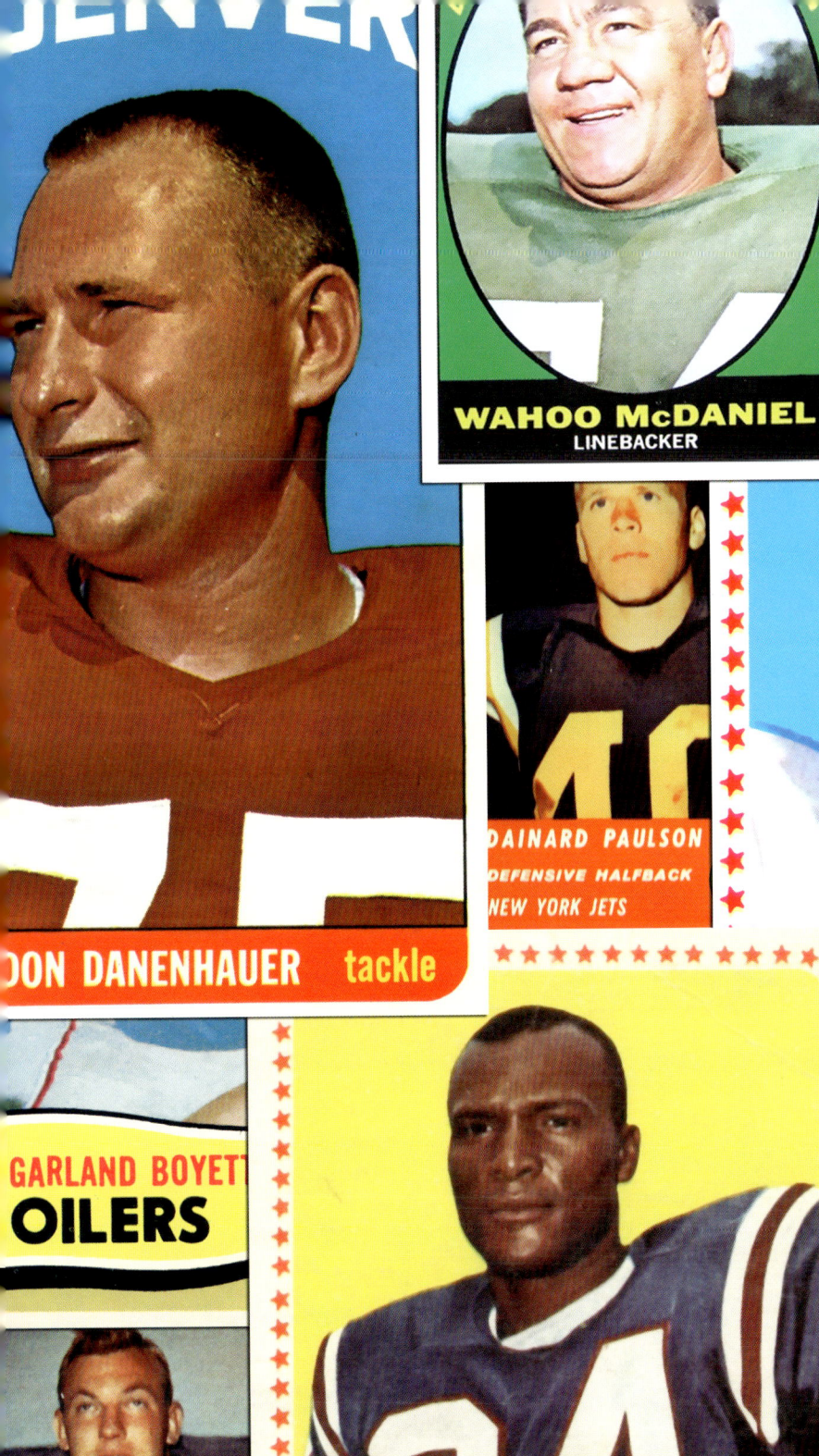

BERT BOBO

MACK YOHO

Remember the AFL

TRIVIA ANSWERS

Not so Foolish
1. A. Sid Gillman
2. G. Lou Saban
3. F. Lou Rymkus
4. E. Buster Ramsey
5. B. Eddie Erdelatz
6. C. Hank Stram
7. H. Frank Filchock
8. D. "Slingin" Sammy Baugh
9. Top row (l-r): A-C-F-B-E-H-G
   Bottom row (l-r): D-I
10. 1. D – Gerhard Schwedes/Syracuse
    2. A – Richie Lucas/Penn State
    3. B – Don Meredith/SMU
    4. H – Roger LeClerc/Trinity
    5. C – Billy Cannon/LSU
    6. E – Monty Stickles/Notre Dame
    7. H – Dale Hackbart/Wisconsin
    8. F – George Izo/Notre Dame
11. Gowdy's was Paul Christman, Buck's was George Ratterman
12. Copper Bowl
13. *Street & Smith College Football* magazine
14. Burt Bell, former Pittsburgh Steelers owner
15. Charlie Flowers of Ole Miss
16. A-8 B-6 C-11 D-2 E-3 F-7 G-1 H-1
    NOTE: *Mile High Stadium did not exist in 1960. It was called Bears Stadium and was later renovated and renamed Mile High Stadium in 1969. The Oilers played in Rice Stadium in 1965, 1966, and 1967 prior to the Astrodome in 1968. The Raiders played the last three home games of 1960 and all of 1961 in Candlestick Park.*
17. Colorado College of the Mines
18. Señor!
19. Joe's Flying Circus
20. South Dakota

The Progress of the Seasons

1960
1. Harvard Stadium, Boston College, Fenway Park
2. The shirts were red and white stripes—the NFL versions were black and white
3. Al Carmichael, Denver Broncos
4. The Chicago Cardinals
5. Denver Broncos
6. Empty seats
7. Tom Harmon, All-American from Michigan—son Mark starred on TV and in movies, daughter Chris appeared with her husband Rick Nelson on *The Adventures of Ozzie and Harriet* in the sixties.
8. Oakland Raiders
9. A. Mike Holovak and Wally Lemm
10. Paul Maguire

1961
11. The office was at 277 Park Avenue—Wismer's apartment. The living room was his office and his bedroom was the ticket office
12. It refers to William F. (Buffalo Bill) Cody
13. The Grocery Bowl
14. C. The white charger stallion influenced Hollywood resident Gerald Courtney's submittal.
15. B. Luther Hayes caught 14 passes, 3 for touchdowns in 1961 for San Diego
16. C. The Seven Pirates

1962
17. Kemp played for the Pittsburgh Steelers and the New York Giants, Raab for the Detroit Lions and Dorow for the Washington Redskins
18. Cookie Gilchrist, who also had interests in other corporate endeavors including drilling for oil and mining copper.
19. A. Miami of Ohio
20. Tom Pennington

1963
21. Los Angeles Chargers
22. George Sauer, New York Jets in 1967
23. Commission Joe Foss postponed all league games on November 24 to morn the assassination of President John F. Kennedy.

1964
24. Cappelletti kicked 6 field goals
25. Keith Kinderman (or Jacque MacKinnon)
26. Jeppeson Stadium, Houston, Texas
27. Gene Heeter

1965
28. Oakland-Alameda County Coliseum '67, and the Gator Bowl in Jacksonville, Florida '68, '69

440

Trivia Answers

29. St. Louis Cardinals
30. The AFL champions (Buffalo) met the league all-stars [this was the only year for this format—all the rest was East vs. West]
31. Ken Herock caught 23 passes as the Raiders tight end in 1964 to finish 5th on the team
32. 1961—the Western Division had three teams with losing records
33. Keith Lincoln

1966

34. 2 more—in 1968 and 1969
35. Dubenion, Bluffton
    L. Taylor, New Mexico Highlands
    Sestak, McNeese State
    Hennigan, NE LA State
    Haynes, N.Texas State
    O. Taylor, Prairie View
    Cheboian, San Fernando State
    Joe, Villanova,
    Moore, Lincoln
    Meredith, Lamar Tech
36. E. Dave Grayson, a cornerback on the All-AFL team was from Oregon

1967

37. Denver Broncos
38. The Sept. 9 game was scheduled for San Diego, while the Oct. 7 game was scheduled for Boston. But the Boston Red Sox were involved in baseball's World Series at Fenway Park, also the home of the Patriots. The game had to be moved, and the teams agreed to play a second game in San Diego.
39. 66
40. A. Emil
41. 1960, 1961, 1964, 1968

1968

42. Guard
43. Bobby Howfield of the Denver Broncos was a soccer player from England
44. Safety Jess Philllips gained 578 yards to lead the Bengals in rushing in 1969
45. Jimmy Hines
46. C. Bill Baird
47. Bake Turner
48. Tom Mitchell
49. Babe Parrilli
50. Greg Cook, chosen by the Cincinnati Bengals

1969

51. The Bachelors III
52. The first-place teams of each division played the second-place teams from the other division in a one-game playoff round to determine who played in the AFL Championship game. This was the first time an AFL Championship game was played by two teams from the same division. Western teams Kansas City and Oakland played for the championship in Oakland.
53. A commemorative patch signifying the AFL's 10 years, at the request of owner Lamar Hunt.
54. C. 697 yards
55. Jeppesen (Houston), Balboa (San Diego), War Memorial (Buffalo), Oakland-Alameda County, Shea (New York)
56. Ray Abruzzese, DB for Buffalo and New York from 1962-1966

Headgear quiz
In what year did each helmet make its debut?

1. 1968	2. 1966	3. 1966
4. 1962	5. 1960	6. 1965
7. 1964	8. 1960	9. 1960
10. 1968	11. 1960	12. 1963
13. 1963	14. 1961	15. 1965
16. 1963	17. 1963	18. 1967
19. 1964	20. 1960*	21. 1962
22. 1967	23. 1960	24. 1960
25. 1966	26. 1960	27. 1962

In the Trenches

1. SMU
2. Oakland
3. George Blanda, Jim Otto, Gino Cappelletti
4. Daryle Lamonica
5. Jim Norton, Houston Oilers
6. Abner Haynes, Dallas
   Earl Faison, San Diego
   Curtis McClinton, Dallas
   Billy Joe, Denver
   Matt Snell, New York
   Joe Namath, New York
   Bobby Burnett, Buffalo
   George Webster, Houston
   Paul Robinson, Cincinnati
   Carl Garrett, Boston
7. Dave Kocourek–Los Angeles, San Diego, Oakland
8. George Blanda and Billy Cannon–Houston and Oakland; Daryle Lamonica–Buffalo and Oakland
9. Austin
10. Danny Thomas

Remember the AFL

11. Flipper tank
12. Oakland
13. Bo Roberson, LA Chargers
14. Carte Blanche
15. Kim Hammond
16. Denver Broncos–gold jerseys
17. Jan Stenerud, Kansas City Chiefs
18. Charlie Waller
19. David
20. Washington Redskins
21. Tucson, Arizona
22. Tri-corner patriot hat
23. Dave Smith
24. Bones Taylor
25. Sammy Baugh
26. Los Angeles Coliseum, Dallas Cotton Bowl, San Francisco Kezar Stadium
27. Fred Arbanas
28. Army
29. Lionel Taylor, Denver Broncos, and Charlie Hennigan, Houston Oilers
30. Señors
31. Brown and Gold
32. Black and Gold
33. Al Davis
34. Cotton Davidson, Dallas Texans
35. Minnesota
36. DT Jess Richardson, Boston Patriots
37. 1967, Daryle Lamonica
38. Pop Ivy and Wally Lemm–St. Louis Cardinals and Houston Oilers
39. George Wilson
40. Oakland Raiders
41. Bill Miller
42. Blue and Silver
43. Ralph Anderson, Los Anglese Chargers
44. Joe Namath, New York Jets–4,007 yards in 1967
45. Mack Lee Hill, Kansas City Chiefs
46. Greg Cook, Cincinnati Bengals
47. Willard Dewveall, Houston Oilers
48. Pete Gogolak, Buffalo Bills
49. Roman Gabriel and John Brodie
50. Villanova
51. Pete Beathard
52. Don Trull and Bob Davis
53. Joe Bellino
54. Billy Cannon 1959, Joe Bellino 1960, John Huarte 1964, Mike Garrett 1965, O.J. Simpson 1968
55. Bob Schwichert, VPI and Cosmo Iaccavazzi, Princeton
56. Buffalo Bills vs. Boston Partiots
57. Clem Daniels
58. Eddie Erdelatz, Oakland Raiders
59. Larry Grantham, Don Maynard, Bill Mathis
60. Tommy Brooker, Dallas Texans
61. Marlin Briscoe, Denver Broncos
62. Atlanta, Georgia
63. San Diego Chargers
64. Len Dawson, Mike Livingston, Jackie Lee, John Huarte, Tom Flores
65. Dallas
66. Jackie Lee
67. Rick Casares
68. Joe Auer
69. Joel Collier
70. Kansas City
71. Lou Saban–Boston Patriots, Buffalo Bills, Denver Broncos
72. Gene Mingo, Denver Broncos
73. Cincinnati
74. Don Maynard, New York Titans/Jets
75. 1. Lionel Taylor, Denver Broncos
    2. Charley Hennigan, Houston Oilers
    3. Lance Alworth, San Diego Chargers
    4. Don Maynard, New York Titans/Jets
    5. Art Powell, New York Jets and Oakland Raiders
    6. Chris Burford, Dallas Texans/Kansas City Chiefs
    7. Elbert Dubenion, Buffalo Bills
    8. Gino Cappelletti, Boston Patriots
76. Bob Johnson, Center, Tennessee
77. Paul Robinson, Cincinnati Bengals
78. Bob Kalsu, Buffalo Bills
79. Jess Phillips, Cincinnati Bengals
80. Rod Sherman, USC, Cincinnati Bengals
81. Dale Livingston, Bengals kicker
82. Dewey Warren of Tennessee
83. Cookie Gilchrist, Billy Joe
84. Bill Bergey
85. Billy Cannon and Hewritt Dixon
86. Oakland Raiders
87. John Stofa
88. Herb Trevenio, George Blair, Keith Lincoln, Ben Agajanian
89. Jack Faulkner, Denver Broncos
90. The Denver Broncos in 1967 wore a blue helmet with a single white stripe
91. 1-E, 2-C, 3-D, 4-B, 5-A
92. New York Jets-winners of that year's Super Bowl III (one of only 3 losses)
93. The Eleven Angry Men
94. Lewis (Bud) McFadin
95. Frank Tripucka, Denver Broncos
96. Jacky Lee
97. Willie Lanier and Jim Lynch, Kansas City Chiefs
98. Curley Culp, Kansas City Chiefs

Trivia Answers

99. Ed Rutkowski, Buffalo Bills-1968
100. Bob Trumpy, Cincinnati Bengals
101. K. C. Jones, Boston Celtics
102. Clyde "Bulldog" Turner, New York Titans, 1962
103. Howard Glenn, New York Titans
104. Stone Johnson, Kansas City Chiefs
105. H. Roe Bartle recruited the Texans and paved the way for their move to Kansas City—his nickname was the "chief." Hunt renamed the Texans as the Chiefs in thanks to and in honor of Bartle.
106. Chet Soda
107. Tobin Rote. He won in 1957 with the NFL Detroit Lions and in 1963 with the San Diego Chargers
108. Sid Gillman, San Diego Chargers; Hank Stram, Dallas Texans
109. Billy Cannon and Johnny Robinson, LSU-1958
110. Buffalo Bill Cody
111. Los Angeles Chargers owner Barron Hilton was starting a credit card business
112. Dallas Texans
113. Miami Dolphins, 1965
114. New York Titans in 1960-1962, renamed Jets in 1963
115. Boston Patriots
116. Oakland Raiders
117. A local undertaker
118. Kezar Stadium, San Francisco—home of the NFL 49ers in 1960 and Candlestick Park home of the major league baseball's San Francisco Giants in 1961
119. Nippert Stadium, University of Cincinnati, 1968
120. Super Bowl I–Los Angeles Coliseum
    Super Bowl II–The Orange Bowl, Miami
    Super Bowl III–The Orange Bowl, Miami
    Super Bowl IV–Tulane Stadium, New Orleans
121. ABC and NBC, January 1967
122. George Wilson Jr.
123. Dick Wood, John Stofa, Rick Norton-1966
124. John Stofa, Dewey Warren, Sam Wyche-1968
125. Curtis McClinton–Super Bowl I
126. Dickie Post and Brad Hubbard-1967
127. John Hadl, San Diego Chargers-1965
128. George Blanda, Oakland Raiders-1967
129. Jack Kemp, Los Angeles/San Diego Chargers and Buffalo Bills
130. John Madden
131. John Madden-1969
    Bill Conkright-1962
    Marty Feldman-1961, 1962
    Al Davis-1963, 1964, 1965
    Eddie Erdelatz-1960, 1961
    John Rauch-1966, 1967, 1968
132. Lou Saban, Boston Patriots
133. Mike Holovak
134. Pop Ivy-1962, 1963
    Wally Lemm-1961, 1966, 1969
    Lou Rymkus-1960, 1961
    Sammy Baugh-1964
    Hugh "Bones" Taylor-1965
135. Carlton "Cookie" Gilchrist, Buffalo Bills-1962, 1964
    Jim Nance, Boston Patriots-1966, 1967
136. Len Dawson, Dallas Texans/Kansas City Chiefs
137. Abner Haynes, Dallas; Charley Tolar, Houston; Cookie Gilchrist, Buffalo; Jim Nance, Boston; Mike Garrett, Kansas City; Hoyle Granger, Houston
138. Paul Lowe and Jim Nance
139. Emmett Thomas
140. Milt Woodard
141. Dick Wood, Jackie Lee, Steve Tensi
142. Tom Flores, Art Powell
143. 1965–Buffalo defeated San Diego 23-0
144. Balboa Stadium, San Diego-1961, 1963, 1965
145. Preston Reidlehuber of the Oakland Raiders
146. Buffalo–War Memorial Stadium, Denver–Bears/Mile High Stadium, Miami–The Orange Bowl, Cincinnati Bengals–Nippert Stadium
147. A-3, B-4, C-2, D-1
148. #78–Bobby Bell, Kansas City linebacker and #42–Johnny Robinson, Kansas City safety
149. Cookie Gilchrist, Buffalo–981 and Dickie Post, San Diego–873
150. Lee Grosscup, New York Titans–1962
151. George Blanda, Houston Oilers and Oakland Raiders
152. Billy Cannon, Houston Oilers and Oakland Raiders
153. Gino Cappelletti, Boston Patriots
154. Larry Grantham, New York Jets
155. Wayne Hawkins, Oakland Raiders
156. Jim Hunt, Boston Patriots
157. Harry Jacobs, Boston Patriots and Buffalo Bills
158. Jack Kemp, Los Angeles/San Diego Chargers and Buffalo Bills
159. Paul Lowe, Los Angeles/San Diego Chargers and Kansas City Chiefs
160. Jacky Lee, Houston Oilers, Denver Broncos and Kansas City Chiefs
161. Bill Mathis, New York Titans/Jets
162. Paul Maguire, Los Angeles/San Diego Chargers and Buffalo Bills
163. Don Maynard, New York Titans/Jets
164. Ron Mix, Los Angeles/San Diego Chargers
165. Jim Otto, Oakland Raiders
166. Babe Parilli, Oakland Raiders, Boston Patriots and New York Jets
167. Johnny Robinson, Dallas Texans/Kansas City Chiefs
168. Paul Rochester, Dallas Texans/Kansas City Chiefs and New York Jets

169. Ernie Wright, Los Angeles/San Diego Chargers and Cincinnati Bengals

170-178:

Gino Cappelletti	Boston Patriots
Larry Grantham	New York Titans/Jets
Wayne Hawkins	Oakland Raiders
Jim Hunt	Boston Patriots
Bill Mathis	New York Titans/Jets
Don Maynard	New York Titans/Jets
Ron Mix	Los Angeles/San Diego Chargers
Jim Otto	Oakland Raiders
Johnny Robinson	Dallas Texans/Kansas City Chiefs

179. Lamar Hunt, Dallas/Kansas City
K.S. "Bud" Adams, Houston
Ralph Wilson, Buffalo
Billy Sullivan, Boston

180. Otis Taylor, Kansas City Chiefs in Super Bowl IV—a 46-yard touchdown pass from Len Dawson in the third quarter. You can also take credit if you said Mike Livingston, who scored on a 12-yard touchdown run in the fourth quarter for the West in the 1969 all-star game.

Faces of the Game

1. Abner Haynes
2. Paul Maguire
3. Dick Wood
4. Dick Westmoreland
5. Wayne Crow
6. Roger Donnahoo
7. Jerrell Wilson
8. Larry Eisenhower
9. Dickie Post
10. Glenn Bass & Elbert Dubenion
11. Don Trull
12. Charlie Flowers
13. E.J. Holub
14. Wilber "Weeb" Ewbank
15. Brad Hubbert
16. Dainard Paulson
17. Bob Reifsnyder
18. Bob Mishak
19. Billy Cannon
20. Wahoo McDaniel
21. Al Dorow
22. Frank Buncom
23. Ernie Barnes
24. Bill Groman
25. Charlie Hennigan
26. Charlie Tolar
27. Howard Twilley
28. Marlin Briscoe
29. Eldon Danenhauer
30. Ed Budde
31. Jim Whalen
32. Fred Williamson
33. Fred Biletnikoff
34. Cosmo Iacavazzi
35. Charlie Powell
36. Art Powell
37. Sonny Bishop
38. Jim Beirne
39. Jack Spikes
40. Ernie Wright
41. Keith Lincoln
42. Thurlow Cooper
43. Jim Turner
44. Bob McLeod
45. Gene Mingo
46. Dennis Partee
47. Jim Nance
48. Floyd Little
49. Gary McDermott
50. Carroll Hardy
51. Dewey Bohling
52. Pete Lammons
53. Don Maynard
54. George Sauer Jr.
55. Pete Duranko
56. Tony Romeo
57. Lee Riley
58. Wray Carlton
59. Johnny Sample
60. Rommie Loudd
61. Jim Kiick
62. Tom Flores
63. Sammy Weir
64. Charlie Frazier
65. Willie Frazier
66. Larry Elkins
67. Bob McLeod
68. Charlie Hennigan
69. Mike Taliaferro
70. Jack Clancy
71. Dave Kocourek
72. Ron Mix
73. Emil Karas
74. Earl Faison
75. Don Norton
76. Keith Lincoln
77. Ernie Ladd
78. George Atkinson
79. Willie Brown
80. Hewritt Dixon

444

Trivia Answers

81. Charlie Smith
82. Gene Upshaw
83. Ben Davidson
84. Buck Buchanan
85. Jim Lynch
86. Willie Lanier
87. Bobby Bell
88. Jerry Mays
89. Dave Hill
90. Jim Tyrer

By the Numbers

00. Jim Otto, Oakland Raiders
1. Nolan Smith, Kansas City Chiefs
2. Cookie Gilchrist, Denver Broncos
3. Jan Stenrud, Kansas City Chiefs
5. Booth Lusteg, Buffalo Bills
6. Warren McVea, Kansas City Chiefs
7. John Huarte, New York Jets/Boston Patriots/Kansas City Chiefs
9. Keith Lincoln, San Diego Chargers (1969)
10. Mike Livingston, Kansas City Chiefs
11. Pete Beathard, Houston Oilers
12. Joe Namath, New York Jets
13. Steve Tensi, San Diego Chargers (1966)
14. Tom Yewcic, Boston Patriots
15. Max Choboian, Denver Broncos
16. George Blanda, Houston Oilers/Oakland Raiders
17. Mike Taliaferro, New York Jets/Boston Patriots
18. Paul Robinson, Cincinnati Bengals
19. Lance Alworth, San Diego Chargers
20. Miller Farr, Houston Oilers
21. John Hadl, San Diego Chargers
22. "Mini" Max Anderson, Buffalo Bills
23. Paul Lowe, San Diego Chargers
24. Dick Felt, Boston Patriots
25. Frank Pitts, Kansas City Chiefs
26. George Saimes, Buffalo Bills
27. Gary Garrison, San Diego Chargers
28. Abner Haynes, Dallas Texans/Kansas City Chiefs, Denver Broncos, Miami Dolphins, New York Jets
29. Ken Houston, Houston Oilers
30. Wray Carlton, Buffalo Bills
31. Bill Mathis, New York Jets
32. Curtis McClinton, Kansas City Chiefs
33. W.K. Hicks, Houston Oilers
34. Ron Sellers, Boston Patriots
35. Jim Nance, Boston Patriots
36. Clem Daniels, Oakland Raiders
37. Alan Miller, Oakland Raiders
38. Wendell Hayes, Kansas City Chiefs
39. Larry Csonka, Miami Dolphins
40. Dainard Paulson, New York Titans/Jets
41. Matt Snell, New York Jets
42. Butch Byrd, Buffalo Bills
43. George "Butch" Atkinson, Oakland Raiders
44. Elbert Dubenion, Buffalo Bills
45. Leslie "Speedie" Duncan, San Diego Chargers
46. Jim Kearney, Kansas City Chiefs
47. Kent McCloughan, Oakland Raiders
48. Cornell Gordon, New York Jets
49. Jim Warren, San Diego Chargers/Miami Dolphins
50. Chuck Allen, San Diego Chargers
51. Jim Lynch, Kansas City Chiefs
52. Garland Boyette, Houston Oilers
53. Tom Addison, Boston Patriots
54. Bob Johnson, Cincinnati Bengals
55. Frank Buncom, San Diego Chargers/Cincinnati Bengals
56. Emil Karas, San Diego Chargers
57. Hubert Bobo, San Diego Chargers/New York Titans
58. Al Beauchamp, Cincinnati Bengals
59. Larry Kaminski, Denver Broncos
60. Len St.Jean, Boston Patriots
61. Bob Talamini, Houston Oilers/New York Jets
62. Al Atkinson, New York Jets
63. Dave Costa, Denver Broncos
64. Harry Jacobs, Buffalo Bills
65. Sam Guneison, San Diego Chargers
66. Billy Shaw, Buffalo Bills
67. Dave Herman, New York Jets
68. Bob Briggs, San Diego Chargers
69. Sherrill Headrick, Kansas City Chiefs/Cincinnati Bengals
70. Glen Ray Hines wore 78 for Houston
71. Sherman Plunkett wore 79 for the New York Jets
72. Dudley Meredith wore 74 and 75 for the Buffalo Bills
73. Manny Fernandez wore 75 for the Miami Dolphins
75. Bob Svihus wore 76 for the Oakland Raiders
76. Dan Birdwell wore 53 for the Oakland Raiders
77. Gordy Holz wore 74 for the Denver Broncos
78. Pat Holmes wore 79 for Houston Oilers
79. Pete Duranko wore 55 for the Denver Broncos
80. John Elliott, New York Jets
81. Warren Wells, Oakland Raiders
82. Paul Costa, Buffalo Bills
83. Ben Davidson, Oakland Raiders
84. Fred Arbanas, Kansas City Chiefs
85. Chuck Hurston, Kansas City Chiefs
86. Earl Faison, San Diego Chargers
87. Lionel Taylor, Denver Broncos/Houston Oilers
88. Don Norton, San Diego Chargers
89. Bob Dee, Boston Patriots
90. George Webster, Houston Oilers
99. Ernie Ladd, Houston Oilers/Kansas City Chiefs

Remember the AFL

For the Record

1. Jacky Lee
2. Willard Dewveall
3. B. 84
4. A. 98 yards
5. George Blanda and Jacky Lee
6. 55 yards
7. Lance Alworth, San Diego Chargers; Art Powell, Oakland Raiders; Charlie Hennigan, Houston Oilers
8. Dave Grayson, Dallas Texans and Oakland Raiders
9. Keith Lincoln, San Diego Chargers
10. Gino Cappelletti, Boston Patriots
11. Sid Blanks, Houston Oilers
12. Cookie Gilchrist, Buffalo Bills
13. Cookie Gilchrist, Buffalo Bills, and Abner Haynes, Dallas Texans
14. C. Lowe, 4.87   D. Daniels, 4.50   F. Lincoln, 4.46
15. Jack Kemp, San Diego Chargers, Buffalo Bills
16. Willie Brown
17. D. 2 completed passes is the AFL's fewest
18. C. 37
19. B. Don Maynard
20. A, Houston 199 in 1967 and C, Kansas City 170 in 1968 and 177 in 1969
21. A. Jim Nance
22. D. Sid Blanks vs. New York Jets, 1964
23. C and F are held by Len Dawson
24. A. Lance Alworth
25. B. Speedy Duncan, 1967 and F, Tom Janik, 1968
26. C. Speedy Duncan
27. D. Jan Stenerud
28. G. Oakland Raiders, '68-'69; H, Los Angeles/San Diego Chargers, '60-'61
29. E. Kansas City vs. Denver, 1963
30. H. San Diego, 1961
31. K. Mike Taliaferro
32. A. Tom Day
33. I. Ernie Ladd
34. R. Mickey Slaughter and Rex Mirich
35. N. Jim Fraser
36. J. Willie Frazier
37. B. Tom Keating
38. L. Art Powell and Tom Flores
39. O. Scott Appleton
40. C. Horst Muhlman
41. T. Abner Haynes
42. D. Bud McFadin
43. G. Sonny Bishop
44. M. Hewritt Dixon
45. E. Billy Joe
46. F. Rich Jackson
47. P. Blanks, Carwell, C. Frazier
48. Q. Dick Hudson
49. S. Dick Christy and Alan Miller
50. H. Jim Colclough
51. FALSE
52. TRUE, 1973
53. TRUE, in Super Bowl VI with the Cowboys
54. TRUE, he carried ten times in 1969 for Kansas City
55. TRUE, in 1962 and 1963
56. FALSE
57. TRUE, in 1968 he carried 12 times for San Francisco
58. TRUE, in 1950 he played one game with Baltimore
59. TRUE, he played 3 games with Denver
60. TRUE, he caught 7 passes in 1970 for Kansas City

It's a Wrap

61. C. 1960 Fleer
62. E. 1961 Fleer
63. I. 1963 Fleer
64. J. 1961 Topps
65. A. 1964 Topps
66. G. 1965 Topps
67. H. 1966 Topps
68. F. 1967 Topps
69. D. 1968 Topps
70. B. 1969 Topps

About the author

DAVE STEIDEL author

Dave Steidel is a high school counselor in Allentown, Pennsylvania. He is a U.S. Navy veteran and holds degrees in elementary and special education, counseling, and school administration. He has been a high school swim coach, school board president, high school and college soccer referee, and softball umpire. He has published several articles for **Baseball Card** magazine and has been an avid fan of the American Football League from its inception.

Comments on this book are welcomed at:

afl6069@gmail.com

More great football books

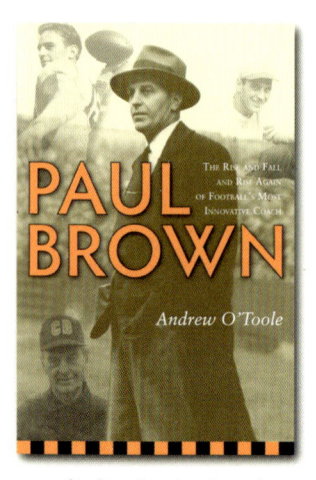

PAUL BROWN
The Rise and Fall and Rise Again of Football's Most Innovative Coach
Andrew O'Toole
Hardcover $24.95 | ISBN-13: 978-1-57860-319-0

Called the "father of the modern offense," Paul Brown invented many aspects of football we now take for granted—from racially integrated rosters to complex passing schemes, classroom instruction, film study, and face masks. His genius led to unsurpassed success, while his authoritarian nature led to conflicts on and off the field.

Paul Brown is the definitive biography of a complicated man, a riveting tale spanning football's rise to become America's most popular sport. An intensely private person, he was generous and caustic, kind and autocratic. Though he rarely raised his voice, players feared his glare. Though uncomfortable in the spotlight, he insisted on complete control.

Paul Brown is a powerful story of one of the most gifted geniuses the game has ever known. Through in-depth research and interviews with the players, coaches, friends, and family members who knew him best, Andrew O'Toole has written what will become a classic book on the history of the game.

THE FOOTBALL UNCYCLOPEDIA
A Highly Opinionated Myth-Busting Guide to America's Most Popular Game
Michael Kun and Adam Hoff
Paperback $15.95 | ISBN-13: 978-1-57860-311-4

With a blend of statistical analysis, opinion (lots of opinion), a love for the game, and a healthy dash of humor, authors Michael Kun and Adam Hoff debunk some of the widely held beliefs about pro football that fans have clung to for generations. No subject is off limits. The 1972 Miami Dolphins? Skewered. America's Team? Put in its place. Joe Namath? Well, he gets a bit of everything. In easy-to-browse alphabetical entries, *The Football Uncyclopedia* covers the gamut, from revered champions to player misbehavior to team uniforms. Sure to spark hours of debate, drunken wagers, and even a few fistfights.

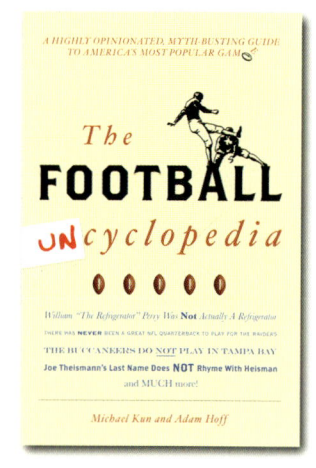

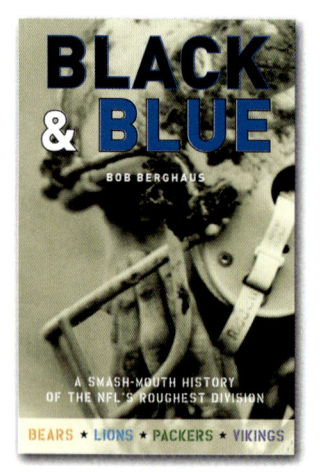

BLACK AND BLUE
A Smash-Mouth History of the NFL's Roughest Division
Bob Berghaus
Paperback $16.95 | ISBN-13: 978-1-57860-320-6

The Chicago Bears, Detroit Lions, Green Bay Packers, and Minnesota Vikings aren't known for their glamour. They're known for playing the roughest brand of football in the league. Through dozens of interviews with players, coaches, team officials, and sportswriters, Bob Berghaus chronicles the 40-year history of the "Black and Blue Division." He profiles each team and its greatest players, while providing behind-the-scenes stories of the biggest games and muddiest moments. *Black and Blue* also includes rare photos, complete division game scores, statistics, playoff-game capsules, and the All-Time Black and Blue team.

Order at www.clerisypress.com